D0417041

THE TIMES

MINI

ATLAS

OF THE WORLD

TIMES BOOKS
LONDON

Published by Times Books
An imprint of HarperCollins Publishers
Westerhill Road
Bishopbriggs
Glasgow G64 2QT
www.harpercollins.co.uk

First published 1991
Published as The Times Atlas
of the World Mini Edition 1994
Second Edition 1999
Third Edition 2006
Fourth Edition 2009
Fifth Edition 2012
Sixth Edition 2015

Seventh Edition 2017

Copyright © Times Books Group Ltd 2017

Maps © Collins Bartholomew Ltd 2017

The Times® is a registered trademark of Times Newspapers Ltd

A catalogue record for this book is available from the British Library

ISBN 978-0-00-826250-1

10 9 8 7 6 5 4 3 2 1
Printed in Hong Kong

All mapping in this atlas is generated from Collins Bartholomew™ digital databases.
Collins Bartholomew™, the UK's leading independent geographical information supplier,
can provide a digital, custom, and premium mapping service to a variety of markets.
For further information:
Tel: +44 (0) 141 306 3752
e-mail: collinsbartholomew@harpercollins.co.uk
or visit our website at: www.collinsbartholomew.com

If you would like to comment on any aspect of this atlas,
please contact us at the above address or online.
www.timesatlas.com
email: timesatlas@harpercollins.co.uk
 facebook.com/thetimesatlas
 @TimesAtlas

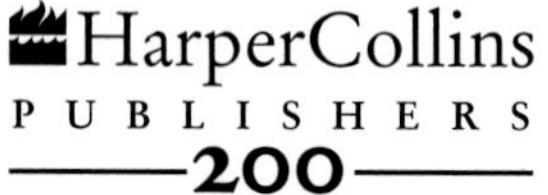

Pages	Title	Scale

GEOGRAPHICAL INFORMATION

6–19	**COUNTRIES of the WORLD**	
20–21	**OCEANIA** Physical Features	
22–23	**ASIA** Physical Features	
24–25	**EUROPE** Physical Features	
26–27	**AFRICA** Physical Features	
28–29	**NORTH AMERICA** Physical Features	
30–31	**SOUTH AMERICA** Physical Features	
32–33	**OCEANS and POLES** Physical Features	
34–35	**CLIMATE**	
36–37	**LAND COVER**	
38–39	**POPULATION**	
40–41	**URBANIZATION**	
42–43	**SYMBOLS and ABBREVIATIONS**	

WORLD

44–45	**WORLD** Physical Features	1:170 000 000
46–47	**WORLD** Countries	1:170 000 000

OCEANIA 1:70 000 000

48–49	OCEANIA	1:70 000 000
50–51	**AUSTRALIA**	1:25 000 000
52–53	**AUSTRALIA** Southeast	1:10 000 000
54	**NEW ZEALAND**	1:10 000 000

ANTARCTICA 1:60 000 000

55	ANTARCTICA	1:60 000 000

ASIA 1:70 000 000

56–57	ASIA	1:70 000 000
58–59	**SOUTHEAST ASIA**	1:30 000 000
60–61	**MALAYSIA and INDONESIA** West	1:15 000 000
62–63	**CONTINENTAL SOUTHEAST ASIA**	1:15 000 000
64	**PHILIPPINES**	1:15 000 000

CONTENTS

Pages	Title	Scale
65	**NORTH KOREA and SOUTH KOREA**	1:9 000 000
66–67	**JAPAN**	1:10 000 000
68–69	**CHINA and MONGOLIA**	1:30 000 000
70–71	**CHINA** Central	1:15 000 000
72–73	**SOUTH ASIA**	1:20 000 000
74–75	**PAKISTAN, INDIA and BANGLADESH**	1:15 000 000
76–77	**CENTRAL ASIA**	1:20 000 000
78–79	**ARABIAN PENINSULA**	1:15 000 000
80–81	**EAST MEDITERRANEAN**	1:15 000 000
82–83	**RUSSIA**	1:42 000 000
84–85	EUROPE	1:40 000 000
86–87	**EUROPEAN RUSSIA**	1:20 000 000
88–89	**NORTHEAST EUROPE**	1:8 000 000
90–91	**UKRAINE and MOLDOVA**	1:8 000 000
92–93	**SCANDINAVIA and ICELAND**	1:10 000 000
94–95	**UNITED KINGDOM and IRELAND**	1:8 000 000
96	**SCOTLAND**	1:4 000 000
97	**IRELAND**	1:4 000 000
98–99	**ENGLAND and WALES**	1:4 000 000
100–101	**NORTHWEST EUROPE**	1:4 000 000
102–103	**CENTRAL EUROPE**	1:8 000 000
104–105	**FRANCE and SWITZERLAND**	1:8 000 000
106–107	**SPAIN and PORTUGAL**	1:8 000 000
108–109	**ITALY and THE BALKANS**	1:8 000 000
110–111	**GREECE, ROMANIA and BULGARIA**	1:8 000 000
112–113	AFRICA	1:60 000 000
114–115	**NORTHWEST AFRICA**	1:26 000 000

CONTENTS

Pages	Title	Scale
116–117	**NORTHEAST AFRICA**	1:26 000 000
118–119	**CENTRAL AFRICA**	1:20 000 000
120–121	**SOUTHERN AFRICA**	1:20 000 000
122–123	**SOUTH AFRICA**	1:10 000 000
124–125	NORTH AMERICA	1:70 000 000
126–127	**CANADA**	1:30 000 000
128–129	**CANADA** West	1:15 000 000
130–131	**CANADA** East	1:15 000 000
132–133	**UNITED STATES OF AMERICA**	1:25 000 000
134–135	**USA** West	1:11 000 000
136–137	**USA** North Central	1:11 000 000
138–139	**USA** South Central	1:11 000 000
140–141	**USA** Northeast	1:11 000 000
142–143	**USA** Southeast	1:11 000 000
144–145	**MEXICO**	1:15 000 000
146–147	**CARIBBEAN**	1:20 000 000
148–149	SOUTH AMERICA	1:70 000 000
150–151	**SOUTH AMERICA** North	1:25 000 000
152–153	**SOUTH AMERICA** South	1:25 000 000
154–155	**BRAZIL** Southeast	1:10 000 000
	OCEANS	
156–157	**PACIFIC OCEAN**	1:120 000 000
158	**ATLANTIC OCEAN**	1:120 000 000
159	**INDIAN OCEAN**	1:120 000 000
160	**ARCTIC OCEAN**	1:60 000 000
161–255	INDEX	

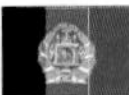

AFGHANISTAN
Islamic Republic of Afghanistan
Capital Kābul

Area sq km	652 225	**Currency**	Afghani
Area sq miles	251 825	**Languages**	Dari, Pashto
Population	32 527 000		(Pashtu), Uzbek,
			Turkmen

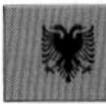

ALBANIA
Republic of Albania
Capital Tirana (Tiranë)

Area sq km	28 748	**Currency**	Lek
Area sq miles	11 100	**Languages**	Albanian, Greek
Population	2 897 000		

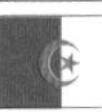

ALGERIA
People's Democratic Republic of Algeria
Capital Algiers (Alger)

Area sq km	2 381 741	**Currency**	Algerian dinar
Area sq miles	919 595	**Languages**	Arabic, French,
Population	39 667 000		Berber

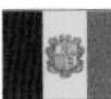

ANDORRA
Principality of Andorra
Capital Andorra la Vella

Area sq km	465	**Currency**	Euro
Area sq miles	180	**Languages**	Catalan, Spanish,
Population	70 000		French

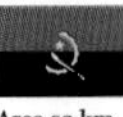

ANGOLA
Republic of Angola
Capital Luanda

Area sq km	1 246 700	**Currency**	Kwanza
Area sq miles	481 354	**Languages**	Portuguese,
Population	25 022 000		Bantu, other local
			lang.

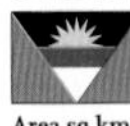

ANTIGUA AND BARBUDA
Capital St John's

Area sq km	442	**Currency**	East Caribbean
Area sq miles	171		dollar
Population	92 000	**Languages**	English, creole

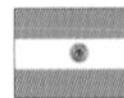

ARGENTINA
Argentine Republic
Capital Buenos Aires

Area sq km	2 766 889	**Currency**	Argentinian peso
Area sq miles	1 068 302	**Languages**	Spanish, Italian,
Population	43 417 000		Amerindian lang.

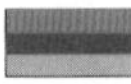

ARMENIA
Republic of Armenia
Capital Yerevan (Erevan)

Area sq km	29 800	**Currency**	Dram
Area sq miles	11 506	**Languages**	Armenian,
Population	3 018 000		Kurdish

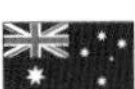

AUSTRALIA
Commonwealth of Australia
Capital Canberra

Area sq km	7 692 024	**Currency**	Australian d
Area sq miles	2 969 907	**Languages**	English, Itali
Population	23 969 000		Greek

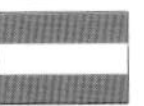

AUSTRIA
Republic of Austria
Capital Vienna (Wien)

Area sq km	83 855	**Currency**	Euro
Area sq miles	32 377	**Languages**	German,
Population	8 545 000		Croatian, Tu

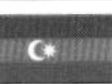

AZERBAIJAN
Republic of Azerbaijan
Capital Baku (Bakı)

Area sq km	86 600	**Currency**	Azerbaijani
Area sq miles	33 436	**Languages**	Azeri, Armen
Population	9 754 000		Russian, Lez

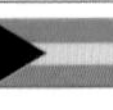

THE BAHAMAS
Commonwealth of The Bahamas
Capital Nassau

Area sq km	13 939	**Currency**	Bahamian d
Area sq miles	5 382	**Languages**	English, cree
Population	388 000		

BAHRAIN
Kingdom of Bahrain
Capital Manama (Al Manāmah)

Area sq km	691	**Currency**	Bahraini din
Area sq miles	267	**Languages**	Arabic, Engl
Population	1 377 000		

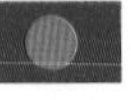

BANGLADESH
People's Republic of Bangladesh
Capital Dhaka (Dacca)

Area sq km	143 998	**Currency**	Taka
Area sq miles	55 598	**Languages**	Bengali, Eng
Population	160 996 000		

BARBADOS
Capital Bridgetown

Area sq km	430	**Currency**	Barbadian d
Area sq miles	166	**Languages**	English, cree
Population	284 000		

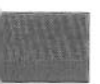

BELARUS
Republic of Belarus
Capital Minsk

Area sq km	207 600	**Currency** Belarusian rouble
Area sq miles	80 155	**Languages** Belarusian, Russian
Population	9 496 000	

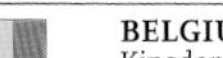

BELGIUM
Kingdom of Belgium
Capital Brussels (Brussel/Bruxelles)

Area sq km	30 520	**Currency** Euro
Area sq miles	11 784	**Languages** Dutch (Flemish), French (Walloon), German
Population	11 299 000	

BELIZE
Capital Belmopan

Area sq km	22 965	**Currency** Belize dollar
Area sq miles	8 867	**Languages** English, Spanish, Mayan, creole
Population	359 000	

BENIN
Republic of Benin
Capital Porto-Novo

Area sq km	112 620	**Currency** CFA franc*
Area sq miles	43 483	**Languages** French, Fon, Yoruba, Adja, other local lang.
Population	10 880 000	

BHUTAN
Kingdom of Bhutan
Capital Thimphu

Area sq km	46 620	**Currency** Ngultrum, Indian rupee
Area sq miles	18 000	
Population	775 000	**Languages** Dzongkha, Nepali, Assamese

BOLIVIA
Plurinational State of Bolivia
Capital La Paz/Sucre

Area sq km	1 098 581	**Currency** Boliviano
Area sq miles	424 164	**Languages** Spanish, Quechua, Aymara
Population	10 725 000	

BOSNIA AND HERZEGOVINA
Capital Sarajevo

Area sq km	51 130	**Currency** Convertible mark
Area sq miles	19 741	**Languages** Bosnian, Serbian, Croatian
Population	3 810 000	

BOTSWANA
Republic of Botswana
Capital Gaborone

Area sq km	581 370	**Currency** Pula
Area sq miles	224 468	**Languages** English, Setswana, Shona, other local lang.
Population	2 262 000	

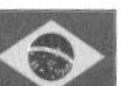

BRAZIL
Federative Republic of Brazil
Capital Brasília

Area sq km	8 514 879	**Currency** Real
Area sq miles	3 287 613	**Languages** Portuguese
Population	207 848 000	

BRUNEI
Brunei Darussalam
Capital Bandar Seri Begawan

Area sq km	5 765	**Currency** Bruneian dollar
Area sq miles	2 226	**Languages** Malay, English, Chinese
Population	423 000	

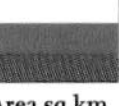

BULGARIA
Republic of Bulgaria
Capital Sofia

Area sq km	110 994	**Currency** Lev
Area sq miles	42 855	**Languages** Bulgarian, Turkish, Romany, Macedonian
Population	7 150 000	

BURKINA FASO
Capital Ouagadougou

Area sq km	274 200	**Currency** CFA franc*
Area sq miles	105 869	**Languages** French, Moore (Mossi), Fulani, other local lang.
Population	18 106 000	

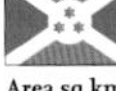

BURUNDI
Republic of Burundi
Capital Bujumbura

Area sq km	27 835	**Currency** Burundian franc
Area sq miles	10 747	**Languages** Kirundi (Hutu, Tutsi), French
Population	11 179 000	

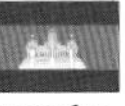

CAMBODIA
Kingdom of Cambodia
Capital Phnom Penh

Area sq km	181 035	**Currency** Riel
Area sq miles	69 884	**Languages** Khmer, Vietnamese
Population	15 578 000	

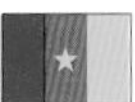

CAMEROON
Republic of Cameroon
Capital Yaoundé

Area sq km	475 442	**Currency**	CFA franc*
Area sq miles	183 569	**Languages**	French, English,
Population	23 344 000		Fang, Bamileke,
			other local lang.

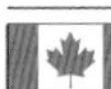

CANADA
Capital Ottawa

Area sq km	9 984 670	**Currency**	Canadian dollar
Area sq miles	3 855 103	**Languages**	English, French,
Population	35 940 000		other local lang.

CAPE VERDE (CABO VERDE)
Republic of Cabo Verde
Capital Praia

Area sq km	4 033	**Currency**	Cape Verdean
Area sq miles	1 557		escudo
Population	521 000	**Languages**	Portuguese, creole

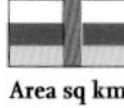

CENTRAL AFRICAN REPUBLIC
Capital Bangui

Area sq km	622 436	**Currency**	CFA franc*
Area sq miles	240 324	**Languages**	French, Sango,
Population	4 900 000		Banda, Baya,
			other local lang.

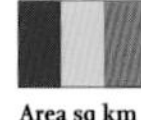

CHAD
Republic of Chad
Capital Ndjamena

Area sq km	1 284 000	**Currency**	CFA franc*
Area sq miles	495 755	**Languages**	Arabic, French,
Population	14 037 000		Sara, other local
			lang.

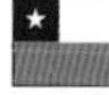

CHILE
Republic of Chile
Capital Santiago

Area sq km	756 945	**Currency**	Chilean peso
Area sq miles	292 258	**Languages**	Spanish,
Population	17 948 000		Amerindian lang.

CHINA
People's Republic of China
Capital Beijing (Peking)

Area sq km	9 606 802	**Currency**	Yuan, HK dollar,
Area sq miles	3 709 186		Macao pataca
Population	1 383 925 000	**Languages**	Mandarin
			(Putonghua), Wu,
			Cantonese, Hsiang,
			regional lang.

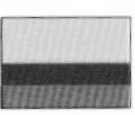

COLOMBIA
Republic of Colombia
Capital Bogotá

Area sq km	1 141 748	**Currency**	Colombian p
Area sq miles	440 831	**Languages**	Spanish,
Population	48 229 000		Amerindian

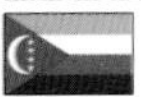

COMOROS
Union of the Comoros
Capital Moroni

Area sq km	1 862	**Currency**	Comorian fra
Area sq miles	719	**Languages**	Shikomor
Population	788 000		(Comorian),
			French, Arab

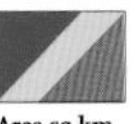

CONGO
Republic of the Congo
Capital Brazzaville

Area sq km	342 000	**Currency**	CFA franc*
Area sq miles	132 047	**Languages**	French, Kong
Population	4 620 000		Monokutuba
			other local la

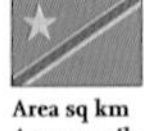

CONGO, DEMOCRATIC REPUBLIC OF THE
Capital Kinshasa

Area sq km	2 345 410	**Currency**	Congolese fra
Area sq miles	905 568	**Languages**	French, Ling
Population	77 267 000		Swahili, Kon
			other local la

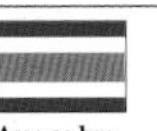

COSTA RICA
Republic of Costa Rica
Capital San José

Area sq km	51 100	**Currency**	Costa Rican
Area sq miles	19 730	**Languages**	Spanish
Population	4 808 000		

CÔTE D'IVOIRE (IVORY COAST)
Republic of Côte d'Ivoire
Capital Yamoussoukro

Area sq km	322 463	**Currency**	CFA franc*
Area sq miles	124 504	**Languages**	French, creol
Population	22 702 000		Akan, other l
			lang.

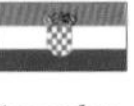

CROATIA
Republic of Croatia
Capital Zagreb

Area sq km	56 538	**Currency**	Kuna
Area sq miles	21 829	**Languages**	Croatian, Ser
Population	4 240 000		

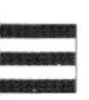

CUBA
Republic of Cuba
Capital Havana (La Habana)

sq km	110 860	**Currency**	Cuban peso
sq miles	42 803	**Languages**	Spanish
lation	11 390 000		

EAST TIMOR (TIMOR-LESTE)
Democratic Republic of Timor-Leste
Capital Dili

Area sq km	14 874	**Currency**	US dollar
Area sq miles	5 743	**Languages**	Portuguese, Tetun, English
Population	1 185 000		

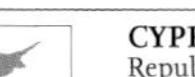

CYPRUS
Republic of Cyprus
Capital Nicosia (Lefkosia)

sq km	9 251	**Currency**	Euro
sq miles	3 572	**Languages**	Greek, Turkish, English
lation	1 165 000		

ECUADOR
Republic of Ecuador
Capital Quito

Area sq km	272 045	**Currency**	US dollar
Area sq miles	105 037	**Languages**	Spanish, Quechua, Amerindian lang.
Population	16 144 000		

CZECHIA
Czech Republic
Capital Prague (Praha)

sq km	78 864	**Currency**	Czech koruna
sq miles	30 450	**Languages**	Czech, Moravian, Slovakian
lation	10 543 000		

EGYPT
Arab Republic of Egypt
Capital Cairo (Al Qāhirah)

Area sq km	1 000 250	**Currency**	Egyptian pound
Area sq miles	386 199	**Languages**	Arabic
Population	91 508 000		

DENMARK
Kingdom of Denmark
Capital Copenhagen (København)

sq km	43 075	**Currency**	Danish krone
sq miles	16 631	**Languages**	Danish
lation	5 669 000		

EL SALVADOR
Republic of El Salvador
Capital San Salvador

Area sq km	21 041	**Currency**	US dollar
Area sq miles	8 124	**Languages**	Spanish
Population	6 127 000		

DJIBOUTI
Republic of Djibouti
Capital Djibouti

sq km	23 200	**Currency**	Djiboutian franc
sq miles	8 958	**Languages**	Somali, Afar, French, Arabic
lation	888 000		

EQUATORIAL GUINEA
Republic of Equatorial Guinea
Capital Malabo

Area sq km	28 051	**Currency**	CFA franc*
Area sq miles	10 831	**Languages**	Spanish, French, Fang
Population	845 000		

DOMINICA
Commonwealth of Dominica
Capital Roseau

sq km	750	**Currency**	East Caribbean dollar
sq miles	290	**Languages**	English, creole
lation	73 000		

ERITREA
State of Eritrea
Capital Asmara

Area sq km	117 400	**Currency**	Nakfa
Area sq miles	45 328	**Languages**	Tigrinya, Tigre
Population	5 228 000		

DOMINICAN REPUBLIC
Capital Santo Domingo

sq km	48 442	**Currency**	Dominican peso
sq miles	18 704	**Languages**	Spanish, creole
lation	10 528 000		

ESTONIA
Republic of Estonia
Capital Tallinn

Area sq km	45 200	**Currency**	Euro
Area sq miles	17 452	**Languages**	Estonian, Russian
Population	1 313 000		

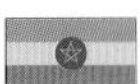

ETHIOPIA
Federal Democratic Republic of Ethiopia
Capital Addis Ababa (Ādīs Ābeba)

Area sq km	1 133 880	**Currency** Birr
Area sq miles	437 794	**Languages** Oromo, Amharic,
Population	99 391 000	Tigrinya, other
		local lang.

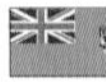

FIJI
Republic of Fiji
Capital Suva

Area sq km	18 330	**Currency** Fijian dollar
Area sq miles	7 077	**Languages** English, Fijian,
Population	892 000	Hindi

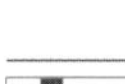

FINLAND
Republic of Finland
Capital Helsinki (Helsingfors)

Area sq km	338 145	**Currency** Euro
Area sq miles	130 559	**Languages** Finnish, Swedish,
Population	5 503 000	Sami

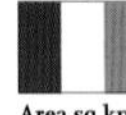

FRANCE
French Republic
Capital Paris

Area sq km	543 965	**Currency** Euro
Area sq miles	210 026	**Languages** French, German
Population	64 395 000	dialects, Italian,
		Arabic, Breton

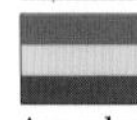

GABON
Gabonese Republic
Capital Libreville

Area sq km	267 667	**Currency** CFA franc*
Area sq miles	103 347	**Languages** French, Fang,
Population	1 725 000	other local lang.

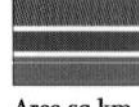

THE GAMBIA
Republic of The Gambia
Capital Banjul

Area sq km	11 295	**Currency** Dalasi
Area sq miles	4 361	**Languages** English, Malinke,
Population	1 991 000	Fulani, Wolof

Gaza
Disputed territory

Area sq km	363	**Currency** Israeli shekel
Area sq miles	140	**Languages** Arabic
Population	1 820 000	

GEORGIA
Capital Tbilisi

Area sq km	69 700	**Currency** Lari
Area sq miles	26 911	**Languages** Georgian, Ru
Population	4 000 000	Armenian, A
		Ossetian, Ab

GERMANY
Federal Republic of Germany
Capital Berlin

Area sq km	357 022	**Currency** Euro
Area sq miles	137 849	**Languages** German, Tu
Population	80 689 000	

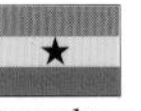

GHANA
Republic of Ghana
Capital Accra

Area sq km	238 537	**Currency** Cedi
Area sq miles	92 100	**Languages** English, Ha
Population	27 410 000	Akan, other
		lang.

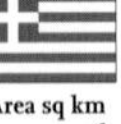

GREECE
Hellenic Republic
Capital Athens (Athina)

Area sq km	131 957	**Currency** Euro
Area sq miles	50 949	**Languages** Greek
Population	10 955 000	

GRENADA
Capital St George's

Area sq km	378	**Currency** East Caribb
Area sq miles	146	dollar
Population	107 000	**Languages** English, cre

GUATEMALA
Republic of Guatemala
Capital Guatemala City

Area sq km	108 890	**Currency** Quetzal
Area sq miles	42 043	**Languages** Spanish,
Population	16 343 000	Mayan lang.

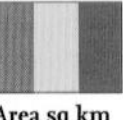

GUINEA
Republic of Guinea
Capital Conakry

Area sq km	245 857	**Currency** Guinean fra
Area sq miles	94 926	**Languages** French, Fula
Population	12 609 000	Malinke, ot
		local lang.

GUINEA-BISSAU
Republic of Guinea-Bissau
Capital Bissau

sq km	36 125	**Currency**	CFA franc*
sq miles	13 948	**Languages**	Portuguese, crioulo, other local lang.
ulation	1 844 000		

GUYANA
Co-operative Republic of Guyana
Capital Georgetown

sq km	214 969	**Currency**	Guyana dollar
sq miles	83 000	**Languages**	English, creole, Amerindian lang.
ulation	767 000		

HAITI
Republic of Haiti
Capital Port-au-Prince

sq km	27 750	**Currency**	Gourde
sq miles	10 714	**Languages**	French, creole
ulation	10 711 000		

HONDURAS
Republic of Honduras
Capital Tegucigalpa

sq km	112 088	**Currency**	Lempira
sq miles	43 277	**Languages**	Spanish, Amerindian lang.
ulation	8 075 000		

HUNGARY
Capital Budapest

sq km	93 030	**Currency**	Forint
sq miles	35 919	**Languages**	Hungarian
ulation	9 855 000		

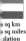

ICELAND
Republic of Iceland
Capital Reykjavík

sq km	102 820	**Currency**	Icelandic króna
sq miles	39 699	**Languages**	Icelandic
ulation	329 000		

INDIA
Republic of India
Capital New Delhi

sq km	3 166 620	**Currency**	Indian rupee
sq miles	1 222 632	**Languages**	Hindi, English, many regional lang.
ulation	1 311 051 000		

INDONESIA
Republic of Indonesia
Capital Jakarta

Area sq km	1 919 445	**Currency**	Rupiah
Area sq miles	741 102	**Languages**	Indonesian, other local lang.
Population	257 564 000		

IRAN
Islamic Republic of Iran
Capital Tehrān

Area sq km	1 648 000	**Currency**	Iranian rial
Area sq miles	636 296	**Languages**	Farsi, Azeri, Kurdish, regional lang.
Population	79 109 000		

IRAQ
Republic of Iraq
Capital Baghdād

Area sq km	438 317	**Currency**	Iraqi dinar
Area sq miles	169 235	**Languages**	Arabic, Kurdish, Turkmen
Population	36 423 000		

IRELAND
Capital Dublin (Baile Átha Cliath)

Area sq km	70 282	**Currency**	Euro
Area sq miles	27 136	**Languages**	English, Irish
Population	4 688 000		

ISRAEL
State of Israel
Capital Jerusalem* (Yerushalayim) (El Quds)

Area sq km	22 072	**Currency**	Shekel
Area sq miles	8 522	**Languages**	Hebrew, Arabic
Population	8 064 000		

* De facto capital. Disputed.

ITALY
Italian Republic
Capital Rome (Roma)

Area sq km	301 245	**Currency**	Euro
Area sq miles	116 311	**Languages**	Italian
Population	59 798 000		

JAMAICA
Capital Kingston

Area sq km	10 991	**Currency**	Jamaican dollar
Area sq miles	4 244	**Languages**	English, creole
Population	2 793 000		

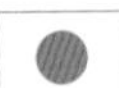

JAPAN
Capital Tōkyō

Area sq km	377 727	Currency	Yen
Area sq miles	145 841	Languages	Japanese
Population	126 573 000		

JORDAN
Hashemite Kingdom of Jordan
Capital 'Ammān

Area sq km	89 206	Currency	Jordanian dinar
Area sq miles	34 443	Languages	Arabic
Population	7 595 000		

KAZAKHSTAN
Republic of Kazakhstan
Capital Astana (Akmola)

Area sq km	2 717 300	Currency	Tenge
Area sq miles	1 049 155	Languages	Kazakh, Russian, Ukrainian, German, Uzbek, Tatar
Population	17 625 000		

KENYA
Republic of Kenya
Capital Nairobi

Area sq km	582 646	Currency	Kenyan shilling
Area sq miles	224 961	Languages	Swahili, English, other local lang.
Population	46 050 000		

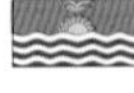

KIRIBATI
Republic of Kiribati
Capital Bairiki, Tarawa Atoll

Area sq km	717	Currency	Australian dollar
Area sq miles	277	Languages	Gilbertese, English
Population	112 000		

KOSOVO
Republic of Kosovo
Capital Pristina (Prishtinë)

Area sq km	10 908	Currency	Euro
Area sq miles	4 212	Languages	Albanian, Serbian
Population	1 805 000		

KUWAIT
State of Kuwait
Capital Kuwait (Al Kuwayt)

Area sq km	17 818	Currency	Kuwaiti dinar
Area sq miles	6 880	Languages	Arabic
Population	3 892 000		

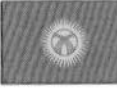

KYRGYZSTAN
Kyrgyz Republic
Capital Bishkek (Frunze)

Area sq km	198 500	Currency	Kyrgyz som
Area sq miles	76 641	Languages	Kyrgyz, Russian, Uzbek
Population	5 940 000		

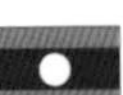

LAOS
Lao People's Democratic Republic
Capital Vientiane (Viangchan)

Area sq km	236 800	Currency	Kip
Area sq miles	91 429	Languages	Lao, other loc lang.
Population	6 802 000		

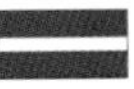

LATVIA
Republic of Latvia
Capital Riga

Area sq km	64 589	Currency	Euro
Area sq miles	24 938	Languages	Latvian, Russ
Population	1 971 000		

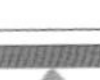

LEBANON
Lebanese Republic
Capital Beirut (Beyrouth)

Area sq km	10 452	Currency	Lebanese po
Area sq miles	4 036	Languages	Arabic, Arme French
Population	5 851 000		

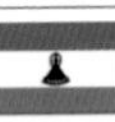

LESOTHO
Kingdom of Lesotho
Capital Maseru

Area sq km	30 355	Currency	Loti, S. African ra
Area sq miles	11 720	Languages	Sesotho, Eng Zulu
Population	2 135 000		

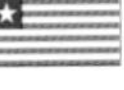

LIBERIA
Republic of Liberia
Capital Monrovia

Area sq km	111 369	Currency	Liberian dol
Area sq miles	43 000	Languages	English, cree other local l
Population	4 503 000		

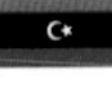

LIBYA
State of Libya
Capital Tripoli (Ṭarābulus)

Area sq km	1 759 540	Currency	Libyan dina
Area sq miles	679 362	Languages	Arabic, Berb
Population	6 278 000		

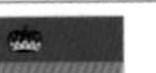

LIECHTENSTEIN
Principality of Liechtenstein
Capital Vaduz

Area sq km	160	Currency	Swiss franc
Area sq miles	62	Languages	German
Population	38 000		

LITHUANIA
Republic of Lithuania
Capital Vilnius

sq km	65 200	**Currency**	Euro
sq miles	25 174	**Languages**	Lithuanian,
lation	2 878 000		Russian, Polish

LUXEMBOURG
Grand Duchy of Luxembourg
Capital Luxembourg

sq km	2 586	**Currency**	Euro
sq miles	998	**Languages**	Letzeburgish,
lation	567 000		German, French

MACEDONIA (F.Y.R.O.M.)
Republic of Macedonia
Capital Skopje

sq km	25 713	**Currency**	Macedonian denar
sq miles	9 928	**Languages**	Macedonian,
lation	2 078 000		Albanian, Turkish

MADAGASCAR
Republic of Madagascar
Capital Antananarivo

sq km	587 041	**Currency**	Ariary
sq miles	226 658	**Languages**	Malagasy, French
lation	24 235 000		

MALAWI
Republic of Malawi
Capital Lilongwe

sq km	118 484	**Currency**	Malawian kwacha
sq miles	45 747	**Languages**	Chichewa,
lation	17 215 000		English, other
			local lang.

MALAYSIA
Capital Kuala Lumpur/Putrajaya

sq km	332 965	**Currency**	Ringgit
sq miles	128 559	**Languages**	Malay, English,
lation	30 331 000		Chinese, Tamil,
			other local lang.

MALDIVES
Republic of the Maldives
Capital Male

sq km	298	**Currency**	Rufiyaa
sq miles	115	**Languages**	Divehi
lation	364 000		(Maldivian)

MALI
Republic of Mali
Capital Bamako

Area sq km	1 240 140	**Currency**	CFA franc*
Area sq miles	478 821	**Languages**	French, Bambara,
Population	17 600 000		other local lang.

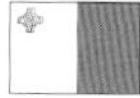

MALTA
Republic of Malta
Capital Valletta

Area sq km	316	**Currency**	Euro
Area sq miles	122	**Languages**	Maltese, English
Population	419 000		

MARSHALL ISLANDS
Republic of the Marshall Islands
Capital Delap-Uliga-Djarrit

Area sq km	181	**Currency**	US dollar
Area sq miles	70	**Languages**	English,
Population	53 000		Marshallese

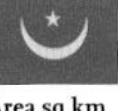

MAURITANIA
Islamic Republic of Mauritania
Capital Nouakchott

Area sq km	1 030 700	**Currency**	Ouguiya
Area sq miles	397 955	**Languages**	Arabic, French,
Population	4 068 000		other local lang.

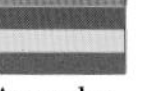

MAURITIUS
Republic of Mauritius
Capital Port Louis

Area sq km	2 040	**Currency**	Mauritius rupee
Area sq miles	788	**Languages**	English, creole,
Population	1 273 000		Hindi, Bhojpurī,
			French

MEXICO
United Mexican States
Capital Mexico City (Ciudad de México)

Area sq km	1 972 545	**Currency**	Mexican peso
Area sq miles	761 604	**Languages**	Spanish,
Population	127 017 000		Amerindian lang.

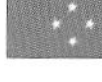

MICRONESIA, FEDERATED STATES OF
Capital Palikir

Area sq km	701	**Currency**	US dollar
Area sq miles	271	**Languages**	English, Chuukese,
Population	104 000		Pohnpeian, other
			local lang.

COUNTRIES OF THE WORLD

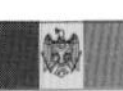

MOLDOVA
Republic of Moldova
Capital Chișinău (Kishinev)

Area sq km	33 700	**Currency**	Moldovan leu
Area sq miles	13 012	**Languages**	Romanian, Ukrainian, Gagauz, Russian
Population	4 069 000		

MONACO
Principality of Monaco
Capital Monaco-Ville

Area sq km	2	**Currency**	Euro
Area sq miles	1	**Languages**	French, Monégasque, Italian
Population	38 000		

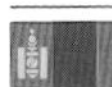

MONGOLIA
Capital Ulan Bator (Ulaanbaatar)

Area sq km	1 565 000	**Currency**	Tugrik (tögrög)
Area sq miles	604 250	**Languages**	Khalka (Mongolian), Kazakh, other local lang.
Population	2 959 000		

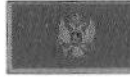

MONTENEGRO
Republic of Montenegro
Capital Podgorica

Area sq km	13 812	**Currency**	Euro
Area sq miles	5 333	**Languages**	Serbian (Montenegrin), Albanian
Population	626 000		

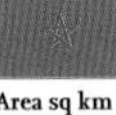

MOROCCO
Kingdom of Morocco
Capital Rabat

Area sq km	446 550	**Currency**	Moroccan dirham
Area sq miles	172 414	**Languages**	Arabic, Berber, French
Population	34 378 000		

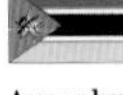

MOZAMBIQUE
Republic of Mozambique
Capital Maputo

Area sq km	799 380	**Currency**	Metical
Area sq miles	308 642	**Languages**	Portuguese, Makua, Tsonga, other local lang.
Population	27 978 000		

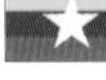

MYANMAR (Burma)
Republic of the Union of Myanmar
Capital Nay Pyi Taw

Area sq km	676 577	**Currency**	Kyat
Area sq miles	261 228	**Languages**	Burmese, Shan, Karen, other local lang.
Population	53 897 000		

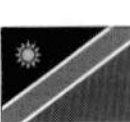

NAMIBIA
Republic of Namibia
Capital Windhoek

Area sq km	824 292	**Currency**	Namibian do
Area sq miles	318 261	**Languages**	English, Afri German, Ova other local la
Population	2 459 000		

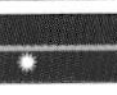

NAURU
Republic of Nauru
Capital Yaren (de facto)

Area sq km	21	**Currency**	Australian de
Area sq miles	8	**Languages**	Nauruan, En
Population	10 000		

NEPAL
Federal Democratic Republic of Nepa
Capital Kathmandu

Area sq km	147 181	**Currency**	Nepalese rup
Area sq miles	56 827	**Languages**	Nepali, Mait Bhojpuri, En other local la
Population	28 514 000		

NETHERLANDS
Kingdom of the Netherlands
Capital Amsterdam/The Hague ('s-Grave

Area sq km	41 526	**Currency**	Euro
Area sq miles	16 033	**Languages**	Dutch, Frisia
Population	16 925 000		

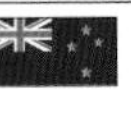

NEW ZEALAND
Capital Wellington

Area sq km	270 534	**Currency**	New Zealand dollar
Area sq miles	104 454		
Population	4 529 000	**Languages**	English, Ma

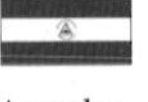

NICARAGUA
Republic of Nicaragua
Capital Managua

Area sq km	130 000	**Currency**	Córdoba
Area sq miles	50 193	**Languages**	Spanish, Amerindian
Population	6 082 000		

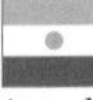

NIGER
Republic of Niger
Capital Niamey

Area sq km	1 267 000	**Currency**	CFA franc*
Area sq miles	489 191	**Languages**	French, Hau Fulani, othe lang.
Population	19 899 000		

NIGERIA
Federal Republic of Nigeria
Capital Abuja

sq km	923 768	**Currency**	Naira
sq miles	356 669	**Languages**	English, Hausa,
lation	182 202 000		Yoruba, Ibo,
			Fulani, other local
			lang.

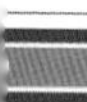

NORTH KOREA
Democratic People's Republic of Korea
Capital P'yŏngyang

sq km	120 538	**Currency**	North Korean won
sq miles	46 540	**Languages**	Korean
lation	25 155 000		

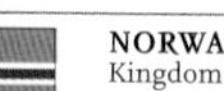

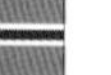

NORWAY
Kingdom of Norway
Capital Oslo

sq km	323 878	**Currency**	Norwegian krone
sq miles	125 050	**Languages**	Norwegian, Sami
ation	5 211 000		

OMAN
Sultanate of Oman
Capital Muscat (Masqaṭ)

sq km	309 500	**Currency**	Omani rial
sq miles	119 499	**Languages**	Arabic, Baluchi,
lation	4 491 000		Indian lang.

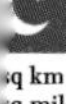

PAKISTAN
Islamic Republic of Pakistan
Capital Islamabad

sq km	881 888	**Currency**	Pakistani rupee
sq miles	340 497	**Languages**	Urdu, Punjabi,
ation	188 925 000		Sindhi, Pashto
			(Pashtu), English,
			Balochi

PALAU
Republic of Palau
Capital Melekeok (Ngerulmud)

sq km	497	**Currency**	US dollar
sq miles	192	**Languages**	Palauan, English
ation	21 000		

PANAMA
Republic of Panama
Capital Panama City

km	77 082	**Currency**	Balboa
q miles	29 762	**Languages**	Spanish, English,
ation	3 929 000		Amerindian lang.

PAPUA NEW GUINEA
Independent State of Papua New Guinea
Capital Port Moresby

Area sq km	462 840	**Currency**	Kina
Area sq miles	178 704	**Languages**	English,
Population	7 619 000		Tok Pisin (creole),
			other local lang.

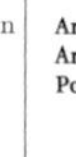

PARAGUAY
Republic of Paraguay
Capital Asunción

Area sq km	406 752	**Currency**	Guaraní
Area sq miles	157 048	**Languages**	Spanish, Guaraní
Population	6 639 000		

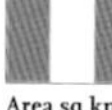

PERU
Republic of Peru
Capital Lima

Area sq km	1 285 216	**Currency**	Nuevo sol
Area sq miles	496 225	**Languages**	Spanish, Quechua,
Population	31 377 000		Aymara

PHILIPPINES
Republic of the Philippines
Capital Manila

Area sq km	300 000	**Currency**	Philippine peso
Area sq miles	115 831	**Languages**	English, Filipino,
Population	100 699 000		Tagalog, Cebuano,
			other local lang.

POLAND
Republic of Poland
Capital Warsaw (Warszawa)

Area sq km	312 683	**Currency**	Złoty
Area sq miles	120 728	**Languages**	Polish, German
Population	38 612 000		

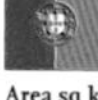

PORTUGAL
Portuguese Republic
Capital Lisbon (Lisboa)

Area sq km	88 940	**Currency**	Euro
Area sq miles	34 340	**Languages**	Portuguese
Population	10 350 000		

QATAR
State of Qatar
Capital Doha (Ad Dawḥah)

Area sq km	11 437	**Currency**	Qatari riyal
Area sq miles	4 416	**Languages**	Arabic
Population	2 235 000		

ROMANIA
Capital Bucharest (București)

Area sq km	237 500	**Currency**	Romanian leu
Area sq miles	91 699	**Languages**	Romanian,
Population	19 511 000		Hungarian

RUSSIA
Russian Federation
Capital Moscow (Moskva)

Area sq km	17 075 400	**Currency**	Russian rouble
Area sq miles	6 592 849	**Languages**	Russian, Tatar,
Population	143 457 000		Ukrainian, other
			local lang.

RWANDA
Republic of Rwanda
Capital Kigali

Area sq km	26 338	**Currency**	Rwandan franc
Area sq miles	10 169	**Languages**	Kinyarwanda,
Population	11 610 000		French, English

ST KITTS AND NEVIS
Federation of St Kitts and Nevis
Capital Basseterre

Area sq km	261	**Currency**	East Caribbean
Area sq miles	101		dollar
Population	56 000	**Languages**	English, creole

ST LUCIA
Capital Castries

Area sq km	616	**Currency**	East Caribbean
Area sq miles	238		dollar
Population	185 000	**Languages**	English, creole

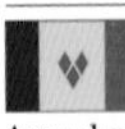

ST VINCENT AND THE GRENADINES
Capital Kingstown

Area sq km	389	**Currency**	East Caribbean
Area sq miles	150		dollar
Population	109 000	**Languages**	English, creole

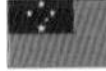

SAMOA
Independent State of Samoa
Capital Apia

Area sq km	2 831	**Currency**	Tala
Area sq miles	1 093	**Languages**	Samoan, English
Population	193 000		

SAN MARINO
Republic of San Marino
Capital San Marino

Area sq km	61	**Currency**	Euro
Area sq miles	24	**Languages**	Italian
Population	32 000		

SÃO TOMÉ AND PRÍNCIPE
Democratic Rep. of São Tomé and Pr
Capital São Tomé

Area sq km	964	**Currency**	Dobra
Area sq miles	372	**Languages**	Portuguese,
Population	190 000		

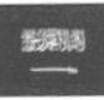

SAUDI ARABIA
Kingdom of Saudi Arabia
Capital Riyadh (Ar Riyāḍ)

Area sq km	2 200 000	**Currency**	Saudi Arabi
Area sq miles	849 425		riyal
Population	31 540 000	**Languages**	Arabic

SENEGAL
Republic of Senegal
Capital Dakar

Area sq km	196 720	**Currency**	CFA franc*
Area sq miles	75 954	**Languages**	French, Wol
Population	15 129 000		Fulani, othe
			lang.

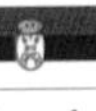

SERBIA
Republic of Serbia
Capital Belgrade (Beograd)

Area sq km	77 453	**Currency**	Serbian dina
Area sq miles	29 904	**Languages**	Serbian,
Population	7 046 000		Hungarian

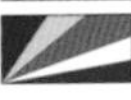

SEYCHELLES
Republic of Seychelles
Capital Victoria

Area sq km	455	**Currency**	Seychelles r
Area sq miles	176	**Languages**	English, Fre
Population	96 000		creole

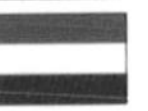

SIERRA LEONE
Republic of Sierra Leone
Capital Freetown

Area sq km	71 740	**Currency**	Leone
Area sq miles	27 699	**Languages**	English, cre
Population	6 453 000		Mende, Ter
			other local

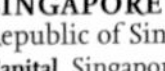

SINGAPORE
Republic of Singapore
Capital Singapore

Area sq km	639	**Currency**	Singapore
Area sq miles	247	**Languages**	Chinese, E
Population	5 604 000		Malay, Tam

SLOVAKIA
Slovak Republic
Capital Bratislava

sq km	49 035	**Currency**	Euro
sq miles	18 933	**Languages**	Slovak,
ation	5 426 000		Hungarian, Czech

SLOVENIA
Republic of Slovenia
Capital Ljubljana

sq km	20 251	**Currency**	Euro
sq miles	7 819	**Languages**	Slovene, Croatian,
ation	2 068 000		Serbian

SOLOMON ISLANDS
Capital Honiara

sq km	28 370	**Currency**	Solomon Islands
sq miles	10 954		dollar
ation	584 000	**Languages**	English, creole,
			other local lang.

SOMALIA
Federal Republic of Somalia
Capital Mogadishu (Muqdisho)

sq km	637 657	**Currency**	Somali shilling
sq miles	246 201	**Languages**	Somali, Arabic
ation	10 787 000		

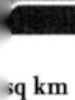

SOUTH AFRICA
Republic of South Africa
Capital Pretoria (Tshwane)/
Cape Town/Bloemfontein

sq km	1 219 090	**Currency**	Rand
sq miles	470 693	**Languages**	Afrikaans,
ation	54 490 000		English, nine
			official local lang.

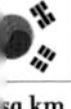

SOUTH KOREA
Republic of Korea
Capital Seoul (Sŏul)

sq km	99 274	**Currency**	South Korean
sq miles	38 330		won
ation	50 293 000	**Languages**	Korean

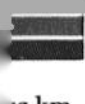

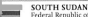

SOUTH SUDAN
Federal Republic of South Sudan
Capital Juba

sq km	644 329	**Currency**	South Sudan
sq miles	248 775		pound
ation	12 340 000	**Languages**	English, Arabic,
			Dinka, Nuer, other
			local lang.

SPAIN
Kingdom of Spain
Capital Madrid

Area sq km	504 782	**Currency**	Euro
Area sq miles	194 897	**Languages**	Spanish (Castilian),
Population	46 122 000		Catalan, Galician,
			Basque

SRI LANKA
Democratic Socialist Republic of Sri Lanka
Capital Sri Jayewardenepura Kotte

Area sq km	65 610	**Currency**	Sri Lankan rupee
Area sq miles	25 332	**Languages**	Sinhalese,
Population	20 715 000		Tamil, English

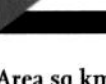

SUDAN
Republic of the Sudan
Capital Khartoum

Area sq km	1 861 484	**Currency**	Sudanese pound
Area sq miles	718 725		(Sudani)
Population	40 235 000	**Languages**	Arabic, English,
			Nubian, Beja, Fur,
			other local lang.

SURINAME
Republic of Suriname
Capital Paramaribo

Area sq km	163 820	**Currency**	Surinamese dollar
Area sq miles	63 251	**Languages**	Dutch,
Population	543 000		Surinamese,
			English, Hindi

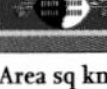

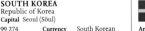

SWAZILAND
Kingdom of Swaziland
Capital Mbabane, Lobamba

Area sq km	17 364	**Currency**	Lilangeni,
Area sq miles	6 704		South African
Population	1 287 000		rand
		Languages	Swazi, English

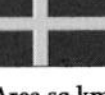

SWEDEN
Kingdom of Sweden
Capital Stockholm

Area sq km	449 964	**Currency**	Swedish krona
Area sq miles	173 732	**Languages**	Swedish, Sami
Population	9 779 000		

SWITZERLAND
Swiss Confederation
Capital Bern (Berne)

Area sq km	41 293	**Currency**	Swiss franc
Area sq miles	15 943	**Languages**	German, French,
Population	8 299 000		Italian, Romansch

17

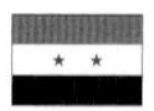

SYRIA
Syrian Arab Republic
Capital Damascus (Dimashq)

Area sq km	184 026	**Currency**	Syrian pound
Area sq miles	71 052	**Languages**	Arabic, Kurdish,
Population	18 502 000		Armenian

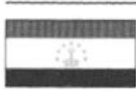

TAIWAN
Republic of China
Capital Taibei

Area sq km	36 179	**Currency**	New Taiwan dollar
Area sq miles	13 969	**Languages**	Mandarin
Population	23 462 000		(Putonghua), Min,
			Hakka, other local
			lang.

The People's Republic of China claims Taiwan as its 23rd province.

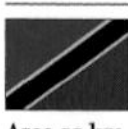

TAJIKISTAN
Republic of Tajikistan
Capital Dushanbe

Area sq km	143 100	**Currency**	Somoni
Area sq miles	55 251	**Languages**	Tajik, Uzbek,
Population	8 482 000		Russian

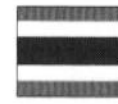

TANZANIA
United Republic of Tanzania
Capital Dodoma

Area sq km	945 087	**Currency**	Tanzanian shilling
Area sq miles	364 900	**Languages**	Swahili, English,
Population	53 470 000		Nyamwezi, other
			local lang.

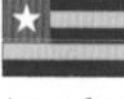

THAILAND
Kingdom of Thailand
Capital Bangkok (Krung Thep)

Area sq km	513 115	**Currency**	Baht
Area sq miles	198 115	**Languages**	Thai, Lao,
Population	67 959 000		Chinese, Malay,
			Mon-Khmer lang.

TOGO
Togolese Republic
Capital Lomé

Area sq km	56 785	**Currency**	CFA franc*
Area sq miles	21 925	**Languages**	French, Ewe,
Population	7 305 000		Kabre, other local
			lang.

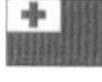

TONGA
Kingdom of Tonga
Capital Nuku'alofa

Area sq km	748	**Currency**	Pa'anga
Area sq miles	289	**Languages**	Tongan, English
Population	106 000		

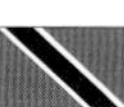

TRINIDAD AND TOBAGO
Republic of Trinidad and Tobago
Capital Port of Spain

Area sq km	5 130	**Currency**	Trinidad an
Area sq miles	1 981	**Languages**	Tobago doll
Population	1 360 000		English, cre
			Hindi

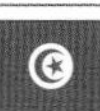

TUNISIA
Tunisian Republic
Capital Tunis

Area sq km	164 150	**Currency**	Tunisian di
Area sq miles	63 379	**Languages**	Arabic, Fren
Population	11 254 000		

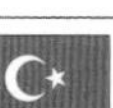

TURKEY
Republic of Turkey
Capital Ankara

Area sq km	779 452	**Currency**	Lira
Area sq miles	300 948	**Languages**	Turkish, Ku
Population	78 666 000		

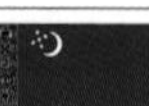

TURKMENISTAN
Capital Ashgabat

Area sq km	488 100	**Currency**	Turkmen m
Area sq miles	188 456	**Languages**	Turkmen, U
Population	5 374 000		Russian

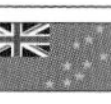

TUVALU
Capital Vaiaku, Funafuti Atoll

Area sq km	25	**Currency**	Australian d
Area sq miles	10	**Languages**	Tuvaluan, E
Population	10 000		

UGANDA
Republic of Uganda
Capital Kampala

Area sq km	241 038	**Currency**	Ugandan sh
Area sq miles	93 065	**Languages**	English, Sw
Population	39 032 000		Luganda, ot
			local lang.

UKRAINE
Capital Kiev (Kyiv)

Area sq km	603 700	**Currency**	Hryvnia
Area sq miles	233 090	**Languages**	Ukrainian,
Population	44 824 000		Russian

UNITED ARAB EMIRATES
Federation of Emirates
Capital Abu Dhabi (Abū Ẓaby)

sq km	77 700	**Currency**	UAE dirham
sq miles	30 000	**Languages**	Arabic, English
Population	9 157 000		

UNITED KINGDOM
United Kingdom of Great Britain and
Northern Ireland
Capital London

sq km	243 609	**Currency**	Pound sterling
sq miles	94 058	**Languages**	English, Welsh,
Population	64 716 000		Gaelic

UNITED STATES OF AMERICA
Capital Washington D.C.

sq km	9 826 635	**Currency**	US dollar
sq miles	3 794 085	**Languages**	English, Spanish
Population	321 774 000		

URUGUAY
Oriental Republic of Uruguay
Capital Montevideo

sq km	176 215	**Currency**	Uruguayan peso
sq miles	68 037	**Languages**	Spanish
Population	3 432 000		

UZBEKISTAN
Republic of Uzbekistan
Capital Tashkent

sq km	447 400	**Currency**	Uzbek som
sq miles	172 742	**Languages**	Uzbek, Russian,
Population	29 893 000		Tajik, Kazakh

VANUATU
Republic of Vanuatu
Capital Port Vila

sq km	12 190	**Currency**	Vatu
sq miles	4 707	**Languages**	English,
Population	265 000		Bislama (creole),
			French

VATICAN CITY
Vatican City State or Holy See
Capital Vatican City

sq km	0.5	**Currency**	Euro
sq miles	0.2	**Languages**	Italian
Population	800		

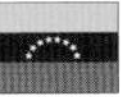

VENEZUELA
Bolivarian Republic of Venezuela
Capital Caracas

Area sq km	912 050	**Currency**	Bolívar
Area sq miles	352 144	**Languages**	Spanish,
Population	31 108 000		Amerindian lang.

VIETNAM
Socialist Republic of Vietnam
Capital Ha Nôi (Hanoi)

Area sq km	329 565	**Currency**	Dong
Area sq miles	127 246	**Languages**	Vietnamese, Thai,
Population	93 448 000		Khmer, Chinese,
			other local lang.

West Bank
Disputed territory

Area sq km	5 860	**Currency**	Jordanian dinar,
Area sq miles	2 263		Israeli shekel
Population	2 862 000	**Languages**	Arabic, Hebrew

Western Sahara
Disputed territory (Morocco)

Area sq km	266 000	**Currency**	Moroccan dirham
Area sq miles	102 703	**Languages**	Arabic
Population	573 000		

YEMEN
Republic of Yemen
Capital Şan'ā'

Area sq km	527 968	**Currency**	Yemeni riyal
Area sq miles	203 850	**Languages**	Arabic
Population	26 832 000		

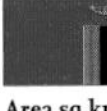

ZAMBIA
Republic of Zambia
Capital Lusaka

Area sq km	752 614	**Currency**	Zambian kwacha
Area sq miles	290 586	**Languages**	English, Bemba,
Population	16 212 000		Nyanja, Tonga,
			other local lang.

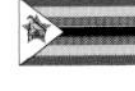

ZIMBABWE
Republic of Zimbabwe
Capital Harare

Area sq km	390 759	**Currency**	US dollar and
Area sq miles	150 873		other currencies
Population	15 603 000	**Languages**	16 local languages
			including English,
			Shona, Ndebele

Total Land Area 8 844 516 sq km / 3 414 868 sq miles
(includes New Guinea and Pacific Island nations)

HIGHEST MOUNTAIN
Puncak Jaya
4 884 m / 16 023 feet

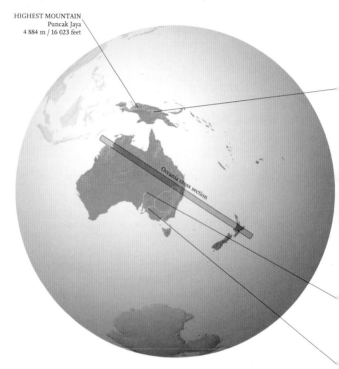

Oceania cross section

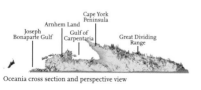

Joseph
Bonaparte Gulf

Arnhem Land

Gulf of
Carpentaria

Cape York
Peninsula

Great Dividing
Range

Oceania cross section and perspective view

Tasman Sea

North Cape

North Island

Cook Strait

HIGHEST MOUNTAINS	metres	feet	Map page
Puncak Jaya, Indonesia	4 884	16 023	59 D3
Puncak Trikora, Indonesia	4 730	15 518	59 D3
Puncak Mandala, Indonesia	4 700	15 420	59 D3
Puncak Yamin, Indonesia	4 595	15 075	—
Mt Wilhelm, Papua New Guinea	4 509	14 793	59 D3
Mt Kubor, Papua New Guinea	4 359	14 301	—

LARGEST ISLAND
New Guinea
808 510 sq km /
312 166 sq miles

LARGEST ISLANDS	sq km	sq miles	Map page
New Guinea	808 510	312 166	59 D3
South Island (Te Waipounamu)	151 215	58 384	54 B2
North Island (Te Ika-a-Māui)	115 777	44 701	54 B1
Tasmania	67 800	26 178	51 D4

LONGEST RIVERS	km	miles	Map page
Murray-Darling	3 672	2 282	52 B2
Darling	2 844	1 767	52 B2
Murray	2 375	1 476	52 B3
Murrumbidgee	1 485	923	52 B2
Lachlan	1 339	832	53 C2
Cooper Creek	1 113	692	52 B1

LARGEST LAKES	sq km	sq miles	Map page
Kati Thanda-Lake Eyre	0–8 900	0–3 436	52 A1
Lake Torrens	0–5 780	0–2 232	52 A1

LARGEST LAKE AND LOWEST POINT
Kati Thanda-Lake Eyre
0-8 900 sq km / 0-3 436 sq miles
16 m / 52 feet below sea level

LONGEST RIVER AND
LARGEST DRAINAGE BASIN
Murray-Darling
3 672 km / 2 282 miles
1 058 000 sq km / 409 000 sq miles

Total Land Area 45 036 492 sq km / 17 388 590 sq miles

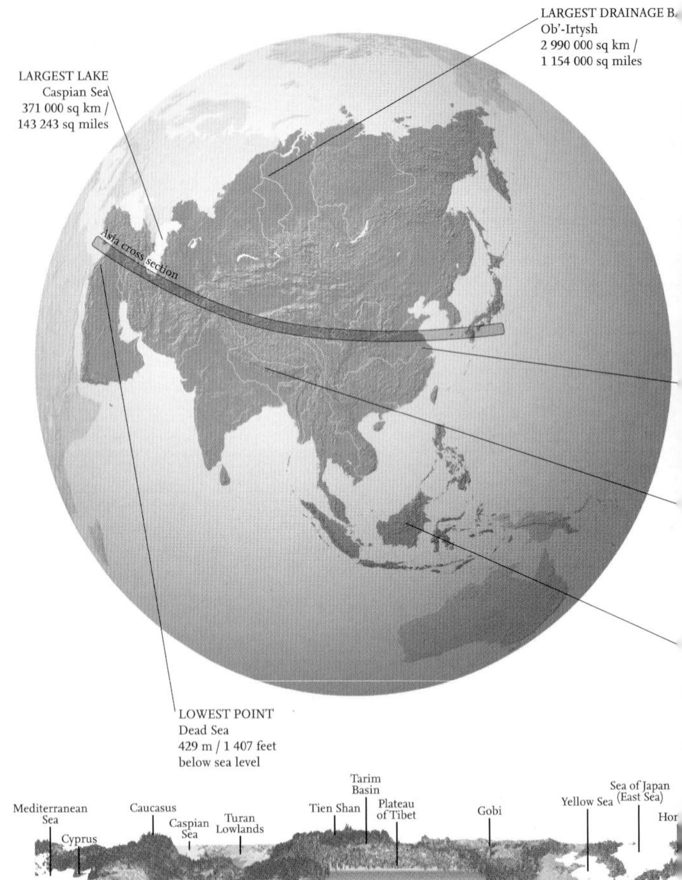

LARGEST DRAINAGE B.
Ob'-Irtysh
2 990 000 sq km /
1 154 000 sq miles

LARGEST LAKE
Caspian Sea
371 000 sq km /
143 243 sq miles

Asia cross section

LOWEST POINT
Dead Sea
429 m / 1 407 feet
below sea level

Mediterranean Sea — Cyprus — Caucasus — Caspian Sea — Turan Lowlands — Tien Shan — Tarim Basin — Plateau of Tibet — Gobi — Yellow Sea — Sea of Japan (East Sea) — Hor

Asia cross section and perspective view

HIGHEST MOUNTAINS	metres	feet	Map page
Mt Everest (Sagarmatha/ Qomolangma Feng), China/Nepal	8 848	29 028	75 C2
K2 (Qogir Feng), China/Pakistan	8 611	28 251	74 B1
Kangchenjunga, India/Nepal	8 586	28 169	75 C2
Lhotse, China/Nepal	8 516	27 939	—
Makalu, China/Nepal	8 463	27 765	—
Cho Oyu, China/Nepal	8 201	26 906	—

LARGEST ISLANDS	sq km	sq miles	Map page
Borneo	745 561	287 861	61 C1
Sumatra (Sumatera)	473 606	182 859	60 A1
Honshū	227 414	87 805	67 B3
Celebes (Sulawesi)	189 216	73 056	58 C3
Java (Jawa)	132 188	51 038	61 B2
Luzon	104 690	40 421	64 B1

LONGEST RIVER
Yangtze (Chang Jiang)
6 380 km /
3 965 miles

LONGEST RIVERS	km	miles	Map page
Yangtze (Chang Jiang)	6 380	3 965	70 C2
Ob'-Irtysh	5 568	3 460	86 F2
Yenisey-Angara-Selenga	5 550	3 449	83 H3
Yellow (Huang He)	5 464	3 395	70 B2
Irtysh	4 440	2 759	86 F2
Mekong	4 425	2 750	63 B2

HIGHEST MOUNTAIN
Mt Everest
8 848 m / 29 028 feet

LARGEST LAKES	sq km	sq miles	Map page
Caspian Sea	371 000	143 243	81 C1
Lake Baikal (Ozero Baykal)	30 500	11 776	69 D1
Lake Balkhash (Ozero Balkash)	17 400	6 718	77 D2
Aral Sea (Aral'skoye More)	17 158	6 625	76 B2
Ysyk-Köl	6 200	2 394	77 D2

LARGEST ISLAND
Borneo
745 561 sq km /
287 861 sq miles

Total Land Area 9 908 599 sq km / 3 825 710 sq miles

LARGEST ISLAND
Great Britain
218 476 sq km /
84 354 sq miles

Europe cross section

HIGHEST MOUNTA
El'brus
5 642 m / 18 510 feet

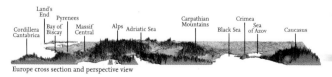

Europe cross section and perspective view

Cordillera
Cantabrica
Land's
End
Bay of
Biscay
Pyrenees
Massif
Central
Alps
Adriatic Sea
Carpathian
Mountains
Black Sea
Crimea
Sea
of Azov
Caucasus

HIGHEST MOUNTAINS	metres	feet	Map pages
El'brus, Russia	5 642	18 510	87 D4
Gora Dykh-Tau, Russia	5 204	17 073	—
Shkhara, Georgia/Russia	5 201	17 063	—
Kazbek, Georgia/Russia	5 047	16 558	76 A2
Mont Blanc, France/Italy	4 810	15 781	105 D2
Dufourspitze, Italy/Switzerland	4 634	15 203	—

LARGEST ISLANDS	sq km	sq miles	Map pages
Great Britain	218 476	84 354	95 C3
Iceland	102 820	39 699	92 A3
Ireland	83 045	32 064	97 C2
Ostrov Severnyy (part of Novaya Zemlya)	47 079	18 177	86 E1
Spitsbergen	37 814	14 600	82 C1

LONGEST RIVER AND
LARGEST DRAINAGE BASIN
Volga
3 688 km / 2 292 miles
1 380 000 sq km / 533 000 sq miles

LONGEST RIVERS	km	miles	Map pages
Volga	3 688	2 292	89 F2
Danube	2 850	1 771	110 A1
Dnieper	2 285	1 420	91 C2
Kama	2 028	1 260	86 E3
Don	1 931	1 200	89 E3
Pechora	1 802	1 120	86 E2

LARGEST LAKE AND LOWEST POINT
Caspian Sea
371 000 sq km / 143 243 sq miles
28m / 92 feet below sea level

LARGEST LAKES	sq km	sq miles	Map pages
Caspian Sea	371 000	143 243	81 C1
Lake Ladoga (Ladozhskoye Ozero)	18 390	7 100	86 C2
Lake Onega (Onezhskoye Ozero)	9 600	3 707	86 C2
Vänern	5 585	2 156	93 F4
Rybinskoye Vodokhranilishche	5 180	2 000	89 E2

Total Land Area 30 343 578 sq km / 11 715 655 sq miles

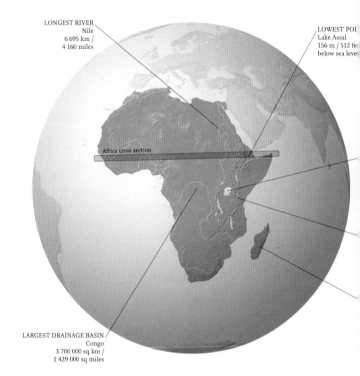

LONGEST RIVER
Nile
6 695 km /
4 160 miles

Africa cross section

LOWEST POI
Lake Assal
156 m / 512 fe
below sea leve

LARGEST DRAINAGE BASIN
Congo
3 700 000 sq km /
1 429 000 sq miles

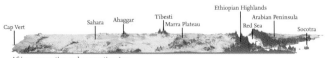

Cap Vert   Sahara   Ahaggar   Tibesti   Marra Plateau   Ethiopian Highlands   Arabian Peninsula   Red Sea   Socotra

Africa cross section and perspective view

HIGHEST MOUNTAINS	metres	feet	Map page
Kilimanjaro, Tanzania	5 892	19 330	119 D3
Mt Kenya (Kirinyaga), Kenya	5 199	17 057	119 D3
Mount Stanley, Democratic Republic of the Congo/Uganda	5 109	16 762	119 C2
Meru, Tanzania	4 565	14 977	119 D3
Ras Dejen, Ethiopia	4 533	14 872	117 B3
Mt Karisimbi, Rwanda	4 510	14 796	—

LARGEST ISLANDS	sq km	sq miles	Map page
Madagascar	587 040	226 656	121 D3

LARGEST LAKE
Lake Victoria
68 870 sq km /
26 591 sq miles

LONGEST RIVERS	km	miles	Map page
Nile	6 695	4 160	116 B1
Congo	4 667	2 900	118 B3
Niger	4 184	2 600	115 C4
Zambezi	2 736	1 700	120 C2
Wabē Shebelē Wenz	2 490	1 547	117 C4
Ubangi	2 250	1 398	118 B3

HIGHEST MOUNTAIN
Kilimanjaro
5 892 m / 19 330 feet

LARGEST LAKES	sq km	sq miles	Map page
Lake Victoria	68 870	26 591	52 B2
Lake Tanganyika	32 600	12 587	119 C3
Lake Nyasa (Lake Malawi)	29 500	11 390	121 C1
Lake Volta	8 482	3 275	114 C4
Lake Turkana	6 500	2 510	119 D2
Lake Albert	5 600	2 162	119 D2

LARGEST ISLAND
Madagascar
587 040 sq km /
226 656 sq miles

Total Land Area 24 680 331 sq km / 9 529 076 sq miles
(including Hawaiian Islands)

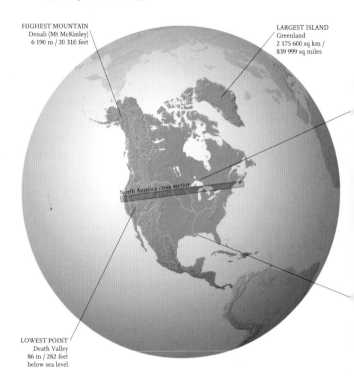

HIGHEST MOUNTAIN
Denali (Mt McKinley)
6 190 m / 20 310 feet

LARGEST ISLAND
Greenland
2 175 600 sq km /
839 999 sq miles

North America cross section

LOWEST POINT
Death Valley
86 m / 282 feet
below sea level

Coast Ranges

Rocky Mountains

Great Plains

Lake Michigan

Lake Huron

Lake Erie

Chesapeake
Bay

Appalachian
Mountains

Long
Island

Cape
Cod

Nova
Scotia

North America cross section and perspective view

HIGHEST MOUNTAINS	metres	feet	Map page
Denali (Mt McKinley), USA	6 190	20 310	124 F2
Mt Logan, Canada	5 959	19 550	126 B2
Pico de Orizaba, Mexico	5 610	18 405	145 C3
Mt St Elias, USA	5 489	18 008	126 B2
Volcán Popocatépetl, Mexico	5 452	17 887	145 C3
Mt Foraker, USA	5 303	17 398	—

LARGEST LAKE
Lake Superior
82 100 sq km /
31 699 sq miles

LARGEST ISLANDS	sq km	sq miles	Map page
Greenland	2 175 600	839 999	127 I2
Baffin Island	507 451	195 927	127 G2
Victoria Island	217 291	83 896	126 D2
Ellesmere Island	196 236	75 767	127 F1
Cuba	110 860	42 803	146 B2
Newfoundland	108 860	42 031	131 E2
Hispaniola	76 192	29 418	147 C2

LONGEST RIVERS	km	miles	Map page
Mississippi-Missouri	5 969	3 709	133 D3
Mackenzie-Peace-Finlay	4 241	2 635	126 C2
Missouri	4 086	2 539	137 E3
Mississippi	3 765	2 340	142 C3
Yukon	3 185	1 979	126 A2
St Lawrence	3 058	1 900	131 D2

LONGEST RIVER AND
LARGEST DRAINAGE BASIN
Mississippi-Missouri
5 969 km / 3 709 miles
3 250 000 sq km / 1 255 000
sq miles

LARGEST LAKES	sq km	sq miles	Map page
Lake Superior	82 100	31 699	140 B1
Lake Huron	59 600	23 012	140 C2
Lake Michigan	57 800	22 317	140 B2
Great Bear Lake	31 328	12 096	126 C2
Great Slave Lake	28 568	11 030	128 C1
Lake Erie	25 700	9 923	140 C2
Lake Winnipeg	24 387	9 416	129 E2
Lake Ontario	18 960	7 320	141 D2

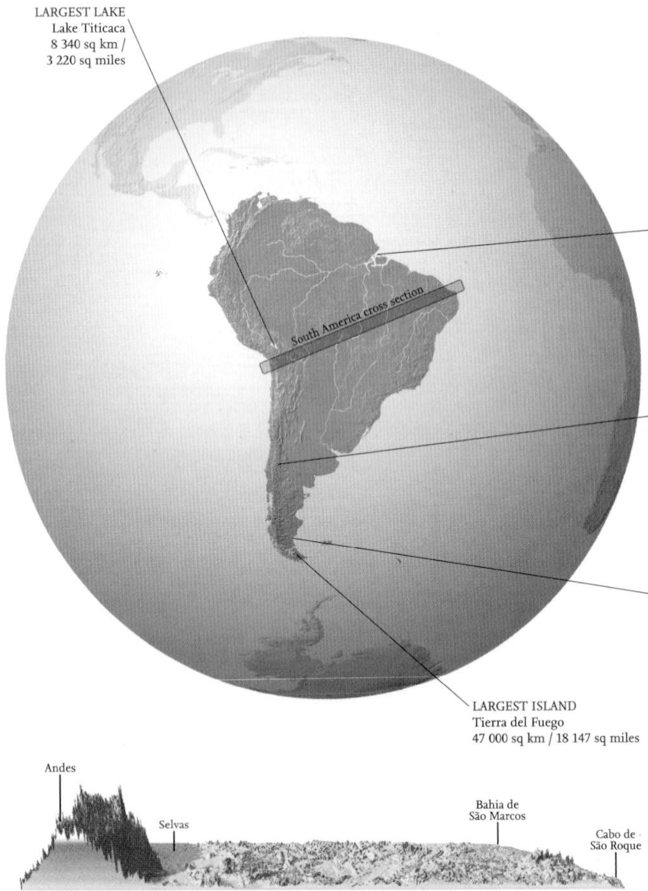

Total Land Area 17 815 420 sq km / 6 878 534 sq miles

LARGEST LAKE
Lake Titicaca
8 340 sq km /
3 220 sq miles

South America cross section

LARGEST ISLAND
Tierra del Fuego
47 000 sq km / 18 147 sq miles

Andes

Selvas

Bahia de
São Marcos

Cabo de
São Roque

South America cross section and perspective view

HIGHEST MOUNTAINS	metres	feet	Map page
Cerro Aconcagua, Argentina	6 961	22 838	153 B4
Cerro Ojos del Salado, Argentina/Chile	6 893	22 615	152 B3
Cerro Bonete, Argentina	6 872	22 546	—
Cerro Pissis, Argentina	6 858	22 500	—
Cerro Tupungato, Argentina/Chile	6 800	22 309	—
Cerro Mercedario, Argentina	6 770	22 211	—

LARGEST ISLANDS	sq km	sq miles	Map page
Tierra del Fuego	47 000	18 147	153 B6
Isla Grande de Chiloé	8 394	3 241	153 A5
East Falkland	6 760	2 610	153 C6
West Falkland	5 413	2 090	153 B6

LONGEST RIVER AND
LARGEST DRAINAGE BASIN
Amazon
6 516 km / 4 049 miles
7 050 000 sq km / 2 722 000 sq miles

LONGEST RIVERS	km	miles	Map page
Amazon (Amazonas)	6 516	4 049	150 C1
Río de la Plata-Paraná	4 500	2 796	153 C4
Purus	3 218	2 000	150 B2
Madeira	3 200	1 988	150 C2
São Francisco	2 900	1 802	151 E3
Tocantins	2 750	1 709	151 D2

HIGHEST MOUNTAIN
Cerro Aconcagua
6 961 m / 22 838 feet

LARGEST LAKES	sq km	sq miles	Map page
Lake Titicaca	8 340	3 220	152 B2

LOWEST POINT
Laguna del Carbón
105 m / 344 feet below sea level

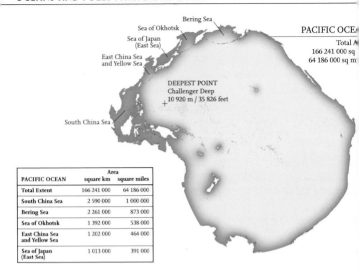

PACIFIC OCE

Total A
166 241 000 sq
64 186 000 sq m

Bering Sea

Sea of Okhotsk

Sea of Japan
(East Sea)

East China Sea
and Yellow Sea

DEEPEST POINT
Challenger Deep
10 920 m / 35 826 feet

South China Sea

PACIFIC OCEAN	Area	
	square km	square miles
Total Extent	166 241 000	64 186 000
South China Sea	2 590 000	1 000 000
Bering Sea	2 261 000	873 000
Sea of Okhotsk	1 392 000	538 000
East China Sea and Yellow Sea	1 202 000	464 000
Sea of Japan (East Sea)	1 013 000	391 000

ANTARCTICA

Total Land Area 12 093 000 sq km /
4 669 107 sq miles (excluding ice shelves)

HIGHEST MOUNTAIN
Mt Vinson
4 897 m / 16 066 feet

HIGHEST MOUNTAINS	Height	
	metres	feet
Mt Vinson	4 897	16 066
Mt Tyree	4 852	15 918
Mt Kirkpatrick	4 528	14 855
Mt Markham	4 351	14 275
Mt Sidley	4 285	14 058
Mt Minto	4 165	13 665

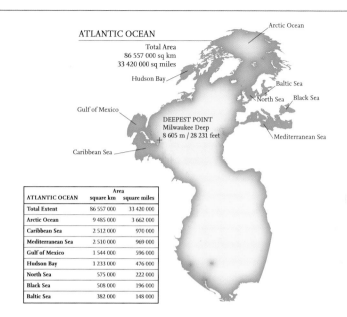

ATLANTIC OCEAN

Total Area
86 557 000 sq km
33 420 000 sq miles

Arctic Ocean

Hudson Bay

Baltic Sea

North Sea   Black Sea

Gulf of Mexico

DEEPEST POINT
Milwaukee Deep
8 605 m / 28 231 feet

Mediterranean Sea

Caribbean Sea

ATLANTIC OCEAN	Area	
	square km	square miles
Total Extent	86 557 000	33 420 000
Arctic Ocean	9 485 000	3 662 000
Caribbean Sea	2 512 000	970 000
Mediterranean Sea	2 510 000	969 000
Gulf of Mexico	1 544 000	596 000
Hudson Bay	1 233 000	476 000
North Sea	575 000	222 000
Black Sea	508 000	196 000
Baltic Sea	382 000	148 000

The Gulf

Red Sea   Bay of Bengal

DEEPEST POINT
Java Trench
7 125 m / 23 376 feet

INDIAN OCEAN	Area	
	square km	square miles
Total Extent	73 427 000	28 350 000
Bay of Bengal	2 172 000	839 000
Red Sea	453 000	175 000
The Gulf	238 000	92 000

INDIAN OCEAN

Total Area
73 427 000 sq km
28 350 000 sq miles

CLIMATE

MAJOR CLIMATIC REGIONS AND SUB-TYPES
Köppen classification system
Winkel Tripel Projection
scale 1:200 000 000

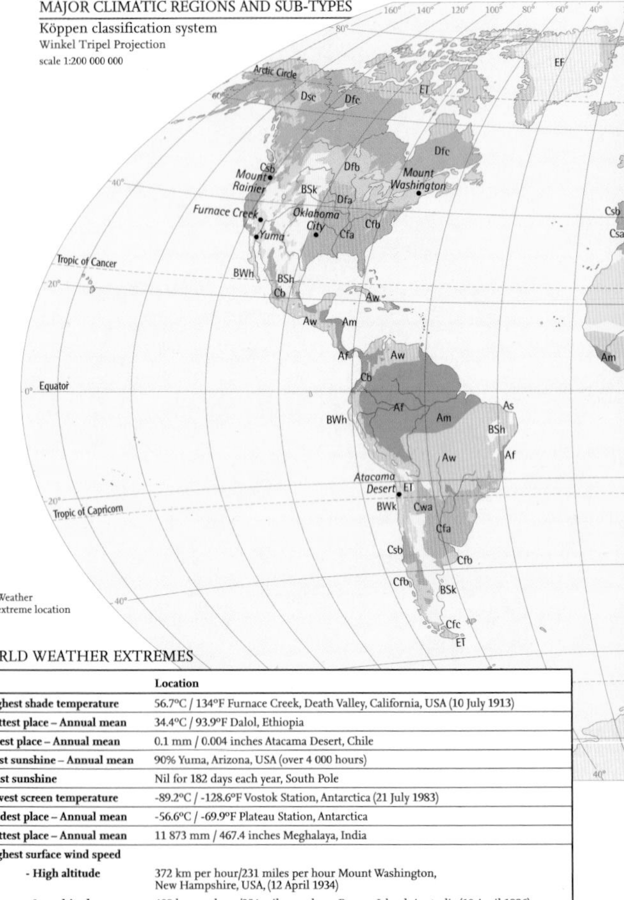

• Weather
  extreme location

WORLD WEATHER EXTREMES

	Location
Highest shade temperature	56.7°C / 134°F Furnace Creek, Death Valley, California, USA (10 July 1913)
Hottest place – Annual mean	34.4°C / 93.9°F Dalol, Ethiopia
Driest place – Annual mean	0.1 mm / 0.004 inches Atacama Desert, Chile
Most sunshine – Annual mean	90% Yuma, Arizona, USA (over 4 000 hours)
Least sunshine	Nil for 182 days each year, South Pole
Lowest screen temperature	-89.2°C / -128.6°F Vostok Station, Antarctica (21 July 1983)
Coldest place – Annual mean	-56.6°C / -69.9°F Plateau Station, Antarctica
Wettest place – Annual mean	11 873 mm / 467.4 inches Meghalaya, India
Highest surface wind speed	
- High altitude	372 km per hour/231 miles per hour Mount Washington, New Hampshire, USA, (12 April 1934)
- Low altitude	408 km per hour/254 miles per hour Barrow Island, Australia (10 April 1996)
- Tornado	512 km per hour / 318 miles per hour in a tornado, Oklahoma City, Oklahoma, USA (3 May 1999)
Greatest snowfall	31 102 mm / 1 224.5 inches Mount Rainier, Washington, USA (19 February 1971 – 18 February 1972)

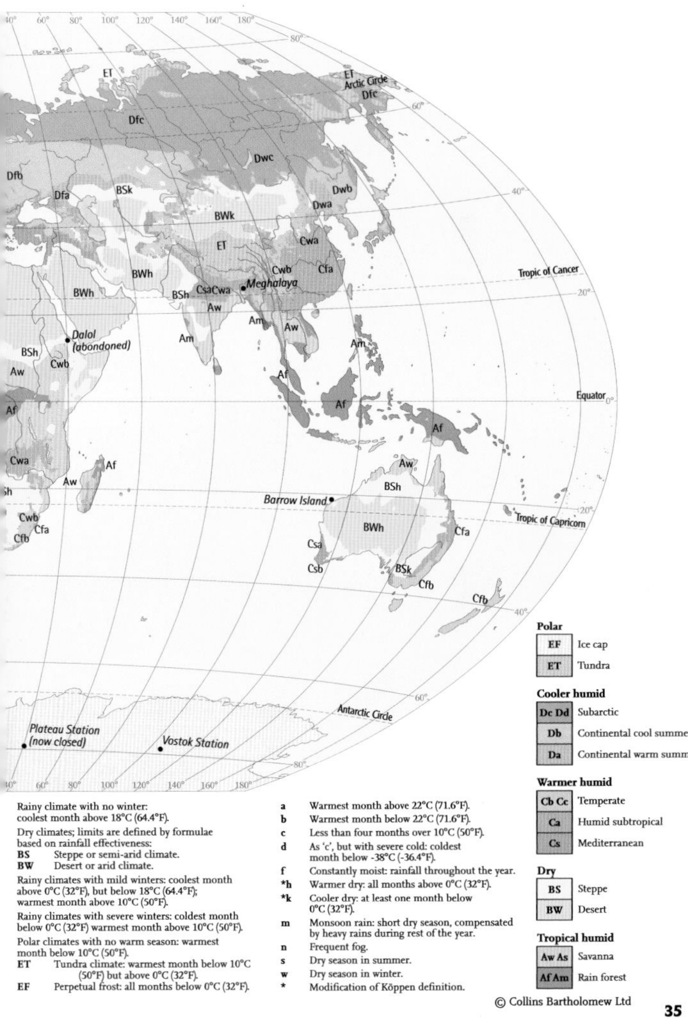

Rainy climate with no winter:
coolest month above 18°C (64.4°F).

Dry climates; limits are defined by formulae
based on rainfall effectiveness:
BS   Steppe or semi-arid climate.
BW   Desert or arid climate.

Rainy climates with mild winters: coolest month
above 0°C (32°F), but below 18°C (64.4°F);
warmest month above 10°C (50°F).

Rainy climates with severe winters: coldest month
below 0°C (32°F) warmest month above 10°C (50°F).

Polar climates with no warm season: warmest
month below 10°C (50°F).
ET   Tundra climate: warmest month below 10°C
       (50°F) but above 0°C (32°F).
EF   Perpetual frost: all months below 0°C (32°F).

a   Warmest month above 22°C (71.6°F).
b   Warmest month below 22°C (71.6°F).
c   Less than four months over 10°C (50°F).
d   As 'c', but with severe cold: coldest
      month below -38°C (-36.4°F).
f   Constantly moist: rainfall throughout the year.
*h   Warmer dry: all months above 0°C (32°F).
*k   Cooler dry: at least one month below
      0°C (32°F).
m   Monsoon rain: short dry season, compensated
      by heavy rains during rest of the year.
n   Frequent fog.
s   Dry season in summer.
w   Dry season in winter.
*   Modification of Köppen definition.

Polar

EF	Ice cap
ET	Tundra

Cooler humid

Dc Dd	Subarctic
Db	Continental cool summer
Da	Continental warm summer

Warmer humid

Cb Cc	Temperate
Ca	Humid subtropical
Cs	Mediterranean

Dry

BS	Steppe
BW	Desert

Tropical humid

Aw As	Savanna
Af Am	Rain forest

© Collins Bartholomew Ltd

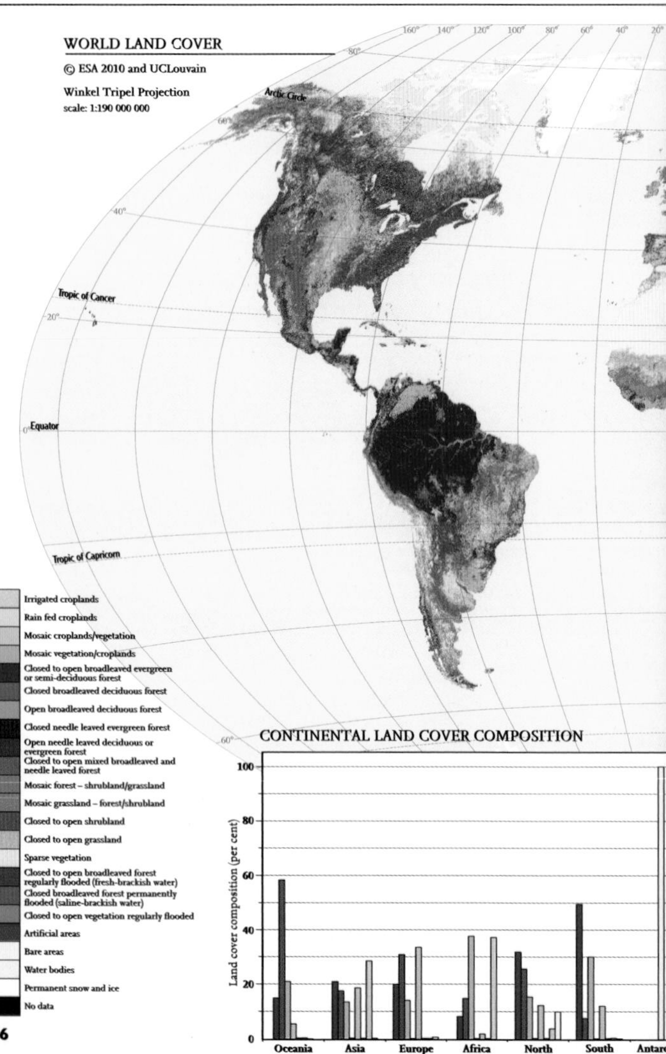

WORLD LAND COVER

© ESA 2010 and UCLouvain

Winkel Tripel Projection
scale: 1:190 000 000

Arctic Circle

Tropic of Cancer

Equator

Tropic of Capricorn

Irrigated croplands
Rain fed croplands
Mosaic croplands/vegetation
Mosaic vegetation/croplands
Closed to open broadleaved evergreen or semi-deciduous forest
Closed broadleaved deciduous forest
Open broadleaved deciduous forest
Closed needle leaved evergreen forest
Open needle leaved deciduous or evergreen forest
Closed to open mixed broadleaved and needle leaved forest
Mosaic forest – shrubland/grassland
Mosaic grassland – forest/shrubland
Closed to open shrubland
Closed to open grassland
Sparse vegetation
Closed to open broadleaved forest regularly flooded (fresh-brackish water)
Closed broadleaved forest permanently flooded (saline-brackish water)
Closed to open vegetation regularly flooded
Artificial areas
Bare areas
Water bodies
Permanent snow and ice
No data

CONTINENTAL LAND COVER COMPOSITION

Land cover composition (per cent)

100

80

60

40

20

0

Oceania | Asia | Europe | Africa | North America | South America | Antarc

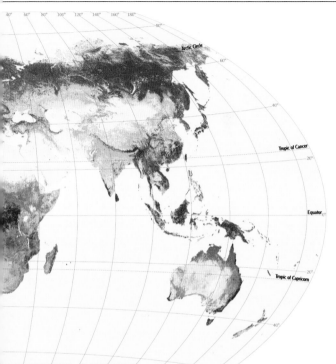

40° 60° 80° 100° 120° 140° 160° 180°

Arctic Circle

Tropic of Cancer

Equator

Tropic of Capricorn

Antarctic Circle

...ND COVER GRAPHS - CLASSIFICATION

Class description	Map classes
Forest/Woodland	Evergreen needleleaf forest
	Evergreen broadleaf forest
	Deciduous needleleaf forest
	Deciduous broadleaf forest
	Mixed forest
Shrubland	Closed shrublands
	Open shrublands
Grass/Savanna	Woody savannas
	Savannas
	Grasslands
Wetland	Permanent wetlands
Crops/Mosaic	Croplands
	Cropland/Natural vegetation mosaic
Urban	Urban and built-up
Snow/Ice	Snow and Ice
Barren	Barren or sparsely vegetated

GLOBAL LAND COVER COMPOSITION

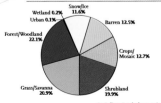

Wetland 0.2%
Urban 0.1%
Snow/Ice 11.6%
Barren 12.5%
Forest/Woodland 22.1%
Crops/Mosaic 12.7%
Grass/Savanna 20.9%
Shrubland 19.9%

© Collins Bartholomew Ltd

37

WORLD POPULATION DISTRIBUTION

Population Density
Winkel Tripel Projection
scale 1:190 000 000

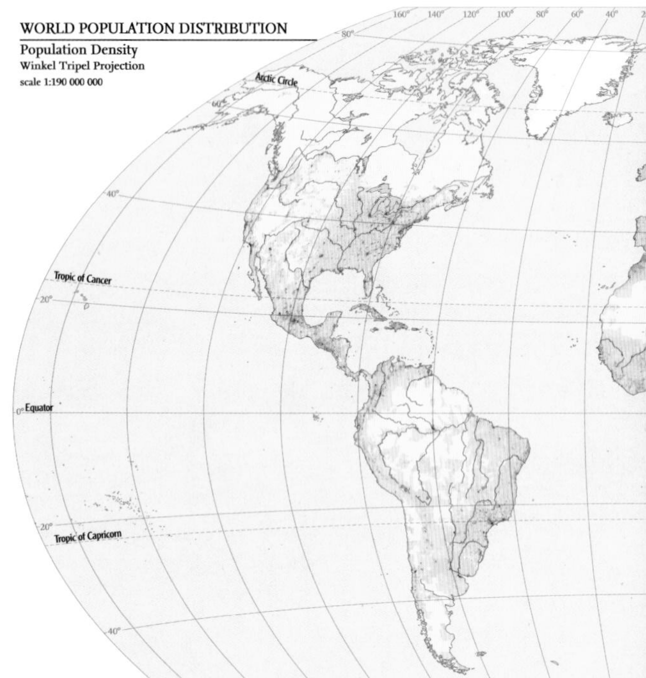

KEY POPULATION STATISTICS FOR MAJOR REGIONS

	Population (millions) 2015	Growth (%) 2010–2015	Infant mortality rate 2010–2015	Total fertility rate 2010–2015	Life expectancy at birth (years) 2010–2015
World	7 349	1.2	36	2.5	70
More developed regions[1]	1 251	0.3	5	1.7	78
Less developed regions[2]	6 098	1.4	39	2.7	69
Africa	1 186	2.6	59	4.7	60
Asia (excluding Russia)	4 393	1	31	2.2	72
Europe (including Russia)	738	0.1	5	1.6	77
Latin America and the Caribbean[3]	634	1.1	20	2.2	75
Northern America[4]	358	0.8	6	1.9	79
Oceania	39	1.5	20	2.4	77

1. Europe, North America, Australia, New Zealand and Japan.
2. Africa, Asia (except Japan), Latin America and the Caribbean, Melanesia, Micronesia and Polynesia.
3. South America, Central America (incl. Mexico) and all Caribbean Islands.
4. Bermuda, Canada, Greenland, Saint Pierre and Miquelon, and United States.

Growth (%) is the average annual rate of population change.
Infant mortality rate is average annual deaths per 1 000 births.
Total fertility rate is births per woman.

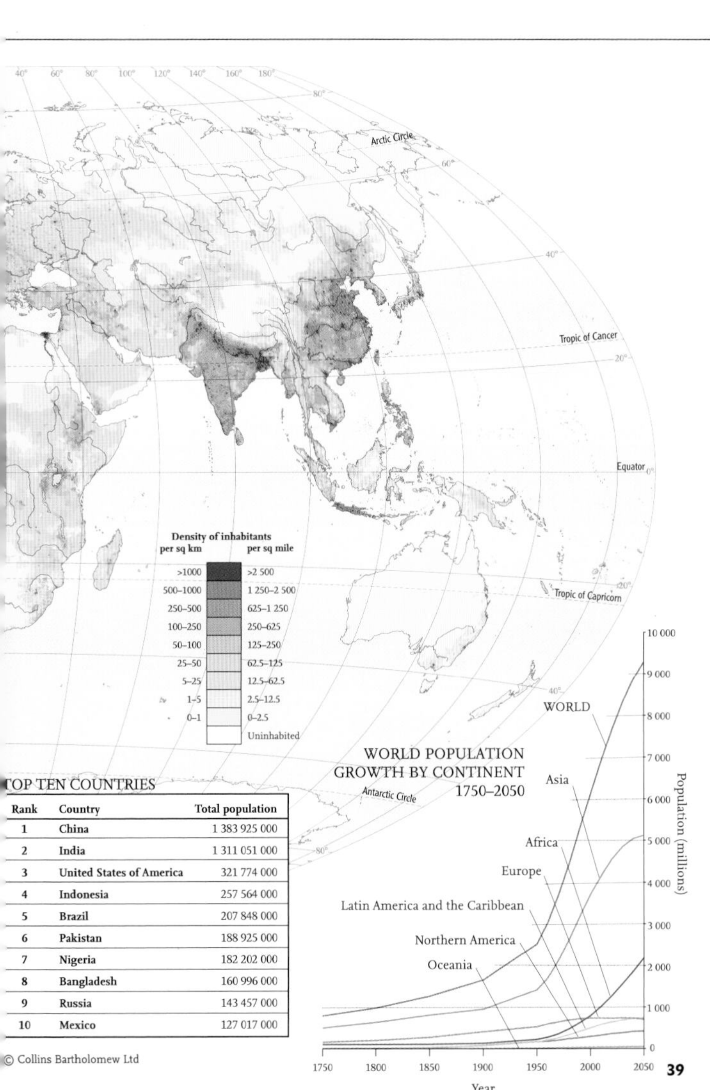

Density of inhabitants

per sq km	per sq mile
>1000	>2 500
500–1000	1 250–2 500
250–500	625–1 250
100–250	250–625
50–100	125–250
25–50	62.5–125
5–25	12.5–62.5
1–5	2.5–12.5
0–1	0–2.5
	Uninhabited

TOP TEN COUNTRIES

Rank	Country	Total population
1	China	1 383 925 000
2	India	1 311 051 000
3	United States of America	321 774 000
4	Indonesia	257 564 000
5	Brazil	207 848 000
6	Pakistan	188 925 000
7	Nigeria	182 202 000
8	Bangladesh	160 996 000
9	Russia	143 457 000
10	Mexico	127 017 000

© Collins Bartholomew Ltd

WORLD POPULATION
GROWTH BY CONTINENT
1750–2050

WORLD

Asia

Africa

Europe

Latin America and the Caribbean

Northern America

Oceania

Population (millions)

Year

THE WORLD'S MAJOR CITIES

Urban agglomerations with over
1 million inhabitants.
Winkel Tripel Projection
scale 1:190 000 000

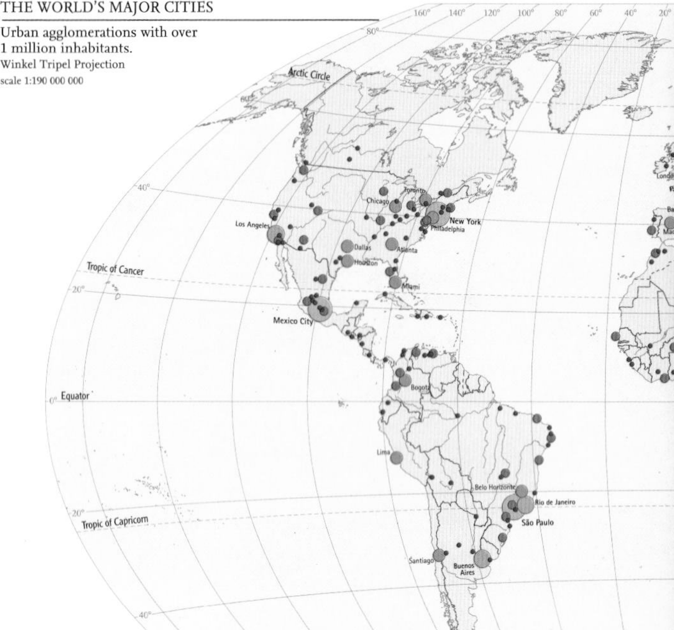

LEVEL OF URBANIZATION BY MAJOR REGION 1970–2030
Urban population as a percentage of total population

	1970	2010	2030
World	36.6	51.6	59.9
More developed regions[1]	66.6	77.5	82.1
Less developed regions[2]	25.3	46.0	55.8
Africa	23.5	39.2	47.7
Asia	23.7	44.4	55.5
Europe[3]	62.8	72.7	77.4
Latin America and the Caribbean[4]	57.1	78.8	83.4
Northern America[5]	73.8	82.0	85.8
Oceania	71.2	70.7	71.4

1. More developed regions comprise Europe, North
America, Australia/New Zealand and Japan.
2. Less developed regions comprise all regions of
Africa, Asia (except Japan), Latin America and the
Caribbean plus Melanesia, Micronesia and Poly
3. Includes Russia (Russian Federation).
4. South America, Central America (inc. Mexico) a
Caribbean Islands.
5. Including Bermuda, Greenland, and Saint Pierr
and Miquelon.

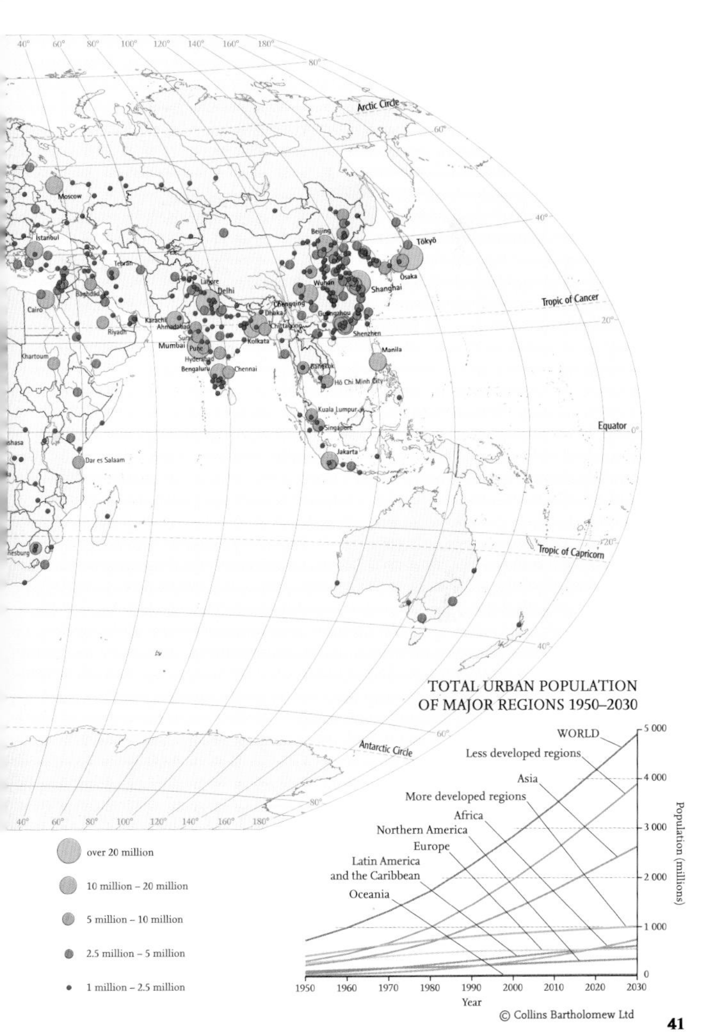

TOTAL URBAN POPULATION OF MAJOR REGIONS 1950–2030

WORLD
Less developed regions
More developed regions
Asia
Africa
Northern America
Europe
Latin America and the Caribbean
Oceania

Population (millions)

5 000
4 000
3 000
2 000
1 000
0

1950 1960 1970 1980 1990 2000 2010 2020 2030
Year

© Collins Bartholomew Ltd

over 20 million

10 million – 20 million

5 million – 10 million

2.5 million – 5 million

1 million – 2.5 million

SYMBOLS

Map symbols used on the map pages are explained here. The depiction of relief follows the tradition of layer-colouring, with colours depicting altitude bands. Ocean pages have a different contour interval. Settlements are classified in terms of both population and administrative significance. The abbreviations listed are those used in place names on the map pages and within the index.

LAND AND WATER FEATURES

	Lake	—	River
	Impermanent lake	– – –	Impermanent rive
	Salt lake or lagoon		Ice cap / Glacier
	Impermanent salt lake	⤙123	Pass height in metres
	Dry salt lake or salt pan	∴	Site of special int
		ᴨᴨᴨᴨ	Wall

RELIEF

Contour intervals used in layer-colouring for land height and sea depth

METRES FEET		Ocean pages METRES FEET
5000 16404		0 0
3000 9843		200 656
2000 6562		2000 6562
1000 3281		3000 9843
500 1640		4000 13124
200 656		5000 16404
0 LAND B.S.L.		6000 19686
200 656		7000 22967
4000 13124		9000 29529
6000 19686		123 Ocean deep In metres.

1234 Summit
△ Height in metres

1234 Volcano
▲ Height in metres

BOUNDARIES

▄▄▄▄	International boundary
·▪️◆	Disputed international boundary or alignment unconfirmed
⟋▪️	Undefined international boundary in the sea. All land within this boundary is part of state or territory named.
▄▄ ▄▄	Disputed territory boundary
——	Administrative boundary Shown for selected countries only.
✳✳✳✳	Ceasefire line or other boundary described on the map

TRANSPORT

═══	Motorway
——	Main road
– – –	Track
——	Main railway
⊥⊥⊥⊥	Canal
✈	Main airport

CITIES AND TOWNS

Built-up area
SCALE 1:4 000 000 only

Population	National Capital	Administrative Capital Shown for selected countries only	Other City or Town
over 10 million	**BEIJING** ▣	**São Paulo** ◉	**New York** ◉
5 to 10 million	**MADRID** ▣	**Toronto** ◉	**Philadelphia** ◉
1 to 5 million	**KUWAIT** ▢	**Sydney** ○	**Seattle** ○
500 000 to 1 million	**BANGUI** ▫	**Winnipeg** ○	**Warangal** ○
100 000 to 500 000	WELLINGTON ▫	Edinburgh ○	Apucarana ○
50 000 to 100 000	PORT OF SPAIN ▫	Bismarck ○	Invercargill ○
under 50 000	MALABO ▫	Charlottetown ○	Ceres ○

ities and towns are explained separately

	Physical features	
ountry	**FRANCE**	
		Island	*Gran Canaria*
verseas Territory/Dependency	**Guadeloupe**	
		Lake	*Lake Erie*
isputed Territory	WESTERN SAHARA	
		Mountain	*Mt Blanc*
dministrative name shown for selected countries only.	**SCOTLAND**	
rea name	PATAGONIA	River	*Thames*
		Region	*LAPPLAND*
istorical area	Kashmir	

CONTINENTAL MAPS

BOUNDARIES

——— International boundary

- - - - - Disputed international boundary

•••••• Ceasefire line

CITIES AND TOWNS

National capital	Other city or town
Kuwait □	Seattle ○

ABBREVIATIONS

Arch.	Archipelago			**Mts**	Mountains Monts	French	hills, mountains
B.	Bay			**N.**	North, Northern		
	Bahia, Baía	Portuguese	bay	**O.**	Ostrov	Russian	island
	Bahía	Spanish	bay	**Pt**	Point		
	Baie	French	bay	**Pta**	Punta	Italian, Spanish	cape, point
C.	Cape			**R.**	River		
	Cabo	Portuguese, Spanish	cape, headland		Rio	Portuguese	river
	Cap	French	cape, headland		Río	Spanish	river
Co	Cerro	Spanish	hill, peak, summit		Rivière	French	river
E.	East, Eastern			**Ra.**	Range		
Est.	Estrecho	Spanish	strait	**S.**	South, Southern		
Gt	Great				Salar, Salina, Salinas	Spanish	saltpan, saltpans
I.	Island, Isle			**Sa**	Serra	Portuguese	mountain range
	Ilha	Portuguese	island		Sierra	Spanish	mountain range
	Islas	Spanish	island	**Sd**	Sound		
Is	Islands, Isles			**S.E.**	Southeast, Southeastern		
	Islas	Spanish	islands	**St**	Saint		
Khr.	Khrebet	Russian	mountain range		Sankt	German	
L.	Lake				Sint	Dutch	saint
	Loch	(Scotland)	lake	**Sta**	Santa	Italian, Portuguese, Spanish	saint
	Lough	(Ireland)	lake				
	Lac	French	lake	**Ste**	Sainte	French	saint
	Lago	Portuguese, Spanish	lake	**Str.**	Strait		
M.	Mys	Russian	cape, point	**W.**	West, Western		
Mt	Mount				Wadi, Wādī	Arabic	watercourse
	Mont	French	hill, mountain				
Mt.	Mountain						

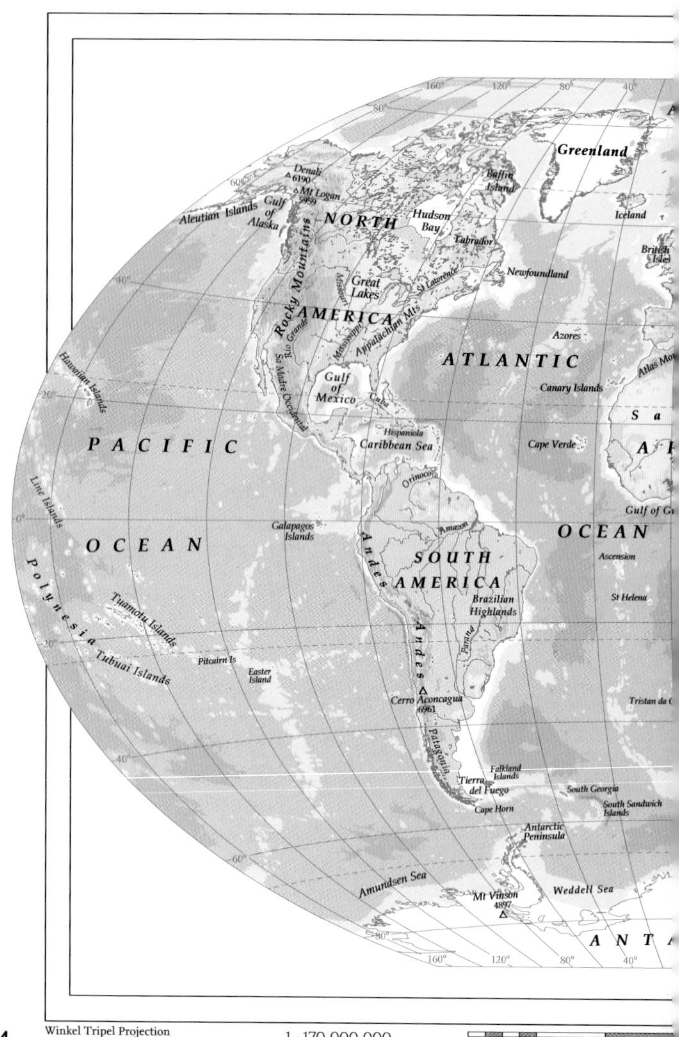

Winkel Tripel Projection

1 : 170 000 000

MILES 0   1000   2000   30

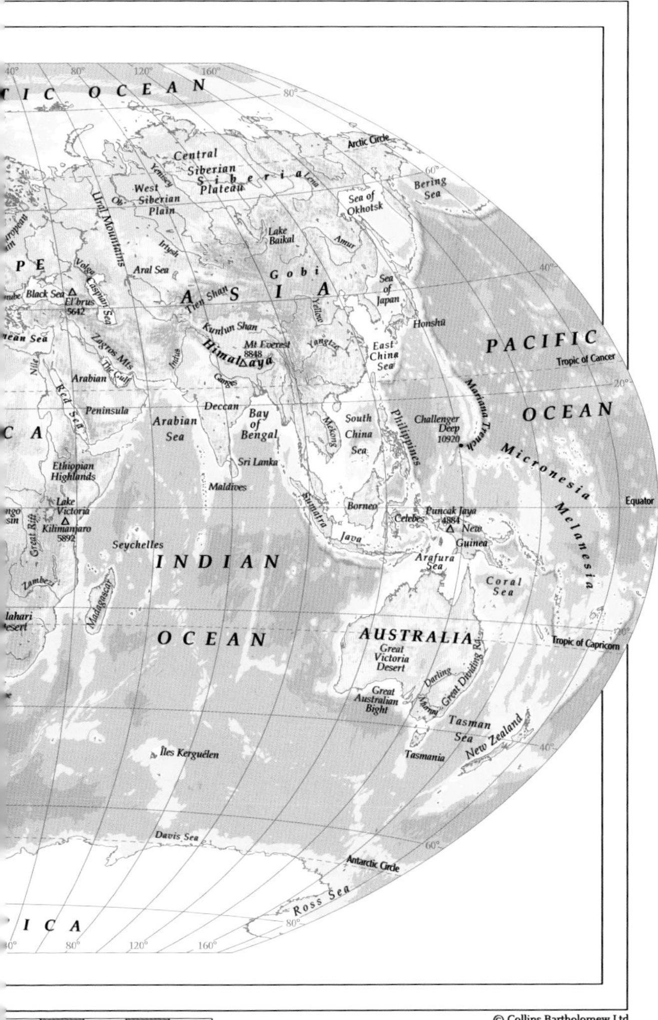

ARCTIC OCEAN

80°

Arctic Circle

Central
Siberian
West Siberia
Siberian Plateau
Plain
Ural Mountains
Sea of
Ob
Okhotsk
Lena
Bering
Sea

40°

Aral Sea
A S I A
Gobi
Sea
of
Japan

Lake Baikal

Amur

PE

Black Sea
Volga
Caspian Sea
El'brus
5642
Tien Shan
Kunlun Shan
Honshū
Mt Everest
8848
East
China
Sea
PACIFIC

Zagros Mts
The Gulf
Himalaya
Yangtze

Tropic of Cancer

ean Sea

Nile
Arabian
Peninsula
Deccan
Ganges
Mekong
South
China
Sea
OCEAN

C A
Arabian
Sea
Bay
of
Bengal
Philippines
Mariana Trench
Challenger
Deep
10920

Red Sea

Ethiopian
Highlands
Sri Lanka
Micronesia

Maldives
Sumatra
Borneo
Celebes
Puncak Jaya
4864
New
Guinea

Equator

ngo
sin
Lake
Victoria
Kilimanjaro
5892
Java

Great Rift
Seychelles
I N D I A N
Arafura
Sea

Zambezi
Coral
Sea

lahari
Desert
Madagascar
O C E A N
AUSTRALIA
Tropic of Capricorn

Great
Victoria
Desert
Great Dividing Range

Darling
Murray
Great
Australian
Bight
Tasman
Sea
New Zealand

Îles Kerguélen

Tasmania

40°

Davis Sea

Antarctic Circle

60°

I C A
Ross Sea

80°

40°   80°   120°   160°

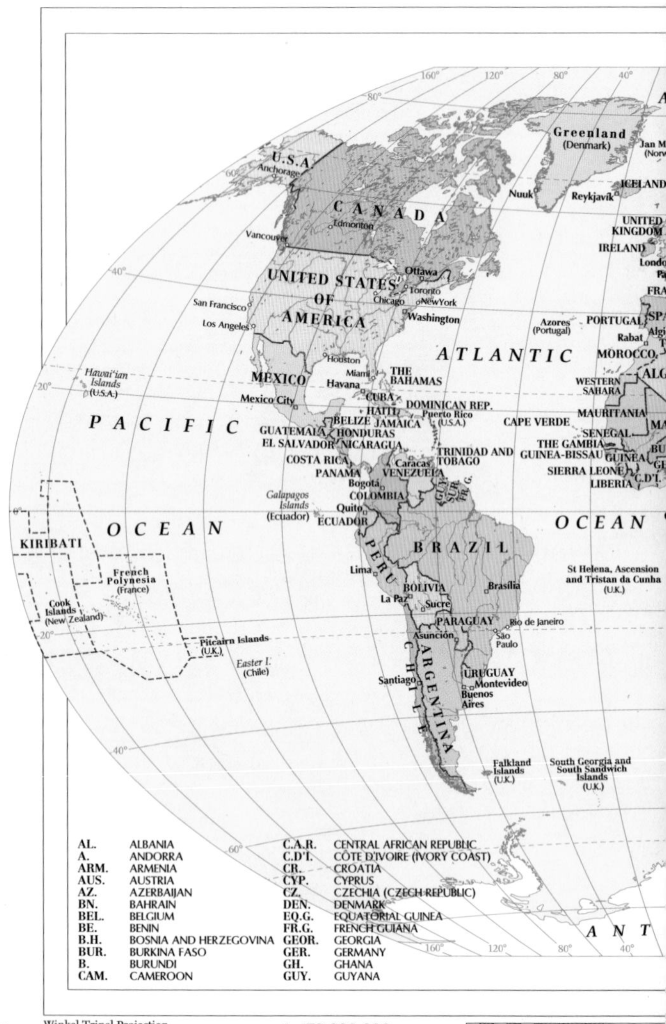

Greenland
(Denmark)

Jan Ma
(Norw

ICELAND

Reykjavík

UNITED
KINGDOM

IRELAND

Londo
Pa

FRA

SP.

Alg

MOROCCO

WESTERN
SAHARA

ALG

MAURITANIA

MA

CAPE VERDE

SENEGAL

THE GAMBIA

GUINEA-BISSAU

BU

GUINEA

GU

SIERRA LEONE

D'I

LIBERIA

U.S.A.

Anchorage

CANADA

Edmonton

Vancouver

UNITED STATES
OF
AMERICA

Ottawa

Toronto

Chicago

New York

Washington

San Francisco

Los Angeles

Houston

MEXICO

Mexico City

Havana

Miami

THE
BAHAMAS

CUBA

DOMINICAN REP.

HAITI

Puerto Rico
(U.S.A.)

BELIZE JAMAICA

GUATEMALA HONDURAS

EL SALVADOR NICARAGUA

COSTA RICA

PANAMA

Caracas

TRINIDAD AND
TOBAGO

VENEZUELA

Bogotá

COLOMBIA

Galapagos
Islands
(Ecuador)

Quito

ECUADOR

GU

PERU

Lima

BRAZIL

Brasília

BOLIVIA

La Paz

Sucre

Rio de Janeiro

São
Paulo

PARAGUAY

Asunción

ARGENTINA

CHILE

URUGUAY

Montevideo

Buenos
Aires

Santiago

St Helena, Ascension
and Tristan da Cunha
(U.K.)

ATLANTIC

OCEAN

Azores
(Portugal)

PORTUGAL

Rabat

PACIFIC

Hawai'ian
Islands
(U.S.A.)

OCEAN

KIRIBATI

French
Polynesia
(France)

Cook
Islands
(New Zealand)

Pitcairn Islands
(U.K.)

Easter I.
(Chile)

OCEAN

Falkland
Islands
(U.K.)

South Georgia and
South Sandwich
Islands
(U.K.)

ANT

AL.	ALBANIA	C.A.R.	CENTRAL AFRICAN REPUBLIC
A.	ANDORRA	C.D'I.	CÔTE D'IVOIRE (IVORY COAST)
ARM.	ARMENIA	CR.	CROATIA
AUS.	AUSTRIA	CYP.	CYPRUS
AZ.	AZERBAIJAN	CZ.	CZECHIA (CZECH REPUBLIC)
BN.	BAHRAIN	DEN.	DENMARK
BEL.	BELGIUM	EQ.G.	EQUATORIAL GUINEA
BE.	BENIN	FR.G.	FRENCH GUIANA
B.H.	BOSNIA AND HERZEGOVINA	GEOR.	GEORGIA
BUR.	BURKINA FASO	GER.	GERMANY
B.	BURUNDI	GH.	GHANA
CAM.	CAMEROON	GUY.	GUYANA

Winkel Tripel Projection

1 : 170 000 000

MILES 0   1000   2000   3

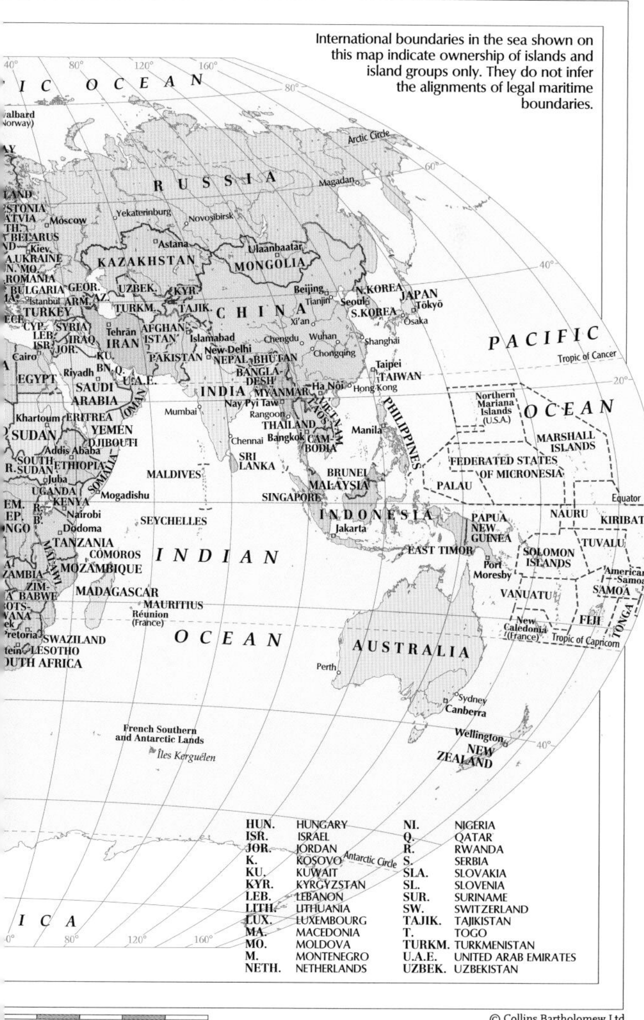

International boundaries in the sea shown on this map indicate ownership of islands and island groups only. They do not infer the alignments of legal maritime boundaries.

HUN.	HUNGARY	NI.	NIGERIA
ISR.	ISRAEL	Q.	QATAR
JOR.	JORDAN	R.	RWANDA
K.	KOSOVO	S.	SERBIA
KU.	KUWAIT	SLA.	SLOVAKIA
KYR.	KYRGYZSTAN	SL.	SLOVENIA
LEB.	LEBANON	SUR.	SURINAME
LITH.	LITHUANIA	SW.	SWITZERLAND
LUX.	LUXEMBOURG	TAJIK.	TAJIKISTAN
MA.	MACEDONIA	T.	TOGO
MO.	MOLDOVA	TURKM.	TURKMENISTAN
M.	MONTENEGRO	U.A.E.	UNITED ARAB EMIRATES
NETH.	NETHERLANDS	UZBEK.	UZBEKISTAN

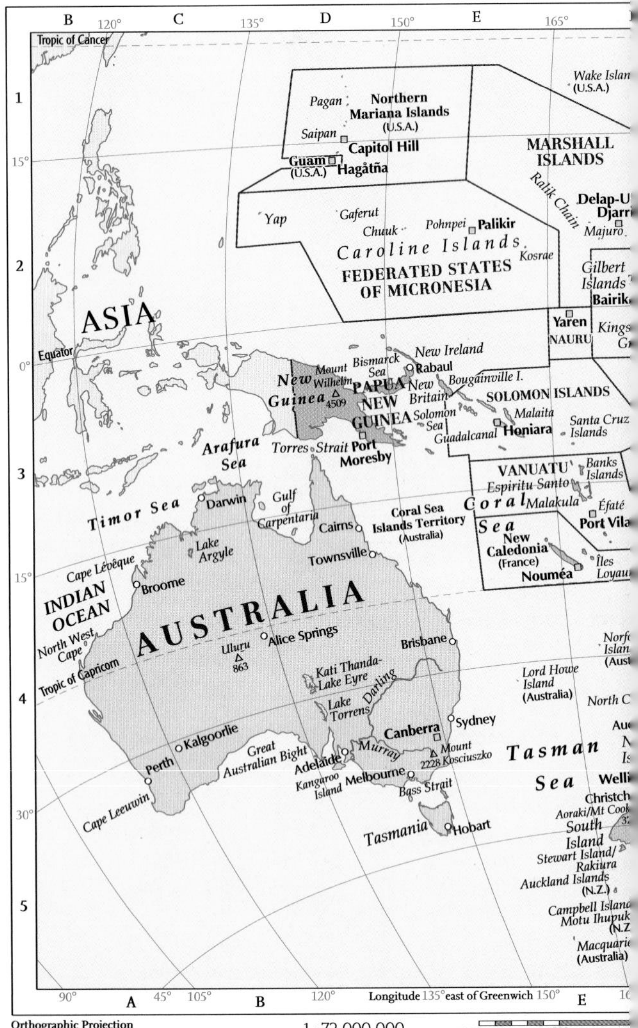

Orthographic Projection

1 : 72 000 000

MILES 0   500

| B | 120° | C | 135° | D | 150° | E | 165° |

Tropic of Cancer

Wake Islan (U.S.A.)

Pagan · **Northern Mariana Islands** (U.S.A.)

Saipan ·

□**Capitol Hill**

□ **Guam** · □**Hagåtña**
(U.S.A.)

MARSHALL ISLANDS

Yap · *Gaferut*

Ralik Chain

Delap-U
Djarr
Majuro ·

Chuuk · *Pohnpei* **Palikir**

Caroline Islands

FEDERATED STATES OF MICRONESIA

Kosrae

Gilbert Islands

Bairik

Yaren
NAURU

Kings G

ASIA

Equator

Bismarck Sea

New Ireland

Mount Wilhelm △ **Rabaul**
4509

New Guinea

PAPUA NEW GUINEA

New Britain

Bougainville I.

SOLOMON ISLANDS

Malaita

Santa Cruz
Islands

Solomon Sea

Guadalcanal **Honiara**

VANUATU *Banks Islands*

Espiritu Santo

Arafura Sea

Torres Strait

Port Moresby

Malakula

△ *Éfaté*

Port Vila

Darwin ○

Gulf of Carpentaria

Cairns ○

Coral Sea Islands Territory
(Australia)

Coral Sea

New Caledonia
(France)

Nouméa

Îles Loyau

Timor Sea

Townsville ○

Cape Lépêque ·

Lake Argyle

INDIAN OCEAN

Broome ○

North West Cape

Tropic of Capricorn

AUSTRALIA

Uluru △ ○ *Alice Springs*
863

Norf Islan (Aust

Lord Howe Island
(Australia)

North C

Brisbane ○

Kati Thanda-
Lake Eyre

Lake Torrens

Darling

○ *Kalgoorlie*

Canberra □ ○ *Sydney*

Murray

△ *Mount*
2228 *Kosciuszko*

Au N Is

Tasman Sea

Perth ○

Great Australian Bight

Adelaide ○

Kangaroo Island

Melbourne ○

Cape Leeuwin

Bass Strait

Well

Christch

Hobart ○

Tasmania

Aoraki/Mt Cook △
5

South Island

Stewart Island/
Rakiura

Auckland Islands
(N.Z.)

Campbell Island
Motu Ihupuk
(N.Z

Macquari
(Australia)

| 90° | A | 45° | 105° | B | 120° | Longitude 135° east of Greenwich 150° | E | 10 |

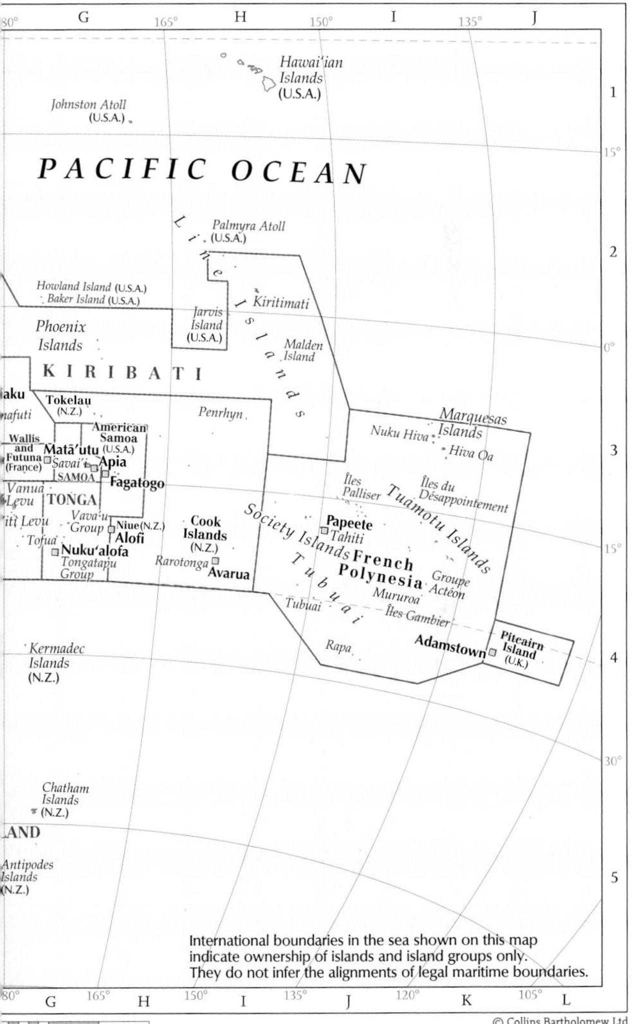

80°

| G | 165° | H | 150° | I | 135° | J |

Hawai'ian Islands (U.S.A.)

1

Johnston Atoll (U.S.A.)

15°

PACIFIC OCEAN

Palmyra Atoll (U.S.A.)

L i n e

2

Howland Island (U.S.A.)
Baker Island (U.S.A.)

Jarvis Island (U.S.A.)

Kiritimati

Phoenix Islands

I s l a n d s

Malden Island

0°

KIRIBATI

iaku
nafuti

Tokelau (N.Z.)

Penrhyn

Marquesas Islands

Nuku Hiva · *Hiva Oa*

3

Wallis and Futuna (France)

American Samoa (U.S.A.)

Matā'utu

Savai'i

Apia

Îles Palliser

Îles du Désappointement

Tuamotu Islands

SAMOA

Vanua Levu

Fagatogo

'iti Levu

TONGA

Vava'u Group

Niue (N.Z.)

Society Islands

Papeete
Tahiti

Tofua ·

Nuku'alofa

Alofi

Cook Islands (N.Z.)

French Polynesia

15°

Tongatapu Group

Rarotonga

Avarua

T u b u a i

Groupe Actéon

Kermadec Islands (N.Z.)

Tubuai

Mururoa

Îles Gambier

Pitcairn Island (U.K.)

4

Rapa

Adamstown

30°

Chatham Islands (N.Z.)

AND

Antipodes Islands (N.Z.)

5

International boundaries in the sea shown on this map indicate ownership of islands and island groups only. They do not infer the alignments of legal maritime boundaries.

80°

| G | 165° | H | 150° | I | 135° | J | 120° | K | 105° | L |

500   1000   1500 KILOMETRES

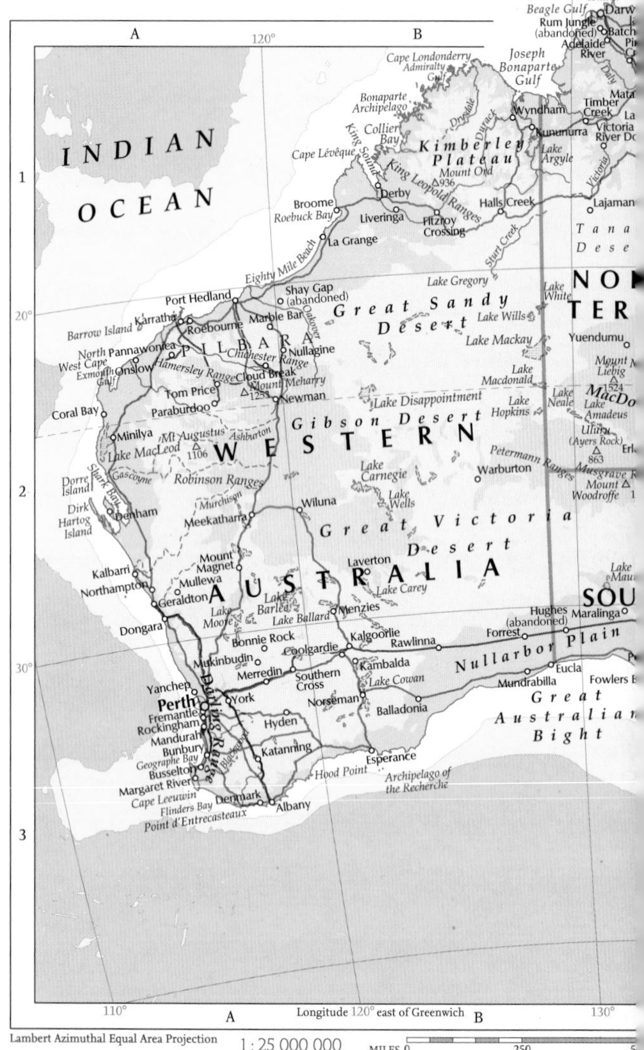

INDIAN

OCEAN

Bathurst Island • *Melville Island*
Beagle Gulf Darw
Rum Jungle (abandoned) Batch
Adelaide Pi
River

Cape Londonderry
Admiralty

Bonaparte Archipelago
Collier Bay
Cape Lévêque
King George

Joseph Bonaparte Gulf

Wyndham
Kununurra
Lake Argyle
Victoria River Do
Mata
Timber Creek
La

Kimberley Plateau
Mount Ord
936
King Leopold Ranges
Halls Creek
Lajaman

Broome
Roebuck Bay
Liveringa
Derby
Fitzroy Crossing
Sturt Creek

NO
TER

La Grange

Eighty Mile Beach

Tana Dese

Port Hedland
Shay Gap (abandoned)
Lake Gregory
Lake White

Barrow Island
Karratha
Roebourne
Marble Bar
Great Sandy Desert
Lake Wills

North Pannawonica
West Cape
Exmouth
Gulf
Onslow
Hamersley Range
Chichester Range
Nullagine
Cloud Break
Lake Mackay

Yuendumu

Coral Bay
Tom Price
Paraburdoo
Mount Meharry
1251
Newman

Lake Macdonald

Mount Liebig
MacDo

PILBARA
△

Lake Disappointment
Gibson Desert
Lake Hopkins
Lake Neale
Lake Amadeus
863
Ulara
(Ayers Rock)
△
Erl

Minilya
Mt Augustus
1106
Ashburton
WESTERN

Lake Carnegie
Warburton
Petermann Ranges
Musgrave R
Mount R
Woodroffe 1

Dorre Island
Lake MacLeod
Gascoyne
Robinson Ranges
Murchison
Meekatharra
Wiluna
Lake Wells

Dirk Hartog Island
Denham
Great Victoria Desert

Lake Mau

Kalbarri
Mount Magnet
Mullewa
AUSTRALIA
Laverton
Lake Carey

Lake
Maralinga
SOU

Northampton
Geraldton
Lake Moore
Lake Barlee
Lake Ballard
Menzies
Hughes
(abandoned)
Forrest

Dongara
Bonnie Rock
Coolgardie
Kalgoorlie
Rawlinna
Nullarbor Plain
Eucla
Mundrabilla
Fowlers B

Mukinbudin
Merredin
Southern Cross
Kambalda
Lake Cowan

Great Australian Bight

Yanchep
Perth
Fremantle
Rockingham
Mandurah
Bunbury
York
Hyden
Norseman
Balladonia

Geographe Bay
Busselton
Margaret River
Cape Leeuwin
Flinders Bay
Point d'Entrecasteaux
Katanning
Hood Point
Esperance
Archipelago of the Recherche
Denmark
Albany

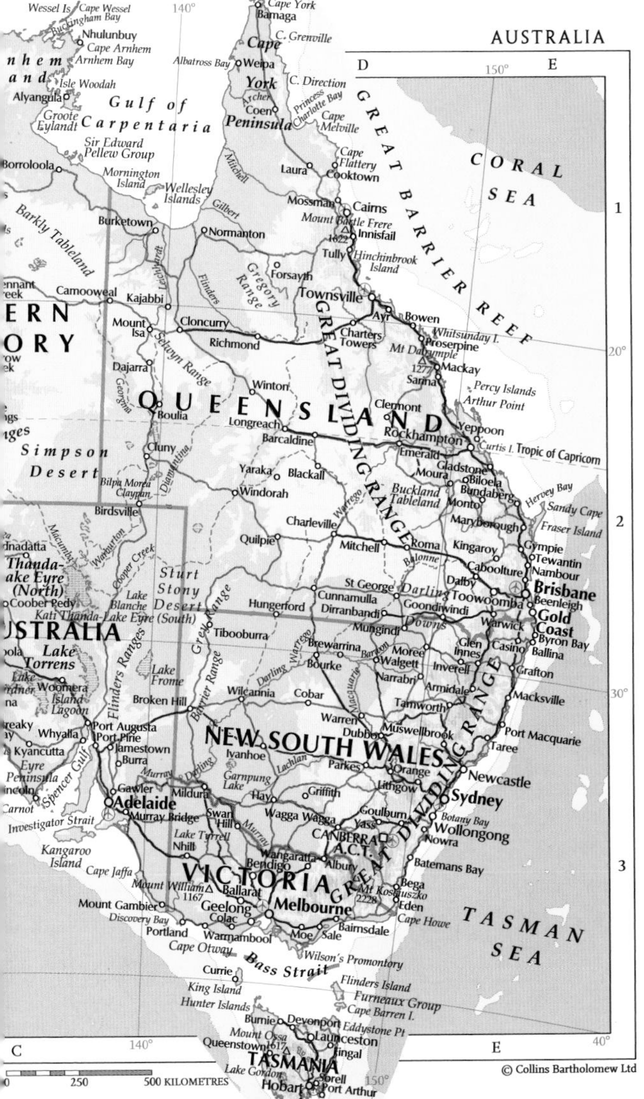

CORAL SEA

TASMAN SEA

GREAT DIVIDING RANGE

QUEENSLAND

NEW SOUTH WALES

VICTORIA

TASMANIA

Gulf of Carpentaria

Cape York Peninsula

Simpson Desert

Sturt Stony Desert

Arnhem Land

Barkly Tableland

Wessel Is
Cape Wessel
Cape Arnhem
Arnhem Bay
Nhulunbuy
Albatross Bay
Weipa
Cape York
Bamaga
C. Grenville
C. Direction
Princess Charlotte Bay
Cape Melville
Cape Flattery
Cooktown
Laura
Mossman
Cairns
Mount Bartle Frere 1622
Innisfail
Tully
Hinchinbrook I.
Townsville
Ayr
Bowen
Whitsunday I.
Proserpine
Mt Dalrymple 1259
Mackay
Percy Islands
Arthur Point
Yeppoon
Rockhampton
Curtis I. Tropic of Capricorn
Gladstone
Biloela
Bundaberg
Monto
Hervey Bay
Sandy Cape
Fraser Island
Maryborough
Gympie
Tewantin
Nambour
Caboolture
Brisbane
Beenleigh
Gold Coast
Byron Bay
Ballina
Casino
Grafton
Macksville
Port Macquarie
Taree
Newcastle
Sydney
Botany Bay
Wollongong
Nowra
Batemans Bay
Bega
Eden
Cape Howe

Charters Towers
Clermont
Emerald
Moura
Buckland Tableland
Samai
Cloncurry
Richmond
Mount Isa
Camooweal
Kajabbi
Burketown
Normanton
Forsayth
Georgetown
Croydon
Winton
Boulia
Dajarra
Longreach
Barcaldine
Blackall
Yaraka
Windorah
Quilpie
Charleville
Mitchell
Roma
Kingaroy
Dalby
Toowoomba
Warwick
Goondiwindi
St George
Dirranbandi
Cunnamulla
Hungerford
Tibooburra
Bourke
Brewarrina
Walgett
Moree
Inverell
Glen Innes
Armidale
Tamworth
Narrabri
Wilcannia
Cobar
Warren
Dubbo
Muswellbrook
Broken Hill
Ivanhoe
Parkes
Orange
Lithgow
Goulburn
CANBERRA
A.C.T.
Yass
Cooma
Mt Kosciuszko 2228
Wagga Wagga
Albury
Wangaratta
Benalla
Bendigo
Ballarat
Mt William 1167
Geelong
Melbourne
Moe
Sale
Bairnsdale
Colac
Warrnambool
Portland
Cape Otway
Mount Gambier
Discovery Bay
Wilson's Promontory
Flinders Island
Furneaux Group
Cape Barren I.
King Island
Hunter Islands
Currie
Burnie
Devonport
Eddystone Pt
Launceston
Queenstown
Mount Ossa 1617
Zeehan
Lake Gordon
Hobart
Strahan
Port Arthur

Mitchell
Gregory Range
Flinders
Gilbert
Gregory Range
Leichhardt
Cloncurry
Selwyn Range
Georgina
Diamantina
Thomson
Barcoo
Cooper Creek
Bulloo
Paroo
Warrego
Condamine
Maranoa
Balonne
Darling
Macintyre
Gwydir
Namoi
Castlereagh
Macquarie
Bogan
Lachlan
Murrumbidgee
Murray
Goulburn
Loddon
Lake Eyre
Lake Torrens
Lake Frome
Lake Blanche
Lake Tyrrell
Gippsland Lakes
Bass Strait
Investigator Strait
Spencer Gulf
Kangaroo Island
Cape Jaffa

© Collins Bartholomew Ltd

0 250 500 KILOMETRES

140°   150°

D   E

C

1

2

3

20°

30°

40°

51

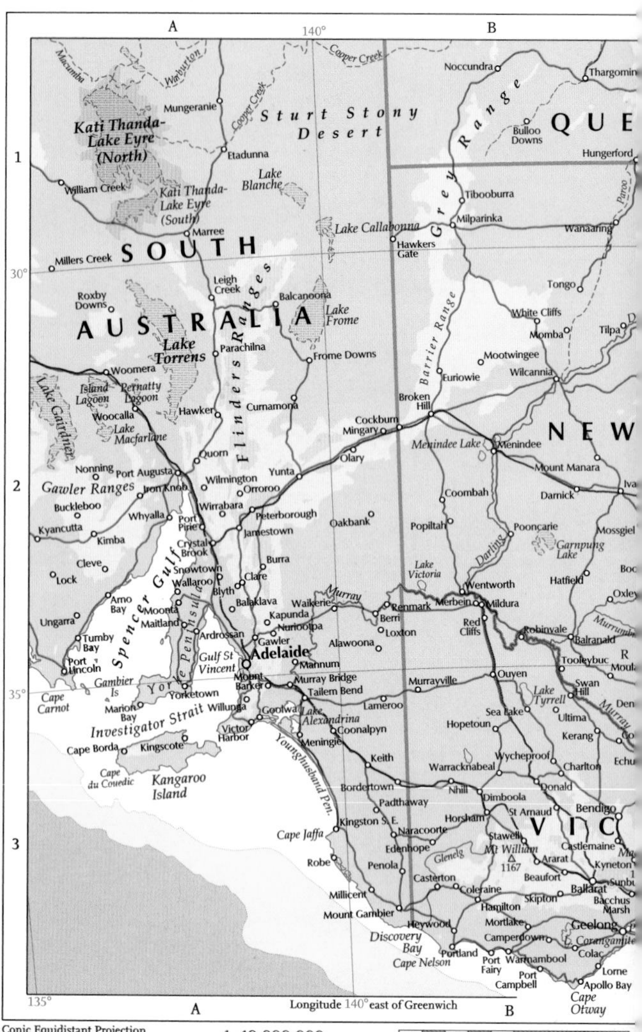

A
140°
B

Macumba
Warburton
Cooper Creek
Noccundra
Thargomindah

Kati Thanda-
Lake Eyre
(North)
Mungeranie
Cooper Creek
Sturt Stony
Desert
Bulloo
Downs
Hungerford

1

William Creek
Etadunna
Lake
Blanche
Tibooburra
Grey Range

Kati Thanda-
Lake Eyre
(South)
Marree
Lake Callabonna
Milparinka
Wanaaring

Millers Creek
Hawkers
Gate
Tongo

SOUTH
Leigh
Creek
White Cliffs
Momba
Tilpa

30°
Roxby
Downs
Balcanoona
Lake
Frome
Mootwingee
Wilcannia

AUSTRALIA
Parachilna
Frome Downs
Euriowie
Barrier Range

Lake
Torrens
Flinders Ranges
Curnamona
Cockburn
Mingary
Broken
Hill

Woomera
Hawker
NEW

Island
Lagoon
Pernatty
Lagoon
Lake
Macfarlane
Quorn
Olary
Menindee Lake
Menindee

Woocalla
Wilmington
Yunta
Mount Manara

2
Nonning
Port Augusta
Orroroo
Coombah
Darnick
Iva

Gawler Ranges
Iron Knob
Wirrabara
Peterborough
Oakbank
Popiltah
Pooncarie
Garnpung
Lake
Mossgiel

Buckleboo
Whyalla
Port
Pirie
Jamestown
Darling
Boc

Kyancutta
Crystal
Brook
Burra
Lake
Victoria
Hatfield

Cleve
Lock
Snowtown
Wallaroo
Blyth
Clare
Walkerie
Murray
Wentworth

Ungarra
Amo
Bay
Moonta
Balaklava
Kapunda
Berri
Renmark
Merbein
Mildura

Tumby
Bay
Maitland
Ardrossan
Nuriootpa
Gawler
Loxton
Red
Cliffs
Robinvale
Balranald

Port
Lincoln
Gulf St
Vincent
Adelaide
Alawoona
Tooleybuc
Moul

Yorke Peninsula
Mannum
Ouyen
Swan
Hill
Den

Cape
Carnot
Gambier
Is
Yorketown
Mount
Barker
Murray Bridge
Tailem Bend
Lameroo
Murrayville
Lake
Tyrrell
Ultima
Murr

35°
Marion
Bay
Willunga
Victor
Harbor
Goolwa
Lake
Alexandrina
Coonalpyn
Hopetoun
Sea Lake
Kerang
Echu

Investigator Strait
Cape Borda
Kingscote
Younghusband Pen.
Meningie
Keith
Warracknabeal
Wycheproof
Charlton

Cape
du Couedic
Kangaroo
Island
Bordertown
Nhill
Dimboola
Donald
Bendigo

Padthaway
Horsham
St Arnaud
Castlemaine
My

Cape Jaffa
Kingston S.E.
Naracoorte
Edenhope
Glenelg
Stawell
Mt William
1167
Beaufort
Ararat
Kyneton
Sunb

3
Robe
Penola
Casterton
Coleraine
Skipton
Ballarat
Bacchus
Marsh

Millicent
Mount Gambier
Hamilton
Mortlake
Camperdown
Geelong
Colac

Heywood
Portland
Warrnambool
Port
Fairy
Discovery
Bay
Cape Nelson
Port
Campbell
Corangamite
Lorne
Apollo Bay
Cape
Otway

VIC

QUE

135°
A
Longitude 140° east of Greenwich
B

52
Conic Equidistant Projection
1 : 10 000 000
MILES 0
100
200

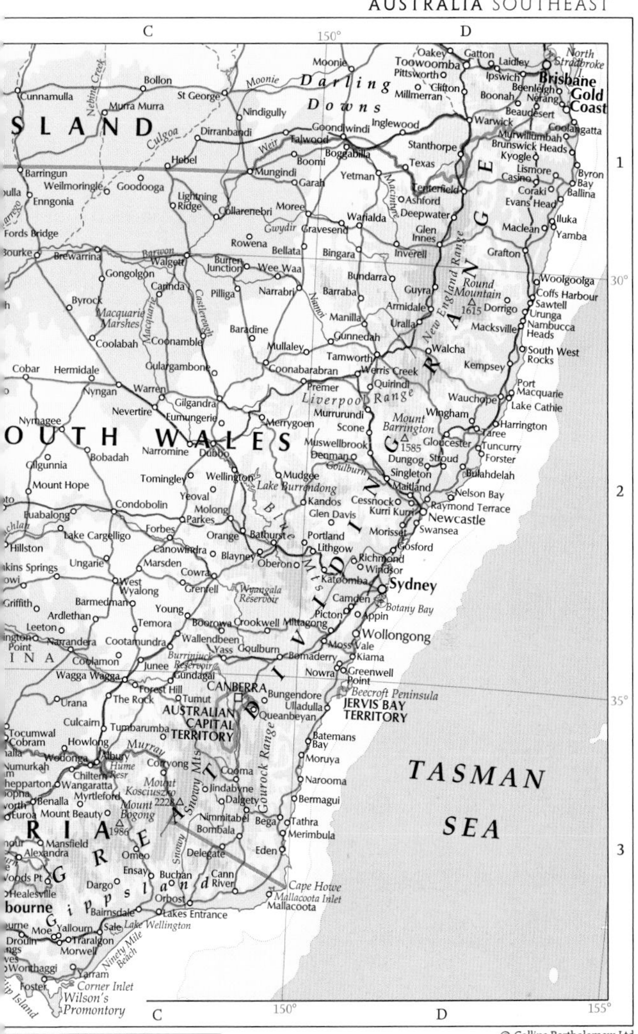

North Stradbroke

Oakey Gatton Laidley Ipswich
Toowoomba
Pittsworth Clifton
Millmerran Brisbane
Gold
Warwick Boonah Beaudesert Coast
Stanthorpe Kyogle Brunswick Heads
Texas Casino Lismore Byron Bay
Emmaville Ashford Coraki Ballina
Deepwater Grafton Iluka
Glen Yamba
Inverell Innes
Maclean
Bundarra Guyra Woolgoolga
Round Coffs Harbour
Mountain Sawtell
Armidale 1615 Dorrigo Urunga
Uralla Macksville Nambucca
Walcha Heads
South West
Kempsey Rocks
Port Macquarie
Lake Cathie

Darling Downs

Moonie
Goondiwindi
Inglewood
Talwood
Boggabilla
Boomi
Garah
Yetman
Mungindi
Moree
Wanalda
Gravesend
Bellata Bingara
Rowena
Wee Waa
Burren Barraba
Junction
Pilliga Narrabri Manilla
Baradine Gunnedah
Mullaley Tamworth
Coonabarabran Werris Creek
Premer Quirindi
Coonamble Murrurundi
Merrygoen Scone
Mount
Barrington
Denman
Muswellbrook 1585 Gloucester
Singleton Dungog Stroud
Kandos Cessnock Maitland
Glen Davis Kurri Kurri Raymond Terrace
Portland Morisset Newcastle
Lithgow Swansea
Richmond Gosford
Katoomba Windsor
Sydney
Camden
Picton Botany Bay
Appin
Mittagong Wollongong
Moss Vale Kiama
Bomaderry Greenwell
Nowra Point
Beecroft Peninsula
Bungendore Ulladulla JERVIS BAY
Queanbeyan TERRITORY
Batemans
Bay
Cooma Moruya
Narooma
Jindabyne
Dalgety Bermagui
Nimmitabel Bega Tathra
Bombala Merimbula
Delegate Eden
Cann
River
Buchan
Orbost Cape Howe
Lakes Entrance Mallacoota Inlet
Mallacoota

TASMAN

SEA

0 100 200 300 KILOMETRES

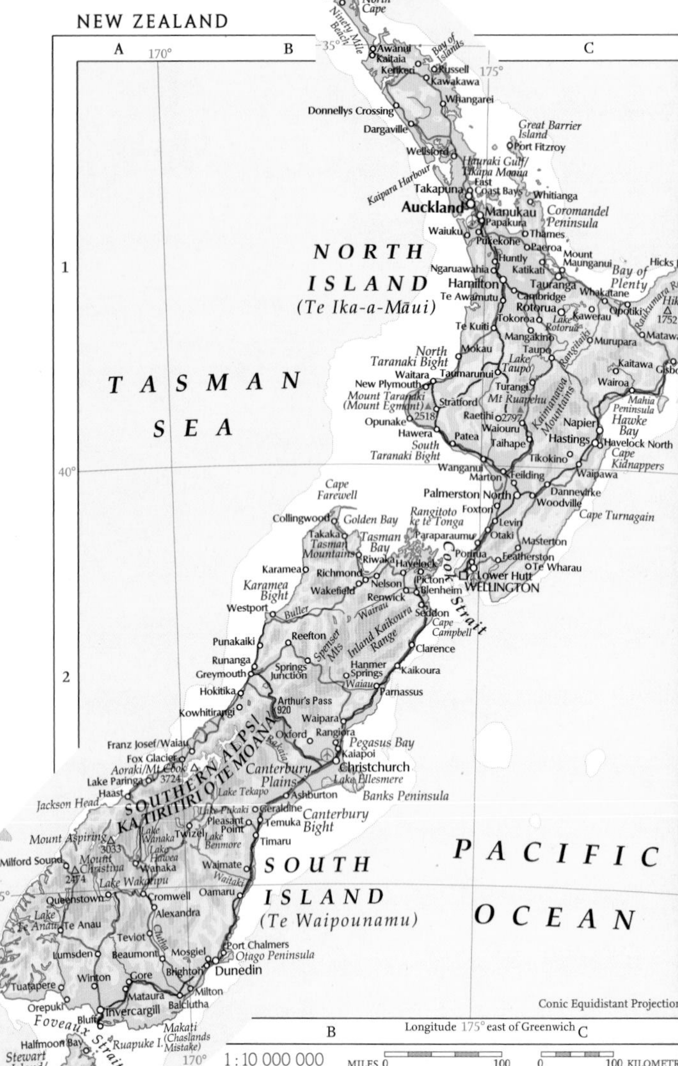

Te Paki
North
Cape
Ninety Mile Beach
Awanui
Kaitaia
Kerikeri
Russell
Kawakawa
Whangarei

Bay of Islands

Donnellys Crossing
Dargaville
Wellsford
Great Barrier
Island
Port Fitzroy
Whitianga

Hauraki Gulf
Tikapa Moana

East
Bays
Coromandel
Peninsula
Takapuna
Auckland
Manukau
Papakura
Thames
Waiuku
Pukekohe
Huntly
Mount
Maunganui
Hicks Ba
Ngaruawahia
Katikati
Tauranga

NORTH
ISLAND
(Te Ika-a-Māui)

Hamilton
Te Awamutu
Cambridge
Rotorua
Whakatane
Matawai
Te Kuiti
Lake Rotorua
Lake Kaweau

North
Taranaki Bight
Mokau
Taumarunui
Lake Taupo
Turangi
Murupara
Kaitaia
Gabon

TASMAN
SEA

New Plymouth
Waitara
Inglewood
Mount Taranaki
(Mount Egmont)
2518
Stratford
Opunake
Hawera
Patea
Raetihi
Waiouru
Mt Ruapehu
2797
Napier
Hastings
Havelock North
Waipawa

Mahia
Peninsula
Hawke
Bay
Cape
Kidnappers

South
Taranaki Bight
Wanganui
Taihape
Tikokino

Marton
Feilding
Dannevirke
Woodville
Cape Turnagain

Cape
Farewell
Collingwood
Golden Bay
Palmerston North
Foxton
Levin
Otaki
Masterton

Rangitoto
ke te Tonga
Paraparaumu
Porirua
Featherston
Te Wharau

Takaka
*Tasman
Mountains*
Riwaka
Havelock
Picton
WELLINGTON
Lower Hutt

Karamea
Richmond
Nelson
Renwick
Blenheim
Cook
Strait

Tasman Bay
Wakefield
Seddon
Cape
Campbell

*Karamea
Bight*
Westport
Wairau
Reefton
Spenser Mts
Inland Kaikoura
Range

Punakaiki
Buller
Hanmer
Springs
Kaikoura

Runanga
Springs
Junction
Greymouth
Clarence
Hokitika
Arthur's Pass
920
Waiau
Parnassus

Kowhitirangi
Waipara
Oxford
Rangiora
Pegasus Bay

Franz Josef/Waiau
Fox Glacier
Kaiapoi
Christchurch
Aoraki/Mt Cook
3724
Canterbury
Plains
Lake Ellesmere
Banks Peninsula

Lake Paringa
Haast
Jackson Head
Lake Tekapo
Ashburton
Geraldine
Temuka
*Canterbury
Bight*

Mount Aspiring
3033
Twizel
Point
Benmore
Timaru

Mount
Christina
2474
Lake Wanaka
*Lake
Hawea*
Wanaka
Waimate
Waitaki
Oamaru

Milford Sound
Lake Wakatipu
Cromwell
Queenstown
Alexandra

SOUTH
ISLAND
(Te Waipounamu)

*Lake
Te Anau*
*Lake
Manapouri*
Teviot
Mosgiel
Port Chalmers
Otago Peninsula

Beaumont
Brighton
Dunedin

PACIFIC
OCEAN

Lumsden
Winton
Tuatapere
Orepuki
Mataura
Gore
Clutha
Balclutha
Milton

Foveaux
Halfmoon Bay
Bluff
Invercargill
Makati
(Chaslands
Mistake)

Stewart
Island/
Rakiura
Ruapuke I

Strait

Longitude 175° east of Greenwich

1 : 10 000 000
MILES 0   100
0   100 KILOMETRES

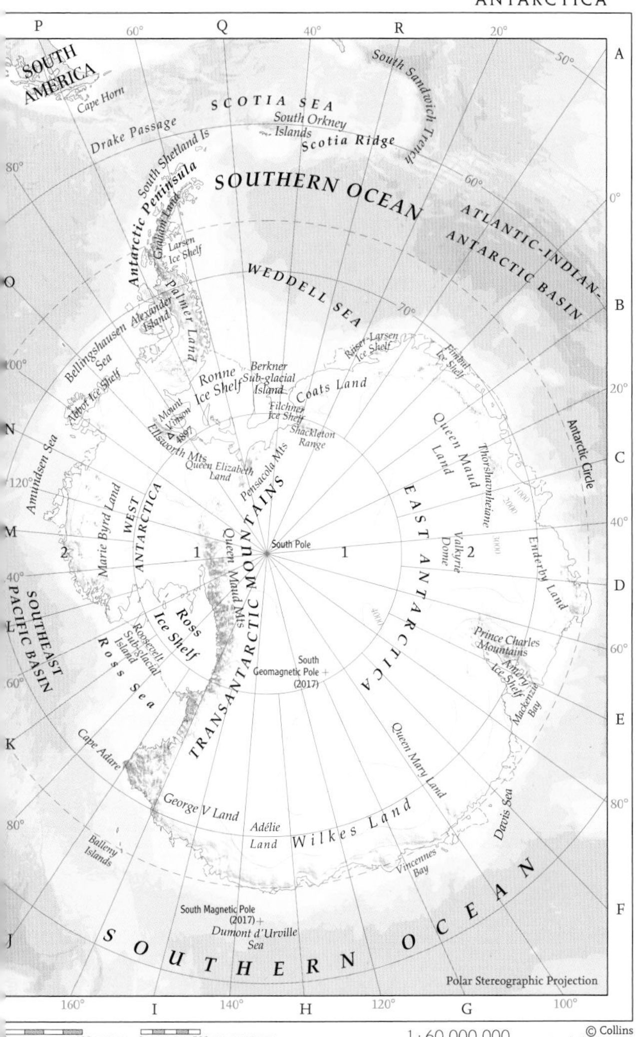

P 60° Q 40° R 20° A 50°

SOUTH AMERICA

Cape Horn

SCOTIA SEA

South Sandwich Trench

South Orkney Islands

Drake Passage

Scotia Ridge

South Shetland Is

SOUTHERN OCEAN

80°

Antarctic Peninsula

ATLANTIC-INDIAN-

ANTARCTIC BASIN

60°

Graham Land

0°

Larsen Ice Shelf

WEDDELL SEA

70°

B

O

Bellingshausen Sea

Alexander Island

Palmer Land

Larsen Ice Shelf

Filchner Ice Shelf

Antarctic Circle

Thurston Island

Ronne Ice Shelf

Berkner Sub-glacial Island

Coats Land

20°

N

100°

Amundsen Sea

Mount Sidley 4181

Ellsworth Mts

Queen Elizabeth Land

Filchner Ice Shelf

Shackleton Range

Pensacola Mts

Queen Maud Land

C

Theron

40°

120°

WEST ANTARCTICA

Marie Byrd Land

Queen Maud Mts

EAST ANTARCTICA

Valkyrie Dome

2

M

2

1

South Pole

TRANSANTARCTIC MOUNTAINS

1

Prince Charles Mountains

Amery Ice Shelf

60°

40°

Ross Ice Shelf

Roosevelt Island

Roosevelt Sub-glacial Island

South Geomagnetic Pole (2017) +

Mackenzie Bay

D

SOUTHEAST PACIFIC BASIN

60°

Ross Sea

Queen Mary Land

E

K

Cape Adare

80°

George V Land

Adélie Land

Wilkes Land

Davis Sea

Balleny Islands

Vincennes Bay

F

J

South Magnetic Pole (2017) +

Dumont d'Urville Sea

SOUTHERN OCEAN

Polar Stereographic Projection

160° I 140° H 120° G 100°

0 400 MILES 0 500 KILOMETRES

1 : 60 000 000

© Collins Bartholomew Ltd

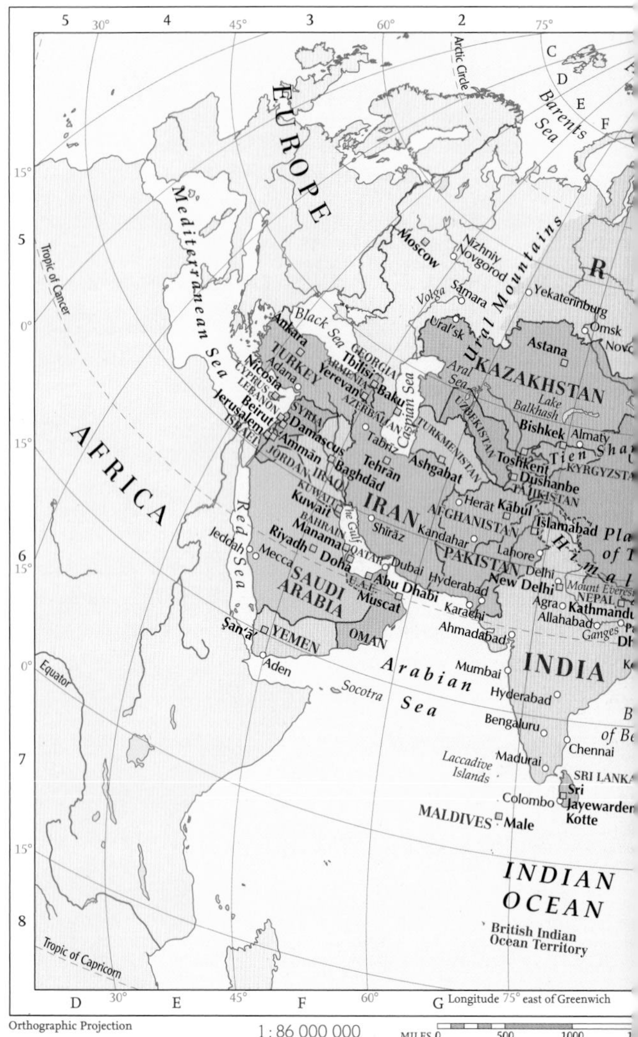

Orthographic Projection

1 : 86 000 000

MILES 0   500   1000

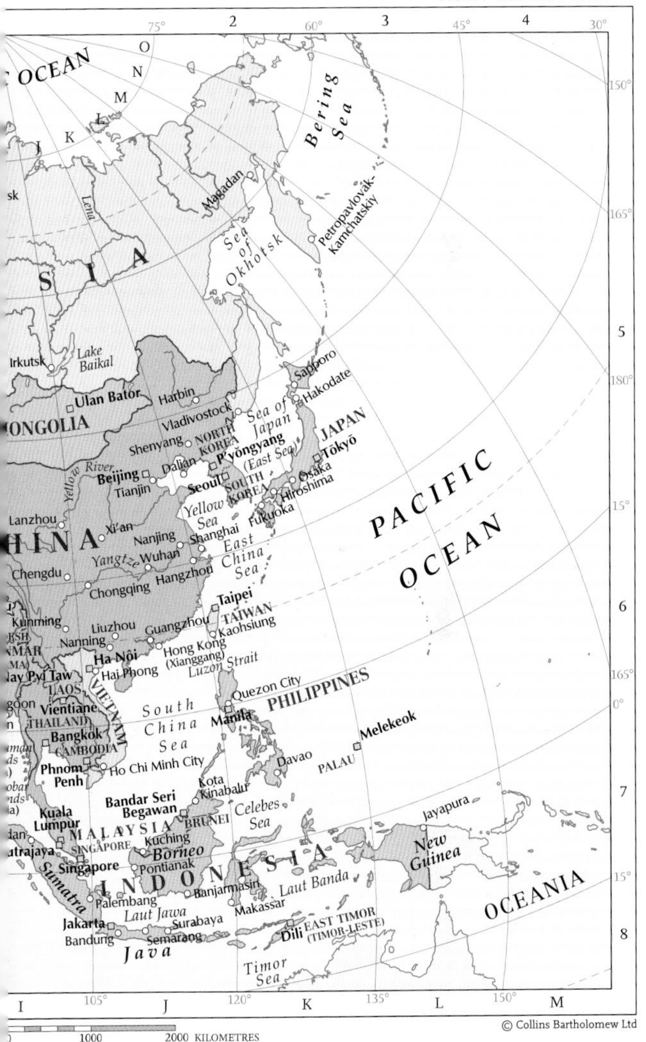

OCEAN

O
N
M
K
A

Bering
Sea

Petropavlovsk-
kamchatskiy

Sea
of
Okhotsk

Lena

Magadan

sk

S I A

Irkutsk   Lake
Baikal

MONGOLIA   Ulan Bator

Sea of
Japan
(East Sea)

Sapporo
Hakodate

Harbin

Shenyang   Vladivostok
NORTH
KOREA   JAPAN
Beijing   Dalian   P'yongyang   Tōkyō
Tianjin   Seoul   SOUTH   Ōsaka
Yellow   KOREA   Hiroshima
Sea   Fukuoka

Yellow River

Lanzhou

CHINA   Xi'an
Nanjing
Chengdu   Yangtze   Wuhan   Shanghai
Chongqing Hangzhou   East
China
Sea

PACIFIC
OCEAN

Kunming
Liuzhou   Guangzhou   TAIPEI
Nanning   Kaohsiung
Hong Kong   TAIWAN
Ha Nôi   (Xianggang)
Hai Phong   Luzon Strait

MYANMAR
Nay Pyi Taw
LAOS
Vientiane
THAILAND

Quezon City
PHILIPPINES
Manila

Melekeok

Bangkok
CAMBODIA
Phnom
Penh

South
China
Sea

Ho Chi Minh City

Davao

PALAU

Jayapura

Kuala
Lumpur   Bandar Seri
Begawan   Kota
Kinabalu

Kuching   BRUNEI   Celebes
Sea

MALAYSIA
SINGAPORE
Putrajaya   Singapore   Borneo
Pontianak

New
Guinea

INDONESIA

OCEANIA

Sumatra

Palembang   Banjarmasin   Makassar   Laut Banda
Jakarta   Laut Jawa   Surabaya   Dili   EAST TIMOR
Bandung   Semarang   (TIMOR-LESTE)
Java

Timor
Sea

I   J   K   L   M

© Collins Bartholomew Ltd

1000   2000 KILOMETRES

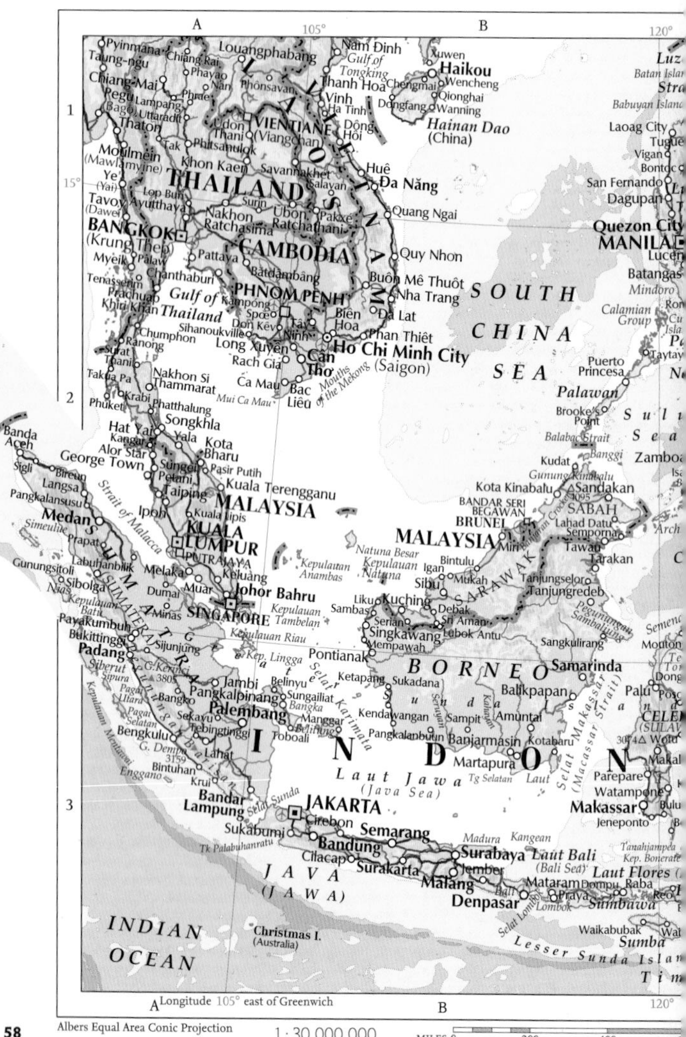

Albers Equal Area Conic Projection

1 : 30 000 000

MILES 0   200   400

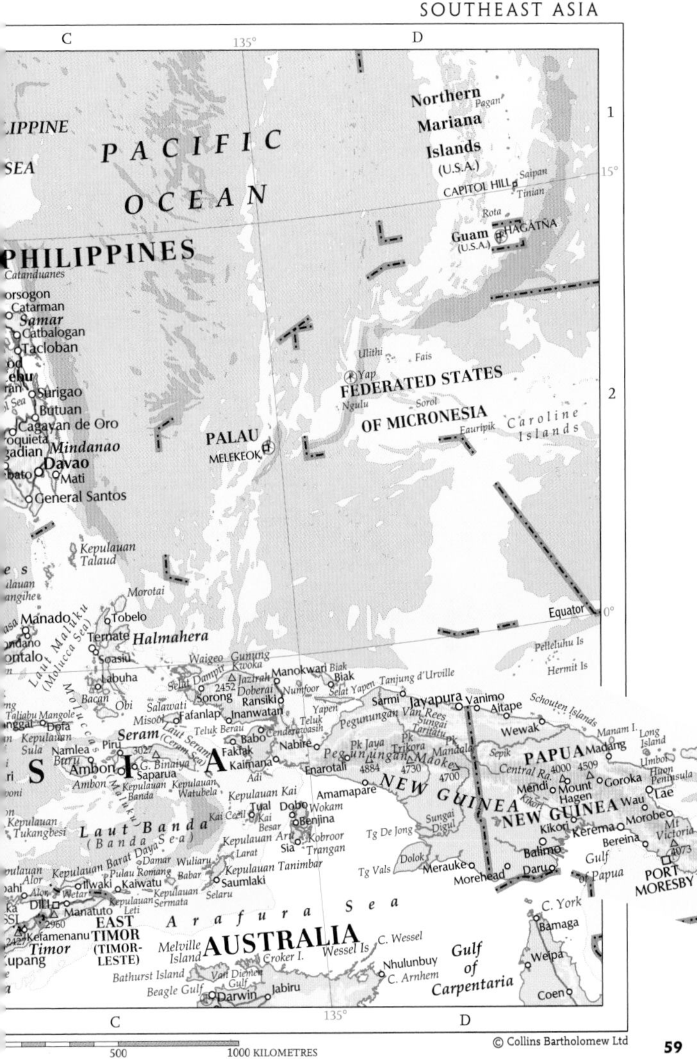

PACIFIC

OCEAN

Northern
Mariana
Islands
(U.S.A.)   15°
CAPITOL HILL ●Saipan
Rota ● Tinian

Guam HAGÅTÑA
(U.S.A.)

PHILIPPINES

Catanduanes

orsogon
○Catarman   Samar
○Catbalogan
○Tacloban

od
ehu
Sea ○Surigao
○Butuan
○Cagayan de Oro
oquieta Mindanao
adian
bato ○Davao ●Mati
○Mati
○General Santos

Ulithi ○:   Fais

⊕Yap
FEDERATED STATES

Ngulu
○Sorol   Caroline
Faurivin   Islands

PALAU
MELEKEOK

OF MICRONESIA

e s

auan
angihe

alauan   Morotai
○Talaud

Manado   Laut Maluku
(Molucca Sea)
○Tobelo

indano ○Ternate Halmahera
ortalo ○Tidore
○Labuha
Bacan Waigeo Gunung
Obi Seasii   Kwoka
Salawati △Jazirah △2452 Manokwari ○Biak
Misool ○Sorong ○Numfoor Ranski Selat Yapen Tanjung d'Urville
○Afanlap   ○Inanwatan ○Yapen ○Sarmi Jayapura○ ○Vanimo

Equator   0°

Pelleluhu Is

Hermit Is

S   I   A

ng
Taliabu Mangole
ngal Sula Opfa
an Kepulauan
Banggai Peru △3027
Namlea Seram ○3027

Piru
○Ambon
Ambon

Seram
K.G. Binaiya
○Saparua △3027
Kepulauan
Watubela

Teluk Berau
Fakfak
Teluk
Kaimana

Nabire○
Peguningan Van Rees Tarikora ○Mandala Wewak○
Enarotali○ ○Nabire Mandala Sepik   Manam I.

PAPUA Madang Long
Island

voni

Kepulauan
Tukangbesi

ulauan
Alor
ahi ○Alor ○Atapupu
Kalabahi

Kai Cecil   ○Tual ○Dobo Wokam
○Saparua Banda ○Tual Dobo ○Wokam Besar
Laut Banda
(Banda Sea)

Kepulauan Kai
Kai ○Kai

Kepulauan Aru
○Benjina

DILI

pulauan
Barat Daya
Kepulauan
○Damar Wuliaru
○Pulau Romang Babar
○Kawatu Kepulauan
Leti Sermata Selaru

○Larat
○Lirat
Kepulauan Tanimbar
Sia ○Trangan

Sungai
Digul Tikora ○Mendi Mount ○Goroka Morobe○
4509 Hagen Kikori ○Wau Lae
NEW GUINEA Kerema Morobe
Bereina○ Mt
4073
○Balimo Gulf Victoria
Daru○ of PORT
○Morehead Papua MORESBY

Tg De Jong
○Dolok
Tg Vals

Morehead

EAST
TIMOR
(TIMOR-
LESTE)

Manatuto
○Manatuto
○Kefamenanu EAST
upang Timor

Melville
Island Croker I.
Bathurst Island Van Diemen
Beagle Gulf ○Darwin Jabiru

○Wessel Is
○Nhulunbuy
C. Arnhem

Arafura   Sea

AUSTRALIA

135°

C. Wessel

C. York
○Bamaga

Gulf
of
Carpentaria

○Welpa

○Coen

500   1000 KILOMETRES

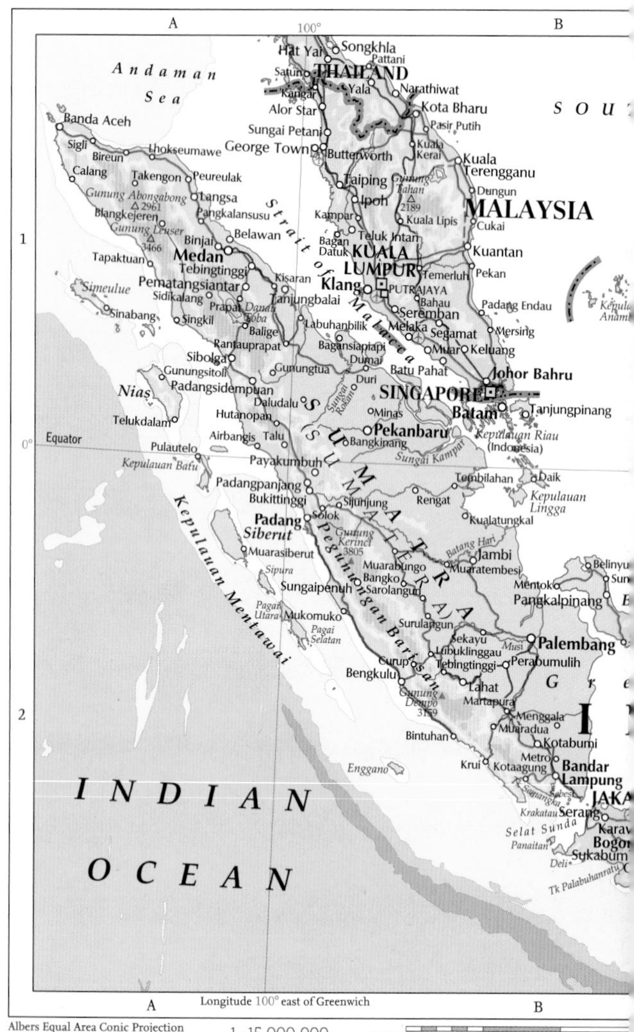

A   100°   B

Andaman
Sea

SOU

Hat Yai   Songkhla
Pattani
Satun   THAILAND
Kangar   Yala   Narathiwat
Alor Star
Banda Aceh
Sigli
Bireun
Calang   Lhokseumawe
Sungai Petani   Pasir Putih
George Town   Butterworth   Kuala Krai   Kuala Terengganu
Takengon   Langsa
Gunung Abongabong   △2961
Blangkejeren   Pangkalansusu
Gunung Leuser △3466
Tapaktuan
Binjai   Belawan
Medan
Tebingtinggi
Pematangsiantar
Sidikalang   Prapa
Simeulue
Sinabang   Singkil
Kisaran   Tanjungbalai
Danau Toba
Rantauprapat   Labuhanbilik
Baligé
Bagansiapiapi
Sibolga   Gunungtua   Duri
Gunungsitoli   Dumai
Padangsidempuan
Nias   Daludalu   Minas
Telukdalam   Hutanopan
Airbangis   Talu   Bangkinang
Pulautelo
Kepulauan Batu
Payakumbuh
Padangpanjang   Sungai Kampar
Bukittinggi   Sijunjung   Rengat
Padang   *Solok*
Siberut   *Gunung Kerinci* △3805
Muarasiberut
Sipura
Sungaipenuh   Bangko   Sarolangun
Muarabungo   Muaratembesi
Pagai Utara
Mukomuko   Surulangun
Pagai Selatan   Sekayu   *Musi*
Lubuklinggau
Gurup   Tebingtinggi   Perabumulih
Bengkulu   Lahat
Gunung Dempo △3159   Martapura
Muaradua
Menggala
Bintuhan   Kotabumi
Enggano   Metro
Krui   Kotaagung   Bandar Lampung
Krakatau   Serang
Selat Sunda

MALAYSIA
Taiping
Tahan △2189
Ipoh   Kuala Lipis
Kampar
Teluk Intan   Temerluh   Pekan
Bagan Datuk   KUALA LUMPUR
Klang   PUTRAJAYA
Bahau   Padang Endau
Seremban
Melaka   Segamat   Mersing
Muar   Keluang
Batu Pahat
Johor Bahru
SINGAPORE
Batam   Tanjungpinang
Pekanbaru
Kepulauan Riau
(Indonesia)
Daik
Kepulauan Lingga
Tembilahan
Kualatungkal
Batang Hari
Jambi   Belinyu
Mentoko   Sun
Pangkalpinang
Palembang

Dungun
Cukai
Kuantan

Kepul Anam

Tanjungpinang

G

I

JAKA
Karav
Bogor
Sukabum
Deli

Gunung
Kerinci

Pesisir

Bukit

Barisan

Kepulauan Mentawai

INDIAN

OCEAN

Equator   0°

1

2

Longitude 100° east of Greenwich

A   B

Albers Equal Area Conic Projection   1 : 15 000 000   MILES 0   100   200

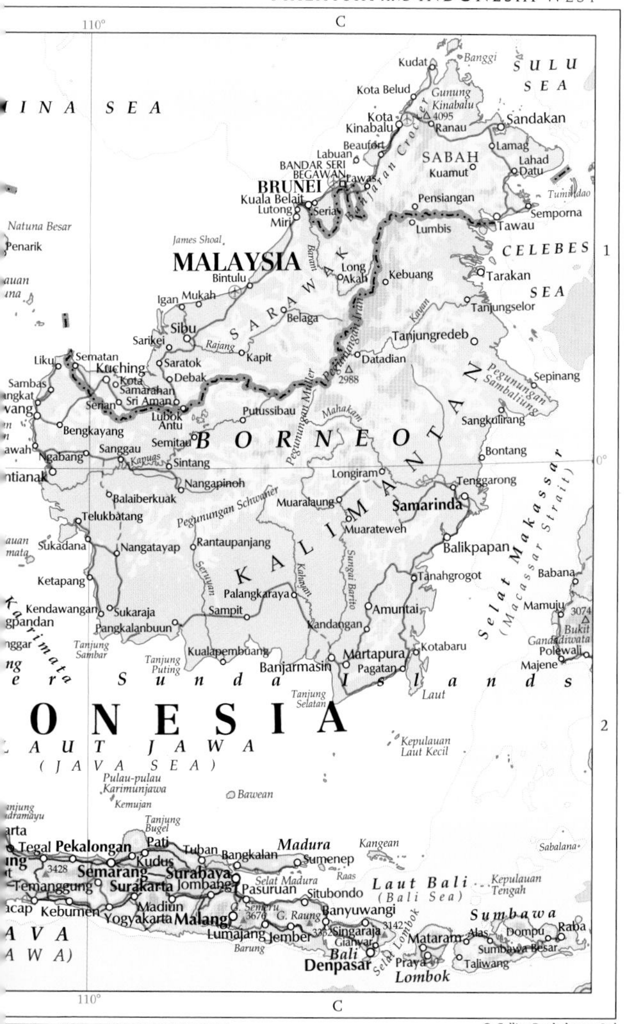

C

110°

NA SEA

Natuna Besar

Penarik

auan
una

L

Liku

Sambas
ngkat
vang
an
awah

Ngabang

ntianak

Sematan

Kuching
Kota
Samarahan
Serian
Sri Aman

Bengkayang

Sanggau

Semitau

Sintang

Balaiberkuak

Telukbatang

Sukadana

Nangatayap
Rantaupanjang

Ketapang

Kendawangan
gpandan

Sukaraja
Pangkalanbuan

Tanjung
Sambar

ngga

Tanjung
Puting

a   Sunda

 O N E S I A

L A U T   J A W A
(J A V A   S E A)

anjung
amayu

arta

Tegal   Pekalongan
Pati
ng
Temanggung   Semarang
cap   Kebumen   Madiun
A V A
(A W A)

Yogyakarta

Tuban
Kudus
Surakarta   Jombang

Malang

Kudat
Banggi

Kota Belud

Kota
Kinabalu

Labuan

Beaufort

Ranau

SABAH

Kuamut

Lamag

Lahad
Datu

Sandakan

SULU
SEA

Gunung
Kinabalu
4095

Tawau

Tunuddao

Semporna

CELEBES

SEA

Tarakan

Sepinang

Bontang

Samarinda

Balikpapan
Babana

Tanahgrogot

Mamuju

Ganda
Polewali
Majene

Kotabaru

1

0°

2

Penyinganan
Sumbatung

Pegunungan

BANDAR SERI
BEGAWAN
Tawas
BRUNEI
Kuala Belait
Lutong   Seria
Miri

MALAYSIA

Igan   Mukah
Bintulu

Sibu
Sarikei
Debak
Saratok
Kapit

Belaga

Long
Akah

Kebuang

Lumbis

Pensiangan

Kinabatangan

Tanjungredeb

Datadian
2988

Putussibau

Lubok
Antu

Sangkulirang

Kanyan
Nangapinoh

Longiram

Muaralaung

Muarateweh

Palangkaraya

Sampit

Kualapembuang

Banjarmasin

Martapura

Pagatan

Laut

Tanjung
Selatan

Kepulauan
Laut Kecil

Pulau-pulau
Karimunjawa

Kemujan

Bawean

Sabalana

Tanjung
Bugel

Bangkalan

Madura

Kangean
Sumenep
Raas

Sabalana

Selat Madura
Pasuruan

Surabaya

Situbondo

Laut Bali
(Bali Sea)

Kepulauan
Tengah

Sumbawa

Alas
Dompu
Raba

Lumajang   Jember
Banyuwangi

Bali

Mataram

Tanjung Besar

Denpasar

Lombok

Praya

Taliwang

S U L A W E S I

B O R N E O

K A L I M A N T A N

S A R A W A K

Selat Makassar
(Macassar Strait)

Selat Lombok

250   500 KILOMETRES

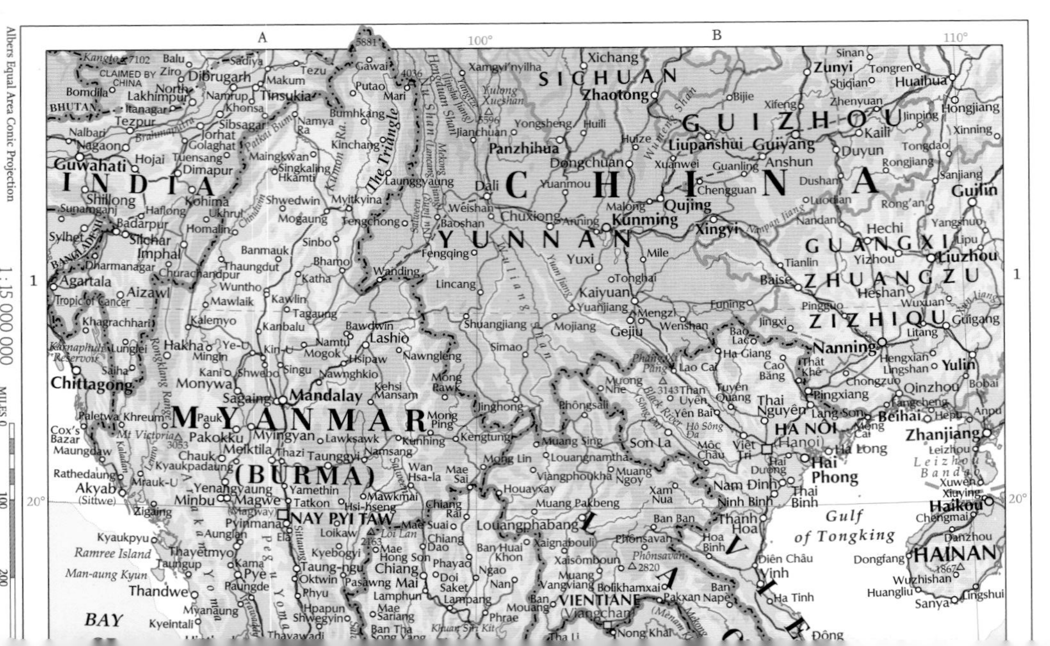

Albers Equal Area Conic Projection   1 : 15 000 000   MILES 0   100   200

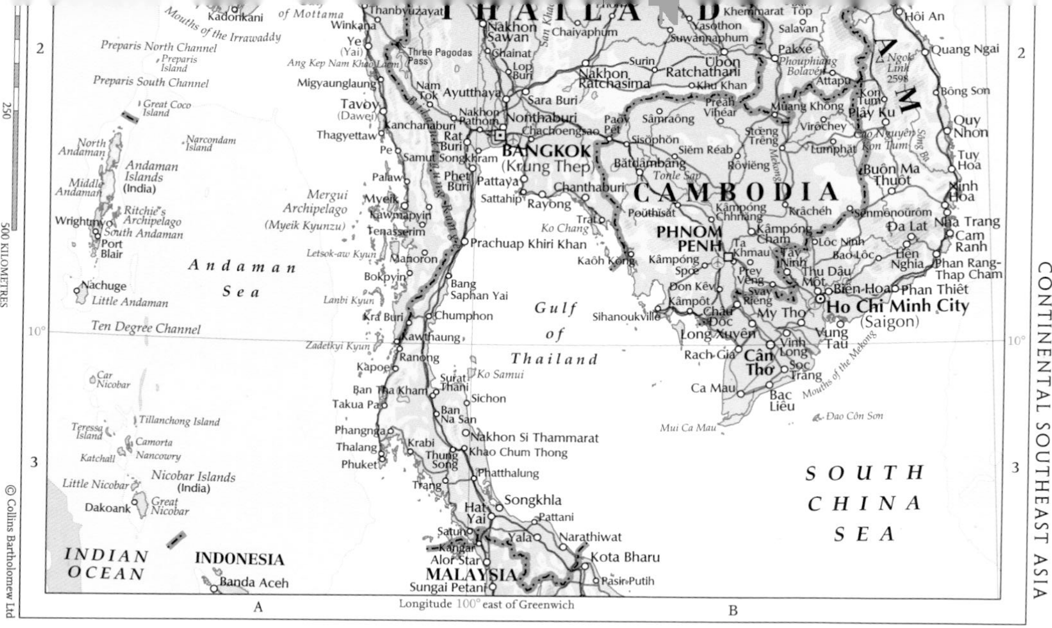
SOUTH
CHINA
SEA
Gulf
of
Thailand
Andaman
Sea
INDIAN
OCEAN
CAMBODIA
MALAYSIA
INDONESIA
Hôi An
Quang Ngai
Bông Son
Quy Nhon
Tuy Hòa
Ninh Hòa
Nha Trang
Cam Ranh
Phan Rang-Thap Cham
Phan Thiêt
Ho Chi Minh City
(Saigon)
Đa Lat
Buôn Ma Thuôt
Play Ku
Kon Tum
Ngok Linh
2598
Sông Ba
Attapu
Salavan
Pakxé
Phouphiang Bolavén
Khemmarat
Yasothon
Ubon Ratchathani
Suwannaphum
Khu Khan
Surin
Nakhon Ratchasima
Chaiyaphum
Nakhon Sawan
Chainat
Lop Buri
Sara Buri
Ayutthaya
Nonthaburi
BANGKOK
(Krung Thep)
Chachoengsao
Nakhon Pathom
Samut Songkhram
Rat Buri
Phet Buri
Pattaya
Sattahip
Rayong
Chanthaburi
Trat
Ko Chang
Prachuap Khiri Khan
Bang Saphan Yai
Chumphon
Kawthaung
Ranong
Surat Thani
Ko Samui
Sichon
Ban Na San
Nakhon Si Thammarat
Khao Chum Thong
Phatthalung
Songkhla
Hat Yai
Pattani
Yala
Narathiwat
Kota Bharu
Pasir Putih
Alor Star
Sungai Petani
Kangar
Satun
Trang
Thung Song
Krabi
Phangnga
Thalang
Phuket
Takua Pa
Ban Tha Kham
Kapoe
Krâ Buri
Bokpyin
Manoron
Tenasserim
Kawmapyin
Myeik
Palaw
Pe
Thagyettaw
Kanchanaburi
Tavoy
(Dawei)
Nam Tok
Three Pagodas Pass
Migyaunglaung
Ang Kep Nam Khao Laem
Ye
(Yai)
Winkana
Thanbyuzayat
Kadonkani
of Mottama
Mouths of the Irrawaddy
Mergui Archipelago
(Myeik Kyunzu)
Letsok-aw Kyun
Lanbi Kyun
Zadetkyi Kyun
PHNOM PENH
Ta Khmau
Kâmpóng Spoe
Kâmpôt
Don Kév
Chau Dôc
Sihanoukville
Kaôh Kong
Poŭthĭsăt
Bătdâmbâng
Sisŏphŏn
Paoy Pet
Siĕm Réab
Tonle Sap
Kâmpóng Chhnăng
Kâmpóng Cham
Krâchéh
Stœng Trêng
Mekong
Rôviĕng
Preăh Vihéar
Sâmraông
Sênmonoŭrôm
Lumphăt
Virochey
Muang Khong
Lôc Ninh
Tây Ninh
Thu Dâu Môt
Biên Hoa
Bao Lôc
Liên Nghia
Vung Tau
My Tho
Vinh Long
Cân Thơ
Soc Trăng
Bac Liêu
Ca Mau
Mui Ca Mau
Rach Gia
Long Xuyên
Prey Vêng
Svay Riĕng
Mouths of the Mekong
Đao Côn Son
Preparis North Channel
Preparis Island
Preparis South Channel
Great Coco Island
Narcondam Island
North Andaman
Andaman Islands
(India)
Middle Andaman
Ritchie's Archipelago
South Andaman
Wrightmyo
Port Blair
Hachuge
Little Andaman
Ten Degree Channel
Car Nicobar
Tillanchong Island
Teressa Island
Camorta
Nancowry
Katchall
Nicobar Islands
(India)
Little Nicobar
Great Nicobar
Dakoank
Banda Aceh
Longitude 100° east of Greenwich
10°
A
B
2
3
250
500 KILOMETRES

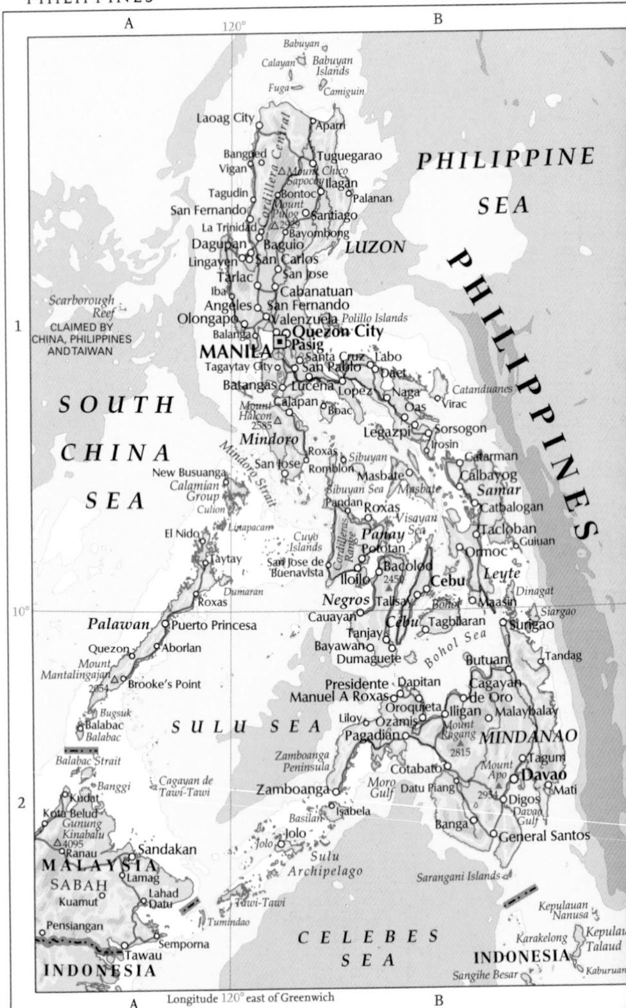

PHILIPPINE
SEA

PHILIPPINES

SOUTH

CHINA

SEA

LUZON

Babuyan
Calayan Babuyan
Islands
Fuga Camiguin
Laoag City Aparri
Banged Tuguegarao
Vigan Mount Chico Ilagan
Tagudin Bontoc Palanan
San Fernando Santiago
La Trinidad Bayombong
Dagupan Baguio
Lingayen San Carlos
Tarlac San Jose
Ibat Cabanatuan
Angeles San Fernando
Olongapo Valenzuela Polillo Islands
Balanga Quezon City
MANILA Pasig
Santa Cruz Labo
Tagaytay City San Pablo Daet
Batangas Lucena Lopez Naga
Calapan Oas Virac
Mount Roxas Legazpi Sorsogon
Halcon Romblon Irosin
Mindoro Masbate Catarman
New Busuanga Sibuyan Sea Calbayog Samar
Calamian Pandan Masbate Catbalogan
Group Roxas Tacloban
Culion Visayan Ormoc Guiuan
El Nido Cuyo Sea
Islands Pototan Leyte
Taytay San Jose de Iloilo Cebu Maasin
Buenavista Bacolod Siargao
Roxas Negros Talisay Bohol Surigao
Dumaran Cauayan Cebu Tagbilaran Dinagat
Palawan Puerto Princesa Tanjay Dapitan Butuan Tandag
Quezon Bayawan Presidente Cagayan
Aborlan Dumaguete Manuel A Roxas de Oro
Mount Oroquieta Malaybalay
Mantalingajan Liloy Ozamiz Iligan
Brooke's Point Pagadian MINDANAO
Bugsuk SULU SEA Cotabato Mount Tagum
Balabac Zamboanga Datu Piang Davao
Balabac Strait Peninsula Banga Digos
Cagayan de Zamboanga Moro Davao Mati
Tawi-Tawi Gulf Gulf
Kudat Basilan Isabela General Santos
Kota Belud Banggi
Gunung Jolo Sulu
Kinabalu Jolo Archipelago Sarangani Islands
Ranau Sandakan
MALAYSIA Lamag
SABAH Lahad Tawi-Tawi Kepulauan
Kuamut Datu Nanusa
Pensiangan Cagayan de
Sempurna Tumindao Karakelong
Tawau Sangihe Besar Talaud
INDONESIA CELEBES INDONESIA Kaburuan
SEA

Scarborough
Reef
CLAIMED BY
CHINA, PHILIPPINES
AND TAIWAN

Cordillera Central

Catanduanes

Sibuyan

Cuyo
Islands

Cordillera
Range

Panay

Bohol Sea

Mindoro Strait

Lutapacam

Luzon

Longitude 120° east of Greenwich

Albers Equal Area Conic
Projection   1 : 15 000 000   MILES 0   100   250 KILOMET

A   120°   B

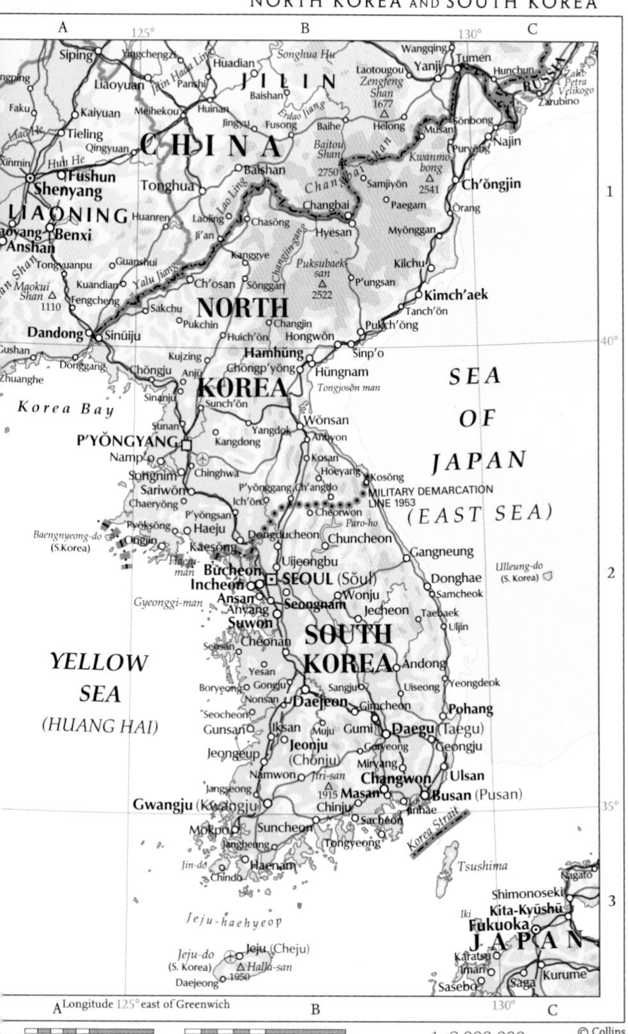
A
B
C
125°
130°
1
2
3
40°
35°
Siping
Yingchengzi
Huadian
Songhua Hu
Wangqing
Yanji
Tumen
Hunchun
RUSSIA
Zaliv Petra Velikogo
Zarubino
Laotougou
Zengfeng Shan
1677
Liaoyuan
Jilin Hada Ling
Panshi
JILIN
Baishan
Erdao Jiang
Faku
Kaiyuan
Meihekou
Huinan
Jingyu
Fusong
Baihe
Helong
Sŏnbong
Musan
Najin
Puryŏng
Tieling
Qingyuan
CHINA
Baitou Shan
2750
Changbai Shan
Kwanmo-bong
2541
Xinmin
Hun He
Fushun
Shenyang
Baishan
Tonghua
Samjiyŏn
Ch'ŏngjin
Paegam
LIAONING
Huanren
Lao Ling
Laoling
Chasŏng
Changbai
Hyesan
Ŏrang
Myŏnggan
Benxi
Anshan
Ji'an
Kanggye
Changjin-gang
Guanshui
Tongyuanpu
Kilchu
Puksubaek-san
2522
P'ungsan
Maokui Shan
1110
Kuandian
Yalu Jiang
Ch'osan
Sŏnggan
Kimch'aek
Fengcheng
Sakchu
NORTH
Tanch'ŏn
Pukchin
Changjin
Pukch'ŏng
Dandong
Sinŭiju
Huich'ŏn
Hongwŏn
Donggang
Kujzing
Hamhŭng
Sinp'o
Chŏngju
Anju
Chŏngp'yŏng
Hŭngnam
Zhuanghe
KOREA
Tongjosŏn man
SEA OF JAPAN (EAST SEA)
Sinanju
Sunch'ŏn
Korea Bay
Wŏnsan
Sunan
Yangdŏk
P'YŎNGYANG
Kangdong
Anbyon
Namp'o
Kosan
Songnim
Chinghwa
Hoeyang
Kosŏng
Sariwŏn
P'yŏnggang
Ch'angdo
MILITARY DEMARCATION LINE 1953
Chaeryŏng
Ich'ŏn
Ch'ŏrwon
P'yŏngsan
Paro-ho
Pyŏksŏng
Haeju
Baengnyeong-do (S.Korea)
Ongjin
Dongducheon
Chuncheon
Kaesŏng
Gangneung
Haeju-man
Uijeongbu
Ulleung-do (S. Korea)
Bucheon
SEOUL (Sŏul)
Donghae
Incheon
Samcheok
Wonju
Ansan
Gyeonggi-man
Anyang
Seongnam
Jecheon
Taebaek
Suwon
Uljin
Seosan
Cheonan
SOUTH KOREA
YELLOW SEA (HUANG HAI)
Andong
Yesan
Boryeong
Gongju
Sangju
Uiseong
Yeongdeok
Nonsan
Daejeon
Gimcheon
Pohang
Seocheon
Gunsan
Iksan
Muju
Gumi
Daegu (Taegu)
Jeonju (Chŏnju)
Gyeongju
Jeongeup
Miryang
Namwon
Jiri-san
1915
Changwon
Ulsan
Jangseong
Masan
Busan (Pusan)
Gwangju (Kwangju)
Chinju
Jinhae
Mokpo
Suncheon
Sacheon
Korea Strait
Jangheung
Tongyeong
Tsushima
Jin-do
Haenam
Chindo
Nagato
Shimonoseki
Kita-Kyūshū
Iki
Fukuoka
JAPAN
Jeju-haehyeop
Jeju (Cheju)
Jeju-do (S. Korea)
Halla-san
1950
Karatsu
Imari
Kurume
Saga
Sasebo
Daejeong
Longitude 125° east of Greenwich

MILES 0 50 100 | 0 100 200 KILOMETRES 1 : 9 000 000

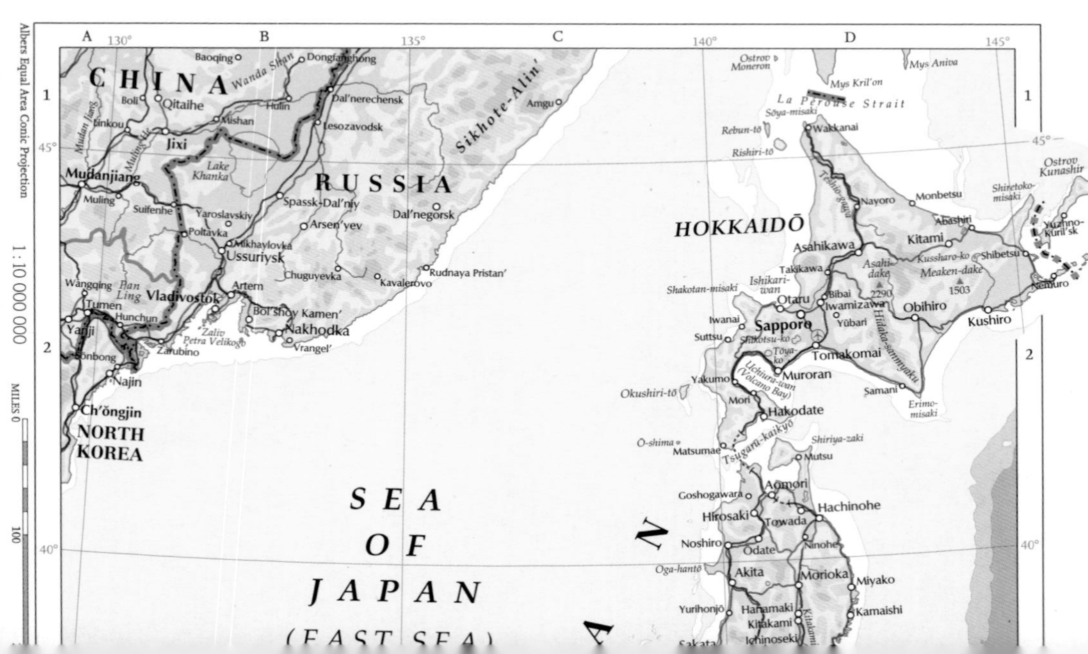

Albers Equal Area Conic Projection

1 : 10 000 000

MILES 0   100

HOKKAIDŌ

RUSSIA

CHINA

NORTH KOREA

SEA OF JAPAN

(EAST SEA)

La Pérouse Strait

Sikhote-Alin'

Wanda Shan

Lake Khanka

Kushiro
Obihiro
Kitami
Monbetsu
Abashiri
Nayoro
Wakkanai
Asahikawa
Iwamizawa
Otaru
Sapporo
Muroran
Tomakomai
Hakodate
Mori
Matsumae
Samani
Hidaka-sanmyaku

Hachinohe
Aomori
Odate
Akita
Morioka
Miyako
Kamaishi
Miyako
Kitakami
Hanamaki
Ichinoseki
Hirosaki
Noshiro
Goshogawara
Mutsu

Vladivostok
Ussuriysk
Nakhodka
Artem
Spassk-Dal'ny
Arsen'yev
Dal'negorsk
Rudnaya Pristan'
Kavalerovo
Chuguyevka
Nakhodka
Vrangel'
Bol'shoy Kamen'

Najin
Ch'ŏngjin
Mudanjiang
Jixi
Qitaihe
Baoqing
Dongning
Hunchun
Tumen
Yanji

Ostrov Kunashir
Yuzhno-Kuril'sk
Shikotan
Shiretoko-misaki

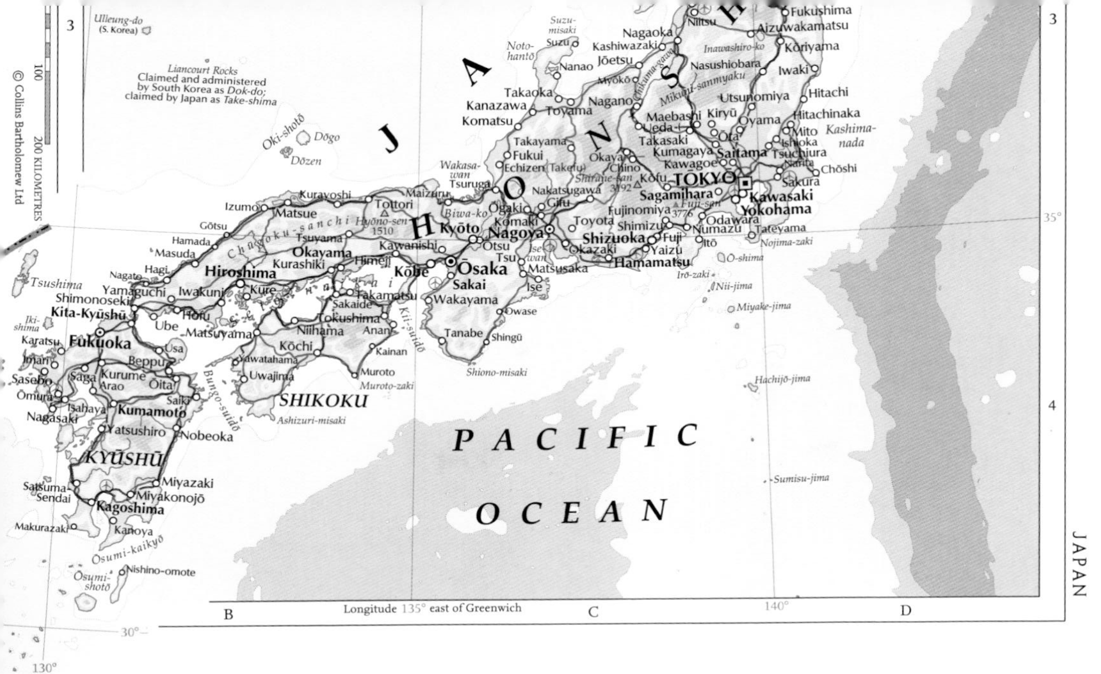

3

35°

D

4

Fukushima
Nimu
Takamatsu
Azuma-san
Kōriyama
Iwaki
Hitachinaka
Hitachi
Inawashiro-ko
Utsunomiya
Mito
Kashima-
Nasushiobara
Kasumiga-ura
nada
Nagaoka
Maebashi
Kiryū
Sakura
Chōshi
Kashiwazaki
Takasaki
Kumagaya
Narita
Jōetsu
Nagano
Kawagoe
Chiba
Nanao
Matsumoto
Kōfu
3192
TOKYO
Kawasaki
Nakatsugawa
Yokohama
Takaoka
Takayama
Gifu
Odawara
Ō-shima
Toyama
Echizen-misaki
Numazu
Kanazawa
Fukui
Ōgaki
Sagamihara
Irō-zaki
Komatsu
Ōtsu
Nagoya Ono
Shizuoka
Ō-shima
Komatsu
Toyoda Fuji
Hamamatsu
Yaizu
Ni-jima
Wakasa-
Kyōto
Ōsaka
Nakatsugawa
Matsusaka
wan
Tsuruga
Ōtsu
Tsu
Ise
Miyake-jima
Tottori
Biwa-ko
Kōbe
Sakai
Owase
Shimo-misaki
Hachijō-jima
Matsue
Himeji
Maizuru
Wakayama
Tanabe
Kurayoshi
Fukuyama
Akashi
Anan
Kainan
Muroto
Izumo
Okayama
Kōbe
Kii-suidō
Muroto-zaki
Gōtsu
Kurashiki
Sakaide
Hiroshima
Kure
Tokushima
Hamada
Iwakuni
Niihama
Kōchi
Masuda
Tokuyama
Kōchi
Ube
Iwata
Watanabe
Hagi
Yamaguchi
Kita-Kyūshū
Ube
Matsuyama
SHIKOKU
Ashizuri-misaki
Nagato
Beppu
Uwajima
Tsushima
Shimonoseki
Ōita
Bungo-suidō
Nobeoka
Fukuoka
Saga
Kurume
Kumamoto
KYŪSHŪ
Karatsu
Ōmuta
Yatsushiro
Miyazaki
Imari
Arao
Miyakonojō
Sasebo
Minamata
Hitoyoshi
Ōmura
Kagoshima
Nagasaki
Kumamoto
Satsuma
Shimabara
Nishino-omote
Isahaya
Sendai

Ullŭng-do (S. Korea)

Liancourt Rocks
Claimed and administered
by South Korea as Dok-do;
claimed by Japan as Take-shima

Oki-shotō
Dōgo
Dōzen

135°

PACIFIC

OCEAN

C

Sumisu-jima

140°

30°

Ōsumi-shotō
Ōsumi-kaikyō

130°

B

Longitude 135° east of Greenwich

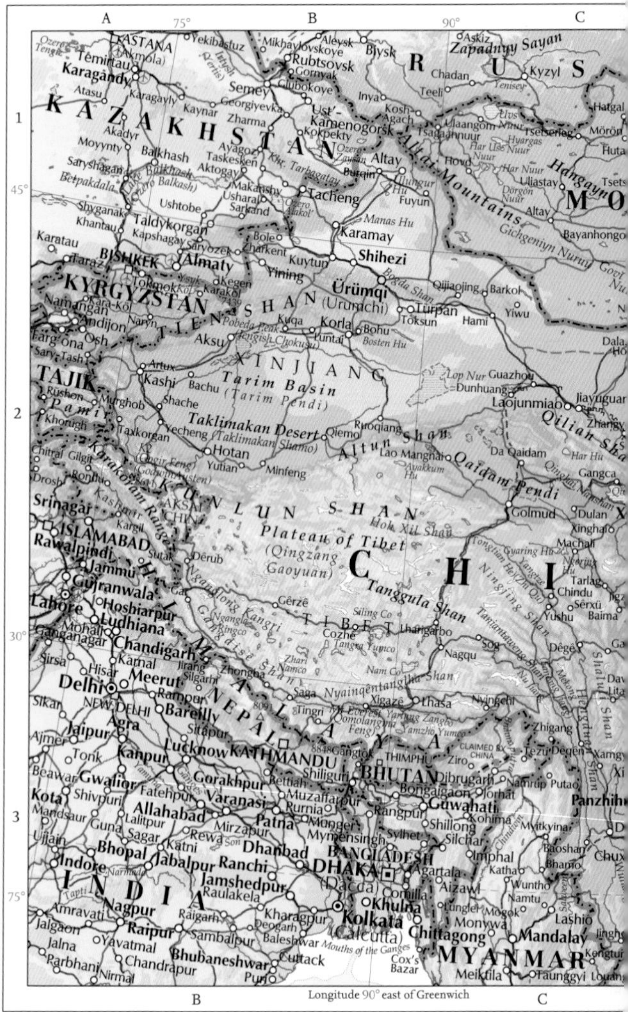

Albers Equal Area Conic Projection

1 : 30 000 000

MILES 0   200   400

Longitude 90° east of Greenwich

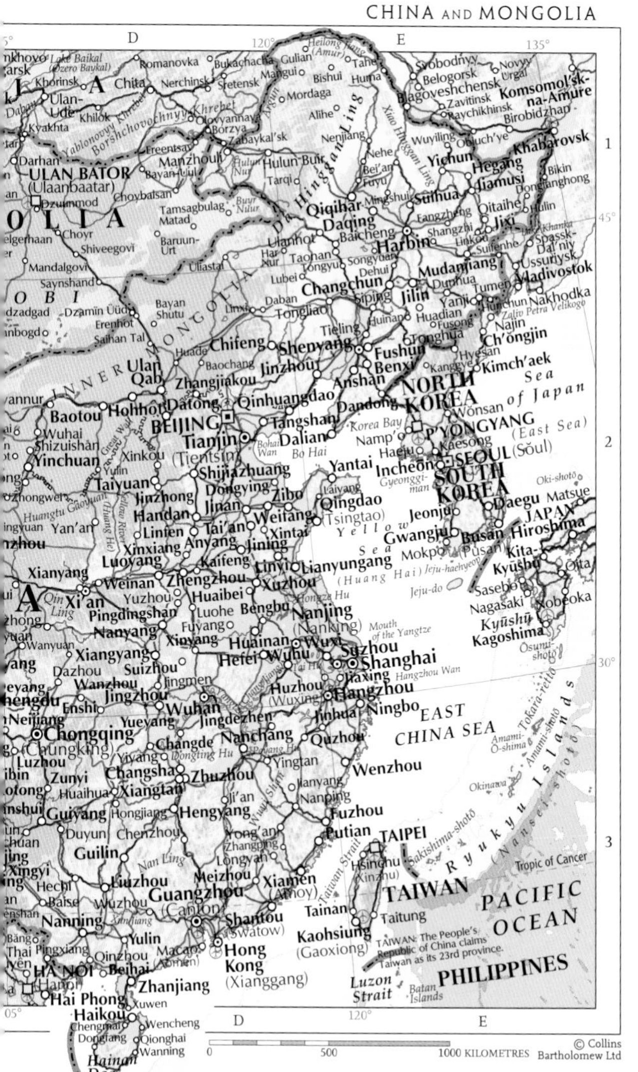
ULAN BATOR
(Ulaanbaatar)
BEIJING
Tianjin
Shenyang
Harbin
Changchun
Dalian
Qingdao
Shanghai
Hangzhou
Nanjing
Wuhan
Chongqing
Guangzhou
(Canton)
Hong Kong
(Xianggang)
TAIPEI
TAIWAN
P'YONGYANG
SEOUL
NORTH KOREA
SOUTH KOREA
JAPAN
Sea of Japan
(East Sea)
Yellow Sea
(Huang Hai)
EAST CHINA SEA
PACIFIC OCEAN
PHILIPPINES
Vladivostok
Khabarovsk
Tropic of Cancer
TAIWAN: The People's Republic of China claims Taiwan as its 23rd province.
HA NOI
(Hanoi)
Hai Phong
Haikou
Hainan Dao
Ryukyu Islands
(Nansei-shotō)
Luzon Strait
Taiwan Strait
1000 KILOMETRES
© Collins Bartholomew Ltd

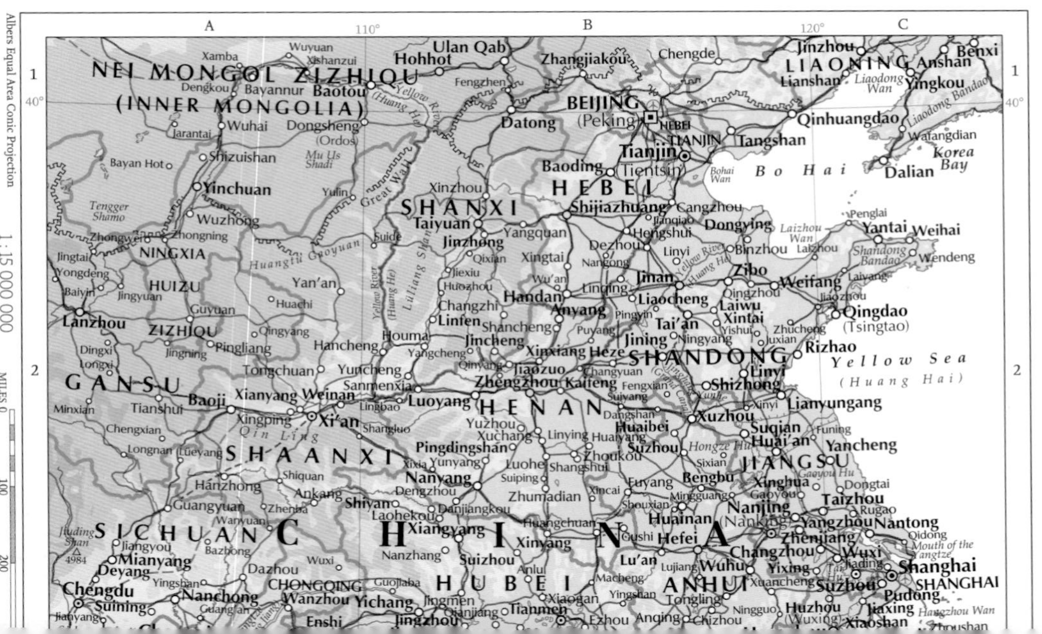

Albers Equal Area Conic Projection   1 : 15 000 000   MILES 0   100   200

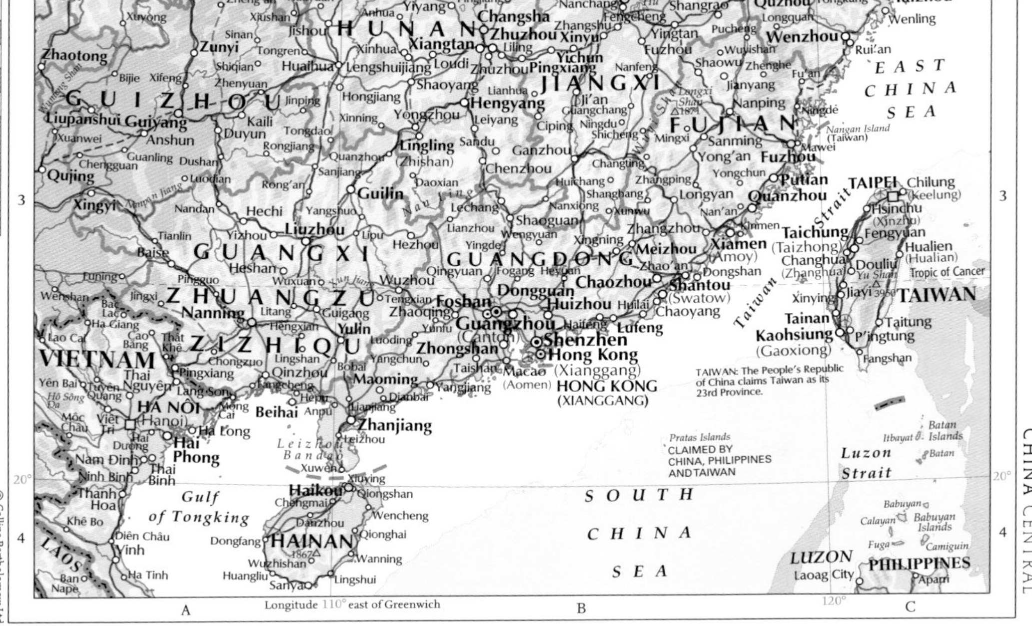

EAST CHINA SEA

Yong'an Fuzhou
Putian Quanzhou
Yongchun
Sanming
Nanping
Zhangzhou Xiamen (Amoy)
Longyan Quanzhou
Meizhou Shantou (Swatow)
Chaozhou Chaoyang

FUJIAN

TAIPEI
Chilung (Keelung)
Hsinchu
Taichung (Taizhong)
Changhua Douliu (Hualian)
Chiai (Zhangyi)
Tainan
Kaohsiung (Gaoxiong)
Pingtung
Taitung

TAIWAN

Tropic of Cancer

Luzon Strait

Batan Islands
Batan
Ibugao
Babuyan Babuyan Islands
Fuga Camiguin
Claveria
Laoag City

PHILIPPINES

LUZON

TAIWAN: The People's Republic
of China claims Taiwan as its
23rd Province.

Pratas Island
CLAIMED BY
CHINA, PHILIPPINES
AND TAIWAN

JIANGXI

Changsha
Zhuzhou Xiangtan
Loudi Zhuzhou Pingxiang
Shaoyang
Hengyang
Lingling Lianhua
Daoxian

HUNAN

Shaoguan
Yingde
Qingyuan
Foshan Guangzhou
Zhaoqing (Canton)
Jiangmen
Taishan

GUANGDONG

Dongguan
Huizhou Haifeng
Shenzhen
Hong Kong
Macao (Xianggang)
(Aomen) HONG KONG
(XIANGGANG)

SOUTH CHINA SEA

GUIZHOU
Zunyi
Guiyang Anshun
Liupanshui Duyun
Xingyi Kaili
Qujing

Guilin
Liuzhou Yangshuo
Hechi
Laibin

GUANGXI

Nanning
Beihai
Zhanjiang

GUANGXI

VIETNAM
HÀ NOI (Hanoi)
Hai Phong

Haikou
HAINAN
Sanya

Gulf of Tongking

LAOS

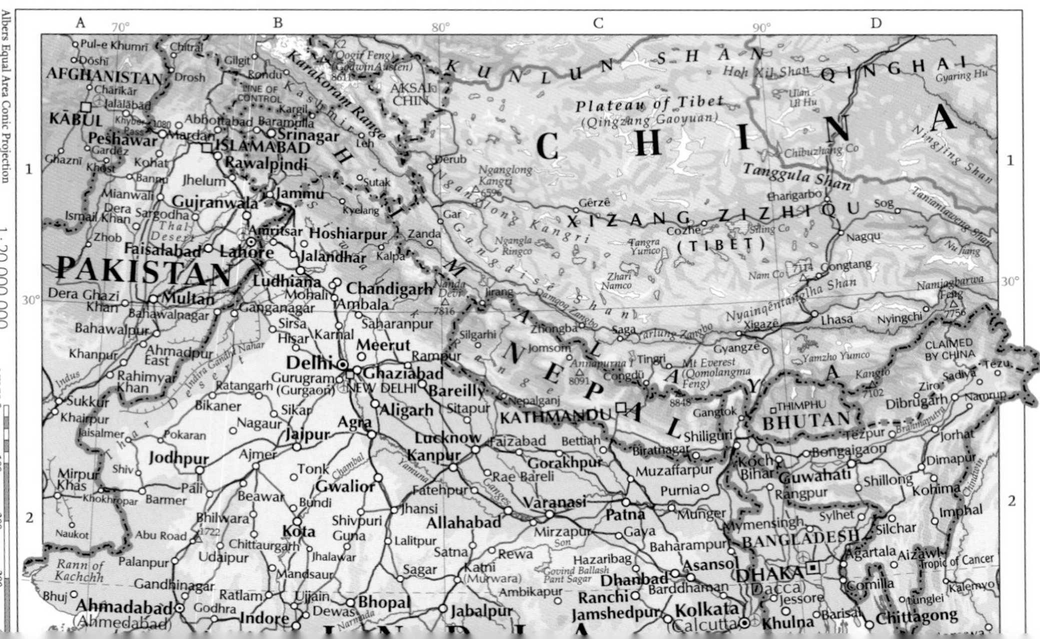

Albers Equal Area Conic Projection   1 : 20 000 000   MILES 0   100   200   300

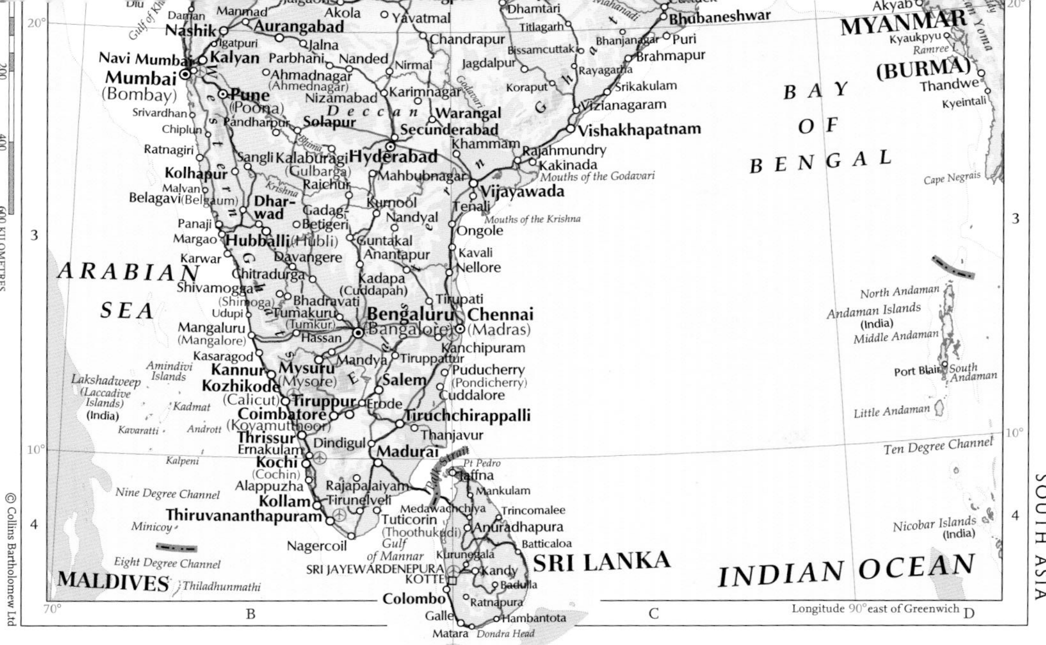

MYANMAR
(BURMA)

Akyab
Kyaukpyu
Ramree
Thandwe
Kyeintali
Cape Negrais

BAY
OF
BENGAL

North Andaman
Andaman Islands
(India)
Middle Andaman
Port Blair
South Andaman
Little Andaman

Ten Degree Channel

Nicobar Islands
(India)

INDIAN OCEAN

Bhubaneshwar
Puri
Bhanjanagar
Brahmapur
Tiklagarh
Bissamcuttack
Sikakulam
Ravagada
Koraput
Vishakhapatnam

Dhamtari
Chandrapur
Jagdalpur
Rajahmundry
Kakinada
Mouths of the Godavari

Yavatmal
Akola
Aurangabad
Jalna
Ahmadnagar
(Ahmednagar)
Nizamabad
Nanded
Parbhani
Karimnagar
Warangal
Nirmal
Nagpur
Deccan
Khammam
Vijayawada
Machilipatnam
Mouths of the Krishna

Nashik
Kalyan
Navi Mumbai
Mumbai
(Bombay)
Pune
(Poona)
Solapur
Chiplun
Srivardhan
Ratnagiri

Sangli
Kolhapur
Malvan
Ratnagiri
Panaji
Margao
Belagavi(Belgaum)
Karwar

Gulbarga
Kalaburagi
Raichur
Gadag
Hubballi-Dharwad
Bagalkot
Bijapur
Dharwad
Shivamogga
(Shimoga)
Chitradurg
Davangere

ARABIAN
SEA

Lakshadweep
Islands
Amindivi
Islands
Laccadive
Islands
(India)
Kadmat
Amini
Kavaratti

Secunderabad
Hyderabad
Mahbubnagar
Gadwal
Kurnool
Nandyal
Kadapa
(Cuddapah)
Anantapur
Tirupati
Nellore
Kavali
Ongole

Bidar
Bhadravati
Tumakuru
(Tumkur)
Hassan
Mysuru
(Mysore)
Mangaluru
(Mangalore)
Udupi
Kasaragod

Bengaluru
Bangalore
Vellore
Chennai
(Madras)
Kanchipuram
Tiruppur
Puducherry
(Pondicherry)
Cuddalore

Salem
Erode
Tiruchirappalli
Thanjavur
Kannur
(Cannanore)
Kozhikode
(Calicut)
Thrissur
(Trichur)
Coimbatore
(Koyambuttoor)
Dindigul
Madurai
Rajapalaiyam
Tirunelveli
Tuticorin
(Thoothukudi)
Nagercoil

Ernakulam
Kochi
(Cochin)
Alappuzha
Kollam
Thiruvananthapuram

MALDIVES
Minicoy
(India)
Kalpeni

SRI LANKA
Jaffna
Pt Pedro
Medawachchiya
Anuradhapura
Trincomalee
Batticaloa
Kurunegala
Kandy
Badulla
SRI JAYEWARDENEPURA KOTTE
Colombo
Ratnapura
Galle
Matara
Dondra Head
Hambantota
Gulf of Mannar

Nine Degree Channel
Eight Degree Channel

Longitude 90° east of Greenwich D

200   400   600 KILOMETRES

© Collins Bartholomew Ltd   73

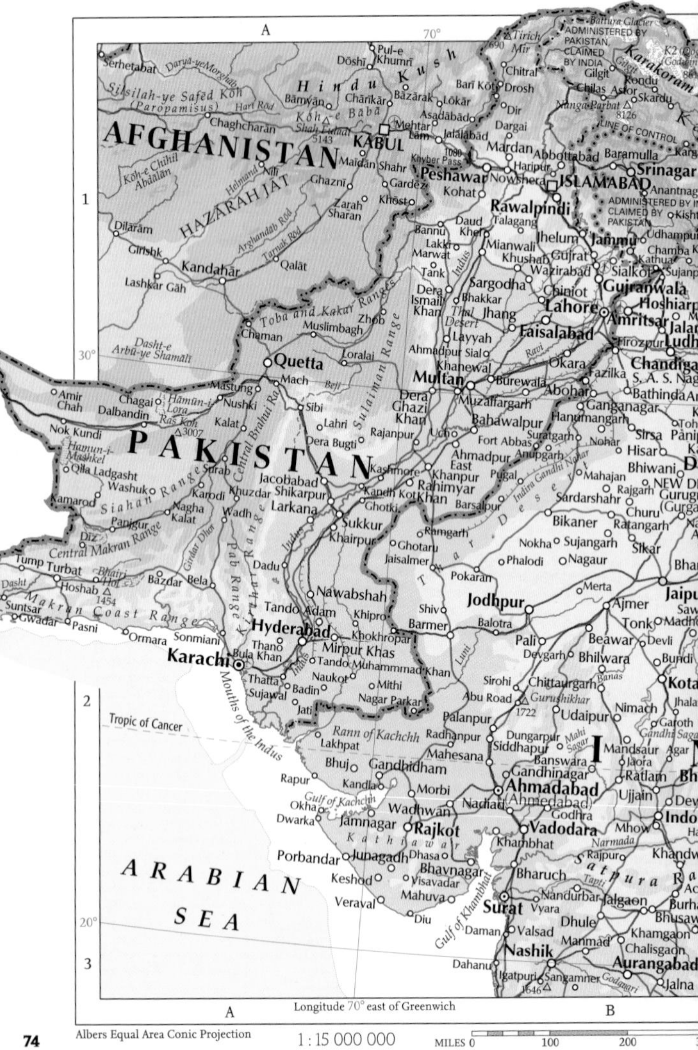

Serhetabat
Silsilah-ye Safed Kōh
(Paropamisus)
Hari Rōd
Chaghcharan
Dōshī
Pul-e Khumrī
Hindu Kush
Tirich Mīr
7690
K2
Godwi
8611
Bāmiyān
Charikār
Bāzārak
Bari Kōṭ
Drosh
Chilas
Skardu
Koh-e Bābā
Shah Fulādī
5143
Mehtarlām
Jalālābād
Dir
Chitral
Nanga Parbat
8126
LINE OF CONTROL
ADMINISTERED BY
PAKISTAN
CLAIMED
BY INDIA
Karakoram

AFGHANISTAN
KABUL
Maidān Shahr
Asadābād
Mardan
Abbottābād
Bāzārak
Peshāwar
Nowshera
Haripur
Baramula
Srīnagar
Anantnag
ISLAMABAD
Rawalpindi
ADMINISTERED BY
CLAIMED BY
PAKISTAN

Koh-e Chihil
Abdalān
Ghaznī
Gardēz
Khōst
Kohat
Daud
Khēl
Talagang
Jhelum
Jammu
Udhampur
Chamba
Kisht

Dīlārām
HAZĀRĀHJĀT
Zarah Sharan
Bannu
Lakki
Marwat
Khushab
Sargodha
Gujrat
Sialkot
Gujranwala
Hoshiarpur
Jalan

Girishk
Arghandab Rūd
3007
Qalāt
Tank
Dera Ismāil Khan
Thal
Jhang
Chiniot
Lahore
Amritsar
Ludh

Kandahār
Tarnak Rūd
Toba and Kakar Ranges
Zhob
Muslimbagh
Ahmadpur Sial
Faisalabad
Okāra
Fazilka
Chandiga
S.A.S. Nag.

Lashkar Gāh
Chaman
Loralai
Khānewāl
Burewāla
Abohar
Bathinda
Ar

Dasht-e
Arbu-ye Shamali
Mastung
Quetta
Mach
Bolan
Sibi
Dera Ghāzi Khan
Multan
Muzaffargarh
Bahāwalpur
Hanumangarh
Sirsa
Panip

PAKISTAN
Kalāt
Lahri
Rājanpur
Dera Bugti
Ahmadpur East
Fort Abbas
Pugal
Nohar
Hisar
Bhiwani
NEW D

Amir Chah
Chāgai
Hamun-i-Lora
Ras Koh
3007
Khuzdar
Jacobābad
Shikārpur
Kashmor
Khānpur
Rahimyar
Khan
Barsalpur
Mahājan
Sardārshahr
Churu
Gurga
Gurga

Nōk Kundi
Dalbandin
Surāb
Central Brahui Range
Karodi
Larkāna
Kandh Kot
Ghōtki
Bīkāner
Sujāngarh
Ratangarh
Bhar

Qila Ladgasht
Humun-i-Mashkel
Wadh
Khudar
Sukkur
Khairpur
Ghotāru
Jaisalmer
Nokha
Nāgaur
Sikar

Kamarod
Siahan *Range*
Panjgūr
Nagha
Kalat
Dādu
Nawābshāh
Pokaran
Phalodi
Merta
Jaipu
Saw

Tump
Turbat
Central Makran Range
1454
Bela
Khipro
Barmer
Balotra
Jodhpur
Ajmer
Tonk
Devli
Bundi

Dasht
Bāzdar
Nawābshāh
Tando Adam
Mirpur Khas
Pāli
Devgarh
Bhilwara

Hoshab
Bhaji
Makran Coast Range
Sonmiāni
Bula Khan
Hyderābād
Tando
Muhammad Khan
Nagar Parkar
Sirohi
Chittaurgarh
Bhilwara
Kota
Jhal

Suntsar
Pasni
Ormara
Thatta
Badin
Naukot
Mithi
Abu Road
Gurushikhar
1722
Udaipur
Dungarpur
Banswara
Mandsaur
Agar

Gwādar
Mouths of the Indus
Karāchi
Sujāwal
Jāti
Rann of Kachchh
Lakhpat
Radhanpur
Siddhpur
Dungarpur
Mahi
Ratlam
Ujjain
Indo

Tropic of Cancer
Bhuj
Gandhidham
Mahesana
Gandhinagar
Godhra
Mhow
Khandw

Rāpar
Kandla
Morbi
Nadiad
Ahmadābad
Vadodara
Narmada
Jathura Ra

Okha
Dwārka
Jāmnagar
Wadhwan
Dhasa
Khambhat
Bharuch

ARABIAN
SEA
Porbandar
Junāgadh
Rajkot
Kathiawar
Visavadar
Bhāvnagar
Gulf of Khambhat
Sūrat
Valsad
Daman
Nandurbar
Jalgaon
Bhusaw

Keshod
Mahuva
Diu
Vyāra
Dhule
Khamgaon

Verāval
Dahanu
Kalyan
Sangamner
Godavari
Manmad
Chalisgaon
Aurangabad

Nāshik
Igatpuri
1646

Albers Equal Area Conic Projection
Longitude 70° east of Greenwich
1 : 15 000 000
MILES 0   100   200

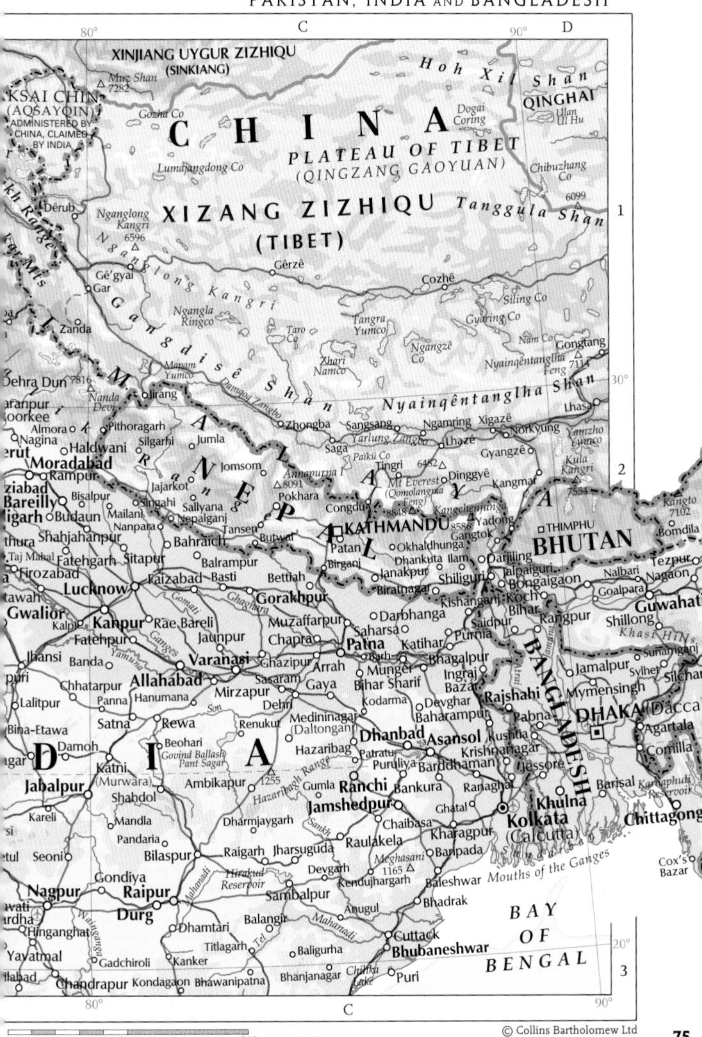

KSAI CHIN
(AQSAYQIN)
ADMINISTERED BY
CHINA, CLAIMED
BY INDIA

XINJIANG UYGUR ZIZHIQU
(SINKIANG)

Muz Shan
728?

Gozha Co

Hoh Xil Shan

QINGHAI

Ulan
Ul Hu

C H I N A

PLATEAU OF TIBET
(QINGZANG GAOYUAN)

Lumajangdong Co

Dogai
Coring

Chibuzhang Co

XIZANG ZIZHIQU
(TIBET)

Tanggula Shan

6099

Nganglong
Kangri
6596

Derub

Ng01

Ge'gyai

Gar

Gerze

Cozhe

Ngangla
Ringco

Tingri

6452

Siling Co

Gyaring Co

Nam Co

Nyainqentanglha
Feng
711

Gongtang

Zanda

Taro
Co

Zhari
Namco

Ngangze
Co

Lhasa

Nyainqentanglha Shan

30°

Manam
Yumco

Dehra Dun
7816

Nanda
Devi

Nanda

Zhongba

Sangsang

Ngamring

Xigaze

Norkyung

Lanzho
Yumco

Almora

Pithoragarh

Silgarhi

Jumla

Saga

Yarlung Zangbo

Lhaze

Gyangze

Kangri
7543

erut

Nagina

Haldwani

Paiku Co

Tingri

Dinggye

Kangma

2

Moradabad

Rampur

Bisalpur

Jajarkot

Annapurna I
8091

Pokhara

Congdo

*Everest
(Qomolangma)
8848*

Kangchenjunga
8586

Yadong

Kanchro
7102

Bareilly

Singhali

Nepalganj

Tansen

KATHMANDU

Dhankuta

Darjiling

THIMPHU

BHUTAN

Bomdila

igarh

Budaun

Mailani

Nanpara

Butwal

Patan

Birganj

Ilam

Shiliguri

Bongaigaon

Nalbari

Tezpur

thura

Shahjahanpur

Bahraich

Balrampur

Janakpur

Biratnagar

Kishanganj

Koch

Rangpur

Goalpara

Nagaon

Guwahati

Taj Mahal

Fatehgarh

Sitapur

Faizabad

Basti

Gorakhpur

Muzaffarpur

Darbhanga

Saidpur

Purnia

Bihar

Shillong

Khasi Hills

Firozabad

Lucknow

Kanpur

Rae Bareli

Jaunpur

Chapra

Patna

Katihar

Bhagalpur

Rajshahi

Jamalpur

Silchar

tawah

Gwalior

Kalpi

Fatehpur

Allahabad

Varanasi

Arrah

Munger

Ingraj
Bazar

Pabna

Mymensingh

DHAKA (Dacca)

Sylhet

Jhansi

Banda

Chhatarpur

Panna

Hanumana

Mirzapur

Sasaram

Gaya

Bihar Sharif

Kodarma

Deoghar

Baharampur

BANGLADESH

Agartala

Comilla

Lalitpur

Bina-Etawa

Satna

Rewa

Dehri

Renukut

Medininagar
(Daltonganj)

Hazaribag

Dhanbad

Asansol

Krishnanagar

Kushtia

Jessore

Barddhaman

Khulna

Barisal

Karnaphuli
Reservoir

Damoh

Katni
(Murwara)

Shahdol

Ambikapur

Gumla

Ranchi

Patratu
Purulia

Jamshedpur

Ranaghat

Chittagong

D I A

Jabalpur

Kareli

Mandla

Dharmjaygarh

Pandaria

Raigarh

Bilaspur

Chaibasa

Raulakela

Jharsuguda

Devgarh

Bampada

Kharagpur

Kolkata
(Calcutta)

Meghasani
1165

Ghatal

Cox's
Bazar

Seoni

Nagpur

Gondiya

Raipur

Durg

Dhamtari

Bhilaspur

Sambalpur

Kendujhargarh

Anugul

Bhadrak

Mouths of the Ganges

vati

rdha

Hinganghat

Kanker

Titlagarh

Balangir

Baligurha

Mahanadi

Cuttack

Bhubaneshwar

BAY

Yavatmal

Gadchiroli

Kondagaon

Bhawanipatna

Bhanjanagar

Chilika
Lake

Puri

20°

OF

labad

Chandrapur

Kondagaon

Bhawanipatna

BENGAL

3

80°

C

90°

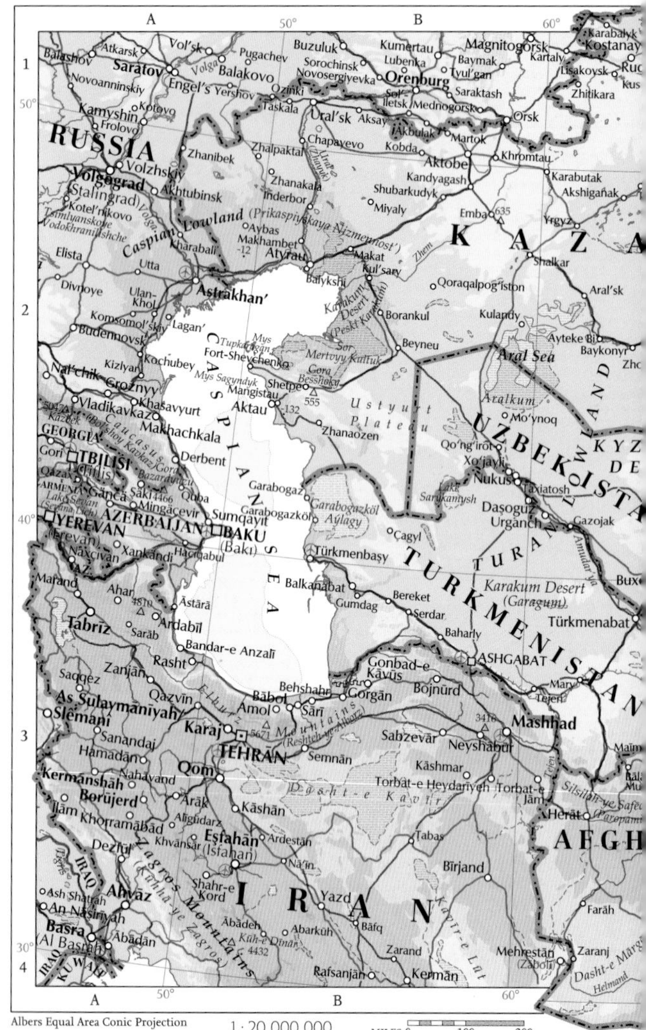

Albers Equal Area Conic Projection   1 : 20 000 000   MILES 0   100   200

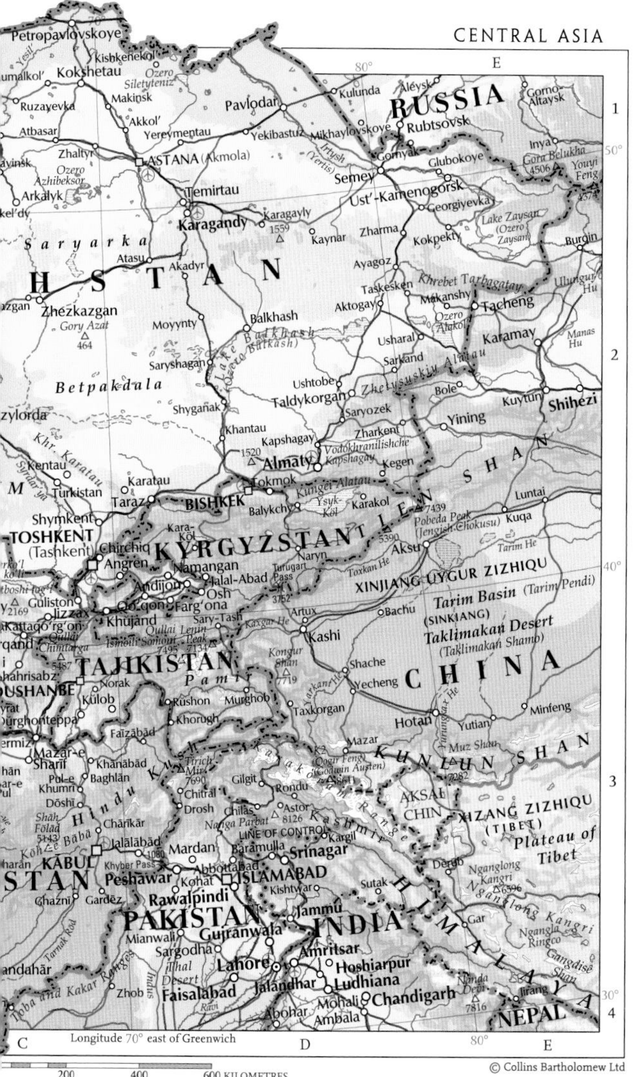

Petropavlovskoye
Kishkenekol'
umalkol' Kokshetau
Ruzayevka Makinsk
'Akkol' Yereymentau
Atbasar Zhaltyr
ASTANA (Akmola)
Arkalyk Ozero Zhiibeksor
kel'dy
Temirtau
Karagandy Karagayly
Saryarka Atasu Akadyr
H S T A N
zgan Zhezkazgan
Gory Azat 464 Moyynty
Betpakdala Balkhash
Saryshagan
zylorda Shyganak
Khantau
Kentau Karatau 1520 Kapshagay
Turkistan Kapshagay
M Taraz Almaty
Shymkent
Tokmok
TOSHKENT BISHKEK Balykchy
(Tashkent) Kara- Kol
Chirchiq Kungey-Alatau Ysyk-Köl
Angren KYRGYZSTAN Kol
Namangan Naryn
Andijon Jalal-Abad
Qŭqon Farg'ona Oš 3762
Khŭjand Sary-Tash
TAJIKISTAN Qullai Lenin 7439
Norak Pamir 7495
USHANBE Kŭlob Murghob
rat Khorugh
Faizabad
Ozero
Balkhash
(Balkash)
Ushtobe
Taldykorgan
Zharkent
Saryozek
Vodokhranilishche
Kapshagay
Kegen
Zhungar Alatau
Bole
Yining
Karamay
Sarkand
Ushoral
Aktogay
Taskesken
Khrebet Tarbagatay
Makanshy
Tacheng
Ayagoz
Ozero Alakol
Kaynar
Zharma
Kokpekty
Burqin
Georgiyevka
Ust'-Kamenogorsk
Lake Zaysan
Ozero Zaysan
Semey
Mikhaylovskoye
Rubtsovsk
Gornyak
RUSSIA
Aleysk
Kulunda
Pavlodar
Yekibastuz Irtysh (Yertis)
Glubokoye
Inya
Gora Belukha 4506
Youyi Feng
Gorno-Altaysk
Shihezi
Kuytun
Kuqa
Aksu
Luntai
TIEN SHAN
Pobeda Peak (Jengish Chokusu) 7439
Taxkan He
Tarim He
Artux
Kashi
Shache
Yecheng
Bachu
XINJIANG UYGUR ZIZHIQU (SINKIANG)
Tarim Basin (Tarim Pendi)
Taklimakan Desert (Taklimakan Shamo)
CHINA
Minfeng
Yutian
Hotan
Muz Tag
Mazar-e Sharif
Khanabad
Balkhan
Pol-e Khumri
Dōshī
Baghlan
Charikar
Jalalabad
KABUL
STAN
Peshawar
Ghazni
Gardez
Khyber Pass
Kohat
Rawalpindi
Mardan
Abbottabad
ISLAMABAD
Mianwali
Sargodha
Gujranwala
Lahore
Faisalabad
PAKISTAN
Tirich Mir 7690
Gilgit
Chitral
Drosh
Rondu
Astor
Chilas
Nanga Parbat 8126
Skardu
K2 (Qogir Feng) (Mount Godwin Austen) 8611
Gasherbrum 8068
HINDU KUSH
AKSAI CHIN
LINE OF CONTROL
Kargil
Srinagar
Baramula
KUNLUN SHAN
XIZANG ZIZHIQU (TIBET)
Plateau of Tibet
Deqen
Ngangolong Kangri
Kangri
Degoe
Ngangla Ringco
Gangdisê Shan
Jammu
Amritsar
Jalandhar
Hoshiarpur
Ludhiana
Chandigarh
Mohali
Ambala
INDIA
HIMALAYA
NEPAL
Kishtwar
Sutak

200   400   600 KILOMETRES

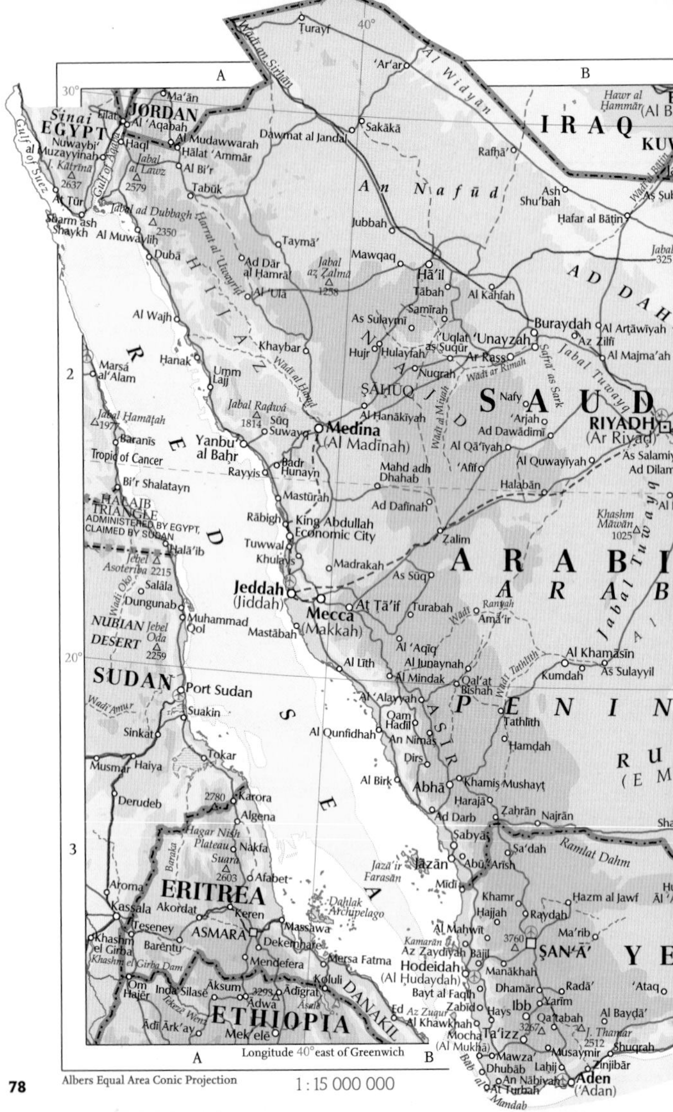
A
B
30°
40°
Ţurayf
'Ar'ar
Wādī as Sirḩān
Al Widyān
Hawr al Ḩammār (Al Ba
IRAQ
KUW
Sinai
EGYPT
JORDAN
Ma'ān
Eilat
Al 'Aqabah
Gulf of Suez
Gulf of Aqaba
Nuwaybi'
al Muzayyinah
Ḩaql
Al Mudawwarah
Ḩālat 'Ammār
Al Bi'r
J. Kātrīnā
2637
Jabal al Lawz
2579
Aţ Ţūr
Sharm ash Shaykh
Tabūk
Sakākā
Dawmat al Jandal
Rafḩā'
An Nafūd
Ash Shu'bah
Ḩafar al Bāţin
Aş Şuba
Wādī al Bāţin
Jabal ad Dubbagh
2350
Ḩarrat al 'Uwayrid
Al Muwayliḩ
Dubā
Taymā'
Jubbah
Mawqaq
Ḩā'il
Jabal-a
325
Ad Dār al Ḩamrā'
Jabal az Zalmā
1258
Al 'Ulā
Ţābah
Al Kahfah
AD DAHN
HIJAZ
Al Wajh
Samīrah
As Sulaymī
Buraydah
Al Arţāwīyah
Az Zilfī
Al Majma'ah
'Uqlat aş Şuqūr
'Unayzah
Khaybar
Hujr
Hulayfah
Ar Rass
Wādī ar Rimah
Şafrā' as Sark
Jabal Ţuwayq
Marsá al 'Alam
Ḩanak
Umm Lajj
Wādī al Ḩamḑ
Nuqrah
NAJD
ŞĀHŪQ
SAUDI
Nafy
'Arjah
RIYADH
(Ar Riyāḑ)
Jabal Radwá
1814
Jabal Ḩamāţah
1977
Sūq Suwayq
Medina
(Al Madīnah)
Al Ḩanākīyah
Wādī al Miyāh
Ad Dawādimī
Al Qā'īyah
Baranīs
Yanbu' al Baḩr
Tropic of Cancer
Badr Ḩunayn
Rayyis
Mahd adh Dhahab
'Afīf
Al Quwayīyah
As Salamiya
Ad Dilam
Bi'r Shalatayn
RED SEA
Mastūrah
Ḩalabān
Al Hi
HALAIB TRIANGLE
ADMINISTERED BY EGYPT, CLAIMED BY SUDAN
Ad Dafīnah
Rābigh
King Abdullah Economic City
Khashm Māwān
1025
Ḩalā'ib
Tuwwal
Zalim
Jebel Asoteriba
2215
Khulays
Madrakah
ARABIAN
Salâla
Wadi Oko
Jeddah
(Jiddah)
As Sūq
ARAB
Dungunab
Mecca
(Makkah)
Aţ Ţā'if
Turabah
Ranyah
Wādī
'Amā'ir
NUBIAN DESERT
Jebel Oda
2259
Muhammad Qol
Mastābah
20°
SUDAN
Al 'Aqīq
Al Khamāsīn
Al Līth
Al Junaynah
Wādī Tathlīth
Kumdah
As Sulayyil
Port Sudan
Al Mindak
Qal'at Bīshah
Wadi Amur
Suakin
Al 'Alayyah
PENIN
Qam Hadīl
Tathlīth
Sinkat
Al Qunfidhah
An Nimāş
Ḩamdah
ASIR
Tokar
RU
(EM
Musmar
Haiya
Dirs
Al Birk
Abhā
Khamīs Mushayţ
Derudeb
2780
Karora
Ḩarajā
Ẓahrān
Najrān
Shara
Algena
Ad Darb
Hagar Nish Plateau
Nakfa
Şabyā
Şa'dah
Ramlat Dahm
Baraka
Suara
2603
Jīzān
Abū 'Arīsh
Jazā'ir Farasān
Afabet
Midi
Aroma
ERITREA
Dahlak Archipelago
Khamr
Ḩazm al Jawf
Hus Āl 'Al
Kassala
Akordat
Keren
Ḩajjah
Raydah
Teseney
ASMARA
Massawa
Al Maḩwīt
Ma'rib
Khashm el Girba
Barentu
Dekemhare
Kamarān
Az Zaydīyah
Bājil
3760
ŞAN'Ā'
YE
Khashm el Girba Dam
Mendefera
Mersa Fatma
Hodeidah
(Al Ḩudaydah)
Manākhah
Om Hajer
Inda Silasē
Āksum
3293
Ādīgrat
Koluli
DANAKIL
Dhamār
Radā'
'Ataq
Tekezē Wenz
Ādwa
Āsalē
Bayt al Faqīh
Zabīd
Ḩays
Ibb
Yarīm
Al Bayḑā'
ETHIOPIA
Az Zuqur
Al Khawkhah
Qa'ţabah
3267
Ādī Ārk'ay
Mek'elē
Mocha (Al Mukhā)
Ta'izz
J. Thamar
2512
Shuqrah
Longitude 40° east of Greenwich
Mawza'
Musaymīr
Dhubāb
Laḩij
Zinjibār
Bab al Mandab
An Nābiyah
Aţ Ţurbah
Aden
('Adan)

Albers Equal Area Conic Projection

1 : 15 000 000

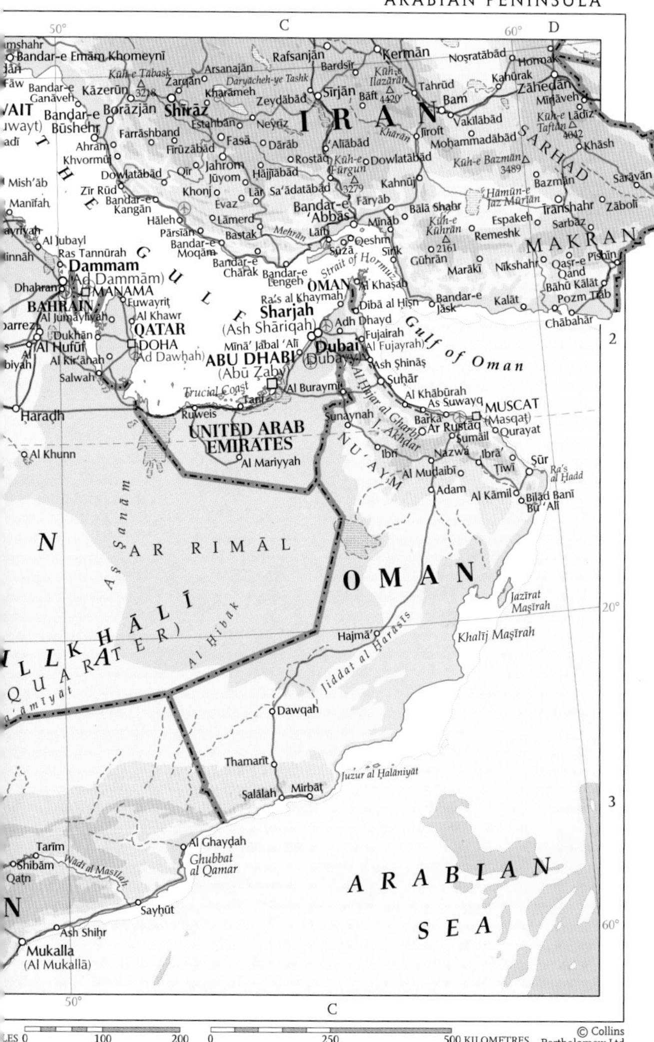

IRAN
Shīrāz
Kermān
Rafsanjān
Sīrjān
Bandar-e 'Abbās
Zāhedān
SARHAD
MAKRAN
Bandar-e Emām Khomeynī
Būshehr
Kāzerūn
Borāzjān
Jahrom
Lār
Mīnāb
Jīroft
Bam
Īrānshahr
Chābahār
Dammam (Ad Dammām)
MANAMA
BAHRAIN
QATAR
DOHA (Ad Dawḩah)
ABU DHABI (Abū Ẕaby)
Dubai (Dubayy)
Sharjah (Ash Shāriqah)
Ra's al Khaymah
Fujairah (Al Fujayrah)
UNITED ARAB EMIRATES
Al Buraymī
Şuḩār
MUSCAT (Masqaţ)
Nazwá
Şūr
Ra's al Ḩadd
OMAN
Strait of Hormuz
Gulf of Oman
THE GULF
AR RIMĀL
RUB' AL KHĀLĪ (EMPTY QUARTER)
Jazīrat Maşīrah
Khalīj Maşīrah
Jiddat al Ḩarāsīs
Hajmā'
Dawqah
Thamarīt
Şalālah
Mirbāţ
Juzur al Ḩalāniyāt
Al Ghayḑah
Sayḩūt
Ash Shiḩr
Mukalla (Al Mukallā)
ARABIAN SEA
Al Hufūf
Ḩaraḑh
Al Khunn
Al Mariyyah

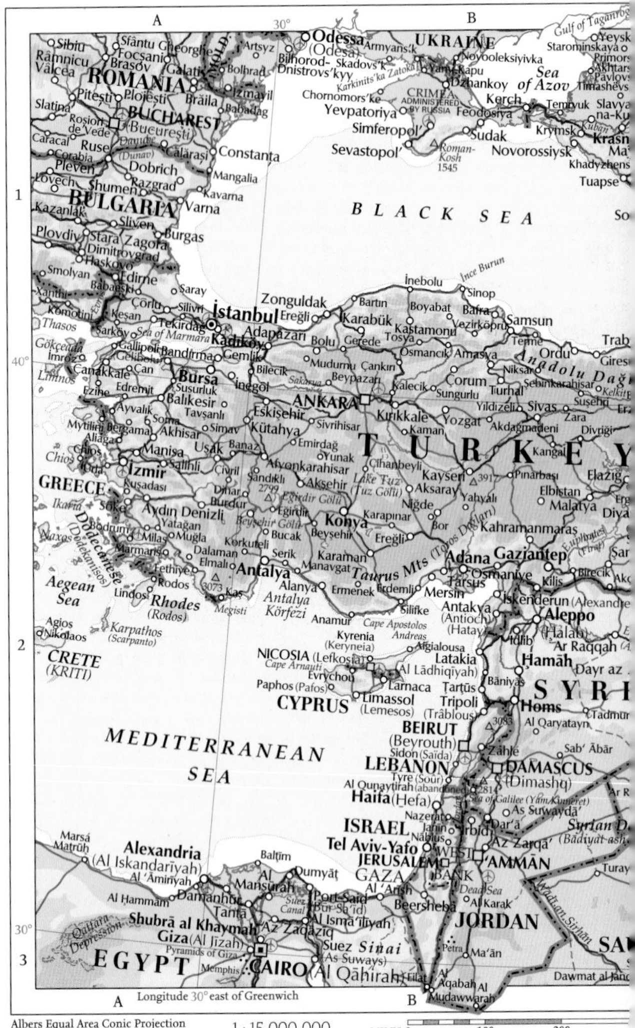

Gulf of Taganrog

UKRAINE
Sibiu Sfântu Gheorghe Artsyz **Odessa** Armyans'k Novo+ Starominskaya Yeysk
Râmnicu Focșani Brasov Bilhorod- Skadovs'k (Odesa) boleksiyivka Sea Primorskaya
Vâlcea Pitești Galați Bolhrad Dnistrovs'kyy Karkinits'ka Zatoka Yany Kapu Dzhankoy Akhtar Timashevsk
Slatina Ploiești Brăila Izmaïl Chornomors'ke CRIMEA ADMINISTERED Kerch Temryuk Slavya-
Roșiori **BUCHAREST** Babadag Yevpatoriya BY RUSSIA Feodosiya na-ku **Krasn**
de Vede Rusev Danube (Dunări) Simferopol' Sudak Novorossiysk Khadyzhens Slavya-
Caracal Corabi Călărași Constanța Sevastopol' Roman- Krymsk
Pleven Shumen Razgrad Mangalia Kosh Tuapse So
BULGARIA Dobrich 1545
Lovech Kazanlŭk Varna
Plovdiv Stara Zagora Burgas **B L A C K S E A**
(Dimitrovgrad)

Smolyan Edirne Şaray Zonguldak Bartin İnebolu İnce Burun Sinop
Babaeski Çorlu Silivri İstanbul Ereğli Karabük Boyabat Bafra Samsun
Thasos Keşan Şarköy Tekirdağ **Kadıköy** Adapazarı Bolu Gerede Tosya Osmancık Amasya Terme Ordu Trab
Gökçeada Gallipoli Bandırma Gemlik Düzce Beypazarı Çorum Niksar Şebinkarahisar Gires
İmroz Çanakkale Can Bilecik Sakarya Çankırı Sungurlu Yıldızeli Sivas
Ezine Biga Edremit **Bursa** İnegöl Eskişehir Ankara Kırıkkale Kaman Yozgat Akdağmadeni Zara Divriği
Ayvalık Balıkesir Tavşanlı Kütahya Sivrihisar Kırşehir Kangal
Mytilíni Bergama Akhisar Simav Banaz Emirdağ Çihanbeyli Lake Tuz Yahyalı Elbistan
Chíos Manisa Salihli Uşak Afyonkarahisar (Tuz Gölü) Aksaray Kahramanmaraş Malatya
GREECE **İzmir** Ödemiş Dinar Sandıklı Akşehir Karapınar Bor Ereğli Osmaniye İskenderun
Kuşadası Aydın Denizli Burdur Beyşehir Eğirdir Gölü Konya Ereğli **Adana** **Gaziantep**
İkaría Söke Nazilli Çivril Tavas Isparta Beyşehir Karaman Taurus Mts (Toros Dağı) Tarsus Antakya Kilis **Aleppo**
Bodrum Milas Muğla Köyceğiz Elmalı Serik Manavgat Mersin (Antioch) (Hatay) (Halab) Ar Raqqah
Kárpathos Fethiye Antalya Alanya Ermenek Erdemli Silifke Kyrenia Hamāh
(Scarpanto) Rhodes Antalya Anamur Cape Apostolos Latakia **SYRIA**
CRETE Lindos (Rodos) Körfezi Andreas Dayr az
(KRITI) Megísti NICOSIA Cape Arnauti Afigalousa Al Lādhiqīyah Baniyas Zawr
Agios (Lefkosía) Kyrenía Larnaca Tartūs Homs Tadmu
Níkólaos Paphos (Pafos) Evrychou Evrychou **CYPRUS** Limassol Tripoli Al Qaryatayn
(Lemesos) (Trâblous) Ḥomṣ

M E D I T E R R A N E A N **BEIRUT** Sab'Ābar
(Beyrouth) **DAMASCUS**
S E A Sidon (Saïda) Zahlé
LEBANON Tyre (Sour) As Suwaydā'
Sea of Galilee (Yām Kinneret) Ḍar'ā Suḥnah
Haifa (Ḥefa) Nazareth Az Zarqā' Surtán Bādiyat ash
Marsá Baltim **ISRAEL** **Tel Aviv-Yafo WEST** **AMMAN** Turay
Maṭrūḥ **Alexandria** Manṣūra **JERUSALEM** **BANK**
(Al Iskandarīyah) Al 'Āmirīyah Dumyāṭ **GAZA** Dead Sea
Al Hammām Damanhūr Port Said Al 'Arīsh Al Karak **JORDAN** SA
Qattara Tanta Būr Sa'īd Beersheba
Depression **Shubrā al Khaymah** Zaqāzīq Suez Canal Ismâ'ilîya Ma'ān
Giza (Al Jīzah) Suez Sinai
Pyramids of Giza As Suways Aqaba Al
Memphis **CAIRO** (Al Qāhirah) Mudawwarah Dawmat al Jan
EGYPT

A Longitude 30° east of Greenwich B

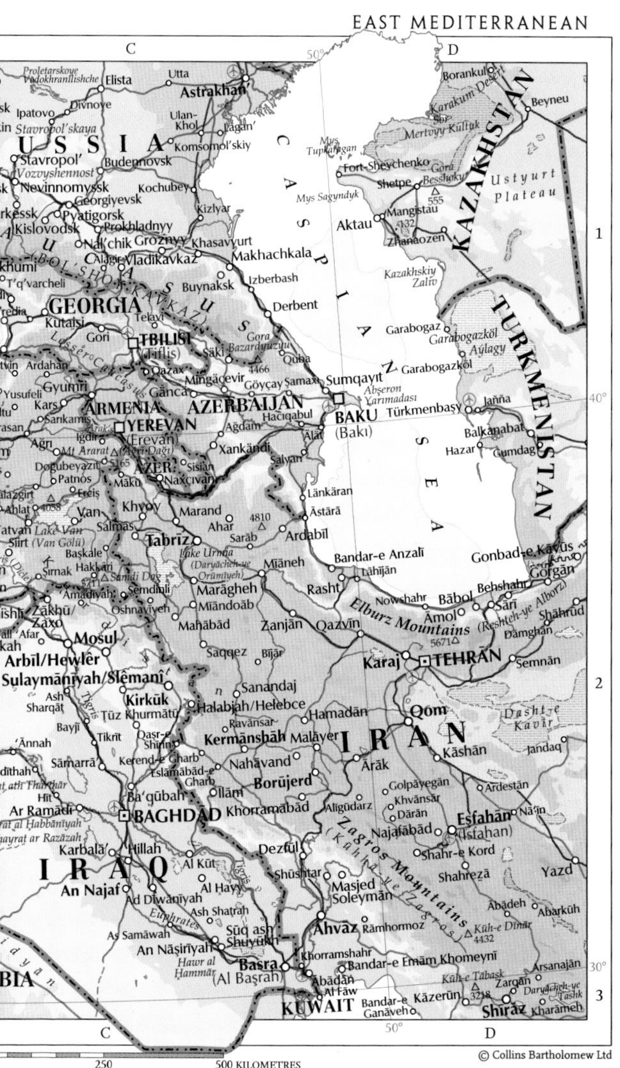
C
D
50°
40°
30°
1
2
3
RUSSIA
GEORGIA
ARMENIA
AZERBAIJAN
KAZAKHSTAN
TURKMENISTAN
IRAN
IRAQ
KUWAIT
CASPIAN SEA
Elista
Utta
Astrakhan'
Ipatovo
Divnoye
Stavropol'skaya
Ulan-Khol
Lagan'
Komsomol'skiy
Stavropol'
Budennovsk
Vozvyshennost'
Nevinnomyssk
Kochubey
Georgiyevsk
Kislovodsk
Pyatigorsk
Prokhladnyy
Kizlyar
Nal'chik
Groznyy
Khasavyurt
Makhachkala
Alagir
Vladikavkaz
T'q'varcheli
Buynaksk
Izberbash
Derbent
Telavi
Kutaisi
Gori
TBILISI
(Tiflis)
Şäki
Quba
Gora Bazardyuzyu
4466
Ardahan
Qazax
Mingäçevir
Göyçay
Şamaxı
Sumqayıt
Gyumri
Gäncä
Yusufeli
Kars
Sarıkamış
YEREVAN
(Erevan)
Ağdam
Hacıqabul
BAKU
(Bakı)
Abşeron Yarımadası
Älät
Iğdır
Ağrı
Mt Ararat
(Ağrı Dağı)
5165
Xankändi
Salyan
Doğubeyazıt
Patnos
AZER.
Sisian
Maku
Naxçıvan
Erciş
Länkäran
Ahlat
4058
Van
Khvoy
Marand
Ästärä
4810
Ahar
Tatvan
Lake Van
(Van Gölü)
Salmas
Siirt
Tabrīz
Sarāb
Ardabīl
Başkale
Lake Urmia
(Daryācheh-ye Orūmīyeh)
Hakkari
Şırnak
Mīāneh
Bandar-e Anzalī
Lāhījān
Rasht
Marāgheh
Amādīyah
Oshnavīyeh
Mīāndoāb
Zākhū/Zaxo
Mahābād
Zanjān
Qazvīn
Nowshahr
Bābol
Āmol
Sārī
Behshahr
Gorgān
Gonbad-e Kāvūs
Elburz Mountains
(Reshteh-ye Alborz)
5671
Shāhrūd
Dāmghān
Tall 'Afar
Mosul
Saqqez
Bījār
Karaj
TEHRĀN
Semnān
Arbīl/Hewlêr
Sulaymānīyah/Slêmanî
Sanandaj
Ash Sharqāṭ
Kirkūk
Halabjah/Helebce
Tigris
Ṭūz Khurmātū
Ravānsar
Hamadān
Qom
Dasht-e Kavīr
Bayjī
Tikrīt
Qaṣr-e Shīrīn
Kermānshāh
Malāyer
Kāshān
Jandaq
'Ānnah
Sāmarrā'
Kerend-e Gharb
Eslāmābād-e Gharb
Nahāvand
Arāk
Borūjerd
Golpāyegān
Ardestān
Hīt
Ba'qūbah
Īlām
Khvānsār
Ar Ramādī
BAGHDĀD
Khorramābād
Alīgūdarz
Dārān
Eşfahān
Nā'īn
Najafābād
(Isfahan)
Zagros Mountains
(Kūhhā-ye Zāgros)
Karbalā'
Ḥillah
Dezfūl
Shahr-e Kord
Al Kūt
Yazd
Shūshtar
Shahreẓā
An Najaf
Al Ḥayy
Masjed Soleymān
Ad Dīwānīyah
Ābādeh
Abarkūh
Euphrates
Ash Shaṭrah
Ahvāz
Rāmhormoz
Kūh-e Dīnār
4432
As Samāwah
Sūq ash Shuyūkh
An Nāşirīyah
Hawr al Ḥammār
Khorramshahr
Basra
(Al Başrah)
Ābādān
Bandar-e Emām Khomeynī
Al Fāw
Arsanajān
Kūh-e Tābask
3218
Zargān
Bandar-e Ganāveh
Kāzerūn
Shīrāz
Kharāmeh
Borankul
Karakum Desert
Beyneu
Sor Mertvyy Kultuk
Mys Tupkaragan
Fort-Shevchenko
Ustyurt Plateau
Shetpe
Gora Besshoky
555
Mys Sagyndyk
Aktau
Mangistau
132
Zhanaozen
Kazakhskiy Zaliv
Garabogaz
Garabogazköl Aýlagy
Garabogazköl
Jaňňa
Türkmenbaşy
Balkanabat
Hazar
Gumdag
Dashtī Kavīr
ABIA
250
500 KILOMETRES

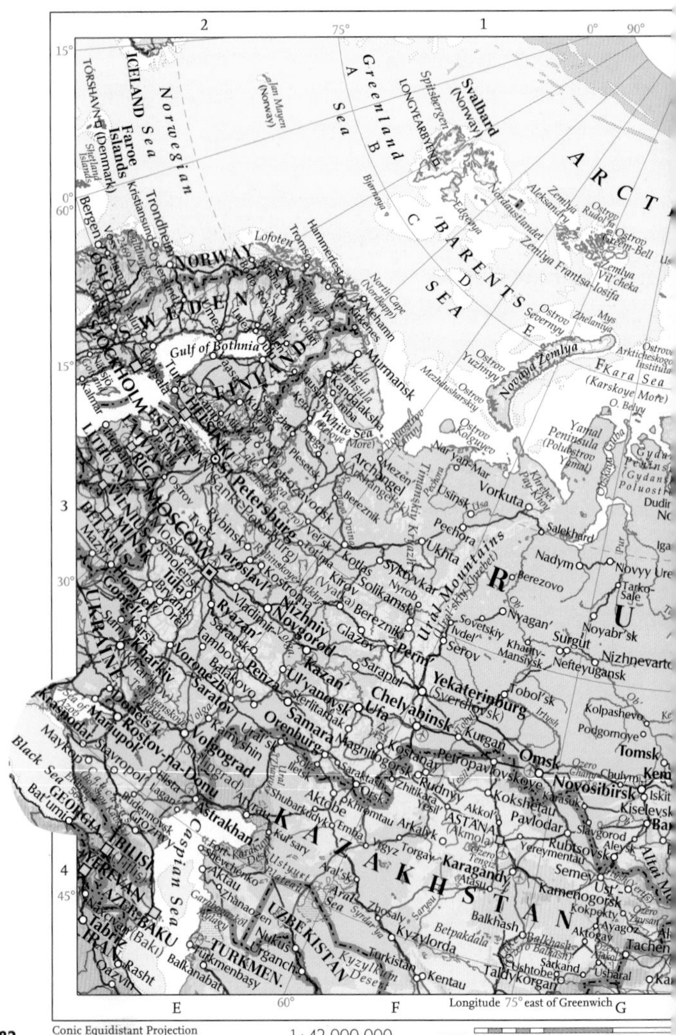

15°

ICELAND
Svalbard
(Norway)

Norwegian
Sea

Jan Mayen
(Norway)

Greenland
Sea

LONGYEARBYEN

Spitsbergen

TÓRSHAVN
Faroe
Islands
(Denmark)

0°
60°

Trondheim
Kristiansund
Bergen

Bjørnøya

NORWAY

ARCTIC

Aleksandry
Ostrov
Rudol'fa
Mys Zhelaniya
Mud
Novaya
Zemlya

BARENTS
SEA

SWEDEN

Lofoten

North Cape
(Nordkapp)

Hammerfest

Murmansk

Nardoand
Alesund

Severnyy

Ostrov Belyy
Yuzhnyy

Novaya
Zemlya

Fkara
(Karskoye More)
Sea

15°

Gulf of Bothnia

FINLAND

Kandalaksha

White Sea
(Beloye More)

Kem'

Mezhdusharskiy

Ostrov
Vaygach

Yamal
Peninsula
(Poluostrov
Yamal)

Gydan
Penin
(Polu
Polu

HELSINKI

St Petersburg

Arkhangel'sk

Mezen'

Nar'yan-Mar

Vorkuta

Salekhard

Novyy Ure

Dudi

LITHUANIA

MINSK

BELARUS

MOSCOW

Vologda

Kotlas

Ukhta

Pechora

Nadym

Berezovo

Novyy Urengoy

Tarko-
Sale

30°

Yaroslavl'

Nizhniy
Novgorod

Kirov

Syktyvkar

Nyrob

Solikamsk

Berezniki

Nyagan'

RU

Noyabr'sk

Surgut

Nizhnevart

UKRAINE

Ryazan'

Vladimir

Glazov

Perm'

Ivdel'

Serov

Khanty-
Mansiysk

Nefteyugansk

Penza

Kazan'

Ul'yanovsk

Sarapul

Sovetskiy

Tobol'sk

Kolpashevo

Podgornoye

Tomsk

Voronezh

Saratov

Samara

Ufa

Yekaterinburg
(Sverdlovsk)

Chelyabinsk

Kurgan

Ishim

Omsk

Kem

Rostov-na-Donu

Volgograd

Orenburg

Magnitogorsk

Kustanay

Petropavlovsk

Novosibirsk

Kiselevsk

Black Sea

GEORGIA

TBILISI

Astrakhan

Atyrau

Aktobe

Arkalyk

Kokshetau

ASTANA

Pavlodar

Rubtsovsk

Semey

Ust-

Kamenogorsk

Caspian
Sea

AZERBAIJAN

BAKU

TURKMEN.

Turkmenbasy

UZBEKISTAN

Aral Sea

Syr Dar'ya

Aral'sk

Zhezkazgan

Karaganda

KAZAKHSTAN

Balkhash

Kyzylorda

Turkistan

Taldykorgan

IRAN

Rasht

Balkanabat

Nukus

Kyzylkum
Desert

Kentau

Betpakdala

Sarysu

Almaty

Ucharal

E   60°   F   Longitude 75° east of Greenwich   G

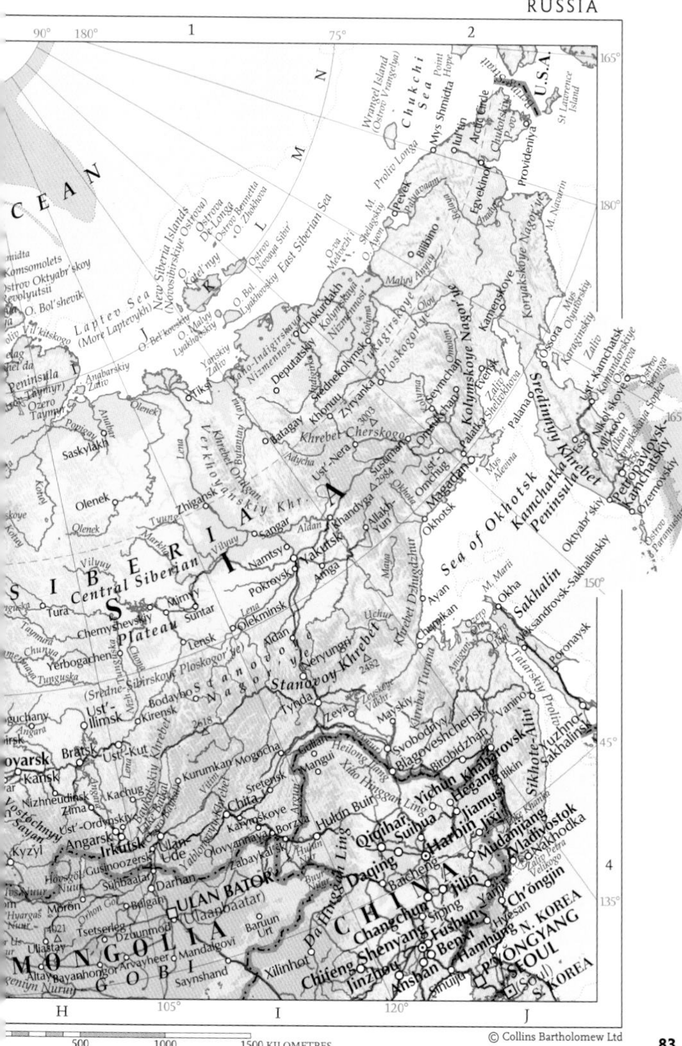

90°   180°   1   75°   2   165°

N

Wrangel Island
(Ostrov Vrangelya)
Mys Shmidta   Chukchi   Mys
Sea   Dezhneva   St Lawrence
Island

M   Ostrova
De Longa   Proliv Longa   Ostrova
Diomida   U.S.A.
Mys Shmidta   Uelen
Amderma
Chukchi   Egvekinot   Lavrentiya   Providence

Komsomolets
Ostrov Oktyabr'skoy   Ostrova
Revolyutsii   De Longa   Novaya Sibir'
O. Bol'shevik   O. Bennetta   O. Bol. Lyakhovskiy   Bilibino   Egvekinot   M. Navarin

New Siberian Islands   East Siberian Sea   Anadyr'
(Novosibirskiye Ostrova)   Markovo   Kamchatskiy Zaliv

Schmidta   O. Begicheva   O. Bol'shoy   Chokurdakh   Kolymskoye   Magistral'noye   Mys
Ostrov Oktyabr'   Lyakhovskiy   Nagorno   Olyutorskiy
revolyutsii   Laptev Sea   Yukagir   Kolymskoye Nagor'ye
(More Laptevykh)   Nizhneyansk   Srednekolymsk   Korryakskoye Nagor'ye   Sora   Kamchatka
O. Bel'kovskiy   Yanskiy   Deputatskiy   Oloy   Ossora   Karaginskiy
Zaliv   Zyryanka   Sredinnyy

Peninsula   Anabarskiy   Olenek   Verkhoyansk   Khonuu   Khrebet Cherskogo   Seymchan   Palana   Klyuchevskaya   Ust'-Kamchatsk
(Taymyr)   Zaliv   Batagay   Ust'-Nera   Omsukchan   Sopka
Taymyr   Paynoy   Anabar   Ola   Magadan   Klyuchi   Petropavlovsk-
Saskylakh   Verkhoyanskiy Khrebet   Zhigansk   Omchak   Mys Omney   Ayan   Okhotsk   Mil'kovo   Kamchatskiy
Koye   Olenek   Tungus   Angar   Aldan   Khandyga   Yur   Srednekolymsk   Petropavlovsk-Kamchatskiy
Olenek   Olenek   Tuoy   Batamay   Namtsy   Ust'-Maya   Okhotsk   Severo-Kuril'sk
Vilyuy   Central Siberian   Mirnyy   Pokrovsk   Amga   M. Marii   Oktyabr'skiy   Ozernovskiy
Tura   Plateau   Suntar   Lena   Olëkminsk   Sea of Okhotsk   Paramushir
S   I   B   E   R   I   A   Kamchatka
Yerbogachen   (Sredne-Sibirskoye Ploskogor'ye)   Uchur   Khrebet Dzhugdzhur   Peninsula   Sakhalin
Chuna   Peleduy   Bodaybo   Neryungri   Chumikan   Tatarskiy
Tunguska   Ust'-   Kirensk   Nagornyy   Stanovoy Khrebet   Aldan   Aleksandrovsk-Sakhalinskiy

oyarsk   Bratsk   Ust'-Kut   Kurumkan Mogocha   Svobodnyy   Amur   Sakhalin   Proliv
Ust'-Ilimsk   Ilimsk   Ust'-Ordynskiy   Chita   Zeya   Shimanovsk   Khabarovsk   Poronaysk
Kansk   Nizhneudinsk   Zima   Bodaybo   Sretensk   Belogorsk   Birobidzhan   150°
Zima   Irkutsk   Kachug   Zabaykal'sk   Borzya   Skovorodino   Blagoveshchensk   Tatarskiy Proliv   45°
Angarsk   Qiqihar   Yichun Khabarovsk   Sikhote Alin'
Kyzyl   Ulan-Ude   Mogoytuy   Xiao Hinggan   Suihua   Heihe   Jiamusi   Yuzhno-Sakhalinsk
Sayan   Gusinoozersk   Kyakhta   Hulun Buir Hu   Nen   Qiqihar   Hegang   Mudanjiang   Vladivostok
Horgo   Darhan   Zabaykal'sk   Daqing   Harbin   Jixi   Nakhodka
Moron   Hövsgöl   Darhan   Xilin Gol   CHINA   Changchun   Jilin   Mudanjiang   135°
Hyargas Nuur   Belgian   ULAN BATOR   Baruun   Fuxin   Shenyang   Benxi   Fushun   Ch'ŏngjin
Uliastay   (Ulaanbaatar)   Urt   Mandalgovi   Jinzhou   Anshan   Benxi   N. KOREA
MONGOLIA   Bayanhongor Arvayheer   Saynshand   Chifeng   Jinzhou   Liaoyang   P'YONGYANG   SEOUL
Altay   G   O   B   I   Xilinhot   Chengde   Dandong   Haeju   S. KOREA
ventiyn Nuruu

H   105°   I   120°   J

500   1000   1500 KILOMETRES   © Collins Bartholomew Ltd   **83**

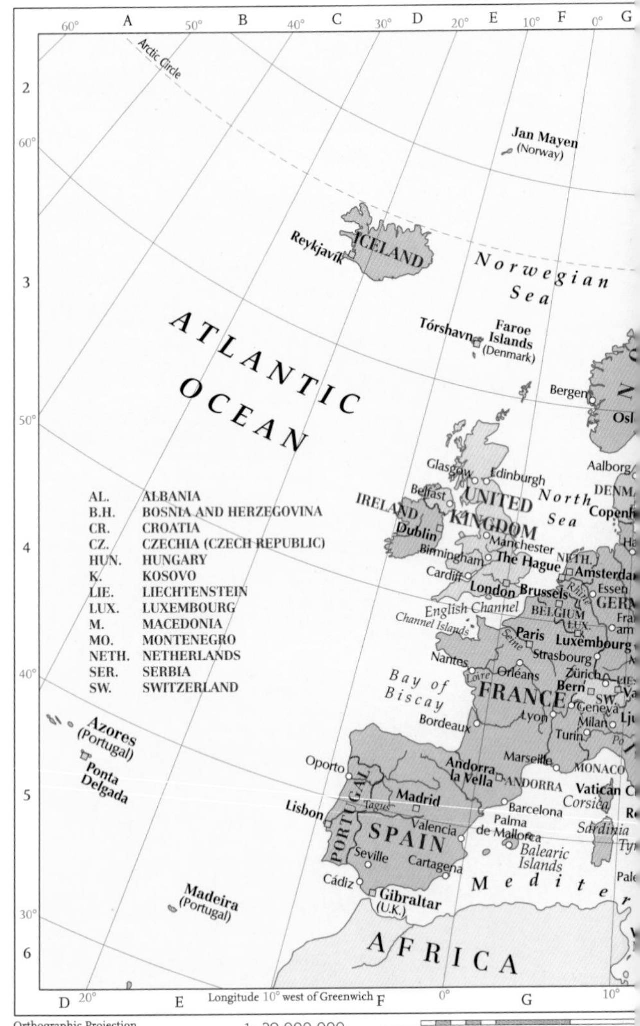

A
B
C
D
E
F
G

60°
50°
40°
30°
20°
10°
0°

Arctic Circle

2

60°

Jan Mayen
(Norway)

Reykjavík
ICELAND
Norwegian
Sea

3

ATLANTIC

OCEAN

Tórshavn
Faroe
Islands
(Denmark)

Bergen
N
Osl

50°

Glasgow
Edinburgh
North
Aalborg

Belfast
UNITED
Sea
DENM.

IRELAND
KINGDOM
Copenh

Dublin
Manchester
NETH.
Amsterdam

Birmingham
The Hague
Essen

Cardiff
London
Brussels
GER

English Channel
BELGIUM
Fra

Channel Islands
LUX.
Luxembourg
am

4

AL.   ALBANIA
B.H.   BOSNIA AND HERZEGOVINA
CR.   CROATIA
CZ.   CZECHIA (CZECH REPUBLIC)
HUN.   HUNGARY
K.   KOSOVO
LIE.   LIECHTENSTEIN
LUX.   LUXEMBOURG
M.   MACEDONIA
MO.   MONTENEGRO
NETH.   NETHERLANDS
SER.   SERBIA
SW.   SWITZERLAND

Paris
Strasbourg
Zürich
LIE.

Nantes
Bern
Va

Bay of
FRANCE
Geneva
Lju

Biscay
Lyon
Milan

Bordeaux
Turin
Po

40°

Marseille
MONACO

Azores
(Portugal)

Andorra
la Vella
ANDORRA
Corsica
Re

Ponta
Delgada

Oporto
Madrid
Barcelona
Ty

Lisbon
Tagus
Valencia
Palma
de Mallorca
Balearic
Islands
Pale

5
PORTUGAL
SPAIN

Seville
Cartagena

Madeira
(Portugal)

Cádiz
Gibraltar
(U.K.)
Medite
r

30°

6

AFRICA

D
20°
E
Longitude 10° west of Greenwich
F
0°
G
10°

84
Orthographic Projection
1 : 39 000 000
MILES 0
250
500

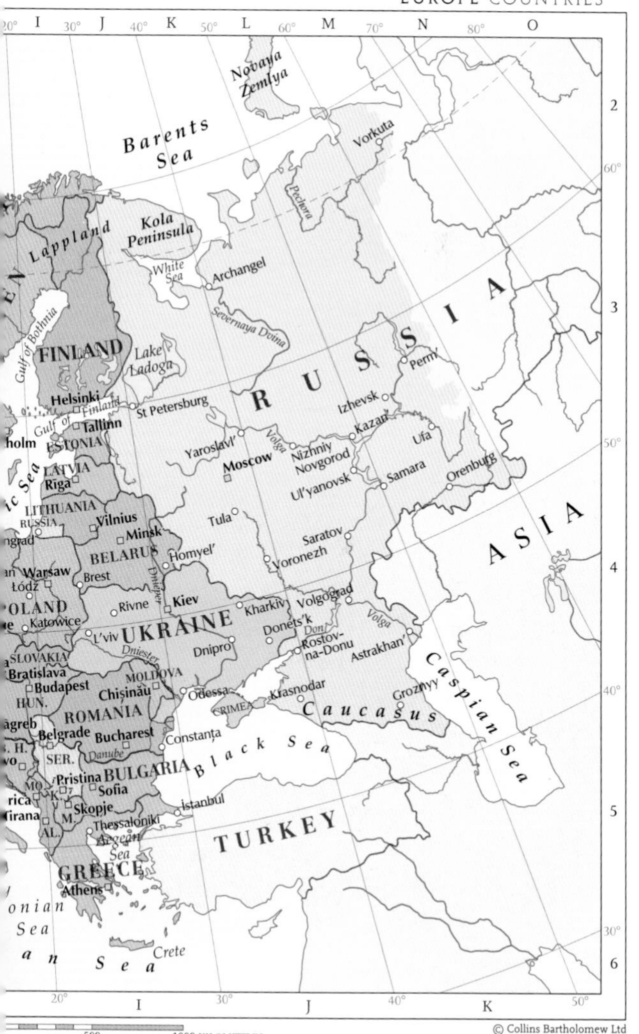

Novaya Zemlya

Barents Sea

Vorkuta

Pechora

Lappland

Kola Peninsula

White Sea

Archangel

Severnaya Dvina

RUSSIA

FINLAND

Lake Ladoga

Helsinki

Gulf of Finland

St Petersburg

Perm'

Tallinn

ESTONIA

holm

Yaroslavl'

Izhevsk

Kazan'

Moscow

Nizhniy Novgorod

Ufa

ic Sea

LATVIA

Riga

Ul'yanovsk

Samara

Orenburg

LITHUANIA

RUSSIA

Vilnius

Minsk

Tula

Saratov

ASIA

grad

Warsaw

BELARUS

Homyel'

Voronezh

Brest

Dnieper

łódź

POLAND

e

Rivne

Kiev

Kharkiv

Volgograd

Katowice

L'viv

UKRAINE

Donets'k

Don

Volga

SLOVAKIA

Dniester

Dnipro

Rostov-na-Donu

Astrakhan'

Caspian Sea

Bratislava

MOLDOVA

Budapest

Chişinău

Odessa

Krasnodar

Grozny

HUN.

CRIMEA

Caucasus

agreb

ROMANIA

Belgrade

Bucharest

Constanţa

Black Sea

S. H.

Danube

vo

SER.

Pristina

BULGARIA

MO.

Sofia

rica

Skopje

İstanbul

Tirana

AL.

Thessaloniki

Aegean Sea

TURKEY

GREECE

Athens

onian Sea

an

Sea

Crete

© Collins Bartholomew Ltd

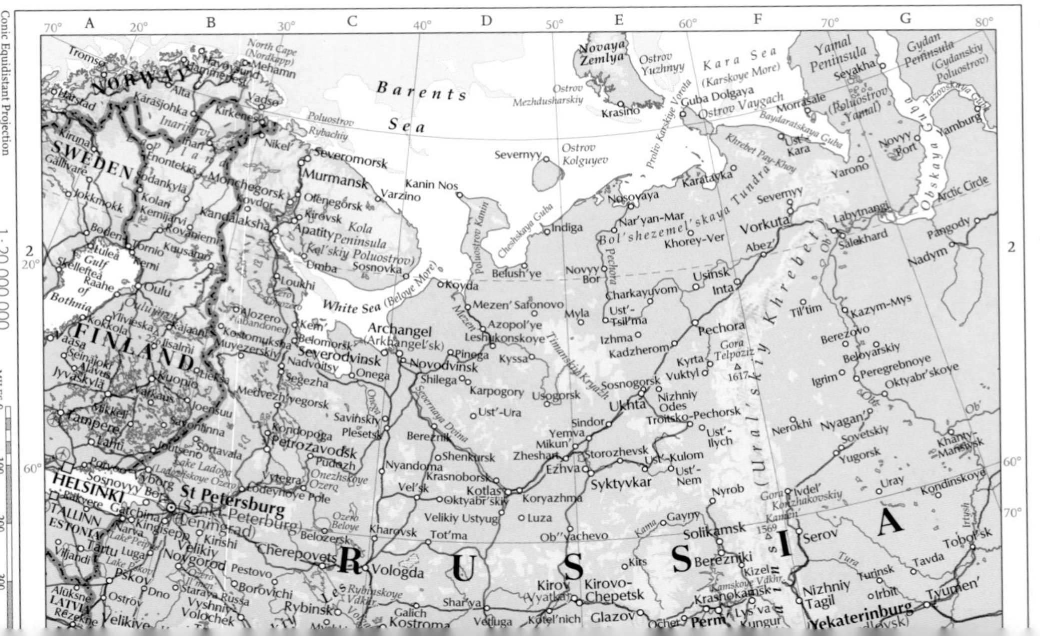

Conic Equidistant Projection

1 : 20 000 000

MILES 0   100   200   300

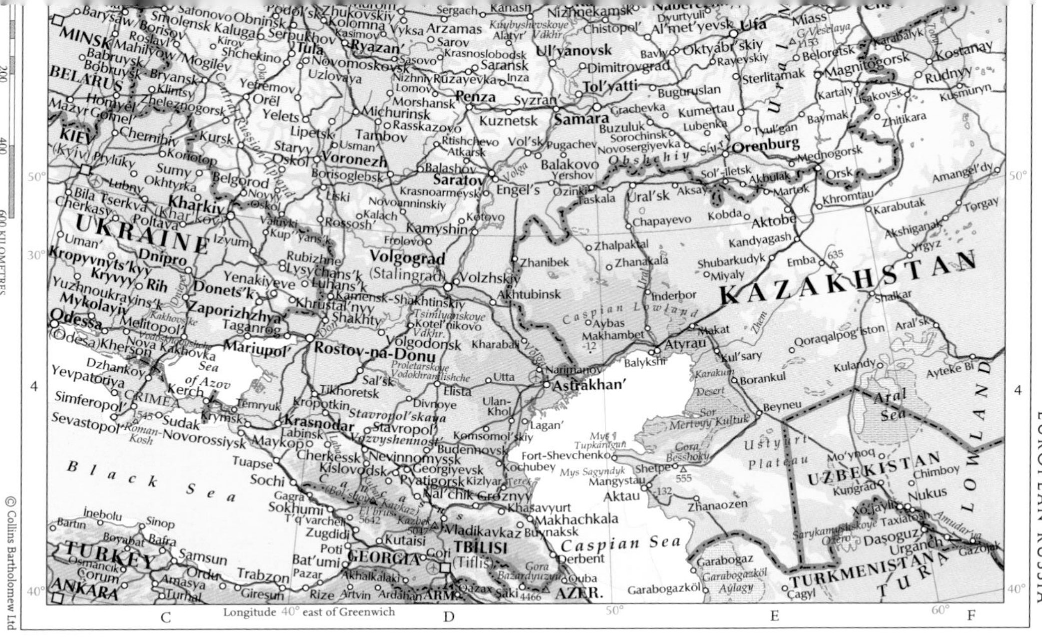
KAZAKHSTAN
UKRAINE
BELARUS
GEORGIA
TURKEY
UZBEKISTAN
TURKMENISTAN
AZER.
ARM.
CRIMEA
Caspian Sea
Black Sea
Sea of Azov
Aral Sea
Caspian Lowland
Central Russian Upland
Ustyurt Plateau
Obshchiy Syrt
TURAN LOWLAND
MINSK
KIEV (Kyiv)
TBILISI (Tiflis)
ANKARA
Volgograd (Stalingrad)
Rostov-na-Donu
Astrakhan'
Saratov
Samara
Tol'yatti
Ul'yanovsk
Penza
Voronezh
Kharkiv
Dnipro
Odessa (Odesa)
Orenburg
Ufa
Aktobe
Atyrau
Aktau
Makhachkala
Krasnodar
Stavropol'
Sochi
Mariupol'
Zaporizhzhya
Donets'k
Kryvyy Rih
Mykolayiv
Kherson
Simferopol'
Sevastopol'
Tula
Ryazan'
Kursk
Belgorod
Orël
Bryansk
Engel's
Ural'sk
Orsk
Magnitogorsk
Kostanay
Longitude 40° east of Greenwich
200
400
600 KILOMETRES

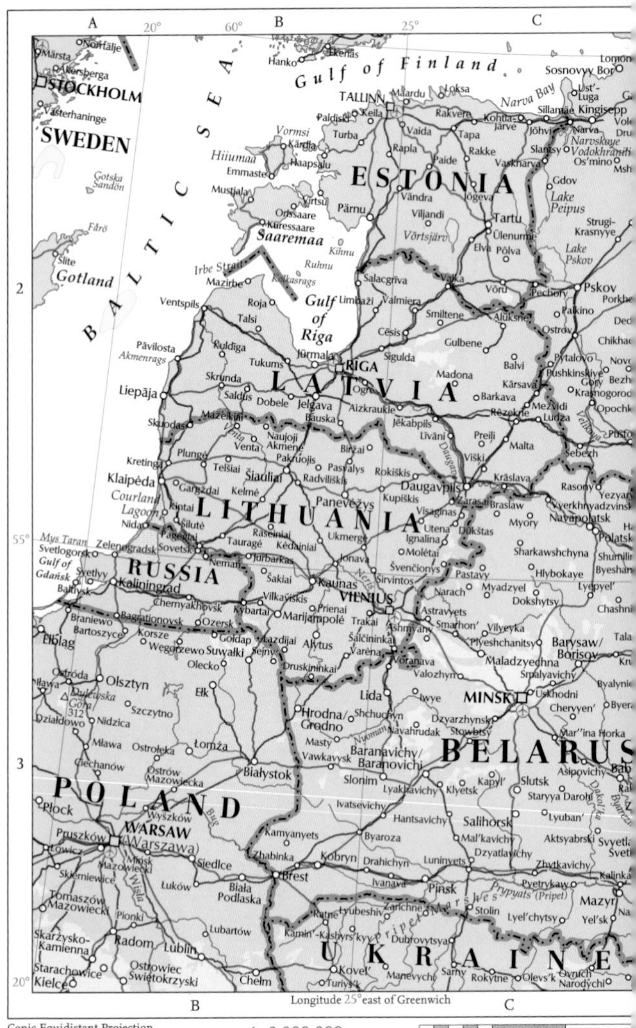

Conic Equidistant Projection

1 : 8 000 000

MILES 0   50   100

Longitude 25° east of Greenwich

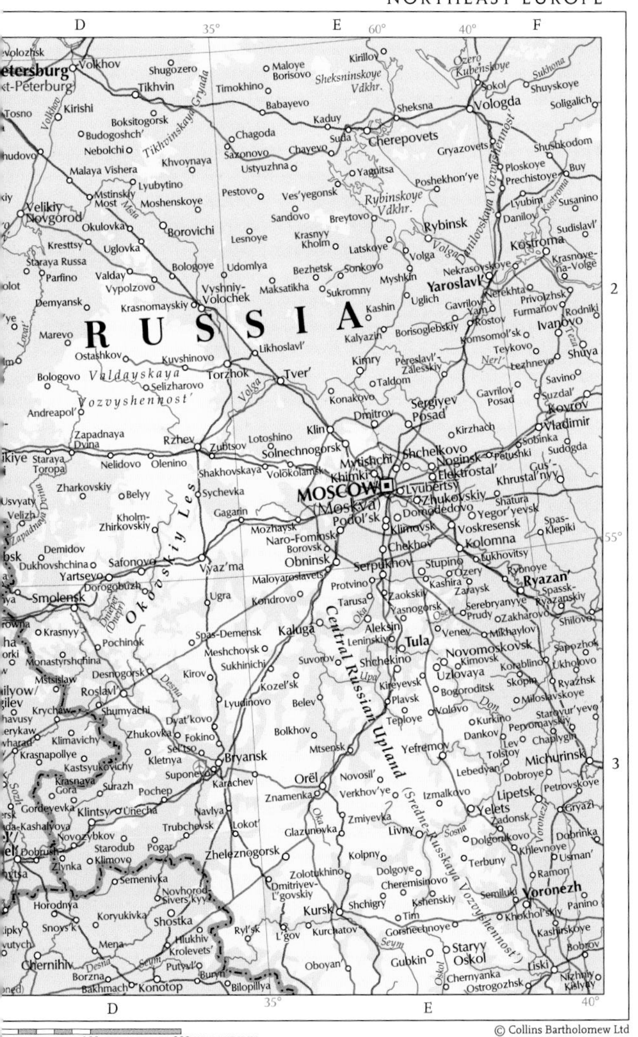

D 35° E 60° 40° F

Voloznsk
Volkhov
etersburg/
 st-Peterburg)
Tosno
Kirishi
Tikhvin
Shugozero
Timokhino
Maloye
Borisovo
Kirillov
Ocero
Kubenskoye
Sokol
Sukhona
Shuyskoye
Soligalich
Vologda

hudovo
Budogosch'
Nebolchi
Boksitogorsk
Malaya Vishera
Chagoda
Khvoynaya
Sazonovo
Kaduy
Suda
Sheksna
Cherepovets
Gryazovets
Poshekhon'ye
Ploskoye
Prechistoye
Buy
Shushkodom

Velikiy
Novgorod
Mstinskiy
Most
Lyubytino
Pestovo
Ustyuzhna
Ves'yegonsk
Yagnitsa
Rubinskoye
Vdkhr.
Danilov
Lyubim
Susanino

Krestsy
Okulovka
Moshenskoye
Sandovo
Breytovo
Rybinsk
Nekrasovskoye
Sudislavl'
Krasnoye-
Volge
Kostroma

Parfino
Staraya Russa
Uglovka
Bologoye
Krasnyy
Kholm
Latskoye
Yaroslavl'
Privolzhsk
Furmanov
2
Valday
Udomlya
Bezhetsk
Sonkovo
Myshkin
Gavrilov-
Yam
Nerekhta
Komsomol'sk
Ivanovo

Demyansk
Vypolzovo
Vyshniy-
Volochek
Maksatikha
Sukromny
Kashin
Borisoglebskiy
Teykovo
Savino
Shuya

R U S S I A
Likhoslavl'
Kimry
Kalyazin
Pereslavl'-
Zaleskiy
Suzdal'
Kovrov

Ostashkov
Kuvshinovo
Torzhok
Tver'
Konakovo
Taldom
Sergiyev
Posad
Gavrilov
Posad
Vladimir

Andreapol'
Valdayskaya
Vozvyshennost'
Selizharovo
Kirzhach
Sobinka

Zapadnaya
Dvina
Rzhev
Zubtsov
Lotoshino
Klin
Solnechnogorsk
Shchelkovo
Noginsk-
Patushki
Gus'-
Khrustal'nyy

ikiye Staraya
Toropa
Nelidovo
Olenino
Shakhovskaya
Volokolamsk
Khimki
Mytishchi
Elektrostal'
Spas-
Klepiki

Zharkovskiy
Sychevka
MOSCOW
Moskva
Lyubertsy
Zhukovskiy
Shatura
Yegor'yevsk

bsk
Demidov
Kholm-
Zhirkovskiy
Gagarin
Mozhaysk
Podol'sk
Domodedovo
Voskresensk
Spas-
Klepiki

Dukhovshchina
Safonovo
Naro-Fominsk
Bronsk
Klimovsk
Kolomna
Lukhovitsy
55°

Smolensk
Yartsevo
Dorogobuzh
Vyaz'ma
Obninsk
Chekhov
Stupino
Ozery
Ryazan'
Spass-
Klepiki

rowna
Krasnyy
Ugra
Maloyaroslavets
Protvino
Serpukhov
Kashira
Zaraysk
Spass-

orki
Pochinok
Spas-Demensk
Kondrovo
Tarusa
Zaoksky
Venev
Mikhaylov
Ryazhsk

illyow/
gilev
Monastyrshchina
Desnogorsk
Kirov
Meshchovsk
Kaluga
Aleksin
Leninskiy
Novomoskovsk
Skopin
Sapozhok

havusy
erykaw
Krychaw
Shumyachi
Roslavl'
Sukhinichi
Suvorov
Shchekino
Uzlovaya
Kimovsk
Korablino
Ukholovo

Klimavichy
Zhukovka
Kozel'sk
Belev
Tula
Bogoroditsk
Miloslavskoye

whatau
Krasnapollye
Klimovichi
Dyat'kovo
Fokino
Plavsk
Teploye
Novosel'skoye
Tovarkovskiy
Mihaylov

Kaskyevichy
Kletnya
Suponevo
Bolkhov
Mtsensk
Kireyevsk
Kurkino
Chaplygin

Surazh
Krasnaya
Gora
Pochep
Bryansk
Karachev
Orël
Novosil'
Efremov
Lebedyan
Dobroye
Michurinsk

Gordeyevka
Klintsy
Unecha
Navlya
Znamenka
Verkhov'ye
Izmalkovo
Lipetsk
Petrovskoye

Novozybkov
Trubchevsk
Lokot'
Glazunovka
Zmiyevka
Livny
Dolgoye
Yelets
Zadonsk
Gryazi

Starodub
Pogar
Zheleznogorsk
Kolpny
Terbuny
Dobrinka
Usman'

Klimovo
Semenivka
Novhorod
Sivers'kyi
Dmitriyev-
L'govskiy
Zolotukhino
Shchigry
Cheremisinovo
Semiluki
Voronezh
3

Horodnya
Koryukivka
Shostka
Ryl'sk
Kursk
Tim
Kshenskiy
Staryy
Oskol
Panino

Snovs'k
Hlukhiv
Krolevets
L'gov
Kurchatov
Oboyan'
Chernyanka
Liski

Chernihiv
Borzna
Bakhmach
Konotop
Putyvl'
Buryn'
Bilopillya
Staryy
Oskol
Ostrogozhsk

D 35° E 40°

100 200 KILOMETRES

© Collins Bartholomew Ltd
89

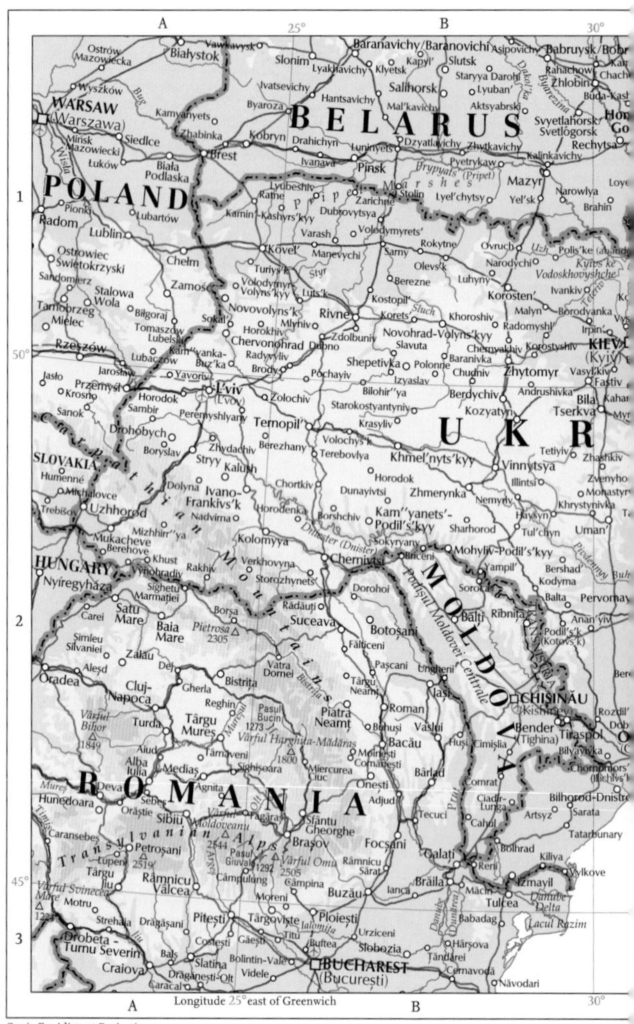

Ostrów
Mazowiecka   Białystok
Wyszków   Baranavichy/Baranovichi Asipovichy Babruysk Bobr
                 Slonim Lyakhavichy Klyetsk   Svyetlahorsk Kar
WARSAW   Ivatsevichy   Kapyl' Starnya Darohi   Rahachow Zhlobin Hom
(Warszawa)   Hantsavichy Mal'kavichy Slutsk Svetlogorsk   Go
Mińsk   Kamyanyets   Aktsyabrski   Rechytsa
Mazowiecki Siedlce   Kobryn Drahichyn   BELARUS
           Zhabinka Brest Ivanava   Pinsk   Pyetrykaw Kalinkavichy
Łuków   Biała   Luninyets Zhytkavichy
POLAND   Podlaska   P   r   i   p   y   a   t   M a r s h e s   Mazyr Narowlya
Radom Lublin Lubartów Ratne Kamin'-Kashyrs'kyy Stolin Zarichne Dubrovytsya Yel'sk Brahin
Ostrowiec   Varash Volodymyrets' Rokytne
Świętokrzyski Chełm Kovel' Turiys'k Sarny Olevs'k Narodychi Ovruch Uzh Polis'ke
Sandomierz Zamość Volodymyr- Volyns'kyy Luts'k Kostopil' Berezne Luhyny Korosten' Ivankiv Vodoskhovyshche
Tarnobrzeg Stalowa Biłgoraj Sokal' Horokhiv Rivne Zdolbuniv Novohrad-Volyns'kyy Malyn Borodyanka Irpin'
Mielec Wola Tomaszów Chervonohrad Radyvyliv Dubno Slavuta Polonne Chernyakhiv Korostyshiv KIEV
Rzeszów Lubelski Sokal'- Brody Pochayiv Izyaslav Baranivka Zhytomyr Andrushivka Vasyl'kiv (KYIV) Kahar
Jasło Jarosław Yavoriv Zolochiv Shepetivka Chudniv Berdychiv Fastiv Bila
Przemyśl Horodok Bilohir'ya Starokostyantyniv Kozyatyn Tserkva Myr
Krosno Sambir Peremyshlyany Ternopil' Krasyliv UKR
Sanok Drohobych Zhydachiv Berezhany Volochys'k Khmel'nyts'kyy Vinnytsya Tetiyiv
SLOVAKIA Boryslav Stryy Kalush Chortkiv Horodok Nemyriv Illintsi Zvenyho
Humenné Michalovce Dolyna Ivano- Dunayivtsi Zhmerynka Khrystynivka Monastyr
Uzhhorod Frankivs'k Nadvirna Kam''yanets'- Sharhorod Tul'chyn Uman'
HUNGARY Mukacheve Mizhhir''ya Kolomyya Podil's'kyy Mohyliv-Podil's'kyy Bershad' Kodyma
Nyíregyháza Berehove Khust Verkhovyna Kosiv Dnister (Dniestr) Skryany Yampil' Pervoma
Rakhiv Storozhynets' Chernivtsi Bârcéni MOLDOVA Balta
Vynohradiv Sighetu Dorohoi Bălţi Ribniţa
Satu Marmaţiei Rădăuţi Pervoma
Mare Borşa Suceava Botoşani Anan'yiv
Carei Baia Pietrosa Soroca Kotovs'k
Şimleu Mare 2305 Vatra Iaşi (Podil's'k)
Silvaniei Zalău Dornei Paşcani Ungheni CHIŞINĂU Rozdil'
Aleşd Bistriţa Roman Bender Tiraspol
Oradea Cluj- Gherla Reghin Piatra (Tighina) Bilyhorod
Napoca Turda Târgu Neamţ Bacău Huşi Cimişlia
Aiud Mureş Târnăveni Buhuşi Vaslui Comrat Chornomors'ke
Alba Mediaş Sighişoara Miercurea Bârlad Bilhorod-Dnistrovs'kyy
Iulia Orăştie Ciuc Adjud Tecuci Comrat Sarata
Hunedoara ROMANIA Oneşti Galaţi Reni Tatarbunary
Caransebeş Slănic Sfântu Focşani   Renni Kiliya
Râmnicu Gheorghe Râmnicu Buzău Brăila Izmayil Danube
Ţupeni Sărat Ianca Măcin Delta
Petroşani Câmpulung Braşov Tulcea Lacul Razim
Râmnicu Vâlcea Câmpina Urziceni Babadag Hârşova
Drobeta- Drăgăşani Piteşti Târgovişte Ploieşti Slobozia Ţăndărei Cernavodă Năvodari
Turnu Severin Costeşti Găeşti Buftea BUCHAREST
Craiova Slatina Bolintin-Vale Videle (Bucureşti)
Caracal Olt

Conic Equidistant Projection

1 : 8 000 000   MILES 0   50   100

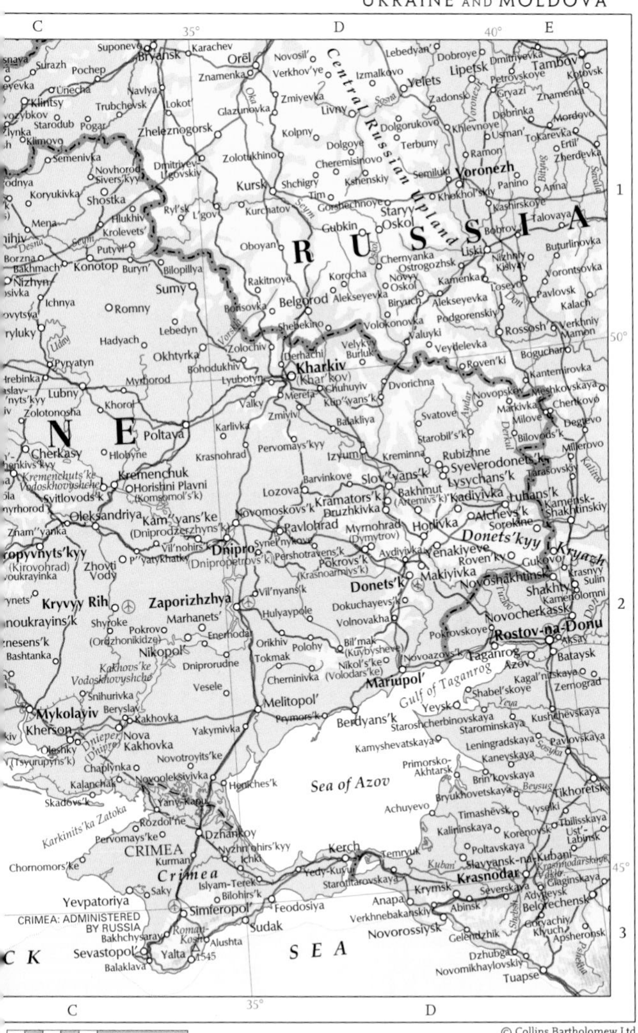

CRIMEA: ADMINISTERED BY RUSSIA

0 100 200 KILOMETRES

© Collins Bartholomew Ltd

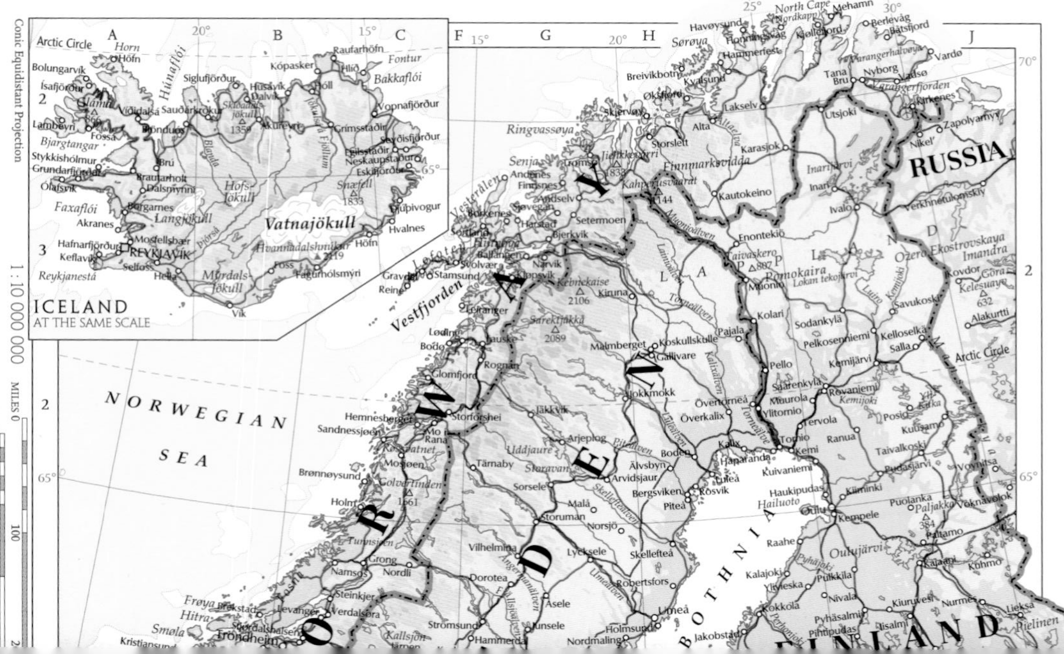

Conic Equidistant Projection

1 : 10 000 000

MILES 0   100   2

KILOMETRES 0   100   200   300

RUSSIA

FINLAND

S W E D E N N O R W A Y

B O T H N I A

N O R W E G I A N S E A

ICELAND
AT THE SAME SCALE

Vatnajökull

North Cape

Arctic Circle

Arctic Circle

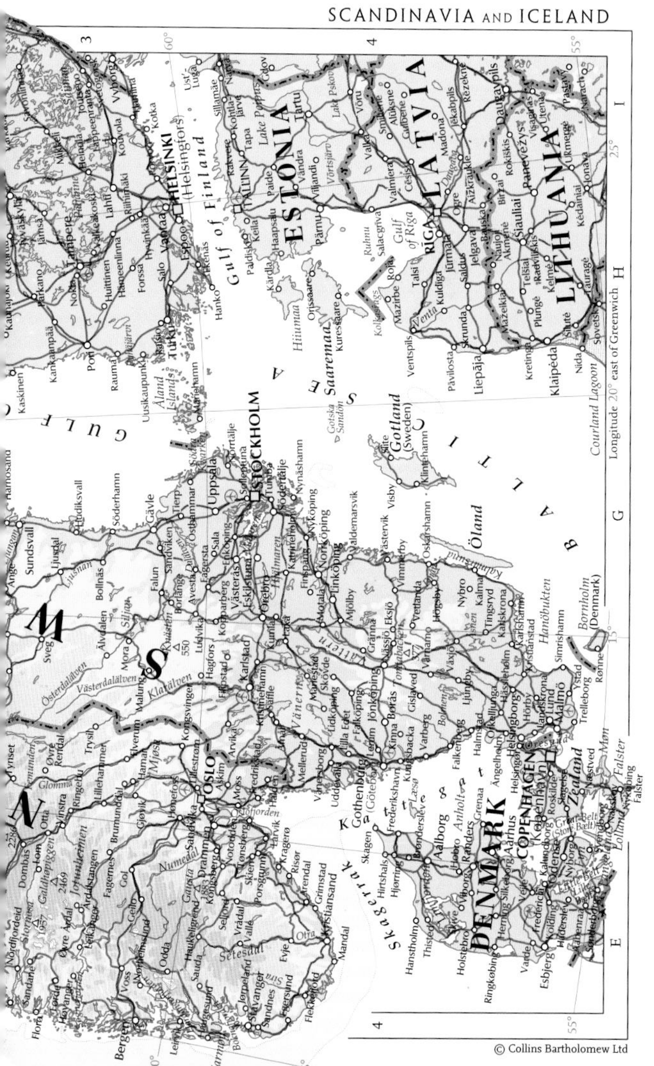
ESTONIA
LATVIA
LITHUANIA
DENMARK
HELSINKI
(Helsingfors)
STOCKHOLM
OSLO
RĪGA
TALLINN
COPENHAGEN
(København)
Gulf of Finland
Gulf of Riga
Gotland
(Sweden)
Öland
Bornholm
(Denmark)
Saaremaa
Hiiumaa
Åland
Islands
Skagerrak
Kattegat
Zealand
Vänern
Vättern
Hjälmaren
Mälaren
Lake Peipus
Gothenburg
(Göteborg)
Courland Lagoon
Longitude 20° east of Greenwich

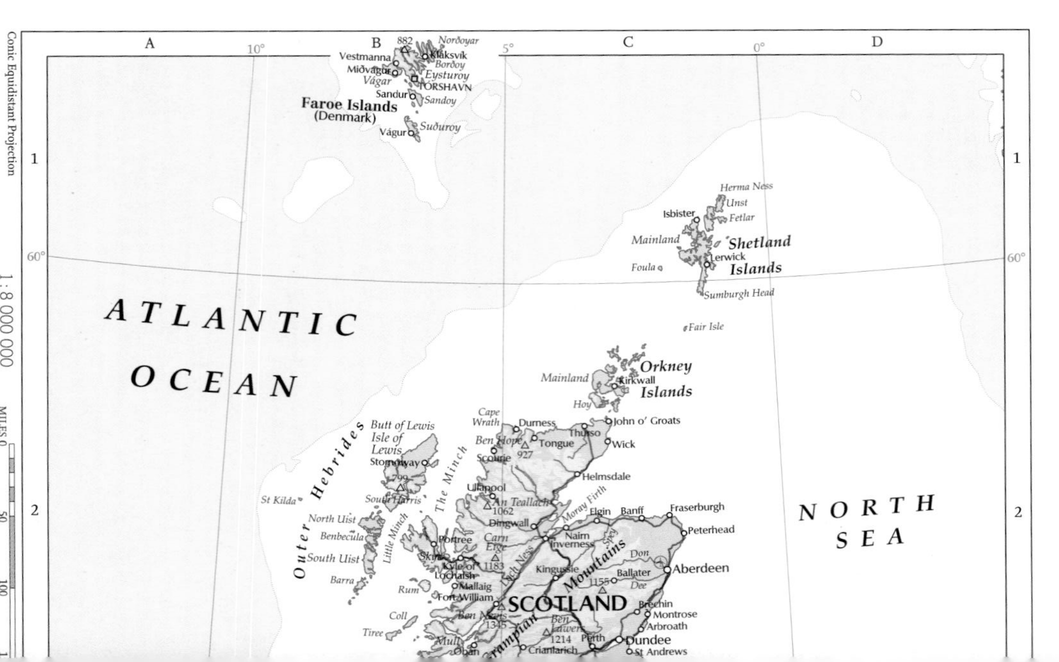

Conic Equidistant Projection

1 : 8 000 000

MILES 0   50   100

ATLANTIC

OCEAN

NORTH

SEA

Faroe Islands
(Denmark)

Vestmanna
Midvágur
Vágur
Sandur
Sandoy
Suduroy

882

Norðragøta
Klaksvík
Eysturoy
TÓRSHAVN

SCOTLAND

Grampian Mountains

Outer Hebrides

The Minch

Little Minch

Butt of Lewis
Isle of
Lewis
Stornoway
North Uist
Benbecula
South Uist
Barra
St Kilda

Shetland
Islands

Herma Ness
Unst
Fetlar
Isbister
Mainland
Foula
Lerwick
Sumburgh Head

Fair Isle

Orkney
Islands

Mainland
Kirkwall
Hoy

John o' Groats
Wick

Helmsdale
Durness
Ben Hope
Tongue
Scourie
Cape
Wrath
Ullapool

Fraserburgh
Peterhead
Banff
Elgin
Nairn
Inverness
Kingussie
Aberdeen
Ballater
Dee
Don

Montrose
Arbroath
Dundee
St Andrews

Rùm
Coll
Tiree

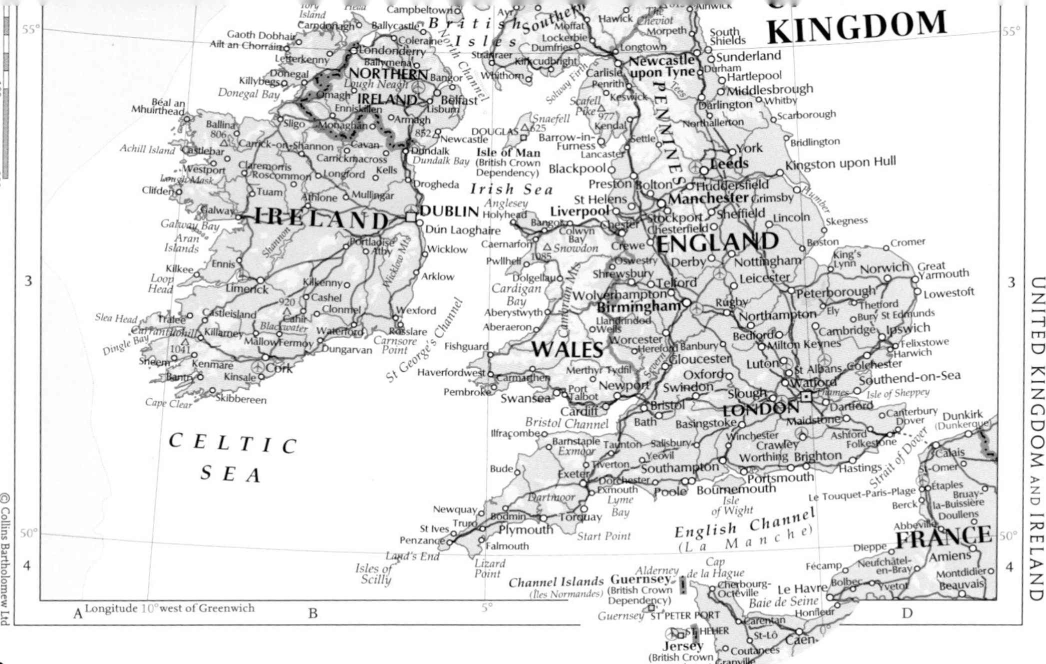

© Collins Bartholomew Ltd

100   200 KILOMETRES

KINGDOM
ENGLAND
WALES
IRELAND
NORTHERN IRELAND
FRANCE
CELTIC SEA
Irish Sea
English Channel
(La Manche)
Bristol Channel
St George's Channel
North Channel
Strait of Dover
PENNINES
Channel Islands
(Îles Normandes)
Isle of Man
(British Crown Dependency)
LONDON
DUBLIN
Birmingham
Manchester
Liverpool
Leeds
Newcastle upon Tyne
Cardiff
Swansea
Bristol
Southampton
Plymouth
Belfast
Cork
Limerick
Galway
Jersey
Guernsey
Longitude 10° west of Greenwich

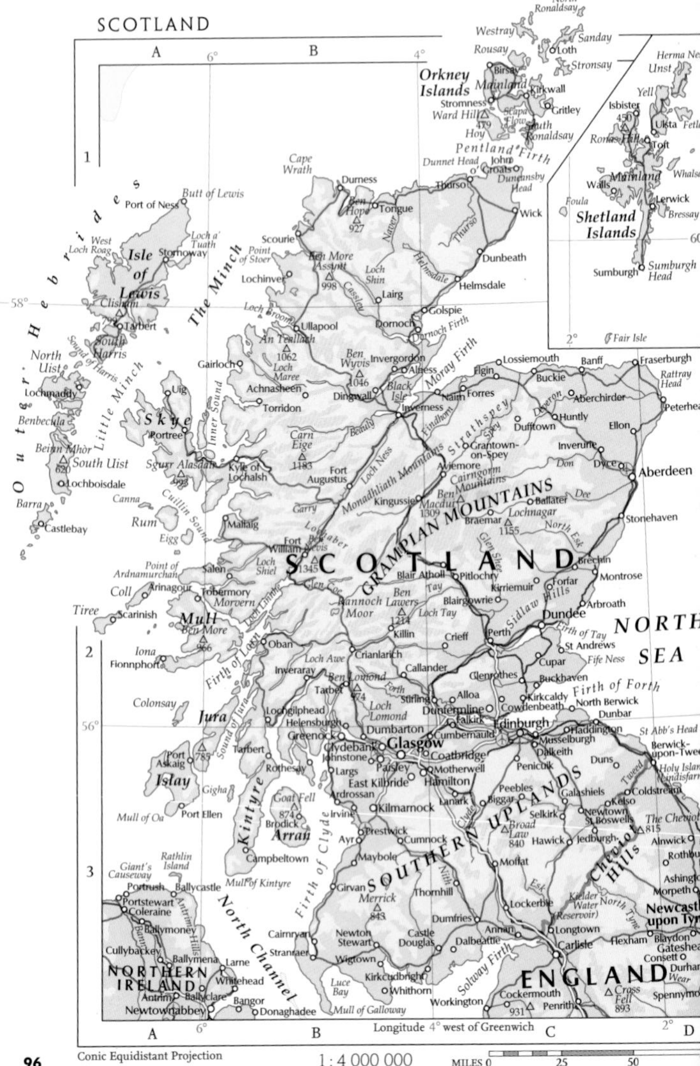

Conic Equidistant Projection

1 : 4 000 000

MILES 0   25   50

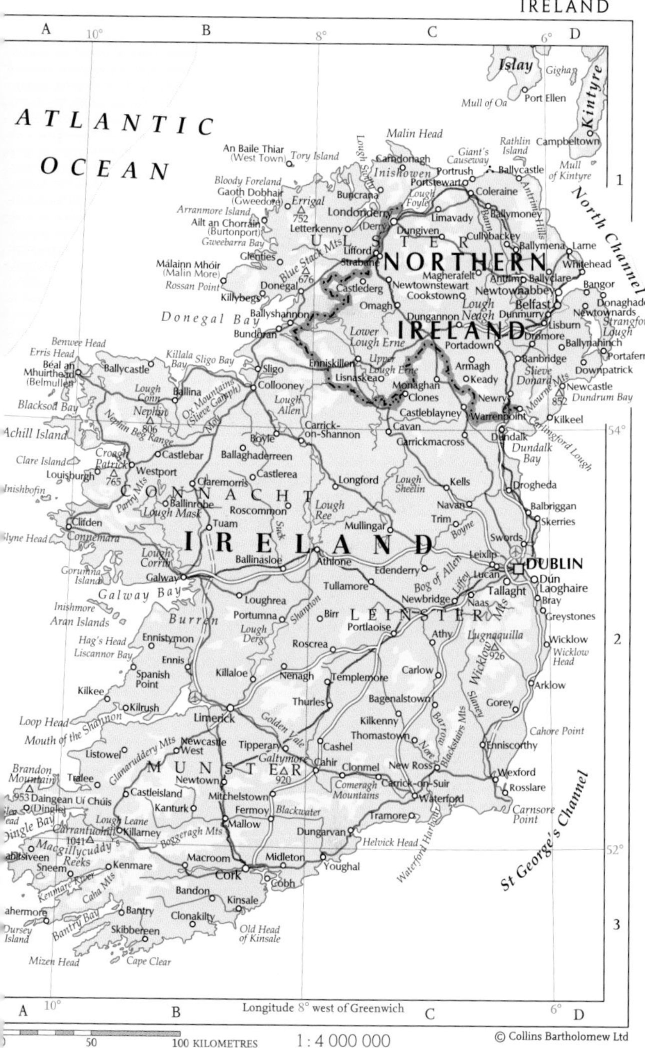

1 : 4 000 000

© Collins Bartholomew Ltd

ATLANTIC OCEAN
NORTHERN IRELAND
IRELAND
ULSTER
CONNACHT
LEINSTER
MUNSTER
DUBLIN
Belfast
Islay
Kintyre
North Channel
St George's Channel
Donegal Bay
Galway Bay
Malin Head
Tory Island
Londonderry (Derry)
Letterkenny
Donegal
Sligo
Galway
Limerick
Cork
Waterford
Wexford
Athlone
Kilkenny
Lough Neagh
Lough Corrib
Lough Derg
Lough Ree
Shannon
Mizen Head
Cape Clear
Old Head of Kinsale
Longitude 8° west of Greenwich
100 KILOMETRES

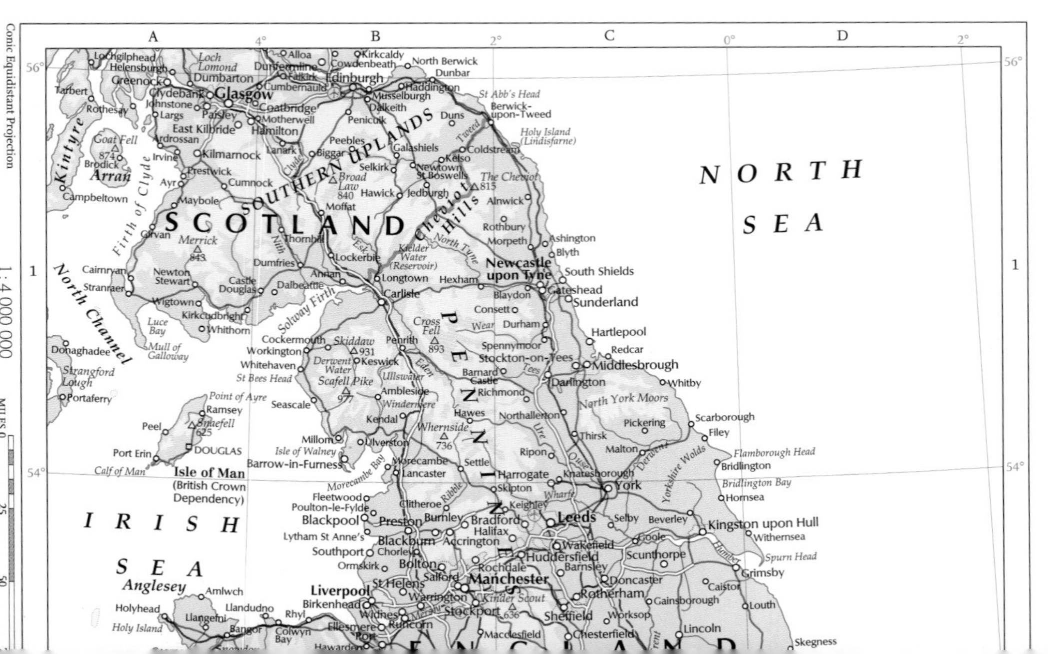

Conic Equidistant Projection

1 : 4 000 000

MILES 0   25   50

FRANCE

Great Yarmouth
Lowestoft
Southwold
Norwich
Dereham
Swaffham
Long Stratton
Thetford
Mildenhall
Ely
Newmarket
Bury St Edmunds
Ipswich
Woodbridge
Orford Ness
Harwich
Clacton-on-Sea
Felixstowe
Colchester
Braintree
Chelmsford
Saffron Walden
Cambridge
Royston
Harlow
Basildon
Southend-on-Sea
Isle of Sheppey
Sittingbourne
Gillingham
Gravesend
Margate
North Foreland
Ramsgate
Canterbury
Whitstable
Dover
Strait of Dover
Hythe
Folkestone
Ashford
Royal Tunbridge Wells
Maidstone
Sevenoaks
Rye
Dungeness
Hastings
Bexhill
Eastbourne
Beachy Head

Huntingdon
Peterborough
St Neots
Bedford
Kettering
Northampton
Milton Keynes
Luton
St Albans
Hertford
Stevenage
Hitchin
Watford
Hemel Hempstead
High Wycombe
LONDON
Slough
Bracknell
Staines
Epsom
Croydon
Reigate
Redhill
Crawley
East Grinstead
Haywards Heath
Lewes
Brighton
Hove
Worthing

Leicester
Loughborough
Coalville
Hinckley
Nuneaton
Tamworth
Sutton Coldfield
Walsall
Wolverhampton
West Bromwich
Dudley
Birmingham
Coventry
Rugby
Daventry
Warwick
Leamington
Stratford-upon-Avon
Redditch
Bromsgrove
Kidderminster
Telford
Shrewsbury
Welshpool
Newtown

Banbury
Bicester
Aylesbury
Oxford
Witney
Abingdon
Wallingford
Newbury
Reading
Basingstoke
Andover
Newport
Winchester
Chichester
Bognor Regis
Portsmouth
Gosport
Havant
Fareham
Southampton
Isle of Wight
Newport
Ventnor
St Catherine's Point

WALES
Cambrian Mountains
Cardigan Bay
Barmouth
Aberystwyth
Aberaeron
Cardigan
Fishguard
St David's Head
St Bride's Bay
Milford Haven
Pembroke
Tenby
Carmarthen Bay
Carmarthen
Llanelli
Swansea
Neath
Port Talbot
Bridgend
Aberdare
Merthyr Tydfil
Brecon
Brecon Beacons
Pontypridd
Abergavenny
Cardiff
Newport
Chepstow
Monmouth
Ross-on-Wye
Hereford
Leominster
Ludlow
Llandrindod Wells
Builth Wells
Llandovery
Llandeilo
Llanidloes
Lampeter

Worcester
Great Malvern
Gloucester
Cheltenham
Stroud
Cirencester
Swindon
Chippenham
Marlborough
Devizes
Trowbridge
Bath
Bristol
Weston-super-Mare
Bridgwater
Glastonbury
Wells
Chard
Yeovil
Shepton Mallet
Frome
Shaftesbury
Blandford Forum
Salisbury
Romsey
Christchurch
Bournemouth
Poole
Dorchester
Weymouth
Bill of Portland
Lyme Bay
Sidmouth
Exmouth
Teignmouth
Torquay
Newton Abbot
Dartmouth
Start Point

Bristol Channel
Minehead
Exmoor
Ilfracombe
Barnstaple
Bideford
Taunton
Tiverton
Exeter
Okehampton
Dartmoor
Tavistock
Plymouth
Launceston
Liskeard
Bodmin
Bodmin Moor
St Austell
Looe
Fowey
Truro
Falmouth
Camborne
Redruth
Penzance
St Ives
Land's End
Lizard Point
Newquay
Perranporth
Bude
Lundy
Hartland Point

ENGLISH CHANNEL
(LA MANCHE)

Boulogne-sur-Mer
Berck
Le Touquet-Paris-Plage
Montreuil
Mers-les-Bains
Le Tréport
Dieppe
FRANCE

Greenwich 0° meridian

© Collins
Bartholomew Ltd

50   100   150 KILOMETRES

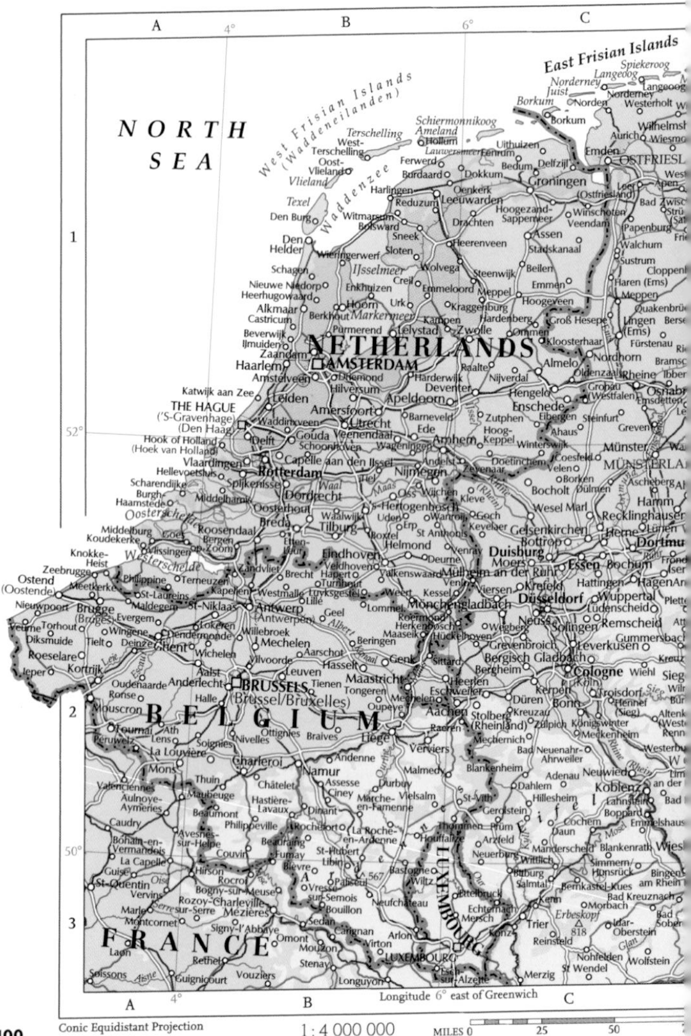

Conic Equidistant Projection   1 : 4 000 000   MILES 0   25   50

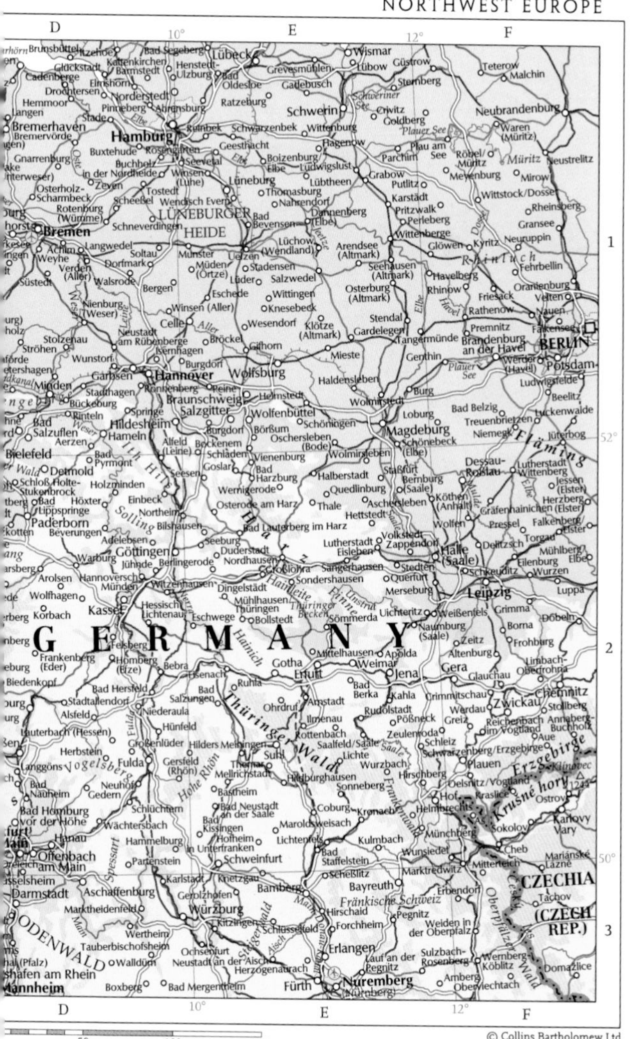
D
E
F
10°
12°
1
2
3
52°
50°
Brunsbüttel
Itzehoe
Bad Segeberg
Lübeck
Wismar
Glückstadt
Kaltenkirchen
Henstedt-Ulzburg
Barmstedt
Bad Oldesloe
Grevesmühlen
Lübow
Güstrow
Teterow
Malchin
Cadenberge
Elmshorn
Gadebusch
Sternberg
Drochtersen
Norderstedt
Schweriner See
Hemmoor
Pinneberg
Ahrensburg
Ratzeburg
Schwerin
Crivitz
Goldberg
Neubrandenburg
Stade
Elbe
Bremerhaven
Bremervörde
Hamburg
Reinbek
Schwarzenbek
Wittenburg
Plauer See
Waren (Müritz)
Geesthacht
Hagenow
Plau am See
Gnarrenburg
Buxtehude
Rosengarten
Boizenburg/Elbe
Parchim
Röbel/Müritz
Müritz
Neustrelitz
Buchholz in der Nordheide
Seevetal
Ludwigslust
Winsen (Luhe)
Grabow
Mirow
Osterholz-Scharmbeck
Zeven
Lüneburg
Lübtheen
Putlitz
Mewenburg
Tostedt
Thomasburg
Wittstock/Dosse
Rotenburg (Wümme)
Scheeßel
Wendisch Evern
Nahrendorf
Karstädt
LÜNEBURGER HEIDE
Bad Bevensen
Dannenberg (Elbe)
Pritzwalk
Rheinsberg
Perleberg
Schneverdingen
Bremen
Gransee
Wittenberge
Dosse
Lüchow (Wendland)
Arendsee (Altmark)
Glöwen
Kyritz
Neuruppin
Langwedel
Achim
Soltau
Munster
Uelzen
Weyhe
Verden (Aller)
Dorfmark
Müden (Örtze)
Stadensen
Seehausen (Altmark)
Rhinluch
Fehrbellin
Walsrode
Lüder
Salzwedel
Havelberg
Süstedt
Bergen
Osterburg (Altmark)
Rhinow
Oranienburg
Weser
Eschede
Wittingen
Friesack
Velten
Nienburg (Weser)
Winsen (Aller)
Knesebeck
Elbe
Havel
Rathenow
Nauen
Leine
Celle
Aller
Wesendorf
Klötze (Altmark)
Stendal
Premnitz
Falkensee
Stolzenau
Neustadt am Rübenberge
Bröckel
Gardelegen
Tangermünde
Brandenburg an der Havel
BERLIN
Ströhen
Isernhagen
Gifhorn
Mieste
Genthin
Werder (Havel)
Potsdam
Wunstorf
Burgdorf
Plauer See
Garbsen
Hannover
Wolfsburg
Haldensleben
Ludwigsfelde
Minden
Stadthagen
Ronnenberg
Peine
Helmstedt
Burg
Beelitz
Bückeburg
Braunschweig
Wolmirstedt
Springe
Salzgitter
Wolfenbüttel
Loburg
Bad Belzig
Luckenwalde
Rinteln
Hildesheim
Schöningen
Treuenbrietzen
Bad Salzuflen
Weser
Hameln
Burgdorf
Börßum
Magdeburg
Niemegk
Jüterbog
Aerzen
Alfeld (Leine)
Bockenem
Oschersleben (Bode)
Schönebeck (Elbe)
Fläming
Bielefeld
Bad Pyrmont
Schladen
Wolmirsleben
Wald
Detmold
Goslar
Vienenburg
Dessau-Roßlau
Lutherstadt Wittenberg
Schloß Holte-Stukenbrock
Holzminden
Seesen
Bad Harzburg
Halberstadt
Staßfurt
Bernburg (Saale)
Jessen (Elster)
Bad Lippspringe
Höxter
Einbeck
Wernigerode
Quedlinburg
Köthen (Anhalt)
Mulde
Herzberg (Elster)
Solling
Northeim
Osterode am Harz
Thale
Aschersleben
Gräfenhainichen
Paderborn
Bilshausen
Harz
Hettstedt
Saale
Wolfen
Pressel
Falkenberg/Elster
Beverungen
Adelebsen
Bad Lauterberg im Harz
Volkstedt
Torgau
Göttingen
Seeburg
Duderstadt
Lutherstadt Eisleben
Zappendorf
Halle (Saale)
Delitzsch
Mühlberg/Elbe
Warburg
Jühnde
Berlingerode
Nordhausen
Sangerhausen
Stedten
Eilenburg
Arolsen
Hannoversch Münden
Großlohra
Sondershausen
Querfurt
Schkeuditz
Wurzen
Witzenhausen
Dingelstädt
Hainleite
Merseburg
Leipzig
Luppa
Wolfhagen
Hessisch Lichtenau
Mühlhausen/Thüringen
Thüringer Becken
Unstrut
Finne
Kassel
Korbach
Eschwege
Bollstedt
Sömmerda
Uichteritz
Weißenfels
Grimma
Döbeln
GERMANY
Naumburg (Saale)
Borna
Felsberg
Zeitz
Frohburg
Frankenberg (Eder)
Homberg (Efze)
Hainich
Mittelhausen
Apolda
Altenburg
Limbach-Oberfrohna
Bebra
Gotha
Erfurt
Weimar
Jena
Gera
Glauchau
Biedenkopf
Eisenach
Ruhla
Bad Berka
Kahla
Crimmitschau
Chemnitz
Bad Hersfeld
Bad Salzungen
Arnstadt
Zwickau
Stollberg
Stadtallendorf
Thüringer Wald
Ohrdruf
Rudolstadt
Werdau
Alsfeld
Niederaula
Ilmenau
Pößneck
Greiz
Reichenbach im Vogtland
Annaberg-Buchholz
Fulda
Hünfeld
Rottenbach
Zeulenroda
Lauterbach (Hessen)
Saalfeld/Saale
Aue
Großenlüder
Hilders
Meiningen
Schleiz
Herbstein
Suhl
Lichte
Schwarzenberg/Erzgebirge
Fulda
Gersfeld (Rhön)
Themar
Wurzbach
Erzgebirge
Langgöns
Vogelsberg
Hohe Rhön
Mellrichstadt
Hirschberg
Plauen
Klínovec
Bad Nauheim
Neuhof
Gedern
Hildburghausen
Sonneberg
Oelsnitz/Vogtland
Krušné hory
Hohe Rhön
Bastheim
Frankenwald
Hof
Kraslice
Ostrov
Schlüchtern
Bad Neustadt an der Saale
Coburg
Kronach
Helmbrechts
Bad Homburg vor der Höhe
Wächtersbach
Bad Kissingen
Maroldsweisach
Sokolov
Karlovy Vary
Hanau
Spessart
Hammelburg
Hofheim in Unterfranken
Lichtenfels
Kulmbach
Münchberg
Offenbach am Main
Partenstein
Schweinfurt
Bad Staffelstein
Wunsiedel
Cheb
Mariánské Lázně
Scheßlitz
Marktredwitz
Mitterteich
Frankenheim
Karlstadt
Knetzgau
Bayreuth
Erbendorf
CZECHIA (CZECH REP.)
Darmstadt
Aschaffenburg
Gerolzhofen
Bamberg
Fränkische Schweiz
Oberpfälzer Wald
Tachov
Marktheidenfeld
Würzburg
Hirschaid
Pegnitz
Český les
Main
Kitzingen
Steigerwald
Forchheim
Weiden in der Oberpfalz
ODENWALD
Wertheim
Schlüsselfeld
Main-Donau-Kanal
Tauberbischofsheim
Ochsenfurt
Aisch
Erlangen
Lauf an der Pegnitz
Sulzbach-Rosenberg
Wernberg-Köblitz
Walldürn
Neustadt an der Aisch
Herzogenaurach
Domažlice
Mannheim
Boxberg
Bad Mergentheim
Fürth
Nuremberg (Nürnberg)
Amberg
Oberviechtach
50
100
150 KILOMETRES

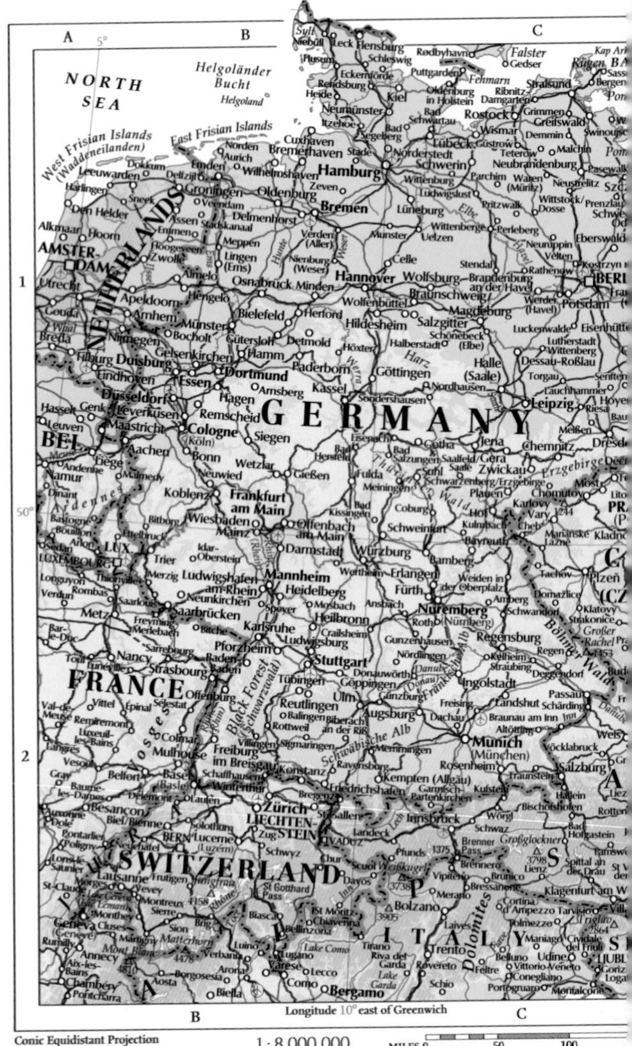

Conic Equidistant Projection

1 : 8 000 000

MILES 0   50   100

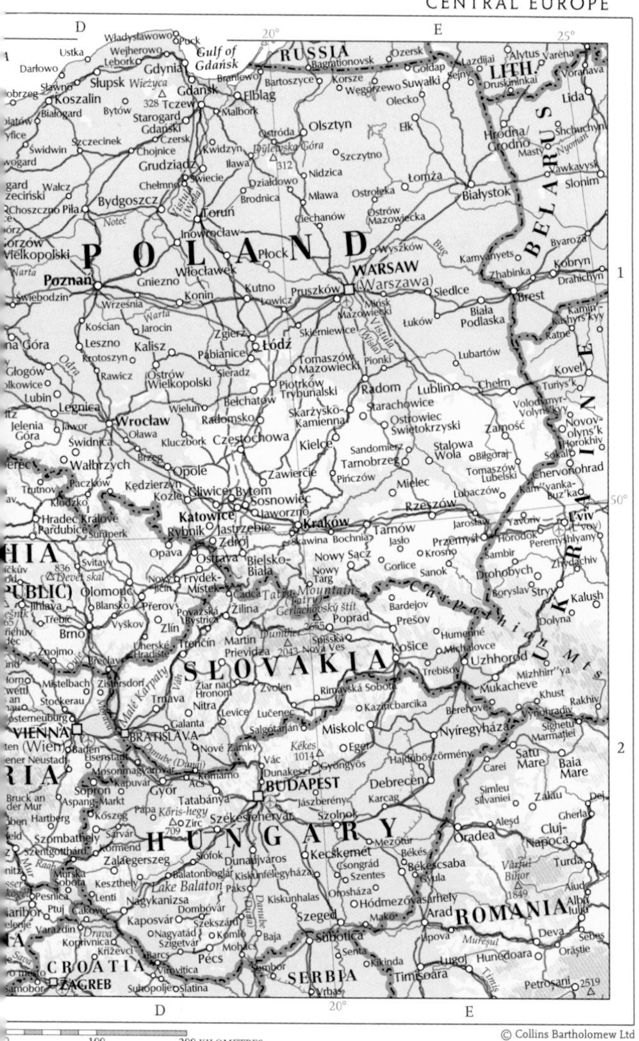

D
E
20°
25°
50°
1
2
POLAND
WARSAW
(Warszawa)
RUSSIA
LITH.
BELARUS
UKRAINE
SLOVAKIA
HUNGARY
BUDAPEST
ROMANIA
SERBIA
CROATIA
ZAGREB
VIENNA
(Wien)
BRATISLAVA
Gulf of Gdańsk
Carpathian Mts
Tatra Mountains
Lake Balaton
Kraków
Łódź
Wrocław
Poznań
Gdańsk
Katowice
Lviv
Brest
Košice
Debrecen
Cluj-Napoca
Danube
Vistula
0
100
200 KILOMETRES

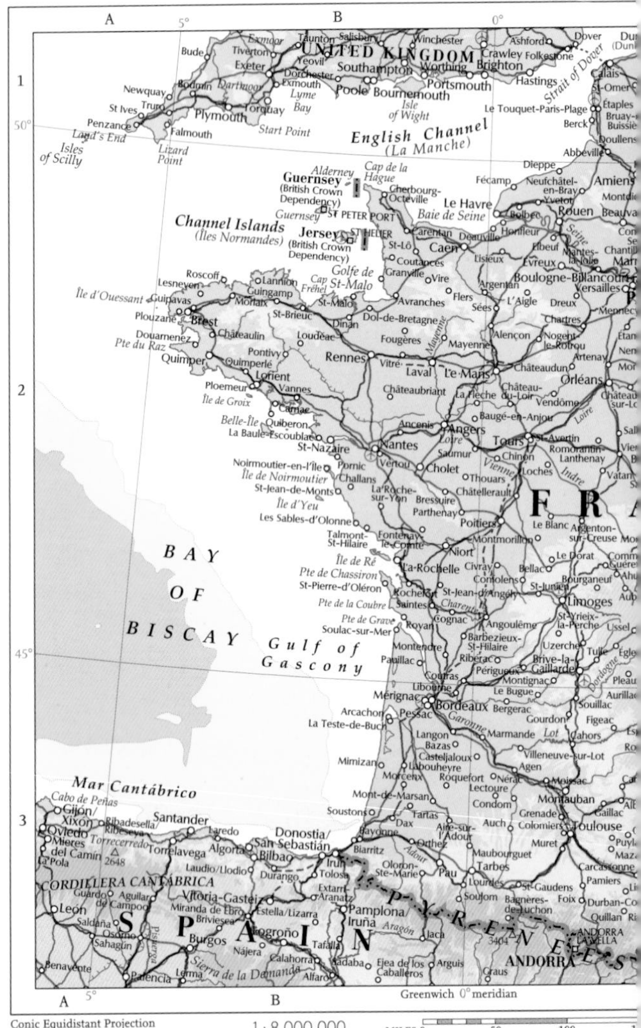

Conic Equidistant Projection   1:8 000 000   MILES 0   50   100

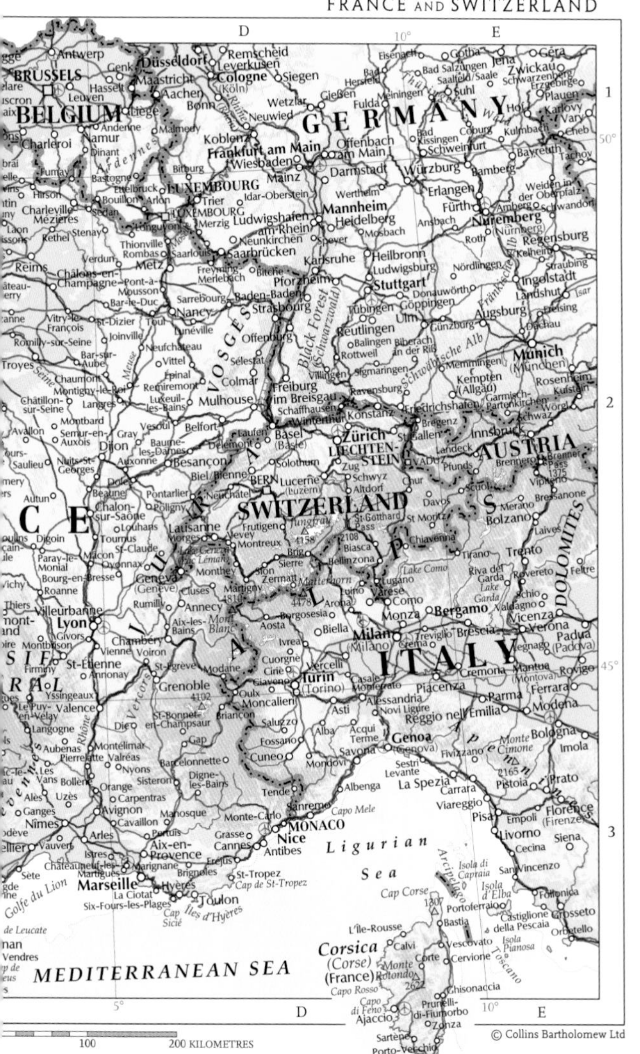

© Collins Bartholomew Ltd

1
2
3
10°
5°
50°
45°
BRUSSELS
BELGIUM
Antwerp
Liège
Namur
Charleroi
Düsseldorf
Remscheid
Leverkusen
Cologne
(Köln)
Siegen
Maastricht
Aachen
Bonn
Koblenz
Frankfurt am Main
Wiesbaden
Mainz
Offenbach am Main
Darmstadt
GERMANY
Eisenach
Gotha
Jena
Gera
Zwickau
Bad Salzungen
Saalfeld/Saale
Suhl
Plauen
Fulda
Meiningen
Gießen
Wetzlar
Neuwied
Bad Kissingen
Schweinfurt
Coburg
Kulmbach
Hof
Bayreuth
Cheb
Karlovy Vary
Würzburg
Bamberg
Erlangen
Fürth
Nuremberg
(Nürnberg)
Regensburg
Mannheim
Heidelberg
Ludwigshafen am Rhein
LUXEMBOURG
Trier
Idar-Oberstein
Saarbrücken
Metz
Verdun
Reims
Châlons-en-Champagne
Nancy
Strasbourg
Karlsruhe
Heilbronn
Ludwigsburg
Stuttgart
Pforzheim
Baden-Baden
Ingolstadt
Augsburg
Ulm
Reutlingen
Munich
(München)
Black Forest
(Schwarzwald)
VOSGES
Colmar
Mulhouse
Freiburg im Breisgau
Troyes
Dijon
Besançon
Belfort
Basel
(Basle)
Zürich
LIECHTENSTEIN
VADUZ
Konstanz
Friedrichshafen
Bregenz
Innsbruck
AUSTRIA
Kempten (Allgäu)
Rosenheim
SWITZERLAND
BERN
Lucerne
(Luzern)
Solothurn
Neuchâtel
Biel/Bienne
Lausanne
Geneva
(Genève)
Lake Geneva
(Lac Léman)
Montreux
Sion
Zermatt
Matterhorn
Jungfrau
St Gotthard Pass
Chur
Davos
St Moritz
Bolzano
Merano
Brenner Pass
DOLOMITES
Trento
Lugano
Como
Lake Como
Varese
Monza
Bergamo
Brescia
Milan
(Milano)
Verona
Vicenza
Padua
(Padova)
ITALY
Cremona
Mantua
(Mantova)
Piacenza
Parma
Reggio nell'Emilia
Modena
Ferrara
Bologna
Turin
(Torino)
Aosta
Mont Blanc
Annecy
Chambéry
Grenoble
Lyon
Villeurbanne
St-Étienne
Valence
Alessandria
Asti
Genoa
(Genova)
La Spezia
Pisa
Livorno
Florence
(Firenze)
Siena
Cuneo
Sanremo
MONACO
Monte-Carlo
Nice
Cannes
Antibes
Avignon
Nîmes
Arles
Aix-en-Provence
Marseille
Toulon
Hyères
Montpellier
Golfe du Lion
Ligurian Sea
MEDITERRANEAN SEA
Corsica
(Corse)
(France)
Bastia
Ajaccio
Bonifacio
Isola d'Elba

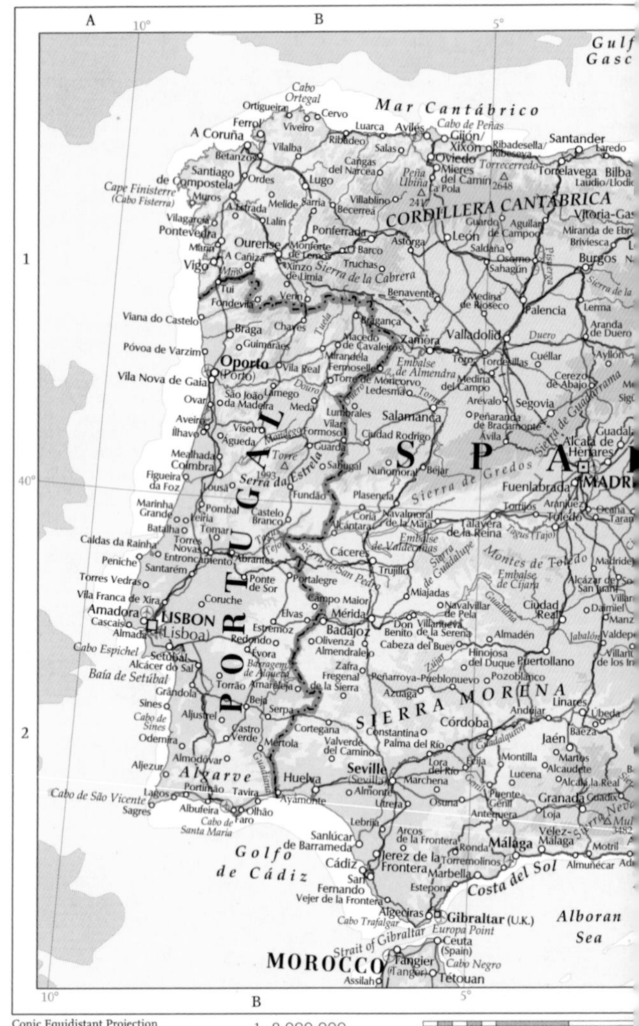

Mar Cantábrico

Cabo Ortegal
Ortigueira Cervo
Ferrol Viveiro Ribadeo Luarca Avilés Cabo de Peñas
A Coruña Vilalba Salas Gijón/Xixón Santander
Betanzos Cangas del Narcea Oviedo Ribadesella Laredo
Santiago Ordes Lugo La Pola Mieres Torrecerredo Torrelavega Bilba
de Compostela Melide Sarria Villablino del Camin 2648 Laudio/Llod
Cape Finisterre Muros A Estrada Becerreá 24V Guardo Aguilar de Vitoria-Ga
(Cabo Fisterra) Lalín Ponferrada Astorga León Campóo Miranda de Ebro
Vilagarcía A Cañiza Monforte El Barco Saldaña Osorno Brivies-ca L
Pontevedra Ourense de Lemos Truchas CORDILLERA CANTÁBRICA Burgos
Marín Ribadavia Xinzo Sierra de la Cabrera Benavente Sahagún Palencia Sierra de
Vigo Tui de Limia Verín Medina Lerma
Fondevila Benavente de Rioseco Aranda de
Viana do Castelo Braga Chaves Bragança Zamora Valladolid Duero Cuéllar Cerezo de Ayllón
Guimarães Macedo Tordesillas Abajo Sigü
Póvoa de Varzim de Cavaleiros Segovia Guadal
Oporto Vila Real Mirando Embalse Tordesillas Peñaranda de Alcalá de
Porto Ferrospelho de Almeida del Campo Bragança Henares
Vila Nova de Gaia São João Lamego Torre de Moncorvo Ledesma Arévalo Ávila A·MADR
da Madeira Meda Lumbrales Salamanca S P A Fuenlabrada MADRI
Ovar Viseu Vilar Ciudad Rodrigo Ávila Sierra de Gredos
Aveiro Águeda Formoso Guarda Nuñomoral Béjar Torrijos Aranju
Ílhavo Meinhado 1993 Sabugal Plasencia Sierra de Gredos Toledo Ocaña Tara
Coimbra Serra da Estrela Navalmoral Talavera Montes de Toledo Madride
Figueira Lousã Fundão Coria de la Mata de la Reina Tajo (Tejo) Alcázar de S
da Foz Marinha Castelo Branco Alcántara Embalse Madridejos San Juan
Grande Pombal Navalmoral Trujillo de Valdecañas Ciudad Villan
Caldas da Rainha Entroncamento Cáceres Miajadas Real Valdepe
Batalha Torres Tomar Guadiana Sierra de Guadalupe Almodóvar Manz
Peniche Novas Santarém Abrantes Embalse de los Ini
Torres Vedras Ponte Portalegre Campo Maior Navalvillar de Cijara
Vila Franca de Xira de Sor Cáceres de Pela Almadén Villan
Amadora Coruche Elvas Mérida Benito de la Serena Hinojosa Puertollano
Cascais LISBON Estremoz Badajoz Don Villarnevo del Duque Linares
Almada (Lisboa) Redondo Olivenza Cabeza del Buey Pozoblanco Úbeda
Cabo Espichel Barragem Almendralejo SIERRA MORENA Andújar
Setúbal de Alqueva Zafra Peñarroya-Pueblonuevo Jaén
Baía de Setúbal Torrão Amareleja Fregenal Azuaga Córdoba Martos Linares
Grândola Beja de la Sierra Guadalquivir Montilla Alcaudete La Rota
Sines Cabo de Aljustel Serpa Cortegana Constantina Lucena Granada Guada
Sines Odemira Castro Valverde Palma del Río Puente Antequera Loja Mul
Aljezur Verde Mértola del Camino Osuna Genil 482
Algarve Huelva Marchena Málaga Motril Ad
Portimão Tavira Ayamonte Almonte Sevilla Vélez- Almuñécar
Lagos Albufeira Olhão Utrera Seville Málaga Costa del Sol
Sagres Cabo de de Barrameda Lebrija Arcos de Ronda Torremolinos
Cabo de São Vicente Santa Maria Cádiz la Frontera Marbella
Golfo San Jerez de la Estepona
de Cádiz Fernando Frontera Algeciras Gibraltar (U.K.)
Vejer de la Frontera Cabo Trafalgar Europa Point
Strait of Gibraltar Ceuta Alboran
(Spain) Cabo Negro Sea
MOROCCO Tangier Tetouan
Tánger Assilah

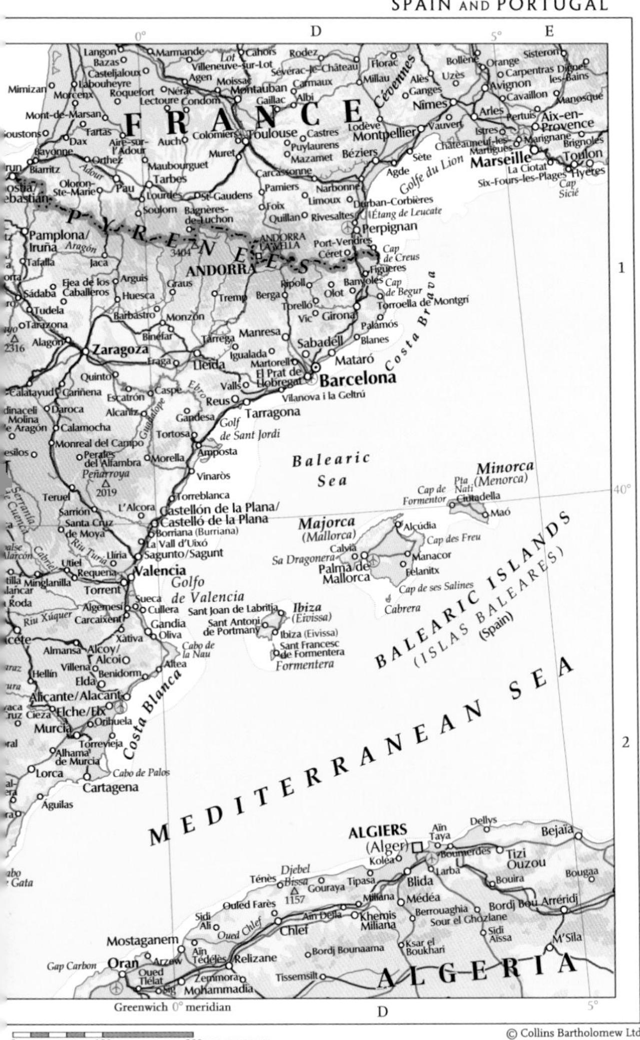

D
E
0°
5°
1
2
40°
FRANCE
Langon
Bazas
Casteljaloux
Marmande
Lot
Cahors
Rodez
Villeneuve-sur-Lot
Sévérac-le-Château
Florac
Cévennes
Bollène
Orange
Sisteron
Carpentras
Digne-les-Bains
Mimizan
Labouheyre
Morcenx
Roquefort
Nérac
Agen
Moissac
Montauban
Carmaux
Millau
Alès
Uzès
Avignon
Cavaillon
Manosque
Lectoure
Condom
Gaillac
Albi
Ganges
Nîmes
Arles
Mont-de-Marsan
Tartas
Dax
Aire-sur-l'Adour
Auch
Colomiers
Toulouse
Castres
Lodève
Montpellier
Vauvert
Istres
Pertuis
Aix-en-Provence
Marignane
Brignoles
Bayonne
Orthez
Muret
Puylaurens
Mazamet
Béziers
Sète
Châteauneuf-les-Martigues
Marseille
Toulon
Biarritz
Adour
Maubourguet
Tarbes
Carcassonne
Agde
Golfe du Lion
La Ciotat
Hyères
Six-Fours-les-Plages
Cap Sicié
Oloron-Ste-Marie
Pau
Lourdes
St-Gaudens
Pamiers
Narbonne
Foix
Limoux
Durban-Corbières
Soulom
Bagnères-de-Luchon
Quillan
Rivesaltes
Étang de Leucate
Perpignan
PYRENEES
Pamplona/ Iruña
Aragón
Jaca
3404
ANDORRA LA VELLA
ANDORRA
Port-Vendres
Céret
Cap de Creus
Tafalla
Figueres
Ejea de los Caballeros
Arguis
Graus
Huesca
Tremp
Berga
Ripoll
Olot
Banyoles
Cap de Begur
Costa Brava
Sádaba
Tudela
Torroella de Montgrí
Barbastro
Monzón
Torelló
Vic
Girona
Tarazona
Binéfar
Tàrrega
Manresa
Palamós
2316
Alagón
Zaragoza
Sabadell
Blanes
Igualada
Fraga
Lleida
Martorell
Mataró
Quinto
El Prat de Llobregat
Barcelona
Calatayud
Cariñena
Caspe
Ebro
Valls
Escatrón
Reus
Vilanova i la Geltrú
Daroca
Alcañiz
Tarragona
Guadalope
Gandesa
Golf de Sant Jordi
Calamocha
Monreal del Campo
Tortosa
Perales del Alfambra
Morella
Amposta
Peñarroya
2019
Vinaròs
Balearic Sea
Teruel
Torreblanca
L'Alcora
Minorca (Menorca)
Cap de Formentor
Pta Nati
Ciutadella
Maó
Sarrión
Castellón de la Plana/ Castelló de la Plana
Santa Cruz de Moya
Borriana (Burriana)
La Vall d'Uixó
Majorca (Mallorca)
Alcúdia
Cap des Freu
Riu Turia
Llíria
Sagunto/Sagunt
Calvià
Manacor
Sa Dragonera
Palma de Mallorca
Felanitx
Utiel
Requena
Valencia
Minglanilla
Golfo de Valencia
Cap de ses Salines
Torrent
Cabrera
Sueca
Algemesí
Cullera
Sant Joan de Labritja
Ibiza (Eivissa)
Riu Xúquer
Carcaixent
Gandia
Sant Antoni de Portmany
Xàtiva
Oliva
Ibiza (Eivissa)
Almansa
Alcoy/ Alcoi
Cabo de la Nau
Sant Francesc de Formentera
Formentera
Villena
Benidorm
Altea
BALEARIC ISLANDS (ISLAS BALEARES) (Spain)
Hellín
Elda
Alicante/Alacant
Costa Blanca
Elche/Elx
Orihuela
Murcia
Torrevieja
Alhama de Murcia
Lorca
Cabo de Palos
Cartagena
Águilas
MEDITERRANEAN SEA
ALGIERS (Alger)
Aïn Taya
Dellys
Bejaïa
Boumerdes
Tizi Ouzou
Koléa
Djebel Bissa
1157
Ténès
Gouraya
Tipasa
Blida
Larba
Bouira
Bougaa
Miliana
Médéa
Ouled Farès
Berrouaghia
Bordj Bou Arréridj
Sidi Ali
Aïn Defla
Khemis Miliana
Sour el Ghozlane
Oued Chlef
Chlef
Sidi Aïssa
M'Sila
Mostaganem
Ksar el Boukhari
Aïn Tédélès
Bordj Bounaama
Gap Carbon
Oran
Arzew
Relizane
ALGERIA
Oued Tlélat
Zemmora
Tissemsilt
Sig
Mohammadia
Greenwich 0° meridian
D
5°
0
100
200 KILOMETRES

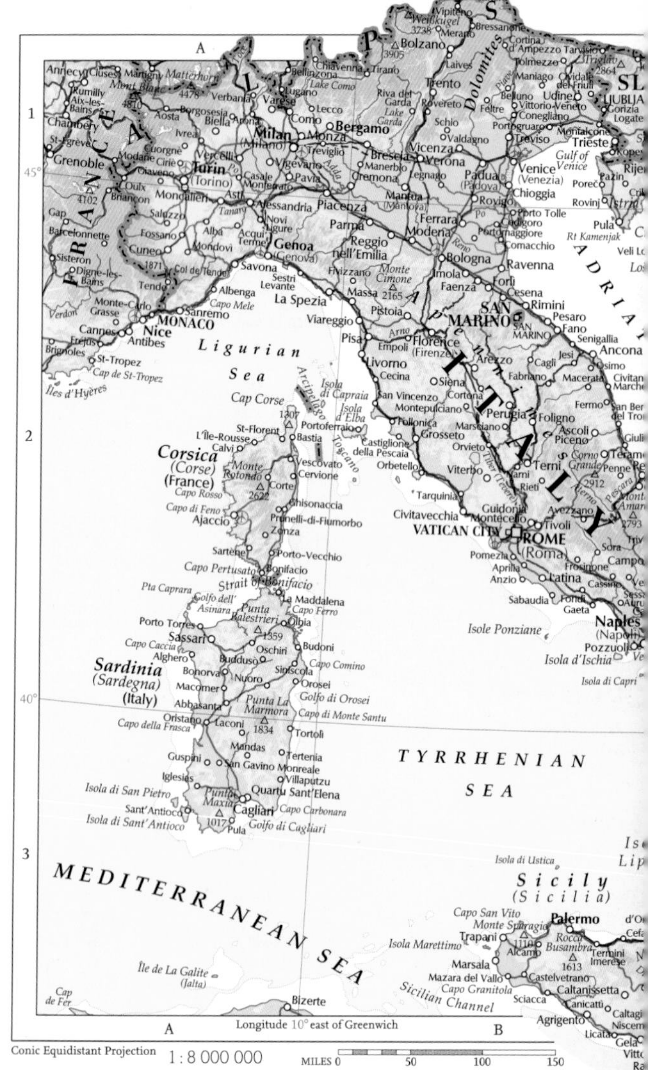

FRANCE

Annecy Cluses Martigny Matterhorn
Rumilly Monte Bianco
Aix-les-Bains St-Gervais Mont Blanc Grand-St-Bernard
Chambéry Verbania Lugano Lecco Lake Como
Grenoble Modane Cirie Ivrea Biella Vercelli
Oulx Susa Aosta Novara
Briançon Monginevro Turin Vigevano Pavia
Gap Chisone (Torino) Asti Casale Monferrato
Barcelonnette Salazzo Alba Acqui Terme
Digne-les- Cuneo Mondovi Fossano Alessandria
Bains Sisteron Col de Tende Novi Ligure
Verdon Tende Capo Mele Acqui Terme
Monte-Carlo Grasse Albenga Savona
MONACO Sanremo Finale Ligure
Cannes Nice Capo Mele
Fréjus Antibes
St-Tropez
Cap de St-Tropez
Iles d'Hyères

ALPS

Chiavenna Tirano
Bellinzona Riva del
Bolzano
Verbania Garda
Como Bergamo Schio
Milan Monza Brescia Rovereto
Magenta Trento
Abbiategrasso Lodi Cremona Legnano Verona
Lecco Vicenza
Mantova Padua
Piacenza Rovigo
Parma Ferrara
Reggio Modena
nell'Emilia
Monte Bologna
Cimone Imola
2165 Faenza
Massa Forli
Pistoia Cesena
Arno
Pisa Florence
Empoli Firenze
Livorno Siena
Cecina San Vincenzo
Montepulciano
Pollonica
Grosseto
Orbetello

Bolzano
3905
Dolomites
Vipiteno
Merano
Belluno
Feltre
Bassano del Grappa
Treviso
Venice
(Venezia)
Gulf of
Venice
Chioggia
Porto Tolle
Comacchio
Ravenna
Rimini
Pesaro
Fano
Senigallia
Ancona
Jesi Osimo
Fabriano Macerata
Perugia Foligno
Assisi
Terni
Rieti

ITALIA

SAN
MARINO
SAN
MARINO

Brenner
Vipiteno
Bressanone
Campo Tures
Dobbiaco
Cortina d'Ampezzo Tarvisio
Tolmezzo
Maniago Gemona Tricesimo
Vittorio-Veneto Udine Cividale
Portogruaro Pordenone
Conegliano Monfalcone
Gorizia
SLOVENIA
LJUBLJANA
Trieste
Rovinj
Pula
Rt Kamenjak

Liguran
Sea

Cap Corse
Isola
di Capraia
Isola
d'Elba
Portoferraio
St-Florent Bastia
Calvi
L'Île-Rousse
Monte
Rotondo Vescovato
2307 Corte Cervione
Corsica
(Corse)
(France)
Capo Rosso
Capo di Feno Ajaccio
Cauro
Sartène
Propriano
Porto-Vecchio
Capo Pertusato
Bonifacio
Strait of Bonifacio
Pta Caprara
Asinara Golfo dell'
Asinara La Maddalena
Porto Torres Palau Capo Ferro
Capo Caccia Sassari Olbia
Alghero Buddusò
Bonorva Oschiri
Macomer Nuoro
Abbasanta Siniscola
Sardinia Orosei
(Sardegna) Golfo di Orosei
(Italy)
Oristano Laconi Capo di Monte Santu
Capo della Frasca 1834
Tortoli
Guspini Mandas Fertenia
Iglesias San Gavino Monreale Villaputzu
Quartu Sant'Elena
Isola di San Pietro Punta Cagliari
Sant'Antioco Maxia Capo Carbonara
Isola di Sant'Antioco 1017 Pula Golfo di Cagliari

Lago
Maggiore
Gulf of
Garda
Monte Baldo

Arcipelago
Toscano

VATICAN CITY
ROME
Roma
Aprilia
Anzio Latina
Sabaudia
Gaeta
Isole Ponziane

Castiglione
della Pescaia
Montalto
di Castro
Tarquinia
Civitavecchia
Viterbo
Guidonia
Montecelio
Tivoli
Pomezia
Frosinone
Cassino
Sora
Avezzano
Frascati
Gran
Sasso
2912

Naples
(Napoli)
Pozzuoli
Isola d'Ischia
Isola di Capri

ADRIAT

San Ben
del Tron
Penne
Pescara
Teramo
Ascoli Piceno
Fermo
Civita
March

TYRRHENIAN
SEA

MEDITERRANEAN SEA

Cap
de Fer

Île de La Galite
(Jalta)

Bizerte

Isola di Ustica

Sicily
(Sicilia)

Palermo
Capo San Vito Rocca
Monte Sparagio Busambra
Trapani Alcamo 1613
Marsala Castelvetrano
Mazara del Vallo Castelvetrano
Capo Granitola Sciacca
Sicilian Channel
Agrigento

Termini
Imerese
Caltanissetta
Canicatti
Caltagirone
Licata Gela

Lip

Isole
Lip

Longitude 10° east of Greenwich
Conic Equidistant Projection   1 : 8 000 000
MILES 0   50   100   150

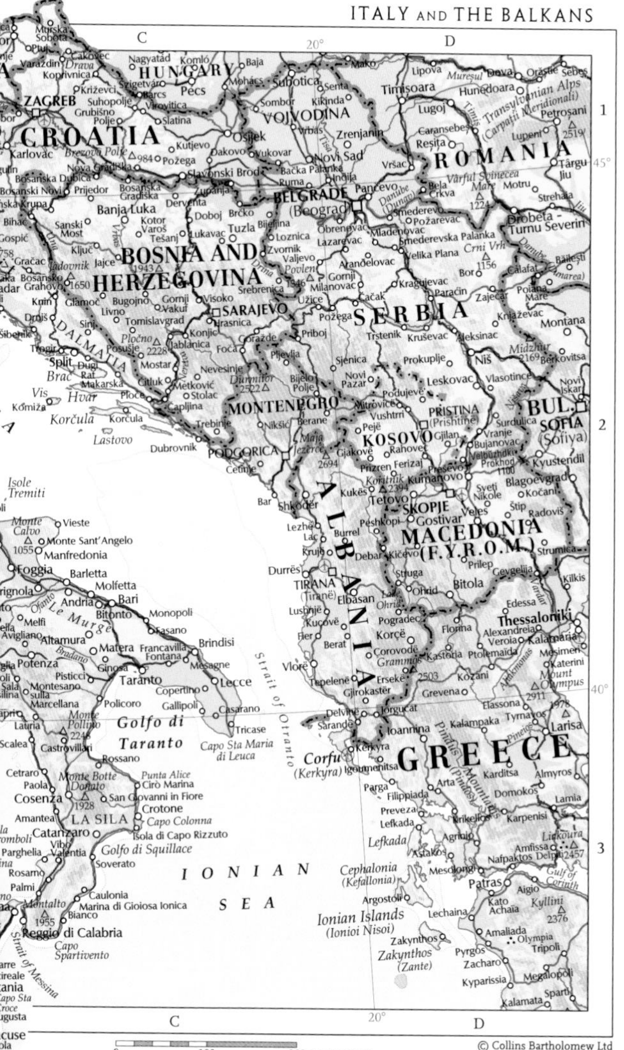
CROATIA
BOSNIA AND HERZEGOVINA
SERBIA
MONTENEGRO
KOSOVO
ALBANIA
MACEDONIA (F.Y.R.O.M.)
ROMANIA
BUL.
GREECE
HUNGARY
VOJVODINA
ZAGREB
BELGRADE (Beograd)
SARAJEVO
PODGORICA
TIRANA (Tiranë)
SKOPJE
SOFIA (Sofiya)
PRISTINA (Prishtinë)
IONIAN SEA
Golfo di Taranto
Strait of Otranto
Golfo di Squillace
Strait of Messina
Ionian Islands (Ionioi Nisoi)
Cephalonia (Kefallonia)
Corfu (Kerkyra)
Zakynthos (Zante)
Lefkada
Pindus Mountains (Pindos)
Mount Olympus
Transylvanian Alps (Carpaţii Meridionali)
DALMATIA
LA SILA
Le Murge
Split
Dubrovnik
Bari
Brindisi
Taranto
Lecce
Thessaloniki
Patras
C
D
1
2
3
20°
45°
40°
0
100
200 KILOMETRES
© Collins Bartholomew Ltd

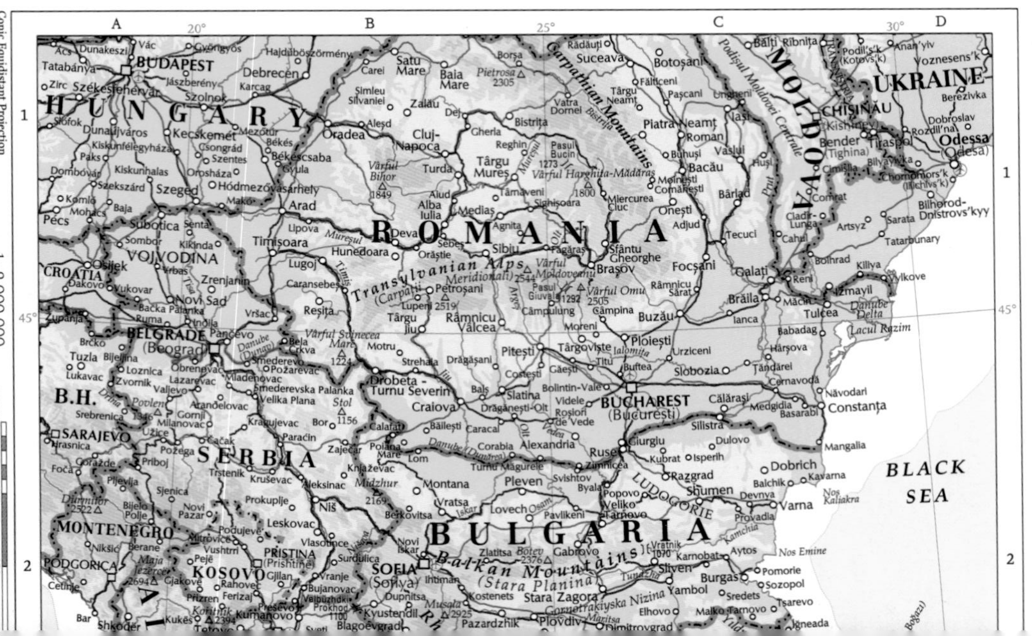

Conic Equidistant Projection

1 : 8 000 000

MILES 0   50   100

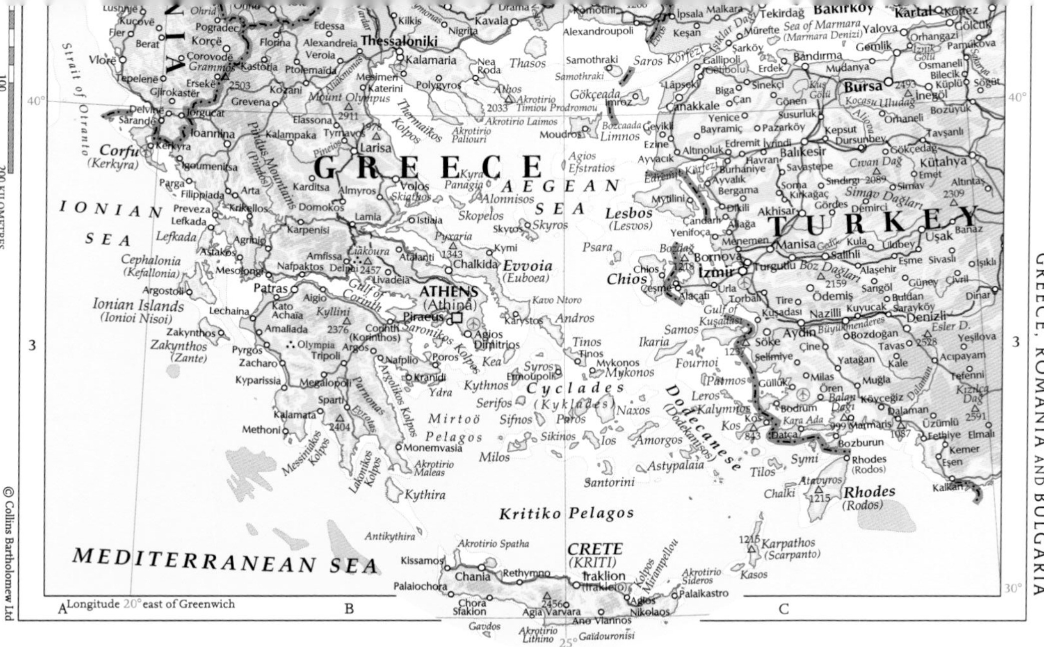

100   200 KILOMETRES

© Collins Bartholomew Ltd

GREECE
TURKEY
AEGEAN SEA
IONIAN SEA
MEDITERRANEAN SEA
Kritiko Pelagos
Mirtoö Pelagos
Strait of Otranto
ATHENS (Athina)
Thessaloniki
Izmir
Bursa
CRETE (KRITI)
Rhodes (Rodos)
Dodecanese (Dodekanisos)
Cyclades (Kyklades)
Lesbos (Lesvos)
Chios
Samos
Evvoia (Euboea)
Corfu (Kerkyra)
Cephalonia (Kefallonia)
Zakynthos (Zante)
Ionian Islands (Ionioi Nisoi)
Pindus Mountains (Pindos)
Sea of Marmara (Marmara Denizi)
Longitude 20° east of Greenwich

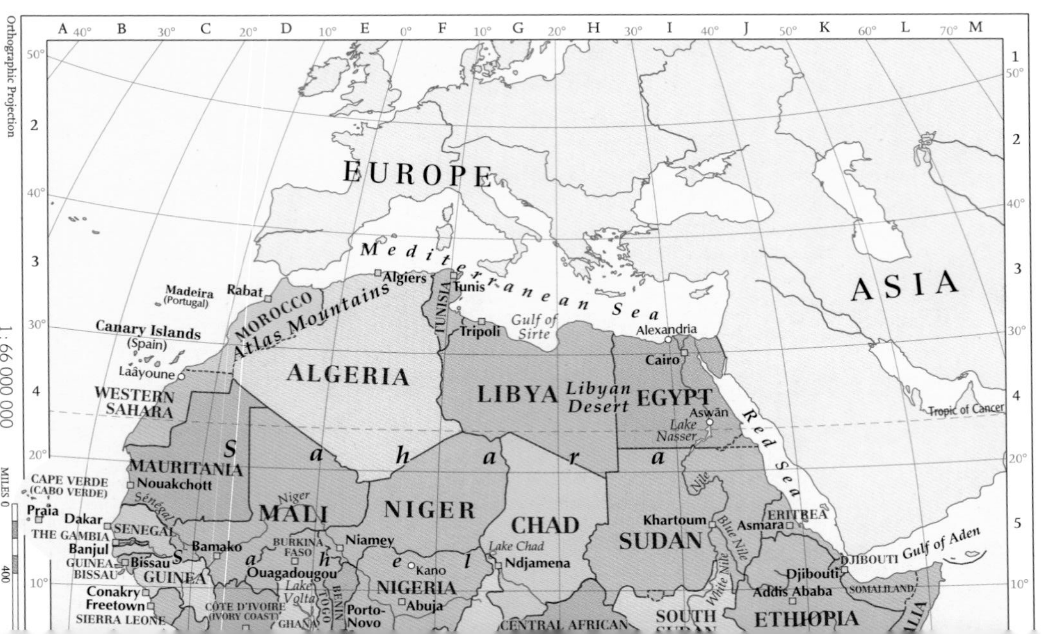
A
B
C
D
E
F
G
H
I
J
K
L
M
1
2
3
4
5
40°
30°
20°
10°
0°
50°
60°
70°
EUROPE
ASIA
Mediterranean Sea
Red Sea
Gulf of Aden
Gulf of Sirte
Tropic of Cancer
Madeira
(Portugal)
Canary Islands
(Spain)
Laâyoune
WESTERN SAHARA
Rabat
MOROCCO
Atlas Mountains
Algiers
ALGERIA
TUNISIA
Tunis
Tripoli
LIBYA
Libyan Desert
Alexandria
Cairo
EGYPT
Aswān
Lake Nasser
Sahara
Sahel
MAURITANIA
Nouakchott
Sénégal
CAPE VERDE
(CABO VERDE)
Praia
Dakar
SENEGAL
THE GAMBIA
Banjul
GUINEA-BISSAU
Bissau
GUINEA
Conakry
Freetown
SIERRA LEONE
Bamako
MALI
Niger
BURKINA FASO
Ouagadougou
Lake Volta
CÔTE D'IVOIRE
(IVORY COAST)
GHANA
TOGO
BENIN
Porto-Novo
Niamey
NIGER
Kano
NIGERIA
Abuja
CHAD
Lake Chad
Ndjamena
CENTRAL AFRICAN
SUDAN
Khartoum
Nile
Blue Nile
White Nile
SOUTH
ERITREA
Asmara
DJIBOUTI
Djibouti
Addis Ababa
ETHIOPIA
SOMALILAND
MILES 0
400

Orthographic Projection

1: 66 000 000

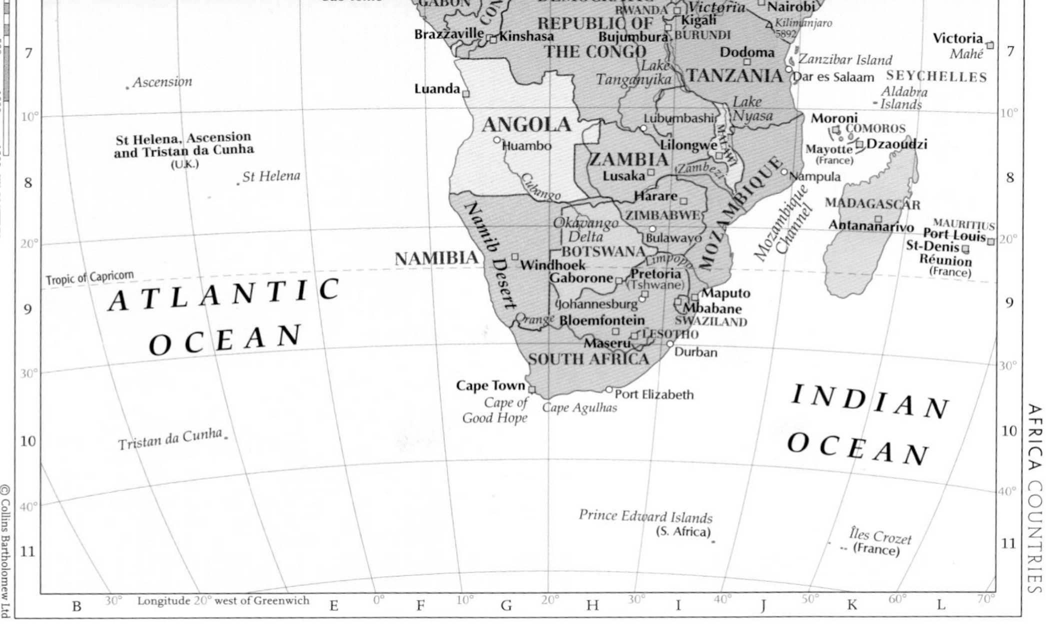

INDIAN OCEAN

ATLANTIC OCEAN

Victoria □
Mahé
SEYCHELLES
Aldabra
Islands
MAURITIUS
Port Louis □
St-Denis □
Réunion
(France)
Zanzibar Island
Dar es Salaam
Moroni
COMOROS
Mayotte □ Dzaoudzi
(France)
MADAGASCAR
Antananarivo □
Nampula
Mozambique Channel

Nairobi □
Kilimanjaro
Dodoma □
TANZANIA
Lake Nyasa
MALAWI
Lilongwe □
Lake Tanganyika
Zambezi
MOZAMBIQUE
Luangwa

RWANDA
Kigali □
BURUNDI
Bujumbura □
DEMOCRATIC REPUBLIC OF THE CONGO
Kinshasa ■
Lubumbashi

GABON
CON...
Brazzaville ■

ZAMBIA
Lusaka ■
Harare ■
ZIMBABWE
Bulawayo
Limpopo
Maputo ■
Mbabane □
SWAZILAND
Pretoria ■ (Tshwane)
Maseru □
LESOTHO
Port Elizabeth

ANGOLA
Luanda ■
Huambo
Cubango
Cuanza
Okavango Delta
BOTSWANA
Gaborone ■
Johannesburg
Bloemfontein ■
Orange
SOUTH AFRICA
Durban

NAMIBIA
Windhoek ■
Namib Desert
Cape Town ■
Cape of Good Hope
Cape Agulhas

Ascension
St Helena
St Helena, Ascension and Tristan da Cunha (U.K.)

Tropic of Capricorn

Tristan da Cunha

Iles Crozet
(France)

Prince Edward Islands
(S. Africa)

Longitude 20° west of Greenwich

500   1000   1500   KILOMETRES

© Collins Bartholomew Ltd

113

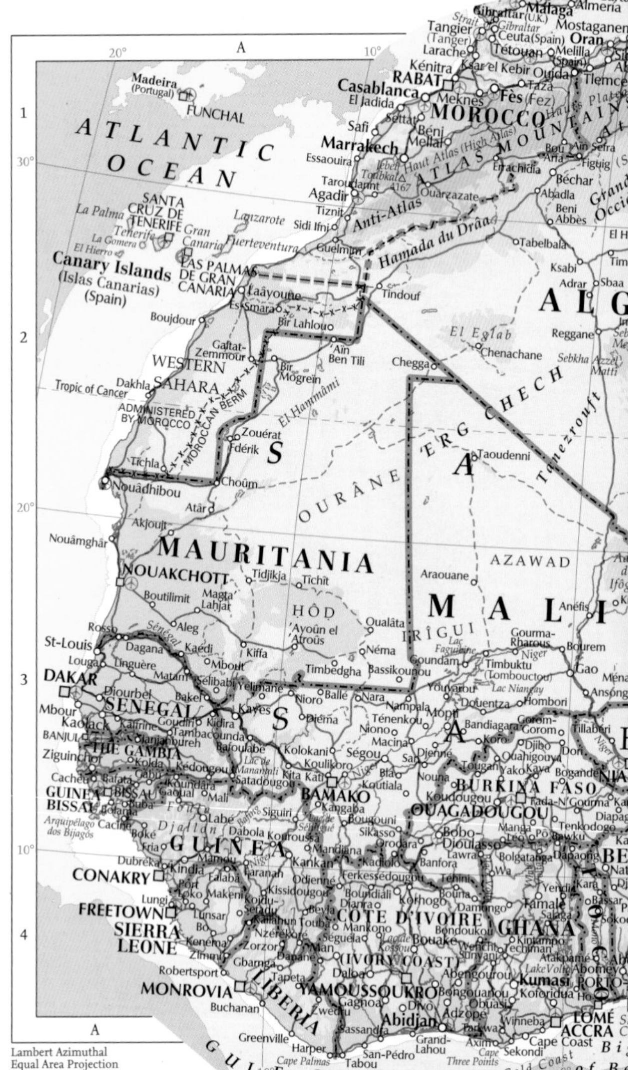
ATLANTIC OCEAN
Madeira (Portugal)
FUNCHAL
SANTA CRUZ DE TENERIFE
LAS PALMAS DE GRAN CANARIA
Canary Islands (Islas Canarias) (Spain)
La Palma
Tenerife
La Gomera
El Hierro
Gran Canaria
Lanzarote
Fuerteventura
SPAIN
Gibraltar (U.K.)
Strait of Gibraltar
Málaga
Almería
Tangier (Tanger)
Ceuta (Spain)
Tétouan
Melilla (Spain)
Larache
Mostaganem
Oran
Kénitra
Ksar el Kebir
Oujda
Tlemcen
RABAT
Casablanca
El Jadida
Meknès
Fès (Fez)
Taza
Settat
MOROCCO
Safi
Béni Mellal
Marrakech
Essaouira
Jebel Toubkal 4167
Haut Atlas (High Atlas)
ATLAS MOUNTAINS
Hauts Plateaux
Bou Arfa
Aïn Sefra
Figuig
Taroudannt
Errachidia
Béchar
Agadir
Ouarzazate
Abadla
Tiznit
Anti-Atlas
Beni Abbès
Grand Erg Occidental
Sidi Ifni
Hamada du Drâa
Guelmim
Tabelbala
El Ho
Ksabi
Timimoun
Adrar
Sbaa
Tindouf
ALG
Laâyoune
Es Smara
Bir Lahlou
Boujdour
Reggane
El Eglab
Chenachane
Sebkha Azzel Matti
Galtat-Zemmour
Aïn Ben Tili
Chegga
WESTERN SAHARA
Bir Mogreïn
ERG CHECH
Tropic of Cancer
Dakhla
ADMINISTERED BY MOROCCO
MOROCCAN BERM
El Hammâmi
Tanezrouft
Zouérat
Fdérik
S
Taoudenni
A
Tichla
Nouâdhibou
Choûm
OUARÂNE
Atâr
Akjoujt
Nouâmghâr
MAURITANIA
AZAWAD
NOUAKCHOTT
Tidjikja
Tîchît
Araouane
Boutilimit
Magta' Lahjar
HÔD
MALI
Anéfis
Rosso
Aleg
Ayoûn el Atroûs
Oualâta
IRÎGUI
Sénégal
St-Louis
Dagana
Kaédi
Kiffa
Néma
Lac Faguibine
Gourma-Rharous
Bourem
Louga
Linguère
Mbout
Timbuktu (Tombouctou)
Niger
Gao
DAKAR
Matam
Sélibabi
Timbedgha
Bassikounou
Goundam
Ménaka
Diourbel
Bakel
Yelimané
Nioro
Ballé
Nara
Youvarou
Lac Niangay
Ansongo
Mbour
SENEGAL
Kayes
Diéma
Nampala
Douentza
Hombori
Kaolack
Kaffrine
Goudiri
Kidira
Ténenkou
Mopti
Gorom-Gorom
BANJUL
Tambacounda
Niono
Bandiagara
Tillabéri
THE GAMBIA
Bafoulabé
Macina
Koro
Djibo
Ziguinchor
Kolda
Kédougou
Kolokani
Ségou
Djenné
Ouahigouya
Dori
Lac de Manantali
Koulikoro
San
Tougan
Yako
Kaya
Cacheu
Bafatá
Gabú
Koundara
Satadougou
Kita
Kati
Bla
Nouna
Bogandé
GUINEA BISSAU
BISSAU
Gaoual
Mali
BAMAKO
Koutiala
BURKINA FASO
Buba
Bolama
Fouta Djallon
Siguiri
Kangaba
Koudougou
Fada-N'Gourma
Labé
Bafing
Bougouni
OUAGADOUGOU
Diapaga
Arquipélago dos Bijagós
Cacine
Boké
Dabola
Kouroussa
Sikasso
Manga
Pô
Tenkodogo
Bawku
Fria
GUINEA
Mandiana
Orodara
Bobo-Dioulasso
Léo
Dubréka
Mamou
Kankan
Kadiolo
Banfora
Lawra
Bolgatanga
Dapaong
CONAKRY
Kindia
Faranah
Odienné
Ferkessédougou
Wa
Falaba
Kissidougou
Boundiali
Téhini
Yendi
Kara
Lungi
Port Loko
Makeni
Koidu-Sefadu
Dianra
Korhogo
Bouna
Damongo
Tamale
Bassar
FREETOWN
Lunsar
Kailahun
Beyla
Touba
CÔTE D'IVOIRE
Salaga
Sokodé
Bo
Nzérékoré
Mankono
Bondoukou
GHANA
SIERRA LEONE
Kenema
Zorzor
Séguéla
Bouaké
Wenchi
Kintampo
Zimmi
Man
Lac de Kossou
Sunyani
Techiman
Gbarnga
Danané
(IVORY COAST)
Atakpamé
Robertsport
Tapeta
Daloa
Abengourou
Lake Volta
Abomey
MONROVIA
LIBERIA
YAMOUSSOUKRO
Bongouanou
Kumasi
Koforidua
Buchanan
Gagnoa
Divo
Obuasi
Zwedru
Adzopé
LOMÉ
Abidjan
Winneba
ACCRA
Sassandra
Tarkwa
Greenville
Grand-Lahou
Axim
Cape Coast
Harper
San-Pédro
Sekondi
Cape Palmas
Tabou
Three Points
Cape
Gold Coast
GULF OF GUINEA
Bight of Benin
20°
10°
30°
0°
A
1
2
3
4

Lambert Azimuthal Equal Area Projection

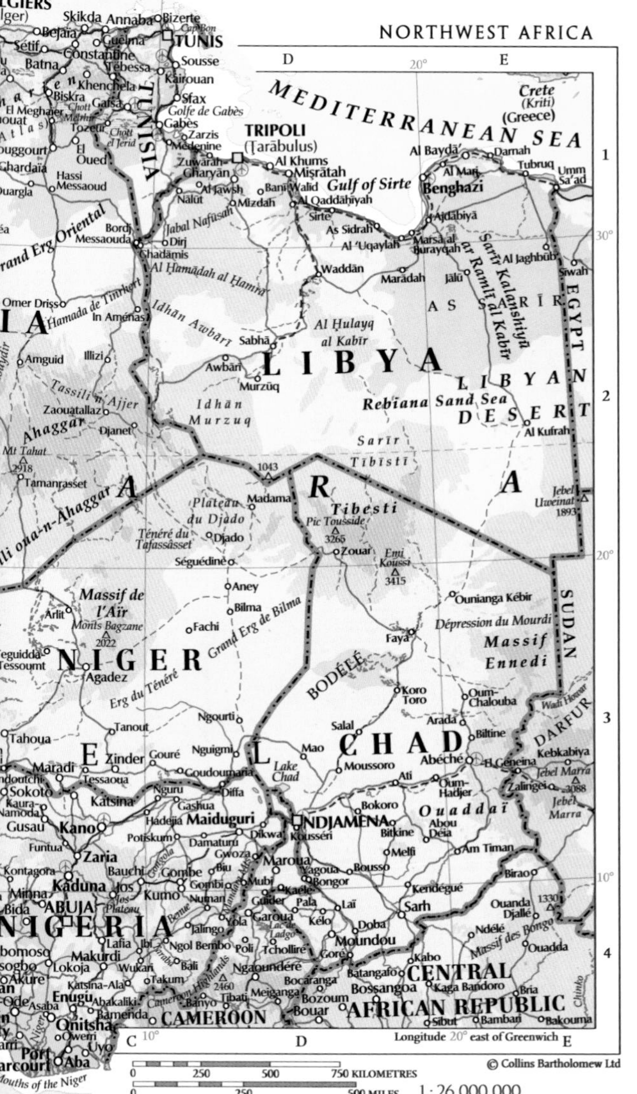

LGIERS
(lger)
Skikda Annaba
Bejaïa Guelma
Sétif Constantine Bizerte
Batna Tébessa TUNIS
Meghteri Khenchela Sousse
Biskra El Oued Kairouan
Touggourt Chott el Jerid Sfax
Ouargla Golfe de Gabès
Grand Erg Oriental Gabès
Hassi Zarzis
Messaoud Medenine

MEDITERRANEAN SEA
Crete
(Kriti)
(Greece)

TRIPOLI
(Ṭarābulus)
Zuwārah Al Khums
Gharyān Miṣrātah
Nālūt Banī Walīd
Jabal Nafūsah Al Qaddāḥiyah
Mizdah As Sidrah
Sirte
Al ʿUqaylah
Waddān Marādah

Omer Driss
Hamada de Tinrhert In Aménas
Illizi
Tassili n'Ajjer
Ahaggar
Mt Tahat
2918
Tamanrasset

LIBYA
Al Bayḍā' Darnah
Al Marj Ţubruq
Benghazi Umm
Ajdābiyā Sa'ad
Marsá al
Burayqah Al Jaghbūb
Jālū Siwah
Sarīr Kalanshiyū
ar Ramlat al Kabīr
EGYPT

Ghadāmis
Dirj
Al Hamādah al Hamrā'
Sabḥā Awbārī
Murzūq
Idhān Murzūq
Idhān Awbārī

Al Ḥulayq
al Kabīr

Rebiana Sand Sea
Al Kufrah

LIBYAN DESERT

Sarīr
Tibistī

Zaouatallaz
Djanet

1043
Madama
Pic Toussidé
3265
Zouar
Emi
Koussi
3415

Tibesti

Jebel
Uwaynāt
1893

SAHARA

ili oua-n-Ahaggar
Plateau
du Djâdo
Ténéré du
Tafassâsset
Djado
Séguédine
Aney

Ouninaga Kébir

Dépression du Mourdi
Massif
Ennedi

SUDAN

Massif de
l'Aïr
Arlit Monts Bagzane
2022
Teguidda-n-
Tessoumt
Agadez
Tahoua

NIGER

Bilma
Grand Erg de Bilma
Fachi

Faya

BODÉLÉ

Koro
Toro
Oum-
Chalouba

Wadi Howar
DARFUR

Zinder Gouré
Goudoumaria
Ngourti
Nguigmi
Mao
Tanout
Erg du Ténéré

Salal

CHAD

Moussoro
Ati
Oum-
Hadjer
Abéché
El Geneina
Kebkabiya
Jebel Marra
3088
Zalingei
Marra

Maradi
Tessaoua
Niguru
Diffa
Lake
Chad
Bokoro

Ouaddaï

Am Timan

Birao
Ouanda
Djallé
1330
Massif des Bongo

Katsina
Kano
Gusau Funtua
Zaria
KADUNA
Minna
Bida
ABUJA

NIGERIA

Sokoto
Ndoutcho
Kaura
Namoda
Hadejia Maiduguri
Potiskum
Damaturu
Dikwa
Kousséri

Bauchi
Gombe
Gombi
Biu
Mubi
Gwoza
Numan
NDJAMENA
Bongor
Bousso
Melfi
Kendégué
Sarh
Ndélé
Kabo
Ouadda
Bria
Bambari

Kontagora
Lafia
Jos
Wukari
Jalingo
Ngol Bembo
Poli
Tcholliré
Garoua
Guider
Pala
Kélo
Laï
Doba
Moundou
Goré
Bocaranga
Bossangoa
Kaga Bandoro
Bakouma

Makurdi
Katsina-Ala
Takum
Bali
2460
Banyo
Tibati
Ngaoundéré
Bozoum
Bouar
Batangafo

Enugu
Onitsha
Owerri
Aba
Port
arcourt
Bamenda
Abakaliki
Mamfe
CAMEROON
Foumban
Bafoussam
Tignère
Menganga
Meiganga

CENTRAL
AFRICAN REPUBLIC

Chinko

Longitude 20° east of Greenwich

0   250   500   750 KILOMETRES
0   250   500 MILES
1 : 26 000 000

© Collins Bartholomew Ltd

115

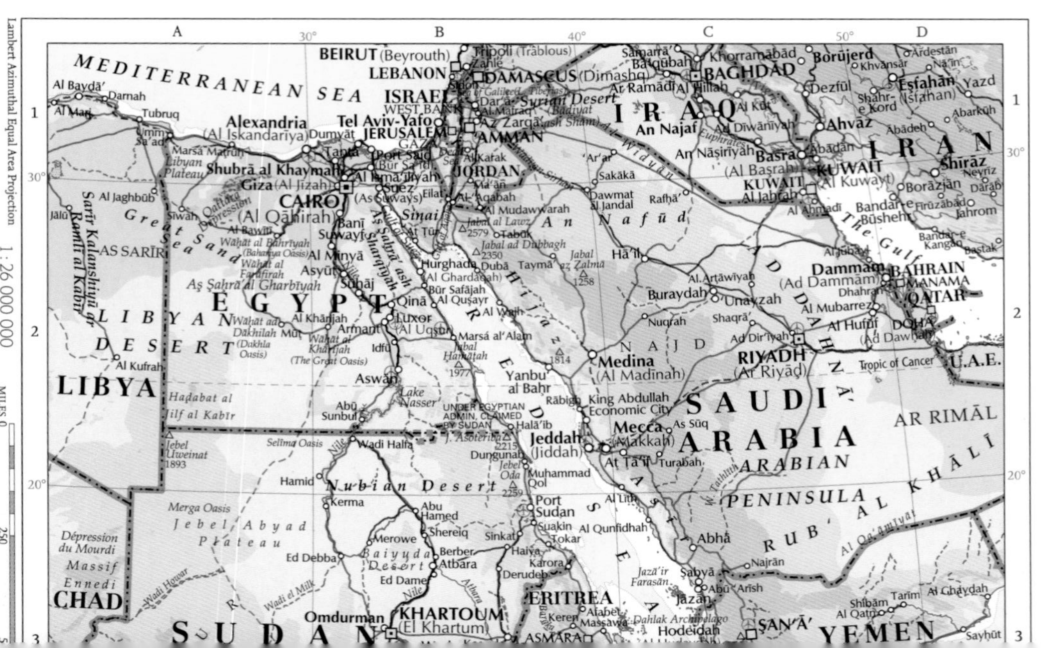

Lambert Azimuthal Equal Area Projection   1 : 26 000 000   MILES 0   250   5

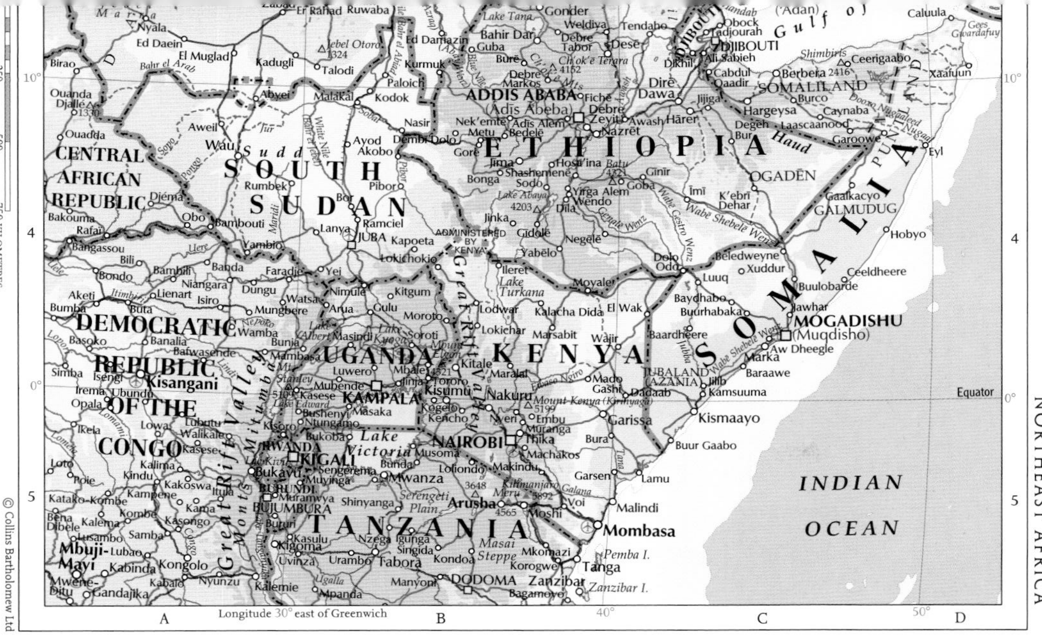

© Collins Bartholomew Ltd

250   500   750 KILOMETRES

INDIAN
OCEAN
SOMALIA
ETHIOPIA
KENYA
TANZANIA
UGANDA
SOUTH SUDAN
CENTRAL AFRICAN REPUBLIC
DEMOCRATIC REPUBLIC OF THE CONGO
RWANDA
BURUNDI
DJIBOUTI
SOMALILAND
PUNTLAND
GALMUDUG
JUBALAND (AZANIA)
OGADĒN
ADDIS ABABA
(Ādīs Ābeba)
MOGADISHU
(Muqdisho)
NAIROBI
KAMPALA
JUBA
KIGALI
BUJUMBURA
DODOMA
Mombasa
Kisangani
Kismaayo
Zanzibar
Tanga
Great Rift Valley
Lake Victoria
Lake Turkana
Lake Tana
Gulf of
Equator
Longitude 30° east of Greenwich

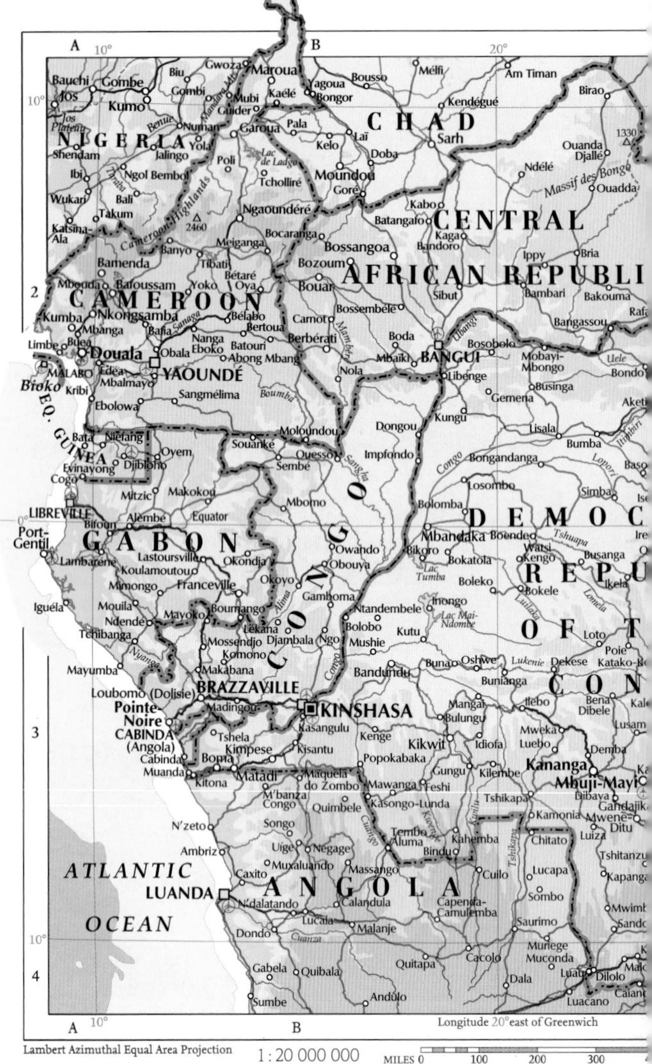

A 10° B 20°

Bauchi JOS Gombe Biu Gwoza Maroua
Kumo Gombi Mubi Kaélé Yagoua Bousso Melfi Am Timan
Los Plateau Guider Bongor Kendégué Birao
NIGERIA Numan Garoua Pala Laï CHAD 1330
Shendam Yola Kelo Doba Sarh Ouanda Djalle
Ibi Ngol Bembol Poli Tcholliré Gore Ndélé Massif des Bongo Ouadda
Wukari Takum Ngaoundéré Kabo Batangafo Kaga Ippy Bria
Katsina-Ala Bali Meiganga Bocaranga Bandoro CENTRAL Bambari Bakouma
Bamenda Tibati Yoko Bozoum Sibut AFRICAN REPUBLI Bangassou Raf
Mbouda Batoussam Banyo Bélabo Bétaré Oya Bouar Bossembélé Boda
Kumba Nkongsamba Bafia Bertoua Carnot Berbérati Bosoboko Mobayi- Bondo
Limbe Buea Obala Eboko Nanga Eboko Abong Mbang Nola Mbaiki BANGUI Mbongo Gemena Businga Aket
MALABO Douala YAOUNDÉ Batouri Libenge Lisala Bumba Simba
Bioko Kribi Sangmelima Moloundou Dongou Kungu Bongandanga
GUINEA Ebolowa Souanké Ouesso Impfondo Losombo Bolomba DEMOC
Bata Djibloho Oyem Sembé Congo Mbandaka Boende Waisi REPU
Evinayong Mitzic Mbomo Bikoro Bokatola Busanga Ikela
LIBREVILLE Bitam Alembé Equator Owando Bokele OF
Port- Makokou Okondja Okoyo Obouya Boleko Loto Dekese Pole
Gentil GABON Lastoursville Oyem Ntandembele Inongo Kutu Mushie Bena Dibele
Lambaréné Koulamoutou Franceville Gamboma Bolobo Bandundu Buniana CON
Iguéla Mouila Mayoko Bourmango Lékana Djambala Ngo Ilebo Mweka Luebo Kananga
Ndendé Mossendjo Komono BRAZZAVILLE KINSHASA Mangaï Bulungu Idiofa Kilembe Mbuji-Mayi
Tchibanga Loubomo (Dolisie) Madingou Kasangulu Kenge Kikwit Gungu Tshikapa Kamonia Mwene- Gandajik
Mayumba Pointe- Tshela Kimpese Kisantu Popokabaka Kasongo-Lunda Luiza Ditu
Noire CABINDA Bopa Matadi Maquela do Zombo Mawanga Feshi Chitato Kapanga
(Angola) Cabinda Kitona M'banza Quimbele Bindu Cuilo Lucapa Sombo
Muanda N'zeto Songo Uíge Negage Massango Capenda- Saurimo Mwim
ATLANTIC Ambriz Caxito Muxaluando Camulemba Muriege Muconda Sando
LUANDA N'dalatando ANGOLA Calandula Cacolo Dilolo Caian
OCEAN Dondo Lucala Malanje Dala Luau Luacano
Gabela Quibala Quitapa Andulo
Sumbe

A 10° B Longitude 20° east of Greenwich

118 Lambert Azimuthal Equal Area Projection 1 : 20 000 000 MILES 0 100 200 300

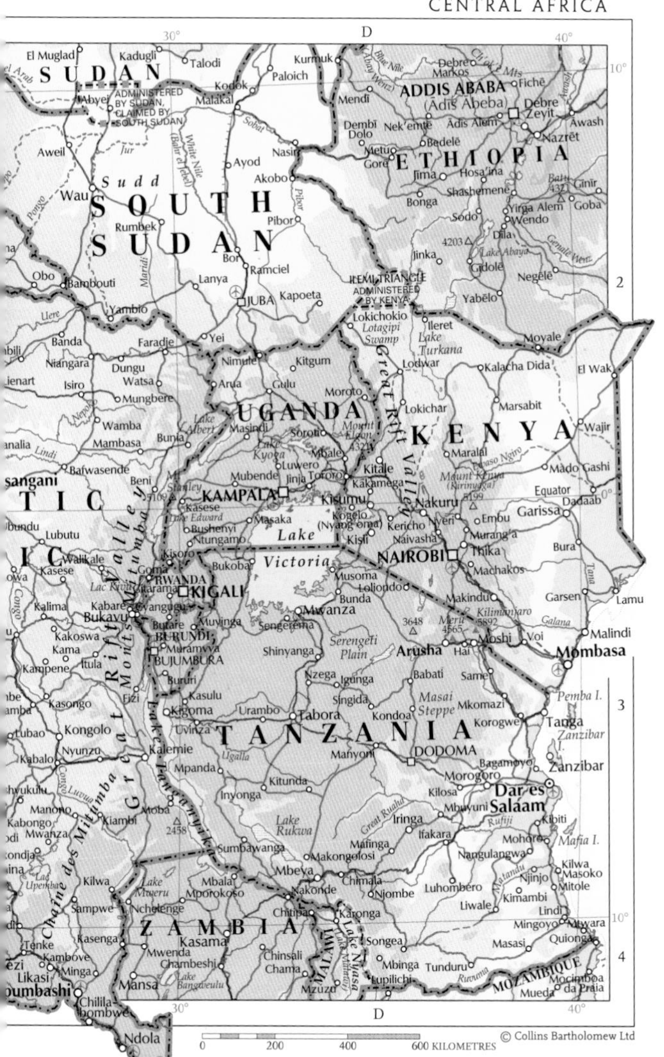

El Muglad · Kadugli · Talodi · Kurmuk · Debre Markos · Fiche · Debre Zeyit · Awash · 10°
SUDAN · ADMINISTERED BY SUDAN, CLAIMED BY SOUTH SUDAN · Abyei · Malakal · Kodok · Paloich · Mendi · ADDIS ABEBA (Adis Abeba) · Nek'emte · Adis Alem · Nazrēt · Awash
Aweil · Wau · White Nile · Ayod · Nasir · Dembi Dolo · Metu · Gore · ETHIOPIA · Hosa'ina · Bati · Ginir · Goba
Sudd · Rumbek · Bor · Pibor · Akobo · Bonga · Jima · Shashemene · Sodo · Yirga Alem · Wendo · Dila
SOUTH SUDAN · Ramciel · Jinka · 4203 · Lake Abaya · Genale Hēnz · 2
Obo · Bambouti · Lanya · JUBA · Kapoeta · REEM TRIANGLE ADMINISTERED BY KENYA · Negele · Yabelo · Moyale · 2
Banda · Faradje · Yei · Nimule · Kitgum · Lokichokio · Lotagipi Swamp · Ileret · Lake Turkana · Kalacha Dida · El Wak
Niangara · Dungu · Watsa · Arua · Gulu · Moroto · Lokichar · Marsabit · Wajir
Isiro · Mungbere · Masindi · UGANDA · Soroti · Mount Elgon 4321 · KENYA · Maralal · Mado Gashi
Wamba · Bunia · Lira · Mbale · Kitale · Mount Kenya (Kirinyaga) 5199 · Equator · Dadaab
Bafwasende · Beni · Lake Edward · KAMPALA · Jinja · Kisumu · Kericho · Nakuru · Embu · Garissa
Lubutu · Kasese · Mubende · Masaka · Kendu · (Nyanza) · Kisii · Naivasha · Murang'a · Thika · Bura
Walikale · Goma · Bukoba · Lake Victoria · Musoma · NAIROBI · Machakos · Garsen · Lamu
Kalima · Kama · RWANDA · KIGALI · Butare · Loliondo · Makindu · Kilimanjaro 5895 · Meru Mount · Mombasa
Kasongo · Bukavu · Cyangugu · Muyinga · Muramvya · Shinyanga · Mwanza · Serengeti Plain · Arusha · Moshi · Voi · Malindi
BURUNDI · BUJUMBURA · Bururi · Nzega · Igunga · Babati · Same · Pemba I. · Zanzibar
Kongolo · Uvira · Kasulu · Urambo · Tabora · Singida · Kondoa · Mkomazi · Korogwe · Tanga · Zanzibar · 3
Kabalo · Kigoma · Nyunzo · Kalemie · Mpanda · Kitunda · Manyoni · TANZANIA · DODOMA · Morogoro · Bagamoyo · Dar es Salaam
Moba · Inyonga · Kilosa · Mbuyuni · Iringa · Mohoro · Mafia I.
Kabongo · Kiambi · Lake Rukwa · Sumbawanga · Mafinga · Ifakara · Nangulangwa · Kilwa Masoko · Mitole
Manono · Kilwa · Lake Mweru · Mbala · Mporokoso · Mbeya · Sakonde · Njombe · Luhombero · Kimambi · Lindi
Upemba · Sampwe · Nchelenge · Chunya · Chimala · Liwale · Mingoyo · Mtwara · 10°
Rasenga · ZAMBIA · Kasama · Mwenda · Chambeshi · Karonga · Songea · Mbinga · Masasi · Quionga
Kambove · Minga · Mansa · Lake Bangweulu · Chinsali · Chama · Tunduru · Ruvuma · MOZAMBIQUE · Mocimboa da Praia
Likasi · Chililabombwe · Mzuzu · Lupilichi · Mued · 4
Lubumbashi · Ndola · 30° · 40° · D

0 · 200 · 400 · 600 KILOMETRES · © Collins Bartholomew Ltd

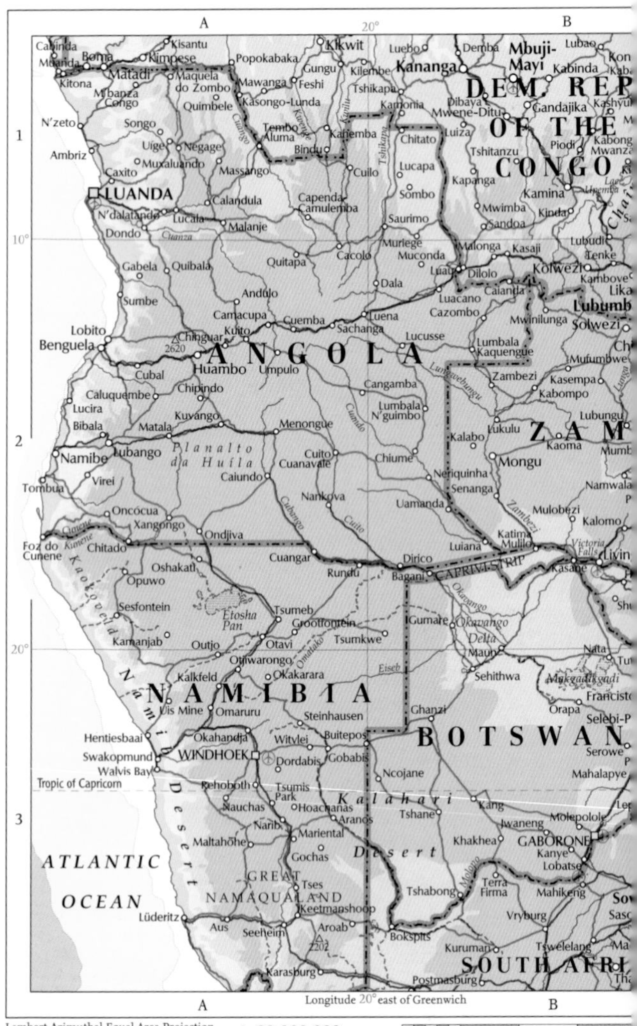

Lambert Azimuthal Equal Area Projection   1 : 20 000 000   MILES 0   100   200   300

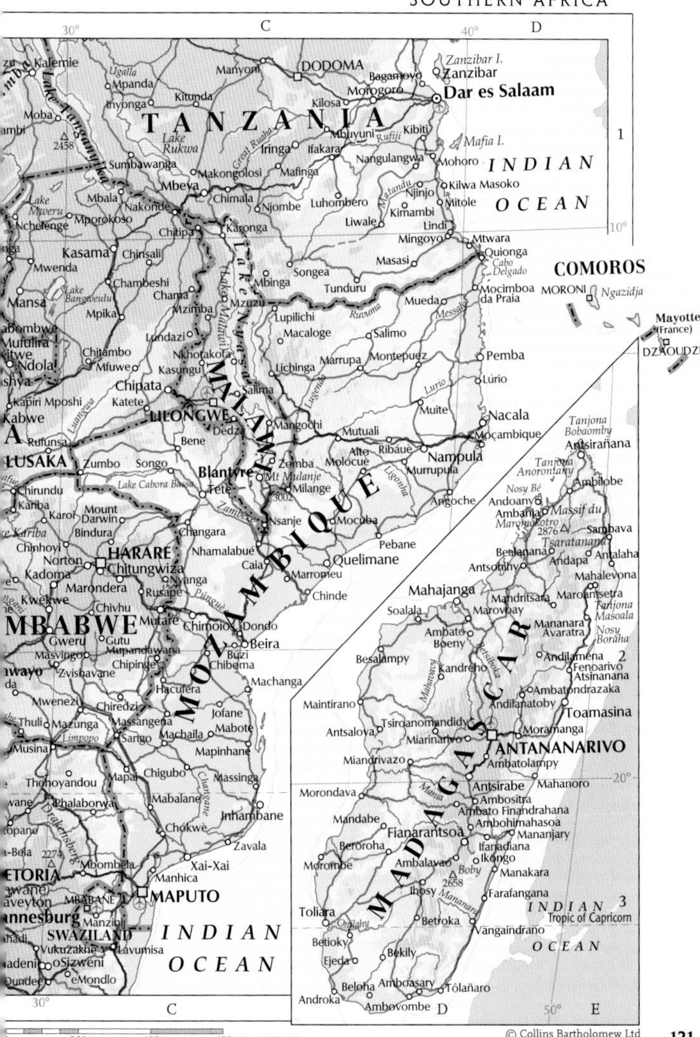

Kalemie
Mpanda
Moba
Ugalla
Manyoni
DODOMA
Bagamoyo
Zanzibar I.
Zanzibar
Dar es Salaam
Inyonga
Kitunda
Kilosa
Morogoro
TANZANIA
2456
Iringa
Ifakara
Muyuni
Rufiji
Kibiti
Mafia I.
INDIAN
Sumbawanga
Makongolosi
Mafinga
Nangulangwa
Mohoro
OCEAN
Mbala
Nakonde
Njombe
Luhombero
Ninjo
Kilwa Masoko
Mporokoso
Chitipa
Karonga
Kimambi
Mitole
Lindi
Nchelenge
Kasama
Chinsali
Mbinga
Songea
Tunduru
Liwale
Mingoyo
Mtwara
Mwenda
Chambeshi
Masasi
Quionga
Cabo
Delgado
Mansa
Chama
Mzimba
Mzuzu
Lupilichi
Mueda
Mocímboa
da Praia
COMOROS
Mpika
Lundazi
Macaloge
Salimo
Montepuez
MORONI
Ngazidja
Chitambo
Nkhotakota
Lichinga
Marrupa
Pemba
Mayotte
(France)
Chipata
Kasungu
Saluma
Lúrio
Muite
Nacala
DZAOUDZI
Kabwe
Katete
LILONGWE
Dedza
Mangochi
Mutuali
Moçambique
Tanjona
Bobaomby
LUSAKA
Zumbo
Songo
Zomba
Alto
Molócuè
Ribáuè
Nampula
Antsirañana
Blantyre
Mt Mulanje
Milange
Murrupula
Ambilobe
Karoi
Mount
Darwin
Tete
Changara
Nsanje
Mocuba
Angoche
Nosy Bé
Andoany
Massif du
Marojejy
Chinhoyi
Bindura
Namabue
Quelimane
Pebane
Benjamona
Antsohihy
Sambava
HARARE
Chitungwiza
Marromeu
Chinde
Mahajanga
Andapa
Antalaha
Kadoma
Marondera
Nyanga
Rusape
Soalala
Marovoay
Mandritsara
Maromandia
Kwekwe
Chivhu
Mutare
Chimoio
Dondo
Beira
Ambato
Boeny
Andilamena
Gweru
Gutu
Buzi
Besalampy
Kandreho
Fenoarivo
Atsinanana
Zvishavane
Chibaba
Maintirano
Sirdanomandidy
ANTANANARIVO
Toamasina
Chivi
Chiredzi
Machanga
Miarinarivo
Moramanga
Mwenezi
Jofane
Mabote
Miandrivazo
Antsirabe
Mahanoro
Thohoyandou
Mapai
Chigubo
Massinga
Morondava
Ambositra
Phalaborwa
Mabalane
Fianarantsoa
Mananjary
Musina
Limpopo
Sango
Machaila
Mapinhane
Mandabe
Beroroha
Ifanadiana
Manakara
Thohoyandou
Chókwè
Inhambane
Ihosy
Farafangana
PRETORIA
Mbombela
Manhiça
Xai-Xai
Zavala
Toliara
Betroka
Vangaindrano
Johannesburg
MAPUTO
MBABANE
SWAZILAND
INDIAN
Bekily
Ejeda
Betioky
Ambovombe
OCEAN
Androka
Beloha
Ambosary
Tôlanaro

MOZAMBIQUE
MALAWI
ZIMBABWE
MADAGASCAR

© Collins Bartholomew Ltd   **121**

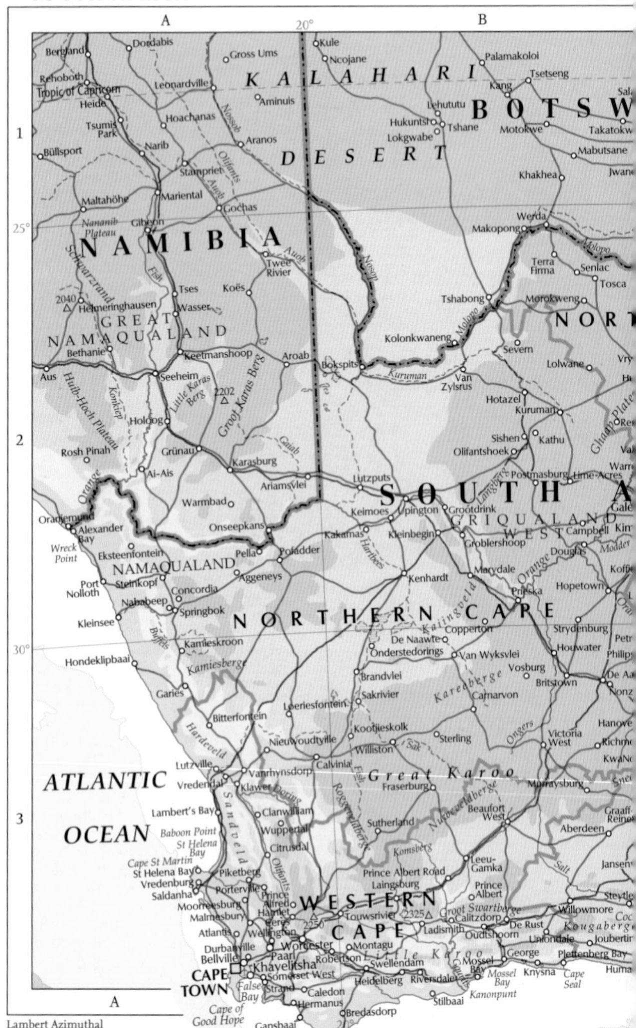

A 20° B

Bergland Dordabis Gross Ums Kule Ncojane Palamakoloi Tsetseng Sal
Rehoboth Leonardville KALAHARI Kang BOTSW
Tropic of Capricorn Aminuis Lehututu
Heide Hoachanas Hukuntsi Tshane Motokwe Takatokwane Mabutsane
Tsumis Narib Aranos DESERT Lokgwabe Jwane
Park Stampriet Khakhea
Büllsport 1 Werda
Gochas Makapong Terra
Mariental Firma
25° Nananib Aub Auob Nossob Senlac Tosca
Plateau Gibeon Tses Twee Tshabong Morokweng NOR
2040 Heinrichshausen Koës Rivier
NAMIBIA Wasser Kolonkwaneng Severn Lowane Vry
GREAT Kuruman
Bethanie NAMAQUALAND Keetmanshoop Aroab Bokspits Van Hotazel Kuruman
Aus Seeheim 2202 Zylsrus Sishen Kathu Val
Holoog Little Karas Berg Groot Karas Berg Olifantshoek Postmasburg Lime-Acres Warr
Rosh Pinah Grünau Karasburg Kakamas Upington Groblershoop SOUTH A Acres Kim
Ai-Ais Ariamsvlei GRIQUALAND Campbell
Warmbad Keimoes WEST Douglas
Orangemund Onseepkans Kleinbegin Hopetown
Alexander Pella Kenhardt Marydale Strydenburg Petr
Bay Steinkopf Aggeneys Copperton Houwater Phillip
Wreck Eksteenfontein Concordia Van Wyksvlei Vosburg Britstown De Nonz
Point Springbok De Naawte Brandvlei Carnarvon Victoria Hanover
Port Nahoep NORTHERN CAPE Onderstedorings West Richm
Nolloth Kamieskroon Sakrivier KWAN
Kleinsee Kamiesberg Sterling Oggers Beaufort Murraysburg
Hondeklipbaai Garies Loeriesfontein Kootjieskolk Karreberge West Aberdeen Jansen
Bitterfontein Nieuwoudtville Williston Great Karoo
ATLANTIC Lutzville Vredendal Calvinia Fraserburg Leeu- steyt
OCEAN Baboon Point Vanrhynsdorp Sutherland Beaufort Gamka Willowmore Coc
St Helena Klawer Prince Albert Road West Prince Kougaberge Joubert
Bay Lambert's Bay Clanwilliam Laingsburg Albert De Rust Plettenberg Bay Hb
Cape St Martin Citrusdal Touwsrivier 2325 Great Swartberg Oudtshoorn Knysna Cape
St Helena Bay Piketberg Prince Little Karoo Calitzdorp Langfontein Seal
Saldanha Porterville Alfred Ladismith Mossel
Vredenburg Moorreesburg Hamlet WESTERN Montagu Riversdale Bay
Malmesbury Wellington CAPE Swellendam Mossel
Atlantis Durbanville Paarl Worcester Robertson Heidelberg Riversdale Kanonpunt Bay
CAPE Bellville Khayelitsha Stellenbosch Caledon Bredasdorp Stilbaai
TOWN False Bay Strand Hermanus
Cape of Gansbaai Struis Bay Cape Agulhas
Good Hope

A

Lambert Azimuthal
Equal Area Projection

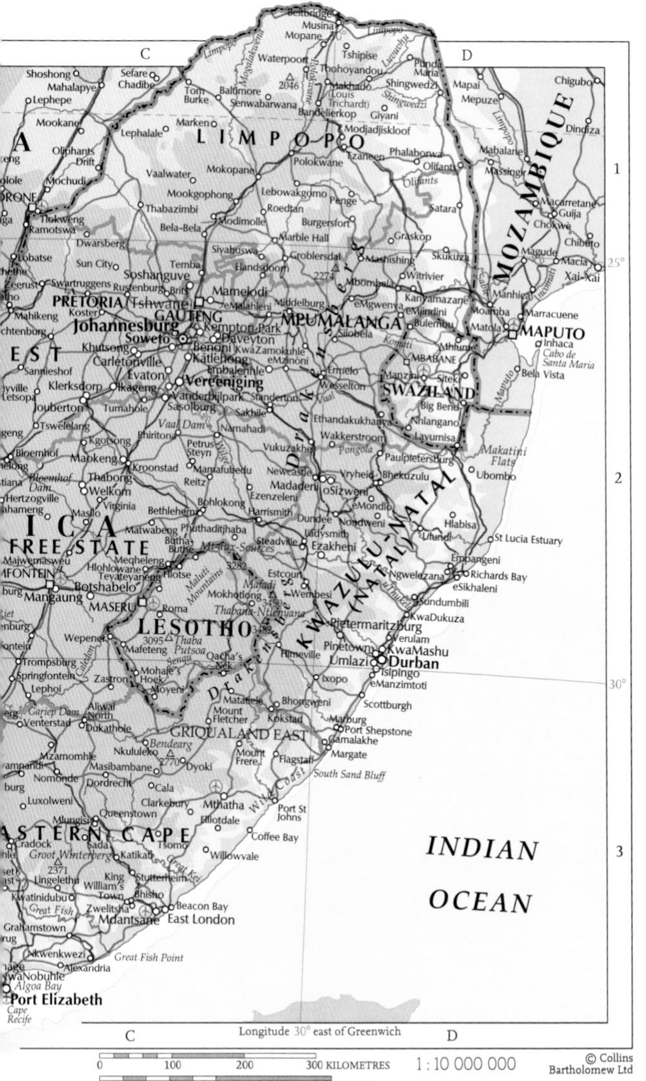

INDIAN OCEAN

Longitude 30° east of Greenwich

| 0 | 100 | 200 | 300 KILOMETRES |

1 : 10 000 000

| 0 | 100 | 200 MILES |

© Collins
Bartholomew Ltd

123

Selected place names and features visible on the map:

Shoshong, Mahalapye, Lephepe, Mookane, Sefare, Chadibwa, Tom Burke, Baltimore, senwabarwana, Bandelierkop, Waterpoort, Thohoyandou, Musina, Mopane, Tshipise, Pondo Maria, Shingwedzi, Mapai, Mepuzze, Chigubo, Dindiza

LIMPOPO, MOZAMBIQUE, Makhado (Louis Trichardt), Giyani, Olifants, Phalaborwa, Mabalane, Massingir, Macarretane, Guija, Chibuto, Chokwe

Olifants Drift, Mochudi, Lephalale, Marken, Vaalwater, Mokopane, Polokwane, Tzaneen, Olifants, Satara, Magude, Xai-Xai, Macia

GABORONE, Thokweng, Ramotswa, Dwarsberg, Thabazimbi, Bela-Bela, Modimolle, Roedtan, Penge, Graskop, Skukuza, Witrivier, Manhiça, Marracuene

Globatse, Swartruggens, Rustenburg, Brits, Soshanguve, Siyabuswa, Elandsdoorn, Groblersdal, Mashishing, Kanyamazane, Mbombela, Matola, MAPUTO, Cabo de Santa Maria, Bela Vista

PRETORIA, Tshwane, Mamelodi, GAUTENG, MPUMALANGA, Middelburg, Witbank, eMgwenya, Mbuzini, Mhinhuti, Moamba

Johannesburg, Soweto, Kempton Park, Katlehong, eMalahleni, Siloela, Ermelo, MBABANE, SWAZILAND, Big Bend

Carletonville, Khutsong, Evaton, Benoni, KwaZamokuhle, eMzinoni, Wesselton, Shlangano, SWAZILAND

Klerksdorp, Okageng, Vereeniging, Vanderbijlpark, Sasolburg, Standerton, Sakhile, Ithandakukhanya, Piet Retief, Pongola, Paulpietersburg, Makatini Flats, Ubombo

EAST, Orkney, Bloemhof, Tumahole, Namahadi, Vukuzakhe, Wakkerstroom, Bhekuzulu, Vryheid, Mondlo, St Lucia Estuary

FREE STATE, Kroonstad, Manafuletsu, Reitz, Madadeni, Newcastle, oSizweni, Nqutu, Ulundi, Hlabisa, Embangeni, Richards Bay, eSikhaleni

Bloemhof, Thabong, Welkom, Virginia, Bethlehem, Bohlokong, Harrismith, Durnacol, Ladysmith, Dundee, Nqwelezana, Ngwelezana, KWAZULU-NATAL

Bultfontein, Matwabeng, Phuthaditjhaba, Ezenzeleni, Steadville, Ezakheni, Estcourt, Wembesi, KWAZULU-NATAL, kwaDukuza, kwaMashu

Hertzogville, Hoopstad, Bethulie, Meqheleng, Kestell, Clarens, Bergville, Weenen, Mooi River, eMondlo, Stanger, Verulam

MANGAUNG, Botshabelo, Thaba Nchu, MASERU, Roma, Thabang, Mokhotlong, Matatiele, Pietermaritzburg, Pinetown, Westville, Durban

Wepener, LESOTHO, Thaba Putsoa, Mohale's Hoek, Matatiele, Mount Fletcher, Kokstad, Umlazi, Isipingo, Amanzimtoti

Zastron, Mafeteng, Moyeni, Mount Frere, Matatiele, Bizana, Harding, Margate, South Sand Bluff

Aliwal North, GRIQUALAND EAST, Nkululeko, Masibambane, Dordrecht, Cala, Flagstaff, Port St Johns

Tarkastad, Mzamomhle, Nomonde, Luxolweni, Queenstown, Clarkebury, Mthatha, Elliotdale, Coffee Bay

EASTERN CAPE, Cradock, Lingelethu, King William's Town, Bhisho, Stutterheim, Willowvale, Beacon Bay

Graaff-Reinet, Zwelitsha, Mdantsane, East London

Port Elizabeth, Algoa Bay, Cape Recife, Alexandra, Great Fish Point

Drakensberg, Thabana Ntlenyana 3482, Thaba Putsoa 3096

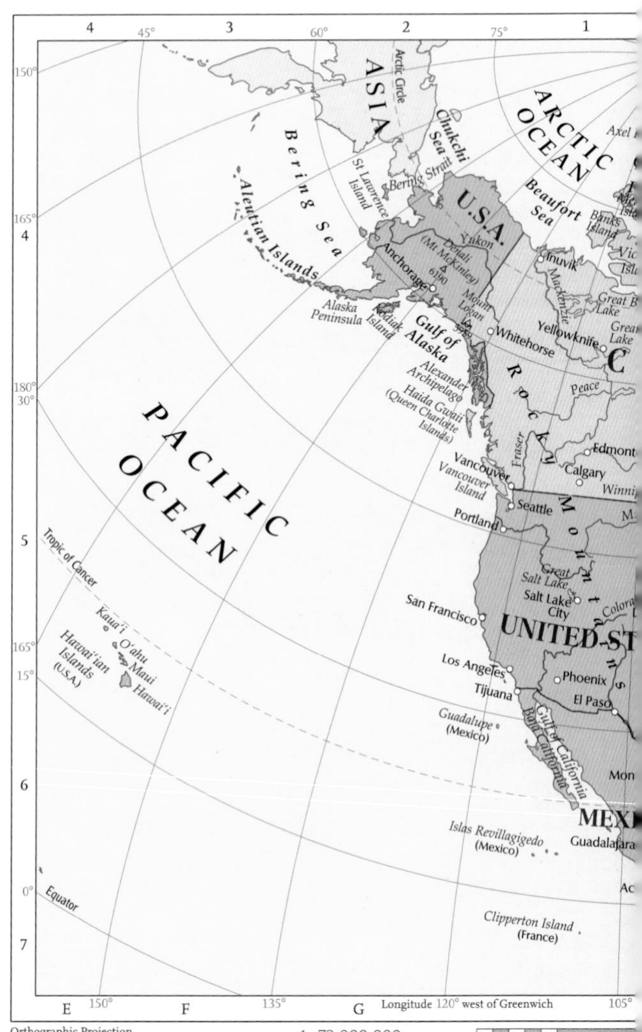

150°

Arctic Circle

ASIA

ARCTIC OCEAN

Axel

Chukchi Sea

St Lawrence Island

Bering Strait

Beaufort Sea

Banks Island

Vic Isl

B e r i n g   S e a

U.S.A.

Yukon

Inuvik

Mackenzie

Great B Lake

Grea Lake

165°

4

Aleutian Islands

Anchorage

Denali (Mt. McKinley) 6190

Mount Logan

Whitehorse

Yellowknife

C

Alaska Peninsula

Kodiak Island

Gulf of Alaska

R

Peace

Alexander Archipelago

180°

30°

Haida Gwaii (Queen Charlotte Islands)

Edmont

P A C I F I C

Fraser

Calgary

Winni

M

Vancouver

Vancouver Island

O C E A N

Seattle

5

Portland

Tropic of Cancer

Great Salt Lake

Salt Lake City

Colora

San Francisco

UNITED-ST

Kaua'i

O'ahu

165°

15°

Hawai'ian Islands (U.S.A.)

Maui

Hawai'i

Los Angeles

Tijuana

Phoenix

El Paso

Guadalupe (Mexico)

Mon

6

Islas Revillagigedo (Mexico)

MEX

Guadalajara

0°

Equator

Ac

Clipperton Island (France)

7

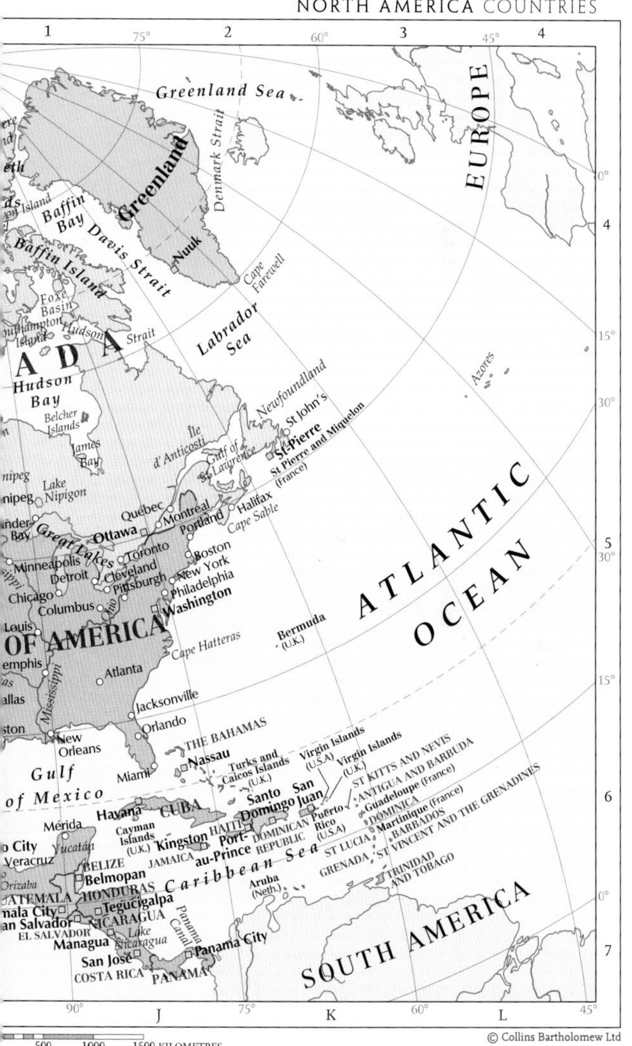

Greenland Sea

Greenland

Denmark Strait

EUROPE

Baffin
Bay

Davis Strait

Baffin Island

Nuuk

Cape
Farewell

Foxe
Basin

Hudson
Strait

Labrador
Sea

Azores

ADA

Hudson
Bay

Belcher
Islands

James
Bay

Île
d'Anticosti

Newfoundland

Gulf of
St Lawrence

St John's

St-Pierre

St Pierre and Miquelon
(France)

nipeg

Lake
Nipigon

Quebec

Montreal

Halifax

ATLANTIC

ander
Bay

Great Lakes

Ottawa

Toronto

Portland

Cape Sable

Minneapolis

Detroit
Cleveland

Boston

New York

OCEAN

Chicago

Pittsburgh

Columbus

Philadelphia

Washington

Louis

OF AMERICA

Cape Hatteras

Bermuda
(U.K.)

emphis

Atlanta

as

Mississippi

allas

Jacksonville

ston

Orlando

THE BAHAMAS

Gulf

New
Orleans

Miami

Nassau

Turks and
Caicos Islands
(U.K.)

Virgin Islands
(U.S.A.)

Virgin Islands
(U.K.)

ST KITTS AND NEVIS

ANTIGUA AND BARBUDA

of Mexico

Mérida

Havana

CUBA

Cayman
Islands
(U.K.)

JAMAICA

Kingston

Santo
Domingo

San
Juan

Puerto
Rico
(U.S.A.)

Guadeloupe (France)

DOMINICA

o City

Yucatán

HAITI

DOMINICAN
REPUBLIC

Port-
au-Prince

Martinique (France)

Veracruz

BELIZE

Belmopan

Caribbean Sea

ST LUCIA

BARBADOS

rizaba

ATEMALA

HONDURAS

Tegucigalpa

Aruba
(Neth.)

GRENADA

ST VINCENT AND THE GRENADINES

mala City

an Salvador

NICARAGUA

Lake
Nicaragua

TRINIDAD
AND TOBAGO

EL SALVADOR

Managua

Panama
Canal

Panama City

SOUTH AMERICA

San José

COSTA RICA

PANAMA

90°

75°

60°

45°

J

K

L

500   1000   1500 KILOMETRES

© Collins Bartholomew Ltd

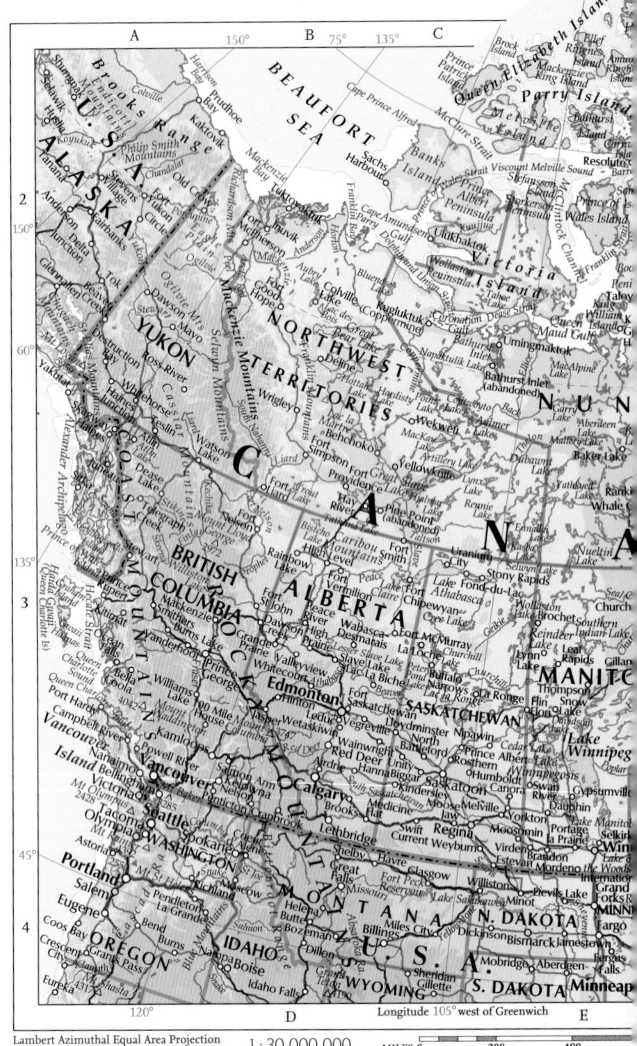

Lambert Azimuthal Equal Area Projection

1 : 30 000 000

MILES 0   200   400

Longitude 105° west of Greenwich

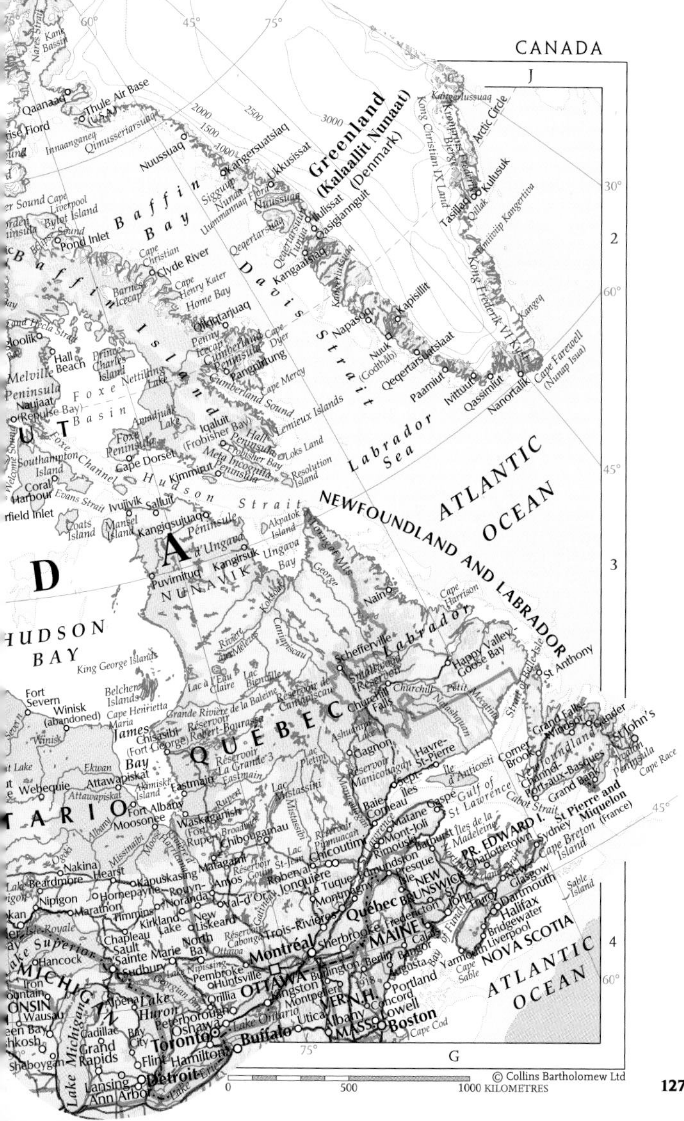

Narès Strait

Qaanaaq
Thule Air Base
(U.S.A.)
Qimusseriarsuaq

Kong Christian IX Land
Kangerlussuaq
Arctic Circle

Greenland
(Kalaallit Nunaat)
Denmark

Nuussuaq

Sisimiut
Ilulissat (Denmark)
Qasigiannguit

Baffin
Bay

Pond Inlet
Clyde River

Cape Christian
Cape Henry Kater
Home Bay

Qeqertarsuaq
Kangaatsiaq
Kangeq

Kong Frederik VI Kyst

Napasoq
Kapisillit

Davis
Strait

Nuuk
(Godthåb)
Qeqertarsuatsiaat

Baffin
Island

Okitaarjuaq

Paamiut

Cape Farewell
(Nunap Isua)

Nanortalik

Ivittuut

Qassimiut

Pangnirtung

Cumberland Sound

Cape Mercy

Labrador
Sea

ATLANTIC

OCEAN

Iqaluit

Lemieux Islands
Oks Land

Cape Dorset
Kimmirut
Resolution
Island

NEWFOUNDLAND AND LABRADOR

Akpatok
Island

Ungava
Bay

C A N A D A

N U N A V I K

Puvirnituq
Kangirsuk

Nain

Cape
Harrison

HUDSON
BAY

King George Islands

Belcher
Islands

Schefferville
Happy Valley-
Goose Bay

St Anthony

Labrador

Churchill
Falls

Gander
Grand Falls-
Windsor

St John's

Grande Rivière de la Baleine

QUEBEC

Gagnon

Havre-
St-Pierre

Anticosti
Island

Corner
Brook

Cape Race

ONTARIO

Moosonee

Baie-
Comeau

Gulf of
St Lawrence

St Pierre and
Miquelon (France)

Cabot
Strait

Sydney

Cape Breton
Island

Chibougamau

Saguenay

Mont-Joli

Îles de la
Madeleine

Charlottetown

P.E. EDWARD I.

Amos

Val-d'Or

La Tuque

NEW BRUNSWICK

Moncton

Halifax

Rouyn

Trois-Rivières

Sherbrooke

MAINE

Fredericton

Yarmouth

NOVA SCOTIA

ATLANTIC
OCEAN

Montréal

Québec

N.H.

Portland

VT.

MASS.

Boston

Cape Cod

OTTAWA

Toronto

Hamilton

Buffalo

Lake
Ontario

Utica

Albany

Detroit

Lake
Erie

Collins Bartholomew Ltd

127

0   500   1000 KILOMETRES

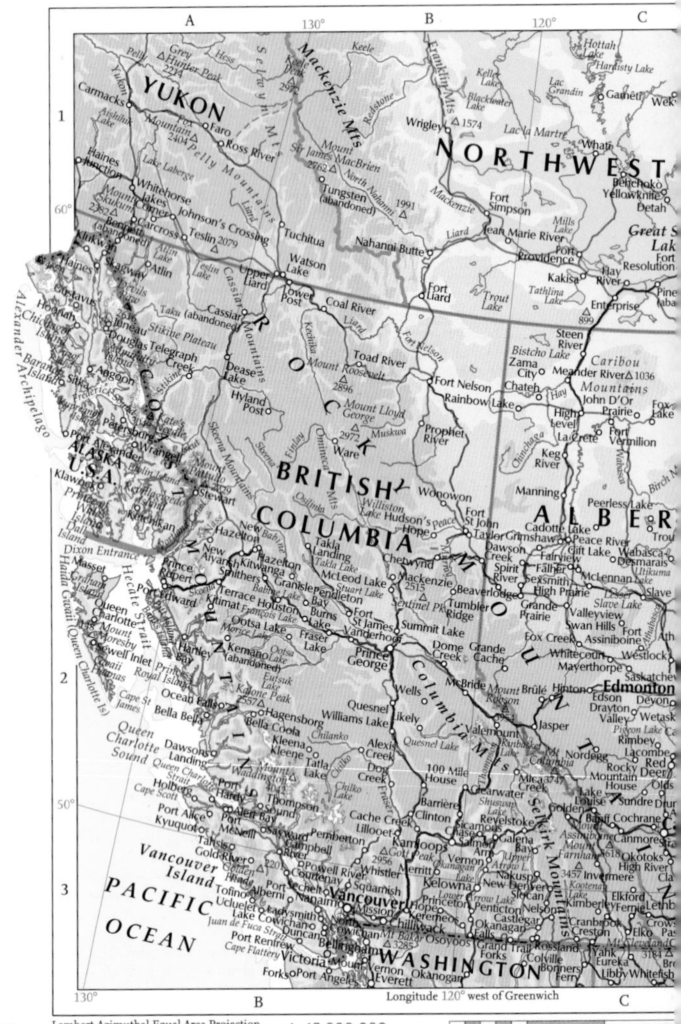

Lambert Azimuthal Equal Area Projection   1 : 15 000 000   MILES 0   100   200

Longitude 120° west of Greenwich

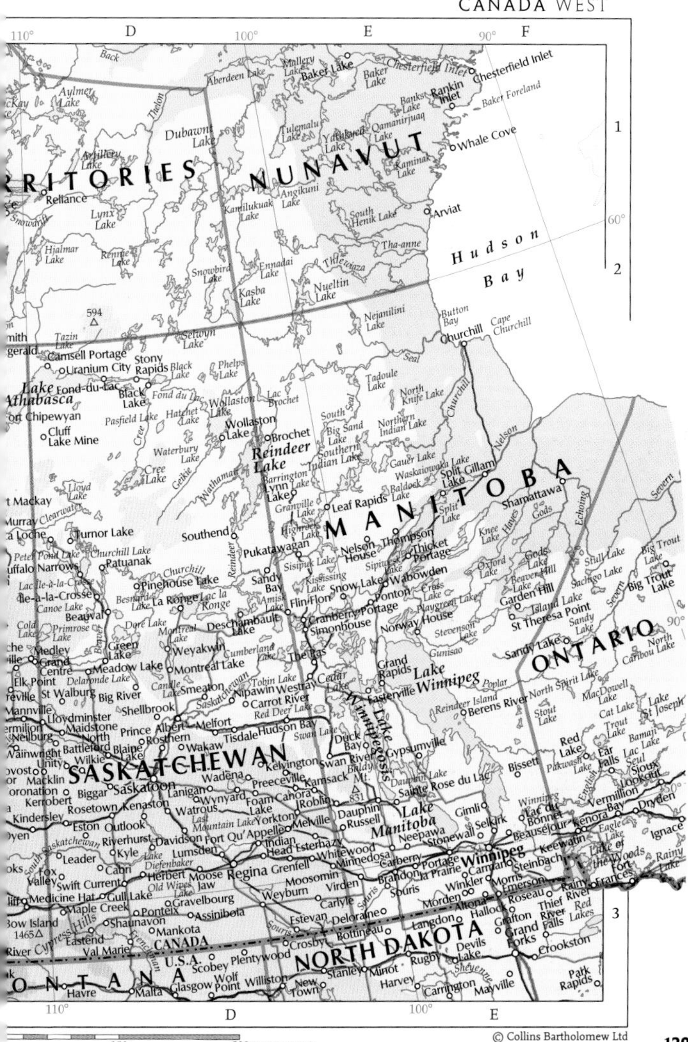

D
E
F
110°
100°
90°
1
2
3
60°
50°
NUNAVUT
MANITOBA
SASKATCHEWAN
ONTARIO
NORTH DAKOTA
CANADA
U.S.A.
Hudson Bay
Chesterfield Inlet
Baker Lake
Baker Foreland
Rankin Inlet
Whale Cove
Arviat
Dubawnt Lake
Reliance
Lynx Lake
Hjalmar Lake
Kasba Lake
Nueltin Lake
Ennadai Lake
Snowbird Lake
Nejanilini Lake
Selwyn Lake
Button Bay
Churchill
Cape Churchill
Tazin Lake
Camsell Portage
Uranium City
Stony Rapids
Black Lake
Fond-du-Lac
Lake Athabasca
Fort Chipewyan
Cluff Lake Mine
Wollaston Lake
Brochet
Lac Brochet
Reindeer Lake
Southern Indian Lake
Tadoule Lake
North Knife Lake
Northern Indian Lake
Gauer Lake
Split Lake
Gillam
Lynn Lake
Leaf Rapids
Shamattawa
Southend
Pukatawagan
Thompson
Nelson House
Thicket Portage
Wabowden
Snow Lake
Flin Flon
Cranberry Portage
Simonhouse
Norway House
Turnor Lake
Patuanak
Pinehouse Lake
La Ronge
Lac la Ronge
Deschambault Lake
The Pas
Beauval
Ile-à-la-Crosse
Green Lake
Meadow Lake
Weyakwin
Montreal Lake
Smeaton
Nipawin
Carrot River
Westray
Easterville
Grand Rapids
Lake Winnipeg
Berens River
North Spirit Lake
Big River
Shellbrook
Prince Albert
Melfort
Tisdale
Hudson Bay
Lloydminster
Maidstone
North Battleford
Wakaw
Rosthern
Swan River
Gypsumville
Kelvington
Wadena
Kamsack
Preeceville
Saskatoon
Lanigan
Wynyard
Watrous
Foam Lake
Canora
Roblin
Dauphin
Lake Winnipegosis
Lake Manitoba
Sainte Rose du Lac
Gimli
Selkirk
Beausejour
Kenora
Dryden
Ignace
Vermillion Bay
Sioux Lookout
Red Lake
Ear Falls
Bissett
Yorkton
Melville
Russell
Neepawa
Stonewall
Winnipeg
Portage la Prairie
Steinbach
Carman
Brandon
Minnedosa
Carberry
Rosetown
Kindersley
Kerrobert
Biggar
Outlook
Kenaston
Davidson
Fort Qu'Appelle
Indian Head
Esterhazy
Whitewood
Regina
Moose Jaw
Grenfell
Moosomin
Virden
Souris
Lumsden
Swift Current
Medicine Hat
Maple Creek
Gull Lake
Gravelbourg
Assiniboia
Weyburn
Carlyle
Estevan
Deloraine
Boissevain
Morden
Winkler
Morris
Emerson
Altona
Shaunavon
Ponteix
Mankota
Eastend
Val Marie
Bow Island
Cypress Hills
1465
831
594
Crosby
Plentywood
Scobey
Wolf Point
Glasgow
Malta
Havre
Williston
New Town
Stanley
Minot
Rugby
Devils Lake
Harvey
Carrington
Mayville
Grand Forks
Crookston
Thief River Falls
Grafton
Langdon
Hallock
Roseau
Bottineau
Park Rapids
Rainy River
Fort Frances
Lake of the Woods
Big Trout Lake
Sandy Lake
Garden Hill
Island Lake
St Theresa Point
Oxford Lake
Gods Lake
Knee Lake

250
500 KILOMETRES

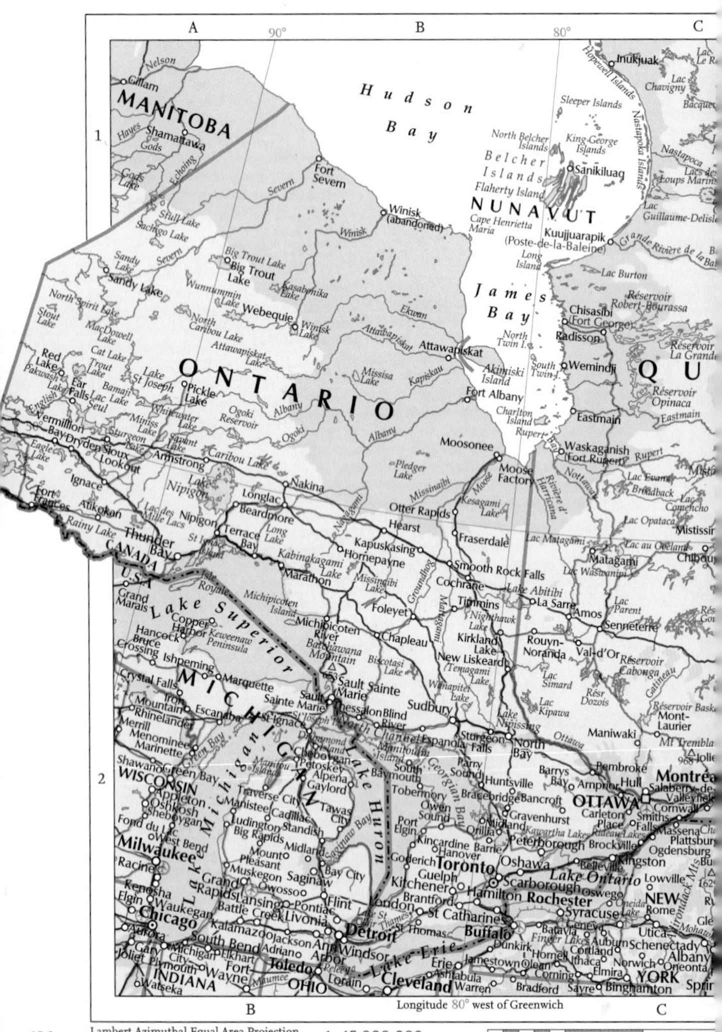

Hudson Bay

MANITOBA

NUNAVUT

Belcher Islands

James Bay

ONTARIO

QU

Lake Superior

MICHIGAN

Lake Huron

WISCONSIN

Lake Ontario

Lake Erie

Chicago

Detroit

Toronto

OTTAWA

Montréal

Cleveland

OHIO

INDIANA

Buffalo

Longitude 80° west of Greenwich

130   Lambert Azimuthal Equal Area Projection   1:15 000 000   MILES 0   100   200

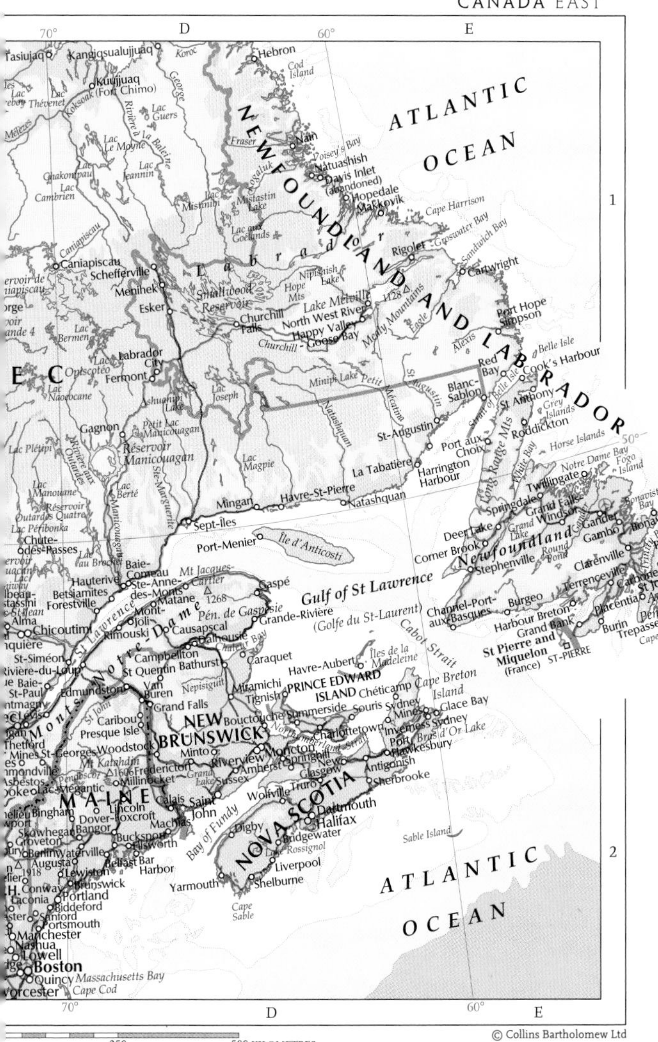

70°

D   60°   E

Tasiujaq Kangiqsualujjuaq Korok Hebron

Kuujjuaq (Fort Chimo) Cod Island

ATLANTIC

OCEAN

Gnaonontsat Lac Nain

Cambrien Natuashish

Davis Inlet (abandoned)

Hopedale

Makkovik

Cape Harrison

1

Caniapiscau Labrador

Schefferville Rigolet Goosewater Bay

Menihek Nipishish Cartwright

Esker Lake Lake Melville Sandwich Bay

Churchill North West River 1128 Port Hope Simpson

Falls Happy Valley- Mealy Mountains

Goose Bay

Churchill Churchill River

Labrador Alexis

Fermont City Red Belle Isle

Bay Cook's Harbour

Joseph Blanc- St Anthony

Ashuanipi Sablon Quirpon Island

Gagnon Petit Lac Port au Roddickton

Manicouagan Choix Horse Islands

Réservoir Lac La Tabatière St-Augustin Notre Dame Bay

Manicouagan Magpie Harrington Twillingate Fogo Island

Harbour Springdale Grand Falls- Gander

QUEBEC Mingan Havre-St-Pierre Natashquan Windsor Bonavista Bay

Sept-Îles Île d'Anticosti Deer Lake Round Bonavista

Corner Brook Pond Couch

Baie- Gulf of St Lawrence Newfoundland Clarenville Cove

Port-Menier Stephenville Gander

Comeau (Golfe du Saint-Laurent) Channel-Port- St John's

Ste-Anne- Mt Jacques- aux-Basques Placentia

des-Monts Cartier Burgeo Grand Bank Bay Avalon

Forestville Gaspé Cabot Strait Harbour Breton Terrenceville Peninsula

Matane Pén. de Gaspésie St Pierre and Burin Trepassey

Mont- Grande-Rivière Miquelon Cape Race

Rimouski Causapscal (France) ST-PIERRE

Campbellton Bathurst Havre-Aubert

St Quentin Caraquet Îles de la

Rivière-du-Loup Van Madeleine

Edmundston Buren Miramichi PRINCE EDWARD

Grand Falls Tignish ISLAND Chéticamp Cape Breton

Caribou Summerside Souris Island

Presque Isle Minto Bouctouche Charlottetown Inverness Sydney

Woodstock Riverview Moncton Glace Bay

MAINE Fredericton NEW Amherst Bras d'Or Lake

Millinocket BRUNSWICK Sussex Wolfville Antigonish

Kahtahdin Saint Truro Shelburne

MT Katahdin John NOVA SCOTIA

Bangor Bay of Fundy Dartmouth

Bucksport Digby Bridgewater Halifax

Belfast Bar Rossignol Sable Island

Augusta Harbor Liverpool

Brunswick Yarmouth Shelburne

Biddeford Cape ATLANTIC

Portland Sable

Portsmouth OCEAN

Manchester

Nashua Massachusetts Bay

Lowell

Quincy Cape Cod

Boston

Worcester

2

70°

D   60°   E

250   500 KILOMETRES   © Collins Bartholomew Ltd   **131**

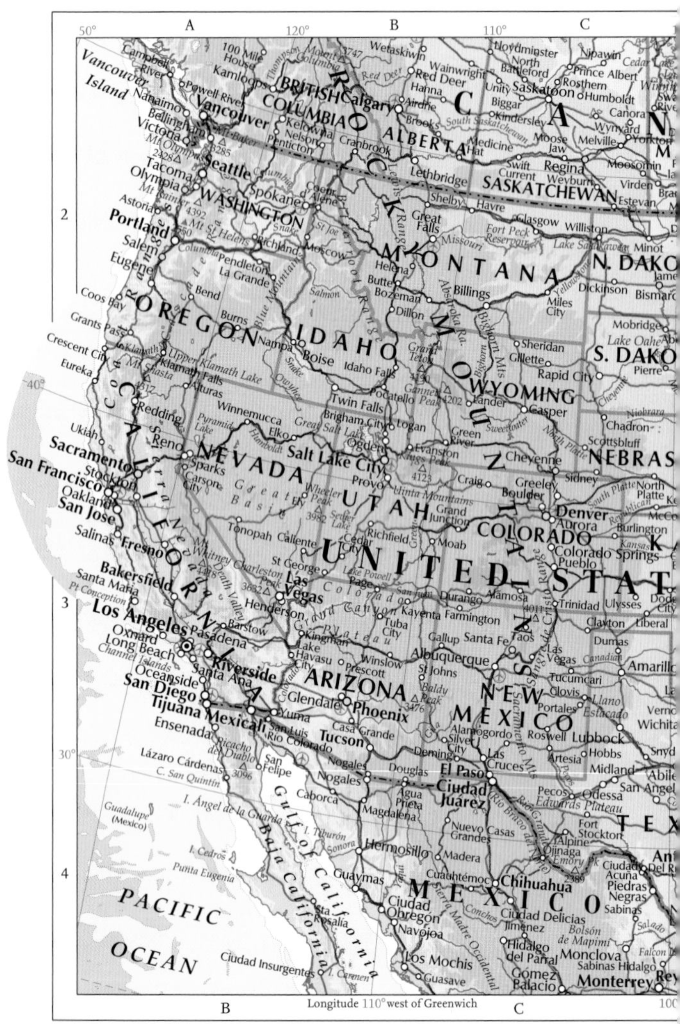

Lambert Azimuthal Equal Area Projection   1 : 25 000 000   MILES 0   250

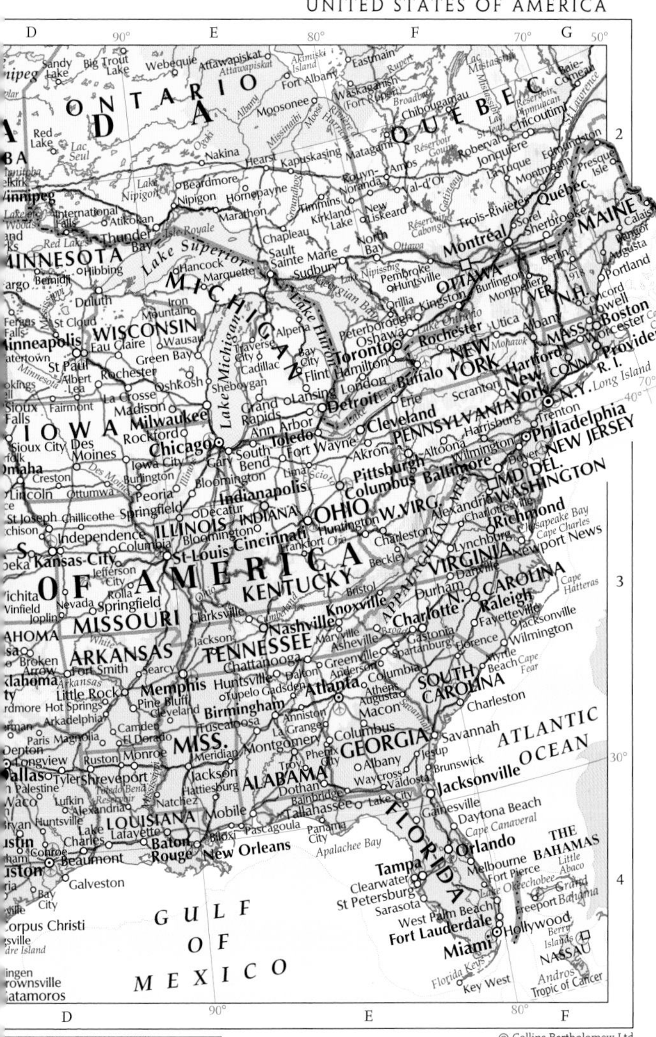
ONTARIO
QUÉBEC
MINNESOTA
WISCONSIN
MICHIGAN
IOWA
ILLINOIS
INDIANA
OHIO
PENNSYLVANIA
NEW YORK
MAINE
VER.
N.H.
MASS.
CONN.
R.I.
NEW JERSEY
DEL.
MD
WASHINGTON
W.VIRG.
VIRGINIA
KENTUCKY
MISSOURI
ARKANSAS
TENNESSEE
N. CAROLINA
SOUTH CAROLINA
GEORGIA
ALABAMA
MISS.
LOUISIANA
FLORIDA
OF AMERICA
ATLANTIC OCEAN
GULF OF MEXICO
THE BAHAMAS
NASSAU
Lake Superior
Lake Michigan
Lake Huron
Montréal
OTTAWA
Toronto
Chicago
Detroit
Cleveland
Pittsburgh
Philadelphia
New York
Boston
Providence
Baltimore
Richmond
Indianapolis
Columbus
Cincinnati
St Louis
Kansas City
Memphis
Nashville
Atlanta
Charlotte
Raleigh
Birmingham
New Orleans
Jacksonville
Orlando
Tampa
Miami
Fort Lauderdale
Milwaukee
Minneapolis
Toledo
Buffalo
Rochester
Hartford
Louisville
Knoxville
Tropic of Cancer
Cape Hatteras
Cape Canaveral
Appalachian Mts

0 250 500 750 KILOMETRES

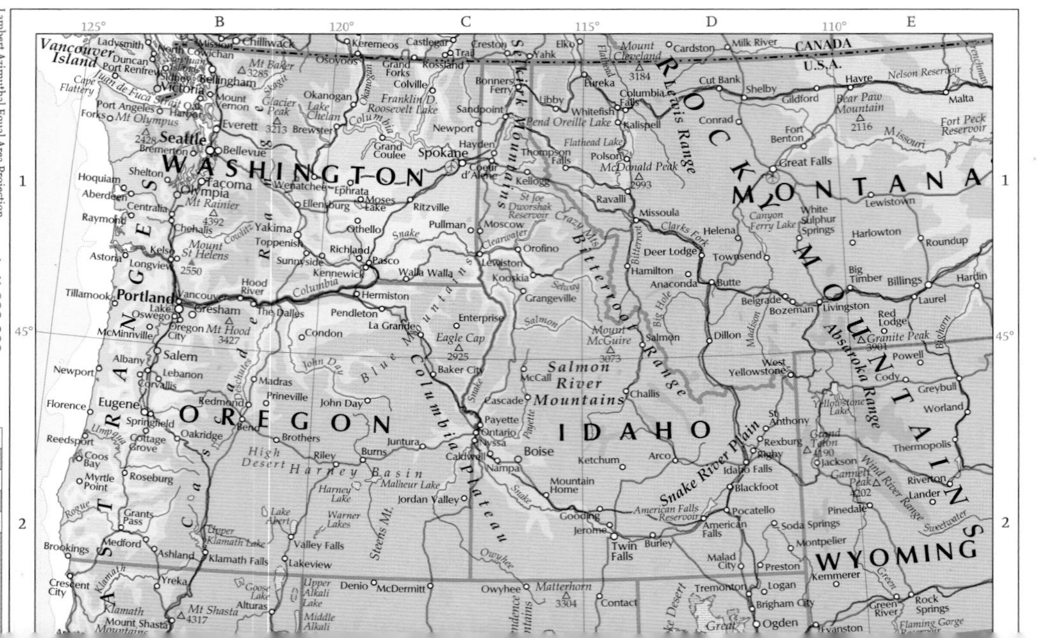

Lambert Azimuthal Equal Area Projection   1 : 11 000 000   MILES 0   100

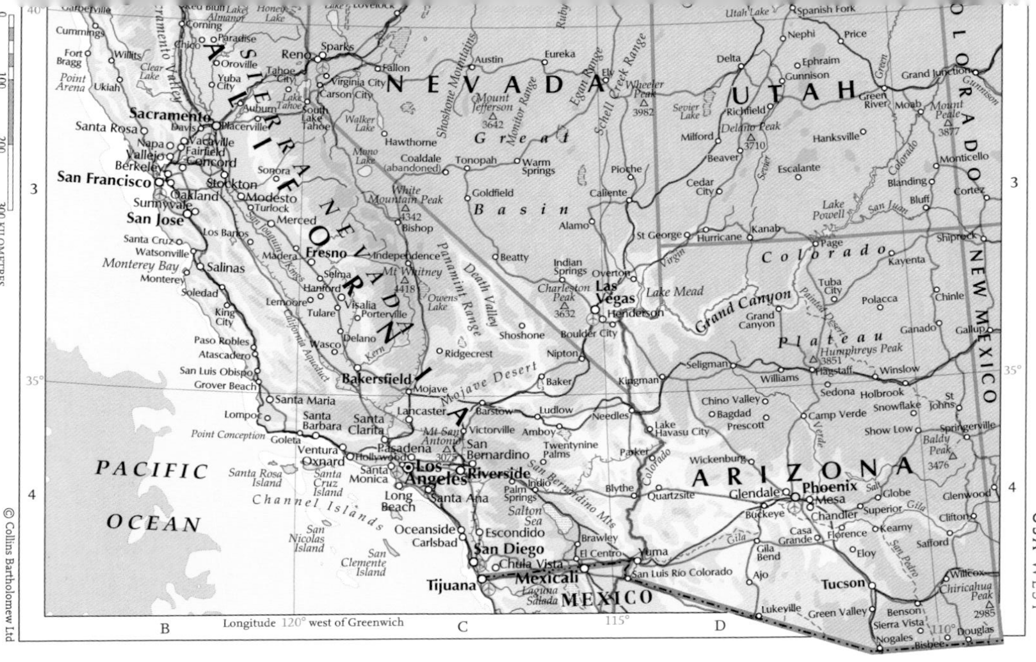

COLORADO
NEW MEXICO
UTAH
NEVADA
ARIZONA
CALIFORNIA
SIERRA NEVADA
MEXICO
PACIFIC OCEAN
Great Basin
Colorado Plateau
Grand Canyon
Death Valley
Mojave Desert
Panamint Range
Lake Mead
Salton Sea
Channel Islands
Sacramento Valley
California Aqueduct
Monterey Bay
Point Conception
Grand Junction
Moab
Price
Nephi
Delta
Richfield
Cedar City
St George
Kanab
Page
Flagstaff
Winslow
Holbrook
Kingman
Prescott
Phoenix
Mesa
Glendale
Tucson
Yuma
Nogales
Bisbee
Douglas
Las Vegas
Henderson
Boulder City
Reno
Sparks
Carson City
Tonopah
Ely
Eureka
Austin
Fallon
Sacramento
San Francisco
Oakland
San Jose
Stockton
Modesto
Fresno
Bakersfield
Santa Barbara
Los Angeles
Long Beach
Riverside
San Bernardino
San Diego
Tijuana
Mexicali
Palm Springs
Barstow
Needles
Santa Rosa
Salinas
Monterey
Santa Maria
Oxnard
Ventura
Lancaster
Longitude 120° west of Greenwich
0
100
200
300 KILOMETRES

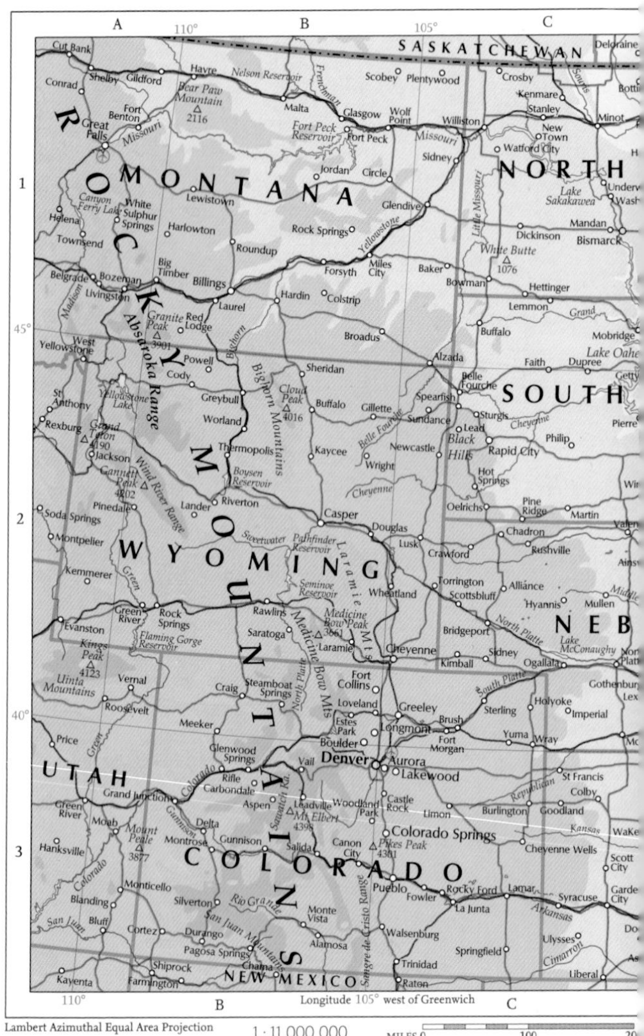

Lambert Azimuthal Equal Area Projection   1 : 11 000 000   MILES 0   100   20

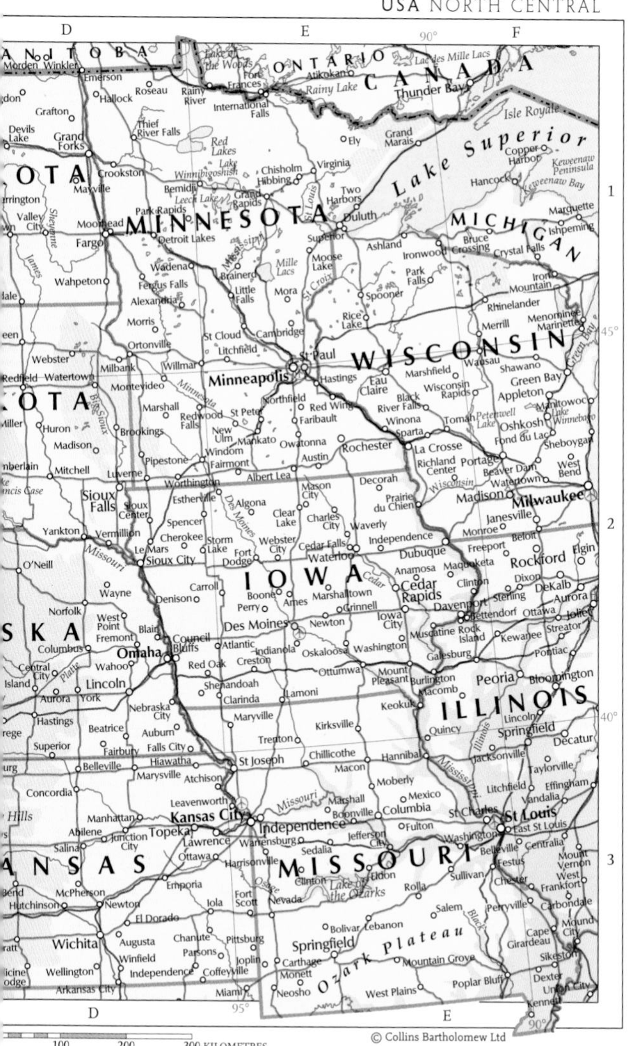

CANADA
ONTARIO
Lake of the Woods
Lake Superior
MINNESOTA
WISCONSIN
MICHIGAN
IOWA
ILLINOIS
MISSOURI
Minneapolis
St Paul
Duluth
Milwaukee
Des Moines
Omaha
Kansas City
St Louis
Springfield
Ozark Plateau
Lake of the Ozarks
Thunder Bay
International Falls
Fargo
Sioux Falls
Sioux City
Madison
Rochester
Cedar Rapids
Davenport
Peoria
Rockford
Topeka
Wichita
Lincoln
100
200
300 KILOMETRES

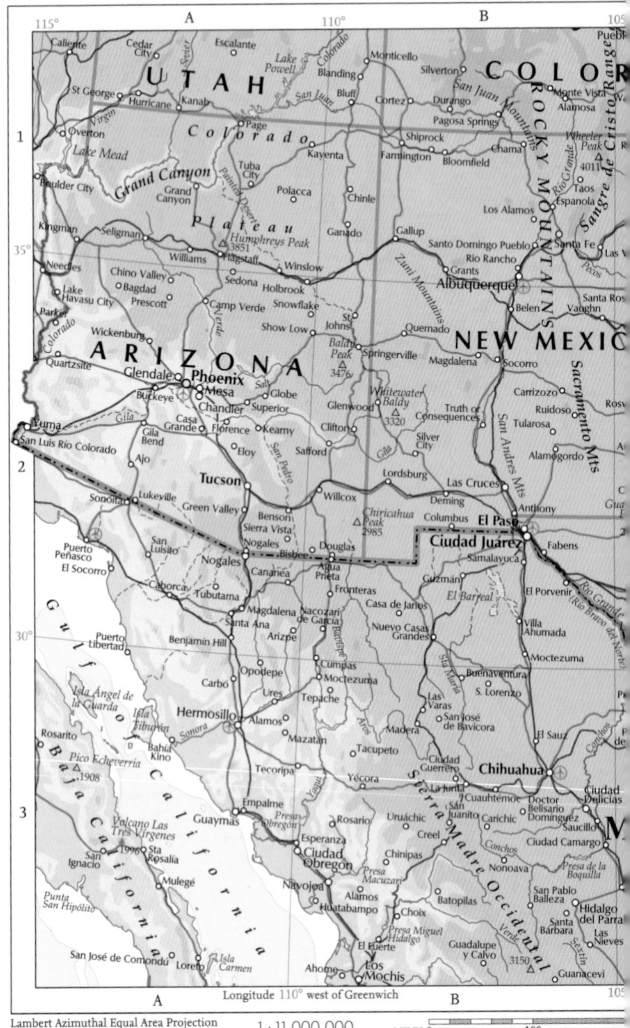

Lambert Azimuthal Equal Area Projection

1 : 11 000 000

MILES 0   100

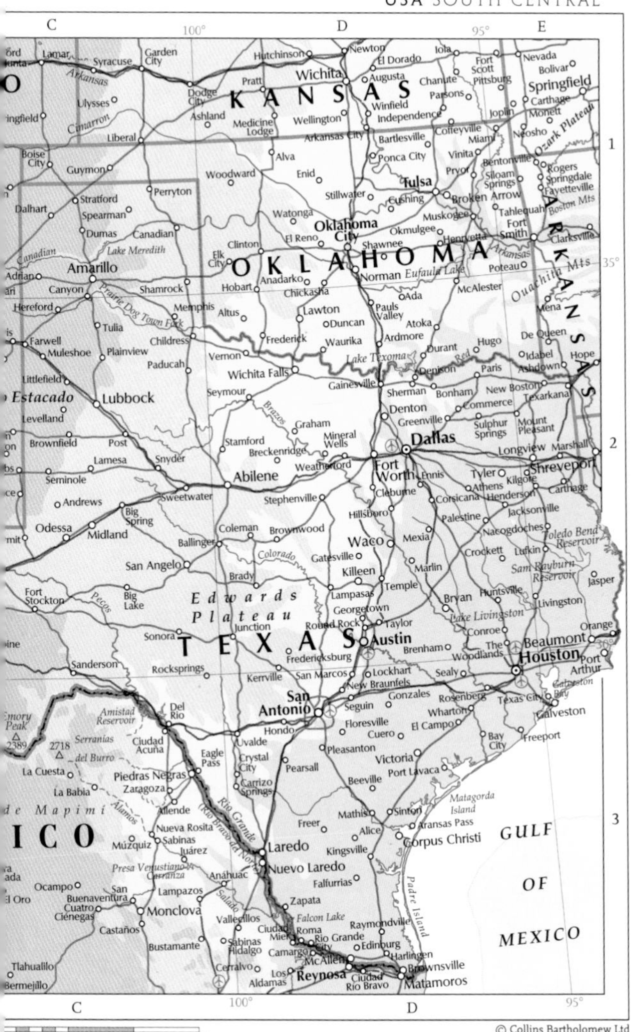

C
100°
D
95°
E
1
2
3
35°
30°
KANSAS
OKLAHOMA
TEXAS
ARKANSAS
GULF
OF
MEXICO
Lamar
Syracuse
Garden City
Hutchinson
Newton
El Dorado
Iola
Fort Scott
Nevada
Bolivar
Arkansas
Pratt
Wichita
Augusta
Chanute
Pittsburg
Springfield
Dodge City
Ulysses
Winfield
Parsons
Carthage
Monett
Ashland
Medicine Lodge
Wellington
Independence
Joplin
Cimarron
Liberal
Arkansas City
Bartlesville
Coffeyville
Miami
Neosho
Ozark Plateau
Boise City
Alva
Ponca City
Vinita
Guymon
Woodward
Enid
Pryor
Bentonville
Rogers
Springdale
Fayetteville
Siloam Springs
Perryton
Tulsa
Stillwater
Cushing
Broken Arrow
Stratford
Dalhart
Spearman
Watonga
Muskogee
Tahlequah
Boston Mts
Dumas
Canadian
Oklahoma City
Okmulgee
Fort Smith
Clarksville
El Reno
Clinton
Shawnee
Henryetta
Canadian
Lake Meredith
Elk City
Amarillo
Adrian
Norman
Eufaula Lake
Poteau
Ouachita Mts
Anadarko
Canyon
Shamrock
Hobart
Chickasha
McAlester
Ada
Prairie Dog Town Fork
Hereford
Memphis
Altus
Lawton
Pauls Valley
Mena
Tulia
Duncan
Atoka
Farwell
Childress
Frederick
Waurika
Ardmore
De Queen
Muleshoe
Plainview
Vernon
Lake Texoma
Durant
Hugo
Idabel
Hope
Red
Paducah
Wichita Falls
Denison
Paris
Ashdown
Littlefield
Gainesville
Sherman
Bonham
New Boston
Estacado
Lubbock
Seymour
Texarkana
Levelland
Brazos
Denton
Commerce
Graham
Greenville
Sulphur Springs
Mount Pleasant
Brownfield
Post
Stamford
Mineral Wells
Dallas
Breckenridge
Longview
Marshall
Lamesa
Snyder
Weatherford
Fort Worth
Shreveport
Seminole
Abilene
Ennis
Tyler
Kilgore
Athens
Carthage
Andrews
Sweetwater
Stephenville
Cleburne
Corsicana
Henderson
Big Spring
Hillsboro
Jacksonville
Palestine
Odessa
Midland
Coleman
Brownwood
Nacogdoches
Toledo Bend Reservoir
Ballinger
Waco
Mexia
Colorado
Gatesville
Crockett
Lufkin
San Angelo
Killeen
Marlin
Sam Rayburn Reservoir
Brady
Jasper
Temple
Fort Stockton
Pecos
Big Lake
Edwards Plateau
Lampasas
Bryan
Huntsville
Livingston
Georgetown
Junction
Round Rock
Taylor
Lake Livingston
Conroe
Orange
Sonora
Austin
Brenham
The Woodlands
Beaumont
Fredericksburg
Houston
Port Arthur
Sanderson
Rocksprings
Kerrville
San Marcos
Lockhart
Sealy
New Braunfels
Galveston Bay
San Antonio
Gonzales
Rosenberg
Texas City
Seguin
Wharton
Galveston
Amistad Reservoir
Del Rio
Hondo
Floresville
El Campo
Emory Peak
Cuero
Bay City
Freeport
Serranías del Burro
Uvalde
2389
2718
Ciudad Acuña
Eagle Pass
Crystal City
Pleasanton
Victoria
La Cuesta
Pearsall
Piedras Negras
Port Lavaca
Zaragoza
Carrizo Springs
Beeville
La Babia
Matagorda Island
Allende
Rio Grande
Mathis
Sinton
de Mapimí
Alamos
(Rio Bravo del Norte)
Freer
Aransas Pass
Nueva Rosita
Alice
ICO
Sabinas
Corpus Christi
Múzquiz
Laredo
Juárez
Kingsville
Presa Venustiano Carranza
Nuevo Laredo
Anáhuac
Falfurrias
Ocampo
San Buenaventura
Lampazos
Padre Island
Salado
Cuatro Ciénegas
Zapata
Monclova
Falcon Lake
Vallecillos
Castaños
Ciudad Mier
Roma
Raymondville
Rio Grande City
Bustamante
Sabinas Hidalgo
Camargo
Edinburg
McAllen
Harlingen
Tlahualilo
Cerralvo
Brownsville
Los Aldamas
Reynosa
Ciudad Río Bravo
Matamoros
Bermejillo
100
200
300 KILOMETRES

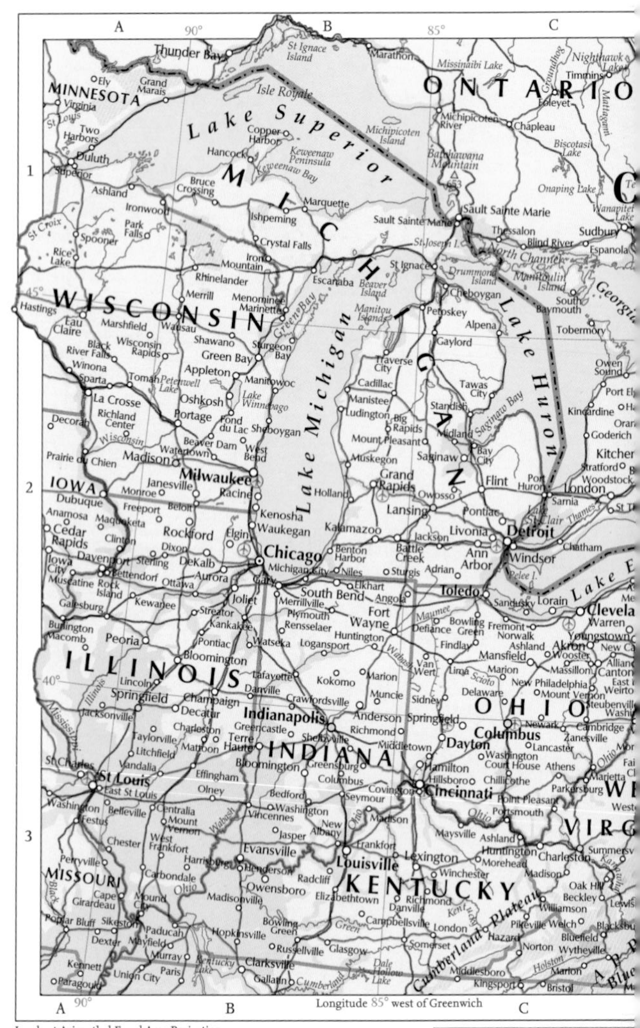

Lambert Azimuthal Equal Area Projection

1 : 11 000 000

MILES 0   100

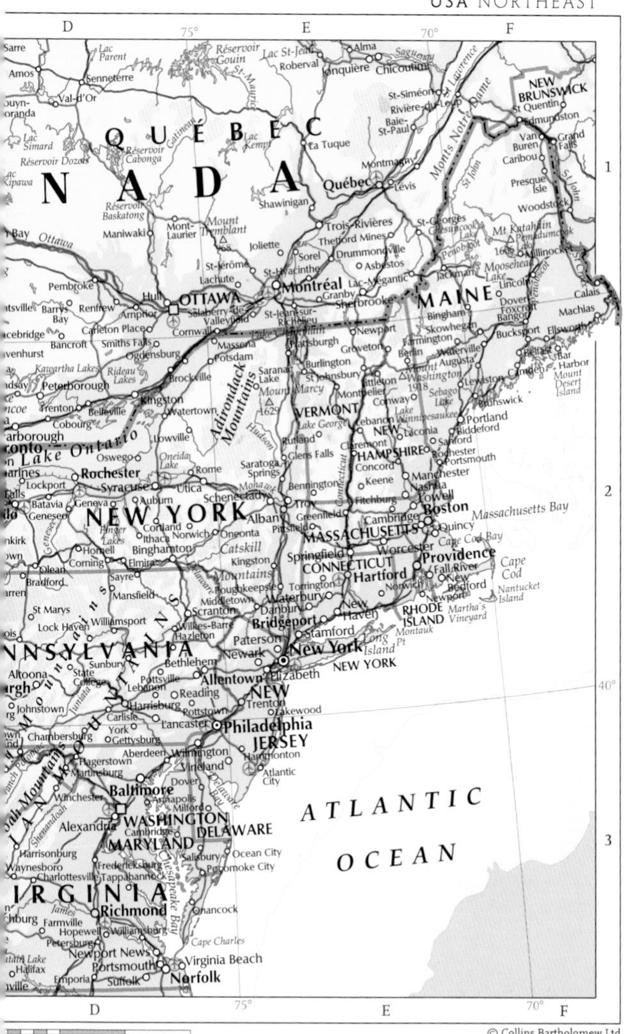
QUÉBEC
CANADA
MAINE
NEW BRUNSWICK
VERMONT
NEW HAMPSHIRE
NEW YORK
MASSACHUSETTS
CONNECTICUT
RHODE ISLAND
PENNSYLVANIA
NEW JERSEY
DELAWARE
MARYLAND
VIRGINIA
WASHINGTON
OTTAWA
Montréal
Québec
Boston
Providence
Hartford
New York
Philadelphia
Baltimore
Richmond
Norfolk
Rochester
Lake Ontario
Adirondack Mountains
Atlantic City
ATLANTIC OCEAN
Massachusetts Bay
Cape Cod
Long Island
Chesapeake Bay
Virginia Beach
100 200 300 KILOMETRES

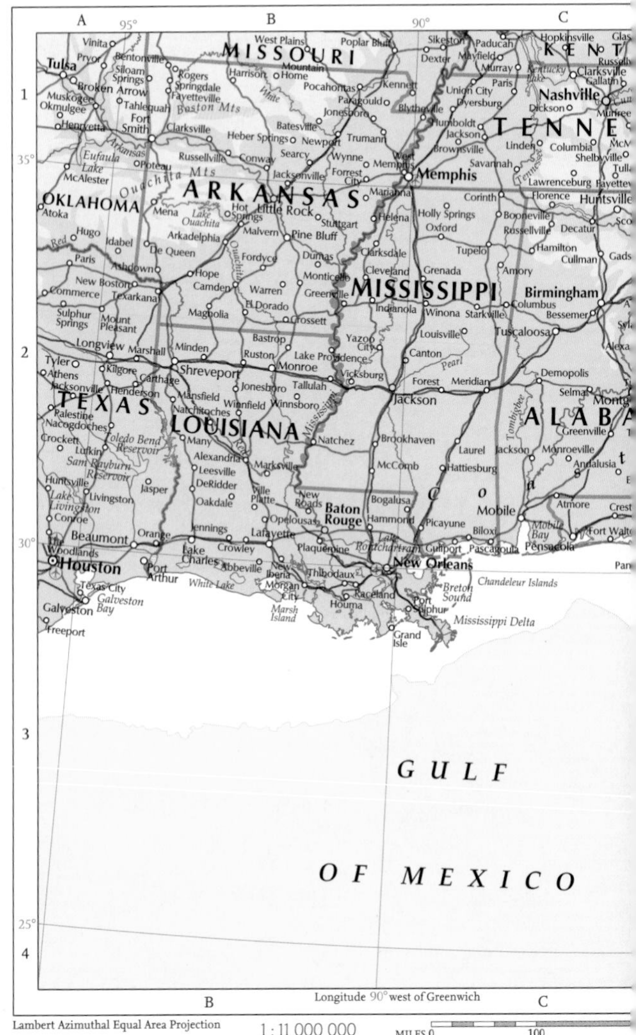

A
95°
B
90°
C

West Plains
Poplar Bluff
Sikeston
Paducah
Hopkinsville
Glas
KENTU
Russe

MISSOURI
Mountain
Home
Dexter
Mayfield
Murray
Kentucky
Lake
Clarksville
Gallatin

Vinita
Bentonville
Harrison

Tulsa
Pryor
Rogers
Springdale
Pocahontas
Kennett
Union City
Paris
Dickson
Nashville
Murfree

Broken Arrow
Siloam Springs
Fayetteville
Paragould
Dyersburg

Muskogee
Tahlequah
Fort Smith
Clarksville
Batesville
Jonesboro
Blytheville
Humboldt

Okmulgee
Henryetta
Heber Springs
Trumann
Jackson
Brownsville
Linden
Columbia
TENNE
Shelbyville
McM

1

35°
Eufaula
Lake
Russellville
Conway
Searcy
Newport
Wynne
Memphis
Savannah
Lawrenceburg
Fayette

McAlester
Protem
ARKANSAS
Forrest City
Marianna
Corinth
Florence
Huntsville
Decatur
Sco

OKLAHOMA
Ouachita Mts
Hot Springs
Little Rock
Helena
Holly Springs
Booneville
Russellville
Hamilton
Cullman
Gads

Atoka
Mena
Lake Ouachita
Malvern
Stuttgart
Oxford
Tupelo
Amory
Birmingham

Hugo
Idabel
Arkadelphia
Pine Bluff
Clarksdale
Grenada
Columbus
Bessemer

Paris
De Queen
Fordyce
Cleveland
Greenwood
MISSISSIPPI
Starkville
Tuscaloosa

New Boston
Ashdown
Hope
Camden
Monticello
Indianola
Winona
Louisville

Commerce
Texarkana
Magnolia
El Dorado
Warren
Crossett
Yazoo City
Canton

2
Sulphur Springs
Mount Pleasant
Bastrop
Greenville
Forest
Meridian
Demopolis

Tyler
Longview
Marshall
Minden
Ruston
Lake Providence
Vicksburg
Pearl
Selma
Mont

Athens
Kilgore
Carthage
Shreveport
Monroe
Tallulah
Jackson
ALABA

Jacksonville
Henderson
Mansfield
Jonesboro
Winnsboro
Greenville

TEXAS
Palestine
Natchitoches
Winnfield
Kinnsboro
Brookhaven
Monroeville
Annalusia

Nacogdoches
LOUISIANA
Many
Natchez
McComb
Laurel
Jackson
Atmore

Crockett
Toledo Bend Reservoir
Alexandria
Marksville
Hattiesburg
Mobile
Crest

Lufkin
Sam Rayburn Reservoir
Leesville
DeRidder
Ville Platte
Bogalusa
Mobile Bay
Fort Walt

Huntsville
Jasper
Oakdale
New Roads
Hammond
Picayune
Pensacola

Lake Livingston
Livingston
Opelousas
Baton Rouge
Biloxi
Pascagoula
Par

30°
Conroe
Orange
Jennings
Lafayette
Plaquemine
Pontchartrain
Gulfport
Chandeleur Islands

Beaumont
Lake Charles
Crowley
Raceland
New Orleans
Breton Sound

Woodlands
Port Arthur
Abbeville
Iberia
Morgan City
Thibodaux
Sulphur
Mississippi Delta

Houston
White Lake
Marsh Island
Houma

Texas City
Galveston
Galveston Bay
Port

Freeport
Grand Isle

3

G U L F

O F   M E X I C O

25°
4

B
Longitude 90° west of Greenwich
C

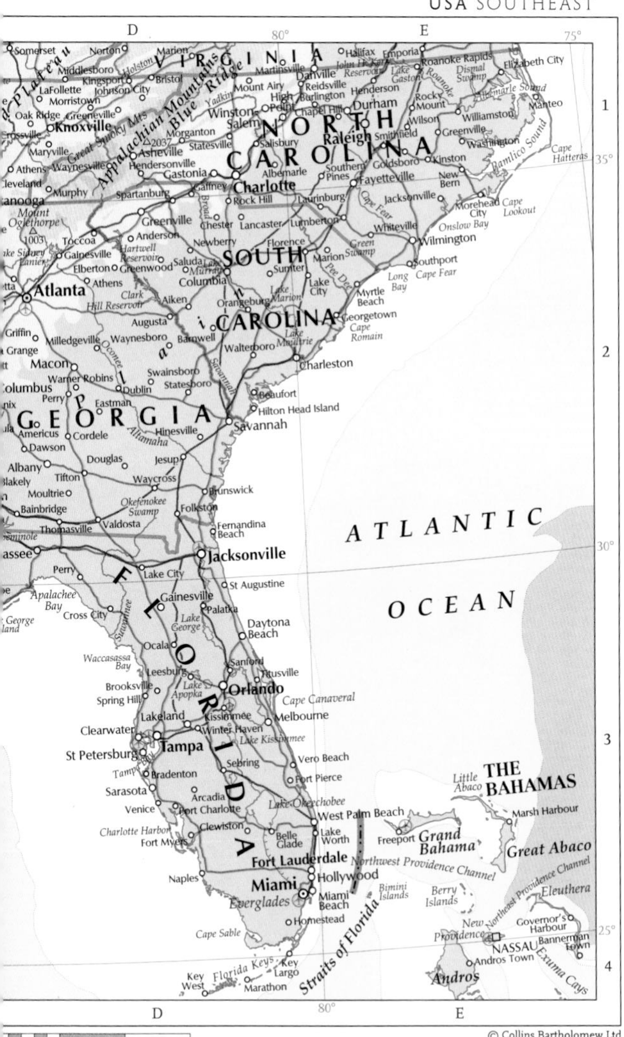
NORTH CAROLINA
SOUTH CAROLINA
GEORGIA
FLORIDA
VIRGINIA
ATLANTIC OCEAN
THE BAHAMAS
Charlotte
Atlanta
Jacksonville
Orlando
Tampa
Miami
Savannah
Charleston
Raleigh
Columbia
Knoxville
Fort Lauderdale
NASSAU
Grand Bahama
Great Abaco
Andros
Eleuthera
Straits of Florida
Florida Keys
Key West
Everglades
Cape Canaveral
Cape Hatteras
Pamlico Sound
Northwest Providence Channel
Northeast Providence Channel
100 200 300 KILOMETRES

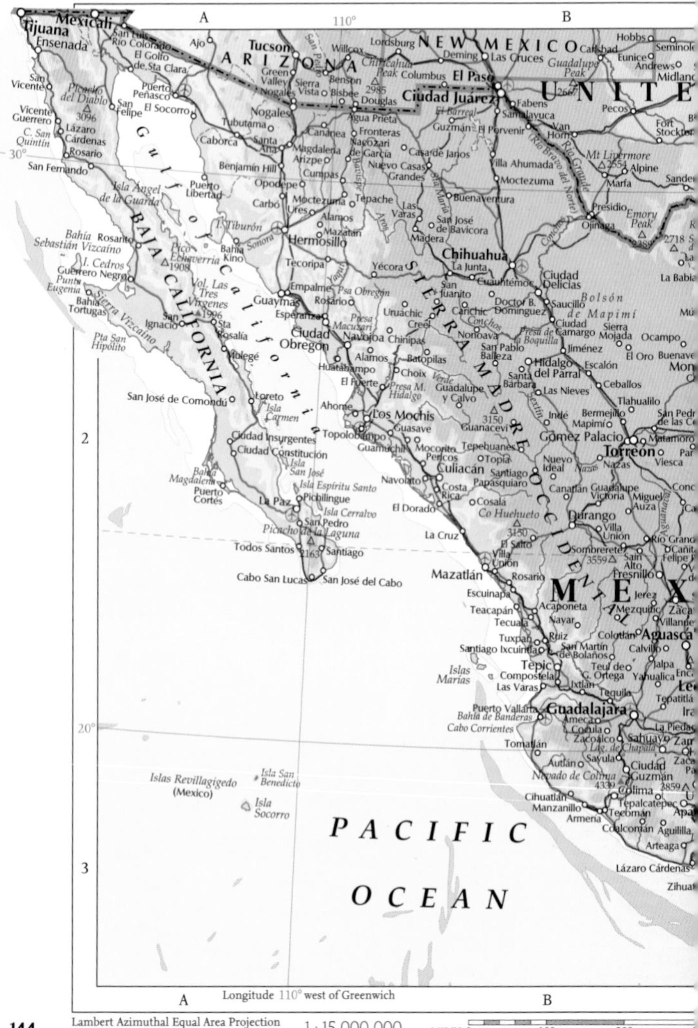

A

B

Mexicali
Tijuana
Ensenada

Ajo Lordsburg Deming Las Cruces Carlsbad Hobbs Seminole

NEW MEXICO

ARIZONA Columbus El Paso UNITE

Tucson Willcox Benson Bisbee Douglas Ciudad Juárez Fabens Pecos Fort Stockton

San Vicente
Guerrero
Lázaro Cárdenas
Rosario
San Fernando

Puerto Peñasco Nogales El Porvenir Mt Livermore Marfa Alpine Sandes

Caborca Fronteras Villa Ahumada Moctezuma Presidio Emory Peak 2718

Benjamín Hill Nuevo Casas Grandes Buenaventura Ojinaga La Babia

BAJA CALIFORNIA

Puerto Libertad Carbó Moctezuma José de Bavicora **Chihuahua** Ciudad Delicias Bolsón de Mapimí

Isla Ángel de la Guarda Tiburón Hermosillo Madera La Junta Cuauhtémoc Sierra Mojada Ocampo

Bahía Rosario Sebastián Vizcaíno Tecoripa Yécora San Juanito Doctor B. Domínguez El Oro Buenave Mon

Guerrero Negro Kino Empalmes Unáchic Creel Santa Bárbara Ceballos

Punta Eugenia Sierra **Guaymas** Rosario Navojoa Chínipas San Pablo Balleza Hidalgo del Parral Tlahualilo San Pedr de las C

Bahía Tortugas Ciudad Obregón Álamos Batopilas Guadalupe y Calvo Las Nieves Indé Bermejillo Gómez Palacio Matamoro

San José de Comondú El Fuerte Choix Mapimí **Torreón** Viesca

Isla Carmen Los Mochis Guasave Guanaceví **MADRE** Nuevo Ideal Cuencamé Santiago Miguel A Auza San Gran

Ciudad Insurgentes Topolobampo Guamúchil Topia Papasquiaro Canatlán Guadalupe Victoria Río Grand

Ciudad Constitución Mocorito Pericos **Culiacán** Santiago **Durango** Sombrerete Villa Unión

La Paz Picchilingue Navolato Costa Rica Cosalá El Salto Fresnillo

Todos Santos Santiago La Cruz Villa Unión **M E X** Jerez Mezquitic Villalde

Cabo San Lucas San José del Cabo **Mazatlán** Rosario Acaponeta Nayar Calvillo **Aguasca**

Escuinapa Teacapán Tecuala Ruiz San Martín de Bolaños Colotlán Yahualica Le

Santiago Ixcuintla Tuxpán **Tepic** Teul deo Jalpa Tepatitlá

Islas Marías Compostela Las Varas Ixtlán San Pedro Ortega Tequila Ameca **Guadalajara**

Puerto Vallarta Bahía de Banderas Cabo Corrientes Cocula Zacoalco La Piedra

Tomatlán Autlán **Nevado de Colima 4330** Ciudad Guzmán Tecalitlán

Cihuatlán Tepalcatepec Colcomán Aguililla

Islas Revillagigedo (Mexico) Isla San Benedicto Manzanillo Tecomán Arteaga

Isla Socorro Lázaro Cárdenas Zihuat

P A C I F I C

O C E A N

30°

20°

110°

2

3

144 Lambert Azimuthal Equal Area Projection

A Longitude 110° west of Greenwich B

1 : 15 000 000 MILES 0 100 200

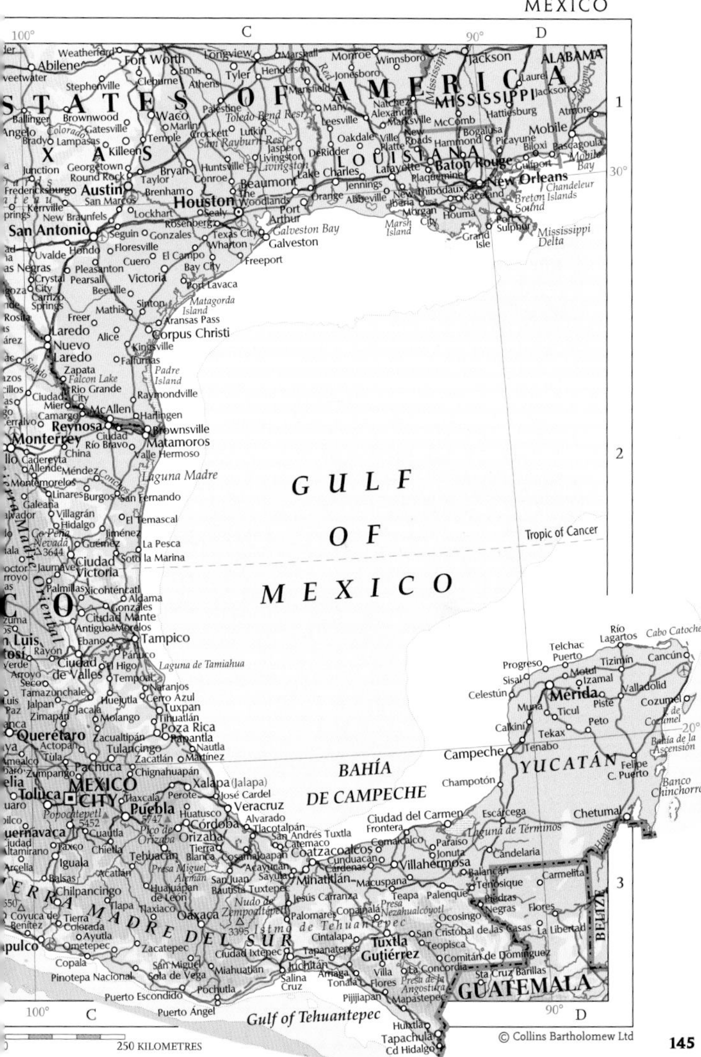

100°
C
90°
D
1
2
3
30°
20°
STATES OF AMERICA
TEXAS
LOUISIANA
MISSISSIPPI
ALABAMA
Abilene
Sweetwater
Weatherford
Fort Worth
Cleburne
Ennis
Athens
Tyler
Longview
Marshall
Henderson
Monroe
Winnsboro
Jackson
Laurel
Jonesboro
Mansfield
Stephenville
Ballinger
Brownwood
Waco
Marlin
Palestine
Toledo Bend Resr
Many
Natchez
Alexandria
Marksville
McComb
Hattiesburg
Atmore
Mobile
Colorado
Gatesville
Temple
Crockett
Lufkin
Leesville
Oakdale
Ville Platte
New Roads
Bogalusa
Hammond
Picayune
Biloxi
Pascagoula
Mobile Bay
Brady
Lampasas
Killeen
Sam Rayburn Resr
Jasper
Livingston
DeRidder
Junction
Georgetown
Round Rock
Bryan
Huntsville
Lake Livingston
Lake Charles
Lafayette
Baton Rouge
Plaquemine
Gulfport
Fredericksburg
Austin
Taylor
Conroe
Beaumont
Jennings
New Orleans
Chandeleur
Kerrville
San Marcos
Brenham
Houston
The Woodlands
Orange
Abbeville
New Iberia
Thibodaux
Raceland
Breton Islands
Breton Sound
New Braunfels
Lockhart
Sealy
Port Arthur
Morgan City
Houma
San Antonio
Seguin
Gonzales
Rosenberg
Texas City
Galveston Bay
Marsh Island
Grand Isle
Port Sulphur
Mississippi Delta
Galveston
Uvalde
Hondo
Floresville
Wharton
El Campo
Freeport
Piedras Negras
Pleasanton
Cuero
Bay City
Crystal City
Pearsall
Victoria
Port Lavaca
Carrizo Springs
Beeville
Matagorda Island
Freer
Mathis
Sinton
Aransas Pass
Laredo
Alice
Corpus Christi
Nuevo Laredo
Kingsville
Falfurrias
Padre Island
Zapata
Falcon Lake
Rio Grande City
Ciudad Mier
Raymondville
Camargo
McAllen
Harlingen
Reynosa
Brownsville
Monterrey
Ciudad Río Bravo
Matamoros
China
Valle Hermoso
Cadereyta
Allende
Méndez
Montemorelos
Conchos
Laguna Madre
Linares
Burgos
San Fernando
Galeana
Villagrán
Hidalgo
El Temascal
Jiménez
Cerro Peña Nevada
3644
Güémez
La Pesca
Soto la Marina
Ciudad Victoria
Jaumave
Sierra Madre Oriental
Palmillas
Xicohténcatl
Aldama
González
Ciudad Mante
Antiguo Morelos
Tampico
Ébano
San Luis Potosí
Rayón
Ciudad Valles
Pánuco
El Higo
Laguna de Tamiahua
Tempoal
Naranjos
Cerro Azul
Tamazunchale
Huejutla
Tuxpan
Jalpan
Jacala
Molango
Tihuatlán
Zimapán
Poza Rica
Querétaro
Zacualtipán
Papantla
Actopan
Tulancingo
Nautla
Tula
Zacatlán
Martínez
Pachuca
Zumpango
Chignahuapan
Toluca
MEXICO CITY
Xalapa (Jalapa)
Perote
José Cardel
Tlaxcala
Puebla
Veracruz
Popocatépetl
5452
Huatusco
Alvarado
Pico de Orizaba
5747
Córdoba
Tlacotalpán
San Andrés Tuxtla
Cuernavaca
Cuautla
Orizaba
Catemaco
Taxco
Chietla
Tierra Blanca
Coatzacoalcos
Iguala
Tehuacán
Cosamaloapan
Acayucan
Presa Miguel Alemán
Sayula
Minatitlán
Balsas
Acatlán
San Juan Bautista Tuxtepec
Chilpancingo
Huajuapan de León
Jesús Carranza
Tlapa
Tlaxiaco
Nudo de Zempoaltépetl
Palomares
Coyuca de Benítez
Tierra Colorada
Oaxaca
3395
SIERRA MADRE DEL SUR
Istmo de Tehuantepec
Ayutla
Acapulco
Ometepec
Zacatepec
Ciudad Ixtepec
Tapanatepec
Copala
San Miguel Sola de Vega
Miahuatlán
Juchitán
Arriaga
Pinotepa Nacional
Salina Cruz
Tonalá
Pochutla
Puerto Escondido
Puerto Ángel
Gulf of Tehuantepec
GULF OF MEXICO
Tropic of Cancer
BAHÍA DE CAMPECHE
Río Lagartos
Cabo Catoche
Telchac Puerto
Progreso
Tizimín
Cancún
Motul
Sisal
Izamal
Celestún
Mérida
Valladolid
Muna
Pisté
Cozumel
Ticul
Isla de Cozumel
Calkiní
Peto
Tekax
Campeche
Tenabo
Bahía de la Ascensión
YUCATÁN
Felipe C. Puerto
Champotón
Banco Chinchorro
Ciudad del Carmen
Escárcega
Chetumal
Frontera
Laguna de Términos
Comalcalco
Paraíso
Jonuta
Candelaria
Cunduacán
Cárdenas
Villahermosa
Balancán
Carmelita
Macuspana
Tenosique
Teapa
Palenque
Piedras Negras
Flores
Copainalá
Presa Nezahualcóyotl
Ocosingo
Cintalapa
Tuxtla Gutiérrez
San Cristóbal de las Casas
La Libertad
BELIZE
Teopisca
Comitán de Domínguez
La Concordia
Villa Flores
Presa de la Angostura
Sta Cruz Barillas
GUATEMALA
Pijijiapan
Mapastepec
Huixtla
Tapachula
Cd Hidalgo
250 KILOMETRES
© Collins Bartholomew Ltd

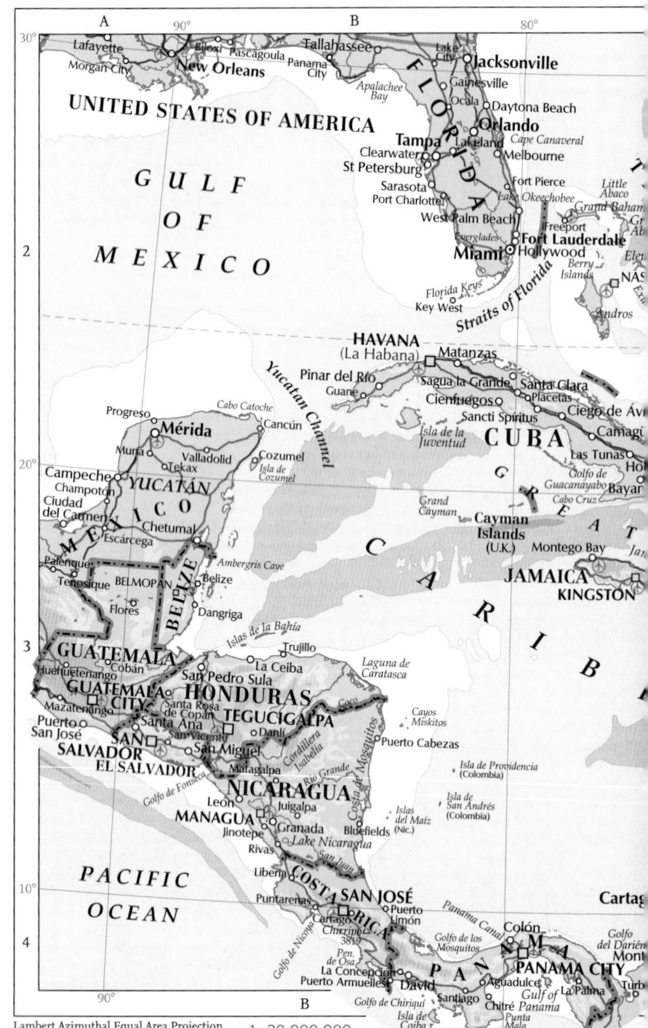

Lambert Azimuthal Equal Area Projection   1 : 20 000 000

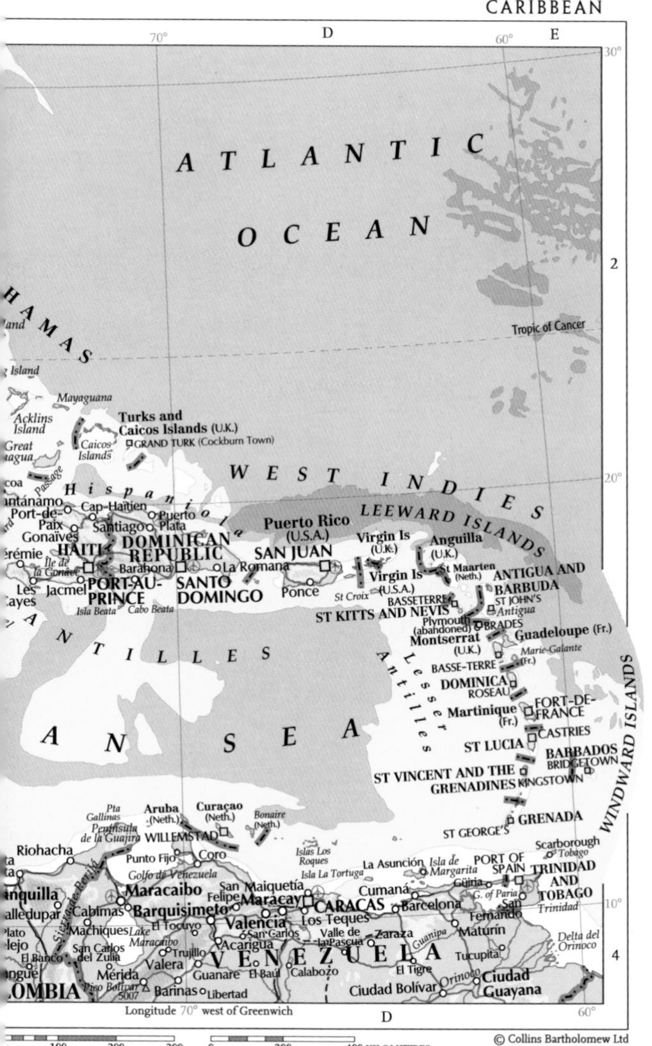

ATLANTIC

OCEAN

Tropic of Cancer

BAHAMAS

Acklins
Island

Great
Inagua

Mayaguana

Caicos
Islands

Turks and
Caicos Islands (U.K.)
◻ GRAND TURK (Cockburn Town)

WEST INDIES

Hispaniola

LEEWARD ISLANDS

Cap-Haïtien
Port-de-
Paix
Gonaïves
Jérémie
Île de
la Gonâve
Les
Cayes
Jacmel

Santiago
Cabo Beata
Isla Beata

DOMINICAN
REPUBLIC

Puerto
Plata

Barahona

PORT-AU-
PRINCE

Puerto Rico
(U.S.A.)

SAN JUAN

La Romana

SANTO
DOMINGO

Ponce

St Croix

Virgin Is
(U.K.)

Virgin Is
(U.S.A.)

Anguilla
(U.K.)

St Maarten
(Neth.)

ANTIGUA AND
BARBUDA

Antigua

ST JOHN'S

BASSE-TERRE

ST KITTS AND NEVIS

Plymouth
(abandoned)

Montserrat
(U.K.)

BRADES

Guadeloupe (Fr.)

Marie-Galante
(Fr.)

BASSE-TERRE

DOMINICA

ROSEAU

Martinique
(Fr.)

FORT-DE-
FRANCE

CASTRIES

ST LUCIA

ST VINCENT AND THE
GRENADINES

BARBADOS

BRIDGETOWN

KINGSTOWN

GRENADA

ST GEORGE'S

WINDWARD ISLANDS

Lesser Antilles

HAITI

ANTILLES

CARIBBEAN SEA

Pta
Gallinas

Peninsula
de la Guajira

Aruba
(Neth.)

WILLEMSTAD

Curaçao
(Neth.)

Bonaire
(Neth.)

Riohacha

Punto Fijo

Coro

Islas Los
Roques

La Asunción

Isla de
Margarita

Scarborough

Tobago

Anguilla

Cabimas

Machiques

San Carlos
del Zulia

Maracaibo

Lake
Maracaibo

Barquisimeto

San
Felipe

Maiquetía

Maracay

Valencia

CARACAS

Los Teques

Cumaná

Golfo de
Venezuela

El Banco

Valera

Trujillo

Mérida

Ocumare

San Carlos

Valle de
La Pascua

Zaraza

Barcelona

G. of Paria

Maturín

Fernando

PORT OF
SPAIN

TRINIDAD
AND
TOBAGO

Trinidad

Delta del
Orinoco

Pino Bolívar
5007

Barinas

Acarigua

El Baúl

Calabozo

Guárico

El Tigre

Orinoco

Ciudad
Guayana

COLOMBIA

Guanare

Libertad

VENEZUELA

Ciudad Bolívar

Tucupita

100   200   300   0   200   400 KILOMETRES

© Collins Bartholomew Ltd

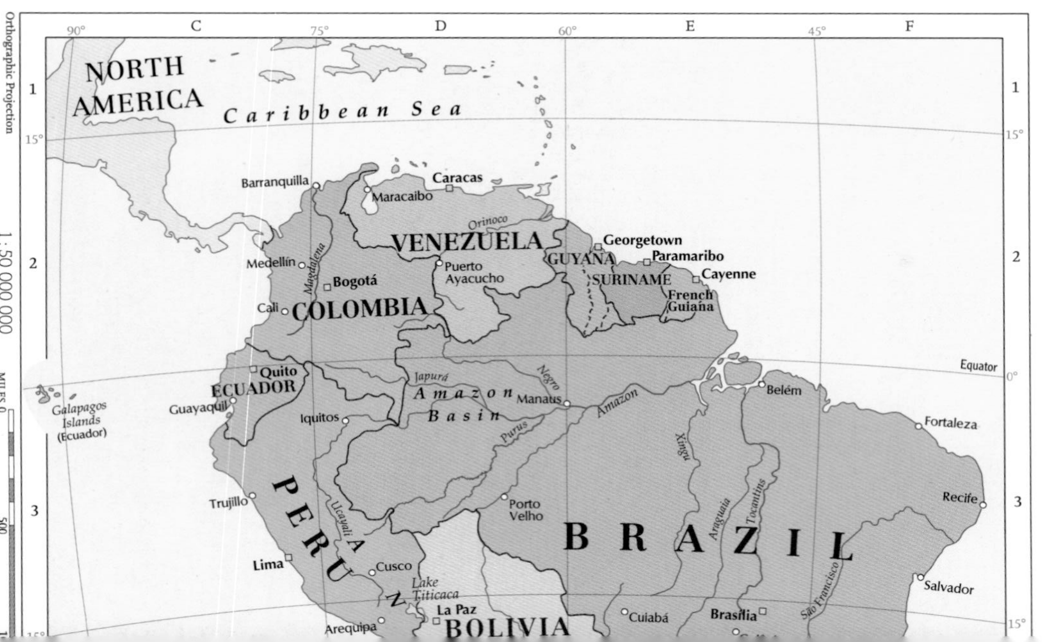

Orthographic Projection   1 : 50 000 000   MILES 0   500   1

1   15°   **2**   0°   **3**   15°

Equator

F

45°

E

60°

D

75°

C

90°

NORTH
AMERICA

Caribbean Sea

Barranquilla

Maracaibo

Caracas

VENEZUELA

Orinoco

Puerto
Ayacucho

Bogotá

Medellín

COLOMBIA

Cali

Magdalena

GUYANA

Georgetown

Paramaribo

SURINAME

Cayenne

French
Guiana

Negro

Manaus

A m a z o n
B a s i n

Japurá

B R A Z I L

Belém

Amazon

Xingu

Tocantins

Araguaia

Fortaleza

Recife

Salvador

São Francisco

Brasília

Cuiabá

Porto
Velho

Madeira

Quito

ECUADOR

Guayaquil

Iquitos

Ucayali

P E R U

Lima

Trujillo

Cusco

Arequipa

Lake
Titicaca

BOLIVIA

La Paz

Galápagos
Islands
(Ecuador)

1   15°   **2**   **3**

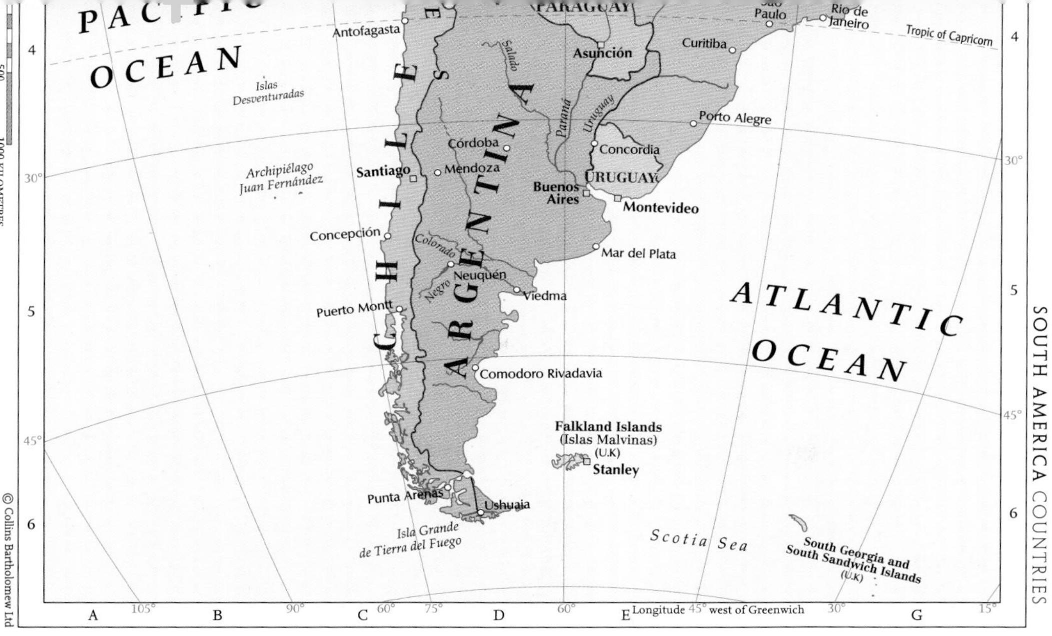

Tropic of Capricorn

Rio de Janeiro

Paulo

Curitiba

Porto Alegre

Concórdia

PARAGUAY

Asunción

Paraná

Uruguay

URUGUAY

Montevideo

Salado

Mar del Plata

Buenos Aires

ATLANTIC

OCEAN

A R G E N T I N A

Antofagasta

Córdoba

Mendoza

Santiago

Salado

Colorado

Negro

Neuquén

Viedma

Comodoro Rivadavia

Falkland Islands
(Islas Malvinas)
(U.K.)
Stanley

Scotia Sea

South Georgia and
South Sandwich Islands
(U.K.)

E Longitude 45° west of Greenwich

C H I L E

Concepción

Puerto Montt

Punta Arenas

Ushuaia

Isla Grande
de Tierra del Fuego

PACIFIC

OCEAN

Islas
Desventuradas

Archipiélago
Juan Fernández

500   1000 KILOMETRES

© Collins Bartholomew Ltd

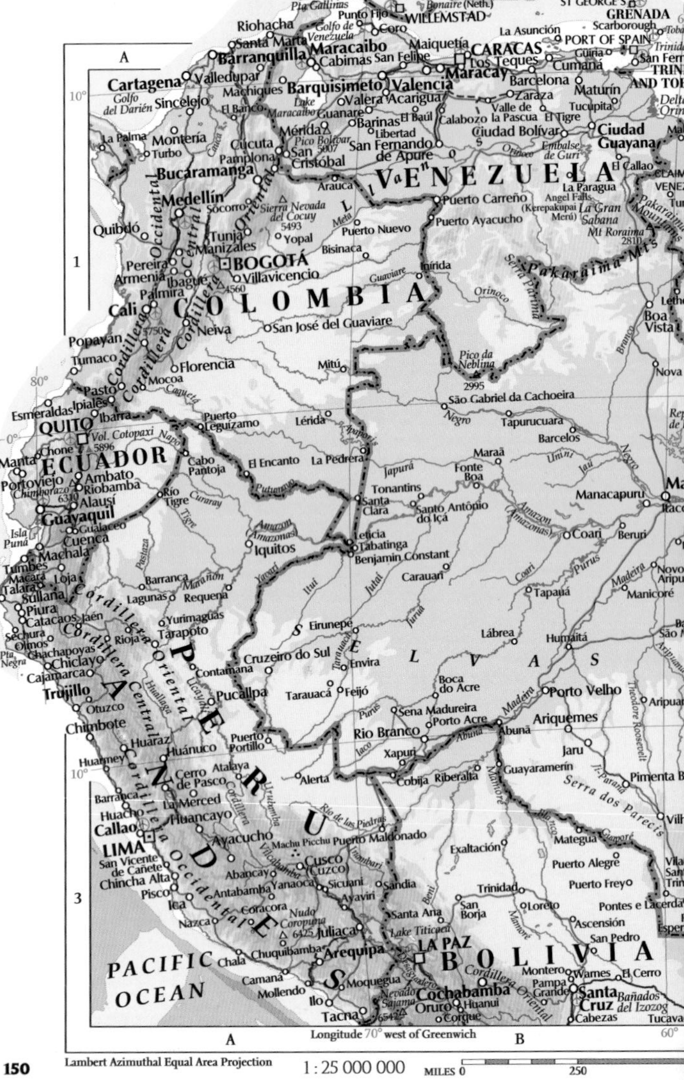

Lambert Azimuthal Equal Area Projection

1 : 25 000 000

MILES 0   250

Longitude 70° west of Greenwich

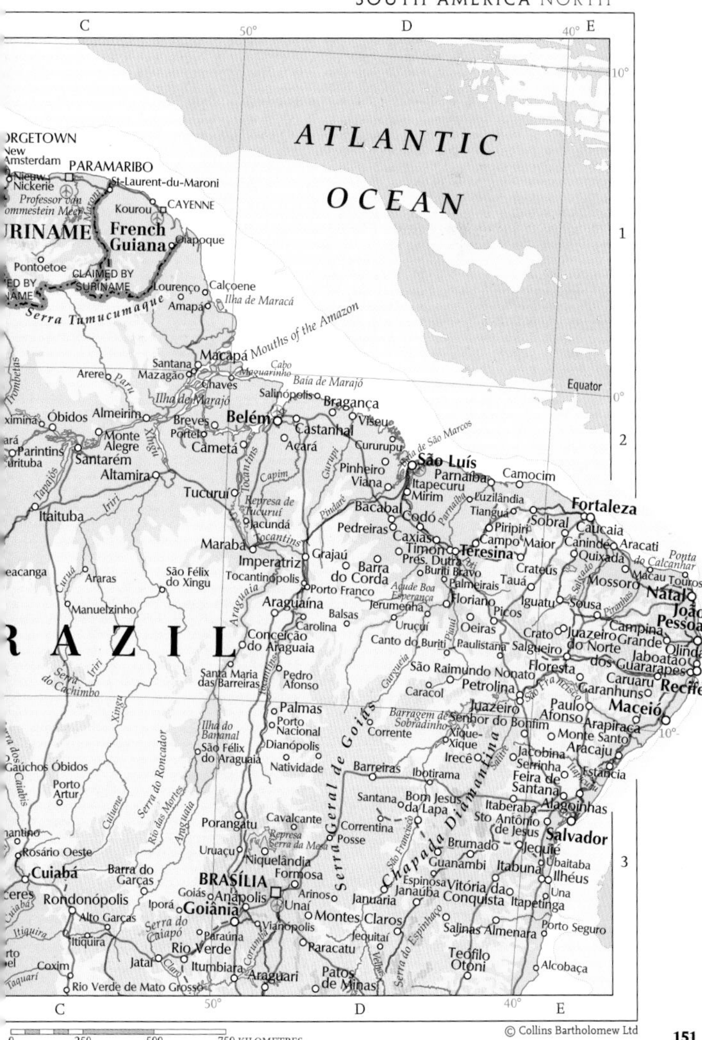

ATLANTIC

OCEAN

RGETOWN
New Amsterdam
Nieuw PARAMARIBO
Nickerie St-Laurent-du-Maroni
Professor con
ommestein Meer Kourou CAYENNE
Pontoetoe
URINAME French
Guiana Oïapoque
ED BY CLAIMED BY
AME SURINAME Lourenço Calçoene
Serra Tumucumaque Amapá Ilha de Maracá

Santana Macapá Mouths of the Amazon
Arere Mazagão Cabo
Paru Chaves Orange
ximina, Óbidos Almeirim Ilha de Marajó Baía de Marajó Equator 0°
pará Monte Breves Belém Bragança
Parintins Alegre Portel Viseu
rituba Santarém Cametá Castanhal
Itaituba Altamira Acará Cururupu
Xingu Pinheiro São Luís
Capim Viana Parnaíba
Tucuruí Bacabal Itapecuru- Camocim
Represa de Jacundá Mirim
Tucuruí Iriri Grajaú Codó Fortaleza
eacanga Marabá Imperatriz Pedreiras Caxias Tianguá Sobral Caucaia
Araras Tocantinópolis Barra Pres. Buriti Bravo Piripiri Canindé Aracati
São Félix do Corda Dutra Teresina Crateús Quixadá do Calcanhar
Manuelzinho do Xingu Araguaína Palmeirais Tauá Mossoró
Carolina Jerumenha Floriano Iguatu Natal
R A Z I L Conceição Balsas Picos Sousa João
do Araguaia Canto do Buriti Oeiras Crato Juazeiro Pessoa
Santa Maria São Raimundo Nonato Paulistana Salgueiro do Norte Jaboatão
das Barreiras Pedro Caracol Floresta Guarabira
Afonso Petrolina Serra Talhada Caruaru Recife
Palmas Paulo Garanhuns
Porto Barragem de Juazeiro Afonso Arapiraca Maceió
Nacional Sobradinho Senhor do Bonfim
Ilha do Dianópolis Corrente Xique- Serrinha Jacobina Feira de São Cristóvão
Bananal Natividade Xique Irecê Santana Aracaju
São Félix Barreiras Ibotirama Itaberaba Sto Antônio Alagoinhas
do Araguaia Ibotirama de Jesus Salvador
Gaúchos Óbidos Porangatu Cavalcante Santana Brumado Valença
Porto Uruaçu da Lapa Guanambi Itabuna Ubaitaba
Artur Represa de Correntina Janaúba Vitória da Ilhéus
antino Serra do Mel Posse Conquista Itapetinga Una
ceres Rosário Oeste Niquelândia Januária Porto Seguro
Cuiabá Barra do Formosa Montes Claros Salinas Almenara
Rondonópolis Garças Uruaçu BRASÍLIA Anápolis Arinos Teófilo Alcobaça
Alto Garças Iporá Goiás Goiânia Unaí Janaúba Otoni
Itiquira Serra do Rio Verde Paracatu
Coxim Caiapó Itumbiara Araguari Patos
Rio Verde de Mato Grosso de Minas

C 50° D 40° E

0 250 500 750 KILOMETRES

© Collins Bartholomew Ltd 151

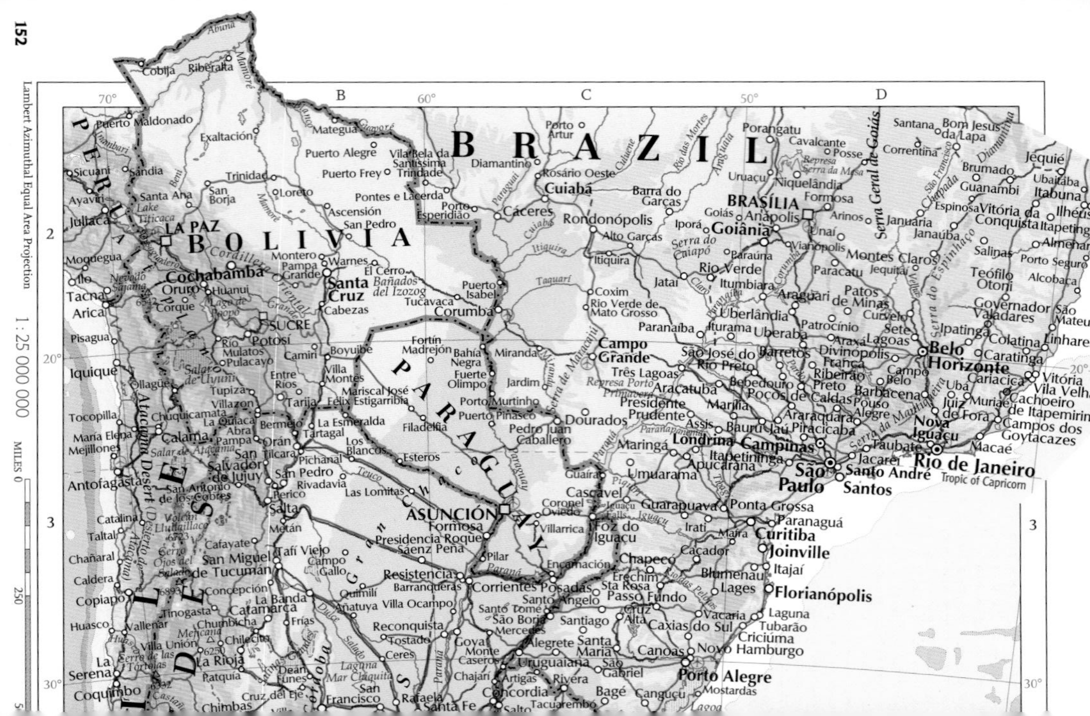

Lambert Azimuthal Equal Area Projection   1 : 25 000 000   MILES 0   250

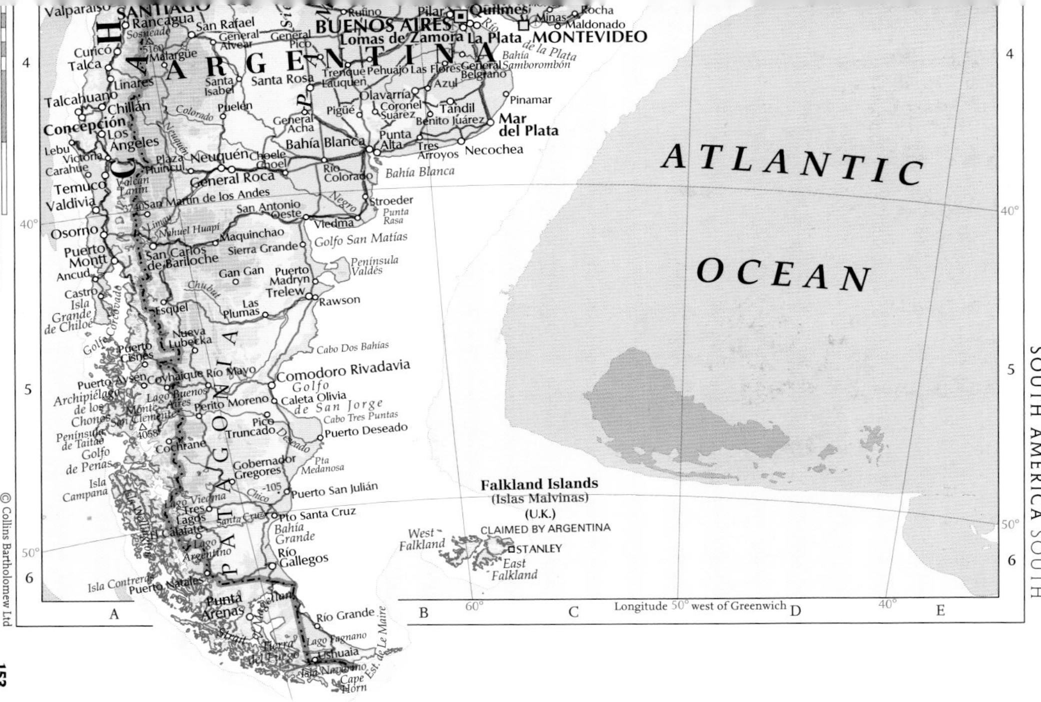

ATLANTIC

OCEAN

Falkland Islands
(Islas Malvinas)
(U.K.)
CLAIMED BY ARGENTINA

West
Falkland

STANLEY

East
Falkland

Longitude 50° west of Greenwich

Pinamar

Mar
del Plata

Necochea

Arroyo

Tres

Azul

Benito Juárez

Tandil

Coronel

Pigüé

Olavarría

Punta Alta

Bahía Blanca

Coronel Suárez

Tornquist

Pehuajó

Carhué

Las Flores

Lomas de Zamora la Plata MONTEVIDEO

BUENOS AIRES

Pergamino

Rosario

Plata del Plata

Sombrerón

Maldonado

Rocha

Quilmes

Bahía Blanca

Santa Rosa

General
Acha

General Roca

Viedma

Río Negro

Colorado

Carmen de Patagones

San Antonio
Oeste

Sierra Grande

Golfo San Matías

Península
Valdés

Punta
Rosa

Puerto
Madryn

Rawson

Trelew

Cabo Dos Bahías

Comodoro Rivadavia

Golfo
San Jorge

Caleta Olivia

Cabo Tres Puntas

Puerto Deseado

Gobernador
Gregores

Río
Chico

Puerto San Julián

Puerto Santa Cruz

Río Santa Cruz

Río Gallegos

Río Grande

Punta Arenas

PATAGONIA

ARGENTINA

San Rafael

Aconcagua

General Alvear

Malargüe

Neuquén

Zapala

Plaza Huincul

Cipolletti

Chos Malal

San Carlos de Bariloche

San Martín de los Andes

Junín de los Andes

Esquel

Puerto Moreno

Lago Buenos Aires

Lago Viedma

Lago
Argentino

Río Mayo

SANTIAGO

Valparaíso

Rancagua

Curicó

Talca

Chillán

Talcahuano

Concepción

Los Ángeles

Victoria

Temuco

Valdivia

Osorno

Puerto
Montt

Ancud

Castro

Isla
Grande
de Chiloé

Archipiélago
de los
Chonos

Golfo
de Penas

Isla
Campana

Puerto Natales

Isla Contreras

Lebu

Cabo
de Hornos

Est. de Le Maire

© Collins Bartholomew Ltd

250   500   750 KILOMETRES

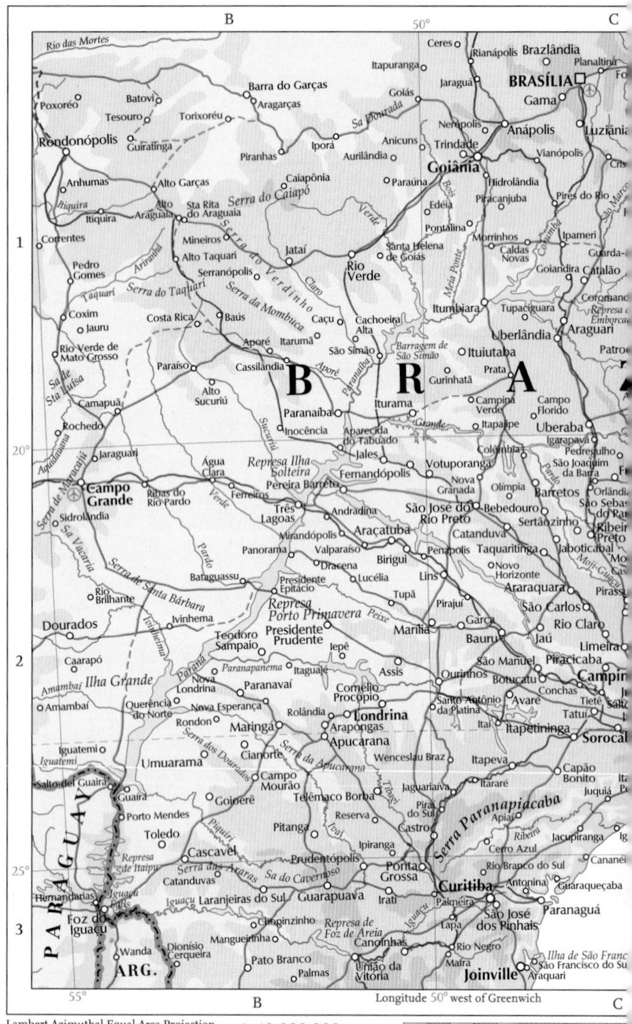

Lambert Azimuthal Equal Area Projection 1 : 10 000 000 MILES 0 100

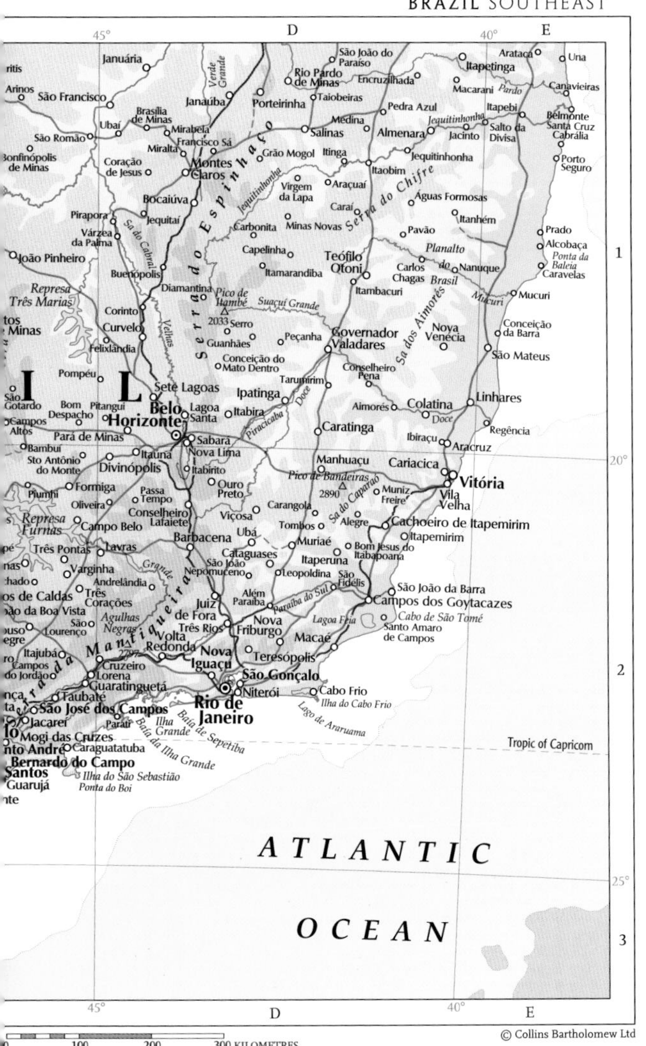

ATLANTIC

OCEAN

Tropic of Capricorn

45° D 40° E

0 100 200 300 KILOMETRES

© Collins Bartholomew Ltd

155

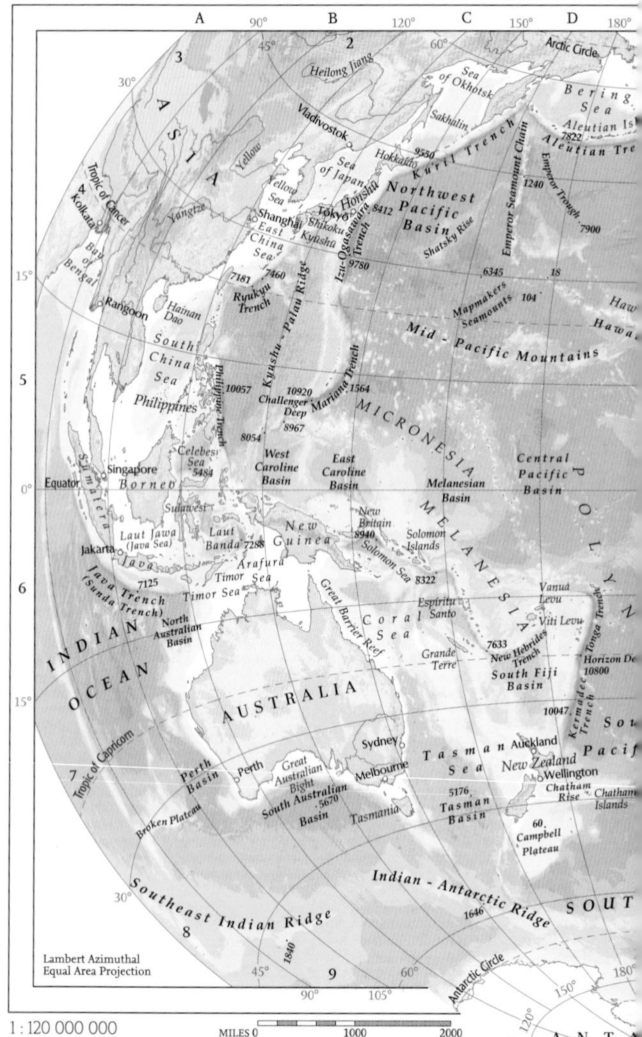

ASIA

Heilong Jiang

Vladivostok

Sea of Okhotsk

Sakhalin

Arctic Circle

Bering Sea

Aleutian Is

Aleutian Tre

Yellow

Yangtze

Kolkata

Bay of Bengal

Rangoon

Hainan Dao

Hokkaido

Honshu

Sea of Japan

Yellow Sea

Shanghai

East China Sea

Tokyo

Kyushu

Ryukyu Trench

South China Sea

Philippines

Philippine Trench

Kyushu–Palau Ridge

Izu-Ogasawara Trench

Mariana Trench

Challenger Deep

Northwest Pacific Basin

Shatsky Rise

Emperor Seamount Chain

Kuril Trench

9550

8412

9780

7181

7460

10057

10920

8054

8967

1564

Mapmakers Seamounts

Mid–Pacific Mountains

6345

104

18

1240

Kuril Trench

7900

7822

Hawa

Hawa

MICRONESIA

West Caroline Basin

East Caroline Basin

Celebes Sea

5484

Singapore

Borneo

Sulawesi

Equator

Sumatra

Melanesian Basin

Central Pacific Basin

POLY

Jakarta

Laut Jawa (Java Sea)

Java

Laut Banda

7288

Arafura Sea

Timor Sea

New Guinea

New Britain

8940

Solomon Sea

Solomon Islands

8322

MELANESIA

Espiritu Santo

Vanua Levu

Viti Levu

Tonga Trench

Java Trench (Sunda Trench)

7125

North Australian Basin

Timor Sea

Great Barrier Reef

Coral Sea

Grande Terre

New Hebrides Trench

7633

South Fiji Basin

Horizon De

10800

INDIAN OCEAN

AUSTRALIA

10047

Perth Basin

Perth

Great Australian Bight

South Australian Basin

5670

Melbourne

Sydney

Tasman Sea

5176

Tasman Basin

Auckland

New Zealand

Wellington

Chatham Rise

Chatham Islands

Pacif

Sou

Broken Plateau

Tasmania

60

Campbell Plateau

Tropic of Capricorn

Southeast Indian Ridge

1356

Indian–Antarctic Ridge

1646

SOUT

Antarctic Circle

ANTA

Lambert Azimuthal
Equal Area Projection

1 : 120 000 000

MILES 0   1000   2000

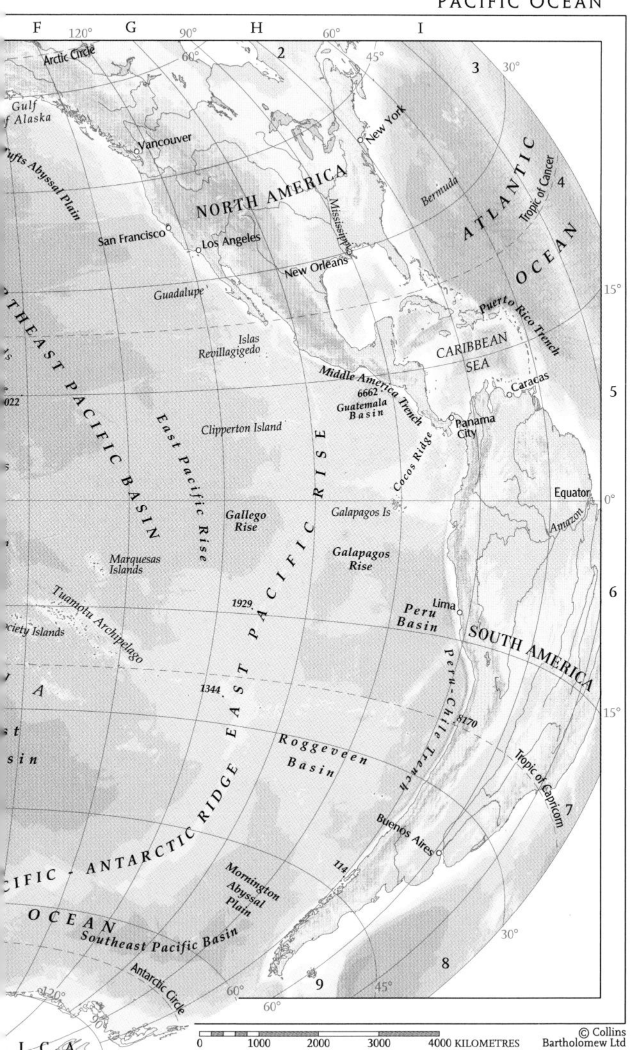

F   120°   G   90°   H   60°   I

Arctic Circle

60°   45°   2   3   30°

Gulf
of Alaska

rufts Abyssal Plain   Vancouver   New York

NORTH AMERICA   Bermuda   4   Tropic of Cancer

San Francisco   Los Angeles   A T L A N T I C   15°

Guadalupe   New Orleans   O C E A N

Islas
Revillagigedo   Middle America Trench   CARIBBEAN
SEA

THEAST PACIFIC BASIN   6662   Caracas   5

022   East Pacific Rise   Clipperton Island   Guatemala
Basin   Panama
City

Cocos Ridge

Gallego
Rise   Galapagos Is   Equator   0°

Marquesas
Islands   Galapagos
Rise   Amazon

1929   Lima   6

Tuamota Archipelago   Peru
Basin   SOUTH AMERICA

ciety Islands   EAST   PACIFIC   RISE   15°

J   A

1344   Peru-Chile Trench   8170

st   Roggeveen
Basin   Tropic of Capricorn

s i n

CIFIC - ANTARCTIC RIDGE   114   Buenos Aires   7

Mornington
Abyssal
Plain

OCEAN   Southeast Pacific Basin   30°

Antarctic Circle

120°   60°   9   8   45°   60°

I   C   A

0   1000   2000   3000   4000 KILOMETRES

© Collins
Bartholomew Ltd   **157**

A 120° 90° B 60° C 30° D E 30° F 60°

Arctic Circle

Greenland

Davis Strait

Hudson Bay

Iceland

Norwegian Basin

Norwegian Sea

Baltic Sea

NORTH AMERICA

45°

Labrador Sea

Reykjanes Ridge

Iceland Basin

Rockall Bank

British Isles

North Sea

London

EUROPE

St Lawrence

Newfoundland

St John's

Grand Banks of Newfoundland

Celtic Shelf 38

2

30°

New York

4556

4938

5943

Lisbon

Mediterranean Sea

5121

Algiers

Bermuda

Azores

Monaco Basin

New Orleans

Tropic of Cancer

3

Nares Deep

Sargasso Sea

5508

Greater Antilles

Cayman Trench

7535

Milwaukee Deep

8605 Deep

Puerto Rico Trench

Canary Is.

5491

Canary Is.

6690

AFRICA

MID-ATLANTIC RIDGE

Caribbean Sea

5523

Lesser Antilles

Panama City

Caracas

4

Cape Verde

Cape Verde Basin

Dakar

Niger

Lagos

Guiana Basin

Amazon Cone

Equator

Amazon

0°

Sierra Leone Basin

Gulf of Guinea

5212

Guinea Basin

5

Lima

SOUTH AMERICA

Ascension

5391

Luanda

Brazil Basin

St Helena

Angola Basin

MID-ATLANTIC RIDGE

6

Tropic of Capricorn

Paraná

Rio de Janeiro

5460

Walvis Ridge

24

Orange Cone

Oran

Rio Grande Rise

Buenos Aires

30°

Tristan da Cunha

Cape of Good Hope

Cape Basin

5520

Cape Tow

Agulhas Basin

619

7

Argentine Basin

6681

Falkland Islands

1530

Atlantic-Indian Ridge

PACIFIC OCEAN

Cape Horn

Drake Passage

Scotia Ridge

South Georgia

Scotia Sea

8325

South Sandwich Trench

Antarctic Peninsula

Antarctic Circle

5750

Atlantic-Indian Antarctic Basin

8

90° 60° 30° 0° 30°

60°

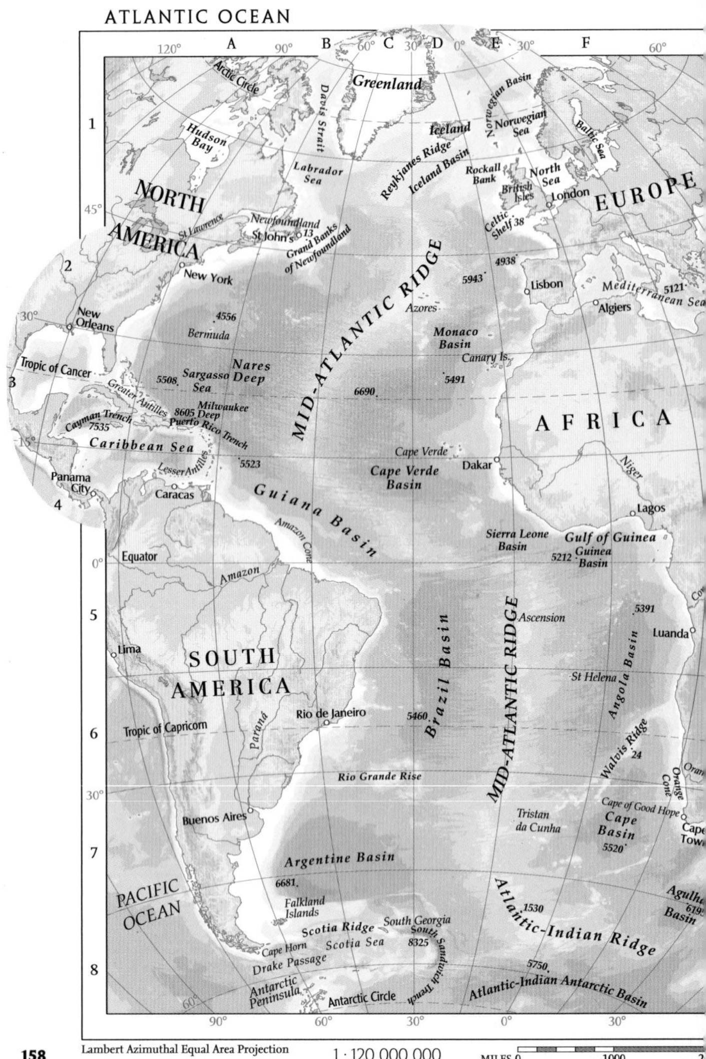

Lambert Azimuthal Equal Area Projection

1 : 120 000 000

MILES 0   1000

2

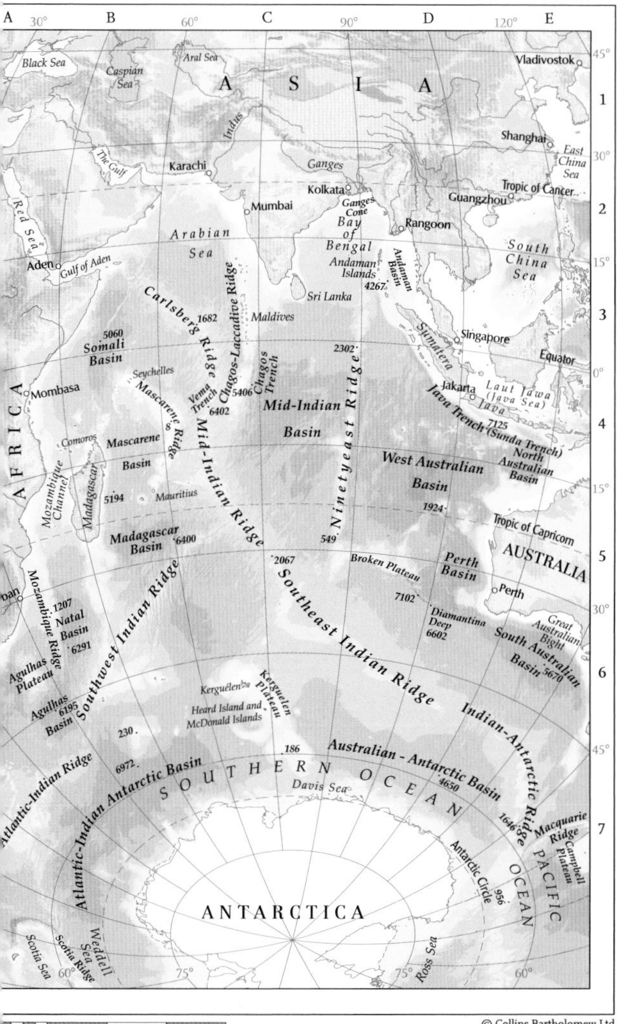

| A | 30° | B | 60° | C | 90° | D | 120° | E |

Black Sea
Caspian Sea
Aral Sea
Vladivostok
45°
1
ASIA
30°
Shanghai
East China Sea
The Gulf
Indus
Karachi
Ganges
Tropic of Cancer
Kolkata
Guangzhou
Mumbai
Ganges Cone
2
Bay of Bengal
Rangoon
Aden
Gulf of Aden
Arabian Sea
South China Sea
Andaman Islands
15°
4267·
Andaman Basin
Sri Lanka
Red Sea
Carlsberg Ridge
1682·
Maldives
3
Sumatra
5060·
Somali Basin
Chagos-Laccadive Ridge
2302·
Singapore
Jakarta
Laut Jawa (Java Sea)
Equator
Mombasa
Seychelles
Mascarene Ridge
Vema Trench
5406·
Chagos Trench
Mid-Indian Basin
Ninetyeast Ridge
Java Trench (Sunda Trench)
7125
Java
North Australian Basin
4
AFRICA
6402·
Mid-Indian Ridge
Comoros
Mascarene Basin
West Australian Basin
Mozambique Channel
5194·
Madagascar
Mauritius
1924·
Tropic of Capricorn
15°
AUSTRALIA
Madagascar Basin
6400·
549·
Broken Plateau
Perth Basin
Perth
5
2067·
Southeast Indian Ridge
7102·
Diamantina Deep 6602·
South Australian Basin
Great Australian Bight
5670·
Dan
1207·
Natal Basin
6291·
Mozambique Ridge
Agulhas Plateau
30°
Agulhas Basin
6195·
Southwest Indian Ridge
Kerguelen Plateau
Kerguelen
Indian-Antarctic Ridge
6
Heard Island and McDonald Islands
186·
Australian - Antarctic Basin
4650·
Macquarie Ridge
Atlantic-Indian Ridge
230·
6972·
Atlantic Indian Antarctic Basin
SOUTHERN OCEAN
Davis Sea
1548·
PACIFIC
Campbell Plateau
45°
OCEAN
7
Scotia Sea
Weddell Sea
956·
Antarctic Circle
Ross Sea
60°
ANTARCTICA
75°
75°
60°

© Collins Bartholomew Ltd

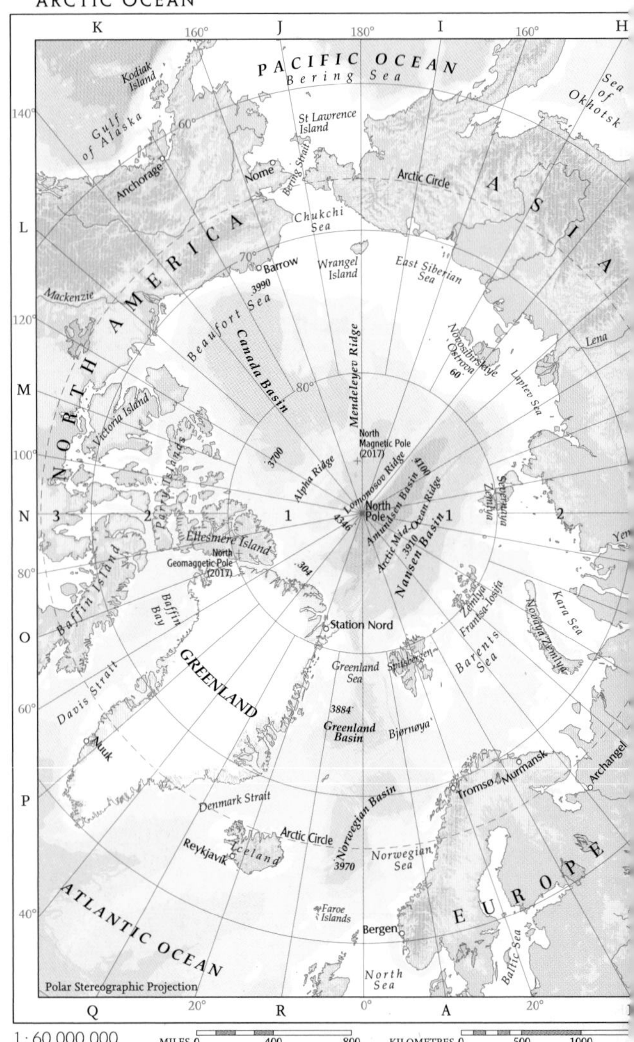

PACIFIC OCEAN
Bering Sea
Sea of Okhotsk
Kodiak Island
Gulf of Alaska
Anchorage
Nome
St Lawrence Island
Bering Strait
Arctic Circle
ASIA
Chukchi Sea
NORTH AMERICA
Barrow
Wrangel Island
East Siberian Sea
Mackenzie
Beaufort Sea
3990
Canada Basin
Mendeleyev Ridge
Novosibirskiye Ostrova
Lena
Laptev Sea
Victoria Island
North Magnetic Pole (2017)
3700
Alpha Ridge
Lomonosov Ridge
4100
Parry Islands
North Pole
Amundsen Basin
Arctic Mid-Ocean Ridge
Severnaya Zemlya
4346
3910
Nansen Basin
Ellesmere Island
North Geomagnetic Pole (2017)
Baffin Island
Baffin Bay
304
Zemlya Frantsa-Iosifa
Novaya Zemlya
Kara Sea
Station Nord
GREENLAND
Davis Strait
Greenland Sea
Spitsbergen
Barents Sea
3884
Greenland Basin
Bjørnøya
Nuuk
Murmansk
Archangel
Tromsø
Norwegian Basin
Denmark Strait
Arctic Circle
Reykjavik
Iceland
3970
Norwegian Sea
EUROPE
ATLANTIC OCEAN
Faroe Islands
Bergen
Baltic Sea
North Sea
Polar Stereographic Projection

1 : 60 000 000

MILES 0 400 800 KILOMETRES 0 500 1000

he index includes all names shown on the
aps in the Atlas of the World. Names are
eferenced by page number and by a grid
eference. The grid reference correlates to
e alphanumeric values which appear within
ch map frame. Each entry also includes the
ountry or geographical area in which the
ature is located. Entries relating to names
ppearing on insets are indicated by a small
ox symbol: □, followed by a grid reference if
e inset has its own alphanumeric values.

ame forms are as they appear on the maps,
ith additional alternative names or name
orms included as cross-references which
efer the user to the entry for the map form
f the name. Names beginning with Mc or
ac are alphabetized exactly as they appear.
he terms Saint, Sainte, etc., are abbreviated
 St, Ste, etc., but alphabetized as if in the
ll form.

Names of physical features beginning with
generic, geographical terms are permuted –
the descriptive term is placed after the main
part of the name. For example, Lake Superior
is indexed as Superior, Lake; Mount Everest
as Everest, Mount. This policy is applied to
all languages.

Entries, other than those for towns and cities,
include a descriptor indicating the type of
geographical feature. Descriptors are not
included where the type of feature is implicit
in the name itself.

Administrative divisions are included to
differentiate entries of the same name and
feature type within the one country. In such
cases, duplicate names are alphabetized in
order of administrative division. Additional
qualifiers are also included for names within
selected geographical areas.

NDEX ABBREVIATIONS

lmin. div.	administrative division	for.	forest	plat.	plateau
fgh.	Afghanistan	Fr.	French	P.N.G.	Papua New Guinea
lg.	Algeria	g.	gulf		
rg.	Argentina	Ger.	Germany	Pol.	Poland
ustr.	Australia	Guat.	Guatemala	Port.	Portugal
t. reg.	autonomous region	h.	hill	prov.	province
zer.	Azerbaijan	hd	head	r.	river
	bay	Hond.	Honduras	reg.	region
angl.	Bangladesh	imp. l.	impermanent lake	resr.	reservoir
ol.	Bolivia	Indon.	Indonesia	S.	South
os. & Herz.	Bosnia and Herzegovina	i.	island	str.	strait
		is	Islands	Switz.	Switzerland
ulg.	Bulgaria	isth.	isthmus	Tajik.	Tajikistan
	cape	Kazakh.	Kazakhstan	Tanz.	Tanzania
an.	Canada	Kyrg.	Kyrgyzstan	terr.	territory
.A.R.	Central African Republic	lag.	lagoon	Thai.	Thailand
		Lith.	Lithuania	Trin. and Tob.	Trinidad and Tobago
han.	channel	Lux.	Luxembourg		
ol.	Colombia	Madag.	Madagascar	Turkm.	Turkmenistan
em. Rep.	Democratic	Maur.	Mauritania	U.A.E.	United Arab Emirates
ongo	Republic of the Congo	Mex.	Mexico	U.K.	United Kingdom
epr.	depression	Moz.	Mozambique	Ukr.	Ukraine
es.	desert	mt.	mountain	Uru.	Uruguay
sp. terr.	disputed territory	mun.	municipality	U.S.A.	United States of America
om. Rep.	Dominican Republic	N.	North		
		Neth.	Netherlands	Uzbek.	Uzbekistan
sc.	escarpment	Nic.	Nicaragua	val.	valley
st.	estuary	N.Z.	New Zealand	Venez.	Venezuela
th.	Ethiopia	Pak.	Pakistan	vol.	volcano
in.	Finland	Para.	Paraguay		
		pen.	peninsula		
		Phil.	Philippines		

1

128 B2 **100 Mile House** Can.

A

93 □E4 **Aabenraa** Denmark
93 E4 **Aabenraa** Denmark
100 C2 **Aachen** Ger.
93 E4 **Aalborg** Denmark
100 B2 **Aalst** Belgium
93 F4 **Aarhus** Denmark
100 B2 **Aarschot** Belgium
68 C2 **Aba** China
115 C4 **Aba** Nigeria
81 C2 **Ābādān** Iran
81 D2 **Ābādeh** Iran
114 B1 **Abadla** Alg.
115 C4 **Abakaliki** Nigeria
83 H3 **Abakan** Russia
150 A3 **Abancay** Peru
81 D2 **Abarkūh** Iran
66 D2 **Abashiri** Japan
117 B4 **Abaya, Lake** Eth.
Ābay Wenz *r.* Eth./Sudan *see* **Blue Nile**
82 G3 **Abaza** Russia
108 A2 **Abbasanta** *Sardinia* Italy
104 C1 **Abbeville** France
142 B3 **Abbeville** U.S.A.
55 O2 **Abbot Ice Shelf** Antarctica
74 B1 **Abbottabad** Pak.
115 E3 **Abéché** Chad
114 B4 **Abengourou** Côte d'Ivoire
114 C4 **Abeokuta** Nigeria
99 A2 **Aberaeron** U.K.
96 C2 **Aberchirder** U.K.
99 B3 **Aberdare** U.K.
99 A2 **Aberdaron** U.K.
122 B3 **Aberdeen** S. Africa
96 C2 **Aberdeen** U.K.
141 D3 **Aberdeen** *MD* U.S.A.
137 D1 **Aberdeen** *SD* U.S.A.
134 B1 **Aberdeen** *WA* U.S.A.
129 E1 **Aberdeen Lake** Can.
134 B2 **Abert, Lake** U.S.A.
99 A2 **Aberystwyth** U.K.
86 F2 **Abez'** Russia
78 B3 **Abhā** Saudi Arabia
Abiad, Bahr el *r.* Sudan/Uganda *see* **White Nile**
114 B4 **Abidjan** Côte d'Ivoire
137 D3 **Abilene** *KS* U.S.A.
139 D2 **Abilene** *TX* U.S.A.
99 C3 **Abingdon** U.K.
91 D3 **Abinsk** Russia
130 B2 **Abitibi, Lake** Can.
81 C1 **Abkhazia** *disp. terr.* Georgia
Åbo Fin. *see* **Turku**
74 B1 **Abohar** India
114 C4 **Abomey** Benin
60 A1 **Abongabong, Gunung** *mt.* Indon.
118 B2 **Abong Mbang** Cameroon
64 A2 **Aborlan** Phil.
115 D3 **Abou Déia** Chad
106 B2 **Abrantes** Port.
152 B3 **Abra Pampa** Arg.
136 A2 **Absaroka Range** *mts* U.S.A.
81 C1 **Abşeron Yarımadası** *pen.* Azer.
78 B3 **Abū 'Arīsh** Saudi Arabia
79 C2 **Abu Dhabi** U.A.E.
116 B3 **Abu Hamed** Sudan
115 C4 **Abuja** Nigeria
81 C2 **Abū Kamāl** Syria
152 B1 **Abunā** *r.* Bol./Brazil
150 B2 **Abunā** Brazil
74 B2 **Abu Road** India
116 B2 **Abū Sunbul** Egypt
117 A3 **Abu Zabad** Sudan
Abū Ẓabī U.A.E. *see* **Abu Dhabi**
117 A4 **Abyei** Sudan
145 B2 **Acambaro** Mex.
106 B1 **A Cañiza** Spain
144 B2 **Acaponeta** Mex.
145 C3 **Acapulco** Mex.
151 D2 **Acará** Brazil
150 B1 **Acarigua** Venez.
145 C3 **Acatlán** Mex.
145 C3 **Acayucán** Mex.
114 B4 **Accra** Ghana
98 B2 **Accrington** U.K.
74 B2 **Achalpur** India
97 A2 **Achill Island** Ireland
101 D1 **Achim** Ger.
96 B2 **Achnasheen** U.K.
91 D2 **Achuyevo** Russia
111 C3 **Acıpayam** Turkey
109 C3 **Acireale** *Sicily* Italy
147 C2 **Acklins Island** Bahamas
153 B4 **Aconcagua, Cerro** *mt.* Arg.
106 B1 **A Coruña** Spain
108 A2 **Acqui Terme** Italy
103 D2 **Ács** Hungary
145 C2 **Actopán** Mex.
139 D2 **Ada** U.S.A.
79 C2 **Adam** Oman
49 J4 **Adamstown** Pitcairn Is
'Adan Yemen *see* **Aden**
80 B2 **Adana** Turkey
111 D2 **Adapazarı** Turkey
Adapazari Turkey *see* **Adapazarı**
108 A1 **Adda** *r.* Italy
78 B2 **Ad Dafīnah** Saudi Arabia
78 B2 **Ad Dahnā'** *des.* Saudi Arabia
78 B2 **Ad Dahnā'** *des.* Saudi Arabia
Ad Dammām Saudi Arabia *see* **Dammam**
78 A2 **Ad Dār al Ḥamrā'** Saudi Arabia
78 B3 **Ad Darb** Saudi Arabia
78 B2 **Ad Dawādimī** Saudi Arabia
Ad Dawḥah Qatar *see* **Doha**
78 B2 **Ad Dilam** Saudi Arabia
116 C2 **Ad Dir'īyah** Saudi Arabia
117 B4 **Addis Ababa** Eth.
81 C2 **Ad Dīwānīyah** Iraq
52 A2 **Adelaide** Austr.
50 C1 **Adelaide River** Austr.
101 D2 **Adelebsen** Ger.
55 J2 **Adélie Land** Antarctica
78 B3 **Aden** Yemen
117 C3 **Aden, Gulf of** Somalia/Yemen
100 C2 **Adenau** Ger.
79 C2 **Adh Dhayd** U.A.E.
59 C3 **Adi** *i.* Indon.
78 A3 **Ādī Ārk'ay** Eth.
116 B3 **Ādīgrat** Eth.
75 B3 **Adilabad** India
141 E2 **Adirondack Mountains** U.S.A.
Ādīs Ābeba Eth. *see* **Addis Ababa**
117 B4 **Ādīs Alem** Eth.
110 C1 **Adjud** Romania
50 B1 **Admiralty Gulf** Austr.
128 A2 **Admiralty Island** U.S.A.
104 B3 **Adour** *r.* France
106 C2 **Adra** Spain
114 B2 **Adrar** Alg.
140 C2 **Adrian** *MI* U.S.A.
139 C1 **Adrian** *TX* U.S.A.
108 B2 **Adriatic Sea** Europe
116 B3 **Ādwa** Eth.
83 K2 **Adycha** *r.* Russia
91 D3 **Adygeysk** Russia
114 B4 **Adzopé** Côte d'Ivoire
111 B3 **Aegean Sea** Greece/Turkey
101 D1 **Aerzen** Ger.
106 B1 **A Estrada** Spain
116 B3 **Afabet** Eritrea
76 C3 **Afghanistan** *country* Asia
78 B2 **'Afīf** Saudi Arabia
80 B2 **Afyonkarahisar** Turkey
115 C3 **Agadez** Niger
114 B1 **Agadir** Morocco
74 B2 **Agar** India
75 D2 **Agartala** India
81 C1 **Ağdam** Azer.
81 C2 **Ağdam (abandoned)** Azer.
105 C3 **Agde** France
104 C3 **Agen** France
122 A2 **Aggeneys** S. Africa
111 C3 **Agia Varvara** Greece
111 B3 **Agios Dimitrios** Greece
111 C3 **Agios Efstratios** *i.* Greece
111 C3 **Agios Nikolaos** Greece
110 B1 **Agnita** Romania
75 B2 **Agra** India
81 C2 **Ağrı** Turkey
Ağrı Dağı *mt.* Turkey *see* **Ararat, Mount**
108 B3 **Agrigento** *Sicily* Italy
111 B3 **Agrinio** Greece
109 B2 **Agropoli** Italy
154 B2 **Água Clara** Brazil
146 B4 **Aguadulce** Panama
144 B2 **Aguanaval** *r.* Mex.
144 B1 **Agua Prieta** Mex.
144 B2 **Aguascalientes** Mex.
155 D1 **Águas Formosas** Brazil
106 B1 **Águeda** Port.
106 C1 **Aguilar de Campoo** Spain
107 C2 **Águilas** Spain
144 B3 **Aguililla** Mex.
122 B3 **Agulhas, Cape** S. Africa
155 D2 **Agulhas Negras** *mt.* Brazil
111 C2 **Ağva** Turkey
115 C2 **Ahaggar** *plat.* Alg.
115 C2 **Ahaggar, Tassili oua-n-** *plat* Alg.
81 C2 **Ahar** Iran
100 C1 **Ahaus** Ger.
81 C2 **Ahlat** Turkey
100 C2 **Ahlen** Ger.
74 B2 **Ahmadabad** India
73 B3 **Ahmadnagar** India
74 B2 **Ahmadpur East** Pak.
74 B1 **Ahmadpur Sial** Pak.
Ahmedabad India *see* **Ahmadabad**
Ahmednagar India *see* **Ahmadnagar**
144 B2 **Ahome** Mex.
79 C2 **Ahram** Iran
101 E1 **Ahrensburg** Ger.
104 C2 **Ahun** France
81 C2 **Ahvāz** Iran
122 A2 **Ai-Ais** Namibia
80 B2 **Aigialousa** Cyprus
111 B3 **Aigio** Greece
143 D2 **Aiken** U.S.A.
97 B1 **Ailt an Chorráin** Ireland
155 D1 **Aimorés** Brazil
155 D1 **Aimorés, Serra dos** *hills* Bra
114 B2 **'Aïn Ben Tili** Maur.
107 D2 **Aïn Defla** Alg.
114 B1 **Aïn Sefra** Alg.
136 D2 **Ainsworth** U.S.A.
Aintab Turkey *see* **Gaziantep**
107 D2 **Aïn Taya** Alg.
107 D2 **Aïn Tédélès** Alg.
115 C3 **Aïr, Massif de l'** *mts* Niger

60 A1 **Airbangis** Indon.
128 C2 **Airdrie** Can.
104 B3 **Aire-sur-l'Adour** France
101 E3 **Aisch** *r.* Ger.
128 A1 **Aishihik Lake** Can.
100 A3 **Aisne** *r.* France
59 D3 **Aitape** P.N.G.
110 B1 **Aiud** Romania
105 D3 **Aix-en-Provence** France
105 D2 **Aix-les-Bains** France
62 A1 **Aizawl** India
88 C2 **Aizkraukle** Latvia
67 C3 **Aizuwakamatsu** Japan
105 D3 **Ajaccio** *Corsica* France
115 E1 **Ajdābiyā** Libya
115 C2 **Ajjer, Tassili n'** *plat.* Alg.
74 B2 **Ajmer** India
138 A2 **Ajo** U.S.A.
77 D2 **Akadyr** Kazakh.
87 E3 **Akbulak** Russia
80 B2 **Akçakale** Turkey
80 B2 **Akdağmadeni** Turkey
88 A2 **Åkersberga** Sweden
118 C2 **Aketi** Dem. Rep. Congo
87 D4 **Akhalkalaki** Georgia
79 C2 **Akhḑar, Jabal** *mts* Oman
111 C3 **Akhisar** Turkey
87 D4 **Akhtubinsk** Russia
130 B1 **Akimiski Island** Can.
66 D3 **Akita** Japan
114 A3 **Akjoujt** Maur.
77 D1 **Akkol'** Kazakh.
88 B2 **Akmenrags** *pt* Latvia
Akmola Kazakh. *see* **Astana**
117 B4 **Akobo** South Sudan
74 B2 **Akola** India
78 A3 **Akordat** Eritrea
127 G2 **Akpatok Island** Can.
92 □A3 **Akranes** Iceland
140 C2 **Akron** U.S.A.
75 B1 **Aksai Chin** *terr.* Asia
80 B2 **Aksaray** Turkey
76 B1 **Aksay** Kazakh.
91 D2 **Aksay** Russia
80 B2 **Akşehir** Turkey
76 C2 **Akshiganak** Kazakh.
77 E2 **Aksu** China
78 A3 **Āksum** Eth.
76 B2 **Aktau** Kazakh.
76 B1 **Aktobe** Kazakh.
77 D2 **Aktogay** Kazakh.
88 C3 **Aktsyabrski** Belarus
115 C4 **Akure** Nigeria
92 □B2 **Akureyri** Iceland
62 A1 **Akyab** Myanmar
142 C2 **Alabama** *r.* U.S.A.
142 C2 **Alabama** *state* U.S.A.
Alacant Spain *see* **Alicante/Alacant**
111 C3 **Alaçatı** Turkey
81 C1 **Alagir** Russia
151 E3 **Alagoinhas** Brazil
107 C1 **Alagón** Spain
79 B2 **Al Aḩmadī** Kuwait
77 E2 **Alakol', Ozero** *salt l.* Kazakh.
92 J2 **Alakurtti** Russia
78 B3 **Al 'Alayyah** Saudi Arabia
80 A2 **Al 'Āmirīyah** Egypt
135 C3 **Alamo** U.S.A.
138 B2 **Alamogordo** U.S.A.
144 A2 **Alamos** *Sonora* Mex.
144 B2 **Alamos** *Sonora* Mex.
144 B2 **Alamos** *r.* Mex.
136 B3 **Alamosa** U.S.A.
93 G3 **Åland Islands** Fin.
80 B2 **Alanya** Turkey
73 B4 **Alappuzha** India
80 B3 **Al 'Aqabah** Jordan
78 B2 **Al 'Aqīq** Saudi Arabia
107 C2 **Alarcón, Embalse de** *resr* Spain
80 B2 **Al 'Arīsh** Egypt
78 B2 **Al Arţāwīyah** Saudi Arabia
61 C2 **Alas** Indon.
111 C3 **Alaşehir** Turkey
128 A2 **Alaska** *state* U.S.A.
124 F3 **Alaska, Gulf of** U.S.A.
81 C2 **Älät** Azer.
87 D3 **Alatyr'** Russia
150 A2 **Alausí** Ecuador
93 H3 **Alavus** Fin.
52 B2 **Alawoona** Austr.
108 A2 **Alba** Italy
107 C2 **Albacete** Spain
110 B1 **Alba Iulia** Romania
109 C2 **Albania** *country* Europe
50 A3 **Albany** Austr.
130 B1 **Albany** *r.* Can.
143 D2 **Albany** *GA* U.S.A.
141 E2 **Albany** *NY* U.S.A.
134 B2 **Albany** *OR* U.S.A.
Al Başrah Iraq *see* **Basra**
51 D1 **Albatross Bay** Austr.
116 A2 **Al Bawīţī** Egypt
115 E1 **Al Bayḑā'** Libya
78 B3 **Al Bayḑā'** Yemen
143 D1 **Albemarle** U.S.A.
143 E1 **Albemarle Sound** *sea chan.* U.S.A.
108 A2 **Albenga** Italy
51 C2 **Alberga** *watercourse* Austr.
119 D2 **Albert, Lake** Dem. Rep. Congo/Uganda
128 C2 **Alberta** *prov.* Can.
100 B2 **Albert Kanaal** *canal* Belgium
137 E2 **Albert Lea** U.S.A.
104 C3 **Albi** France
78 A2 **Al Bi'r** Saudi Arabia
78 B3 **Al Birk** Saudi Arabia
78 B2 **Al Biyāḑh** *reg.* Saudi Arabia
106 C2 **Alboran Sea** Europe
Alborz, Reshteh-ye *mts* Iran *see* **Elburz Mountains**
106 B2 **Albufeira** Port.
138 B1 **Albuquerque** U.S.A.
79 C2 **Al Buraymī** Oman
53 C3 **Albury** Austr.
106 B2 **Alcácer do Sal** Port.
106 C1 **Alcalá de Henares** Spain
106 C2 **Alcalá la Real** Spain
108 B3 **Alcamo** *Sicily* Italy
107 C1 **Alcañiz** Spain
106 B2 **Alcántara** Spain
106 C2 **Alcaraz** Spain
106 C2 **Alcaraz, Sierra de** *mts* Spain
106 C2 **Alcaudete** Spain
106 C2 **Alcázar de San Juan** Spain
91 D2 **Alchevs'k** Ukr.
155 E1 **Alcobaça** Brazil
Alcoi Spain *see* **Alcoy/Alcoi**
107 C2 **Alcoy/Alcoi** Spain
107 D2 **Alcúdia** Spain
145 C2 **Aldama** Mex.
83 J3 **Aldan** Russia
83 J2 **Aldan** *r.* Russia
95 C4 **Alderney** *i.* Channel Is
114 A3 **Aleg** Maur.
155 D2 **Alegre** Brazil
152 C3 **Alegrete** Brazil
83 K3 **Aleksandrovsk-Sakhalinskiy** Russia
91 D1 **Alekseyevka** *Belgorodskaya Oblast'* Russia
91 D1 **Alekseyevka** *Belgorodskaya Oblast'* Russia
89 E3 **Aleksin** Russia
109 D2 **Aleksinac** Serbia
118 B3 **Alèmbé** Gabon
155 D2 **Além Paraíba** Brazil
93 F3 **Ålen** Norway
104 C2 **Alençon** France
80 B2 **Aleppo** Syria
150 A3 **Alerta** Peru
128 B2 **Alert Bay** Can.
105 C3 **Alès** France
110 B1 **Aleşd** Romania
108 A2 **Alessandria** Italy
93 E3 **Ålesund** Norway
124 C3 **Aleutian Islands** U.S.A.
83 L3 **Alevina, Mys** *c.* Russia
128 A2 **Alexander Archipelago** *is* U.S.A.
122 A2 **Alexander Bay** S. Africa
142 C2 **Alexander City** U.S.A.
55 O2 **Alexander Island** Antarctica
53 C3 **Alexandra** Austr.
54 A3 **Alexandra** N.Z.
111 B2 **Alexandreia** Greece
Alexandretta Turkey *see* **İskenderun**
116 A1 **Alexandria** Egypt
110 C2 **Alexandria** Romania
123 C3 **Alexandria** S. Africa
142 B2 **Alexandria** *LA* U.S.A.
137 D1 **Alexandria** *MN* U.S.A.
141 D3 **Alexandria** *VA* U.S.A.
52 A3 **Alexandrina, Lake** Austr.
111 C2 **Alexandroupoli** Greece
131 E1 **Alexis** *r.* Can.
128 B2 **Alexis Creek** Can.
77 E1 **Aleysk** Russia
107 C1 **Alfaro** Spain
81 C3 **Al Fāw** Iraq
101 D2 **Alfeld (Leine)** Ger.
155 C2 **Alfenas** Brazil
Al Fujayrah U.A.E. *see* **Fujairah**
Al Furāt *r.* Iraq/Syria *see* **Euphrates**
106 B2 **Algeciras** Spain
107 C2 **Algemesí** Spain
78 A3 **Algena** Eritrea
Alger Alg. *see* **Algiers**
114 C2 **Algeria** *country* Africa
Al Ghardaqah Egypt *see* **Hurghada**
79 C3 **Al Ghayḑah** Yemen
108 A2 **Alghero** *Sardinia* Italy
79 B2 **Al Ghwaybiyah** Saudi Arabia
115 C1 **Algiers** Alg.
123 C3 **Algoa Bay** S. Africa
137 E2 **Algona** U.S.A.
106 C1 **Algorta** Spain
79 C2 **Al Ḩajar al Gharbī** *mts* Oman
107 C2 **Alhama de Murcia** Spain
80 A2 **Al Ḩammām** Egypt
78 B2 **Al Ḩanākīyah** Saudi Arabia
81 C2 **Al Ḩasakah** Syria
81 C2 **Al Ḩayy** Iraq
79 C3 **Al Ḩibāk** *des.* Saudi Arabia
78 B2 **Al Ḩillah** Saudi Arabia
79 B2 **Al Ḩinnāh** Saudi Arabia
Al Ḩudaydah Yemen *see* **Hodeidah**
79 B2 **Al Hufūf** Saudi Arabia
115 D2 **Al Ḩulayq al Kabīr** *hills* Libya
79 C2 **'Alīābād** Iran
111 C3 **Aliağa** Turkey
111 B2 **Aliakmonas** *r.* Greece
107 C2 **Alicante/Alacant** Spain
139 D3 **Alice** U.S.A.
109 C3 **Alice, Punta** *pt* Italy
51 C2 **Alice Springs** Austr.
75 B2 **Aligarh** India
81 C2 **Alīgūdarz** Iran

69 E1 **Alihe** China
118 B3 **Alima** *r.* Congo
111 C3 **Aliova** *r.* Turkey
117 C3 **Ali Sabieh** Djibouti
Al Iskandarīyah Egypt *see* **Alexandria**
116 B1 **Al Ismā'īlīyah** Egypt
123 C3 **Aliwal North** S. Africa
115 E2 **Al Jaghbūb** Libya
78 B2 **Al Jahrah** Kuwait
115 D1 **Al Jawsh** Libya
106 B2 **Aljezur** Port.
Al Jīzah Egypt *see* **Giza**
79 B2 **Al Jubayl** Saudi Arabia
79 C2 **Al Jumaylīyah** Qatar
78 B2 **Al Junaynah** Saudi Arabia
106 B2 **Aljustrel** Port.
78 B2 **Al Kahfah** Saudi Arabia
79 C2 **Al Kāmil** Oman
80 B2 **Al Karak** Jordan
79 C2 **Al Khābūrah** Oman
78 B2 **Al Khamāsīn** Saudi Arabia
116 B2 **Al Khārijah** Egypt
79 C2 **Al Khaşab** Oman
78 B3 **Al Khawkhah** Yemen
79 C2 **Al Khawr** Qatar
115 D1 **Al Khums** Libya
79 B2 **Al Khunn** Saudi Arabia
79 C2 **Al Kir'ānah** Qatar
100 B1 **Alkmaar** Neth.
115 E2 **Al Kufrah** Libya
81 C2 **Al Kūt** Iraq
Al Kuwayt Kuwait *see* **Kuwait**
Al Lādhiqīyah Syria *see* **Latakia**
75 C2 **Allahabad** India
83 K2 **Allakh-Yun'** Russia
141 D2 **Allegheny** *r.* U.S.A.
140 C3 **Allegheny Mountains** U.S.A.
97 B1 **Allen, Lough** *l.* Ireland
145 B2 **Allende** *Coahuila* Mex.
145 B2 **Allende** *Nuevo León* Mex.
141 D2 **Allentown** U.S.A.
101 D1 **Aller** *r.* Ger.
136 C2 **Alliance** *NE* U.S.A.
140 C2 **Alliance** *OH* U.S.A.
78 B2 **Al Līth** Saudi Arabia
96 C2 **Alloa** U.K.
131 C2 **Alma** Can.
Alma-Ata Kazakh. *see* **Almaty**
106 B2 **Almada** Port.
106 C2 **Almadén** Spain
Al Madīnah Saudi Arabia *see* **Medina**
116 B1 **Al Mafraq** Jordan
78 B3 **Al Maḩwīt** Yemen
78 B2 **Al Majma'ah** Saudi Arabia
135 B2 **Almanor, Lake** U.S.A.
107 C2 **Almansa** Spain
80 B2 **Al Manşūrah** Egypt
79 C2 **Al Mariyyah** U.A.E.
115 E1 **Al Marj** Libya
77 D2 **Almaty** Kazakh.
106 C1 **Almazán** Spain
151 C2 **Almeirim** Brazil
100 C1 **Almelo** Neth.
155 D1 **Almenara** Brazil
106 B1 **Almendra, Embalse de** *resr* Spain
106 B2 **Almendralejo** Spain
106 C2 **Almería** Spain
106 C2 **Almería, Golfo de** *b.* Spain
87 E3 **Al'met'yevsk** Russia
78 B2 **Al Mindak** Saudi Arabia
116 B2 **Al Minyā** Egypt
79 B2 **Al Mish'āb** Saudi Arabia
106 B2 **Almodôvar** Port.
106 B2 **Almonte** Spain
75 B2 **Almora** India
79 B2 **Al Mubarrez** Saudi Arabia
79 C2 **Al Muḑaibī** Oman
80 B3 **Al Mudawwarah** Jordan
Al Mukallā Yemen *see* **Mukalla**
Al Mukhā Yemen *see* **Mocha**
106 C2 **Almuñécar** Spain
78 A2 **Al Muwayliḩ** Saudi Arabia
111 B3 **Almyros** Greece
96 B2 **Alness** U.K.
98 C1 **Alnwick** U.K.
49 G4 **Alofi** Niue
111 B3 **Alonnisos** *i.* Greece
59 C3 **Alor** *i.* Indon.
59 C3 **Alor, Kepulauan** *is* Indon.
60 B1 **Alor Star** Malaysia
Alost Belgium *see* **Aalst**
86 C2 **Alozero (abandoned)** Russia
140 C1 **Alpena** U.S.A.
139 C2 **Alpine** U.S.A.
105 D2 **Alps** *mts* Europe
79 B3 **Al Qa'āmīyāt** *reg.* Saudi Arabia
115 D1 **Al Qaddāḩīyah** Libya
Al Qāhirah Egypt *see* **Cairo**
78 B2 **Al Qā'īyah** Saudi Arabia
81 C2 **Al Qāmishlī** Syria
80 B2 **Al Qaryatayn** Syria
79 B3 **Al Qaţn** Yemen
106 B2 **Alqueva, Barragem de** *resr* Port.
80 B2 **Al Qunayţirah (abandoned)** Syria
78 B3 **Al Qunfidhah** Saudi Arabia
116 B2 **Al Quşayr** Egypt
78 B2 **Al Quwayīyah** Saudi Arabia
101 D2 **Alsfeld** Ger.
92 H2 **Alta** Norway
92 H2 **Altaelva** *r.* Norway
68 B1 **Altai Mountains** Asia
143 D2 **Altamaha** *r.* U.S.A.
151 C2 **Altamira** Brazil
109 C2 **Altamura** Italy
68 B1 **Altay** China
68 C1 **Altay** Mongolia
105 D2 **Altdorf** Switz.
107 C2 **Altea** Spain
101 F2 **Altenburg** Ger.
100 C2 **Altenkirchen (Westerwald)** Ger.
111 C3 **Altınoluk** Turkey
111 D3 **Altıntaş** Turkey
152 B2 **Altiplano** *plain* Bol.
154 B1 **Alto Araguaia** Brazil
154 B1 **Alto Garças** Brazil
121 C2 **Alto Molócuè** Moz.
129 E3 **Altona** Can.
141 D2 **Altoona** U.S.A.
154 B1 **Alto Sucuriú** Brazil
154 B1 **Alto Taquari** Brazil
102 C2 **Altötting** Ger.
68 B2 **Altun Shan** *mts* China
134 B2 **Alturas** U.S.A.
139 D2 **Altus** U.S.A.
88 C2 **Alūksne** Latvia
78 A2 **Al 'Ulā** Saudi Arabia
115 D1 **Al 'Uqaylah** Libya
Al Uqşur Egypt *see* **Luxor**
91 C3 **Alushta** Ukr.
139 D1 **Alva** U.S.A.
145 C3 **Alvarado** Mex.
93 F3 **Älvdalen** Sweden
93 F3 **Älvdalen** *val.* Sweden
92 H2 **Älvsbyn** Sweden
78 A2 **Al Wajh** Saudi Arabia
74 B2 **Alwar** India
81 C2 **Al Widyān** *plat.* Iraq/Saudi Arabia
Alxa Youqi China *see* **Ehen Hudag**
Alxa Zuoqi China *see* **Bayan Hot**
51 C1 **Alyangula** Austr.
88 B3 **Alytus** Lith.
136 C1 **Alzada** U.S.A.
100 D3 **Alzey** Ger.
50 C2 **Amadeus, Lake** *imp. l.* Austr.
81 C2 **'Amādīyah/Amêdî** Iraq
127 G2 **Amadjuak Lake** Can.
106 B2 **Amadora** Port.
78 B2 **Amā'ir** Saudi Arabia
93 F4 **Åmål** Sweden
111 B3 **Amaliada** Greece
59 D3 **Amamapare** Indon.
154 A2 **Amambaí** Brazil
154 B2 **Amambaí** *r.* Brazil
69 E3 **Amami-Ō-shima** *i.* Japan
69 E3 **Amami-shotō** *is* Japan
77 C1 **Amankel'dy** Kazakh.
109 C3 **Amantea** Italy
151 C1 **Amapá** Brazil
106 B2 **Amareleja** Port.
139 C1 **Amarillo** U.S.A.
108 B2 **Amaro, Monte** *mt.* Italy
80 B1 **Amasya** Turkey
150 C1 **Amazon** *r.* S. America
151 D1 **Amazon, Mouths of the** Brazi
Amazonas *r.* S. America *see* **Amazon**
74 B1 **Ambala** India
121 □D3 **Ambalavao** Madag.
121 □D2 **Ambanja** Madag.
150 A2 **Ambato** Ecuador
121 □D2 **Ambato Boeny** Madag.
121 □D3 **Ambato Finandrahana** Madag
121 □D2 **Ambatolampy** Madag.
121 □D2 **Ambatondrazaka** Madag.
101 E3 **Amberg** Ger.
146 B3 **Ambergris Caye** *i.* Belize
75 C2 **Ambikapur** India
121 □D2 **Ambilobe** Madag.
98 B1 **Ambleside** U.K.
121 □D3 **Amboasary** Madag.
121 □D3 **Ambohimahasoa** Madag.
59 C3 **Ambon** Indon.
59 C3 **Ambon** *i.* Indon.
121 □D3 **Ambositra** Madag.
121 □D3 **Ambovombe** Madag.
135 C4 **Amboy** U.S.A.
120 A1 **Ambriz** Angola
145 B2 **Amealco** Mex.
144 B2 **Ameca** Mex.
Amêdî Iraq *see* **'Amādīyah/Amêdî**
100 B1 **Ameland** *i.* Neth.
134 D2 **American Falls** U.S.A.
134 D2 **American Falls Reservoir** U.S.A.
135 D2 **American Fork** U.S.A.
49 G3 **American Samoa** *terr.* S. Pacific Ocean
143 D2 **Americus** U.S.A.
100 B1 **Amersfoort** Neth.
55 F2 **Amery Ice Shelf** Antarctica
137 E2 **Ames** U.S.A.
111 B3 **Amfissa** Greece
83 J2 **Amga** Russia
66 C1 **Amgu** Russia
115 C2 **Amguid** Alg.
83 K3 **Amgun'** *r.* Russia
131 D2 **Amherst** Can.
104 C2 **Amiens** France
73 B3 **Amindivi Islands** India
122 A1 **Aminuis** Namibia
74 A2 **Amir Chah** Pak.
129 D2 **Amisk Lake** Can.

139 C3 **Amistad Reservoir** Mex./U.S.A.
98 A2 **Amlwch** U.K.
80 B2 **'Ammān** Jordan
81 D2 **Āmol** Iran
111 C3 **Amorgos** *i.* Greece
142 C2 **Amory** U.S.A.
130 C2 **Amos** Can.
Amoy China *see* **Xiamen**
155 C2 **Amparo** Brazil
107 D1 **Amposta** Spain
75 B2 **Amravati** India
74 B1 **Amritsar** India
100 B1 **Amstelveen** Neth.
100 B1 **Amsterdam** Neth.
103 C2 **Amstetten** Austria
115 E3 **Am Timan** Chad
76 B2 **Amudar'ya** *r.* Asia
126 E1 **Amund Ringnes Island** Can.
126 C2 **Amundsen Gulf** Can.
55 M2 **Amundsen Sea** Antarctica
61 C2 **Amuntai** Indon.
Amur *r.* China *see* **Heilong Jiang**
78 A3 **'Amur, Wadi** *watercourse* Sudan
83 I2 **Anabar** *r.* Russia
83 I2 **Anabarskiy Zaliv** *b.* Russia
134 D1 **Anaconda** U.S.A.
139 D1 **Anadarko** U.S.A.
80 B1 **Anadolu Dağları** *mts* Turkey
83 M2 **Anadyr'** *r.* Russia
145 B2 **Anáhuac** Mex.
60 B1 **Anambas, Kepulauan** *is* Indon.
137 E2 **Anamosa** U.S.A.
80 B2 **Anamur** Turkey
67 B4 **Anan** Japan
73 B3 **Anantapur** India
74 B1 **Anantnag** India
90 B2 **Anan'yiv** Ukr.
91 D3 **Anapa** Russia
154 C1 **Anápolis** Brazil
152 B3 **Añatuya** Arg.
97 B1 **An Baile Thiar** Ireland
65 B2 **Anbyon** N. Korea
104 B2 **Ancenis** France
108 B2 **Ancona** Italy
153 A5 **Ancud** Chile
Anda China *see* **Daqing**
93 E3 **Åndalsnes** Norway
142 C2 **Andalusia** U.S.A.
73 D3 **Andaman Islands** India
63 A2 **Andaman Sea** Indian Ocean
121 □D2 **Andapa** Madag.
100 B2 **Andelst** Neth.
92 G2 **Andenes** Norway
100 B2 **Andenne** Belgium
100 B2 **Anderlecht** Belgium
126 C2 **Anderson** *r.* Can.
126 B2 **Anderson** *AK* U.S.A.
140 B2 **Anderson** *IN* U.S.A.
143 D2 **Anderson** *SC* U.S.A.
148 D3 **Andes** *mts* S. America
77 D2 **Andijon** Uzbek.
121 □D2 **Andilamena** Madag.
121 □D2 **Andilanatoby** Madag.
121 □D2 **Andoany** Madag.
Andong China *see* **Dandong**
65 B2 **Andong** S. Korea
107 D1 **Andorra** *country* Europe
107 D1 **Andorra la Vella** Andorra
99 C3 **Andover** U.K.
154 B2 **Andradina** Brazil
89 D2 **Andreapol'** Russia
155 D2 **Andrelândia** Brazil
139 C2 **Andrews** U.S.A.
109 C2 **Andria** Italy
121 □D3 **Androka** Madag.
146 C2 **Andros** *i.* Bahamas
111 B3 **Andros** *i.* Greece
143 E4 **Andros Town** Bahamas
73 B3 **Andrott** *i.* India
90 B1 **Andrushivka** Ukr.
92 G2 **Andselv** Norway
106 C2 **Andújar** Spain
120 A2 **Andulo** Angola
114 C3 **Anéfis** Mali
115 D3 **Aney** Niger
83 H3 **Angara** *r.* Russia
69 C1 **Angarsk** Russia
93 G3 **Ånge** Sweden
144 A2 **Ángel de la Guarda, Isla** *i.* Mex.
64 B1 **Angeles** Phil.
150 B1 **Angel Falls** Venez.
93 F4 **Ängelholm** Sweden
92 G3 **Ångermanälven** *r.* Sweden
104 B2 **Angers** France
129 E1 **Angikuni Lake** Can.
98 A2 **Anglesey** *i.* U.K.
121 C2 **Angoche** Moz.
120 A2 **Angola** *country* Africa
140 C2 **Angola** U.S.A.
128 A2 **Angoon** U.S.A.
104 C2 **Angoulême** France
77 D2 **Angren** Uzbek.
147 D3 **Anguilla** *terr.* West Indies
93 F4 **Anholt** *i.* Denmark
71 B3 **Anhua** China
70 B2 **Anhui** *prov.* China
154 B1 **Anhumas** Brazil
154 C1 **Anicuns** Brazil
66 D1 **Aniva, Mys** *c.* Russia
65 B2 **Anjŭ** N. Korea
70 A2 **Ankang** China
80 B2 **Ankara** Turkey
70 B2 **Anlu** China
91 E1 **Anna** Russia
115 C1 **Annaba** Alg.
101 F2 **Annaberg-Buchholz** Ger.
78 B3 **An Nābiyah** Yemen
78 B2 **An Nafūd** *des.* Saudi Arabia
81 C2 **'Annah** Iraq
81 C2 **An Najaf** Iraq
96 C3 **Annan** U.K.
141 D3 **Annapolis** U.S.A.
75 C2 **Annapurna I** *mt.* Nepal
140 C2 **Ann Arbor** U.S.A.
150 C1 **Anna Regina** Guyana
81 C2 **An Nāşirīyah** Iraq
105 D2 **Annecy** France
78 B3 **An Nimāş** Saudi Arabia
62 B1 **Anning** China
142 C2 **Anniston** U.S.A.
105 C2 **Annonay** France
79 B2 **An Nu'ayrīyah** Saudi Arabia
121 □D2 **Anorontany, Tanjona** *hd* Madag.
111 C3 **Ano Viannos** Greece
71 B3 **Anpu** China
70 B2 **Anqing** China
102 C2 **Ansbach** Ger.
70 C1 **Anshan** China
71 A3 **Anshun** China
114 C3 **Ansongo** Mali
150 A3 **Antabamba** Peru
80 B2 **Antakya** Turkey
121 □E2 **Antalaha** Madag.
80 B2 **Antalya** Turkey
80 B2 **Antalya Körfezi** *g.* Turkey
121 □D2 **Antananarivo** Madag.
55 Q3 **Antarctic Peninsula** Antarctica
96 B2 **An Teallach** *mt.* U.K.
106 C2 **Antequera** Spain
138 B2 **Anthony** U.S.A.
114 B2 **Anti-Atlas** *mts* Morocco
105 D3 **Antibes** France
131 D2 **Anticosti, Île d'** *i.* Can.
131 D2 **Antigonish** Can.
147 D3 **Antigua** *i.* Antigua
147 D3 **Antigua and Barbuda** *country* West Indies
145 C2 **Antiguo-Morelos** Mex.
111 B3 **Antikythira** *i.* Greece
Antioch Turkey *see* **Antakya**
49 F6 **Antipodes Islands** N.Z.
152 A3 **Antofagasta** Chile
154 C3 **Antonina** Brazil
97 C1 **Antrim** U.K.
97 C1 **Antrim Hills** U.K.
121 □D2 **Antsalova** Madag.
121 □D2 **Antsirabe** Madag.
121 □D2 **Antsirañana** Madag.
121 □D2 **Antsohihy** Madag.
100 B2 **Antwerp** Belgium
Antwerpen Belgium *see* **Antwerp**
An Uaimh Ireland *see* **Navan**
75 C2 **Anugul** India
74 B2 **Anupgarh** India
73 C4 **Anuradhapura** Sri Lanka
51 C3 **Anxious Bay** Austr.
70 B2 **Anyang** China
65 B2 **Anyang** S. Korea
108 B2 **Anzio** Italy
Aomen *aut. reg.* China *see* **Macao**
66 D2 **Aomori** Japan
54 B2 **Aoraki/Mount Cook** *mt.* N.Z.
108 A1 **Aosta** Italy
143 D3 **Apalachee Bay** U.S.A.
150 B2 **Apaporis** *r.* Col.
154 B2 **Aparecida do Tabuado** Brazil
64 B1 **Aparri** Phil.
86 C2 **Apatity** Russia
144 B3 **Apatzingán** Mex.
100 B1 **Apeldoorn** Neth.
100 C1 **Apen** Ger.
108 A2 **Apennines** *mts* Italy
49 G3 **Apia** Samoa
154 C2 **Apiaí** Brazil
64 B2 **Apo, Mount** *vol.* Phil.
101 E2 **Apolda** Ger.
52 B3 **Apollo Bay** Austr.
143 D3 **Apopka, Lake** U.S.A.
154 B1 **Aporé** Brazil
154 B1 **Aporé** *r.* Brazil
80 B2 **Apostolos Andreas, Cape** Cyprus
133 E3 **Appalachian Mountains** U.S.A.
53 D2 **Appin** Austr.
140 B2 **Appleton** U.S.A.
108 B2 **Aprilia** Italy
91 D3 **Apsheronsk** Russia
154 B2 **Apucarana** Brazil
154 B2 **Apucarana, Serra da** *hills* Brazil
78 A2 **Aqaba, Gulf of** Asia
Aqsayqin *terr.* Asia *see* **Aksai Chin**
154 A1 **Aquidauana** *r.* Brazil
117 A4 **Arab, Bahr el** *watercourse* Sudan
Arabian Gulf Asia *see* **The Gulf**
78 B2 **Arabian Peninsula** Asia
56 G5 **Arabian Sea** Indian Ocean
151 E3 **Aracaju** Brazil
151 E2 **Aracati** Brazil
154 B2 **Araçatuba** Brazil
155 D1 **Aracruz** Brazil
155 D1 **Araçuaí** Brazil
110 B1 **Arad** Romania
115 E3 **Arada** Chad
156 C6 **Arafura Sea** Austr./Indon.
154 B1 **Aragarças** Brazil

107 C1 **Aragón** *r.* Spain
151 D2 **Araguaia** *r.* Brazil
151 D2 **Araguaína** Brazil
154 C1 **Araguari** Brazil
115 C2 **Arak** Alg.
81 C2 **Ārāk** Iran
62 A1 **Arakan Yoma** *mts* Myanmar
81 C1 **Arak's** *r.* Armenia
76 B2 **Aralkum** *des.* Kazakh./Uzbek.
76 C2 **Aral Sea** *salt l.* Kazakh./Uzbek.
76 C2 **Aral'sk** Kazakh.
Aral'skoye More *salt l.* Kazakh./Uzbek. *see* **Aral Sea**
106 C1 **Aranda de Duero** Spain
109 D2 **Aranđelovac** Serbia
97 B2 **Aran Islands** Ireland
106 C1 **Aranjuez** Spain
122 A1 **Aranos** Namibia
139 D3 **Aransas Pass** U.S.A.
67 B4 **Arao** Japan
114 B3 **Araouane** Mali
151 E2 **Arapiraca** Brazil
154 B2 **Arapongas** Brazil
154 C3 **Araquari** Brazil
78 B1 **'Ar'ar** Saudi Arabia
154 C2 **Araraquara** Brazil
151 C2 **Araras** Brazil
154 B3 **Araras, Serra das** *mts* Brazil
52 B3 **Ararat** Austr.
81 C2 **Ararat, Mount** Turkey
155 D2 **Araruama, Lago de** *lag.* Brazil
155 E1 **Arataca** Brazil
Aratürük China *see* **Yiwu**
150 A1 **Arauca** Col.
154 C1 **Araxá** Brazil
81 C2 **Arbīl/Hewlêr** Iraq
96 C2 **Arbroath** U.K.
74 A2 **Arbū-ye Shamālī, Dasht-e** *des.* Afgh.
104 B3 **Arcachon** France
143 D3 **Arcadia** U.S.A.
134 B2 **Arcata** U.S.A.
145 B3 **Arcelia** Mex.
86 D2 **Archangel** Russia
51 D1 **Archer** *r.* Austr.
134 D2 **Arco** U.S.A.
106 B2 **Arcos de la Frontera** Spain
127 F2 **Arctic Bay** Can.
160 **Arctic Ocean** World
126 C2 **Arctic Red** *r.* Can.
81 C2 **Ardabīl** Iran
81 C1 **Ardahan** Turkey
93 E3 **Årdalstangen** Norway
100 B3 **Ardennes** *plat.* Belgium
81 D2 **Ardestān** Iran
53 C2 **Ardlethan** Austr.
139 D2 **Ardmore** U.S.A.
96 A2 **Ardnamurchan, Point of** U.K.
52 A2 **Ardrossan** Austr.
96 B3 **Ardrossan** U.K.
135 B3 **Arena, Point** U.S.A.
93 E4 **Arendal** Norway
101 E1 **Arendsee (Altmark)** Ger.
150 A3 **Arequipa** Peru
151 C2 **Arere** Brazil
106 C1 **Arévalo** Spain
108 B2 **Arezzo** Italy
104 B2 **Argentan** France
153 B4 **Argentina** *country* S. America
153 A6 **Argentino, Lago** *l.* Arg.
104 C2 **Argenton-sur-Creuse** France
110 C2 **Argeş** *r.* Romania
74 A1 **Arghandāb Rōd** *r.* Afgh.
111 B3 **Argolikos Kolpos** *b.* Greece
111 B3 **Argos** Greece
111 B3 **Argostoli** Greece
107 C1 **Arguis** Spain
69 E1 **Argun'** *r.* China/Russia
50 B1 **Argyle, Lake** Austr.
122 A2 **Ariamsvlei** Namibia
152 A2 **Arica** Chile
96 A2 **Arinagour** U.K.
155 C1 **Arinos** Brazil
150 C3 **Aripuanã** Brazil
150 B2 **Aripuanã** *r.* Brazil
150 B2 **Ariquemes** Brazil
154 B1 **Ariranhá** *r.* Brazil
138 A2 **Arizona** *state* U.S.A.
144 A1 **Arizpe** Mex.
78 B2 **'Arjah** Saudi Arabia
92 G2 **Arjeplog** Sweden
142 B2 **Arkadelphia** U.S.A.
77 C1 **Arkalyk** Kazakh.
142 B2 **Arkansas** *r.* U.S.A.
142 B1 **Arkansas** *state* U.S.A.
137 D3 **Arkansas City** U.S.A.
Arkhangel'sk
97 C2 **Arklow** Ireland
102 C1 **Arkona, Kap** *c.* Ger.
82 G1 **Arkticheskogo Instituta, Ostrova** *is* Russia
105 C3 **Arles** France
115 C3 **Arlit** Niger
100 B3 **Arlon** Belgium
97 C1 **Armagh** U.K.
116 B2 **Armant** Egypt
81 C1 **Armavir** Russia
81 C1 **Armenia** *country* Asia
150 A1 **Armenia** Col.
144 B3 **Armería** Mex.
53 D2 **Armidale** Austr.
130 B1 **Armstrong** Can.
80 B1 **Armyans'k** Ukr.
80 B2 **Arnauti, Cape** Cyprus
100 B2 **Arnhem** Neth.
51 C1 **Arnhem, Cape** Austr.
51 C1 **Arnhem Bay** Austr.
51 C1 **Arnhem Land** *reg.* Austr.
108 B2 **Arno** *r.* Italy
52 A2 **Arno Bay** Austr.
130 C2 **Arnprior** Can.
100 D2 **Arnsberg** Ger.
101 E2 **Arnstadt** Ger.
122 A2 **Aroab** Namibia
101 D2 **Arolsen** Ger.
78 A3 **Aroma** Sudan
108 A1 **Arona** Italy
144 B2 **Aros** *r.* Mex.
75 C2 **Arrah** India
81 C2 **Ar Ramādī** Iraq
96 B3 **Arran** *i.* U.K.
97 B1 **Arranmore Island** Ireland
80 B2 **Ar Raqqah** Syria
104 C1 **Arras** France
78 B2 **Ar Rass** Saudi Arabia
145 C3 **Arriaga** Mex.
79 C2 **Ar Rimāl** *reg.* Saudi Arabia
Ar Riyāḍ Saudi Arabia *see* **Riyadh**
145 C2 **Arroyo Seco** Mex.
79 C2 **Ar Rustāq** Oman
80 C2 **Ar Ruṭbah** Iraq
81 D3 **Arsanajān** Iran
66 B2 **Arsen'yev** Russia
111 B3 **Arta** Greece
144 B3 **Arteaga** Mex.
66 B2 **Artem** Russia
Artemivs'k Ukr. *see* **Bakhmut**
104 C2 **Artenay** France
138 C2 **Artesia** U.S.A.
51 E2 **Arthur Point** Austr.
54 B2 **Arthur's Pass** N.Z.
152 C4 **Artigas** Uru.
129 D1 **Artillery Lake** Can.
90 B2 **Artsyz** Ukr.
77 D3 **Artux** China
81 C1 **Artvin** Turkey
59 C3 **Aru, Kepulauan** *is* Indon.
119 D2 **Arua** Uganda
147 D3 **Aruba** *terr.* West Indies
119 D3 **Arusha** Tanz.
69 C1 **Arvayheer** Mongolia
129 E1 **Arviat** Can.
92 G2 **Arvidsjaur** Sweden
93 F4 **Arvika** Sweden
87 D3 **Arzamas** Russia
107 C2 **Arzew** Alg.
100 C2 **Arzfeld** Ger.
101 F2 **Aš** Czechia
115 C4 **Asaba** Nigeria
74 B1 **Asadābād** Afgh.
66 D2 **Asahi-dake** *vol.* Japan
66 D2 **Asahikawa** Japan
78 B3 **Āsalē** *l.* Eth.
75 C2 **Asansol** India
131 C2 **Asbestos** Can.
109 C2 **Ascea** Italy
152 B2 **Ascensión** Bol.
113 D7 **Ascension** *i.* S. Atlantic Ocean
145 D3 **Ascensión, Bahía de la** *b.* Mex.
101 D3 **Aschaffenburg** Ger.
100 C2 **Ascheberg** Ger.
101 E2 **Aschersleben** Ger.
108 B2 **Ascoli Piceno** Italy
92 G3 **Åsele** Sweden
110 B2 **Asenovgrad** Bulg.
76 B3 **Aşgabat** Turkm.
50 A2 **Ashburton** *watercourse* Austr.
54 B2 **Ashburton** N.Z.
142 B2 **Ashdown** U.S.A.
143 D1 **Asheville** U.S.A.
53 D1 **Ashford** Austr.
99 D3 **Ashford** U.K.
Ashgabat Turkm. *see* **Aşgabat**
98 C1 **Ashington** U.K.
67 B4 **Ashizuri-misaki** *pt* Japan
136 D3 **Ashland** *KS* U.S.A.
140 C3 **Ashland** *KY* U.S.A.
140 C2 **Ashland** *OH* U.S.A.
134 B2 **Ashland** *OR* U.S.A.
140 A1 **Ashland** *WI* U.S.A.
88 C3 **Ashmyany** Belarus
78 B3 **Ash Sharawrah** Saudi Arabia
Ash Shāriqah U.A.E. *see* **Sharjah**
81 C2 **Ash Sharqāţ** Iraq
81 C2 **Ash Shaţrah** Iraq
79 B3 **Ash Shiḥr** Yemen
79 C2 **Ash Şhināş** Oman
78 B2 **Ash Shu'bah** Saudi Arabia
78 B2 **Ash Shumlūl** Saudi Arabia
140 C2 **Ashtabula** U.S.A.
131 D1 **Ashuanipi Lake** Can.
108 A2 **Asinara, Golfo dell'** *b. Sardinia* Italy
82 G3 **Asino** Russia
88 C3 **Asipovichy** Belarus
78 B2 **'Asīr** *reg.* Saudi Arabia
93 F4 **Askim** Norway
68 C1 **Askiz** Russia
116 B3 **Asmara** Eritrea
93 F4 **Åsnen** *l.* Sweden
116 B2 **Asoteriba, Jebel** *mt.* Sudan
103 D2 **Aspang-Markt** Austria
136 B3 **Aspen** U.S.A.
54 A2 **Aspiring, Mount** N.Z.
117 C3 **Assab** Eritrea
Aş Şaḥrā' al Gharbīyah *des.* Egypt *see* **Western Desert**
Aş Şaḥrā' ash Sharqīyah *des.* Egypt *see* **Eastern Desert**
78 B2 **As Salamiyah** Saudi Arabia
81 C2 **As Samāwah** Iraq
79 C2 **Aş Şanām** *reg.* Saudi Arabia

115 E2 **As Sarīr** reg. Libya
100 C1 **Assen** Neth.
100 B2 **Assesse** Belgium
115 D1 **As Sidrah** Libya
106 B2 **Assilah** Morocco
129 D3 **Assiniboia** Can.
128 C2 **Assiniboine, Mount** Can.
154 B2 **Assis** Brazil
81 C2 **Aş Şubayḩīyah** Kuwait
81 C2 **As Sulaymānīyah/Slêmanî** Iraq

78 B2 **As Sulaymī** Saudi Arabia
78 B2 **As Sulayyil** Saudi Arabia
78 B2 **As Sūq** Saudi Arabia
80 B2 **As Suwaydā'** Syria
79 C2 **As Suwayq** Oman
83 **As Suways** Egypt see Suez
111 B3 **Astakos** Greece
77 D1 **Astana** Russia
81 C2 **Āstārā** Iran
108 A2 **Asti** Italy
74 B1 **Astor** Pak.
106 B1 **Astorga** Spain
126 B2 **Astoria** U.S.A.
87 D4 **Astrakhan'** Russia
111 C3 **Astravyets** Belarus
111 C3 **Astypalaia** i. Greece
152 C3 **Asunción** Para.
116 B2 **Aswān** Egypt
116 B2 **Aswān** Egypt

152 B3 **Atacama, Desierto de** des. Chile see **Atacama Desert**
152 B3 **Atacama, Salar de** salt flat Chile
152 B3 **Atacama Desert** Chile
114 C4 **Atakpamé** Togo
111 B3 **Atalanti** Greece
150 A3 **Atalaya** Peru
77 C2 **Atamyrat** Turkm.
78 B3 **'Ataq** Yemen
114 A2 **Atâr** Maur.
135 B3 **Atascadero** U.S.A.
77 D2 **Atasu** Kazakh.
111 C3 **Atavyros** mt. Greece
116 B3 **Atbara** Sudan
116 B3 **Atbara** r. Sudan
77 C1 **Atbasar** Kazakh.
137 D3 **Atchison** U.S.A.
108 B2 **Aterno** r. Italy
108 B2 **Atessa** Italy
100 A2 **Ath** Belgium
128 C2 **Athabasca** Can.
129 C2 **Athabasca** r. Can.
129 D2 **Athabasca, Lake** Can.
111 B3 **Athens** Greece
143 D2 **Athens** GA U.S.A.
140 C3 **Athens** OH U.S.A.
143 D1 **Athens** TN U.S.A.
139 D2 **Athens** TX U.S.A.
Athina Greece see **Athens**
97 C2 **Athlone** Ireland
111 B3 **Athos** mt. Greece
97 C2 **Athy** Ireland
115 D3 **Ati** Chad
128 A2 **Atikokan** Can.
87 D3 **Atkarsk** Russia
143 D2 **Atlanta** U.S.A.
137 D2 **Atlantic** U.S.A.
141 E3 **Atlantic City** U.S.A.
158 **Atlantic Ocean** World
152 A3 **Atlantis** S. Africa
114 C1 **Atlas Mountains** Africa
114 C1 **Atlas Saharien** mts Alg.
128 A2 **Atlin** Can.
128 A2 **Atlin Lake** Can.
142 C2 **Atmore** U.S.A.
139 D2 **Atoka** U.S.A.
75 C2 **Atrai** r. India

78 B2 **Aţ Ţā'if** Saudi Arabia
63 B2 **Attapu** Laos
130 B1 **Attawapiskat** Can.
130 B1 **Attawapiskat** r. Can.
130 B1 **Attawapiskat Lake** Can.
100 C2 **Attendorn** Ger.
116 B2 **Aţ Ţūr** Egypt
78 B3 **At Turbah** Yemen
76 B2 **Atyrau** Kazakh.
105 C3 **Aubenas** France
126 C2 **Aubry Lake** Can.
142 C2 **Auburn** AL U.S.A.
135 B3 **Auburn** CA U.S.A.
137 D2 **Auburn** NE U.S.A.
141 D2 **Auburn** NY U.S.A.
104 C2 **Aubusson** France
104 C3 **Auch** France
54 B1 **Auckland** N.Z.
48 C4 **Auckland Islands** is N.Z.
101 F2 **Aue** Ger.
102 C2 **Augsburg** Ger.
109 C3 **Augusta** Sicily Italy
143 D2 **Augusta** GA U.S.A.
137 D3 **Augusta** KS U.S.A.
141 F2 **Augusta** ME U.S.A.
50 A2 **Augustus, Mount** Austr.
100 A2 **Aulnoye-Aymeries** France
62 A2 **Aunglan** Myanmar
122 B2 **Auob** watercourse Namibia/S. Africa
74 B3 **Aurangabad** India
100 C1 **Aurich** Ger.
154 B1 **Aurilândia** Brazil
104 C3 **Aurillac** France
136 C3 **Aurora** CO U.S.A.
140 B2 **Aurora** IL U.S.A.
137 D2 **Aurora** NE U.S.A.
122 A2 **Aus** Namibia
137 E2 **Austin** MN U.S.A.
135 C3 **Austin** NV U.S.A.
139 D2 **Austin** TX U.S.A.
50 **Australia** country Oceania
159 D7 **Australian–Antarctic Basin** Southern Ocean
53 C3 **Australian Capital Territory** admin. div. Austr.
102 C2 **Austria** country Europe
144 B3 **Autlán** Mex.
105 C2 **Autun** France
105 C2 **Auxerre** France
105 D2 **Auxonne** France
105 C2 **Avallon** France
131 E2 **Avalon Peninsula** Can.
154 C2 **Avaré** Brazil
49 H4 **Avarua** Cook Is
91 D2 **Avdiyivka** Ukr.
106 B1 **Aveiro** Port.
109 B2 **Avellino** Italy
100 A2 **Avesnes-sur-Helpe** France
93 G3 **Avesta** Sweden
108 B2 **Avezzano** Italy
96 C2 **Aviemore** U.K.
109 C2 **Avigliano** Italy
105 C3 **Avignon** France
106 C1 **Ávila** Spain
106 B1 **Avilés** Spain
109 C3 **Avola** Sicily Italy
99 C3 **Avon** r. England U.K.
99 C3 **Avon** r. England U.K.
104 B2 **Avranches** France
54 B1 **Awanui** N.Z.
117 C4 **Āwash** Eth.
117 C3 **Āwash** r. Eth.
115 D2 **Awbārī** Libya
115 D2 **Awbārī, Idhān** des. Libya
117 C4 **Aw Dheegle** Somalia
96 B2 **Awe, Loch** l. U.K.
117 A4 **Aweil** South Sudan

126 E1 **Axel Heiberg Island** Can.
114 B4 **Axim** Ghana
150 A3 **Ayacucho** Peru
77 E2 **Ayagoz** Kazakh.
68 B2 **Ayakkum Hu** salt l. China
106 B2 **Ayamonte** Spain
83 K3 **Ayan** Russia
150 A3 **Ayaviri** Peru
76 A2 **Aybas** Kazakh.
91 D2 **Aydar** r. Ukr.
77 C2 **Aydarko'l ko'li** l. Uzbek.
111 C3 **Aydın** Turkey
Ayers Rock h. Austr. see **Uluru/Ayers Rock**
99 C3 **Aylesbury** U.K.
106 C1 **Ayllón** Spain
129 D1 **Aylmer Lake** Can.
117 B4 **Ayod** South Sudan
83 M2 **Ayon, Ostrov** i. Russia
114 B3 **'Ayoûn el 'Atroûs** Maur.
51 D1 **Ayr** Austr.
96 B3 **Ayr** U.K.
98 A1 **Ayre, Point of** Isle of Man
76 C2 **Ayteke Bi** Kazakh.
110 C2 **Aytos** Bulg.
145 C3 **Ayutla** Mex.
63 B2 **Ayutthaya** Thai.
111 C3 **Ayvacık** Turkey
111 C3 **Ayvalık** Turkey
Azania reg. Somalia see **Jubaland**
114 C3 **Azaouagh, Vallée de** watercourse Mali/Niger
77 C2 **Azat, Gory** h. Kazakh.
114 B3 **Azawad** reg. Mali
Azbine mts Niger see **Aïr, Massif de l'**
81 C1 **Azerbaijan** country Asia
77 C1 **Azhibeksor, Ozero** salt l. Kazakh.
86 D2 **Azopol'ye** Russia
84 D5 **Azores** aut. reg. Port.
91 D2 **Azov** Russia
91 D2 **Azov, Sea of** Russia/Ukr.
Azraq, Bahr el r. Eth./Sudan see **Blue Nile**
106 B2 **Azuaga** Spain
146 B4 **Azuero, Península de** pen. Panama
153 C4 **Azul** Arg.
80 B2 **Az Zaqāzīq** Egypt
80 B2 **Az Zarqā'** Jordan
78 B3 **Az Zaydīyah** Yemen
114 C2 **Azzel Matti, Sebkha** salt pan Alg.
78 B2 **Az Zilfī** Saudi Arabia
78 B3 **Az Zuqur** i. Yemen

B

63 B2 **Ba, Sông** r. Vietnam
117 C4 **Baardheere** Somalia
77 C3 **Bābā, Kōh-e** mts Afgh.
110 C2 **Babadag** Romania
111 C2 **Babaeski** Turkey
117 C3 **Bāb al Mandab** str. Africa/Asia
61 C2 **Babana** Indon.
59 C3 **Babar** i. Indon.
119 D3 **Babati** Tanz.
89 E2 **Babayevo** Russia
128 B2 **Babine** r. Can.
128 B2 **Babine Lake** Can.
59 C3 **Babo** Indon.
81 D2 **Bābol** Iran
122 A3 **Baboon Point** S. Africa
88 C3 **Babruysk/Bobruysk** Belarus
64 B1 **Babuyan** i. Phil.
64 B1 **Babuyan Islands** Phil.

151 D2 **Bacabal** Brazil
59 C3 **Bacan** *i.* Indon.
110 C1 **Bacău** Romania
52 B3 **Bacchus Marsh** Austr.
77 D3 **Bachu** China
129 E1 **Back** *r.* Can.
109 C1 **Bačka Palanka** Serbia
63 B3 **Bac Liêu** Vietnam
64 B1 **Bacolod** Phil.
130 C1 **Bacqueville, Lac** *l.* Can.
106 B2 **Badajoz** Spain
62 A1 **Badarpur** India
101 F1 **Bad Belzig** Ger.
101 E2 **Bad Berka** Ger.
101 D2 **Bad Berleburg** Ger.
101 E1 **Bad Bevensen** Ger.
100 C2 **Bad Ems** Ger.
103 D2 **Baden** Austria
102 B2 **Baden-Baden** Ger.
101 E2 **Bad Harzburg** Ger.
101 D2 **Bad Hersfeld** Ger.
102 C2 **Bad Hofgastein** Austria
101 D2 **Bad Homburg vor der Höhe** Ger.
74 A2 **Badin** Pak.
Bādiyat ash Shām *des.* Asia *see* **Syrian Desert**
101 E2 **Bad Kissingen** Ger.
100 C3 **Bad Kreuznach** Ger.
101 E2 **Bad Lauterberg im Harz** Ger.
101 D2 **Bad Lippspringe** Ger.
101 D3 **Bad Mergentheim** Ger.
101 D2 **Bad Nauheim** Ger.
100 C2 **Bad Neuenahr-Ahrweiler** Ger.
101 E2 **Bad Neustadt an der Saale** Ger.
101 E1 **Bad Oldesloe** Ger.
101 D2 **Bad Pyrmont** Ger.
78 A2 **Badr Ḥunayn** Saudi Arabia
101 D1 **Bad Salzuflen** Ger.
101 E2 **Bad Salzungen** Ger.
102 C1 **Bad Schwartau** Ger.
101 E1 **Bad Segeberg** Ger.
100 C3 **Bad Sobernheim** Ger.
101 E2 **Bad Staffelstein** Ger.
73 C4 **Badulla** Sri Lanka
100 D1 **Bad Zwischenahn** Ger.
65 A2 **Baengnyeong-do** *i.* S. Korea
106 C2 **Baeza** Spain
114 A3 **Bafatá** Guinea-Bissau
160 O2 **Baffin Bay** *sea* Can./Greenland
127 G2 **Baffin Island** Can.
118 B2 **Bafia** Cameroon
114 A3 **Bafing** *r.* Africa
114 A3 **Bafoulabé** Mali
118 B2 **Bafoussam** Cameroon
76 B3 **Bāfq** Iran
80 B1 **Bafra** Turkey
79 C2 **Bāft** Iran
119 C2 **Bafwasende** Dem. Rep. Congo
119 D3 **Bagamoyo** Tanz.
60 B1 **Bagan Datuk** Malaysia
120 B2 **Bagani** Namibia
60 B1 **Bagansiapiapi** Indon.
138 A2 **Bagdad** U.S.A.
152 C4 **Bagé** Brazil
97 C2 **Bagenalstown** Ireland
81 C2 **Baghdād** Iraq
77 C3 **Baghlān** Afgh.
104 C3 **Bagnères-de-Luchon** France
Bago Myanmar *see* **Pegu**
88 B3 **Bagrationovsk** Russia
Bagrax China *see* **Bohu**
64 B1 **Baguio** Phil.
115 C3 **Bagzane, Monts** *mts* Niger
Bahamas *country* West Indies *see* **The Bahamas**
146 C2 **Bahamas, The** *country* West Indies
75 C2 **Baharampur** India
Bahariya Oasis Egypt *see* **Bahrīyah, Wāḥāt al**
76 B3 **Baharly** Turkm.
60 B1 **Bahau** Malaysia
72 B2 **Bahawalnagar** Pak.
74 B2 **Bahawalpur** Pak.
153 B4 **Bahía Blanca** Arg.
144 A2 **Bahía Kino** Mex.
152 C3 **Bahía Negra** Para.
144 A2 **Bahía Tortugas** Mex.
117 B3 **Bahir Dar** Eth.
75 C2 **Bahraich** India
79 C2 **Bahrain** *country* Asia
116 A2 **Bahrīyah, Wāḥāt al** *oasis* Egypt
79 D2 **Bāhū Kālāt** Iran
110 B1 **Baia Mare** Romania
69 E1 **Baicheng** China
131 D2 **Baie-Comeau** Can.
Baie-du-Poste Can. *see* **Mistissini**
131 C2 **Baie-St-Paul** Can.
65 B1 **Baihe** China
69 D1 **Baikal, Lake** Russia
110 B2 **Băileşti** Romania
68 C2 **Baima** China
143 D2 **Bainbridge** U.S.A.
48 F2 **Bairiki** Kiribati
Bairin Youqi China *see* **Daban**
53 C3 **Bairnsdale** Austr.
71 A3 **Baise** China
65 B1 **Baishan** *Jilin* China
65 B1 **Baishan** *Jilin* China
65 B1 **Baitou Shan** *mt.* China/N. Korea
70 A2 **Baiyin** China
116 B3 **Baiyuda Desert** Sudan
103 D2 **Baja** Hungary
144 A1 **Baja California** *pen.* Mex.
78 B3 **Bājil** Yemen
114 A3 **Bakel** Senegal
135 C3 **Baker** *CA* U.S.A.
136 C1 **Baker** *MT* U.S.A.
134 B1 **Baker, Mount** *vol.* U.S.A.
134 C2 **Baker City** U.S.A.
129 E1 **Baker Foreland** *hd* Can.
49 G2 **Baker Island** N. Pacific Ocean
129 E1 **Baker Lake** Can.
129 E1 **Baker Lake** Can.
135 C3 **Bakersfield** U.S.A.
91 C3 **Bakhchysaray** Ukr.
91 C1 **Bakhmach** Ukr.
91 D2 **Bakhmut** Ukr.
Bākhtarān Iran *see* **Kermānshāh**
Bakı Azer. *see* **Baku**
111 C2 **Bakırköy** Turkey
92 □C2 **Bakkaflói** *b.* Iceland
118 C2 **Bakouma** C.A.R.
81 C1 **Baku** Azer.
64 A2 **Balabac** Phil.
64 A2 **Balabac** *i.* Phil.
64 A2 **Balabac Strait** Malaysia/Phil.
61 C2 **Balaiberkuak** Indon.
52 A2 **Balaklava** Austr.
91 C3 **Balaklava** Ukr.
91 D2 **Balakliya** Ukr.
87 D3 **Balakovo** Russia
76 C3 **Bālā Murghāb** Afgh.
145 C3 **Balancán** Mex.
111 C3 **Balan Dağı** *h.* Turkey
64 B1 **Balanga** Phil.
75 C2 **Balangir** India
79 C2 **Bālā Shahr** Iran
87 D3 **Balashov** Russia
103 D2 **Balaton, Lake** Hungary
103 D2 **Balatonboglár** Hungary
150 C2 **Balbina, Represa de** *resr* Brazi
97 C2 **Balbriggan** Ireland
52 A2 **Balcanoona** Austr.
110 C2 **Balchik** Bulg.
54 A3 **Balclutha** N.Z.
129 E2 **Baldock Lake** Can.
129 D2 **Baldy Mountain** *h.* Can.
138 B2 **Baldy Peak** U.S.A.
Baleares, Islas *is* Spain *see* **Balearic Islands**
107 D2 **Balearic Islands** Spain
107 D1 **Balearic Sea** Spain
155 E1 **Baleia, Ponta da** *pt* Brazil
130 C1 **Baleine, Grande Rivière de la** *r.* Can.
131 D1 **Baleine, Rivière à la** *r.* Can.
75 C2 **Baleshwar** India
108 A2 **Balestrieri, Punta** *mt.* *Sardinia* Italy
61 C2 **Bali** *i.* Indon.
115 D4 **Bali** Nigeria
60 A1 **Balige** Indon.
75 C2 **Baligurha** India
111 C3 **Balıkesir** Turkey
61 C2 **Balikpapan** Indon.
59 D3 **Balimo** P.N.G.
102 B2 **Balingen** Ger.
Bali Sea Indon. *see* **Laut Bali**
76 B3 **Balkanabat** Turkm.
110 B2 **Balkan Mountains** Bulgaria/Serbia
77 D2 **Balkhash** Kazakh.
77 D2 **Balkhash, Lake** Kazakh.
Balkhash, Ozero *l.* Kazakh. *se* **Balkhash, Lake**
50 B3 **Balladonia** Austr.
97 B2 **Ballaghaderreen** Ireland
92 G2 **Ballangen** Norway
52 B3 **Ballarat** Austr.
50 B2 **Ballard, Lake** *imp. l.* Austr.
96 C2 **Ballater** U.K.
114 B3 **Ballé** Mali
53 D1 **Ballina** Austr.
97 B1 **Ballina** Ireland
97 B2 **Ballinasloe** Ireland
139 D2 **Ballinger** U.S.A.
97 B2 **Ballinrobe** Ireland
97 B1 **Ballycastle** Ireland
97 C1 **Ballycastle** U.K.
97 D1 **Ballyclare** U.K.
97 C1 **Ballymena** U.K.
97 C1 **Ballymoney** U.K.
97 D1 **Ballynahinch** U.K.
97 B1 **Ballyshannon** Ireland
95 B2 **Ballyvoy** U.K.
51 D2 **Balonne** *r.* Austr.
74 B2 **Balotra** India
75 C2 **Balrampur** India
52 B2 **Balranald** Austr.
110 B2 **Balş** Romania
151 D2 **Balsas** Brazil
145 C3 **Balsas** Mex.
90 B2 **Balta** Ukr.
90 B2 **Bălţi** Moldova
93 G4 **Baltic Sea** *g.* Europe
80 B2 **Balṭīm** Egypt
123 C1 **Baltimore** S. Africa
141 D3 **Baltimore** U.S.A.
88 A3 **Baltiysk** Russia
62 A1 **Balu** India
88 C2 **Balvi** Latvia
77 D2 **Balykchy** Kyrg.
87 E4 **Balykshi** Kazakh.
79 C2 **Bam** Iran
51 D1 **Bamaga** Austr.
130 A1 **Bamaji Lake** Can.

114 B3	Bamako Mali	
118 C2	Bambari C.A.R.	
101 E3	Bamberg Ger.	
119 C2	Bambili Dem. Rep. Congo	
119 C2	Bambouti C.A.R.	
155 C2	Bambuí Brazil	
118 B2	Bamenda Cameroon	
74 A1	Bāmyān Afgh.	
119 C2	Banalia Dem. Rep. Congo	
151 E3	Bananal, Ilha do i. Brazil	
74 A2	Banas r. India	
111 C3	Banaz Turkey	
62 B2	Ban Ban Laos	
97 C1	Banbridge U.K.	
97 C2	Banbury U.K.	
130 C2	Bancroft Can.	
119 C2	Banda Dem. Rep. Congo	
75 C2	Banda India	
59 C3	Banda, Kepulauan is Indon.	
59 C3	Banda, Laut sea Indon.	
60 A1	Banda Aceh Indon.	
79 C2	Bandar-e 'Abbās Iran	
81 C2	Bandar-e Anzalī Iran	
79 C2	Bandar-e Büshehr Iran	
79 C2	Bandar-e Chārak Iran	
79 C2	Bandar-e Emām Khomeynī Iran	
81 D3	Bandar-e Ganāveh Iran	
79 C2	Bandar-e Jāsk Iran	
79 C2	Bandar-e Kangān Iran	
79 C2	Bandar-e Lengeh Iran	
79 C2	Bandar-e Moqām Iran	
60 B1	Bandar Lampung Indon.	
61 C1	Bandar Seri Begawan Brunei	
	Banda Sea Indon. see Banda, Laut	
155 C2	Bandeiras, Pico de mt. Brazil	
123 C1	Bandelierkop S. Africa	
114 B3	Banderas, Bahía de b. Mex.	
114 B3	Bandiagara Mali	
111 C2	Bandırma Turkey	
97 B3	Bandon Ireland	
118 B3	Bandundu Dem. Rep. Congo	
61 B2	Bandung Indon.	
128 C2	Banff Can.	
96 C2	Banff U.K.	
114 B3	Banfora Burkina Faso	
64 B2	Banga Phil.	
	Bangalore India see Bengaluru	
118 C2	Bangassou C.A.R.	
59 C3	Banggai Indon.	
59 C3	Banggai, Kepulauan is Indon.	
61 C1	Banggi i. Sabah Malaysia	
60 B2	Bangka i. Indon.	
61 C2	Bangkalan Indon.	
60 B1	Bangkinang Indon.	
60 B2	Bangko Indon.	
63 B2	Bangkok Thai.	
75 C2	Bangladesh country Asia	
97 D1	Bangor Northern Ireland U.K.	
98 A2	Bangor Wales U.K.	
141 F2	Bangor U.S.A.	
63 A2	Bang Saphan Yai Thai.	
64 B1	Bangued Phil.	
118 B2	Bangui C.A.R.	
121 B2	Bangweulu, Lake Zambia	
62 B2	Ban Huai Khon Thai.	
116 B2	Banī Suwayf Egypt	
115 D1	Banī Walīd Libya	
80 B2	Bāniyās Syria	
109 C2	Banja Luka Bos. & Herz.	
61 C2	Banjarmasin Indon.	
114 A3	Banjul Gambia	
128 A2	Banks Island B.C. Can.	
126 C2	Banks Island N.W.T. Can.	
48 F3	Banks Islands Vanuatu	
129 E1	Banks Lake Can.	
54 B2	Banks Peninsula N.Z.	

75 C2	Bankura India	
62 A1	Banmauk Myanmar	
62 B2	Ban Mouang Laos	
97 C1	Bann r. U.K.	
63 A2	Ban Napè Laos	
63 A3	Ban Na San Thai.	
143 E4	Bannerman Town Bahamas	
74 B1	Bannu Pak.	
74 B2	Banswara India	
63 A3	Ban Tha Kham Thai.	
62 A2	Ban Tha Song Yang Thai.	
63 B2	Ban Tôp Laos	
97 B3	Bantry Ireland	
97 B3	Bantry Bay Ireland	
118 B2	Banyo Cameroon	
107 D1	Banyoles Spain	
61 C2	Banyuwangi Indon.	
	Bao'an China see Shenzhen	
69 D2	Baochang China	
70 B2	Baoding China	
70 A2	Baoji China	
62 B1	Bao Lac Vietnam	
63 B2	Bao Lôc Vietnam	
66 B1	Baoqing China	
62 A1	Baoshan China	
70 B1	Baotou China	
81 C2	Ba'qūbah Iraq	
109 C2	Bar Montenegro	
117 C4	Baraawe Somalia	
147 C2	Baracoa Cuba	
53 C2	Baradine Austr.	
147 C3	Barahona Dom. Rep.	
116 B3	Baraka watercourse Eritrea/ Sudan	
61 C1	Baram r. Sarawak Malaysia	
74 B1	Baramulla India	
88 C3	Baranavichy/Baranovichi Belarus	
78 A2	Baranis Egypt	
90 B1	Baranivka Ukr.	
128 A2	Baranof Island U.S.A.	
	Baranovichi Belarus see Baranavichy/Baranovichi	
59 C3	Barat Daya, Kepulauan is Indon.	
155 D2	Barbacena Brazil	
147 E3	Barbados country West Indies	
107 D1	Barbastro Spain	
104 B2	Barbezieux-St-Hilaire France	
51 D2	Barcaldine Austr.	
107 D1	Barcelona Spain	
150 B1	Barcelona Venez.	
105 D3	Barcelonnette France	
150 B2	Barcelos Brazil	
	Barcoo Creek watercourse Austr. see Cooper Creek	
103 D2	Barcs Hungary	
75 C2	Barddhaman India	
103 E2	Bardejov Slovakia	
79 C2	Bardsīr Iran	
75 B2	Bareilly India	
160 B2	Barents Sea Arctic Ocean	
78 A3	Barentu Eritrea	
75 C2	Barh India	
141 F2	Bar Harbor U.S.A.	
109 C2	Bari Italy	
74 B1	Bari Kōt Afgh.	
150 A1	Barinas Venez.	
75 C2	Baripada India	
75 D2	Barisal Bangl.	
60 B2	Barisan, Pegunungan mts Indon.	
79 C2	Barkā Oman	
88 C2	Barkava Latvia	
51 C1	Barkly Tableland reg. Austr.	
68 C2	Barkol China	
110 C1	Bârlad Romania	
105 D2	Bar-le-Duc France	

50 A2	Barlee, Lake imp. l. Austr.	
109 C2	Barletta Italy	
53 C2	Barmedman Austr.	
74 B2	Barmer India	
99 A2	Barmouth U.K.	
101 D1	Barmstedt Ger.	
98 C1	Barnard Castle U.K.	
53 B2	Barnato Austr.	
82 G3	Barnaul Russia	
127 G2	Barnes Icecap Can.	
100 B1	Barneveld Neth.	
98 C2	Barnsley U.K.	
99 A3	Barnstaple U.K.	
99 A3	Barnstaple Bay U.K.	
143 D2	Barnwell U.S.A.	
	Baroda India see Vadodara	
150 B1	Barquisimeto Venez.	
96 A2	Barra i. U.K.	
53 D2	Barraba Austr.	
151 D2	Barra do Corda Brazil	
154 B1	Barra do Garças Brazil	
150 C2	Barra do São Manuel Brazil	
150 A3	Barranca Lima Peru	
150 A2	Barranca Loreto Peru	
152 C3	Barranqueras Arg.	
150 A1	Barranquilla Col.	
151 D2	Barreiras Brazil	
154 C2	Barretos Brazil	
130 C2	Barrie Can.	
128 B2	Barrière Can.	
52 B2	Barrier Range hills Austr.	
53 D2	Barrington, Mount Austr.	
129 D2	Barrington Lake Can.	
53 C1	Barringun Austr.	
97 C2	Barrow r. Ireland	
51 C2	Barrow Creek Austr.	
98 B1	Barrow-in-Furness U.K.	
50 A2	Barrow Island Austr.	
126 E2	Barrow Strait Can.	
99 B3	Barry U.K.	
130 C2	Barrys Bay Can.	
74 B2	Barsalpur India	
135 C4	Barstow U.S.A.	
105 C2	Bar-sur-Aube France	
80 B1	Bartın Turkey	
51 D1	Bartle Frere, Mount Austr.	
139 D1	Bartlesville U.S.A.	
103 E1	Bartoszyce Pol.	
61 C2	Barung i. Indon.	
69 D1	Baruun-Urt Mongolia	
91 D2	Barvinkove Ukr.	
53 C2	Barwon r. Austr.	
88 C3	Barysaw/Borisov Belarus	
110 C2	Basarabi Romania	
105 D2	Basel Switz.	
91 C2	Bashtanka Ukr.	
64 B2	Basilan i. Phil.	
99 D3	Basildon U.K.	
99 C3	Basingstoke U.K.	
81 C2	Başkale Turkey	
130 C2	Baskatong, Réservoir resr Can.	
	Basle Switz. see Basel	
118 C2	Basoko Dem. Rep. Congo	
81 C2	Basra Iraq	
128 C2	Bassano Can.	
114 C4	Bassar Togo	
63 A2	Bassein Myanmar	
147 D3	Basse-Terre Guadeloupe	
147 D3	Basseterre St Kitts and Nevis	
114 B3	Bassikounou Maur.	
51 D3	Bass Strait Austr.	
79 C2	Bastak Iran	
101 E2	Bastheim Ger.	
75 C2	Basti India	
105 D3	Bastia Corsica France	
100 B2	Bastogne Belgium	
142 B2	Bastrop U.S.A.	
	Basuo China see Dongfang	

118 A2 **Bata** Equat. Guinea
83 J2 **Batagay** Russia
154 B2 **Bataguassu** Brazil
106 B2 **Batalha** Port.
60 B1 **Batam** Indon.
71 C3 **Batan** *i.* Phil.
118 B2 **Batangafo** C.A.R.
64 B1 **Batangas** Phil.
60 B2 **Batang Hari** *r.* Indon.
71 C3 **Batan Islands** Phil.
141 D2 **Batavia** U.S.A.
91 D2 **Bataysk** Russia
130 B2 **Batchawana Mountain** *h.* Can.
50 C1 **Batchelor** Austr.
63 B2 **Bătdâmbâng** Cambodia
53 D3 **Batemans Bay** Austr.
142 B1 **Batesville** U.S.A.
89 D2 **Batetskiy** Russia
99 B3 **Bath** U.K.
74 B1 **Bathinda** India
53 C2 **Bathurst** Austr.
131 D2 **Bathurst** Can.
126 D2 **Bathurst Inlet** Can.
126 D2 **Bathurst Inlet (abandoned)** Can.
50 C1 **Bathurst Island** Austr.
126 E1 **Bathurst Island** Can.
78 B1 **Bāṭin, Wādī al** *watercourse* Asia
81 C2 **Batman** Turkey
115 C1 **Batna** Alg.
142 B2 **Baton Rouge** U.S.A.
144 B2 **Batopilas** Mex.
118 B2 **Batouri** Cameroon
154 B1 **Batovi** Brazil
92 I1 **Båtsfjord** Norway
73 C4 **Batticaloa** Sri Lanka
109 B2 **Battipaglia** Italy
129 D2 **Battle** *r.* Can.
140 B2 **Battle Creek** U.S.A.
135 C2 **Battle Mountain** U.S.A.
74 B1 **Battura Glacier** Pak.
117 B4 **Batu** *mt.* Eth.
60 A2 **Batu, Kepulauan** *is* Indon.
81 C1 **Bat'umi** Georgia
60 B1 **Batu Pahat** Malaysia
59 C3 **Baubau** Indon.
115 C3 **Bauchi** Nigeria
104 B2 **Baugé-en-Anjou** France
105 D2 **Baume-les-Dames** France
154 C2 **Bauru** Brazil
154 B1 **Baús** Brazil
88 B2 **Bauska** Latvia
102 C1 **Bautzen** Ger.
144 B2 **Bavispe** *r.* Mex.
87 E3 **Bavly** Russia
62 A1 **Bawdwin** Myanmar
61 C2 **Bawean** *i.* Indon.
114 B3 **Bawku** Ghana
146 C2 **Bayamo** Cuba
Bayan Gol China *see* **Dengkou**
68 C1 **Bayanhongor** Mongolia
70 A2 **Bayan Hot** China
70 A1 **Bayannur** China
69 D2 **Bayan Shutu** China
69 D1 **Bayan-Uul** Mongolia
64 B2 **Bayawan** Phil.
80 C1 **Bayburt** Turkey
140 C2 **Bay City** *MI* U.S.A.
139 D3 **Bay City** *TX* U.S.A.
86 F2 **Baydaratskaya Guba** Russia
117 C4 **Baydhabo** Somalia
81 C2 **Bayjī** Iraq
Baykal, Ozero *l.* Russia *see* **Baikal, Lake**
83 I3 **Baykal'skiy Khrebet** *mts* Russia
76 C2 **Baykonyr** Kazakh.
87 E3 **Baymak** Russia
64 B1 **Bayombong** Phil.
104 B3 **Bayonne** France
111 C3 **Bayramiç** Turkey
101 E3 **Bayreuth** Ger.
78 B3 **Bayt al Faqīh** Yemen
106 C2 **Baza** Spain
106 C2 **Baza, Sierra de** *mts* Spain
74 A1 **Bāzārak** Afgh.
76 A2 **Bazardyuzyu, Gora** *mt.* Azer./Russia
104 B3 **Bazas** France
74 A2 **Bazdar** Pak.
70 A2 **Bazhong** China
79 D2 **Bazmān** Iran
79 D2 **Bazmān, Kūh-e** *mt.* Iran
121 □D2 **Bé, Nosy** *i.* Madag.
99 D3 **Beachy Head** U.K.
123 C3 **Beacon Bay** S. Africa
50 B1 **Beagle Gulf** Austr.
121 □D2 **Bealanana** Madag.
97 B1 **Béal an Mhuirthead** Ireland
130 B2 **Beardmore** Can.
Bear Island Arctic Ocean *see* **Bjørnøya**
134 E1 **Bear Paw Mountain** U.S.A.
147 C3 **Beata, Cabo** *c.* Dom. Rep.
147 C3 **Beata, Isla** *i.* Dom. Rep.
137 D2 **Beatrice** U.S.A.
135 C3 **Beatty** U.S.A.
53 D1 **Beaudesert** Austr.
52 B3 **Beaufort** Austr.
61 C1 **Beaufort** *Sabah* Malaysia
143 D2 **Beaufort** U.S.A.
160 L2 **Beaufort Sea** Can./U.S.A.
122 B3 **Beaufort West** S. Africa
96 B2 **Beauly** *r.* U.K.
100 B2 **Beaumont** Belgium
54 A3 **Beaumont** N.Z.
139 E2 **Beaumont** U.S.A.
105 C2 **Beaune** France
100 B2 **Beauraing** Belgium
129 E2 **Beauséjour** Can.
104 C2 **Beauvais** France
129 D2 **Beauval** Can.
129 D2 **Beaver** *r.* Can.
135 D3 **Beaver** U.S.A.
126 B2 **Beaver Creek** Can.
140 B2 **Beaver Dam** U.S.A.
129 E2 **Beaver Hill Lake** Can.
140 B1 **Beaver Island** U.S.A.
128 C2 **Beaverlodge** Can.
74 B2 **Beawar** India
154 C2 **Bebedouro** Brazil
101 D2 **Bebra** Ger.
106 B1 **Becerreá** Spain
114 B1 **Béchar** Alg.
140 C3 **Beckley** U.S.A.
117 B4 **Bedelē** Eth.
99 C2 **Bedford** U.K.
140 B3 **Bedford** U.S.A.
100 C1 **Bedum** Neth.
53 D2 **Beecroft Peninsula** Austr.
101 F1 **Beelitz** Ger.
53 D1 **Beenleigh** Austr.
80 B2 **Beersheba** Israel
139 D3 **Beeville** U.S.A.
53 C3 **Bega** Austr.
107 D1 **Begur, Cap de** *c.* Spain
128 C1 **Behchokò** Can.
81 D2 **Behshahr** Iran
69 E1 **Bei'an** China
71 A3 **Beihai** China
70 B2 **Beijing** China
100 C1 **Beilen** Neth.
96 A2 **Beinn Mhòr** *h.* U.K.
121 C2 **Beira** Moz.
80 B2 **Beirut** Lebanon
123 C1 **Beitbridge** Zimbabwe
106 B2 **Beja** Port.
115 C1 **Bejaïa** Alg.
106 B1 **Béjar** Spain
74 A2 **Beji** *r.* Pak.
103 E2 **Békés** Hungary
103 E2 **Békéscsaba** Hungary
121 □D3 **Bekily** Madag.
74 A2 **Bela** Pak.
123 C1 **Bela-Bela** S. Africa
118 B2 **Bélabo** Cameroon
109 D2 **Bela Crkva** Serbia
61 C1 **Belaga** *Sarawak* Malaysia
73 B3 **Belagavi** India
88 C3 **Belarus** *country* Europe
Belau *country* N. Pacific Ocea *see* **Palau**
123 D2 **Bela Vista** Moz.
60 A1 **Belawan** Indon.
83 M2 **Belaya** *r.* Russia
103 D1 **Bełchatów** Pol.
130 C1 **Belcher Islands** Can.
117 C4 **Beledweyne** Somalia
151 D2 **Belém** Brazil
138 B2 **Belen** U.S.A.
89 E3 **Belev** Russia
97 D1 **Belfast** U.K.
141 F2 **Belfast** U.S.A.
105 D2 **Belfort** France
Belgaum India *see* **Belagavi**
100 B2 **Belgium** *country* Europe
91 D1 **Belgorod** Russia
109 D2 **Belgrade** Serbia
134 D1 **Belgrade** U.S.A.
60 B2 **Belinyu** Indon.
61 B2 **Belitung** *i.* Indon.
146 B3 **Belize** Belize
146 B3 **Belize** *country* Central Americ
83 K1 **Bel'kovskiy, Ostrov** *i.* Russia
128 B2 **Bella Bella** Can.
104 C2 **Bellac** France
128 B2 **Bella Coola** Can.
53 C1 **Bellata** Austr.
136 C2 **Belle Fourche** U.S.A.
136 C2 **Belle Fourche** *r.* U.S.A.
143 D3 **Belle Glade** U.S.A.
104 B2 **Belle-Île** *i.* France
131 E1 **Belle Isle** *i.* Can.
131 E1 **Belle Isle, Strait of** Can.
130 C2 **Belleville** Can.
140 B3 **Belleville** *IL* U.S.A.
137 D3 **Belleville** *KS* U.S.A.
134 B1 **Bellevue** U.S.A.
134 B1 **Bellingham** U.S.A.
55 O2 **Bellingshausen Sea** Antarcti
105 D2 **Bellinzona** Switz.
108 B1 **Belluno** Italy
122 A3 **Bellville** S. Africa
155 E1 **Belmonte** Brazil
146 B3 **Belmopan** Belize
69 E1 **Belogorsk** Russia
121 □D3 **Beloha** Madag.
155 D1 **Belo Horizonte** Brazil
140 B2 **Beloit** U.S.A.
86 C2 **Belomorsk** Russia
91 D3 **Belorechensk** Russia
87 E3 **Beloretsk** Russia
Belorussia *country* Europe *se* **Belarus**
86 F2 **Beloyarskiy** Russia
86 C2 **Beloye, Ozero** *l.* Russia
Beloye More *sea* Russia *see* **White Sea**
86 C2 **Belozersk** Russia
77 E2 **Belukha, Gora** *mt.* Kazakh./Russia
86 D2 **Belush'ye** Russia
89 D2 **Belyy** Russia

82 F2	Belyy, Ostrov i. Russia	
87 E1	Bemidji U.S.A.	
48 C2	Bena Dibele Dem. Rep. Congo	
63 C3	Benalla Austr.	
36 B1	Benavente Spain	
96 A2	Benbecula i. U.K.	
34 B2	Bend U.S.A.	
43 C3	Bendearg mt. S. Africa	
90 B2	Bender Moldova	
52 B3	Bendigo Austr.	
21 C2	Bene Moz.	
39 D2	Benešov Czechia	
59 C2	Benevento Italy	
59 C2	Bengal, Bay of sea Indian Ocean	
73 B3	Bengaluru India	
70 B2	Bengbu China	
45 E1	Benghazi Libya	
61 B1	Bengkayang Indon.	
60 B2	Bengkulu Indon.	
20 A2	Benguela Angola	
96 B1	Ben Hope h. U.K.	
62 B2	Beni r. Bol.	
48 C2	Beni Dem. Rep. Congo	
44 B1	Beni Abbès Alg.	
36 B2	Benidorm Spain	
44 B1	Béni Mellal Morocco	
44 C4	Benin country Africa	
44 C4	Benin, Bight of g. Africa	
45 C4	Benin City Nigeria	
63 D2	Benito Juárez Arg.	
60 B2	Benjamin Constant Brazil	
42 A2	Benjamín Hill Mex.	
59 C1	Benjina Indon.	
96 B2	Ben Lawers mt. U.K.	
96 B2	Ben Lomond h. U.K.	
96 C2	Ben Macdui mt. U.K.	
96 A2	Ben More h. U.K.	
64 B2	Benmore, Lake N.Z.	
96 B2	Ben More Assynt h. U.K.	
28 A2	Bennett (abandoned) Can.	
43 K1	Bennetta, Ostrov i. Russia	
96 B2	Ben Nevis mt. U.K.	
41 E2	Bennington U.S.A.	
23 C3	Benoni S. Africa	
41 D3	Bensheim Ger.	
38 A2	Benson U.S.A.	
61 C2	Benteng Indon.	
40 B2	Benton Harbor U.S.A.	
40 B3	Bentonville U.S.A.	
45 C4	Benue r. Nigeria	
97 B1	Benwee Head Ireland	
96 B2	Ben Wyvis mt. U.K.	
70 C1	Benxi China	
	Beograd Serbia see Belgrade	
75 C2	Beohari India	
34 B1	Beppu Japan	
59 C2	Berane Montenegro	
37 A2	Berat Albania	
59 C3	Berau, Teluk b. Indon.	
16 B3	Berber Sudan	
17 C3	Berbera Somalia	
48 B2	Berbérati C.A.R.	
34 C1	Berck France	
91 D2	Berdyans'k Ukr.	
90 C2	Berdychiv Ukr.	
90 A2	Berehove Ukr.	
59 D3	Bereina P.N.G.	
76 B1	Bereket Turkm.	
92 D3	Berens River Can.	
90 A2	Berezhany Ukr.	
90 C1	Berezivka Ukr.	
90 B1	Berezne Ukr.	
86 D2	Bereznik Russia	
86 E3	Berezniki Russia	
86 F2	Berezovo Russia	
37 D1	Berga Spain	
41 C3	Bergama Turkey	
108 A1	Bergamo Italy	
101 D1	Bergen Ger.	
93 E3	Bergen Norway	
102 C1	Bergen auf Rügen Ger.	
100 B2	Bergen op Zoom Neth.	
104 C3	Bergerac France	
100 C2	Bergheim Ger.	
100 C2	Bergisch Gladbach Ger.	
122 A1	Bergland Namibia	
92 H2	Bergsviken Sweden	
83 M3	Beringa, Ostrov i. Russia	
100 B2	Beringen Belgium	
124 C3	Bering Sea N. Pacific Ocean	
83 N2	Bering Strait Russia/U.S.A.	
135 B3	Berkeley U.S.A.	
100 B1	Berkhout Neth.	
55 Q2	Berkner Sub-glacial Island Antarctica	
110 B2	Berkovitsa Bulg.	
92 I1	Berlevåg Norway	
101 F1	Berlin Ger.	
141 E2	Berlin U.S.A.	
101 E2	Berlingerode Ger.	
53 D3	Bermagui Austr.	
144 B2	Bermejillo Mex.	
152 B3	Bermejo Bol.	
131 D1	Bermen, Lac l. Can.	
125 K4	Bermuda terr. N. Atlantic Ocean	
105 D2	Bern Switz.	
101 E2	Bernburg (Saale) Ger.	
127 F2	Bernier Bay Can.	
100 C3	Bernkastel-Kues Ger.	
121 □D2	Beroroha Madag.	
52 B2	Berri Austr.	
107 D2	Berrouaghia Alg.	
146 C2	Berry Islands Bahamas	
100 C1	Bersenbrück Ger.	
90 B2	Bershad' Ukr.	
131 D1	Berté, Lac l. Can.	
118 B2	Bertoua Cameroon	
150 B2	Beruri Brazil	
98 B1	Berwick-upon-Tweed U.K.	
91 C2	Beryslav Ukr.	
121 □D2	Besalampy Madag.	
105 D2	Besançon France	
129 D2	Besnard Lake Can.	
142 C2	Bessemer U.S.A.	
76 B2	Besshoky, Gora h. Kazakh.	
106 B1	Betanzos Spain	
118 B2	Bétaré Oya Cameroon	
122 A2	Bethanie Namibia	
123 C2	Bethlehem S. Africa	
141 D2	Bethlehem U.S.A.	
121 □D3	Betioky Madag.	
77 D2	Betpakdala plain Kazakh.	
121 □D3	Betroka Madag.	
131 D2	Betsiamites Can.	
121 □D2	Betsiboka r. Madag.	
137 E2	Bettendorf U.S.A.	
75 C2	Bettiah India	
75 B2	Betul India	
75 B2	Betwa r. India	
98 B2	Betws-y-Coed U.K.	
98 C2	Beverley U.K.	
101 D2	Beverungen Ger.	
100 B1	Beverwijk Neth.	
99 D3	Bexhill U.K.	
111 C2	Beykoz Turkey	
114 B4	Beyla Guinea	
76 B2	Beyneu Kazakh.	
80 B1	Beypazarı Turkey	
	Beyrouth Lebanon see Beirut	
80 B2	Beyşehir Turkey	
80 B2	Beyşehir Gölü l. Turkey	
91 D2	Beysug r. Russia	
88 C2	Bezhanitsy Russia	
89 E2	Bezhetsk Russia	
105 C3	Béziers France	
75 C2	Bhadrak India	
73 B3	Bhadravati India	
75 C2	Bhagalpur India	
74 A2	Bhairi Hol mt. Pak.	
74 B1	Bhakkar Pak.	
62 A1	Bhamo Myanmar	
75 C3	Bhanjanagar India	
74 B2	Bharatpur India	
74 B2	Bharuch India	
75 C3	Bhavnagar India	
75 C2	Bhawanipatna India	
123 D2	Bhekuzulu S. Africa	
74 B2	Bhilwara India	
73 B3	Bhima r. India	
123 C3	Bhisho S. Africa	
74 B2	Bhiwani India	
123 C3	Bhongweni S. Africa	
74 B2	Bhopal India	
75 C2	Bhubaneshwar India	
74 A2	Bhuj India	
74 B2	Bhusawal India	
75 D2	Bhutan country Asia	
59 D3	Biak Indon.	
59 D3	Biak i. Indon.	
103 E1	Biała Podlaska Pol.	
103 D1	Białogard Pol.	
103 E1	Białystok Pol.	
109 C3	Bianco Italy	
104 B3	Biarritz France	
105 D2	Biasca Switz.	
66 D2	Bibai Japan	
120 A2	Bibala Angola	
102 B2	Biberach an der Riß Ger.	
115 C4	Bida Nigeria	
141 E2	Biddeford U.S.A.	
99 A3	Bideford U.K.	
101 D2	Biedenkopf Ger.	
105 D2	Biel/Bienne Switz.	
101 D1	Bielefeld Ger.	
108 A1	Biella Italy	
103 D1	Bielsko-Biała Pol.	
63 B2	Biên Hoa Vietnam	
	Bienne Switz. see Biel/Bienne	
130 C1	Bienville, Lac l. Can.	
100 B3	Bièvre Belgium	
118 B3	Bifoun Gabon	
111 C2	Biga Turkey	
123 D2	Big Bend Swaziland	
129 D2	Biggar Can.	
96 C2	Biggar U.K.	
134 D1	Big Hole r. U.S.A.	
136 B1	Bighorn r. U.S.A.	
136 B2	Bighorn Mountains U.S.A.	
139 C2	Big Lake U.S.A.	
140 B2	Big Rapids U.S.A.	
129 D2	Big River Can.	
129 E2	Big Sand Lake Can.	
137 D2	Big Sioux r. U.S.A.	
139 C2	Big Spring U.S.A.	
134 E1	Big Timber U.S.A.	
130 B1	Big Trout Lake Can.	
130 A1	Big Trout Lake Can.	
109 C2	Bihać Bos. & Herz.	
75 C2	Bihar Sharif India	
110 B1	Bihor, Vârful mt. Romania	
114 A3	Bijagós, Arquipélago dos is Guinea-Bissau	
81 C2	Bijār Iran	
109 C2	Bijeljina Bos. & Herz.	
109 C2	Bijelo Polje Montenegro	
71 A3	Bijie China	
74 B2	Bikaner India	
69 E1	Bikin Russia	
118 B3	Bikoro Dem. Rep. Congo	
79 C2	Bilād Banī Bū 'Alī Oman	
75 C2	Bilaspur India	
90 B2	Bila Tserkva Ukr.	

63 A2 **Bilauktaung Range** *mts* Myanmar/Thai.
106 C1 **Bilbao** Spain
111 C2 **Bilecik** Turkey
103 E1 **Biłgoraj** Pol.
90 C2 **Bilhorod-Dnistrovs'kyy** Ukr.
119 C2 **Bili** Dem. Rep. Congo
83 M2 **Bilibino** Russia
134 E1 **Billings** U.S.A.
99 B3 **Bill of Portland** *hd* U.K.
115 D3 **Bilma** Niger
115 D3 **Bilma, Grand Erg de** *des.* Niger
91 D2 **Bil'mak** Ukr.
51 E2 **Biloela** Austr.
91 C2 **Bilohirs'k** Ukr.
90 B1 **Bilohir"ya** Ukr.
91 C1 **Bilopillya** Ukr.
91 D2 **Bilovods'k** Ukr.
142 C2 **Biloxi** U.S.A.
51 C2 **Bilpa Morea Claypan** *salt flat* Austr.
101 E2 **Bilshausen** Ger.
115 E3 **Biltine** Chad
90 C2 **Bilyayivka** Ukr.
143 E3 **Bimini Islands** Bahamas
75 B2 **Bina-Etawa** India
59 C3 **Binaiya, Gunung** *mt.* Indon.
118 B3 **Bindu** Dem. Rep. Congo
121 C2 **Bindura** Zimbabwe
107 D1 **Binéfar** Spain
53 D1 **Bingara** Austr.
100 C3 **Bingen am Rhein** Ger.
141 F1 **Bingham** U.S.A.
141 D2 **Binghamton** U.S.A.
81 C2 **Bingöl** Turkey
60 A1 **Binjai** Indon.
60 B2 **Bintuhan** Indon.
61 C1 **Bintulu** *Sarawak* Malaysia
70 B2 **Binzhou** China
109 C2 **Biograd na Moru** Croatia
118 A2 **Bioko** *i.* Equat. Guinea
118 C1 **Birao** C.A.R.
75 C2 **Biratnagar** Nepal
128 C2 **Birch Mountains** Can.
51 C2 **Birdsville** Austr.
80 B2 **Birecik** Turkey
60 A1 **Bireun** Indon.
75 C2 **Birganj** Nepal
154 B2 **Birigui** Brazil
76 B3 **Bīrjand** Iran
98 B2 **Birkenhead** U.K.
114 B2 **Bir Lahlou** Western Sahara
99 C2 **Birmingham** U.K.
142 C2 **Birmingham** U.S.A.
114 A2 **Bîr Mogreïn** Maur.
115 C3 **Birnin Kebbi** Nigeria
115 C3 **Birnin Konni** Niger
69 E1 **Birobidzhan** Russia
97 C2 **Birr** Ireland
96 C1 **Birsay** U.K.
78 A2 **Bi'r Shalatayn** Egypt
91 D1 **Biryuch** Russia
88 B2 **Biržai** Lith.
75 B2 **Bisalpur** India
138 B2 **Bisbee** U.S.A.
104 A2 **Biscay, Bay of** *sea* France/Spain
102 C2 **Bischofshofen** Austria
130 B2 **Biscotasi Lake** Can.
77 D2 **Bishkek** Kyrg.
135 C3 **Bishop** U.S.A.
69 E1 **Bishui** China
150 B1 **Bisinaca** Col.
115 C1 **Biskra** Alg.
136 C1 **Bismarck** U.S.A.
48 D3 **Bismarck Sea** *sea* P.N.G.
107 D2 **Bissa, Djebel** *mt.* Alg.
114 A3 **Bissau** Guinea-Bissau
129 E2 **Bissett** Can.
128 C2 **Bistcho Lake** Can.
110 B1 **Bistrița** Romania
110 C1 **Bistrița** *r.* Romania
100 C3 **Bitburg** Ger.
105 D2 **Bitche** France
115 D3 **Bitkine** Chad
109 D2 **Bitola** Macedonia
109 C2 **Bitonto** Italy
122 A3 **Bitterfontein** S. Africa
134 D1 **Bitterroot** *r.* U.S.A.
134 C1 **Bitterroot Range** *mts* U.S.A.
91 D1 **Bityug** *r.* Russia
115 D3 **Biu** Nigeria
67 C3 **Biwa-ko** *l.* Japan
68 B1 **Biysk** Russia
115 C1 **Bizerte** Tunisia
92 □A2 **Bjargtangar** *hd* Iceland
92 G3 **Bjästa** Sweden
92 G2 **Bjerkvik** Norway
Björneborg Fin. *see* **Pori**
82 C2 **Bjørnøya** *i.* Arctic Ocean
114 B3 **Bla** Mali
137 E3 **Black** *r.* U.S.A.
51 D2 **Blackall** Austr.
98 B2 **Blackburn** U.K.
134 D2 **Blackfoot** U.S.A.
102 B2 **Black Forest** *mts* Ger.
136 C2 **Black Hills** U.S.A.
96 B2 **Black Isle** *pen.* U.K.
129 D2 **Black Lake** Can.
129 D2 **Black Lake** Can.
99 B3 **Black Mountains** *hills* U.K.
98 B2 **Blackpool** U.K.
62 B1 **Black River** *r.* Vietnam
140 A2 **Black River Falls** U.S.A.
140 C3 **Blacksburg** U.S.A.
80 B1 **Black Sea** Asia/Europe
97 A1 **Blacksod Bay** Ireland
97 C2 **Blackstairs Mountains** *hills* Ireland
114 B4 **Black Volta** *r.* Africa
97 C2 **Blackwater** *r.* Ireland
128 B1 **Blackwater Lake** Can.
50 A3 **Blackwood** *r.* Austr.
76 A2 **Blagodarnyy** Russia
110 B2 **Blagoevgrad** Bulg.
69 E1 **Blagoveshchensk** Russia
129 D2 **Blaine Lake** Can.
137 D2 **Blair** U.S.A.
96 C2 **Blair Atholl** U.K.
96 C2 **Blairgowrie** U.K.
143 D2 **Blakely** U.S.A.
105 D2 **Blanc, Mont** *mt.* France/Italy
153 B4 **Blanca, Bahía** *b.* Arg.
52 A1 **Blanche, Lake** *imp. l.* Austr.
152 B2 **Blanco** *r.* Bol.
131 E1 **Blanc-Sablon** Can.
92 □A2 **Blanda** *r.* Iceland
99 B3 **Blandford Forum** U.K.
135 E3 **Blanding** U.S.A.
107 D1 **Blanes** Spain
60 A1 **Blangkejeren** Indon.
100 C2 **Blankenheim** Ger.
100 C2 **Blankenrath** Ger.
103 D2 **Blansko** Czechia
121 C2 **Blantyre** Malawi
98 C1 **Blaydon** U.K.
53 C2 **Blayney** Austr.
54 B2 **Blenheim** N.Z.
115 C1 **Blida** Alg.
130 B2 **Blind River** Can.
123 C2 **Bloemfontein** S. Africa
123 C2 **Bloemhof** S. Africa
123 C2 **Bloemhof Dam** S. Africa
92 □A2 **Blönduós** Iceland
97 B1 **Bloody Foreland** *pt* Ireland
138 B1 **Bloomfield** U.S.A.
140 B2 **Bloomington** *IL* U.S.A.
140 B3 **Bloomington** *IN* U.S.A.
140 C3 **Bluefield** U.S.A.
146 B3 **Bluefields** Nic.
53 C2 **Blue Mountains** Austr.
134 C1 **Blue Mountains** U.S.A.
116 B3 **Blue Nile** *r.* Eth./Sudan
126 D2 **Bluenose Lake** Can.
140 C3 **Blue Ridge** *mts* U.S.A.
97 B1 **Blue Stack Mountains** *hills* Ireland
54 A3 **Bluff** N.Z.
135 E3 **Bluff** U.S.A.
152 D3 **Blumenau** Brazil
52 A2 **Blyth** Austr.
98 C1 **Blyth** U.K.
135 D4 **Blythe** U.S.A.
142 C1 **Blytheville** U.S.A.
114 A4 **Bo** Sierra Leone
64 B1 **Boac** Phil.
151 D2 **Boa Esperança, Açude** *resr* Brazil
150 B1 **Boa Vista** Brazil
53 C2 **Bobadah** Austr.
71 B3 **Bobai** China
121 □D2 **Bobaomby, Tanjona** *c.* Mad
114 B3 **Bobo-Dioulasso** Burkina F
89 F3 **Bobrov** Russia
91 C1 **Bobrovytsya** Ukr.
Bobruysk Belarus *see* **Babruysk/Bobruysk**
91 C2 **Bobrynets'** Ukr.
121 □D3 **Boby** *mt.* Madag.
150 B2 **Boca do Acre** Brazil
155 D1 **Bocaiúva** Brazil
118 B2 **Bocaranga** C.A.R.
103 E2 **Bochnia** Pol.
100 C2 **Bocholt** Ger.
100 C2 **Bochum** Ger.
101 E1 **Bockenem** Ger.
118 B2 **Boda** C.A.R.
83 I3 **Bodaybo** Russia
115 D3 **Bodélé** *reg.* Chad
92 H2 **Boden** Sweden
99 A3 **Bodmin** U.K.
99 A3 **Bodmin Moor** *moorland* U.K
92 F2 **Bodø** Norway
111 C3 **Bodrum** Turkey
118 C3 **Boende** Dem. Rep. Congo
142 C2 **Bogalusa** U.S.A.
114 B3 **Bogandé** Burkina Faso
68 B2 **Bogda Shan** *mts* China
53 D1 **Boggabilla** Austr.
97 B2 **Boggeragh Mountains** *hills* Ireland
100 B3 **Bogny-sur-Meuse** France
97 C2 **Bog of Allen** *reg.* Ireland
53 C3 **Bogong, Mount** Austr.
60 B2 **Bogor** Indon.
89 E3 **Bogoroditsk** Russia
150 A1 **Bogotá** Col.
82 G3 **Bogotol** Russia
83 H3 **Boguchany** Russia
91 E2 **Boguchar** Russia
70 B2 **Bo Hai** *g.* China
100 A3 **Bohain-en-Vermandois** France
70 B2 **Bohai Wan** *b.* China
123 C2 **Bohlokong** S. Africa
102 C2 **Böhmer Wald** *mts* Ger.
91 D1 **Bohodukhiv** Ukr.
64 B2 **Bohol** *i.* Phil.
64 B2 **Bohol Sea** Phil.
68 B2 **Bohu** China
155 C2 **Boi, Ponta do** *pt* Brazil
154 B1 **Bois** *r.* Brazil
126 C2 **Bois, Lac des** *l.* Can.

34 C2 **Boise** U.S.A.
39 C1 **Boise City** U.S.A.
23 C2 **Boitumelong** S. Africa
01 E1 **Boizenburg/Elbe** Ger.
76 B3 **Bojnūrd** Iran
18 B3 **Bokatola** Dem. Rep. Congo
14 A3 **Boké** Guinea
18 C3 **Bokele** Dem. Rep. Congo
93 E4 **Boknafjorden** *sea chan.* Norway
15 D3 **Bokoro** Chad
63 A2 **Bokpyin** Myanmar
89 D2 **Boksitogorsk** Russia
22 B2 **Bokspits** Botswana
14 A3 **Bolama** Guinea-Bissau
63 B2 **Bolavén, Phouphiang** *plat.* Laos
04 C2 **Bolbec** France
77 E2 **Bole** China
18 B3 **Boleko** Dem. Rep. Congo
14 B3 **Bolgatanga** Ghana
90 B2 **Bolhrad** Ukr.
66 B1 **Boli** China
62 B2 **Bolikhamxai** Laos
10 C2 **Bolintin-Vale** Romania
37 E3 **Bolivar** U.S.A.
50 A1 **Bolívar, Pico** *mt.* Venez.
52 B2 **Bolivia** *country* S. America
89 E3 **Bolkhov** Russia
05 C3 **Bollène** France
93 G3 **Bollnäs** Sweden
53 C1 **Bollon** Austr.
01 E2 **Bollstedt** Ger.
93 F4 **Bolmen** *l.* Sweden
18 B3 **Bolobo** Dem. Rep. Congo
08 B2 **Bologna** Italy
89 D2 **Bologovo** Russia
89 D2 **Bologoye** Russia
18 B2 **Bolomba** Dem. Rep. Congo
83 H1 **Bol'shevik, Ostrov** *i.* Russia
86 E2 **Bol'shezemel'skaya Tundra** *lowland* Russia
66 B2 **Bol'shoy Kamen'** Russia
Bol'shoy Kavkaz *mts* Asia/Europe *see* **Caucasus**
83 K2 **Bol'shoy Lyakhovskiy, Ostrov** *i.* Russia
00 B1 **Bolsward** Neth.
98 B2 **Bolton** U.K.
80 B1 **Bolu** Turkey
92 □A2 **Bolungarvík** Iceland
08 B1 **Bolzano** Italy
18 B3 **Boma** Dem. Rep. Congo
53 D2 **Bomaderry** Austr.
53 C3 **Bombala** Austr.
Bombay India *see* **Mumbai**
55 C1 **Bom Despacho** Brazil
75 D2 **Bomdila** India
51 D3 **Bom Jesus da Lapa** Brazil
55 D2 **Bom Jesus do Itabapoana** Brazil
15 D1 **Bon, Cap** *c.* Tunisia
47 D3 **Bonaire** *i.* West Indies
47 D3 **Bonaire** *mun.* West Indies
50 B1 **Bonaparte Archipelago** *is* Austr.
31 E2 **Bonavista** Can.
31 E2 **Bonavista Bay** Can.
18 C2 **Bondo** Dem. Rep. Congo
14 B4 **Bondoukou** Côte d'Ivoire
58 C3 **Bonerate, Kepulauan** *is* Indon.
55 C1 **Bonfinópolis de Minas** Brazil
17 B4 **Bonga** Eth.
75 D2 **Bongaigaon** India
18 C2 **Bongandanga** Dem. Rep. Congo
18 C2 **Bongo, Massif des** *mts* C.A.R.
15 D3 **Bongor** Chad
114 B4 **Bongouanou** Côte d'Ivoire
63 B2 **Bông Sơn** Vietnam
139 D2 **Bonham** U.S.A.
105 D3 **Bonifacio** *Corsica* France
108 A2 **Bonifacio, Strait of** France/Italy
100 C2 **Bonn** Ger.
134 C1 **Bonners Ferry** U.S.A.
50 A3 **Bonnie Rock** Austr.
129 C2 **Bonnyville** Can.
108 A2 **Bonorva** *Sardinia* Italy
61 C1 **Bontang** Indon.
64 B1 **Bontoc** Phil.
123 C3 **Bontrug** S. Africa
52 B2 **Booligal** Austr.
53 C1 **Boomi** Austr.
53 D1 **Boonah** Austr.
137 E2 **Boone** U.S.A.
142 C2 **Booneville** U.S.A.
137 E3 **Boonville** U.S.A.
53 C2 **Boorowa** Austr.
126 F2 **Boothia, Gulf of** Can.
126 E2 **Boothia Peninsula** Can.
100 C2 **Boppard** Ger.
144 B2 **Boquilla, Presa de la** *resr* Mex.
109 D2 **Bor** Serbia
117 B4 **Bor** South Sudan
80 B2 **Bor** Turkey
121 □E2 **Boraha, Nosy** *i.* Madag.
76 B2 **Borankul** Kazakh.
93 F4 **Borås** Sweden
79 C2 **Borāzjān** Iran
150 C2 **Borba** Brazil
104 B3 **Bordeaux** France
127 F2 **Borden Peninsula** Can.
52 B3 **Bordertown** Austr.
107 D2 **Bordj Bou Arréridj** Alg.
107 D2 **Bordj Bounaama** Alg.
115 C1 **Bordj Messaouda** Alg.
115 C2 **Bordj Omer Driss** Alg.
94 B1 **Borðoy** *i.* Faroe Is
92 □A3 **Borgarnes** Iceland
108 A1 **Borgosesia** Italy
87 D3 **Borisoglebsk** Russia
89 E2 **Borisoglebskiy** Russia
Borisov Belarus *see* **Barysaw/Borisov**
91 D1 **Borisovka** Russia
100 C2 **Borken** Ger.
92 G2 **Borkenes** Norway
100 C1 **Borkum** Ger.
100 C1 **Borkum** *i.* Ger.
93 G3 **Borlänge** Sweden
101 F2 **Borna** Ger.
61 C1 **Borneo** *i.* Asia
93 F4 **Bornholm** *i.* Denmark
111 C3 **Bornova** Turkey
90 B1 **Borodyanka** Ukr.
89 D2 **Borovichi** Russia
89 E2 **Borovsk** Russia
107 C2 **Borriana** Spain
51 C1 **Borroloola** Austr.
110 B1 **Borșa** Romania
90 B2 **Borshchiv** Ukr.
69 D1 **Borshchovochnyy Khrebet** *mts* Russia
101 E1 **Börßum** Ger.
Bortala China *see* **Bole**
81 C2 **Borūjerd** Iran
65 B2 **Boryeong** S. Korea
90 A2 **Boryslav** Ukr.
90 C1 **Boryspil'** Ukr.
91 C1 **Borzna** Ukr.
69 D1 **Borzya** Russia
109 C1 **Bosanska Dubica** Bos. & Herz.
109 C1 **Bosanska Gradiška** Bos. & Herz.
109 C2 **Bosanska Krupa** Bos. & Herz.
109 C1 **Bosanski Novi** Bos. & Herz.
109 C2 **Bosansko Grahovo** Bos. & Herz.
123 C2 **Boshof** S. Africa
109 C2 **Bosnia and Herzegovina** *country* Europe
118 B2 **Bosobolo** Dem. Rep. Congo
110 C2 **Bosporus** *str.* Turkey
118 B2 **Bossangoa** C.A.R.
118 B2 **Bossembélé** C.A.R.
68 B2 **Bosten Hu** *l.* China
98 C2 **Boston** U.K.
141 E2 **Boston** U.S.A.
142 B1 **Boston Mountains** U.S.A.
53 D2 **Botany Bay** Austr.
110 B2 **Botev** *mt.* Bulg.
93 G3 **Bothnia, Gulf of** Fin./Sweden
110 C1 **Botoșani** Romania
123 C2 **Botshabelo** S. Africa
120 B3 **Botswana** *country* Africa
109 C3 **Botte Donato, Monte** *mt.* Italy
136 C1 **Bottineau** U.S.A.
100 C2 **Bottrop** Ger.
154 C2 **Botucatu** Brazil
114 B4 **Bouaké** Côte d'Ivoire
118 B2 **Bouar** C.A.R.
114 B1 **Bou Arfa** Morocco
131 D2 **Bouctouche** Can.
107 E2 **Bougaa** Alg.
114 B3 **Bougouni** Mali
100 B3 **Bouillon** Belgium
107 D2 **Bouira** Alg.
114 A2 **Boujdour** Western Sahara
136 B2 **Boulder** U.S.A.
135 D3 **Boulder City** U.S.A.
51 C2 **Boulia** Austr.
104 C2 **Boulogne-Billancourt** France
99 D3 **Boulogne-sur-Mer** France
118 B3 **Boumango** Gabon
118 B2 **Boumba** *r.* Cameroon
107 D2 **Boumerdès** Alg.
114 B4 **Bouna** Côte d'Ivoire
114 B4 **Boundiali** Côte d'Ivoire
134 D2 **Bountiful** U.S.A.
114 B3 **Bourem** Mali
104 C2 **Bourganeuf** France
105 D2 **Bourg-en-Bresse** France
104 C2 **Bourges** France
53 C2 **Bourke** Austr.
99 C3 **Bournemouth** U.K.
115 C1 **Bou Saâda** Alg.
115 D3 **Bousso** Chad
114 A3 **Boutilimit** Maur.
129 C3 **Bow** *r.* Can.
51 D2 **Bowen** Austr.
129 C3 **Bow Island** Can.
140 B3 **Bowling Green** *KY* U.S.A.
140 C2 **Bowling Green** *OH* U.S.A.
136 C1 **Bowman** U.S.A.
101 D3 **Boxberg** Ger.
100 B2 **Boxtel** Neth.
80 B1 **Boyabat** Turkey
Boyang China *see* **Poyang**
97 B2 **Boyle** Ireland
97 C2 **Boyne** *r.* Ireland
136 B2 **Boysen Reservoir** U.S.A.
152 B3 **Boyuibe** Bol.
111 C3 **Bozburun** Turkey
111 C3 **Bozcaada** *i.* Turkey
111 C3 **Bozdağ** *mt.* Turkey
111 C3 **Boz Dağları** *mts* Turkey
111 C3 **Bozdoğan** Turkey
134 D1 **Bozeman** U.S.A.
118 B2 **Bozoum** C.A.R.
111 D3 **Bozüyük** Turkey
109 C2 **Brač** *i.* Croatia
130 C2 **Bracebridge** Can.
99 C3 **Bracknell** U.K.

109 C2 **Bradano** *r.* Italy
143 D3 **Bradenton** U.S.A.
98 C2 **Bradford** U.K.
141 D2 **Bradford** U.S.A.
139 D2 **Brady** U.S.A.
96 C2 **Braemar** U.K.
106 B1 **Braga** Port.
151 D2 **Bragança** Brazil
106 B1 **Bragança** Port.
155 C2 **Bragança Paulista** Brazil
89 D3 **Brahin** Belarus
73 C3 **Brahmapur** India
62 A1 **Brahmaputra** *r.* China/India
110 C1 **Brăila** Romania
137 E1 **Brainerd** U.S.A.
99 D3 **Braintree** U.K.
100 B2 **Braives** Belgium
101 D1 **Brake (Unterweser)** Ger.
100 D1 **Bramsche** Ger.
150 B2 **Branco** *r.* Brazil
101 F1 **Brandenburg an der Havel** Ger.
129 E3 **Brandon** Can.
97 A2 **Brandon Mountain** *h.* Ireland
122 B3 **Brandvlei** S. Africa
103 D1 **Braniewo** Pol.
130 B2 **Brantford** Can.
131 D2 **Bras d'Or Lake** Can.
155 D1 **Brasil, Planalto do** *plat.* Brazil
154 C1 **Brasília** Brazil
155 D1 **Brasília de Minas** Brazil
88 C2 **Braslaw** Belarus
110 C1 **Braşov** Romania
103 D2 **Bratislava** Slovakia
83 H3 **Bratsk** Russia
102 C2 **Braunau am Inn** Austria
101 E1 **Braunschweig** Ger.
92 □A2 **Brautarholt** Iceland
Bravo del Norte, Río *r.* Mex./U.S.A. *see* **Rio Grande**
135 C4 **Brawley** U.S.A.
97 C2 **Bray** Ireland
150 C2 **Brazil** *country* S. America
154 C1 **Brazlândia** Brazil
139 D3 **Brazos** *r.* U.S.A.
118 B3 **Brazzaville** Congo
109 C2 **Brčko** Bos. & Herz.
96 C2 **Brechin** U.K.
100 B2 **Brecht** Belgium
139 D2 **Breckenridge** U.S.A.
103 D2 **Břeclav** Czechia
99 B3 **Brecon** U.K.
99 B3 **Brecon Beacons** *reg.* U.K.
100 B2 **Breda** Neth.
122 B3 **Bredasdorp** S. Africa
102 B2 **Bregenz** Austria
92 H1 **Breivikbotn** Norway
92 E3 **Brekstad** Norway
101 D1 **Bremen** Ger.
101 D1 **Bremerhaven** Ger.
134 B1 **Bremerton** U.S.A.
101 D1 **Bremervörde** Ger.
139 D2 **Brenham** U.S.A.
108 B1 **Brennero** Italy
102 C2 **Brenner Pass** Austria/Italy
99 D3 **Brentwood** U.K.
108 B1 **Brescia** Italy
108 B1 **Bressanone** Italy
96 □ **Bressay** *i.* U.K.
104 B2 **Bressuire** France
88 B3 **Brest** Belarus
104 B2 **Brest** France
142 C3 **Breton Sound** *b.* U.S.A.
151 C2 **Breves** Brazil
53 C1 **Brewarrina** Austr.
134 C1 **Brewster** U.S.A.
89 E2 **Breytovo** Russia
109 C1 **Brezovo Polje** *plain* Croatia
118 C2 **Bria** C.A.R.
105 D3 **Briançon** France
90 B2 **Briceni** Moldova
99 B3 **Bridgend** U.K.
141 E2 **Bridgeport** *CT* U.S.A.
136 C2 **Bridgeport** *NE* U.S.A.
147 E3 **Bridgetown** Barbados
131 D2 **Bridgewater** Can.
99 B3 **Bridgwater** U.K.
98 C1 **Bridlington** U.K.
98 C1 **Bridlington Bay** U.K.
105 D2 **Brig** Switz.
134 D2 **Brigham City** U.S.A.
54 B3 **Brighton** N.Z.
99 C3 **Brighton** U.K.
105 D3 **Brignoles** France
101 D2 **Brilon** Ger.
109 C2 **Brindisi** Italy
91 D2 **Brin'kovskaya** Russia
53 D1 **Brisbane** Austr.
99 B3 **Bristol** U.K.
143 D1 **Bristol** U.S.A.
99 A3 **Bristol Channel** *est.* U.K.
128 B2 **British Columbia** *prov.* Can.
56 G7 **British Indian Ocean Territory** *terr.* Indian Ocean
95 B2 **British Isles** *is* Europe
123 C2 **Brits** S. Africa
122 B3 **Britstown** S. Africa
104 C2 **Brive-la-Gaillarde** France
106 C1 **Briviesca** Spain
103 D2 **Brno** Czechia
143 D2 **Broad** *r.* U.S.A.
130 C1 **Broadback** *r.* Can.
96 C3 **Broad Law** *h.* U.K.
136 B1 **Broadus** U.S.A.
129 D2 **Brochet** Can.
129 D2 **Brochet, Lac** *l.* Can.
131 D2 **Brochet, Lac au** *l.* Can.
101 E1 **Bröckel** Ger.
126 D1 **Brock Island** Can.
130 C2 **Brockville** Can.
127 F2 **Brodeur Peninsula** Can.
96 B3 **Brodick** U.K.
103 D1 **Brodnica** Pol.
90 B1 **Brody** Ukr.
139 D1 **Broken Arrow** U.S.A.
137 D2 **Broken Bow** U.S.A.
52 B2 **Broken Hill** Austr.
99 B2 **Bromsgrove** U.K.
93 E4 **Brønderslev** Denmark
92 F2 **Brønnøysund** Norway
64 A2 **Brooke's Point** Phil.
142 B2 **Brookhaven** U.S.A.
134 B2 **Brookings** *OR* U.S.A.
137 D2 **Brookings** *SD* U.S.A.
129 C2 **Brooks** Can.
126 B2 **Brooks Range** *mts* U.S.A.
143 D3 **Brooksville** U.S.A.
96 B2 **Broom, Loch** *inlet* U.K.
50 B1 **Broome** Austr.
134 B2 **Brothers** U.S.A.
Broughton Island Can. *see* **Qikiqtarjuaq**
90 C1 **Brovary** Ukr.
139 C2 **Brownfield** U.S.A.
128 C3 **Browning** U.S.A.
142 C1 **Brownsville** *TN* U.S.A.
139 D3 **Brownsville** *TX* U.S.A.
139 D2 **Brownwood** U.S.A.
92 □A2 **Brú** Iceland
104 C1 **Bruay-la-Buissière** France
140 B1 **Bruce Crossing** U.S.A.
103 D2 **Bruck an der Mur** Austria
Bruges Belgium *see* **Brugge**
100 A2 **Brugge** Belgium
128 C2 **Brûlé** Can.
151 D3 **Brumado** Brazil
93 F3 **Brumunddal** Norway
61 C1 **Brunei** *country* Asia
102 C2 **Brunico** Italy
101 D1 **Brunsbüttel** Ger.
143 D2 **Brunswick** *GA* U.S.A.
141 F2 **Brunswick** *ME* U.S.A.
53 D1 **Brunswick Heads** Austr.
136 C2 **Brush** U.S.A.
Brussel Belgium *see* **Bruss**
100 B2 **Brussels** Belgium
Bruxelles Belgium *see* **Brussels**
139 D2 **Bryan** U.S.A.
89 D3 **Bryansk** Russia
91 D2 **Bryukhovetskaya** Russia
103 D1 **Brzeg** Pol.
114 A3 **Buba** Guinea-Bissau
80 B2 **Bucak** Turkey
150 A1 **Bucaramanga** Col.
53 C3 **Buchan** Austr.
114 A4 **Buchanan** Liberia
110 C2 **Bucharest** Romania
65 B2 **Bucheon** S. Korea
101 D1 **Buchholz in der Nordheid** Ger.
110 C1 **Bucin, Pasul** *pass* Romani
101 D1 **Bückeburg** Ger.
138 A2 **Buckeye** U.S.A.
96 C2 **Buckhaven** U.K.
96 C2 **Buckie** U.K.
51 C1 **Buckingham Bay** Austr.
51 D2 **Buckland Tableland** *reg.* A
52 A2 **Buckleboo** Austr.
141 F2 **Bucksport** U.S.A.
Bucureşti Romania *see* **Bucharest**
89 D3 **Buda-Kashalyova** Belarus
103 D2 **Budapest** Hungary
75 B2 **Budaun** India
108 A2 **Buddusò** *Sardinia* Italy
99 A3 **Bude** U.K.
87 D4 **Budennovsk** Russia
89 D2 **Budogoshch'** Russia
108 A2 **Budoni** *Sardinia* Italy
118 A2 **Buea** Cameroon
144 B2 **Buenaventura** Mex.
106 C1 **Buendía, Embalse de** *resr* Spain
155 D1 **Buenópolis** Brazil
153 C4 **Buenos Aires** Arg.
153 A5 **Buenos Aires, Lago** *l.* Arg./Chile
141 D2 **Buffalo** *NY* U.S.A.
136 C1 **Buffalo** *SD* U.S.A.
136 B2 **Buffalo** *WY* U.S.A.
129 D2 **Buffalo Narrows** Can.
122 A2 **Buffels** *watercourse* S. Afri
110 C2 **Buftea** Romania
103 E1 **Bug** *r.* Pol.
61 C2 **Bugel, Tanjung** *pt* Indon.
109 C2 **Bugojno** Bos. & Herz.
64 A2 **Bugsuk** *i.* Phil.
87 E3 **Buguruslan** Russia
110 C1 **Buhuşi** Romania
99 B2 **Builth Wells** U.K.
120 A3 **Buitepos** Namibia
109 D2 **Bujanovac** Serbia
119 C3 **Bujumbura** Burundi
69 D1 **Bukachacha** Russia
119 C3 **Bukavu** Dem. Rep. Congo
60 B2 **Bukittinggi** Indon.
119 D3 **Bukoba** Tanz.
53 D2 **Bulahdelah** Austr.
121 B3 **Bulawayo** Zimbabwe
111 C3 **Buldan** Turkey
123 D2 **Bulembu** Swaziland
69 C1 **Bulgan** Mongolia
110 C2 **Bulgaria** *country* Europe

54 B2 **Buller** *r.* N.Z.
52 B1 **Bulloo Downs** Austr.
122 A1 **Büllsport** Namibia
58 C3 **Bulukumba** Indon.
118 B3 **Bulungu** Dem. Rep. Congo
118 C2 **Bumba** Dem. Rep. Congo
62 A1 **Bumhkang** Myanmar
118 B3 **Buna** Dem. Rep. Congo
50 A3 **Bunbury** Austr.
97 C1 **Buncrana** Ireland
119 D3 **Bunda** Tanz.
51 E2 **Bundaberg** Austr.
53 D2 **Bundarra** Austr.
74 B2 **Bundi** India
97 B1 **Bundoran** Ireland
53 C3 **Bungendore** Austr.
67 B4 **Bungo-suidō** *sea chan.* Japan
119 D2 **Bunia** Dem. Rep. Congo
118 C3 **Bunianga** Dem. Rep. Congo
63 B2 **Buôn Ma Thuôt** Vietnam
119 D3 **Bura** Kenya
78 B2 **Buraydah** Saudi Arabia
100 D2 **Burbach** Ger.
117 C4 **Burco** Somalia
100 B1 **Burdaard** Neth.
80 B2 **Burdur** Turkey
117 B3 **Burē** Eth.
99 D2 **Bure** *r.* U.K.
74 B1 **Burewala** Pak.
101 E1 **Burg** Ger.
110 C2 **Burgas** Bulg.
101 E1 **Burgdorf** *Niedersachsen* Ger.
101 E1 **Burgdorf** *Niedersachsen* Ger.
131 E2 **Burgeo** Can.
123 D1 **Burgersfort** S. Africa
100 A2 **Burgh-Haamstede** Neth.
145 C2 **Burgos** Mex.
106 C1 **Burgos** Spain
111 C3 **Burhaniye** Turkey
74 B2 **Burhanpur** India
101 D1 **Burhave (Butjadingen)** Ger.
131 E2 **Burin** Can.
151 D2 **Buriti Bravo** Brazil
155 C1 **Buritis** Brazil
51 C1 **Burketown** Austr.
114 B3 **Burkina Faso** *country* Africa
134 D2 **Burley** U.S.A.
136 C3 **Burlington** *CO* U.S.A.
137 E2 **Burlington** *IA* U.S.A.
143 E1 **Burlington** *NC* U.S.A.
141 E2 **Burlington** *VT* U.S.A.
Burma *country* Asia *see* **Myanmar**
134 B2 **Burney** U.S.A.
51 D4 **Burnie** Austr.
98 B2 **Burnley** U.K.
134 C2 **Burns** U.S.A.
128 B2 **Burns Lake** Can.
77 E2 **Burqin** China
52 A2 **Burra** Austr.
109 D2 **Burrel** Albania
97 B2 **Burren** *reg.* Ireland
53 C2 **Burrendong, Lake** *resr* Austr.
53 C2 **Burren Junction** Austr.
Burriana Spain *see* **Borriana**
53 C2 **Burrinjuck Reservoir** Austr.
144 B2 **Burro, Serranías del** *mts* Mex.
111 C2 **Bursa** Turkey
116 B2 **Būr Safājah** Egypt
Būr Sa'īd Egypt *see* **Port Said**
130 C1 **Burton, Lac** *l.* Can.
99 C2 **Burton upon Trent** U.K.
59 C3 **Buru** *i.* Indon.
119 C3 **Burundi** *country* Africa
119 C3 **Bururi** Burundi
91 C1 **Buryn'** Ukr.
99 D2 **Bury St Edmunds** U.K.
108 B3 **Busambra, Rocca** *mt. Sicily* Italy
65 B2 **Busan** S. Korea
118 C3 **Busanga** Dem. Rep. Congo
119 D3 **Bushenyi** Uganda
118 C2 **Businga** Dem. Rep. Congo
50 A3 **Busselton** Austr.
139 C3 **Bustamante** Mex.
118 C2 **Buta** Dem. Rep. Congo
119 C3 **Butare** Rwanda
123 C2 **Butha-Buthe** Lesotho
140 D2 **Butler** U.S.A.
59 C3 **Buton** *i.* Indon.
134 D1 **Butte** U.S.A.
60 B1 **Butterworth** Malaysia
96 A1 **Butt of Lewis** *hd* U.K.
129 E2 **Button Bay** Can.
64 B2 **Butuan** Phil.
91 E1 **Buturlinovka** Russia
75 C2 **Butwal** Nepal
101 D2 **Butzbach** Ger.
117 C4 **Buulobarde** Somalia
117 C5 **Buur Gaabo** Somalia
117 C4 **Buurhabaka** Somalia
76 C3 **Buxoro** Uzbek.
101 D1 **Buxtehude** Ger.
89 F2 **Buy** Russia
87 D4 **Buynaksk** Russia
69 D1 **Buyr Nuur** *l.* Mongolia
111 C3 **Büyükmenderes** *r.* Turkey
110 C1 **Buzău** Romania
121 C2 **Búzi** Moz.
87 E3 **Buzuluk** Russia
110 C2 **Byala** Bulg.
88 C3 **Byalynichy** Belarus
88 D3 **Byarezina** *r.* Belarus
88 B3 **Byaroza** Belarus
103 D1 **Bydgoszcz** Pol.
88 C3 **Byerazino** Belarus
88 C2 **Byeshankovichy** Belarus
89 D3 **Bykhaw** Belarus
127 F2 **Bylot Island** Can.
53 C2 **Byrock** Austr.
53 D1 **Byron Bay** Austr.
83 J2 **Bytantay** *r.* Russia
103 D1 **Bytom** Pol.
103 D1 **Bytów** Pol.

C

154 B2 **Caarapó** Brazil
64 B1 **Cabanatuan** Phil.
117 C3 **Cabdul Qaadir** Somalia
106 B2 **Cabeza del Buey** Spain
152 B2 **Cabezas** Bol.
150 A1 **Cabimas** Venez.
120 A1 **Cabinda** Angola
118 B3 **Cabinda** *prov.* Angola
155 D2 **Cabo Frio** Brazil
155 D2 **Cabo Frio, Ilha do** *i.* Brazil
130 C2 **Cabonga, Réservoir** *resr* Can.
51 E2 **Caboolture** Austr.
150 A2 **Cabo Pantoja** Peru
144 A1 **Caborca** Mex.
144 B2 **Cabo San Lucas** Mex.
131 D2 **Cabot Strait** Can.
155 D1 **Cabral, Serra do** *mts* Brazil
107 D2 **Cabrera** *i.* Spain
106 B1 **Cabrera, Sierra de la** *mts* Spain
129 D2 **Cabri** Can.
107 C2 **Cabriel** *r.* Spain
152 C3 **Caçador** Brazil
109 D2 **Čačak** Serbia
108 A2 **Caccia, Capo** *c. Sardinia* Italy
151 C3 **Cáceres** Brazil
106 B2 **Cáceres** Spain
128 B2 **Cache Creek** Can.
114 A3 **Cacheu** Guinea-Bissau
151 C2 **Cachimbo, Serra do** *hills* Brazil
154 B1 **Cachoeira Alta** Brazil
155 D2 **Cachoeiro de Itapemirim** Brazil
114 A3 **Cacine** Guinea-Bissau
120 A2 **Cacolo** Angola
154 B1 **Caçu** Brazil
103 D2 **Čadca** Slovakia
101 D1 **Cadenberge** Ger.
145 B2 **Cadereyta** Mex.
140 B2 **Cadillac** U.S.A.
106 B2 **Cádiz** Spain
106 B2 **Cádiz, Golfo de** *g.* Spain
128 C2 **Cadotte Lake** Can.
104 B2 **Caen** France
98 A2 **Caernarfon** U.K.
98 A2 **Caernarfon Bay** U.K.
152 B3 **Cafayate** Arg.
64 B2 **Cagayan de Oro** Phil.
64 A2 **Cagayan de Tawi-Tawi** *i.* Phil.
108 B2 **Cagli** Italy
108 A3 **Cagliari** *Sardinia* Italy
108 A3 **Cagliari, Golfo di** *b. Sardinia* Italy
76 B2 **Çagyl** Turkm.
97 B3 **Caha Mountains** *hills* Ireland
97 A3 **Cahermore** Ireland
97 C2 **Cahir** Ireland
97 A3 **Cahirsiveen** Ireland
97 C2 **Cahore Point** Ireland
104 C3 **Cahors** France
90 B2 **Cahul** Moldova
121 C2 **Caia** Moz.
151 C3 **Caiabis, Serra dos** *hills* Brazil
120 B2 **Caianda** Angola
154 B1 **Caiapó, Serra do** *mts* Brazil
154 B1 **Caiapônia** Brazil
147 C2 **Caicos Islands** Turks and Caicos Is
96 C2 **Cairngorm Mountains** U.K.
98 A1 **Cairnryan** U.K.
51 D1 **Cairns** Austr.
116 B1 **Cairo** Egypt
98 C2 **Caistor** U.K.
120 A2 **Caiundo** Angola
150 A2 **Cajamarca** Peru
109 C1 **Čakovec** Croatia
123 C3 **Cala** S. Africa
150 B1 **Calabozo** Venez.
110 B2 **Calafat** Romania
107 C1 **Calahorra** Spain
104 C1 **Calais** France
141 F1 **Calais** U.S.A.
152 B3 **Calama** Chile
64 A1 **Calamian Group** *is* Phil.
107 C1 **Calamocha** Spain
120 A1 **Calandula** Angola
60 A1 **Calang** Indon.
64 B1 **Calapan** Phil.
110 C2 **Călărași** Romania
107 C1 **Calatayud** Spain
64 B1 **Calayan** *i.* Phil.
64 B1 **Calbayog** Phil.
151 E2 **Calcanhar, Ponta do** *pt* Brazil
151 C1 **Calçoene** Brazil
Calcutta India *see* **Kolkata**
106 B2 **Caldas da Rainha** Port.
154 C1 **Caldas Novas** Brazil
152 A3 **Caldera** Chile
134 C2 **Caldwell** U.S.A.
123 C3 **Caledon** *r.* Lesotho/S. Africa
122 A3 **Caledon** S. Africa
153 B5 **Caleta Olivia** Arg.
98 A1 **Calf of Man** *i.* Isle of Man
128 C2 **Calgary** Can.
150 A1 **Cali** Col.

Calicut

Calicut India see Kozhikode
135 D3 Calicut U.S.A.
135 B2 California state U.S.A.
144 A1 California, Gulf of Mex.
135 B3 California Aqueduct canal U.S.A.
122 B3 Calitzdorp S. Africa
145 C2 Calkiní Mex.
52 B1 Callabonna, Lake imp. l. Austr.
96 B2 Callander U.K.
150 A3 Callao Peru
108 B3 Caltagirone Sicily Italy
108 B3 Caltanissetta Sicily Italy
120 A2 Caluquembe Angola
117 D3 Caluula Somalia
105 D3 Calvi Corsica France
107 D2 Calvià Spain
144 B2 Calvillo Mex.
122 A3 Calvinia S. Africa
109 C2 Calvo, Monte mt. Italy
144 B2 Camacho Mex.
120 A2 Camacupa Angola
146 C2 Camagüey Cuba
150 A3 Camaná Peru
154 B1 Camapuã Brazil
145 C2 Camargo Mex.
63 B3 Ca Mau Vietnam
63 B3 Ca Mau, Mui c. Vietnam
63 B2 Cambodia country Asia
99 A3 Camborne U.K.
105 C1 Cambrai France
99 B2 Cambrian Mountains hills U.K.
54 C1 Cambridge N.Z.
99 D2 Cambridge U.K.
141 E2 Cambridge MA U.S.A.
141 D3 Cambridge MD U.S.A.
137 E1 Cambridge MN U.S.A.
140 C2 Cambridge OH U.S.A.
131 D1 Cambrien, Lac l. Can.
53 D2 Camden Austr.
142 B2 Camden AR U.S.A.
141 F2 Camden ME U.S.A.
118 B3 Cameroon country Africa
118 B2 Cameroon Highlands slope Cameroon/Nigeria
151 D2 Cametá Brazil
64 B1 Camiguin i. Phil.
152 B3 Camiri Bol.
151 D2 Camocim Brazil
51 C1 Camooweal Austr.
63 A3 Camorta i. India
153 A5 Campana, Isla i. Chile
122 B2 Campbell S. Africa
54 B2 Campbell, Cape N.Z.
48 F6 Campbell Island/Motu Ihupuku N.Z.
128 B2 Campbell River Can.
140 B3 Campbellsville U.S.A.
131 D2 Campbellton Can.
96 B3 Campbeltown U.K.
145 C3 Campeche Mex.
145 C3 Campeche, Bahía de g. Mex.
52 B3 Camperdown Austr.
110 C1 Câmpina Romania
151 E2 Campina Grande Brazil
154 C2 Campinas Brazil
154 C1 Campina Verde Brazil
108 B2 Campobasso Italy
155 C2 Campo Belo Brazil
154 C1 Campo Florido Brazil
152 B3 Campo Gallo Arg.
154 B2 Campo Grande Brazil
151 D2 Campo Maior Brazil
106 B2 Campo Maior Port.
154 B2 Campo Mourão Brazil
155 C2 Campos Altos Brazil
155 C2 Campos do Jordão Brazil

155 D2 Campos dos Goytacazes Brazil
110 C1 Câmpulung Romania
138 A2 Camp Verde U.S.A.
63 B2 Cam Ranh Vietnam
128 C2 Camrose Can.
129 D2 Camsell Portage Can.
111 C2 Çan Turkey
126 F2 Canada country N. America
139 C1 Canadian U.S.A.
139 D1 Canadian r. U.S.A.
111 C2 Çanakkale Turkey
144 A1 Cananea Mex.
154 C2 Cananéia Brazil
Canarias, Islas terr. N. Atlantic Ocean see Canary Islands
114 A2 Canary Islands terr. N. Atlantic Ocean
155 C1 Canastra, Serra da mts Brazil
144 B2 Canatlán Mex.
143 D3 Canaveral, Cape U.S.A.
155 E1 Canavieiras Brazil
53 C3 Canberra Austr.
145 D2 Cancún Mex.
111 C3 Çandarlı Turkey
145 C3 Candelaria Mex.
129 D2 Candle Lake Can.
120 A2 Cangamba Angola
106 B1 Cangas del Narcea Spain
152 C4 Canguçu Brazil
70 B2 Cangzhou China
131 D1 Caniapiscau Can.
131 D1 Caniapiscau r. Can.
131 C1 Caniapiscau, Réservoir de resr Can.
108 B3 Canicattì Sicily Italy
151 E2 Canindé Brazil
144 B2 Cañitas de Felipe Pescador Mex.
80 B1 Çankırı Turkey
128 C2 Canmore Can.
96 A2 Canna i. U.K.
Cannanore India see Kannur
105 D3 Cannes France
99 D3 Cannock U.K.
53 C3 Cann River Austr.
152 C3 Canoas Brazil
129 D2 Canoe Lake Can.
154 B3 Canoinhas Brazil
136 B3 Canon City U.S.A.
129 D2 Canora Can.
53 C2 Canowindra Austr.
106 C1 Cantábrica, Cordillera mts Spain
106 B1 Cantábrico, Mar sea Spain
99 D3 Canterbury U.K.
54 B2 Canterbury Bight b. N.Z.
54 B2 Canterbury Plains N.Z.
63 B2 Cần Thơ Vietnam
151 D2 Canto do Buriti Brazil
Canton China see Guangzhou
142 C2 Canton MS U.S.A.
140 C2 Canton OH U.S.A.
139 C1 Canyon U.S.A.
134 D1 Canyon Ferry Lake U.S.A.
62 B1 Cao Bằng Vietnam
154 C2 Capão Bonito Brazil
155 D2 Caparaó, Serra do mts Brazil
51 D4 Cape Barren Island Austr.
52 A3 Cape Borda Austr.
131 D2 Cape Breton Island Can.
114 B4 Cape Coast Ghana
141 E2 Cape Cod Bay U.S.A.
127 F2 Cape Dorset Can.
143 E2 Cape Fear r. U.S.A.
137 F3 Cape Girardeau U.S.A.
155 D1 Capelinha Brazil
100 B2 Capelle aan den IJssel Neth.

120 A1 Capenda-Camulemba Ango
122 A3 Cape Town S. Africa
112 C5 Cape Verde country Africa
51 D1 Cape York Peninsula Austr.
147 C3 Cap-Haïtien Haiti
151 D2 Capim r. Brazil
58 D1 Capitol Hill N. Mariana Is
109 C2 Čapljina Bos. & Herz.
109 B3 Capo d'Orlando Sicily Italy
108 A2 Capraia, Isola di i. Italy
108 A2 Caprara, Punta pt Sardinia Italy
108 B2 Capri, Isola di i. Italy
120 B2 Caprivi Strip reg. Namibia
150 B2 Caquetá r. Col.
110 B2 Caracal Romania
150 B1 Caracas Venez.
151 D2 Caracol Brazil
155 C2 Caraguatatuba Brazil
153 A4 Carahue Chile
155 D1 Caraí Brazil
155 D2 Carangola Brazil
110 B1 Caransebeş Romania
131 D2 Caraquet Can.
146 B3 Caratasca, Laguna de lag. Hond.
155 D1 Caratinga Brazil
150 B2 Carauari Brazil
107 C2 Caravaca de la Cruz Spain
155 E1 Caravelas Brazil
129 E3 Carberry Can.
144 A2 Carbó Mex.
107 C2 Carbon, Cap c. Alg.
153 B5 Carbón, Laguna del l. Arg.
108 A3 Carbonara, Capo c. Sardinia Italy
136 B3 Carbondale CO U.S.A.
140 B3 Carbondale IL U.S.A.
131 E2 Carbonear Can.
155 D1 Carbonita Brazil
107 C2 Carcaixent Spain
104 C3 Carcassonne France
128 A1 Carcross Can.
145 C3 Cárdenas Mex.
99 B3 Cardiff U.K.
99 A2 Cardigan U.K.
99 A2 Cardigan Bay U.K.
128 C3 Cardston Can.
110 B1 Carei Romania
104 B2 Carentan France
50 B2 Carey, Lake imp. l. Austr.
155 D2 Cariacica Brazil
146 B3 Caribbean Sea N. Atlantic Ocean
141 F1 Caribou U.S.A.
130 B1 Caribou Lake Can.
128 C2 Caribou Mountains Can.
144 B2 Carichic Mex.
100 B3 Carignan France
53 C2 Carinda Austr.
107 C1 Cariñena Spain
130 C2 Carleton Place Can.
123 C2 Carletonville S. Africa
97 C1 Carlingford Lough inlet Ireland/U.K.
98 B1 Carlisle U.K.
141 D2 Carlisle U.S.A.
155 D1 Carlos Chagas Brazil
97 C2 Carlow Ireland
135 C4 Carlsbad CA U.S.A.
138 C2 Carlsbad NM U.S.A.
129 D3 Carlyle Can.
128 A1 Carmacks Can.
129 E3 Carman Can.
99 A3 Carmarthen U.K.
99 A3 Carmarthen Bay U.K.
104 C3 Carmaux France
145 C3 Carmelita Guat.

144 A2 **Carmen, Isla** i. Mex.
104 B2 **Carnac** France
122 B3 **Carnarvon** S. Africa
97 C1 **Carndonagh** Ireland
105 D3 **Carnegie, Lake** imp. l. Austr.
96 B2 **Carn Eige** mt. U.K.
63 A3 **Car Nicobar** i. India
118 B2 **Carnot** C.A.R.
52 A2 **Carnot, Cape** Austr.
97 C2 **Carnsore Point** Ireland
151 D2 **Carolina** Brazil
48 D2 **Caroline Islands**
N. Pacific Ocean
103 D3 **Carpathian Mountains** Europe
Carpaţii Meridionali
mts Romania see
Transylvanian Alps
51 C1 **Carpentaria, Gulf of** Austr.
105 D3 **Carpentras** France
97 B3 **Carrantuohill** mt. Ireland
105 E3 **Carrara** Italy
97 C2 **Carrickmacross** Ireland
97 C1 **Carrick-on-Shannon** Ireland
97 C2 **Carrick-on-Suir** Ireland
137 D1 **Carrington** U.S.A.
138 B2 **Carrizo Springs** U.S.A.
137 E2 **Carrizozo** U.S.A.
137 E2 **Carroll** U.S.A.
143 C2 **Carrollton** U.S.A.
129 D2 **Carrot River** Can.
135 C3 **Carson City** U.S.A.
150 A1 **Cartagena** Col.
107 C2 **Cartagena** Spain
146 B4 **Cartago** Costa Rica
137 E3 **Carthage** MO U.S.A.
139 E2 **Carthage** TX U.S.A.
131 E1 **Cartwright** Can.
151 E2 **Caruaru** Brazil
114 B1 **Casablanca** Morocco
151 D2 **Casa Branca** Brazil
144 B3 **Casa de Janos** Mex.
138 A2 **Casa Grande** U.S.A.
108 A1 **Casale Monferrato** Italy
109 C2 **Casarano** Italy
134 C2 **Cascade** U.S.A.
134 B2 **Cascade Range** mts Can./
U.S.A.
106 B2 **Cascais** Port.
154 B2 **Cascavel** Brazil
108 B2 **Caserta** Italy
97 C2 **Cashel** Ireland
53 D1 **Casino** Austr.
107 C1 **Caspe** Spain
136 B2 **Casper** U.S.A.
76 A2 **Caspian Lowland** Kazakh./
Russia
81 C1 **Caspian Sea** Asia/Europe
154 C2 **Cássia** Brazil
128 B2 **Cassiar (abandoned)** Can.
128 A2 **Cassiar Mountains** Can.
151 B1 **Cassilândia** Brazil
108 B2 **Cassino** Italy
96 B2 **Cassley** r. U.K.
151 E2 **Castanhal** Brazil
152 B3 **Castaño** r. Arg.
144 B2 **Castaños** Mex.
104 C3 **Casteljaloux** France
Castelló de la Plana Spain
see **Castellón de la Plana/
Castelló de la Plana**
107 C2 **Castellón de la Plana/Castelló
de la Plana** Spain
106 B2 **Castelo Branco** Port.
108 B3 **Castelvetrano** Sicily Italy
52 B3 **Casterton** Austr.
108 B2 **Castiglione della Pescaia** Italy
97 B2 **Castlebar** Ireland
96 A2 **Castlebay** U.K.

97 C1 **Castleblayney** Ireland
97 C1 **Castlederg** U.K.
96 C3 **Castle Douglas** U.K.
128 C3 **Castlegar** Can.
97 B2 **Castleisland** Ireland
52 B3 **Castlemaine** Austr.
97 B2 **Castlerea** Ireland
53 C2 **Castlereagh** r. Austr.
136 C3 **Castle Rock** U.S.A.
129 C2 **Castor** Can.
104 C3 **Castres** France
100 B1 **Castricum** Neth.
147 D3 **Castries** St Lucia
154 C2 **Castro** Brazil
153 A5 **Castro** Chile
106 B2 **Castro Verde** Port.
109 C3 **Castrovillari** Italy
150 A2 **Catacaos** Peru
155 D2 **Cataguases** Brazil
154 C1 **Catalão** Brazil
152 B3 **Catalina** Chile
152 B3 **Catamarca** Arg.
64 B1 **Catanduanes** i. Phil.
154 C2 **Catanduva** Brazil
154 B3 **Catanduvas** Brazil
109 C3 **Catania** Sicily Italy
109 C3 **Catanzaro** Italy
64 B1 **Catarman** Phil.
64 B1 **Catbalogan** Phil.
145 C3 **Catemaco** Mex.
147 C2 **Cat Island** Bahamas
130 A1 **Cat Lake** Can.
145 D2 **Catoche, Cabo** c. Mex.
141 E2 **Catskill Mountains** U.S.A.
64 B2 **Cauayan** Phil.
150 A1 **Cauca** r. Col.
151 E2 **Caucaia** Brazil
81 C1 **Caucasus** mts Asia/Europe
100 A2 **Caudry** France
109 C3 **Caulonia** Italy
131 D2 **Causapscal** Can.
105 D3 **Cavaillon** France
151 D3 **Cavalcante** Brazil
97 C2 **Cavan** Ireland
154 B3 **Cavernoso, Serra do**
Brazil
151 D2 **Caxias** Brazil
152 C3 **Caxias do Sul** Brazil
120 A1 **Caxito** Angola
151 C1 **Cayenne** Fr. Guiana
146 B3 **Cayman Islands** terr.
West Indies
117 C4 **Caynaba** Somalia
120 B2 **Cazombo** Angola
144 B2 **Ceballos** Mex.
64 B1 **Cebu** Phil.
64 B1 **Cebu** i. Phil.
108 B2 **Cecina** Italy
137 F2 **Cedar** r. U.S.A.
135 D3 **Cedar City** U.S.A.
137 E2 **Cedar Falls** U.S.A.
129 D2 **Cedar Lake** Can.
137 E2 **Cedar Rapids** U.S.A.
144 A2 **Cedros, Isla** i. Mex.
51 C3 **Ceduna** Austr.
117 C4 **Ceeldheere** Somalia
117 C3 **Ceerigaabo** Somalia
108 B3 **Cefalù** Sicily Italy
145 B2 **Celaya** Mex.
58 C3 **Celebes** i. Indon.
156 B5 **Celebes Sea** Indon./Phil.
145 C2 **Celestún** Mex.
101 E1 **Celle** Ger.
95 B3 **Celtic Sea** Ireland/U.K.
59 D3 **Cenderawasih, Teluk** b. Indon.
150 A1 **Central, Cordillera** mts Col.
150 A3 **Central, Cordillera** mts Peru
64 B1 **Central, Cordillera** mts Phil.

118 C2 **Central African Republic**
country Africa
74 A2 **Central Brahui Range** mts
Pak.
137 D2 **Central City** U.S.A.
140 B3 **Centralia** IL U.S.A.
134 B1 **Centralia** WA U.S.A.
74 A2 **Central Makran Range** mts
Pak.
59 D3 **Central Range** mts P.N.G.
89 E3 **Central Russian Upland** hills
Russia
83 I2 **Central Siberian Plateau**
Russia
111 B3 **Cephalonia** i. Greece
Ceram Sea Indon. see
Seram, Laut
152 B3 **Ceres** Arg.
154 C1 **Ceres** Brazil
122 A3 **Ceres** S. Africa
104 C3 **Céret** France
106 C1 **Cerezo de Abajo** Spain
109 C2 **Cerignola** Italy
110 C2 **Cernavodă** Romania
145 C2 **Cerralvo** Mex.
144 B2 **Cerralvo, Isla** i. Mex.
145 B2 **Cerritos** Mex.
154 C2 **Cerro Azul** Brazil
145 C2 **Cerro Azul** Mex.
150 A3 **Cerro de Pasco** Peru
106 B1 **Cervione** Corsica France
108 B2 **Cesena** Italy
88 C2 **Cēsis** Latvia
102 C2 **České Budějovice** Czechia
101 F3 **Český les** mts Czechia
111 C3 **Çeşme** Turkey
53 D2 **Cessnock** Austr.
109 C2 **Cetinje** Montenegro
109 C3 **Cetraro** Italy
106 B2 **Ceuta** N. Africa
105 C3 **Cévennes** mts France
Ceylon country Asia see
Sri Lanka
79 D2 **Chābahār** Iran
150 A2 **Chachapoyas** Peru
89 D3 **Chachersk** Belarus
63 B2 **Chachoengsao** Thai.
115 D3 **Chad** country Africa
115 D3 **Chad, Lake** Africa
69 C1 **Chadaasan** Mongolia
68 C1 **Chadan** Russia
123 C1 **Chadibe** Botswana
136 C2 **Chadron** U.S.A.
65 B2 **Chaeryŏng** N. Korea
74 A2 **Chagai** Pak.
89 E2 **Chaghcharān** Afgh.
89 E2 **Chagoda** Russia
75 C2 **Chaibasa** India
63 B2 **Chainat** Thai.
63 B2 **Chaiyaphum** Thai.
152 C4 **Chajarí** Arg.
131 D1 **Chakonipau, Lac** l. Can.
150 A3 **Chala** Peru
131 D2 **Chaleur Bay** inlet Can.
74 B2 **Chalisgaon** India
111 C3 **Chalki** i. Greece
111 B3 **Chalkida** Greece
104 B2 **Challans** France
134 D2 **Challis** U.S.A.
105 C2 **Châlons-en-Champagne**
France
105 C2 **Chalon-sur-Saône** France
138 B1 **Chama** U.S.A.
121 C2 **Chama** Zambia
74 A1 **Chaman** Pak.
74 B1 **Chamba** India
74 B2 **Chambal** r. India

137 D2 **Chamberlain** U.S.A.
141 D3 **Chambersburg** U.S.A.
105 D2 **Chambéry** France
121 C2 **Chambeshi** Zambia
140 B2 **Champaign** U.S.A.
141 E2 **Champlain, Lake** Can./U.S.A.
145 C3 **Champotón** Mex.
152 A3 **Chañaral** Chile
126 B2 **Chandalar** *r.* U.S.A.
142 C3 **Chandeleur Islands** U.S.A.
74 B1 **Chandigarh** India
138 A2 **Chandler** U.S.A.
75 B3 **Chandrapur** India
63 B2 **Chang, Ko** *i.* Thai.
Chang'an China *see* **Rong'an**
121 C3 **Changane** *r.* Moz.
121 C2 **Changara** Moz.
65 B1 **Changbai** China
65 B1 **Changbai Shan** *mts* China/N. Korea
69 E2 **Changchun** China
71 B3 **Changde** China
65 B2 **Ch'angdo** N. Korea
71 C3 **Changhua** Taiwan
Chang Jiang *r.* China *see* **Yangtze**
65 B1 **Changjin** N. Korea
65 B1 **Changjin-gang** *r.* N. Korea
71 B3 **Changsha** China
71 B3 **Changting** China
65 B2 **Changwon** S. Korea
70 B2 **Changyuan** China
70 B2 **Changzhi** China
70 B2 **Changzhou** China
111 B3 **Chania** Greece
95 C4 **Channel Islands** English Chan.
135 C4 **Channel Islands** U.S.A.
131 E2 **Channel-Port-aux-Basques** Can.
63 B2 **Chanthaburi** Thai.
104 C2 **Chantilly** France
137 D3 **Chanute** U.S.A.
82 G3 **Chany, Ozero** *salt l.* Russia
71 B3 **Chaoyang** *Guangdong* China
Chaoyang *Jilin* China *see* **Huinan**
71 B3 **Chaozhou** China
144 B2 **Chapala, Laguna de** *l.* Mex.
76 B1 **Chapayevo** Kazakh.
152 C3 **Chapecó** Brazil
143 E1 **Chapel Hill** U.S.A.
130 B2 **Chapleau** Can.
89 E3 **Chaplygin** Russia
91 C2 **Chaplynka** Ukr.
75 C2 **Chapra** India
145 B2 **Charcas** Mex.
99 B3 **Chard** U.K.
104 B2 **Charente** *r.* France
77 C3 **Chārīkār** Afgh.
86 E2 **Charkayuvom** Russia
100 B2 **Charleroi** Belgium
141 D3 **Charles, Cape** U.S.A.
137 E2 **Charles City** U.S.A.
140 B3 **Charleston** *IL* U.S.A.
143 E2 **Charleston** *SC* U.S.A.
140 C3 **Charleston** *WV* U.S.A.
135 C3 **Charleston Peak** U.S.A.
51 D2 **Charleville** Austr.
105 C2 **Charleville-Mézières** France
143 D1 **Charlotte** U.S.A.
143 D3 **Charlotte Harbor** *b.* U.S.A.
141 D3 **Charlottesville** U.S.A.
131 D2 **Charlottetown** Can.
52 B3 **Charlton** Austr.
130 C1 **Charlton Island** Can.
51 D2 **Charters Towers** Austr.
104 C2 **Chartres** France
128 C2 **Chase** Can.
88 C3 **Chashniki** Belarus
Chaslands Mistake *c.* N.Z. *see* **Makati**
65 B1 **Chasŏng** N. Korea
104 B2 **Chassiron, Pointe de** *pt* France
104 B2 **Châteaubriant** France
104 C2 **Château-du-Loir** France
104 C2 **Châteaudun** France
104 B2 **Châteaulin** France
105 D3 **Châteauneuf-les-Martigues** France
104 C2 **Châteauneuf-sur-Loire** France
105 C2 **Château-Thierry** France
128 C2 **Chateh** Can.
100 B2 **Châtelet** Belgium
104 C2 **Châtellerault** France
140 C2 **Chatham** Can.
49 G5 **Chatham Islands** *is* N.Z.
105 C2 **Châtillon-sur-Seine** France
143 D2 **Chattahoochee** *r.* U.S.A.
143 C1 **Chattanooga** U.S.A.
63 B2 **Châu Đốc** Vietnam
62 A1 **Chauk** Myanmar
105 D2 **Chaumont** France
105 C2 **Chauny** France
151 D2 **Chaves** Brazil
106 B1 **Chaves** Port.
130 C1 **Chavigny, Lac** *l.* Can.
89 D3 **Chavusy** Belarus
89 E2 **Chayevo** Russia
86 E3 **Chaykovskiy** Russia
102 C1 **Cheb** Czechia
87 D3 **Cheboksary** Russia
140 C1 **Cheboygan** U.S.A.
114 B2 **Chegga** Maur.
134 B1 **Chehalis** U.S.A.
Cheju S. Korea *see* **Jeju**
Cheju-do *i.* S. Korea *see* **Jeju-do**
89 E2 **Chekhov** Russia
134 B1 **Chelan, Lake** U.S.A.
103 E1 **Chełm** Pol.
99 D3 **Chelmer** *r.* U.K.
103 D1 **Chełmno** Pol.
99 D3 **Chelmsford** U.K.
99 B3 **Cheltenham** U.K.
87 F3 **Chelyabinsk** Russia
101 F2 **Chemnitz** Ger.
114 B2 **Chenachane** Alg.
70 B1 **Chengde** China
70 A2 **Chengdu** China
71 A3 **Chengguan** China
71 B4 **Chengmai** China
Chengshou China *see* **Yingshan**
70 A2 **Chengxian** China
Chengyang China *see* **Juxian**
73 C3 **Chennai** India
71 B3 **Chenzhou** China
65 B2 **Cheonan** S. Korea
65 B2 **Cheorwon** S. Korea
99 B3 **Chepstow** U.K.
104 B2 **Cherbourg-Octeville** France
89 E3 **Cheremisinovo** Russia
69 C1 **Cheremkhovo** Russia
89 E2 **Cherepovets** Russia
91 C2 **Cherkasy** Ukr.
87 D4 **Cherkessk** Russia
91 C1 **Chernihiv** Ukr.
91 D2 **Cherninivka** Ukr.
90 B2 **Chernivtsi** Ukr.
90 B1 **Chernyakhiv** Ukr.
88 B3 **Chernyakhovsk** Russia
89 E3 **Chernyanka** Russia
83 I2 **Chernyshevskiy** Russia
137 D2 **Cherokee** U.S.A.
83 K2 **Cherskogo, Khrebet** *mts* Russia
91 E2 **Chertkovo** Russia
90 A1 **Chervonohrad** Ukr.
88 C3 **Chervyen'** Belarus
89 D3 **Cherykaw** Belarus
141 D3 **Chesapeake Bay** U.S.A.
86 D2 **Cheshskaya Guba** *b.* Russia
98 B2 **Chester** U.K.
140 B3 **Chester** *IL* U.S.A.
143 D2 **Chester** *SC* U.S.A.
98 C2 **Chesterfield** U.K.
129 E1 **Chesterfield Inlet** Can.
129 E1 **Chesterfield Inlet** Can.
141 F1 **Chesuncook Lake** U.S.A.
131 D2 **Chéticamp** Can.
145 D3 **Chetumal** Mex.
128 B2 **Chetwynd** Can.
98 B1 **Cheviot Hills** U.K.
136 C2 **Cheyenne** U.S.A.
136 C2 **Cheyenne** *r.* U.S.A.
136 C3 **Cheyenne Wells** U.S.A.
75 B2 **Chhatarpur** India
62 A2 **Chiang Dao** Thai.
62 A2 **Chiang Mai** Thai.
62 A2 **Chiang Rai** Thai.
108 A1 **Chiavenna** Italy
70 B3 **Chibi** China
121 C3 **Chiboma** Moz.
130 C2 **Chibougamau** Can.
123 D1 **Chibuto** Moz.
75 D1 **Chibuzhang Co** *l.* China
140 B2 **Chicago** U.S.A.
128 A2 **Chichagof Island** U.S.A.
99 C3 **Chichester** U.K.
50 A2 **Chichester Range** *mts* Austr
139 D1 **Chickasha** U.S.A.
150 A2 **Chiclayo** Peru
153 B5 **Chico** *r.* Arg.
135 B3 **Chico** U.S.A.
131 C2 **Chicoutimi** Can.
108 B2 **Chieti** Italy
145 C3 **Chietla** Mex.
69 D2 **Chifeng** China
155 D1 **Chifre, Serra do** *mts* Brazil
145 C3 **Chignahuapán** Mex.
121 C3 **Chigubo** Moz.
74 A1 **Chihil Abdālān, Kōh-e** *mts* Afgh.
144 B2 **Chihuahua** Mex.
88 C2 **Chikhachevo** Russia
67 C3 **Chikuma-gawa** *r.* Japan
128 B2 **Chilanko** *r.* Can.
74 B1 **Chilas** Pak.
139 C2 **Childress** U.S.A.
153 A4 **Chile** *country* S. America
152 B3 **Chilecito** Arg.
75 C3 **Chilika Lake** India
121 B2 **Chililabombwe** Zambia
128 B2 **Chilko** *r.* Can.
128 B2 **Chilko Lake** Can.
153 A4 **Chillán** Chile
137 E3 **Chillicothe** *MO* U.S.A.
140 C3 **Chillicothe** *OH* U.S.A.
128 B3 **Chilliwack** Can.
153 A5 **Chiloé, Isla Grande de** *i.* Cl
145 C3 **Chilpancingo** Mex.
53 C3 **Chiltern** Austr.
71 C3 **Chilung** Taiwan
119 D3 **Chimala** Tanz.
152 B4 **Chimbas** Arg.
150 A2 **Chimborazo** *mt.* Ecuador
150 A2 **Chimbote** Peru
87 E4 **Chimboy** Uzbek.
Chimkent Kazakh. *see* **Shymkent**
121 C2 **Chimoio** Moz.
77 C3 **Chimtargha, Qullai** *mt.* Taj

68 C2 China *country* Asia
145 C2 China Mex.
150 A3 Chincha Alta Peru
128 C2 Chinchaga *r.* Can.
145 D3 Chinchorro, Banco Mex.
121 C2 Chinde Moz.
65 B3 Chindo S. Korea
68 C2 Chindu China
62 A1 Chindwin *r.* Myanmar
65 B2 Chinghwa N. Korea
120 B2 Chingola Zambia
120 A2 Chinguar Angola
121 C2 Chinhoyi Zimbabwe
74 B1 Chiniot Pak.
144 B2 Chinipas Mex.
65 B2 Chinju S. Korea
118 C2 Chinko *r.* C.A.R.
138 B1 Chinle U.S.A.
67 C3 Chino Japan
104 C2 Chinon France
138 A2 Chino Valley U.S.A.
121 C2 Chinsali Zambia
108 B1 Chioggia Italy
111 C3 Chios Greece
111 C3 Chios *i.* Greece
121 C2 Chipata Zambia
120 A2 Chipindo Angola
121 C3 Chipinge Zimbabwe
73 B3 Chiplun India
99 B3 Chippenham U.K.
99 C3 Chipping Norton U.K.
77 C2 Chirchiq Uzbek.
121 C3 Chiredzi Zimbabwe
138 B2 Chiricahua Peak U.S.A.
146 B4 Chiriquí, Golfo de *b.* Panama
146 B4 Chirripó *mt.* Costa Rica
121 B2 Chirundu Zimbabwe
130 C1 Chisasibi Can.
137 E1 Chisholm U.S.A.
90 B2 Chişinău Moldova
87 E3 Chistopol' Russia
69 D1 Chita Russia
120 A2 Chitado Angola
121 C2 Chitambo Zambia
120 B1 Chitato Angola
121 C1 Chitipa Malawi
73 B3 Chitradurga India
74 B1 Chitral Pak.
146 B4 Chitré Panama
75 D2 Chittagong Bangl.
74 B2 Chittaurgarh India
121 C2 Chitungwiza Zimbabwe
120 B2 Chiume Angola
121 C2 Chivhu Zimbabwe
70 B2 Chizhou China
114 C1 Chlef Alg.
107 D2 Chlef, Oued *r.* Alg.
153 B4 Choele Choel Arg.
144 B2 Choix Mex.
103 D1 Chojnice Pol.
117 B3 Ch'ok'ē Mountains Eth.
117 B3 Ch'ok'ē Terara *mt.* Eth.
83 K2 Chokurdakh Russia
121 C3 Chókwè Moz.
104 B2 Cholet France
102 C1 Chomutov Czechia
83 I2 Chona *r.* Russia
150 A2 Chone Ecuador
65 B1 Ch'ŏngjin N. Korea
65 B2 Chŏngju N. Korea
65 B2 Chŏngp'yŏng N. Korea
70 A3 Chongqing China
70 A2 Chongqing *mun.* China
71 A3 Chongzuo China
Chŏnju S. Korea *see* Jeonju
153 A5 Chonos, Archipiélago de los *is* Chile
154 B3 Chopinzinho Brazil
111 B3 Chora Sfakion Greece
98 B2 Chorley U.K.
90 C2 Chornomors'k Ukr.
91 C2 Chornomors'ke Ukr.
90 B2 Chortkiv Ukr.
65 B1 Ch'osan N. Korea
67 D3 Chōshi Japan
103 D1 Choszczno Pol.
114 A2 Choûm Maur.
69 D1 Choybalsan Mongolia
69 D1 Choyr Mongolia
54 B2 Christchurch N.Z.
99 C3 Christchurch U.K.
127 G2 Christian, Cape Can.
123 C2 Christiana S. Africa
54 A2 Christina, Mount N.Z.
153 B5 Chubut *r.* Arg.
90 B1 Chudniv Ukr.
89 D2 Chudovo Russia
Chudskoye Ozero *l.* Estonia/Russia *see* Peipus, Lake
126 B2 Chugach Mountains U.S.A.
67 B4 Chūgoku-sanchi *mts* Japan
66 B2 Chuguyevka Russia
91 D2 Chuhuyiv Ukr.
160 J3 Chukchi Sea Russia/U.S.A.
83 N2 Chukotskiy Poluostrov *pen.* Russia
135 C4 Chula Vista U.S.A.
82 G3 Chulym Russia
152 B3 Chumbicha Arg.
83 K3 Chumikan Russia
63 A2 Chumphon Thai.
65 B2 Chuncheon S. Korea
Chungking China *see* Chongqing
83 H2 Chunya *r.* Russia
150 A3 Chuquibamba Peru
152 B3 Chuquicamata Chile
105 D2 Chur Switz.
62 A1 Churachandpur India
129 E2 Churchill Can.
129 E2 Churchill *r. Man.* Can.
131 D1 Churchill *r. Nfld. and Lab.* Can.
129 E2 Churchill, Cape Can.
131 D1 Churchill Falls Can.
129 D2 Churchill Lake Can.
74 B2 Churu India
131 C2 Chute-des-Passes Can.
62 B1 Chuxiong China
90 B2 Ciadîr-Lunga Moldova
61 B2 Ciamis Indon.
60 B2 Cianjur Indon.
154 B2 Cianorte Brazil
103 E1 Ciechanów Pol.
146 C2 Ciego de Ávila Cuba
146 B2 Cienfuegos Cuba
107 C2 Cieza Spain
106 C2 Cigüela *r.* Spain
80 B2 Cihanbeyli Turkey
144 B3 Cihuatlán Mex.
106 C2 Cíjara, Embalse de *resr* Spain
61 B2 Cilacap Indon.
139 C1 Cimarron *r.* U.S.A.
90 B2 Cimişlia Moldova
108 B2 Cimone, Monte *mt.* Italy
140 C3 Cincinnati U.S.A.
111 C3 Çine Turkey
100 B2 Ciney Belgium
145 C3 Cintalapa Mex.
71 B3 Ciping China
126 B2 Circle *AK* U.S.A.
136 B1 Circle *MT* U.S.A.
58 B3 Cirebon Indon.
99 C3 Cirencester U.K.
108 A1 Ciriè Italy
109 C3 Cirò Marina Italy
109 C2 Čitluk Bos. & Herz.
122 A3 Citrusdal S. Africa
145 B2 Ciudad Acuña Mex.
145 B3 Ciudad Altamirano Mex.
150 B1 Ciudad Bolívar Venez.
144 B2 Ciudad Camargo Mex.
144 A2 Ciudad Constitución Mex.
145 C3 Ciudad del Carmen Mex.
144 B2 Ciudad Delicias Mex.
145 C2 Ciudad de Valles Mex.
150 B1 Ciudad Guayana Venez.
138 B3 Ciudad Guerrero Mex.
144 B3 Ciudad Guzmán Mex.
145 C3 Ciudad Hidalgo Mex.
144 A2 Ciudad Insurgentes Mex.
145 C3 Ciudad Ixtepec Mex.
144 B1 Ciudad Juárez Mex.
145 C2 Ciudad Mante Mex.
145 C2 Ciudad Mier Mex.
144 B2 Ciudad Obregón Mex.
106 C2 Ciudad Real Spain
145 C2 Ciudad Río Bravo Mex.
106 B1 Ciudad Rodrigo Spain
145 C2 Ciudad Victoria Mex.
107 D1 Ciutadella Spain
111 C3 Civan Dağ *mt.* Turkey
108 B1 Cividale del Friuli Italy
108 B2 Civitanova Marche Italy
108 B2 Civitavecchia Italy
104 C2 Civray France
111 C3 Çivril Turkey
70 C2 Cixi China
99 D3 Clacton-on-Sea U.K.
128 C2 Claire, Lake Can.
105 C2 Clamecy France
122 A3 Clanwilliam S. Africa
52 A2 Clare Austr.
97 A2 Clare Island Ireland
141 E2 Claremont U.S.A.
97 B2 Claremorris Ireland
54 B2 Clarence N.Z.
131 E2 Clarenville Can.
128 C2 Claresholm Can.
137 D2 Clarinda U.S.A.
123 C3 Clarkebury S. Africa
143 D2 Clark Hill Reservoir U.S.A.
140 C3 Clarksburg U.S.A.
142 B2 Clarksdale U.S.A.
134 C1 Clarks Fork *r.* U.S.A.
142 B1 Clarksville *AR* U.S.A.
142 C1 Clarksville *TN* U.S.A.
154 B1 Claro *r.* Brazil
139 C1 Clayton U.S.A.
97 B3 Clear, Cape Ireland
137 E2 Clear Lake U.S.A.
135 B3 Clear Lake U.S.A.
128 C2 Clearwater Can.
129 C2 Clearwater *r.* Can.
143 D3 Clearwater U.S.A.
134 C1 Clearwater *r.* U.S.A.
139 D2 Cleburne U.S.A.
51 D2 Clermont Austr.
105 C2 Clermont-Ferrand France
52 A2 Cleve Austr.
142 B2 Cleveland *MS* U.S.A.
140 C2 Cleveland *OH* U.S.A.
143 D1 Cleveland *TN* U.S.A.
134 D1 Cleveland, Mount U.S.A.
143 D3 Clewiston U.S.A.
97 A2 Clifden Ireland
53 D1 Clifton Austr.
138 B2 Clifton U.S.A.
128 B2 Clinton Can.
137 E2 Clinton *IA* U.S.A.
137 E3 Clinton *MO* U.S.A.
139 D1 Clinton *OK* U.S.A.
96 A2 Clisham *h.* U.K.
98 B2 Clitheroe U.K.

97 B3 **Clonakilty** Ireland
51 D2 **Cloncurry** Austr.
97 C1 **Clones** Ireland
97 C2 **Clonmel** Ireland
100 D1 **Cloppenburg** Ger.
50 A2 **Cloud Break** Austr.
136 B2 **Cloud Peak** U.S.A.
139 C2 **Clovis** U.S.A.
129 D2 **Cluff Lake Mine** Can.
110 B1 **Cluj-Napoca** Romania
51 C2 **Cluny** Austr.
105 D2 **Cluses** France
54 A3 **Clutha** *r.* N.Z.
96 B3 **Clyde** *r.* U.K.
96 B3 **Clyde, Firth of** *est.* U.K.
96 B3 **Clydebank** U.K.
127 G2 **Clyde River** Can.
144 B3 **Coalcomán** Mex.
135 C3 **Coaldale (abandoned)** U.S.A.
128 B2 **Coal River** Can.
150 B2 **Coari** Brazil
150 B2 **Coari** *r.* Brazil
142 B2 **Coastal Plain** U.S.A.
128 B2 **Coast Mountains** Can.
135 B2 **Coast Ranges** *mts* U.S.A.
96 B3 **Coatbridge** U.K.
127 F2 **Coats Island** Can.
55 R2 **Coats Land** *reg.* Antarctica
145 C3 **Coatzacoalcos** Mex.
146 A3 **Cobán** Guat.
53 C2 **Cobar** Austr.
97 B3 **Cobh** Ireland
152 B2 **Cobija** Bol.
141 D2 **Cobourg** Can.
50 C1 **Cobourg Peninsula** Austr.
53 C3 **Cobram** Austr.
101 E2 **Coburg** Ger.
152 B2 **Cochabamba** Bol.
100 C2 **Cochem** Ger.
Cochin India *see* **Kochi**
128 C2 **Cochrane** *Alta* Can.
130 B2 **Cochrane** *Ont.* Can.
153 A5 **Cochrane** Chile
52 B2 **Cockburn** Austr.
Cockburn Town Turks and Caicos Is *see* **Grand Turk**
98 B1 **Cockermouth** U.K.
122 B3 **Cockscomb** *mt.* S. Africa
146 B3 **Coco** *r.* Hond./Nic.
144 B2 **Cocula** Mex.
150 A1 **Cocuy, Sierra Nevada del** *mt.* Col.
141 E2 **Cod, Cape** U.S.A.
108 B2 **Codigoro** Italy
131 D1 **Cod Island** Can.
151 D2 **Codó** Brazil
136 B2 **Cody** U.S.A.
51 D1 **Coen** Austr.
100 C2 **Coesfeld** Ger.
134 C1 **Coeur d'Alene** U.S.A.
123 C3 **Coffee Bay** S. Africa
137 D3 **Coffeyville** U.S.A.
53 D2 **Coffs Harbour** Austr.
104 B2 **Cognac** France
118 A2 **Cogo** Equat. Guinea
52 B3 **Cohuna** Austr.
146 B4 **Coiba, Isla de** *i.* Panama
73 B3 **Coimbatore** India
106 B1 **Coimbra** Port.
52 B3 **Colac** Austr.
155 D1 **Colatina** Brazil
136 C3 **Colby** U.S.A.
99 D3 **Colchester** U.K.
129 C2 **Cold Lake** Can.
96 C3 **Coldstream** U.K.
139 D2 **Coleman** U.S.A.
52 B3 **Coleraine** Austr.
97 C1 **Coleraine** U.K.
123 C3 **Colesberg** S. Africa
144 B3 **Colima** Mex.
144 B3 **Colima, Nevado de** *vol.* Mex.
96 A2 **Coll** *i.* U.K.
53 C1 **Collarenebri** Austr.
50 B1 **Collier Bay** Austr.
54 B2 **Collingwood** N.Z.
97 B1 **Collooney** Ireland
105 D2 **Colmar** France
100 C2 **Cologne** Ger.
154 C2 **Colômbia** Brazil
150 A1 **Colombia** *country* S. America
73 B4 **Colombo** Sri Lanka
104 C3 **Colomiers** France
152 C4 **Colón** Arg.
146 C4 **Colón** Panama
109 C3 **Colonna, Capo** *c.* Italy
96 A2 **Colonsay** *i.* U.K.
153 B4 **Colorado** *r.* Arg.
138 A2 **Colorado** *r.* Mex./U.S.A.
139 D3 **Colorado** *r.* U.S.A.
136 B3 **Colorado** *state* U.S.A.
135 E3 **Colorado Plateau** U.S.A.
136 C3 **Colorado Springs** U.S.A.
144 B2 **Colotlán** Mex.
136 B1 **Colstrip** U.S.A.
137 E3 **Columbia** *MO* U.S.A.
143 D2 **Columbia** *SC* U.S.A.
142 C1 **Columbia** *TN* U.S.A.
134 B1 **Columbia** *r.* U.S.A.
128 C2 **Columbia, Mount** Can.
134 D1 **Columbia Falls** U.S.A.
128 B2 **Columbia Mountains** Can.
134 C1 **Columbia Plateau** U.S.A.
143 D2 **Columbus** *GA* U.S.A.
140 B3 **Columbus** *IN* U.S.A.
142 C2 **Columbus** *MS* U.S.A.
137 D2 **Columbus** *NE* U.S.A.
138 B2 **Columbus** *NM* U.S.A.
140 C3 **Columbus** *OH* U.S.A.
134 C1 **Colville** U.S.A.
126 A2 **Colville** *r.* U.S.A.
126 C2 **Colville Lake** Can.
98 B2 **Colwyn Bay** U.K.
108 B2 **Comacchio** Italy
145 C3 **Comalcalco** Mex.
110 C1 **Comănești** Romania
130 C1 **Comencho, Lac** *l.* Can.
97 C2 **Comeragh Mountains** *hills* Ireland
75 D2 **Comilla** Bangl.
108 A2 **Comino, Capo** *c. Sardinia* Italy
145 C3 **Comitán de Domínguez** Mex.
104 C2 **Commentry** France
139 D2 **Commerce** U.S.A.
127 F2 **Committee Bay** Can.
108 A1 **Como** Italy
153 B5 **Comodoro Rivadavia** Arg.
121 D2 **Comoros** *country* Africa
104 C2 **Compiègne** France
144 B2 **Compostela** Mex.
90 B2 **Comrat** Moldova
114 A4 **Conakry** Guinea
155 E1 **Conceição da Barra** Brazil
151 D2 **Conceição do Araguaia** Brazil
155 D1 **Conceição do Mato Dentro** Brazil
152 B3 **Concepción** Arg.
153 A4 **Concepción** Chile
144 B2 **Concepción** Mex.
135 B4 **Conception, Point** U.S.A.
154 C2 **Conchas** Brazil
138 C1 **Conchas Lake** U.S.A.
144 B2 **Conchos** *r. Chihuahua* Mex.
145 C2 **Conchos** *r. Nuevo León/Tamaulipas* Mex.
135 B3 **Concord** *CA* U.S.A.
141 E2 **Concord** *NH* U.S.A.
152 C4 **Concordia** Arg.
122 A2 **Concordia** S. Africa
137 D3 **Concordia** U.S.A.
53 C2 **Condobolin** Austr.
104 C3 **Condom** France
134 B1 **Condon** U.S.A.
108 B1 **Conegliano** Italy
104 C2 **Confolens** France
75 C2 **Congdü** China
118 B3 **Congo** *country* Africa
118 B3 **Congo** *r.* Congo/Dem. Rep. Congo
118 C3 **Congo, Democratic Republi[c] of the** *country* Africa
129 C2 **Conklin** Can.
97 B1 **Conn, Lough** *l.* Ireland
97 B2 **Connacht** *reg.* Ireland
141 E2 **Connecticut** *r.* U.S.A.
141 E2 **Connecticut** *state* U.S.A.
97 B2 **Connemara** *reg.* Ireland
134 D1 **Conrad** U.S.A.
139 D2 **Conroe** U.S.A.
155 D2 **Conselheiro Lafaiete** Brazil
155 D1 **Conselheiro Pena** Brazil
98 C1 **Consett** U.K.
63 B3 **Côn Sơn, Đao** *i.* Vietnam
110 C2 **Constanța** Romania
106 B2 **Constantina** Spain
115 C1 **Constantine** Alg.
134 D2 **Contact** U.S.A.
150 A2 **Contamana** Peru
153 A6 **Contreras, Isla** *i.* Chile
126 D2 **Contwoyto Lake** Can.
142 B1 **Conway** *AR* U.S.A.
141 E2 **Conway** *NH* U.S.A.
51 C2 **Coober Pedy** Austr.
Cook, Mount *mt.* N.Z. *see* **Aoraki/Mount Cook**
143 C1 **Cookeville** U.S.A.
49 H4 **Cook Islands** S. Pacific Oce[an]
131 E1 **Cook's Harbour** Can.
97 C1 **Cookstown** U.K.
54 B2 **Cook Strait** N.Z.
51 D1 **Cooktown** Austr.
53 C2 **Coolabah** Austr.
53 C2 **Coolamon** Austr.
53 D1 **Coolangatta** Austr.
50 B3 **Coolgardie** Austr.
53 C3 **Cooma** Austr.
52 B2 **Coombah** Austr.
53 C2 **Coonabarabran** Austr.
52 A3 **Coonalpyn** Austr.
53 C2 **Coonamble** Austr.
52 A1 **Cooper Creek** *watercourse* Austr.
134 B2 **Coos Bay** U.S.A.
53 C2 **Cootamundra** Austr.
145 C3 **Copainalá** Mex.
145 C3 **Copala** Mex.
93 F4 **Copenhagen** Denmark
109 C2 **Copertino** Italy
152 A3 **Copiapó** Chile
140 B1 **Copper Harbor** U.S.A.
Coppermine Can. *see* **Kugluktuk**
126 D2 **Coppermine** *r.* Can.
122 B2 **Copperton** S. Africa
152 A3 **Coquimbo** Chile
110 B2 **Corabia** Romania
155 D1 **Coração de Jesus** Brazil
150 A3 **Coracora** Peru
53 D1 **Coraki** Austr.
50 A2 **Coral Bay** Austr.
127 F2 **Coral Harbour** Can.
156 D7 **Coral Sea** S. Pacific Ocean
48 D4 **Coral Sea Islands Territor[y]** Austr.

52 B3 **Corangamite, Lake** Austr.
99 C2 **Corby** U.K.
153 A5 **Corcovado, Golfo** *sea chan.* Chile
143 D2 **Cordele** U.S.A.
64 B1 **Cordilleras Range** *mts* Phil.
152 B4 **Córdoba** Arg.
145 C3 **Córdoba** Mex.
106 C2 **Córdoba** Spain
153 B4 **Córdoba, Sierras de** *mts* Arg.
111 A3 **Corfu** *i.* Greece
106 B2 **Coria** Spain
111 B3 **Corinth** Greece
142 C2 **Corinth** U.S.A.
155 D1 **Corinto** Brazil
97 B3 **Cork** Ireland
111 C2 **Çorlu** Turkey
154 B2 **Cornélio Procópio** Brazil
131 E2 **Corner Brook** Can.
53 C3 **Corner Inlet** *b.* Austr.
135 B3 **Corning** *CA* U.S.A.
141 D2 **Corning** *NY* U.S.A.
Corn Islands *is* Nic. *see* **Maíz, Islas del**
108 B2 **Corno Grande** *mt.* Italy
130 C2 **Cornwall** Can.
126 E1 **Cornwallis Island** Can.
150 B1 **Coro** Venez.
154 C1 **Coromandel** Brazil
54 C1 **Coromandel Peninsula** N.Z.
129 C2 **Coronation** Can.
126 D2 **Coronation Gulf** Can.
152 C3 **Coronel Oviedo** Para.
153 B4 **Coronel Suárez** Arg.
150 A3 **Coropuna, Nudo** *mt.* Peru
109 D2 **Çorovodë** Albania
139 D3 **Corpus Christi** U.S.A.
152 B2 **Corque** Bol.
151 D3 **Corrente** Brazil
154 B1 **Correntes** Brazil
151 D3 **Correntina** Brazil
97 B2 **Corrib, Lough** *l.* Ireland
152 C3 **Corrientes** Arg.
144 B2 **Corrientes, Cabo** *c.* Mex.
53 C3 **Corryong** Austr.
Corse *i.* France *see* **Corsica**
105 D3 **Corse, Cap** *c. Corsica* France
105 D3 **Corsica** *i.* France
139 D2 **Corsicana** U.S.A.
105 D3 **Corte** *Corsica* France
106 B2 **Cortegana** Spain
136 B3 **Cortez** U.S.A.
108 B1 **Cortina d'Ampezzo** Italy
141 D2 **Cortland** U.S.A.
108 B2 **Cortona** Italy
106 B2 **Coruche** Port.
Çoruh Turkey *see* **Artvin**
80 B1 **Çorum** Turkey
152 C2 **Corumbá** Brazil
154 C1 **Corumbá** *r.* Brazil
134 B2 **Corvallis** U.S.A.
98 B2 **Corwen** U.K.
144 B2 **Cosalá** Mex.
145 C3 **Cosamaloapan** Mex.
109 C3 **Cosenza** Italy
105 C2 **Cosne-Cours-sur-Loire** France
107 C2 **Costa Blanca** *coastal area* Spain
107 D1 **Costa Brava** *coastal area* Spain
106 B2 **Costa del Sol** *coastal area* Spain
154 B1 **Costa Rica** Brazil
146 B3 **Costa Rica** *country* Central America
144 B2 **Costa Rica** Mex.
110 B2 **Costești** Romania
64 B2 **Cotabato** Phil.
114 B4 **Côte d'Ivoire** *country* Africa
150 A2 **Cotopaxi, Volcán** *vol.* Ecuador
99 B3 **Cotswold Hills** U.K.
134 B2 **Cottage Grove** U.S.A.
102 C1 **Cottbus** Ger.
104 B2 **Coubre, Pointe de la** *pt* France
52 A3 **Couedic, Cape du** Austr.
137 D2 **Council Bluffs** U.S.A.
88 B2 **Courland Lagoon** *b.* Lith./Russia
128 B3 **Courtenay** Can.
104 B2 **Coutances** France
104 B2 **Coutras** France
100 B2 **Couvin** Belgium
99 C2 **Coventry** U.K.
140 C3 **Covington** U.S.A.
50 B3 **Cowan, Lake** *imp. l.* Austr.
96 C2 **Cowdenbeath** U.K.
53 C3 **Cowes** Austr.
134 B1 **Cowlitz** *r.* U.S.A.
53 C2 **Cowra** Austr.
154 B1 **Coxim** Brazil
75 D2 **Cox's Bazar** Bangl.
153 A5 **Coyhaique** Chile
145 B3 **Coyuca de Benítez** Mex.
75 C1 **Cozhê** China
145 D2 **Cozumel** Mex.
145 D2 **Cozumel, Isla de** *i.* Mex.
123 C3 **Cradock** S. Africa
136 B2 **Craig** U.S.A.
102 C2 **Crailsheim** Ger.
110 B2 **Craiova** Romania
129 D2 **Cranberry Portage** Can.
53 C3 **Cranbourne** Austr.
128 C3 **Cranbrook** Can.
151 D2 **Crateús** Brazil
151 E2 **Crato** Brazil
136 C2 **Crawford** U.S.A.
140 B2 **Crawfordsville** U.S.A.
99 C3 **Crawley** U.K.
134 D1 **Crazy Mountains** U.S.A.
129 D2 **Cree** *r.* Can.
144 B2 **Creel** Mex.
129 D2 **Cree Lake** Can.
100 B1 **Creil** Neth.
105 D2 **Crema** Italy
108 B1 **Cremona** Italy
108 B2 **Cres** *i.* Croatia
134 B2 **Crescent City** U.S.A.
128 C3 **Creston** Can.
137 E2 **Creston** U.S.A.
142 C2 **Crestview** U.S.A.
111 B3 **Crete** *i.* Greece
107 D1 **Creus, Cap de** *c.* Spain
98 B2 **Crewe** U.K.
96 B2 **Crianlarich** U.K.
152 D3 **Criciúma** Brazil
96 C2 **Crieff** U.K.
108 B1 **Crikvenica** Croatia
91 C2 **Crimea** *disp. terr.* Europe
91 C2 **Crimea** *pen.* Ukr.
101 F2 **Crimmitschau** Ger.
154 C1 **Cristalina** Brazil
101 E1 **Crivitz** Ger.
Crna Gora *country* Europe *see* **Montenegro**
109 D2 **Crni Vrh** *h.* Serbia
109 C1 **Črnomelj** Slovenia
97 B2 **Croagh Patrick** *h.* Ireland
109 C1 **Croatia** *country* Europe
61 C1 **Crocker, Banjaran** *mts* Malaysia
139 D2 **Crockett** U.S.A.
59 C3 **Croker Island** Austr.
99 D2 **Cromer** U.K.
54 A3 **Cromwell** N.Z.
137 D1 **Crookston** U.S.A.
53 C2 **Crookwell** Austr.
136 C1 **Crosby** U.S.A.
143 D3 **Cross City** U.S.A.
142 B2 **Crossett** U.S.A.
98 B1 **Cross Fell** *h.* U.K.
129 E2 **Cross Lake** Can.
143 C1 **Crossville** U.S.A.
109 C3 **Crotone** Italy
99 D3 **Crowborough** U.K.
142 B2 **Crowley** U.S.A.
128 C3 **Crowsnest Pass** Can.
146 C3 **Cruz, Cabo** *c.* Cuba
152 C3 **Cruz Alta** Brazil
152 B4 **Cruz del Eje** Arg.
155 D2 **Cruzeiro** Brazil
150 A2 **Cruzeiro do Sul** Brazil
52 A2 **Crystal Brook** Austr.
139 D3 **Crystal City** U.S.A.
140 B1 **Crystal Falls** U.S.A.
103 E2 **Csongrád** Hungary
120 B2 **Cuando** *r.* Angola/Zambia
120 A2 **Cuangar** Angola
118 B3 **Cuango** *r.* Angola/Dem. Rep. Congo
120 A1 **Cuanza** *r.* Angola
139 C3 **Cuatro Ciénegas** Mex.
144 B2 **Cuauhtémoc** Mex.
145 C3 **Cuautla** Mex.
146 B2 **Cuba** *country* West Indies
120 A2 **Cubal** Angola
120 B2 **Cubango** *r.* Angola/Namibia
150 A1 **Cúcuta** Col.
73 B3 **Cuddalore** India
Cuddapah India *see* **Kadapa**
106 C1 **Cuéllar** Spain
120 A2 **Cuemba** Angola
150 A2 **Cuenca** Ecuador
107 C1 **Cuenca** Spain
107 C1 **Cuenca, Serranía de** *mts* Spain
145 C3 **Cuernavaca** Mex.
139 D3 **Cuero** U.S.A.
151 C3 **Cuiabá** Brazil
151 C3 **Cuiabá** *r.* Brazil
96 A2 **Cuillin Sound** *sea chan.* U.K.
120 A1 **Cuilo** Angola
120 B2 **Cuito** *r.* Angola
120 A2 **Cuito Cuanavale** Angola
60 B1 **Cukai** Malaysia
53 C3 **Culcairn** Austr.
53 C1 **Culgoa** *r.* Austr.
144 B2 **Culiacán** Mex.
64 A1 **Culion** *i.* Phil.
107 C2 **Cullera** Spain
142 C2 **Cullman** U.S.A.
97 C1 **Cullybackey** U.K.
151 C3 **Culuene** *r.* Brazil
150 B1 **Cumaná** Venez.
141 D3 **Cumberland** U.S.A.
140 B3 **Cumberland** *r.* U.S.A.
129 D2 **Cumberland Lake** Can.
127 G2 **Cumberland Peninsula** Can.
142 C1 **Cumberland Plateau** U.S.A.
127 G2 **Cumberland Sound** *sea chan.* Can.
96 C3 **Cumbernauld** U.K.
135 B3 **Cummings** U.S.A.
96 B3 **Cumnock** U.K.
144 B1 **Cumpas** Mex.
145 C3 **Cunduacán** Mex.
120 A2 **Cunene** *r.* Angola
108 A2 **Cuneo** Italy
53 C1 **Cunnamulla** Austr.
108 A1 **Cuorgnè** Italy
96 C2 **Cupar** U.K.
147 D3 **Curaçao** *i.* West Indies
147 D3 **Curaçao** *terr.* West Indies
150 A2 **Curaray** *r.* Ecuador
153 A4 **Curicó** Chile
154 C3 **Curitiba** Brazil

Curnamona

52	A2	Curnamona Austr.
51	D3	Currie Austr.
51	E2	Curtis Island Austr.
151	C2	Curuá r. Brazil
60	B2	Curup Indon.
151	D2	Cururupu Brazil
155	D1	Curvelo Brazil
150	A3	Cusco Peru
139	D1	Cushing U.S.A.
134	D1	Cut Bank U.S.A.
75	C2	Cuttack India
101	D1	Cuxhaven Ger.
64	B1	Cuyo Islands Phil.

52 A2 Curnamona Austr.
51 D3 Currie Austr.
51 E2 Curtis Island Austr.
151 C2 Curuá r. Brazil
60 B2 Curup Indon.
151 D2 Cururupu Brazil
155 D1 Curvelo Brazil
150 A3 Cusco Peru
139 D1 Cushing U.S.A.
134 D1 Cut Bank U.S.A.
75 C2 Cuttack India
101 D1 Cuxhaven Ger.
64 B1 Cuyo Islands Phil.
  Cuzco Peru see Cusco
119 C3 Cyangugu Rwanda
111 B3 Cyclades is Greece
129 C3 Cypress Hills Can.
80 B2 Cyprus country Asia
102 C1 Czechia country Europe
103 C1 Czersk Pol.
103 D1 Częstochowa Pol.

D

  Đa, Sông r. Vietnam see Black River
69 D3 Daban China
114 A3 Dabola Guinea
  Dacca Bangl. see Dhaka
102 C2 Dachau Ger.
117 C4 Dadaab Kenya
74 A2 Dadu Pak.
65 B2 Daegu S. Korea
65 B2 Daejeon S. Korea
65 B3 Daejeong S. Korea
64 B1 Daet Phil.
114 A3 Dagana Senegal
64 B1 Dagupan Phil.
74 B3 Dahanu India
69 D2 Da Hinggan Ling mts China
116 C3 Dahlak Archipelago is Eritrea
100 C2 Dahlem Ger.
78 B3 Dahm, Ramlat des. Saudi Arabia/Yemen
60 B2 Daik Indon.
106 C2 Daimiel Spain
97 A2 Daingean Uí Chúis Ireland
51 C2 Dajarra Austr.
114 A3 Dakar Senegal
116 A2 Dākhilah, Wāḩat ad oasis Egypt
114 A2 Dakhla Western Sahara
  Dakhla Oasis Egypt see Dākhilah, Wāḩat ad
63 A3 Dakoank India
88 C3 Dakol'ka r. Belarus
  Dakovica Kosovo see Gjakovë
109 C1 Đakovo Croatia
120 B2 Dala Angola
68 C2 Dalain Hob China
93 G3 Dalälven r. Sweden
111 C3 Dalaman Turkey
111 C3 Dalaman r. Turkey
69 C2 Dalandzadgad Mongolia
63 B2 Đa Lat Vietnam
74 A2 Dalbandin Pak.
96 C3 Dalbeattie U.K.
51 E2 Dalby Austr.
143 C1 Dale Hollow Lake U.S.A.
53 C3 Dalgety Austr.
139 C1 Dalhart U.S.A.
131 D2 Dalhousie Can.
62 B1 Dali China
70 C2 Dalian China
96 C3 Dalkeith U.K.
139 D2 Dallas U.S.A.
128 A2 Dall Island U.S.A.

109 C2 Dalmatia reg. Bos. & Herz./Croatia
66 C2 Dal'negorsk Russia
66 B1 Dal'nerechensk Russia
114 B4 Daloa Côte d'Ivoire
51 D2 Dalrymple, Mount Austr.
92 □A3 Dalsmynni Iceland
143 D2 Dalton U.S.A.
  Daltonganj India see Medininagar
60 B1 Daludalu Indon.
92 □B2 Dalvík Iceland
50 C1 Daly r. Austr.
51 C1 Daly Waters Austr.
74 B2 Daman India
80 B2 Damanhūr Egypt
59 C3 Damar i. Indon.
80 B2 Damascus Syria
115 D3 Damaturu Nigeria
76 B3 Damāvand, Qolleh-ye mt. Iran
81 D2 Dāmghān Iran
79 C2 Dammam Saudi Arabia
101 D1 Damme Ger.
75 B2 Damoh India
114 B4 Damongo Ghana
59 C3 Dampir, Selat sea chan. Indon.
75 C2 Damqoq Zangbo r. China
117 C3 Danakil reg. Africa
114 B4 Danané Côte d'Ivoire
63 B2 Da Nang Vietnam
141 E2 Danbury U.S.A.
65 A1 Dandong China
146 B3 Dangriga Belize
70 B2 Dangshan China
89 F2 Danilov Russia
89 E2 Danilovskaya Vozvyshennost' hills Russia
70 B2 Danjiangkou China
89 E3 Dankov Russia
146 B3 Danlí Hond.
101 E1 Dannenberg (Elbe) Ger.
54 C2 Dannevirke N.Z.
62 B2 Dan Sai Thai.
  Dantu China see Zhenjiang
110 A1 Danube r. Europe
110 C1 Danube Delta Romania/Ukr.
140 B2 Danville IL U.S.A.
140 C3 Danville KY U.S.A.
141 D3 Danville VA U.S.A.
71 A4 Danzhou China
71 B3 Daoxian China
114 C3 Dapaong Togo
64 B2 Dapitan Phil.
68 C2 Da Qaidam China
69 E1 Daqing China
80 B2 Dar'ā Syria
79 C2 Dārāb Iran
81 D2 Dārān Iran
75 C2 Darbhanga India
119 D3 Dar es Salaam Tanz.
117 A3 Darfur reg. Sudan
74 B1 Dargai Pak.
54 B1 Dargaville N.Z.
53 C3 Dargo Austr.
69 D1 Darhan Mongolia
150 A1 Darién, Golfo del g. Col.
75 C2 Darjiling India
53 C2 Darling r. Austr.
53 C1 Darling Downs hills Austr.
50 A3 Darling Range hills Austr.
98 C1 Darlington U.K.
53 C2 Darlington Point Austr.
103 D1 Darłowo Pol.
101 D3 Darmstadt Ger.
115 E1 Darnah Libya
52 B2 Darnick Austr.
107 C1 Daroca Spain
99 D3 Dartford U.K.

99 A3 Dartmoor hills U.K.
131 D2 Dartmouth Can.
99 B3 Dartmouth U.K.
59 D3 Daru P.N.G.
50 C1 Darwin Austr.
74 A2 Dasht r. Pak.
76 B2 Daşoguz Turkm.
61 C1 Datadian Indon.
111 C3 Datça Turkey
70 B1 Datong China
64 B2 Datu Piang Phil.
74 B1 Daud Khel Pak.
88 B2 Daugava r. Latvia
88 C2 Daugavpils Latvia
100 C2 Daun Ger.
129 D2 Dauphin Can.
129 E2 Dauphin Lake Can.
73 B3 Davangere India
64 B2 Davao Phil.
64 B2 Davao Gulf Phil.
137 E2 Davenport U.S.A.
99 C2 Daventry U.K.
123 C2 Daveyton S. Africa
146 B4 David Panama
129 D2 Davidson Can.
126 E3 Davidson Lake Can.
135 B3 Davis U.S.A.
131 D1 Davis Inlet (abandoned) Can.
159 F3 Davis Sea Antarctica
160 P3 Davis Strait Can./Greenland
105 D2 Davos Switz.
  Dawei Myanmar see Tavoy
78 A2 Dawmat al Jandal Saudi Arabia
79 C3 Dawqah Oman
126 B2 Dawson Can.
143 D2 Dawson U.S.A.
128 B2 Dawson Creek Can.
128 B2 Dawsons Landing Can.
68 C2 Dawu China
  Dawukou China see Shizuishan
104 B3 Dax France
68 C2 Da Xueshan mts China
80 C2 Dayr az Zawr Syria
140 C3 Dayton U.S.A.
143 D3 Daytona Beach U.S.A.
70 A2 Dazhou China
122 B3 De Aar S. Africa
80 B2 Dead Sea salt l. Asia
71 B3 De'an China
152 B4 Deán Funes Arg.
128 B2 Dease Lake Can.
126 D2 Dease Strait Can.
135 C3 Death Valley depr. U.S.A.
104 C2 Deauville France
61 C1 Debak Sarawak Malaysia
109 D2 Debar Macedonia
103 E2 Debrecen Hungary
117 B3 Debre Markos Eth.
117 B3 Debre Tabor Eth.
117 B4 Debre Zeyit Eth.
142 C2 Decatur AL U.S.A.
140 B3 Decatur IL U.S.A.
73 B3 Deccan plat. India
111 D2 Děčín Czechia
137 E2 Decorah U.S.A.
88 C2 Dedovichi Russia
121 C2 Dedza Malawi
98 B2 Dee r. England/Wales U.K.
96 C2 Dee r. Scotland U.K.
53 D1 Deepwater Austr.
131 E2 Deer Lake Can.
134 D1 Deer Lodge U.S.A.
140 C2 Defiance U.S.A.
68 C2 Dêgê China
117 C4 Degeh Bur Eth.
102 C2 Deggendorf Ger.
91 E2 Degtevo Russia

75 B1 **Dehra Dun** India
75 C2 **Dehri** India
69 E2 **Dehui** China
100 A2 **Deinze** Belgium
110 B1 **Dej** Romania
59 D3 **De Jongs, Tanjung** *pt* Indon.
140 B2 **DeKalb** U.S.A.
78 A3 **Dekemhare** Eritrea
118 C3 **Dekese** Dem. Rep. Congo
135 C3 **Delano** U.S.A.
135 D3 **Delano Peak** U.S.A.
123 C2 **Delareyville** S. Africa
129 D2 **Delaronde Lake** Can.
140 C2 **Delaware** U.S.A.
141 D3 **Delaware** *r.* U.S.A.
141 D3 **Delaware** *state* U.S.A.
141 D3 **Delaware Bay** U.S.A.
53 C3 **Delegate** Austr.
105 D2 **Delémont** Switz.
100 B1 **Delft** Neth.
100 C1 **Delfzijl** Neth.
121 D2 **Delgado, Cabo** *c.* Moz.
69 C1 **Delgerhaan** Mongolia
75 B2 **Delhi** India
60 B2 **Deli** *i.* Indon.
126 C2 **Délįne** Can.
101 F2 **Delitzsch** Ger.
107 D2 **Dellys** Alg.
101 D1 **Delmenhorst** Ger.
109 B1 **Delnice** Croatia
83 L1 **De-Longa, Ostrova** *is* Russia
129 D3 **Deloraine** Can.
111 B3 **Delphi** *tourist site* Greece
139 C3 **Del Rio** U.S.A.
136 B3 **Delta** *CO* U.S.A.
135 D3 **Delta** *UT* U.S.A.
126 B2 **Delta Junction** U.S.A.
109 D3 **Delvinë** Albania
106 C1 **Demanda, Sierra de la** *mts* Spain
118 C3 **Demba** Dem. Rep. Congo
117 B4 **Dembī Dolo** Eth.
89 D2 **Demidov** Russia
138 B2 **Deming** U.S.A.
111 C3 **Demirci** Turkey
110 C2 **Demirköy** Turkey
102 C1 **Demmin** Ger.
142 C2 **Demopolis** U.S.A.
60 B2 **Dempo, Gunung** *vol.* Indon.
89 D2 **Demyansk** Russia
122 B3 **De Naawte** S. Africa
124 E2 **Denali** *mt.* U.S.A.
100 B1 **Den Burg** Neth.
100 B2 **Dendermonde** Belgium
70 A1 **Dengkou** China
70 B2 **Dengzhou** China
Den Haag Neth. *see* **The Hague**
50 A2 **Denham** Austr.
100 B1 **Den Helder** Neth.
52 B3 **Deniliquin** Austr.
134 C2 **Denio** U.S.A.
137 D2 **Denison** *IA* U.S.A.
139 D2 **Denison** *TX* U.S.A.
111 C3 **Denizli** Turkey
53 D2 **Denman** Austr.
50 A3 **Denmark** Austr.
93 E4 **Denmark** *country* Europe
160 Q3 **Denmark Strait** Greenland/Iceland
61 C2 **Denpasar** Indon.
139 D2 **Denton** U.S.A.
50 A3 **D'Entrecasteaux, Point** Austr.
136 B3 **Denver** U.S.A.
75 C2 **Deogarh** India
83 K2 **Deputatskiy** Russia
68 C3 **Dêqên** China
142 B2 **De Queen** U.S.A.
74 A2 **Dera Bugti** Pak.
74 B1 **Dera Ghazi Khan** Pak.
74 B1 **Dera Ismail Khan** Pak.
87 D4 **Derbent** Russia
50 B1 **Derby** Austr.
99 C2 **Derby** U.K.
99 D2 **Dereham** U.K.
97 B2 **Derg, Lough** *l.* Ireland
91 D1 **Derhachi** Ukr.
142 B2 **DeRidder** U.S.A.
91 D2 **Derkul** *r.* Russia/Ukr.
Derry U.K. *see* **Londonderry**
75 B1 **Dêrub** China
116 B3 **Derudeb** Sudan
122 B3 **De Rust** S. Africa
109 C2 **Derventa** Bos. & Herz.
98 C2 **Derwent** *r.* U.K.
98 B1 **Derwent Water** *l.* U.K.
77 C1 **Derzhavinsk** Kazakh.
152 B2 **Desaguadero** *r.* Bol.
129 D2 **Deschambault Lake** Can.
134 B1 **Deschutes** *r.* U.S.A.
117 B3 **Desē** Eth.
153 B5 **Deseado** *r.* Arg.
137 E2 **Des Moines** U.S.A.
137 E2 **Des Moines** *r.* U.S.A.
91 C1 **Desna** *r.* Russia/Ukr.
89 D3 **Desnogorsk** Russia
101 F2 **Dessau-Roßlau** Ger.
126 B2 **Destruction Bay** Can.
149 C3 **Desventuradas, Islas** *is* S. Pacific Ocean
128 C1 **Detah** Can.
101 D2 **Detmold** Ger.
140 C2 **Detroit** U.S.A.
137 D1 **Detroit Lakes** U.S.A.
100 B2 **Deurne** Neth.
110 B1 **Deva** Romania
100 C1 **Deventer** Neth.
96 C2 **Deveron** *r.* U.K.
103 D2 **Devét skal** *h.* Czechia
74 B2 **Devgarh** India
75 C2 **Devghar** India
137 D1 **Devils Lake** U.S.A.
128 A2 **Devils Paw** *mt.* U.S.A.
99 C3 **Devizes** U.K.
74 B2 **Devli** India
110 C2 **Devnya** Bulg.
128 C2 **Devon** Can.
126 E1 **Devon Island** Can.
51 D4 **Devonport** Austr.
74 B2 **Dewas** India
137 F3 **Dexter** U.S.A.
70 A2 **Deyang** China
81 C2 **Dezfūl** Iran
70 B2 **Dezhou** China
79 C2 **Dhahran** Saudi Arabia
75 D2 **Dhaka** Bangl.
78 B3 **Dhamār** Yemen
75 C2 **Dhamtari** India
75 C2 **Dhanbad** India
75 C2 **Dhankuta** Nepal
62 A1 **Dharmanagar** India
75 C2 **Dharmjaygarh** India
73 B3 **Dharwad** India
74 B2 **Dhasa** India
78 B3 **Dhubāb** Yemen
74 B2 **Dhule** India
144 A1 **Diablo, Picacho del** *mt.* Mex.
51 C2 **Diamantina** *watercourse* Austr.
155 D1 **Diamantina** Brazil
151 D3 **Diamantina, Chapada** *plat.* Brazil
151 C3 **Diamantino** Brazil
71 B3 **Dianbai** China
151 D3 **Dianópolis** Brazil
114 B4 **Dianra** Côte d'Ivoire
114 C3 **Diapaga** Burkina Faso
79 C2 **Dibā al Ḥiṣn** U.A.E.
118 C3 **Dibaya** Dem. Rep. Congo
62 A1 **Dibrugarh** India
136 C1 **Dickinson** U.S.A.
142 C1 **Dickson** U.S.A.
Dicle *r.* Turkey *see* **Tigris**
105 D3 **Die** France
129 D2 **Diefenbaker, Lake** Can.
114 B3 **Diéma** Mali
62 B2 **Diên Châu** Vietnam
101 D1 **Diepholz** Ger.
104 C2 **Dieppe** France
115 D3 **Diffa** Niger
131 D2 **Digby** Can.
105 D3 **Digne-les-Bains** France
105 C2 **Digoin** France
64 B2 **Digos** Phil.
Dihang *r.* China/India *see* **Brahmaputra**
Dihang *r.* China/India *see* **Yarlung Zangbo**
105 D2 **Dijon** France
117 C3 **Dikhil** Djibouti
111 C3 **Dikili** Turkey
100 A2 **Diksmuide** Belgium
115 D3 **Dikwa** Nigeria
117 B4 **Dīla** Eth.
74 A1 **Dilārām** Afgh.
59 C3 **Dili** East Timor
101 D2 **Dillenburg** Ger.
134 D1 **Dillon** U.S.A.
118 C4 **Dilolo** Dem. Rep. Congo
72 D2 **Dimapur** India
Dimashq Syria *see* **Damascus**
52 B3 **Dimboola** Austr.
110 C2 **Dimitrovgrad** Bulg.
87 D3 **Dimitrovgrad** Russia
64 B1 **Dinagat** *i.* Phil.
104 B2 **Dinan** France
100 B2 **Dinant** Belgium
111 D3 **Dinar** Turkey
81 D2 **Dīnār, Kūh-e** *mt.* Iran
73 B3 **Dindigul** India
123 D1 **Dindiza** Moz.
101 E2 **Dingelstädt** Ger.
75 C2 **Dinggyê** China
Dingle Ireland *see* **Daingean Uí Chúis**
97 A2 **Dingle Bay** Ireland
96 B2 **Dingwall** U.K.
70 A2 **Dingxi** China
154 B3 **Dionísio Cerqueira** Brazil
114 A3 **Diourbel** Senegal
74 B1 **Dir** Pak.
51 D1 **Direction, Cape** Austr.
117 C4 **Dirē Dawa** Eth.
120 B2 **Dirico** Angola
115 D1 **Dirj** Libya
50 A2 **Dirk Hartog Island** Austr.
53 C1 **Dirranbandi** Austr.
78 B3 **Ḍirs** Saudi Arabia
50 B2 **Disappointment, Lake** *imp. l.* Austr.
52 B3 **Discovery Bay** Austr.
143 E1 **Dismal Swamp** U.S.A.
99 D2 **Diss** U.K.
108 B3 **Dittaino** *r.* *Sicily* Italy
74 B2 **Diu** India
155 D2 **Divinópolis** Brazil
87 D4 **Divnoye** Russia
114 B4 **Divo** Côte d'Ivoire
80 B2 **Divriği** Turkey
140 B2 **Dixon** U.S.A.
128 A2 **Dixon Entrance** *sea chan.* Can./U.S.A.
80 C2 **Diyarbakır** Turkey
74 A2 **Diz** Pak.
115 D2 **Djado** Niger

115	D2	**Djado, Plateau du** Niger
118	B3	**Djambala** Congo
115	C2	**Djanet** Alg.
115	C1	**Djelfa** Alg.
119	C2	**Djéma** C.A.R.
114	B3	**Djenné** Mali
118	B2	**Djibloho** Equat. Guinea
114	B3	**Djibo** Burkina Faso
117	C3	**Djibouti** country Africa
117	C3	**Djibouti** Djibouti
114	C4	**Djougou** Benin
92	⊔C3	**Djúpivogur** Iceland
91	E1	**Dmitriyevka** Russia
89	E3	**Dmitriyev-L'govskiy** Russia
89	E2	**Dmitrov** Russia
91	C2	**Dnieper** r. Ukr.
90	B2	**Dniester** r. Ukr.
91	D2	**Dnipro** Ukr.
		Dnipro r. Ukr. see **Dnieper**
		Dniprodzerzhyns'k Ukr. see
		Kam"yans'ke
		Dnipropetrovs'k Ukr. see
		Dnipro
91	C2	**Dniprorudne** Ukr.
		Dnister r. Ukr. see **Dniester**
88	C2	**Dno** Russia
115	D4	**Doba** Chad
88	B2	**Dobele** Latvia
101	F2	**Döbeln** Ger.
59	C3	**Doberai, Jazirah** pen. Indon.
59	C3	**Dobo** Indon.
109	C2	**Doboj** Bos. & Herz.
110	C2	**Dobrich** Bulg.
89	F3	**Dobrinka** Russia
90	B2	**Dobroslav** Ukr.
89	E3	**Dobroye** Russia
89	D3	**Dobrush** Belarus
155	E1	**Doce** r. Brazil
145	B2	**Doctor Arroyo** Mex.
144	B2	**Doctor Belisario Domínguez** Mex.
111	C3	**Dodecanese** is Greece
		Dodekanisos is Greece see
		Dodecanese
136	C3	**Dodge City** U.S.A.
119	D3	**Dodoma** Tanz.
100	C2	**Doetinchem** Neth.
59	C3	**Dofa** Indon.
75	C1	**Dogai Coring** salt l. China
128	B2	**Dog Creek** Can.
67	B3	**Dōgo** i. Japan
115	C3	**Dogondoutchi** Niger
81	C2	**Doğubeyazıt** Turkey
79	C2	**Doha** Qatar
62	A2	**Doi Saket** Thai.
100	B1	**Dokkum** Neth.
88	C3	**Dokshytsy** Belarus
91	D2	**Dokuchayevs'k** Ukr.
59	D3	**Dolak** i. Indon.
131	C2	**Dolbeau-Mistassini** Can.
104	B2	**Dol-de-Bretagne** France
105	D2	**Dole** France
99	B2	**Dolgellau** U.K.
89	E3	**Dolgorukovo** Russia
89	E3	**Dolgoye** Russia
		Dolisie Congo see **Loubomo**
108	B1	**Dolomites** mts Italy
117	C4	**Dolo Odo** Eth.
126	D2	**Dolphin and Union Strait** Can.
90	A2	**Dolyna** Ukr.
102	C2	**Domažlice** Czechia
93	E3	**Dombås** Norway
103	D2	**Dombóvár** Hungary
128	B2	**Dome Creek** Can.
147	D3	**Dominica** country West Indies
147	C3	**Dominican Republic** country West Indies
89	E2	**Domodedovo** Russia
111	B3	**Domokos** Greece
61	C2	**Dompu** Indon.
89	E3	**Don** r. Russia
96	C2	**Don** r. U.K.
97	D1	**Donaghadee** U.K.
52	B3	**Donald** Austr.
		Donau r. Austria/Ger. see **Danube**
102	C2	**Donauwörth** Ger.
106	B2	**Don Benito** Spain
98	C2	**Doncaster** U.K.
120	A1	**Dondo** Angola
121	C2	**Dondo** Moz.
73	C4	**Dondra Head** Sri Lanka
97	B1	**Donegal** Ireland
97	B1	**Donegal Bay** Ireland
91	D2	**Donets'k** Ukr.
91	D2	**Donets'kyy Kryazh** hills Russia/Ukr.
50	A2	**Dongara** Austr.
62	B1	**Dongchuan** China
65	B2	**Dongducheon** S. Korea
71	A4	**Dongfang** China
66	B1	**Dongfanghong** China
58	B3	**Donggala** Indon.
65	A2	**Donggang** China
71	B3	**Dongguan** China
62	B2	**Đông Ha** Vietnam
65	B2	**Donghae** S. Korea
		Dong Hai sea N. Pacific Ocean see **East China Sea**
62	B2	**Đông Hội** Vietnam
118	B2	**Dongou** Congo
71	B3	**Dongshan** China
70	B2	**Dongsheng** China
70	C2	**Dongtai** China
71	B3	**Dongting Hu** l. China
		Dong Ujimqin Qi China see **Uliastai**
70	B2	**Dongying** China
63	B2	**Don Kêv** Cambodia
54	B1	**Donnellys Crossing** N.Z.
107	C1	**Donostia/San Sebastián** Spain
99	B3	**Dorchester** U.K.
122	A1	**Dordabis** Namibia
104	B2	**Dordogne** r. France
100	B2	**Dordrecht** Neth.
123	C3	**Dordrecht** S. Africa
129	D2	**Doré Lake** Can.
101	D1	**Dorfmark** Ger.
68	C1	**Dörgön Nuur** salt l. Mongolia
114	B3	**Dori** Burkina Faso
122	A3	**Doring** r. S. Africa
96	B2	**Dornoch** U.K.
96	B2	**Dornoch Firth** est. U.K.
89	D3	**Dorogobuzh** Russia
90	B2	**Dorohoi** Romania
92	G3	**Dorotea** Sweden
50	A2	**Dorre Island** Austr.
53	D2	**Dorrigo** Austr.
100	C2	**Dortmund** Ger.
100	C2	**Dortmund-Ems-Kanal** canal Ger.
153	B5	**Dos Bahías, Cabo** c. Arg.
77	C3	**Dōshi** Afgh.
101	F1	**Dosse** r. Ger.
114	C3	**Dosso** Niger
143	C2	**Dothan** U.S.A.
101	D1	**Dötlingen** Ger.
105	C1	**Douai** France
118	A2	**Douala** Cameroon
104	B2	**Douarnenez** France
114	B3	**Douentza** Mali
98	A1	**Douglas** Isle of Man
122	B2	**Douglas** S. Africa
128	A2	**Douglas** AK U.S.A.
138	B2	**Douglas** AZ U.S.A.
143	D2	**Douglas** GA U.S.A.
136	B2	**Douglas** WY U.S.A.
71	C3	**Douliu** Taiwan
104	C1	**Doullens** France
154	B1	**Dourada, Serra** hills Brazil
154	B2	**Dourados** Brazil
154	B2	**Dourados, Serra dos** hills Brazil
106	B1	**Douro** r. Port.
99	D3	**Dover** U.K.
141	D3	**Dover** U.S.A.
95	D3	**Dover, Strait of** France/U.K.
141	F1	**Dover-Foxcroft** U.S.A.
79	C2	**Dowlatābād** Būshehr Iran
79	C2	**Dowlatābād** Kermān Iran
97	D1	**Downpatrick** U.K.
67	B3	**Dōzen** is Japan
130	C2	**Dozois, Réservoir** resr Can.
114	B2	**Drâa, Hamada du** plat. Alg.
154	B2	**Dracena** Brazil
100	C1	**Drachten** Neth.
110	B2	**Drăgănești-Olt** Romania
110	B2	**Drăgășani** Romania
88	C3	**Drahichyn** Belarus
123	C2	**Drakensberg** mts Lesotho/S. Africa
123	C2	**Drakensberg** mts S. Africa
158	B8	**Drake Passage** S. Atlantic Ocean
111	B2	**Drama** Greece
93	F4	**Drammen** Norway
109	C1	**Drava** r. Europe
128	C2	**Drayton Valley** Can.
101	D2	**Dreieich** Ger.
102	C1	**Dresden** Ger.
104	C2	**Dreux** France
100	B1	**Driemond** Neth.
109	C2	**Drina** r. Bos. & Herz./Serbia
109	C2	**Drniš** Croatia
110	B2	**Drobeta-Turnu Severin** Romania
101	D1	**Drochtersen** Ger.
97	C2	**Drogheda** Ireland
90	A2	**Drohobych** Ukr.
97	C1	**Dromore** U.K.
74	B1	**Drosh** Pak.
53	C3	**Drouin** Austr.
128	C2	**Drumheller** Can.
140	C1	**Drummond Island** U.S.A.
131	C2	**Drummondville** Can.
88	B3	**Druskininkai** Lith.
91	D2	**Druzhkivka** Ukr.
88	D2	**Druzhnaya Gorka** Russia
130	A2	**Dryden** Can.
50	B1	**Drysdale** r. Austr.
78	A2	**Dubā** Saudi Arabia
79	C2	**Dubai** U.A.E.
129	D1	**Dubawnt Lake** Can.
		Dubayy U.A.E. see **Dubai**
78	A2	**Dubbagh, Jabal ad** mt. Saudi Arabia
53	C2	**Dubbo** Austr.
97	C2	**Dublin** Ireland
143	D2	**Dublin** U.S.A.
90	B1	**Dubno** Ukr.
141	D2	**Du Bois** U.S.A.
114	A4	**Dubréka** Guinea
109	C2	**Dubrovnik** Croatia
90	B1	**Dubrovytsya** Ukr.
89	D3	**Dubrowna** Belarus
137	E2	**Dubuque** U.S.A.
129	D2	**Duck Bay** Can.
101	E2	**Duderstadt** Ger.
82	G2	**Dudinka** Russia
99	B2	**Dudley** U.K.
106	B1	**Duero** r. Spain
131	C1	**Duffreboy, Lac** l. Can.

96 C2 **Dufftown** U.K.
109 C2 **Dugi Rat** Croatia
100 C2 **Duisburg** Ger.
123 C3 **Dukathole** S. Africa
79 C2 **Dukhān** Qatar
89 D2 **Dukhovshchina** Russia
Dukou China *see* **Panzhihua**
88 C2 **Dūkštas** Lith.
68 C2 **Dulan** China
152 B4 **Dulce** *r.* Arg.
100 C2 **Dülmen** Ger.
110 C2 **Dulovo** Bulg.
137 E1 **Duluth** U.S.A.
64 B2 **Dumaguete** Phil.
60 B1 **Dumai** Indon.
64 B1 **Dumaran** *i.* Phil.
142 B2 **Dumas** *AR* U.S.A.
139 C1 **Dumas** *TX* U.S.A.
96 B3 **Dumbarton** U.K.
103 D2 **Ďumbier** *mt.* Slovakia
96 C3 **Dumfries** U.K.
55 J3 **Dumont d'Urville Sea** Antarctica
116 B1 **Dumyāţ** Egypt
Duna *r.* Hungary *see* **Danube**
Dunaj *r.* Slovakia *see* **Danube**
103 D2 **Dunakeszi** Hungary
Dunărea *r.* Romania *see* **Danube**
103 D2 **Dunaújváros** Hungary
Dunav *r.* Serbia *see* **Danube**
90 B2 **Dunayivtsi** Ukr.
96 C2 **Dunbar** U.K.
96 C1 **Dunbeath** U.K.
128 B3 **Duncan** Can.
139 D2 **Duncan** U.S.A.
96 C1 **Duncansby Head** U.K.
97 C1 **Dundalk** Ireland
97 C2 **Dundalk Bay** Ireland
123 D2 **Dundee** S. Africa
96 C2 **Dundee** U.K.
97 D1 **Dundrum Bay** U.K.
54 B3 **Dunedin** N.Z.
96 C2 **Dunfermline** U.K.
97 C1 **Dungannon** U.K.
74 B2 **Dungarpur** India
97 C2 **Dungarvan** Ireland
99 D3 **Dungeness** *hd* U.K.
97 C1 **Dungiven** U.K.
53 D2 **Dungog** Austr.
119 C2 **Dungu** Dem. Rep. Congo
60 B1 **Dungun** Malaysia
116 B2 **Dungunab** Sudan
69 E2 **Dunhua** China
68 C2 **Dunhuang** China
Dunkerque France *see* **Dunkirk**
104 C1 **Dunkirk** France
141 D2 **Dunkirk** U.S.A.
97 C2 **Dún Laoghaire** Ireland
97 D1 **Dunmurry** U.K.
96 C1 **Dunnet Head** U.K.
96 C3 **Duns** U.K.
99 C3 **Dunstable** U.K.
110 B2 **Dupnitsa** Bulg.
136 C1 **Dupree** U.S.A.
50 B1 **Durack** *r.* Austr.
144 B2 **Durango** Mex.
106 C1 **Durango** Spain
136 B3 **Durango** U.S.A.
139 D2 **Durant** U.S.A.
153 C4 **Durazno** Uru.
123 D2 **Durban** S. Africa
104 C3 **Durban-Corbières** France
122 A3 **Durbanville** S. Africa
100 B2 **Durbuy** Belgium
100 C2 **Düren** Ger.
73 C2 **Durg** India
98 C1 **Durham** U.K.
143 E1 **Durham** U.S.A.
60 B1 **Duri** Indon.
109 C2 **Durmitor** *mt.* Montenegro
96 B1 **Durness** U.K.
109 C2 **Durrës** Albania
97 A3 **Dursey Island** Ireland
111 C3 **Dursunbey** Turkey
59 D3 **D'Urville, Tanjung** *pt* Indon.
D'Urville Island N.Z. *see* **Rangitoto ke te Tonga**
71 A3 **Dushan** China
77 C3 **Dushanbe** Tajik.
100 C2 **Düsseldorf** Ger.
71 A3 **Duyun** China
91 D2 **Dvorichna** Ukr.
74 A2 **Dwarka** India
123 C1 **Dwarsberg** S. Africa
134 C1 **Dworshak Reservoir** U.S.A.
89 D3 **Dyat'kovo** Russia
96 C2 **Dyce** U.K.
127 G2 **Dyer, Cape** Can.
142 C1 **Dyersburg** U.S.A.
103 D2 **Dyje** *r.* Austria/Czechia
103 D1 **Dylewska Góra** *h.* Pol.
Dymytrov Ukr. *see* **Myrnohrad**
123 C3 **Dyoki** S. Africa
87 E3 **Dyurtyuli** Russia
69 D2 **Dzamïn Üüd** Mongolia
120 D2 **Dzaoudzi** Mayotte
Dzhambul Kazakh. *see* **Taraz**
91 C2 **Dzhankoy** Ukr.
91 D3 **Dzhubga** Russia
83 K3 **Dzhugdzhur, Khrebet** *mts* Russia
103 E1 **Działdowo** Pol.
69 D1 **Dzuunmod** Mongolia
88 C3 **Dzyarzhynsk** Belarus
88 C3 **Dzyatlavichy** Belarus

E

131 E1 **Eagle** *r.* Can.
134 C1 **Eagle Cap** *mt.* U.S.A.
130 A2 **Eagle Lake** Can.
134 B2 **Eagle Lake** U.S.A.
139 C3 **Eagle Pass** U.S.A.
126 B2 **Eagle Plain** Can.
130 A1 **Ear Falls** Can.
99 D3 **Eastbourne** U.K.
156 C3 **East China Sea** N. Pacific Ocean
54 B1 **East Coast Bays** N.Z.
129 D3 **Eastend** Can.
123 C3 **Eastern Cape** *prov.* S. Africa
116 B2 **Eastern Desert** Egypt
73 B3 **Eastern Ghats** *mts* India
129 E2 **Easterville** Can.
153 C6 **East Falkland** *i.* Falkland Is
100 C1 **East Frisian Islands** Ger.
96 B3 **East Kilbride** U.K.
99 C3 **Eastleigh** U.K.
140 C2 **East Liverpool** U.S.A.
123 C3 **East London** S. Africa
130 C1 **Eastmain** Can.
130 C1 **Eastmain** *r.* Can.
143 D2 **Eastman** U.S.A.
140 A3 **East St Louis** U.S.A.
East Sea N. Pacific Ocean *see* **Japan, Sea of**
83 K2 **East Siberian Sea** Russia
59 C3 **East Timor** *country* Asia
140 A2 **Eau Claire** U.S.A.
130 C1 **Eau Claire, Lac à l'** *l.* Can.
59 D2 **Eauripik** *atoll* Micronesia
145 C2 **Ebano** Mex.
99 B3 **Ebbw Vale** U.K.
102 C1 **Eberswalde** Ger.
109 C2 **Eboli** Italy
118 B2 **Ebolowa** Cameroon
107 D1 **Ebro** *r.* Spain
144 A2 **Echeverría, Pico** *mt.* Mex.
67 C3 **Echizen** Japan
129 E2 **Echoing** *r.* Can.
100 C3 **Echternach** Lux.
52 B3 **Echuca** Austr.
106 B2 **Écija** Spain
102 B1 **Eckernförde** Ger.
127 F2 **Eclipse Sound** *sea chan.* Can.
150 A2 **Ecuador** *country* S. America
116 C3 **Ed** Eritrea
117 A3 **Ed Daein** Sudan
117 B3 **Ed Damazin** Sudan
116 B3 **Ed Damer** Sudan
116 B3 **Ed Debba** Sudan
116 B3 **Ed Dueim** Sudan
51 D4 **Eddystone Point** Austr.
100 B1 **Ede** Neth.
118 B2 **Edéa** Cameroon
154 C1 **Edéia** Brazil
53 C3 **Eden** Austr.
98 B1 **Eden** *r.* U.K.
123 C2 **Edenburg** S. Africa
97 C2 **Edenderry** Ireland
52 B3 **Edenhope** Austr.
111 B2 **Edessa** Greece
82 C1 **Edgeøya** *i.* Svalbard
139 D3 **Edinburg** U.S.A.
96 C3 **Edinburgh** U.K.
110 C2 **Edirne** Turkey
128 C2 **Edmonton** Can.
131 D2 **Edmundston** Can.
111 C3 **Edremit** Turkey
111 C3 **Edremit Körfezi** *b.* Turkey
128 C2 **Edson** Can.
119 C3 **Edward, Lake** Dem. Rep. Congo/Uganda
139 C2 **Edwards Plateau** U.S.A.
100 C1 **Eenrum** Neth.
48 F4 **Éfaté** *i.* Vanuatu
140 B3 **Effingham** U.S.A.
135 C3 **Egan Range** *mts* U.S.A.
103 E2 **Eger** Hungary
93 E4 **Egersund** Norway
92 □C2 **Egilsstaðir** Iceland
80 B2 **Eğirdir** Turkey
80 B2 **Eğirdir Gölü** *l.* Turkey
104 C2 **Égletons** France
Egmont, Mount *vol.* N.Z. *see* **Taranaki, Mount**
83 M2 **Egvekinot** Russia
116 A2 **Egypt** *country* Africa
68 C2 **Ehen Hudag** China
100 C1 **Eibergen** Neth.
100 C2 **Eifel** *hills* Ger.
96 A2 **Eigg** *i.* U.K.
73 B4 **Eight Degree Channel** India/Maldives
50 B1 **Eighty Mile Beach** Austr.
80 B3 **Eilat** Israel
101 F2 **Eilenburg** Ger.
101 D2 **Einbeck** Ger.
100 B2 **Eindhoven** Neth.
150 B2 **Eirunepé** Brazil
120 B2 **Eiseb** *watercourse* Namibia
101 E2 **Eisenach** Ger.
102 C1 **Eisenhüttenstadt** Ger.
103 D2 **Eisenstadt** Austria
101 E2 **Eisleben, Lutherstadt** Ger.
Eivissa Spain *see* **Ibiza**
Eivissa *i.* Spain *see* **Ibiza**
107 C1 **Ejea de los Caballeros** Spain
121 □D3 **Ejeda** Madag.
Ejin Qi China *see* **Dalain Hob**
93 H4 **Ekenäs** Fin.
92 J2 **Ekostrovskaya Imandra, Ozero** *l.* Russia

93 F4 **Eksjö** Sweden
122 A2 **Eksteenfontein** S. Africa
130 B1 **Ekwan** *r.* Can.
62 A2 **Ela** Myanmar
123 C2 **Elandsdoorn** S. Africa
111 B3 **Elassona** Greece
80 B2 **Elazığ** Turkey
108 B2 **Elba, Isola d'** *i.* Italy
150 A1 **El Banco** Col.
138 B2 **El Barreal** *salt l.* Mex.
109 D2 **Elbasan** Albania
150 B1 **El Baúl** Venez.
114 C1 **El Bayadh** Alg.
101 D1 **Elbe** *r.* Ger.
136 B3 **Elbert, Mount** U.S.A.
143 D2 **Elberton** U.S.A.
104 C2 **Elbeuf** France
80 B2 **Elbistan** Turkey
103 D1 **Elbląg** Pol.
87 D4 **El'brus** *mt.* Russia
81 C2 **Elburz Mountains** Iran
153 A6 **El Calafate** Arg.
150 B1 **El Callao** Venez.
139 D3 **El Campo** U.S.A.
135 C4 **El Centro** U.S.A.
152 B2 **El Cerro** Bol.
107 C2 **Elche/Elx** Spain
107 C2 **Elda** Spain
137 E3 **Eldon** U.S.A.
144 B2 **El Dorado** Mex.
142 B2 **El Dorado** *AR* U.S.A.
137 D3 **El Dorado** *KS* U.S.A.
114 B2 **El Eglab** *plat.* Alg.
106 C2 **El Ejido** Spain
89 E2 **Elektrostal'** Russia
150 A2 **El Encanto** Col.
146 C2 **Eleuthera** *i.* Bahamas
117 A3 **El Fasher** Sudan
144 B2 **El Fuerte** Mex.
117 A3 **El Geneina** Sudan
116 B3 **El Geteina** Sudan
96 C2 **Elgin** U.K.
140 B2 **Elgin** U.S.A.
115 C1 **El Goléa** Alg.
144 A1 **El Golfo de Santa Clara** Mex.
119 D2 **Elgon, Mount** Kenya/Uganda
114 A2 **El Ḥammâmi** *reg.* Maur.
114 A2 **El Hierro** *i.* Canary Islands
145 C2 **El Higo** Mex.
114 C2 **El Homr** Alg.
110 C2 **Elhovo** Bulg.
87 D4 **Elista** Russia
141 E2 **Elizabeth** U.S.A.
143 E1 **Elizabeth City** U.S.A.
140 B3 **Elizabethtown** U.S.A.
114 B1 **El Jadida** Morocco
103 E1 **Ełk** Pol.
139 D1 **Elk City** U.S.A.
128 C2 **Elkford** Can.
140 B2 **Elkhart** U.S.A.
El Khartum Sudan *see* **Khartoum**
140 D3 **Elkins** U.S.A.
128 C3 **Elko** Can.
134 C2 **Elko** U.S.A.
129 C2 **Elk Point** Can.
126 E1 **Ellef Ringnes Island** Can.
137 D1 **Ellendale** U.S.A.
134 B1 **Ellensburg** U.S.A.
54 B2 **Ellesmere, Lake** N.Z.
127 F1 **Ellesmere Island** Can.
98 B2 **Ellesmere Port** U.K.
126 E2 **Ellice** *r.* Can.
Ellice Islands *country* S. Pacific Ocean *see* **Tuvalu**
123 C3 **Elliotdale** S. Africa
96 C2 **Ellon** U.K.
141 F2 **Ellsworth** U.S.A.
55 O2 **Ellsworth Mountains** Antarctica
111 C3 **Elmalı** Turkey
115 C1 **El Meghaïer** Alg.
141 D2 **Elmira** U.S.A.
107 C2 **El Moral** Spain
101 D1 **Elmshorn** Ger.
117 A3 **El Muglad** Sudan
64 A1 **El Nido** Phil.
117 B3 **El Obeid** Sudan
144 B2 **El Oro** Mex.
115 C1 **El Oued** Alg.
138 A2 **Eloy** U.S.A.
138 B2 **El Paso** U.S.A.
144 B1 **El Porvenir** Mex.
107 D1 **El Prat de Llobregat** Spain
139 D1 **El Reno** U.S.A.
145 B2 **El Salado** Mex.
144 B2 **El Salto** Mex.
146 B3 **El Salvador** *country* Central America
145 B2 **El Salvador** Mex.
138 B3 **El Sauz** Mex.
144 A1 **El Socorro** Mex.
145 C2 **El Temascal** Mex.
150 B1 **El Tigre** Venez.
147 D4 **El Tocuyo** Venez.
88 C2 **Elva** Estonia
106 B2 **Elvas** Port.
93 F3 **Elverum** Norway
119 E2 **El Wak** Kenya
Elx Spain *see* **Elche/Elx**
99 D2 **Ely** U.K.
137 E1 **Ely** *MN* U.S.A.
135 D3 **Ely** *NV* U.S.A.
123 C2 **eMalahleni** S. Africa
93 G4 **Emån** *r.* Sweden
123 D3 **eManzimtoti** S. Africa
76 B2 **Emba** Kazakh.
123 C2 **Embalenhle** S. Africa
154 C1 **Emborcação, Represa de** *resr* Brazil
119 D3 **Embu** Kenya
100 C1 **Emden** Ger.
51 D2 **Emerald** Austr.
129 E3 **Emerson** Can.
111 C3 **Emet** Turkey
123 D2 **eMgwenya** S. Africa
115 D3 **Emi Koussi** *mt.* Chad
110 C2 **Emine, Nos** *pt* Bulg.
80 B2 **Emirdağ** Turkey
123 D2 **eMjindini** S. Africa
88 B2 **Emmaste** Estonia
100 B1 **Emmeloord** Neth.
100 C2 **Emmelshausen** Ger.
100 C1 **Emmen** Neth.
123 D2 **eMondlo** S. Africa
139 C3 **Emory Peak** U.S.A.
144 A2 **Empalme** Mex.
123 D2 **Empangeni** S. Africa
108 B2 **Empoli** Italy
137 D3 **Emporia** *KS* U.S.A.
141 D3 **Emporia** *VA* U.S.A.
Empty Quarter *des.* Saudi Arabia *see* **Rub' al Khālī**
100 C1 **Ems** *r.* Ger.
100 C1 **Emsdetten** Ger.
123 C2 **eMzinoni** S. Africa
59 D3 **Enarotali** Indon.
144 B2 **Encarnación** Mex.
152 C3 **Encarnación** Para.
155 D1 **Encruzilhada** Brazil
58 C3 **Ende** Indon.
126 A2 **Endicott Mountains** U.S.A.
91 C2 **Enerhodar** Ukr.
87 D3 **Engel's** Russia
60 B2 **Enggano** *i.* Indon.
98 C2 **England** *admin. div.* U.K.
130 A1 **English** *r.* Can.
95 C4 **English Channel** France/U.K.
139 D1 **Enid** U.S.A.
100 B1 **Enkhuizen** Neth.
93 G4 **Enköping** Sweden
108 B3 **Enna** *Sicily* Italy
129 D1 **Ennadai Lake** Can.
117 A3 **En Nahud** Sudan
115 E3 **Ennedi, Massif** *mts* Chad
53 C1 **Enngonia** Austr.
97 B2 **Ennis** Ireland
139 D2 **Ennis** U.S.A.
97 C2 **Enniscorthy** Ireland
97 C1 **Enniskillen** U.K.
97 B2 **Ennistymon** Ireland
102 C2 **Enns** *r.* Austria
92 H2 **Enontekiö** Fin.
53 C3 **Ensay** Austr.
100 C1 **Enschede** Neth.
144 A1 **Ensenada** Mex.
70 A2 **Enshi** China
128 C1 **Enterprise** Can.
142 C2 **Enterprise** *AL* U.S.A.
134 C1 **Enterprise** *OR* U.S.A.
152 B3 **Entre Ríos** Bol.
106 B2 **Entroncamento** Port.
115 C4 **Enugu** Nigeria
150 A2 **Envira** Brazil
135 D3 **Ephraim** U.S.A.
134 C1 **Ephrata** U.S.A.
105 D2 **Épinal** France
99 C3 **Epsom** U.K.
118 A2 **Equatorial Guinea** *country* Africa
101 F3 **Erbendorf** Ger.
100 C3 **Erbeskopf** *h.* Ger.
81 C2 **Erciş** Turkey
65 B1 **Erdao Jiang** *r.* China
111 C2 **Erdek** Turkey
80 B2 **Erdemli** Turkey
152 C3 **Erechim** Brazil
69 D1 **Ereentsav** Mongolia
80 B2 **Ereğli** *Konya* Turkey
80 B1 **Ereğli** *Zonguldak* Turkey
69 D2 **Erenhot** China
Erevan Armenia *see* **Yerevan**
101 E2 **Erfurt** Ger.
80 B2 **Ergani** Turkey
114 B2 **'Erg Chech** *des.* Alg./Mali
111 C2 **Ergene** *r.* Turkey
140 C2 **Erie** U.S.A.
140 C2 **Erie, Lake** Can./U.S.A.
66 D2 **Erimo-misaki** *c.* Japan
116 B3 **Eritrea** *country* Africa
101 E3 **Erlangen** Ger.
50 C2 **Erldunda** Austr.
123 C2 **Ermelo** S. Africa
80 B2 **Ermenek** Turkey
111 B3 **Ermoupoli** Greece
73 B4 **Ernakulam** India
73 B3 **Erode** India
100 B2 **Erp** Neth.
114 B1 **Errachidia** Morocco
117 B3 **Er Rahad** Sudan
97 B1 **Errigal** *h.* Ireland
97 A1 **Erris Head** Ireland
109 D2 **Ersekë** Albania
91 E1 **Ertil'** Russia
101 D2 **Erwitte** Ger.
101 F2 **Erzgebirge** *mts* Czechia/Ger.
80 B2 **Erzincan** Turkey
81 C2 **Erzurum** Turkey
93 E4 **Esbjerg** Denmark
135 D3 **Escalante** U.S.A.
144 B2 **Escalón** Mex.
140 B1 **Escanaba** U.S.A.
145 C3 **Escárcega** Mex.
107 C1 **Escatrón** Spain

100 A2 **Escaut** *r.* Belgium/France
101 E1 **Eschede** Ger.
100 B3 **Esch-sur-Alzette** Lux.
101 E2 **Eschwege** Ger.
100 C2 **Eschweiler** Ger.
135 C4 **Escondido** U.S.A.
144 B2 **Escuinapa** Mex.
111 C3 **Eşen** Turkey
81 D2 **Eşfahān** Iran
123 D2 **eSikhaleni** S. Africa
98 B1 **Esk** *r.* U.K.
131 D1 **Esker** Can.
92 □C2 **Eskifjörður** Iceland
93 G4 **Eskilstuna** Sweden
Eskimo Point Can. *see* **Arviat**
80 B2 **Eskişehir** Turkey
81 C2 **Eslāmābād-e Gharb** Iran
111 C3 **Esler Dağı** *mt.* Turkey
111 C3 **Eşme** Turkey
150 A1 **Esmeraldas** Ecuador
79 D2 **Espakeh** Iran
104 C3 **Espalion** France
130 B2 **Espanola** Can.
138 B1 **Espanola** U.S.A.
50 B3 **Esperance** Austr.
144 B2 **Esperanza** Mex.
106 B2 **Espichel, Cabo** *c.* Port.
155 D1 **Espinhaço, Serra do** *mts* Brazil
151 D3 **Espinosa** Brazil
48 F4 **Espiritu Santo** *i.* Vanuatu
144 A2 **Espíritu Santo, Isla** *i.* Mex.
93 H3 **Espoo** Fin.
153 A5 **Esquel** Arg.
114 B1 **Essaouira** Morocco
100 C2 **Essen** Ger.
150 C1 **Essequibo** *r.* Guyana
114 A2 **Es-Smara** Western Sahara
83 L3 **Esso** Russia
79 C2 **Estahbān** Iran
151 E3 **Estância** Brazil
123 C2 **Estcourt** S. Africa
107 C1 **Estella/Lizarra** Spain
106 B2 **Estepona** Spain
106 C1 **Esteras de Medinaceli** Spain
129 D2 **Esterhazy** Can.
152 B3 **Esteros** Para.
136 B2 **Estes Park** U.S.A.
129 D3 **Estevan** Can.
137 E2 **Estherville** U.S.A.
129 D2 **Eston** Can.
88 C2 **Estonia** *country* Europe
106 B1 **Estrela, Serra da** *mts* Port.
106 B2 **Estremoz** Port.
52 A1 **Etadunna** Austr.
104 C2 **Étampes** France
104 C1 **Étaples** France
75 B2 **Etawah** India
123 D2 **Ethandakukhanya** S. Africa
117 B4 **Ethiopia** *country* Africa
109 C3 **Etna, Mount** *vol. Sicily* Italy
128 A2 **Etolin Island** U.S.A.
120 A2 **Etosha Pan** *salt pan* Namibia
100 C3 **Ettelbruck** Lux.
100 B2 **Etten-Leur** Neth.
107 C1 **Etxarri-Aranatz** Spain
99 D3 **Eu** France
53 C2 **Euabalong** Austr.
Euboea *i.* Greece *see* **Evvoia**
50 B3 **Eucla** Austr.
143 C2 **Eufaula** U.S.A.
139 D1 **Eufaula Lake** *resr* U.S.A.
134 B2 **Eugene** U.S.A.
144 A2 **Eugenia, Punta** *pt* Mex.
53 C1 **Eulo** Austr.
53 C2 **Eumungerie** Austr.
139 C2 **Eunice** U.S.A.
80 C2 **Euphrates** *r.* Asia
134 B2 **Eureka** *CA* U.S.A.
134 C1 **Eureka** *MT* U.S.A.
135 C3 **Eureka** *NV* U.S.A.
52 B2 **Euriowie** Austr.
53 C3 **Euroa** Austr.
106 B2 **Europa Point** Gibraltar
128 B2 **Eutsuk Lake** Can.
130 C1 **Evans, Lac** *l.* Can.
53 D1 **Evans Head** Austr.
127 F2 **Evans Strait** Can.
136 A2 **Evanston** U.S.A.
140 B3 **Evansville** U.S.A.
123 C2 **Evaton** S. Africa
79 C2 **Evaz** Iran
83 L2 **Evensk** Russia
50 C2 **Everard Range** *hills* Austr.
75 C2 **Everest, Mount** China/Nepal
134 B1 **Everett** U.S.A.
100 A2 **Evergem** Belgium
143 D3 **Everglades** *swamp* U.S.A.
118 B2 **Evinayong** Equat. Guinea
93 E4 **Evje** Norway
106 B2 **Évora** Port.
104 C2 **Évreux** France
111 C2 **Evros** *r.* Greece/Turkey
111 B3 **Evrotas** *r.* Greece
80 B2 **Evrychou** Cyprus
111 B3 **Evvoia** *i.* Greece
119 E2 **Ewaso Ngiro** *r.* Kenya
152 B2 **Exaltación** Bol.
99 B3 **Exe** *r.* U.K.
99 B3 **Exeter** U.K.
99 B3 **Exmoor** *hills* U.K.
99 B3 **Exmouth** U.K.
50 A2 **Exmouth Gulf** Austr.
146 C2 **Exuma Cays** *is* Bahamas
117 C4 **Eyl** Somalia
51 C3 **Eyre Peninsula** Austr.
94 B1 **Eysturoy** *i.* Faroe Is
123 D2 **Ezakheni** S. Africa
123 C2 **Ezenzeleni** S. Africa
70 B2 **Ezhou** China
86 E2 **Ezhva** Russia
111 C3 **Ezine** Turkey

F

138 B2 **Fabens** U.S.A.
108 B2 **Fabriano** Italy
115 D3 **Fachi** Niger
114 C3 **Fada-N'Gourma** Burkina Faso
108 B2 **Faenza** Italy
59 C3 **Fafanlap** Indon.
110 B1 **Făgăraş** Romania
49 G3 **Fagatogo** American Samoa
93 E3 **Fagernes** Norway
93 G4 **Fagersta** Sweden
153 B6 **Fagnano, Lago** *l.* Arg./Chile
114 B3 **Faguibine, Lac** *l.* Mali
92 □B3 **Fagurhólsmýri** Iceland
126 B2 **Fairbanks** U.S.A.
137 D2 **Fairbury** U.S.A.
135 B3 **Fairfield** U.S.A.
96 □ **Fair Isle** *i.* U.K.
137 E2 **Fairmont** *MN* U.S.A.
140 C3 **Fairmont** *WV* U.S.A.
128 C2 **Fairview** Can.
59 D2 **Fais** *i.* Micronesia
74 B1 **Faisalabad** Pak.
136 C1 **Faith** U.S.A.
77 D3 **Faīzābād** Afgh.
75 C2 **Faizabad** India
59 C3 **Fakfak** Indon.
65 A1 **Faku** China
114 A4 **Falaba** Sierra Leone
139 D3 **Falcon Lake** Mex./U.S.A.
139 D3 **Falfurrias** U.S.A.
128 C2 **Falher** Can.
93 F4 **Falkenberg** Sweden
101 F2 **Falkenberg/Elster** Ger.
101 F1 **Falkensee** Ger.
96 C3 **Falkirk** U.K.
153 C6 **Falkland Islands** *terr.* S. Atlantic Ocean
93 F4 **Falköping** Sweden
135 C3 **Fallon** U.S.A.
141 E2 **Fall River** U.S.A.
137 D2 **Falls City** U.S.A.
99 A3 **Falmouth** U.K.
122 A3 **False Bay** S. Africa
93 F4 **Falster** *i.* Denmark
110 C1 **Fălticeni** Romania
93 G3 **Falun** Sweden
71 A3 **Fangcheng** China
71 C3 **Fangshan** Taiwan
69 E1 **Fangzheng** China
108 B2 **Fano** Italy
119 C2 **Faradje** Dem. Rep. Congo
121 □D3 **Farafangana** Madag.
116 A2 **Farāfirah, Wāḥāt al** *oasis* Egypt
76 C3 **Farāh** Afgh.
114 A3 **Faranah** Guinea
78 B3 **Farasān, Jazā'ir** *is* Saudi Arabia
127 J3 **Farewell, Cape** Greenland
54 B2 **Farewell, Cape** N.Z.
137 D1 **Fargo** U.S.A.
77 D2 **Farg'ona** Uzbek.
137 E2 **Faribault** U.S.A.
141 E2 **Farmington** *ME* U.S.A.
138 B1 **Farmington** *NM* U.S.A.
141 D3 **Farmville** U.S.A.
99 C3 **Farnborough** U.K.
128 C2 **Farnham, Mount** Can.
128 A1 **Faro** Can.
106 B2 **Faro** Port.
88 A2 **Fårö** *i.* Sweden
94 B1 **Faroe Islands** *terr.* N. Atlantic Ocean
79 C2 **Farrāshband** Iran
139 C2 **Farwell** U.S.A.
79 C2 **Fāryāb** Iran
79 C2 **Fasā** Iran
109 C2 **Fasano** Italy
90 B1 **Fastiv** Ukr.
75 B2 **Fatehgarh** India
75 C2 **Fatehpur** India
92 G2 **Fauske** Norway
92 □A3 **Faxaflói** *b.* Iceland
92 G3 **Faxälven** *r.* Sweden
115 D3 **Faya** Chad
142 B1 **Fayetteville** *AR* U.S.A.
143 E1 **Fayetteville** *NC* U.S.A.
142 C1 **Fayetteville** *TN* U.S.A.
74 B1 **Fazilka** India
114 A2 **Fdérik** Maur.
143 E2 **Fear, Cape** U.S.A.
54 C2 **Featherston** N.Z.
104 C2 **Fécamp** France
102 C1 **Fehmarn** *i.* Ger.
101 F1 **Fehrbellin** Ger.
155 D2 **Feia, Lagoa** *lag.* Brazil
150 A2 **Feijó** Brazil
54 C2 **Feilding** N.Z.
151 E3 **Feira de Santana** Brazil
107 D2 **Felanitx** Spain
145 D3 **Felipe C. Puerto** Mex.
155 D1 **Felixlândia** Brazil
99 D3 **Felixstowe** U.K.
101 D2 **Felsberg** Ger.
108 B1 **Feltre** Italy
93 F3 **Femunden** *l.* Norway
71 B3 **Fengcheng** *Jiangxi* China
65 A1 **Fengcheng** *Liaoning* China
62 A1 **Fengqing** China
70 B2 **Fengxian** China
Fengxiang China *see* **Lincang**

71 C3 **Fengyuan** Taiwan
70 B1 **Fengzhen** China
105 D3 **Feno, Capo di** *c.* *Corsica* France
121 □D2 **Fenoarivo Atsinanana** Madag.
91 D2 **Feodosiya** Ukr.
108 A3 **Fer, Cap de** *c.* Alg.
137 D1 **Fergus Falls** U.S.A.
109 D2 **Ferizaj** Kosovo
114 B4 **Ferkessédougou** Côte d'Ivoire
108 B2 **Fermo** Italy
131 D1 **Fermont** Can.
106 B1 **Fermoselle** Spain
97 B2 **Fermoy** Ireland
143 D2 **Fernandina Beach** U.S.A.
154 B2 **Fernandópolis** Brazil
128 C3 **Fernie** Can.
108 B2 **Ferrara** Italy
154 B2 **Ferreiros** Brazil
108 A2 **Ferro, Capo** *c.* *Sardinia* Italy
106 B1 **Ferrol** Spain
100 B1 **Ferwerd** Neth.
114 B1 **Fès** Morocco
118 B3 **Feshi** Dem. Rep. Congo
137 E3 **Festus** U.S.A.
111 C3 **Fethiye** Turkey
96 □ **Fetlar** *i.* U.K.
130 C1 **Feuilles, Rivière aux** *r.* Can.
Fez Morocco *see* **Fès**
121 □D3 **Fianarantsoa** Madag.
117 B4 **Fichē** Eth.
109 C2 **Fier** Albania
96 C2 **Fife Ness** *pt* U.K.
104 C3 **Figeac** France
106 B1 **Figueira da Foz** Port.
107 D1 **Figueres** Spain
114 B1 **Figuig** Morocco
48 F3 **Fiji** *country* S. Pacific Ocean
152 B3 **Filadelfia** Para.
55 Q2 **Filchner Ice Shelf** Antarctica
98 C1 **Filey** U.K.
111 B3 **Filippiada** Greece
93 F4 **Filipstad** Sweden
96 C2 **Findhorn** *r.* U.K.
140 C2 **Findlay** U.S.A.
51 D4 **Fingal** Austr.
141 D2 **Finger Lakes** U.S.A.
106 B1 **Finisterre, Cape** Spain
92 I3 **Finland** *country* Europe
93 H4 **Finland, Gulf of** Europe
128 B2 **Finlay** *r.* Can.
53 C3 **Finley** Austr.
101 E2 **Finne** *ridge* Ger.
92 H2 **Finnmarksvidda** *reg.* Norway
92 G2 **Finnsnes** Norway
93 G4 **Finspång** Sweden
96 A2 **Fionnphort** U.K.
Fırat *r.* Turkey *see* **Euphrates**
Firenze Italy *see* **Florence**
105 C2 **Firminy** France
75 B2 **Firozabad** India
74 B1 **Firozpur** India
79 C2 **Fīrūzābād** Iran
122 A2 **Fish** *watercourse* Namibia
122 B3 **Fish** *r.* S. Africa
99 A3 **Fishguard** U.K.
105 C2 **Fismes** France
Fisterra, Cabo *c.* Spain *see* **Finisterre, Cape**
141 E2 **Fitchburg** U.S.A.
129 C2 **Fitzgerald** Can.
50 B1 **Fitzroy Crossing** Austr.
108 B2 **Fivizzano** Italy
119 C3 **Fizi** Dem. Rep. Congo
92 G3 **Fjällsjöälven** *r.* Sweden
123 C3 **Flagstaff** S. Africa
138 A1 **Flagstaff** U.S.A.
130 C1 **Flaherty Island** Can.
98 C1 **Flamborough Head** U.K.
101 F1 **Fläming** *hills* Ger.
136 B2 **Flaming Gorge Reservoir** U.S.A.
134 D1 **Flathead** *r.* U.S.A.
134 D1 **Flathead Lake** U.S.A.
51 D1 **Flattery, Cape** Austr.
134 B1 **Flattery, Cape** U.S.A.
98 B2 **Fleetwood** U.K.
93 E4 **Flekkefjord** Norway
102 B1 **Flensburg** Ger.
104 B2 **Flers** France
51 D1 **Flinders** *r.* Austr.
50 A3 **Flinders Bay** Austr.
51 D3 **Flinders Island** Austr.
52 A2 **Flinders Ranges** *mts* Austr.
129 D2 **Flin Flon** Can.
140 C2 **Flint** U.S.A.
107 D1 **Florac** France
108 B2 **Florence** Italy
142 C2 **Florence** *AL* U.S.A.
138 A2 **Florence** *AZ* U.S.A.
134 B2 **Florence** *OR* U.S.A.
143 E2 **Florence** *SC* U.S.A.
150 A1 **Florencia** Col.
146 B3 **Flores** Guat.
58 C3 **Flores** *i.* Indon.
58 B3 **Flores, Laut** *sea* Indon.
Flores Sea Indon. *see* **Flores, Laut**
151 E2 **Floresta** Brazil
139 D3 **Floresville** U.S.A.
151 D2 **Floriano** Brazil
152 D3 **Florianópolis** Brazil
153 C4 **Florida** Uru.
143 D2 **Florida** *state* U.S.A.
143 D4 **Florida, Straits of** N. Atlantic Ocean
143 D4 **Florida Keys** *is* U.S.A.
111 B2 **Florina** Greece
93 E3 **Florø** Norway
129 D2 **Foam Lake** Can.
109 C2 **Foča** Bos. & Herz.
110 C1 **Focșani** Romania
71 B3 **Fogang** China
109 C2 **Foggia** Italy
131 E2 **Fogo Island** Can.
104 C3 **Foix** France
89 D3 **Fokino** Russia
130 B2 **Foleyet** Can.
108 B2 **Foligno** Italy
99 D3 **Folkestone** U.K.
143 D2 **Folkston** U.S.A.
108 B2 **Follonica** Italy
129 D2 **Fond-du-Lac** Can.
129 D2 **Fond du Lac** *r.* Can.
140 B2 **Fond du Lac** U.S.A.
106 B1 **Fondevila** Spain
108 B2 **Fondi** Italy
146 B3 **Fonseca, Golfo do** *b.* Central America
150 B2 **Fonte Boa** Brazil
104 B2 **Fontenay-le-Comte** France
92 □C2 **Fontur** *pt* Iceland
53 C2 **Forbes** Austr.
101 E3 **Forchheim** Ger.
93 E3 **Førde** Norway
53 C1 **Fords Bridge** Austr.
142 B2 **Fordyce** U.S.A.
142 C2 **Forest** U.S.A.
53 C3 **Forest Hill** Austr.
131 D2 **Forestville** Can.
96 C2 **Forfar** U.K.
134 B1 **Forks** U.S.A.
108 B2 **Forlì** Italy
107 D2 **Formentera** *i.* Spain
107 D2 **Formentor, Cap de** *c.* Spain
155 C2 **Formiga** Brazil
152 C3 **Formosa** Arg.
Formosa *country* Asia *see* **Taiwan**
154 C1 **Formosa** Brazil
96 C2 **Forres** U.K.
50 B3 **Forrest** Austr.
142 B1 **Forrest City** U.S.A.
51 D1 **Forsayth** Austr.
93 H3 **Forssa** Fin.
53 D2 **Forster** Austr.
136 B1 **Forsyth** U.S.A.
74 B2 **Fort Abbas** Pak.
130 B1 **Fort Albany** Can.
151 E2 **Fortaleza** Brazil
128 C2 **Fort Assiniboine** Can.
96 B2 **Fort Augustus** U.K.
134 D1 **Fort Benton** U.S.A.
135 B3 **Fort Bragg** U.S.A.
Fort Chimo Can. *see* **Kuujjua**
129 C2 **Fort Chipewyan** Can.
136 B2 **Fort Collins** U.S.A.
147 D3 **Fort-de-France** Martinique
137 E2 **Fort Dodge** U.S.A.
130 A2 **Fort Frances** Can.
Fort Franklin Can. *see* **Délin**
Fort George Can. *see* **Chisas**
126 C2 **Fort Good Hope** Can.
96 C2 **Forth** *r.* U.K.
96 C2 **Forth, Firth of** *est.* U.K.
152 C3 **Fortín Madrejón** Para.
143 D3 **Fort Lauderdale** U.S.A.
128 B1 **Fort Liard** Can.
129 C2 **Fort Mackay** Can.
129 C2 **Fort McMurray** Can.
126 C2 **Fort McPherson** Can.
136 C2 **Fort Morgan** U.S.A.
143 D3 **Fort Myers** U.S.A.
128 B2 **Fort Nelson** Can.
128 B2 **Fort Nelson** *r.* Can.
142 C2 **Fort Payne** U.S.A.
136 B1 **Fort Peck** U.S.A.
136 B1 **Fort Peck Reservoir** U.S.A.
143 D3 **Fort Pierce** U.S.A.
128 C1 **Fort Providence** Can.
129 D2 **Fort Qu'Appelle** Can.
128 C1 **Fort Resolution** Can.
Fort Rupert Can. *see* **Waskaganish**
128 B2 **Fort St James** Can.
128 B2 **Fort St John** Can.
128 C2 **Fort Saskatchewan** Can.
137 E3 **Fort Scott** U.S.A.
130 B1 **Fort Severn** Can.
76 B2 **Fort-Shevchenko** Kazakh.
128 B1 **Fort Simpson** Can.
129 C1 **Fort Smith** Can.
142 B1 **Fort Smith** U.S.A.
139 C2 **Fort Stockton** U.S.A.
138 C2 **Fort Sumner** U.S.A.
128 C2 **Fort Vermilion** Can.
142 C2 **Fort Walton Beach** U.S.A.
140 B2 **Fort Wayne** U.S.A.
96 B2 **Fort William** U.K.
139 D2 **Fort Worth** U.S.A.
126 B2 **Fort Yukon** U.S.A.
71 B3 **Foshan** China
92 F3 **Fosna** *pen.* Norway
93 E3 **Fosnavåg** Norway
92 □B3 **Foss** Iceland
92 □A2 **Fossá** Iceland
108 A2 **Fossano** Italy
53 C3 **Foster** Austr.
104 B2 **Fougères** France
96 □ **Foula** *i.* U.K.
111 C3 **Fournoi** *i.* Greece
114 A3 **Fouta Djallon** *reg.* Guinea
54 A3 **Foveaux Strait** N.Z.
136 C3 **Fowler** U.S.A.

50 C3 **Fowlers Bay** Austr.
128 C2 **Fox Creek** Can.
127 F2 **Foxe Basin** *g.* Can.
127 F2 **Foxe Channel** Can.
127 F2 **Foxe Peninsula** Can.
54 B2 **Fox Glacier** N.Z.
128 C2 **Fox Lake** Can.
128 A1 **Fox Mountain** Can.
54 C2 **Foxton** N.Z.
129 D2 **Fox Valley** Can.
97 C1 **Foyle, Lough** *b.* Ireland/U.K.
154 B3 **Foz de Areia, Represa de** *resr* Brazil
120 A2 **Foz do Cunene** Angola
154 B3 **Foz do Iguaçu** Brazil
107 D1 **Fraga** Spain
154 C2 **Franca** Brazil
109 C2 **Francavilla Fontana** Italy
104 C2 **France** *country* Europe
118 B3 **Franceville** Gabon
137 D2 **Francis Case, Lake** U.S.A.
155 D1 **Francisco Sá** Brazil
120 B3 **Francistown** Botswana
128 B2 **François Lake** Can.
101 D2 **Frankenberg (Eder)** Ger.
101 D3 **Frankenthal (Pfalz)** Ger.
101 E2 **Frankenwald** *mts* Ger.
140 C3 **Frankfort** U.S.A.
102 C1 **Frankfurt (Oder)** Ger.
101 D2 **Frankfurt am Main** Ger.
102 C2 **Fränkische Alb** *hills* Ger.
101 E3 **Fränkische Schweiz** *reg.* Ger.
141 D2 **Franklin** U.S.A.
126 C2 **Franklin Bay** Can.
134 C1 **Franklin D. Roosevelt Lake** U.S.A.
128 B1 **Franklin Mountains** Can.
126 E2 **Franklin Strait** Can.
82 E1 **Frantsa-Iosifa, Zemlya** *is* Russia
Franz Josef Land *is* Russia *see* **Frantsa-Iosifa, Zemlya**
54 B2 **Franz Josef/Waiau** N.Z.
108 A3 **Frasca, Capo della** *c. Sardinia* Italy
128 B3 **Fraser** *r. B.C.* Can.
131 D1 **Fraser** *r. Nfld. and Lab.* Can.
122 B3 **Fraserburg** S. Africa
96 C2 **Fraserburgh** U.K.
130 B2 **Fraserdale** Can.
51 E2 **Fraser Island** Austr.
128 B2 **Fraser Lake** Can.
153 C4 **Fray Bentos** Uru.
93 E4 **Fredericia** Denmark
139 D2 **Frederick** U.S.A.
139 D2 **Fredericksburg** *TX* U.S.A.
141 D3 **Fredericksburg** *VA* U.S.A.
128 A2 **Frederick Sound** *sea chan.* U.S.A.
131 D2 **Fredericton** Can.
93 F4 **Frederikshavn** Denmark
Fredrikshamn Fin. *see* **Hamina**
93 F4 **Fredrikstad** Norway
146 C2 **Freeport** Bahamas
140 B2 **Freeport** *IL* U.S.A.
139 D3 **Freeport** *TX* U.S.A.
139 D3 **Freer** U.S.A.
123 C2 **Free State** *prov.* S. Africa
114 A4 **Freetown** Sierra Leone
106 B2 **Fregenal de la Sierra** Spain
104 B2 **Fréhel, Cap** *c.* France
102 B2 **Freiburg im Breisgau** Ger.
102 C2 **Freising** Ger.
102 C2 **Freistadt** Austria
105 D3 **Fréjus** France
50 A3 **Fremantle** Austr.
137 D2 **Fremont** *NE* U.S.A.
140 C2 **Fremont** *OH* U.S.A.
151 C1 **French Guiana** *terr.* S. America
134 E1 **Frenchman** *r.* U.S.A.
49 I4 **French Polynesia** *terr.* S. Pacific Ocean
144 B2 **Fresnillo** Mex.
135 C3 **Fresno** U.S.A.
107 D2 **Freu, Cap des** *c.* Spain
105 D2 **Freyming-Merlebach** France
114 A3 **Fria** Guinea
152 B3 **Frías** Arg.
102 B2 **Friedrichshafen** Ger.
101 F1 **Friesack** Ger.
100 C1 **Friesoythe** Ger.
Frobisher Bay Can. *see* **Iqaluit**
127 G2 **Frobisher Bay** Can.
101 F2 **Frohburg** Ger.
87 D4 **Frolovo** Russia
52 A2 **Frome, Lake** *imp. l.* Austr.
52 A2 **Frome Downs** Austr.
100 C2 **Fröndenberg/Ruhr** Ger.
145 C3 **Frontera** Mex.
144 B1 **Fronteras** Mex.
108 B2 **Frosinone** Italy
92 E3 **Frøya** *i.* Norway
Frunze Kyrg. *see* **Bishkek**
105 D2 **Frutigen** Switz.
103 D2 **Frýdek-Místek** Czechia
71 B3 **Fu'an** China
106 C1 **Fuenlabrada** Spain
152 C3 **Fuerte Olimpo** Para.
114 A2 **Fuerteventura** *i.* Canary Islands
64 B1 **Fuga** *i.* Phil.
79 C2 **Fujairah** U.A.E.
67 C3 **Fuji** Japan
71 B3 **Fujian** *prov.* China
67 C3 **Fujinomiya** Japan
67 C3 **Fuji-san** *vol.* Japan
67 C3 **Fukui** Japan
67 B4 **Fukuoka** Japan
67 D3 **Fukushima** Japan
101 D2 **Fulda** Ger.
101 D2 **Fulda** *r.* Ger.
70 A3 **Fuling** China
137 E3 **Fulton** U.S.A.
105 C2 **Fumay** France
49 F3 **Funafuti** *atoll* Tuvalu
114 A1 **Funchal** Madeira
106 B1 **Fundão** Port.
131 D2 **Fundy, Bay of** *g.* Can.
70 B2 **Funing** *Jiangsu* China
71 A3 **Funing** *Yunnan* China
115 C3 **Funtua** Nigeria
79 C2 **Fürgun, Kūh-e** *mt.* Iran
89 F2 **Furmanov** Russia
155 C2 **Furnas, Represa** *resr* Brazil
51 D4 **Furneaux Group** *is* Austr.
100 C1 **Fürstenau** Ger.
101 E3 **Fürth** Ger.
127 F2 **Fury and Hecla Strait** Can.
65 A1 **Fushun** China
65 B1 **Fusong** China
79 C2 **Fuwayriț** Qatar
70 B2 **Fuyang** China
69 E1 **Fuyu** China
68 B1 **Fuyun** China
71 B3 **Fuzhou** *Fujian* China
71 B3 **Fuzhou** *Jiangxi* China
93 F4 **Fyn** *i.* Denmark
F.Y.R.O.M. *country* Europe *see* **Macedonia**

G

117 C4 **Gaalkacyo** Somalia
120 A2 **Gabela** Angola
115 D1 **Gabès** Tunisia
115 D1 **Gabès, Golfe de** *g.* Tunisia
118 B3 **Gabon** *country* Africa
123 C1 **Gaborone** Botswana
110 C2 **Gabrovo** Bulg.
114 A3 **Gabú** Guinea-Bissau
73 B3 **Gadag-Betigeri** India
75 C2 **Gadchiroli** India
101 E1 **Gadebusch** Ger.
142 C2 **Gadsden** U.S.A.
110 C2 **Găești** Romania
108 B2 **Gaeta** Italy
143 D1 **Gaffney** U.S.A.
115 C1 **Gafsa** Tunisia
89 E2 **Gagarin** Russia
114 B4 **Gagnoa** Côte d'Ivoire
131 D1 **Gagnon** Can.
81 C1 **Gagra** Georgia
122 A2 **Gaiab** *watercourse* Namibia
111 C3 **Gaïdouronisi** *i.* Greece
104 C3 **Gaillac** France
143 D3 **Gainesville** *FL* U.S.A.
143 D2 **Gainesville** *GA* U.S.A.
139 D2 **Gainesville** *TX* U.S.A.
98 C2 **Gainsborough** U.K.
52 A2 **Gairdner, Lake** *imp. l.* Austr.
96 B2 **Gairloch** U.K.
119 E3 **Galana** *r.* Kenya
103 D2 **Galanta** Slovakia
148 B3 **Galapagos Islands** Ecuador
96 C3 **Galashiels** U.K.
110 C1 **Galați** Romania
93 E3 **Galdhøpiggen** *mt.* Norway
145 B2 **Galeana** Mex.
128 C2 **Galena Bay** Can.
140 A2 **Galesburg** U.S.A.
122 B2 **Galeshewe** S. Africa
86 D3 **Galich** Russia
116 B1 **Galilee, Sea of** *l.* Israel
142 C1 **Gallatin** U.S.A.
73 C4 **Galle** Sri Lanka
150 A1 **Gallinas, Punta** *pt* Col.
109 C2 **Gallipoli** Italy
111 C2 **Gallipoli** Turkey
92 H2 **Gällivare** Sweden
138 B1 **Gallup** U.S.A.
117 C4 **Galmudug** *reg.* Somalia
114 A2 **Galtat-Zemmour** Western Sahara
97 B2 **Galtymore** *h.* Ireland
139 E3 **Galveston** U.S.A.
139 E3 **Galveston Bay** U.S.A.
97 B2 **Galway** Ireland
97 B2 **Galway Bay** Ireland
154 C1 **Gama** Brazil
123 D3 **Gamalakhe** S. Africa
114 A3 **Gambia, The** *country* Africa
52 A3 **Gambier Islands** Austr.
131 E2 **Gambo** Can.
118 B3 **Gamboma** Congo
128 C1 **Gamêtî** Can.
138 B1 **Ganado** U.S.A.
81 C1 **Gäncä** Azer.
Gand Belgium *see* **Ghent**
61 C2 **Gandadiwata, Bukit** *mt.* Indon.
118 C3 **Gandajika** Dem. Rep. Congo
131 E2 **Gander** Can.
131 E2 **Gander** *r.* Can.
101 D1 **Ganderkesee** Ger.
107 D1 **Gandesa** Spain
74 B2 **Gandhidham** India
74 B2 **Gandhinagar** India
74 B2 **Gandhi Sagar** *resr* India
107 C2 **Gandia** Spain
Ganga *r.* Bangl./India *see* **Ganges**
153 B5 **Gan Gan** Arg.

74 B2 Ganganagar India
68 C2 Gangca China
75 C1 Gangdisê Shan mts China
75 D2 Ganges r. Bangl./India
105 C3 Ganges France
75 C2 Ganges, Mouths of the Bangl./India
65 B3 Gangneung S. Korea
75 C2 Gangtok India
105 C2 Gannat France
136 B2 Gannett Peak U.S.A.
122 A3 Gansbaai S. Africa
70 A1 Gansu prov. China
71 B3 Ganzhou China
114 B3 Gao Mali
97 B1 Gaoth Dobhair Ireland
114 A3 Gaoual Guinea
Gaoxiong Taiwan see Kaohsiung
70 B2 Gaoyou China
70 B2 Gaoyou Hu l. China
105 D3 Gap France
75 C1 Gar China
76 B2 Garabogaz Turkm.
76 B2 Garabogazköl Turkm.
76 B2 Garabogazköl Aýlagy b. Turkm.
53 C1 Garah Austr.
151 E2 Garanhuns Brazil
135 B2 Garberville U.S.A.
101 D1 Garbsen Ger.
154 C2 Garça Brazil
101 E1 Gardelegen Ger.
136 C3 Garden City U.S.A.
129 E2 Garden Hill Can.
77 C3 Gardēz Afgh.
88 B2 Gargždai Lith.
123 C3 Gariep Dam dam S. Africa
122 A3 Garies S. Africa
119 D3 Garissa Kenya
102 C2 Garmisch-Partenkirchen Ger.
52 B2 Garnpung Lake imp. l. Austr.
104 B3 Garonne r. France
117 C4 Garoowe Somalia
74 B2 Garoth India
118 B2 Garoua Cameroon
96 B2 Garry r. U.K.
126 E2 Garry Lake Can.
119 E3 Garsen Kenya
61 B2 Garut Indon.
140 B2 Gary U.S.A.
145 B2 Garza García Mex.
68 C2 Garzê China
104 B2 Gascony, Gulf of France
50 A2 Gascoyne r. Austr.
115 D3 Gashua Nigeria
131 D2 Gaspé Can.
131 D2 Gaspésie, Péninsule de la pen. Can.
143 E1 Gaston, Lake U.S.A.
143 D1 Gastonia U.S.A.
107 C2 Gata, Cabo de c. Spain
88 D2 Gatchina Russia
98 C1 Gateshead U.K.
139 D2 Gatesville U.S.A.
130 C2 Gatineau r. Can.
53 D1 Gatton Austr.
129 E2 Gauer Lake Can.
93 E4 Gausta mt. Norway
123 C2 Gauteng prov. S. Africa
111 B3 Gavdos i. Greece
93 G3 Gävle Sweden
89 F2 Gavrilov Posad Russia
89 E2 Gavrilov-Yam Russia
62 A1 Gawai Myanmar
52 A2 Gawler Austr.
52 A2 Gawler Ranges hills Austr.
75 C2 Gaya India

114 C3 Gaya Niger
140 C1 Gaylord U.S.A.
86 E2 Gayny Russia
80 B2 Gaza disp. terr. Asia
80 B2 Gaziantep Turkey
76 C2 Gazojak Turkm.
114 B4 Gbarnga Liberia
103 D1 Gdańsk Pol.
88 A3 Gdańsk, Gulf of Pol./Russia
88 C2 Gdov Russia
103 D1 Gdynia Pol.
116 B3 Gedaref Sudan
101 D2 Gedern Ger.
111 C3 Gediz r. Turkey
102 C1 Gedser Denmark
100 B2 Geel Belgium
52 B3 Geelong Austr.
101 E1 Geesthacht Ger.
129 D2 Gê'gyai China
93 E3 Geikie r. Can.
62 B1 Geilo Norway
62 B1 Gejiu China
91 D3 Gela Sicily Italy
91 D3 Gelendzhik Russia
Gelibolu Turkey see Gallipoli
100 C2 Gelsenkirchen Ger.
118 B2 Gemena Dem. Rep. Congo
111 C2 Gemlik Turkey
117 C4 Genalē Wenz r. Eth.
153 B4 General Acha Arg.
153 B4 General Alvear Arg.
153 B4 General Belgrano Arg.
144 B2 General Cepeda Mex.
153 B4 General Pico Arg.
153 B4 General Roca Arg.
64 B2 General Santos Phil.
141 D2 Genesee r. U.S.A.
141 D2 Geneseo U.S.A.
105 D2 Geneva Switz.
141 D2 Geneva U.S.A.
105 D2 Geneva, Lake France/Switz.
Genève Switz. see Geneva
106 B2 Genil r. Spain
100 B2 Genk Belgium
108 A2 Genoa Italy
Genova Italy see Genoa
101 F1 Genthin Ger.
50 A3 Geographe Bay Austr.
65 B2 Geongju S. Korea
131 D1 George r. Can.
122 B3 George S. Africa
143 D3 George, Lake FL U.S.A.
141 E2 George, Lake NY U.S.A.
151 C1 Georgetown Guyana
60 B1 George Town Malaysia
143 E2 Georgetown SC U.S.A.
139 D2 Georgetown TX U.S.A.
55 I2 George V Land reg. Antarctica
81 C1 Georgia country Asia
143 D2 Georgia state U.S.A.
130 B2 Georgian Bay Can.
51 C2 Georgina watercourse Austr.
77 E2 Georgiyevka Kazakh.
87 D4 Georgiyevsk Russia
101 F2 Gera Ger.
151 D3 Geral de Goiás, Serra hills Brazil
54 B2 Geraldine N.Z.
50 A2 Geraldton Austr.
80 B1 Gerede Turkey
103 E2 Gerlach U.S.A.
103 E2 Gerlachovský štít mt. Slovakia
102 C1 Germany country Europe
100 C2 Gerolstein Ger.
101 E3 Gerolzhofen Ger.
101 D2 Gersfeld (Rhön) Ger.
75 C1 Gêrzê China
117 C4 Gestro Wenz, Wabē r. Eth.

141 D3 Gettysburg PA U.S.A.
136 D1 Gettysburg SD U.S.A.
109 D2 Gevgelija Macedonia
111 C3 Geyikli Turkey
122 B2 Ghaap Plateau S. Africa
115 C1 Ghadāmis Libya
75 C2 Ghaghara r. India
114 B4 Ghana country Africa
120 B3 Ghanzi Botswana
115 C1 Ghardaïa Alg.
115 D1 Gharyān Libya
75 C2 Ghatal India
75 B2 Ghaziabad India
75 C2 Ghazipur India
77 C3 Ghaznī Afgh.
100 A2 Ghent Belgium
110 B1 Gherla Romania
105 D3 Ghisonaccia Corsica France
74 B2 Ghotaru India
74 A2 Ghotki Pak.
91 E3 Giaginskaya Russia
97 C1 Giant's Causeway lava field U.K.
61 C2 Gianyar Indon.
109 C3 Giarre Sicily Italy
108 A1 Giaveno Italy
122 A2 Gibeon Namibia
106 B2 Gibraltar Gibraltar
106 B2 Gibraltar, Strait of Morocco/Spain
50 B2 Gibson Desert Austr.
68 C1 Gichgeniyn Nuruu mts Mongolia
117 B4 Gidolē Eth.
104 C2 Gien France
101 D2 Gießen Ger.
101 E1 Gifhorn Ger.
128 C2 Gift Lake Can.
67 C3 Gifu Japan
96 B3 Gigha i. U.K.
106 B1 Gijón/Xixón Spain
138 A2 Gila r. U.S.A.
138 A2 Gila Bend U.S.A.
51 D1 Gilbert r. Austr.
49 F2 Gilbert Islands is Kiribati
134 D1 Gildford U.S.A.
53 C2 Gilgandra Austr.
74 B1 Gilgit Pak.
74 B1 Gilgit r. Pak.
53 C2 Gilgunnia Austr.
129 E2 Gillam Can.
136 B2 Gillette U.S.A.
99 D3 Gillingham U.K.
65 B2 Gimcheon S. Korea
129 E2 Gimli Can.
117 C4 Ginir Eth.
109 C2 Ginosa Italy
53 C3 Gippsland reg. Austr.
74 A2 Girdar Dhor r. Pak.
80 B1 Giresun Turkey
74 A1 Girishk Afgh.
107 D1 Girona Spain
96 B3 Girvan U.K.
54 C1 Gisborne N.Z.
93 F4 Gislaved Sweden
119 C3 Gitarama Rwanda
108 B2 Giulianova Italy
110 C2 Giurgiu Romania
110 C1 Giuvala, Pasul pass Romania
105 C2 Givors France
123 D1 Giyani S. Africa
116 B2 Giza Egypt
109 D2 Gjakovë Kosovo
109 D2 Gjilan Kosovo
109 D2 Gjirokastër Albania
126 E2 Gjoa Haven Can.
93 F3 Gjøvik Norway
131 E2 Glace Bay Can.

134	B1	Glacier Peak vol. U.S.A.
51	E2	Gladstone Austr.
92	⬜A2	Gláma mts Iceland
109	C2	Glamoč Bos. & Herz.
100	C3	Glan r. Ger.
97	B2	Glanaruddery Mountains hills Ireland
96	B3	Glasgow U.K.
140	B3	Glasgow KY U.S.A.
136	B1	Glasgow MT U.S.A.
99	B3	Glastonbury U.K.
101	F2	Glauchau Ger.
86	E3	Glazov Russia
89	E3	Glazunovka Russia
96	B2	Glen Coe val. U.K.
138	A2	Glendale U.S.A.
96	B3	Glasgow U.K.
53	D2	Glen Davis Austr.
136	C1	Glendive U.S.A.
52	B3	Glenelg r. Austr.
53	D1	Glen Innes Austr.
126	B2	Glennallen U.S.A.
141	E2	Glenrothes U.K.
97	B1	Glens Falls U.S.A.
97	B1	Glen Shee val. U.K.
97	B1	Glenties Ireland
138	B2	Glenwood U.S.A.
136	B3	Glenwood Springs U.S.A.
103	D1	Gliwice Pol.
138	A2	Globe U.S.A.
103	D1	Głogów Pol.
92	F2	Glomfjord Norway
93	F4	Glomma r. Norway
51	D4	Gloucester Austr.
99	B3	Gloucester U.K.
101	F1	Glöwen Ger.
77	E1	Glubokoye Kazakh.
101	E2	Glückstadt Ger.
103	C2	Gmünd Austria
102	C2	Gmunden Austria
101	D1	Gnarrenburg Ger.
103	D1	Gniezno Pol.
75	D2	Goalpara India
96	B3	Goat Fell h. U.K.
117	C4	Goba Eth.
120	A3	Gobabis Namibia
153	A5	Gobernador Gregores Arg.
69	D2	Gobi des. China/Mongolia
100	C2	Goch Ger.
122	A1	Gochas Namibia
74	B3	Godavari r. India
73	C3	Godavari, Mouths of the India
74	B2	Goderich Can.
74	B2	Godhra India
129	E2	Gods r. Can.
129	E2	Gods Lake Can.
		Godthåb Greenland see Nuuk
		Godwin-Austen, Mount China/Pak. see K2
130	C2	Goéland, Lac au l. Can.
131	D1	Goélands, Lac aux l. Can.
100	A2	Goes Neth.
154	C1	Goiandira Brazil
154	B1	Goiânia Brazil
154	B1	Goiás Brazil
154	B2	Goioerê Brazil
111	C2	Gökçeada i. Turkey
111	C3	Gökçedağ Turkey
123	D3	Gokwe Zimbabwe
93	E3	Gol Norway
62	A1	Golaghat India
111	C2	Gölcük Turkey
103	E1	Gołdap Pol.
101	F1	Goldberg Ger.
53	D2	Golden Austr.
114	B4	Gold Coast Ghana
54	B2	Golden Bay N.Z.
128	B3	Golden Hinde mt. Can.
97	B2	Golden Vale lowland Ireland
135	C3	Goldfield U.S.A.
128	B3	Gold River Can.
143	E1	Goldsboro U.S.A.
135	C4	Goleta U.S.A.
68	C2	Golmud China
81	D2	Golpāyegān Iran
96	C2	Golspie U.K.
92	F2	Golvertinden mt. Norway
119	C3	Goma Dem. Rep. Congo
75	C2	Gomati r. India
115	D3	Gombe Nigeria
115	D3	Gombi Nigeria
		Gomel' Belarus see Homyel'/Gomel'
144	B2	Gómez Palacio Mex.
147	C3	Gonaïves Haiti
147	C3	Gonâve, Île de la i. Haiti
81	D2	Gonbad-e Kāvūs Iran
117	B3	Gonder Eth.
75	C2	Gondiya India
111	C2	Gönen Turkey
65	B2	Gongju S. Korea
115	D4	Gongola r. Nigeria
53	C2	Gongolgon Austr.
75	D1	Gongtang China
145	C2	Gonzáles Mex.
139	D3	Gonzales U.S.A.
122	A3	Good Hope, Cape of S. Africa
134	D2	Gooding U.S.A.
136	C3	Goodland U.S.A.
53	C1	Goodooga Austr.
98	C2	Goole U.K.
53	C2	Goolgowi Austr.
52	A3	Goolwa Austr.
53	D1	Goondiwindi Austr.
134	B2	Goose Lake U.S.A.
102	B2	Göppingen Ger.
75	C2	Gorakhpur India
109	C2	Goražde Bos. & Herz.
111	C3	Gördes Turkey
89	E3	Gordeyevka Russia
51	D4	Gordon, Lake Austr.
115	D4	Goré Chad
117	B4	Gorē Eth.
54	A3	Gore N.Z.
97	C2	Gorey Ireland
81	D2	Gorgān Iran
81	C1	Gori Georgia
108	B1	Gorizia Italy
		Gor'kiy Russia see Nizhniy Novgorod
103	E2	Gorlice Pol.
103	C1	Görlitz Ger.
109	D2	Gornji Milanovac Serbia
109	C2	Gornji Vakuf Bos. & Herz.
77	E1	Gorno-Altaysk Russia
110	C2	Gornotrakiyska Nizina lowland Bulg.
77	E1	Gornyak Russia
59	D3	Goroka P.N.G.
114	B3	Gorom-Gorom Burkina Faso
59	C2	Gorontalo Indon.
89	E3	Gorshechnoye Russia
97	B2	Gorumna Island Ireland
91	D3	Goryachiy Klyuch Russia
65	B2	Goryeong S. Korea
103	D1	Gorzów Wielkopolski Pol.
53	D2	Gosford Austr.
66	D2	Goshogawara Japan
101	E2	Goslar Ger.
109	C2	Gospić Croatia
99	C3	Gosport U.K.
109	D2	Gostivar Macedonia
		Göteborg Sweden see Gothenburg
101	E2	Gotha Ger.
93	F4	Gothenburg Sweden
136	C2	Gothenburg U.S.A.
93	G4	Gotland i. Sweden
111	B2	Gotse Delchev Bulg.
93	G4	Gotska Sandön i. Sweden
67	B4	Gōtsu Japan
101	D2	Göttingen Ger.
128	B2	Gott Peak Can.
100	B1	Gouda Neth.
114	A3	Goudiri Senegal
115	D3	Goudoumaria Niger
130	C2	Gouin, Réservoir resr Can.
53	C2	Goulburn Austr.
53	B3	Goulburn r. N.S.W. Austr.
53	B3	Goulburn r. Vic. Austr.
114	B3	Goundam Mali
107	D2	Gouraya Alg.
104	C3	Gourdon France
115	D3	Gouré Niger
122	B3	Gourits r. S. Africa
114	B3	Gourma-Rharous Mali
53	C3	Gourock Range mts Austr.
155	D1	Governador Valadares Brazil
143	E3	Governor's Harbour Bahamas
68	C2	Govĭ Altayn Nuruu mts Mongolia
75	C2	Govind Ballash Pant Sagar resr India
99	A3	Gower pen. U.K.
152	C3	Goya Arg.
81	C1	Göyçay Azer.
75	C1	Gozha Co salt l. China
122	B3	Graaff-Reinet S. Africa
101	E1	Grabow Ger.
109	C2	Gračac Croatia
87	E3	Grachevka Russia
101	F2	Gräfenhainichen Ger.
53	D1	Grafton Austr.
137	D1	Grafton U.S.A.
139	D2	Graham U.S.A.
128	A2	Graham Island Can.
55	P3	Graham Land pen. Antarctica
123	C3	Grahamstown S. Africa
152	C2	Grajaú Brazil
111	B2	Grammos mt. Greece
96	B2	Grampian Mountains U.K.
146	B3	Granada Nic.
106	C2	Granada Spain
141	E1	Granby Can.
114	A2	Gran Canaria i. Canary Islands
152	B3	Gran Chaco reg. Arg./Para.
136	C1	Grand r. U.S.A.
146	C2	Grand Bahama i. Bahamas
131	E2	Grand Bank Can.
158	C2	Grand Banks of Newfoundland N. Atlantic Ocean
		Grand Canal canal China see Jinghang Yunhe
138	A1	Grand Canyon U.S.A.
138	A1	Grand Canyon gorge U.S.A.
146	B3	Grand Cayman i. Cayman Is
129	C2	Grand Centre Can.
134	C1	Grand Coulee U.S.A.
152	B2	Grande r. Bol.
154	B2	Grande r. Brazil
153	B6	Grande, Bahía b. Arg.
155	D2	Grande, Ilha i. Brazil
128	C2	Grande Cache Can.
128	C2	Grande Prairie Can.
114	B1	Grand Erg Occidental des. Alg.
115	C2	Grand Erg Oriental des. Alg.
131	D2	Grande-Rivière Can.
152	B4	Grandes, Salinas salt flat Arg.
156	D7	Grand Terre i. S. Pacific Ocean
131	D2	Grand Falls Can.
131	E2	Grand Falls-Windsor Can.
128	C3	Grand Forks Can.

137	D1	Grand Forks U.S.A.
128	C1	Grandin, Lac i. Can.
137	D2	Grand Island U.S.A.
142	B3	Grand Isle U.S.A.
136	B3	Grand Junction U.S.A.
114	B4	Grand-Lahou Côte d'Ivoire
131	D2	Grand Lake N.B. Can.
131	E2	Grand Lake Nfld. and Lab. Can.
137	E1	Grand Marais U.S.A.
106	B2	Grândola Port.
129	E2	Grand Rapids Can.
140	B2	Grand Rapids MI U.S.A.
137	E1	Grand Rapids MN U.S.A.
136	A2	Grand Teton mt. U.S.A.
147	C2	Grand Turk Turks and Caicos Is
134	C1	Grangeville U.S.A.
128	B2	Granisle Can.
134	E1	Granite Peak U.S.A.
108	B3	Granitola, Capo c. Sicily Italy
93	F4	Gränna Sweden
101	F1	Gransee Ger.
99	C2	Grantham U.K.
96	C2	Grantown-on-Spey U.K.
138	B1	Grants U.S.A.
134	B2	Grants Pass U.S.A.
104	C2	Granville France
129	D2	Granville Lake Can.
155	D1	Grão Mogol Brazil
123	D1	Graskop S. Africa
105	D3	Grasse France
107	D1	Graus Spain
92	F2	Gravdal Norway
104	B2	Grave, Pointe de pt France
129	D3	Gravelbourg Can.
130	C2	Gravenhurst Can.
53	D1	Gravesend Austr.
99	D3	Gravesend U.K.
105	D2	Gray France
103	D2	Graz Austria
146	C2	Great Abaco i. Bahamas
50	B3	Great Australian Bight g. Austr.
54	C1	Great Barrier Island N.Z.
51	D1	Great Barrier Reef Austr.
135	C3	Great Basin U.S.A.
126	D2	Great Bear Lake Can.
93	F4	Great Belt sea chan. Denmark
137	D3	Great Bend U.S.A.
63	A2	Great Coco Island Cocos Is
53	B3	Great Dividing Range mts Austr.
146	B2	Greater Antilles is Caribbean Sea
60	B2	Greater Sunda Islands is Indon.
134	D1	Great Falls U.S.A.
123	C3	Great Fish r. S. Africa
123	C3	Great Fish Point S. Africa
147	C2	Great Inagua i. Bahamas
122	B3	Great Karoo plat. S. Africa
123	C3	Great Kei r. S. Africa
99	B2	Great Malvern U.K.
122	A2	Great Namaqualand reg. Namibia
63	A3	Great Nicobar i. India
99	D2	Great Ouse r. U.K.
119	D3	Great Rift Valley Africa
119	D3	Great Ruaha r. Tanz.
134	D2	Great Salt Lake U.S.A.
135	D2	Great Salt Lake Desert U.S.A.
116	A2	Great Sand Sea des. Egypt/ Libya
50	B2	Great Sandy Desert Austr.
128	C1	Great Slave Lake Can.
143	D1	Great Smoky Mountains U.S.A.
50	B2	Great Victoria Desert Austr.
70	B1	Great Wall tourist site China
99	D2	Great Yarmouth U.K.
106	B1	Gredos, Sierra de mts Spain
111	B3	Greece country Europe
136	C2	Greeley U.S.A.
82	F1	Greem-Bell, Ostrov i. Russia
140	B3	Green r. KY U.S.A.
136	B3	Green r. WY U.S.A.
140	B2	Green Bay U.S.A.
140	B1	Green Bay b. U.S.A.
140	C3	Greenbrier r. U.S.A.
140	B3	Greencastle U.S.A.
143	D1	Greeneville U.S.A.
141	E2	Greenfield U.S.A.
129	D2	Green Lake Can.
127	I2	Greenland terr. N. America
160	R2	Greenland Sea Greenland/ Svalbard
96	B3	Greenock U.K.
135	D3	Green River UT U.S.A.
136	B2	Green River WY U.S.A.
140	B3	Greensburg IN U.S.A.
141	D2	Greensburg PA U.S.A.
143	E2	Green Swamp U.S.A.
138	A2	Green Valley U.S.A.
114	B4	Greenville Liberia
142	C2	Greenville MI U.S.A.
142	B3	Greenville MS U.S.A.
143	E1	Greenville NC U.S.A.
143	D2	Greenville SC U.S.A.
139	D2	Greenville TX U.S.A.
53	D2	Greenwell Point Austr.
143	D2	Greenwood U.S.A.
50	B2	Gregory, Lake imp. l. Austr.
51	D1	Gregory Range hills Austr.
102	C1	Greifswald Ger.
101	F2	Greiz Ger.
93	F4	Grenaa Denmark
142	C2	Grenada U.S.A.
147	D3	Grenada country West Indies
104	C3	Grenade France
53	C2	Grenfell Austr.
129	D2	Grenfell Can.
105	D2	Grenoble France
51	D1	Grenville, Cape Austr.
134	B1	Gresham U.S.A.
100	C1	Greven Ger.
111	B2	Grevena Greece
100	C2	Grevenbroich Ger.
101	E1	Grevesmühlen Ger.
136	B2	Greybull U.S.A.
128	A1	Grey Hunter Peak Can.
131	E1	Grey Islands Can.
54	B2	Greymouth N.Z.
52	B1	Grey Range hills Austr.
97	C2	Greystones Ireland
143	D2	Griffin U.S.A.
53	C2	Griffith Austr.
101	F2	Grimma Ger.
102	C1	Grimmen Ger.
98	C2	Grimsby U.K.
128	C2	Grimshaw Can.
92	OB2	Grímsstaðir Iceland
93	E4	Grimstad Norway
137	E2	Grinnell U.S.A.
123	C3	Griqualand East reg. S. Africa
122	B2	Griqualand West reg. S. Africa
127	F1	Grise Fiord Can.
96	C1	Gritley U.K.
123	C2	Groblersdal S. Africa
122	B2	Groblershoop S. Africa
		Grodno Belarus see Hrodna/ Grodno
104	B2	Groix, Île de i. France
100	C1	Gronau (Westfalen) Ger.
92	F3	Grong Norway
100	C1	Groningen Neth.
122	B2	Grootdrink S. Africa
51	C1	Groote Eylandt i. Austr.
120	A2	Grootfontein Namibia
122	A2	Groot Karas Berg plat. Namibia
122	B3	Groot Swartberge mts S. Afri
123	C3	Groot Winterberg mt. S. Afri
101	D2	Großenlüder Ger.
102	C2	Großer Rachel mt. Ger.
103	C2	Grosser Speikkogel mt. Austria
108	B2	Grosseto Italy
101	D3	Groß-Gerau Ger.
102	C2	Großglockner mt. Austria
100	C1	Groß Hesepe Ger.
101	E2	Großlohra Ger.
122	A1	Gross Ums Namibia
131	E1	Groswater Bay Can.
130	B2	Groundhog r. Can.
49	I4	Groupe Actéon is Fr. Polynes
135	B3	Grover Beach U.S.A.
141	E2	Groveton U.S.A.
87	D4	Groznyy Russia
109	C1	Grubišno Polje Croatia
103	D1	Grudziądz Pol.
122	A2	Grünau Namibia
92	☐A3	Grundarfjörður Iceland
89	E3	Gryazi Russia
89	F2	Gryazovets Russia
103	D1	Gryfice Pol.
102	C1	Gryfino Pol.
146	C2	Guacanayabo, Golfo de b. Cuba
144	B2	Guadalajara Mex.
106	C1	Guadalajara prov. Spain
49	E3	Guadalcanal i. Solomon Is
107	C1	Guadalope r. Spain
106	B2	Guadalquivir r. Spain
132	B4	Guadalupe i. Mex.
106	B2	Guadalupe, Sierra de mts Spain
138	C2	Guadalupe Peak U.S.A.
144	B2	Guadalupe Victoria Mex.
144	B2	Guadalupe y Calvo Mex.
106	C1	Guadarrama, Sierra de mts Spain
147	D3	Guadeloupe terr. West Indies
106	B2	Guadiana r. Port./Spain
106	C2	Guadix Spain
154	B2	Guaíra Brazil
147	C3	Guajira, Península de la pen. Col.
150	A2	Gualaceo Ecuador
59	D2	Guam terr. N. Pacific Ocean
144	B2	Guamúchil Mex.
144	B2	Guanacevi Mex.
151	D3	Guanambi Brazil
150	B1	Guanare Venez.
146	B2	Guane Cuba
70	A2	Guang'an China
71	B3	Guangchang China
71	B3	Guangdong prov. China
71	A3	Guangxi Zhuangzu Zizhiqu aut. reg. China
70	A2	Guangyuan China
71	B3	Guangzhou China
155	D1	Guanhães Brazil
147	C4	Guanipa r. Venez.
71	A3	Guanling China
65	A1	Guanshui China
		Guansuo China see Guanling
147	C2	Guantánamo Cuba
150	B3	Guaporé r. Bol./Brazil
154	B3	Guarapuava Brazil
154	C3	Guaraqueçaba Brazil
155	C2	Guaratinguetá Brazil
106	B1	Guarda Port.
154	C1	Guarda-Mor Brazil

106 C1 Guardo Spain
155 C2 Guarujá Brazil
144 B2 Guasave Mex.
146 A3 Guatemala country Central America
146 A3 Guatemala City Guat.
150 B1 Guaviare r. Col.
155 C2 Guaxupé Brazil
150 A3 Guayaquil Ecuador
150 B3 Guayaramerín Bol.
144 A2 Guaymas Mex.
68 C2 Guazhou China
117 B3 Guba Eth.
86 E1 Guba Dolgaya Russia
89 E3 Gubkin Russia
115 C1 Guelma Alg.
114 A2 Guelmim Morocco
104 E2 Guelph Can.
145 C2 Guémez Mex.
104 C2 Guéret France
95 C4 Guernsey terr. Channel Is
144 A2 Guerrero Negro Mex.
131 D1 Guers, Lac l. Can.
121 C2 Gühran Iran
118 B2 Guider Cameroon
108 B2 Guidonia Montecelio Italy
71 A4 Guigang China
100 A3 Guignicourt France
123 D1 Guija Moz.
99 C3 Guildford U.K.
71 B3 Guilin China
130 C1 Guillaume-Delisle, Lac l. Can.
106 B1 Guimarães Port.
114 A3 Guinea country Africa
114 C4 Guinea, Gulf of Africa
114 A3 Guinea-Bissau country Africa
104 B2 Guingamp France
104 B2 Guipavas France
154 B1 Guiratinga Brazil
150 B1 Güiria Venez.
100 A3 Guise France
71 A3 Guiuan Phil.
71 A3 Guixi China
71 B3 Guizhou prov. China
74 B1 Gujranwala Pak.
74 B1 Gujrat Pak.
91 D2 Gukovo Russia
53 C2 Gulargambone Austr.
Gulbarga India see Kalaburagi
88 C2 Gulbene Latvia
79 C2 Gulf, The Asia
71 B3 Gulf of Corinth sea chan. Greece
142 C2 Gulfport U.S.A.
69 E1 Gulian China
77 C2 Guliston Uzbek.
Gulja China see Yining
129 D2 Gull Lake Can.
111 A1 Güllük Turkey
119 D2 Gulu Uganda
120 B2 Gumare Botswana
76 B3 Gumdag Turkm.
65 B2 Gumi S. Korea
75 C2 Gumla India
100 C2 Gummersbach Ger.
74 B2 Guna India
53 C3 Gundagai Austr.
111 C3 Güney Turkey
118 B3 Gungu Dem. Rep. Congo
129 E2 Gunisao r. Can.
53 D2 Gunnedah Austr.
136 B3 Gunnison CO U.S.A.
135 D3 Gunnison UT U.S.A.
136 B3 Gunnison r. U.S.A.
65 B2 Gunsan S. Korea
73 B3 Guntakal India
59 C3 Gunung Kwoka mt. Indon.
60 A1 Gunungsitoli Indon.

60 A1 Gunungtua Indon.
102 C2 Günzburg Ger.
102 C2 Gunzenhausen Ger.
70 B2 Guojiaba China
Gurgaon India see Gurugram
151 D2 Gurgueia r. Brazil
150 B1 Guri, Embalse de resr Venez.
154 C1 Gurinhatã Brazil
74 B2 Gurugram India
151 D2 Gurupi r. Brazil
74 B2 Gurupi Brazil
74 B2 Gurushikhar mt. India
Gur'yev Kazakh. see Atyrau
115 C3 Gusau Nigeria
65 A2 Gushan China
70 B2 Gushi China
83 I3 Gusinoozersk Russia
89 F2 Gus'-Khrustal'nyy Russia
108 A3 Guspini Sardinia Italy
128 A2 Gustavus U.S.A.
101 F1 Güstrow Ger.
101 D2 Gütersloh Ger.
121 C2 Gutu Mupandawana Zimbabwe
75 D2 Guwahati India
150 C1 Guyana country S. America
Guyi China see Sanjiang
139 C1 Guymon U.S.A.
53 D2 Guyra Austr.
71 A3 Guyuan China
144 B1 Guzmán, Mex.
74 A2 Gwadar Pak.
128 A2 Gwaii Haanas Can.
75 B2 Gwalior India
121 B3 Gwanda Zimbabwe
65 B2 Gwangju S. Korea
117 D3 Gwardafuy, Gees c. Somalia
97 B1 Gweebarra Bay Ireland
121 B2 Gweru Zimbabwe
115 D3 Gwoza Nigeria
53 D2 Gwydir r. Austr.
75 C2 Gyangzê China
75 C1 Gyaring Co l. China
68 C2 Gyaring Hu l. China
86 G1 Gydan Peninsula Russia
Gydanskiy Poluostrov pen. Russia see Gydan Peninsula
Gyêgu China see Yushu
65 B2 Gyeonggi-man b. S. Korea
51 E2 Gympie Austr.
103 D2 Gyöngyös Hungary
103 D2 Győr Hungary
129 E2 Gypsumville Can.
103 E2 Gyula Hungary
81 C1 Gyumri Armenia

H

88 B2 Haapsalu Estonia
100 B1 Haarlem Neth.
101 C2 Haarstrang ridge Ger.
54 A2 Haast N.Z.
78 B3 Ḩabbān Yemen
81 C2 Ḩabbānīyah, Buḩayrat al l. Iraq
67 C4 Hachijō-jima i. Japan
66 D2 Hachinohe Japan
81 C1 Hacıqabul Azer.
121 C3 Hacufera Moz.
79 C2 Hadd, Ra's al pt Oman
96 C3 Haddington U.K.
115 D3 Hadejia Nigeria
93 E4 Haderslev Denmark
81 C2 Hadithah Iraq
91 C1 Hadyach Ukr.
65 B2 Haeju N. Korea
65 B2 Haeju-man b. N. Korea
65 B3 Haenam S. Korea
78 B2 Ḩafar al Bāţin Saudi Arabia

62 A1 Haflong India
92 □A3 Hafnarfjörður Iceland
78 D2 Hagar Nish Plateau Eritrea/Sudan
48 D2 Hagåtña Guam
100 C2 Hagen Ger.
101 E1 Hagenow Ger.
128 B2 Hagensborg Can.
141 D3 Hagerstown U.S.A.
93 F3 Hagfors Sweden
67 B4 Hagi Japan
62 B1 Ha Giang Vietnam
97 B2 Hag's Head Ireland
104 B2 Hague, Cap de la c. France
119 D3 Hai Tanz.
128 A2 Haida Gwaii Can.
62 B1 Hai Dương Vietnam
80 B2 Haifa Israel
71 B3 Haifeng China
71 B3 Haikou China
78 B2 Ḩā'il Saudi Arabia
92 H2 Hailuoto i. Fin.
71 B4 Hainan prov. China
69 D3 Hainan Dao i. China
128 A1 Haines U.S.A.
128 A1 Haines Junction Can.
101 E2 Hainich ridge Ger.
101 E2 Hainleite ridge Ger.
62 B1 Hai Phong Vietnam
147 C3 Haiti country West Indies
116 B3 Haiya Sudan
103 E2 Hajdúböszörmény Hungary
78 B3 Ḩajjah Yemen
79 C2 Ḩājjīābād Iran
62 A1 Hakha Myanmar
81 C2 Hakkâri Turkey
66 D2 Hakodate Japan
Ḩalab Syria see Aleppo
78 B2 Ḩalabān Saudi Arabia
81 C2 Ḩalabjah/Helebce Iraq
116 B2 Ḩalā'ib Sudan
78 A2 Halaib Triangle terr. Egypt
79 C3 Ḩalāniyat, Juzur al is Oman
78 A2 Ḩalat 'Ammār Saudi Arabia
101 E2 Halberstadt Ger.
64 B1 Halcon, Mount Phil.
93 F4 Halden Norway
101 E1 Haldensleben Ger.
75 B2 Haldwani India
79 C2 Ḩāleh Iran
54 A3 Halfmoon Bay N.Z.
131 D2 Halifax Can.
98 C2 Halifax U.K.
141 D3 Halifax U.S.A.
65 B3 Halla-san mt. S. Korea
127 F2 Hall Beach Can.
100 B2 Halle Belgium
101 E2 Halle (Saale) Ger.
102 C2 Hallein Austria
137 D1 Hallock U.S.A.
127 G2 Hall Peninsula Can.
50 B1 Halls Creek Austr.
59 C2 Halmahera i. Indon.
93 F4 Halmstad Sweden
62 B1 Ha Long Vietnam
67 B4 Hamada Japan
81 C2 Hamadān Iran
80 B2 Ḩamāh Syria
67 C4 Hamamatsu Japan
93 F3 Hamar Norway
116 B2 Ḩamātah, Jabal mt. Egypt
73 C4 Hambantota Sri Lanka
101 D1 Hamburg Ger.
78 A2 Ḩamḑ, Wādī al watercourse Saudi Arabia
78 B3 Ḩamdah Saudi Arabia
93 H3 Hämeenlinna Fin.
101 D1 Hameln Ger.

Hamersley Range

50 A2 Hamersley Range *mts* Austr.
65 B2 Hamhŭng N. Korea
68 C2 Hami China
118 B2 Hamid Sudan
52 B3 Hamilton Austr.
130 C2 Hamilton Can.
54 C1 Hamilton N.Z.
96 B3 Hamilton U.K.
142 C2 Hamilton AL U.S.A.
134 D1 Hamilton MT U.S.A.
140 C3 Hamilton OH U.S.A.
93 I3 Hamina Fin.
100 C2 Hamm Ger.
81 C2 Ḩammār, Hawr al *imp. l.* Iraq
101 D2 Hammelburg Ger.
92 G3 Hammerdal Sweden
92 H1 Hammerfest Norway
142 B2 Hammond U.S.A.
141 E3 Hammonton U.S.A.
115 D2 Ḩamrā', Al Ḩamādah al *plat.* Libya

78 A2 Ḩanak Saudi Arabia
66 D3 Hanamaki Japan
101 D2 Hanau Ger.
69 D2 Hanbogd Mongolia
70 B2 Hancheng China
140 B1 Hancock U.S.A.
70 B2 Handan China
135 C3 Hanford U.S.A.
68 C1 Hangayn Nuruu *mts* Mongolia
Hanggin Houqi China see Xamba
Hangö Fin. see Hanko
70 C2 Hangzhou China
70 C2 Hangzhou Wan *b.* China
Hanjia China see Pengshui
Hanjiang China see Yangzhou
93 H4 Hanko Fin.
135 D3 Hanksville U.S.A.
54 B2 Hanmer Springs N.Z.
129 C2 Hanna Can.
137 E3 Hannibal U.S.A.
101 D1 Hannover Ger.
101 D2 Hannoversch Münden Ger.
93 F4 Hanöbukten *b.* Sweden
62 B1 Ha Nôi Vietnam
Hanoi Vietnam see Ha Nôi
130 B2 Hanover Can.
122 B3 Hanover S. Africa
93 E4 Hanstholm Denmark
88 C3 Hantsavichy Belarus
75 C2 Hanumana India
74 B2 Hanumangarh India
70 A2 Hanzhong China
92 H2 Haparanda Sweden
100 B2 Hapert Neth.
131 D1 Happy Valley-Goose Bay Can.

78 A2 Ḩaql Saudi Arabia
79 B2 Ḩaraḍh Saudi Arabia
88 C2 Haradok Belarus
78 B3 Ḩarajā Saudi Arabia
121 C2 Harare Zimbabwe
79 C3 Ḩarāsīs, Jiddat al *des.* Oman
69 E1 Harbin China
131 E2 Harbour Breton Can.
74 B2 Harda India
Hardangerfjorden *sea chan.* Norway
100 C1 Hardenberg Neth.
100 B1 Harderwijk Neth.
122 A3 Hardeveld *mts* S. Africa
134 E1 Hardin U.S.A.
128 C1 Hardisty Lake Can.
100 C1 Haren (Ems) Ger.
117 C4 Härer Eth.
117 C4 Hargeysa Somalia

110 C1 Harghita-Mădăraș, Vârful *mt.* Romania
68 C2 Har Hu *l.* China
74 B1 Haripur Pak.
74 A1 Hari Rud *r.* Afgh./Iran
100 B1 Harlingen Neth.
139 D3 Harlingen U.S.A.
99 D3 Harlow U.K.
134 E1 Harlowton U.S.A.
110 C2 Harmanli Bulg.
134 C2 Harney Basin U.S.A.
134 C2 Harney Lake U.S.A.
93 G3 Härnösand Sweden
69 E1 Har Nur China
68 C1 Har Nuur *l.* Mongolia
114 B4 Harper Liberia
101 D1 Harpstedt Ger.
130 C1 Harricana, Rivière d' *r.* Can.
53 D2 Harrington Austr.
131 E1 Harrington Harbour Can.
96 A2 Harris, Sound of *sea chan.* U.K.

140 B3 Harrisburg IL U.S.A.
141 D2 Harrisburg PA U.S.A.
123 C2 Harrismith S. Africa
142 B1 Harrison U.S.A.
131 E1 Harrison, Cape Can.
126 A3 Harrison Bay U.S.A.
141 D3 Harrisonburg U.S.A.
137 E3 Harrisonville U.S.A.
98 C2 Harrogate U.K.
110 C2 Hârșova Romania
92 G2 Harstad Norway
122 B2 Hartbees *watercourse* S. Africa
103 D2 Hartberg Austria
141 E2 Hartford U.S.A.
99 A3 Hartland Point U.K.
98 C1 Hartlepool U.K.
128 B2 Hartley Bay Can.
123 B2 Harts *r.* S. Africa
143 D2 Hartwell Reservoir U.S.A.
68 C1 Har Us Nuur *l.* Mongolia
136 C1 Harvey U.S.A.
99 D3 Harwich U.K.
101 E2 Harz *hills* Ger.
110 C2 Haskovo Bulg.
73 B3 Hassan India
100 B2 Hasselt Belgium
115 C1 Hassi Messaoud Alg.
93 F4 Hässleholm Sweden
100 B2 Hastière-Lavaux Belgium
53 C3 Hastings Austr.
54 C1 Hastings N.Z.
99 D3 Hastings U.K.
137 E2 Hastings MN U.S.A.
137 D2 Hastings NE U.S.A.
Hatay Turkey see Antakya
129 D2 Hatchet Lake Can.
52 B2 Hatfield Austr.
68 C1 Hatgal Mongolia
62 B2 Ha Tinh Vietnam
143 E1 Hatteras, Cape U.S.A.
142 C2 Hattiesburg U.S.A.
100 C2 Hattingen Ger.
63 B3 Hat Yai Thai.
117 C4 Haud *reg.* Eth.
93 E4 Haugesund Norway
93 E4 Haukeligrend Norway
92 I2 Haukipudas Fin.
54 C1 Hauraki Gulf/Tikapa Moana N.Z.
114 B1 Haut Atlas *mts* Morocco
131 D2 Hauterive Can.
114 B1 Hauts Plateaux Alg.
146 B2 Havana Cuba
99 C3 Havant U.K.
101 E1 Havel *r.* Ger.
101 F1 Havelberg Ger.

54 B2 Havelock N.Z.
54 C1 Havelock North N.Z.
99 A3 Haverfordwest U.K.
103 D2 Havlíčkův Brod Czechia
92 H1 Havøysund Norway
111 C3 Havran Turkey
134 E1 Havre U.S.A.
131 D2 Havre-Aubert Can.
131 D1 Havre-St-Pierre Can.
124 E5 Hawai'i *i.* U.S.A.
124 E5 Hawai'ian Islands N. Pacific Ocean
98 B2 Hawarden U.K.
54 A2 Hawea, Lake N.Z.
54 B1 Hawera N.Z.
98 B1 Hawes U.K.
96 C3 Hawick U.K.
54 C1 Hawke Bay N.Z.
52 A2 Hawker Austr.
52 B1 Hawkers Gate Austr.
135 C3 Hawthorne U.S.A.
52 B2 Hay Austr.
128 C1 Hay *r.* Can.
134 C1 Hayden U.S.A.
129 E2 Hayes *r. Man.* Can.
126 E2 Hayes *r. Nunavut* Can.
79 C3 Haymā' Oman
77 C2 Hayotboshi tog'i *mt.* Uzbek.
111 C2 Hayrabolu Turkey
128 C1 Hay River Can.
137 D3 Hays U.S.A.
78 B3 Ḩays Yemen
90 B2 Haysyn Ukr.
99 C3 Haywards Heath U.K.
81 D2 Hazar Turkm.
74 A1 Hazārah Jāt *reg.* Afgh.
140 C3 Hazard U.S.A.
75 C2 Hazaribag India
75 C2 Hazaribagh Range *mts* India
128 B2 Hazelton Can.
141 D2 Hazleton U.S.A.
78 B3 Ḩazm al Jawf Yemen
53 C3 Healesville Austr.
130 B2 Hearst Can.
70 B2 Hebei *prov.* China
53 C1 Hebel Austr.
142 B1 Heber Springs U.S.A.
131 D1 Hebron Can.
128 A2 Hecate Strait Can.
71 A3 Hechi China
93 F3 Hede Sweden
100 B1 Heerenveen Neth.
100 B1 Heerhugowaard Neth.
100 B2 Heerlen Neth.
Hefa Israel see Haifa
70 B2 Hefei China
70 B3 Hefeng China
69 E1 Hegang China
102 B1 Heide Ger.
122 A1 Heide Namibia
102 B2 Heidelberg Ger.
123 B3 Heidelberg S. Africa
102 B2 Heilbronn Ger.
69 E1 Heilong Jiang *r.* China
93 I3 Heinola Fin.
92 F3 Helagsfjället *mt.* Sweden
Helebce Iraq see Ḩalabjah/ Helebce
142 B2 Helena AR U.S.A.
134 D1 Helena MT U.S.A.
96 B2 Helensburgh U.K.
102 B1 Helgoland *i.* Ger.
102 B1 Helgoländer Bucht *g.* Ger.
Helixi China see Ningguo
92 □A3 Hella Iceland
100 B2 Hellevoetsluis Neth.
107 C2 Hellín Spain
76 C3 Helmand *r.* Afgh.

101 E2 **Helmbrechts** Ger.
122 A2 **Helmeringhausen** Namibia
100 B2 **Helmond** Neth.
96 C1 **Helmsdale** U.K.
96 C1 **Helmsdale** *r.* U.K.
101 E1 **Helmstedt** Ger.
65 B1 **Helong** China
93 F4 **Helsingborg** Sweden
Helsingfors Fin. *see* **Helsinki**
93 F4 **Helsingør** Denmark
93 H3 **Helsinki** Fin.
97 C2 **Helvick Head** Ireland
99 C3 **Hemel Hempstead** U.K.
101 D1 **Hemmoor** Ger.
92 F2 **Hemnesberget** Norway
70 B2 **Henan** *prov.* China
140 B3 **Henderson** *KY* U.S.A.
143 E1 **Henderson** *NC* U.S.A.
135 D3 **Henderson** *NV* U.S.A.
139 E2 **Henderson** *TX* U.S.A.
143 D1 **Hendersonville** U.S.A.
99 C3 **Hendon** U.K.
62 A1 **Hengduan Shan** *mts* China
100 C1 **Hengelo** Neth.
70 B2 **Hengshui** China
71 A3 **Hengxian** China
71 B3 **Hengyang** China
Hengzhou China *see* **Hengxian**
91 C2 **Heniches'k** Ukr.
100 C2 **Hennef (Sieg)** Ger.
130 B1 **Henrietta Maria, Cape** Can.
139 D1 **Henryetta** U.S.A.
127 G2 **Henry Kater, Cape** Can.
101 D1 **Henstedt-Ulzburg** Ger.
120 A3 **Hentiesbaai** Namibia
71 A3 **Hepu** China
76 C3 **Herāt** Afgh.
129 D2 **Herbert** Can.
101 D2 **Herbstein** Ger.
99 B2 **Hereford** U.K.
139 C2 **Hereford** U.S.A.
101 D1 **Herford** Ger.
100 C2 **Herkenbosch** Neth.
96 □ **Herma Ness** *hd* U.K.
122 A3 **Hermanus** S. Africa
53 C2 **Hermidale** Austr.
134 C1 **Hermiston** U.S.A.
59 D3 **Hermit Islands** P.N.G.
144 A2 **Hermosillo** Mex.
154 B3 **Hernandarias** Para.
100 C2 **Herne** Ger.
93 E4 **Herning** Denmark
99 C3 **Hertford** U.K.
123 C2 **Hertzogville** S. Africa
51 E2 **Hervey Bay** Austr.
101 F2 **Herzberg (Elster)** Ger.
101 E3 **Herzogenaurach** Ger.
71 A3 **Heshan** China
128 A1 **Hess** *r.* Can.
101 D2 **Hessisch Lichtenau** Ger.
136 C1 **Hettinger** U.S.A.
101 E2 **Hettstedt** Ger.
Hewlêr Iraq *see* **Arbīl/Hewlêr**
98 B1 **Hexham** U.K.
71 B3 **Heyuan** China
52 B3 **Heywood** Austr.
70 B2 **Heze** China
71 B3 **Hezhou** China
137 D3 **Hiawatha** U.S.A.
137 E1 **Hibbing** U.S.A.
54 C1 **Hicks Bay** N.Z.
66 D2 **Hidaka-sanmyaku** *mts* Japan
145 C2 **Hidalgo** Mex.
144 B2 **Hidalgo del Parral** Mex.
154 C1 **Hidrolândia** Brazil
High Atlas *mts* Morocco *see* **Haut Atlas**
134 B2 **High Desert** U.S.A.
128 C2 **High Level** Can.
143 E1 **High Point** U.S.A.
128 C2 **High Prairie** Can.
128 C2 **High River** Can.
129 D2 **Highrock Lake** Can.
99 C3 **High Wycombe** U.K.
88 B2 **Hiiumaa** *i.* Estonia
78 A2 **Hijaz** *reg.* Saudi Arabia
54 C1 **Hikurangi** *mt.* N.Z.
101 E2 **Hildburghausen** Ger.
101 E2 **Hilders** Ger.
101 D1 **Hildesheim** Ger.
81 C2 **Hillah** Iraq
100 C2 **Hillesheim** Ger.
140 C3 **Hillsboro** *OH* U.S.A.
139 D2 **Hillsboro** *TX* U.S.A.
53 C2 **Hillston** Austr.
143 D2 **Hilton Head Island** U.S.A.
100 B1 **Hilversum** Neth.
68 B2 **Himalaya** *mts* Asia
67 B4 **Himeji** Japan
123 C2 **Himeville** S. Africa
51 D1 **Hinchinbrook Island** Austr.
74 A1 **Hindu Kush** *mts* Afgh./Pak.
143 D2 **Hinesville** U.S.A.
75 B2 **Hinganghat** India
81 C2 **Hınıs** Turkey
92 G2 **Hinnøya** *i.* Norway
106 B2 **Hinojosa del Duque** Spain
62 A2 **Hinthada** Myanmar
128 C2 **Hinton** Can.
75 C2 **Hirakud Reservoir** India
66 D2 **Hirosaki** Japan
67 B4 **Hiroshima** Japan
101 E3 **Hirschaid** Ger.
101 E2 **Hirschberg** Ger.
105 C2 **Hirson** France
93 E4 **Hirtshals** Denmark
74 B2 **Hisar** India
147 C2 **Hispaniola** *i.* Caribbean Sea
81 C2 **Hīt** Iraq
67 D3 **Hitachi** Japan
67 D3 **Hitachinaka** Japan
92 E3 **Hitra** *i.* Norway
49 I3 **Hiva Oa** *i.* Fr. Polynesia
93 G4 **Hjälmaren** *l.* Sweden
129 D1 **Hjalmar Lake** Can.
93 F4 **Hjørring** Denmark
123 D2 **Hlabisa** S. Africa
92 □B2 **Hlíð** Iceland
91 C2 **Hlobyne** Ukr.
123 C2 **Hlohlowane** S. Africa
123 C2 **Hlotse** Lesotho
91 C1 **Hlukhiv** Ukr.
88 C2 **Hlybokaye** Belarus
114 C4 **Ho** Ghana
62 B2 **Hoa Binh** Vietnam
122 A1 **Hoachanas** Namibia
51 D4 **Hobart** Austr.
139 D1 **Hobart** U.S.A.
139 C2 **Hobbs** U.S.A.
93 E4 **Hobro** Denmark
117 C4 **Hobyo** Somalia
63 B2 **Ho Chi Minh City** Vietnam
114 B3 **Ḥôḍ** *reg.* Maur.
78 B3 **Hodeidah** Yemen
103 E2 **Hódmezővásárhely** Hungary
Hoek van Holland Neth. *see* **Hook of Holland**
65 B2 **Hoeyang** N. Korea
101 E2 **Hof** Ger.
101 E2 **Hofheim in Unterfranken** Ger.
92 □B3 **Höfn** *Austurland* Iceland
92 □A2 **Höfn** *Vestfirðir* Iceland
92 □B3 **Hofsjökull** Iceland
67 B4 **Hōfu** Japan
93 G4 **Högsby** Sweden
101 D2 **Hohe Rhön** *mts* Ger.
70 B1 **Hohhot** China
75 C1 **Hoh Xil Shan** *mts* China
63 B2 **Hôi An** Vietnam
62 A1 **Hojai** India
54 B2 **Hokitika** N.Z.
66 D2 **Hokkaidō** *i.* Japan
128 B2 **Holberg** Can.
138 A2 **Holbrook** U.S.A.
137 D2 **Holdrege** U.S.A.
146 C2 **Holguín** Cuba
92 □B2 **Hóll** Iceland
Holland *country* Europe *see* **Netherlands**
140 B2 **Holland** U.S.A.
100 B1 **Hollum** Neth.
142 C2 **Holly Springs** U.S.A.
134 C4 **Hollywood** *CA* U.S.A.
143 D3 **Hollywood** *FL* U.S.A.
92 F2 **Holm** Norway
92 H3 **Holmsund** Sweden
122 A2 **Holoog** Namibia
93 E4 **Holstebro** Denmark
143 D1 **Holston** *r.* U.S.A.
98 A2 **Holyhead** U.K.
98 C1 **Holy Island** *England* U.K.
98 A2 **Holy Island** *Wales* U.K.
136 C2 **Holyoke** U.S.A.
101 D2 **Holzminden** Ger.
62 A1 **Homalin** Myanmar
101 D2 **Homberg (Efze)** Ger.
114 B3 **Hombori** Mali
127 G2 **Home Bay** Can.
143 D3 **Homestead** U.S.A.
92 F3 **Hommelvik** Norway
80 B2 **Homs** Syria
89 D3 **Homyel'/Gomel'** Belarus
122 A3 **Hondeklipbaai** S. Africa
145 D3 **Hondo** *r.* Belize/Mex.
139 D3 **Hondo** U.S.A.
146 B3 **Honduras** *country* Central America
93 F3 **Hønefoss** Norway
135 B2 **Honey Lake** U.S.A.
104 C2 **Honfleur** France
70 B3 **Honghu** China
71 A3 **Hongjiang** China
69 D3 **Hong Kong** China
71 B3 **Hong Kong** *aut. reg.* China
65 B1 **Hongwŏn** N. Korea
70 B2 **Hongze Hu** *l.* China
49 E3 **Honiara** Solomon Is
92 I1 **Honningsvåg** Norway
67 B3 **Honshū** *i.* Japan
134 B1 **Hood, Mount** *vol.* U.S.A.
50 A3 **Hood Point** Austr.
134 B1 **Hood River** U.S.A.
100 C1 **Hoogeveen** Neth.
100 C1 **Hoogezand-Sappemeer** Neth.
100 C2 **Hoog-Keppel** Neth.
100 B2 **Hook of Holland** Neth.
128 A2 **Hoonah** U.S.A.
100 B1 **Hoorn** Neth.
128 B3 **Hope** Can.
142 B2 **Hope** U.S.A.
83 N2 **Hope, Point** U.S.A.
131 D1 **Hopedale** Can.
131 D1 **Hope Mountains** Can.
52 B3 **Hopetoun** Austr.
122 B2 **Hopetown** S. Africa
141 D3 **Hopewell** U.S.A.
130 C1 **Hopewell Islands** Can.
50 B2 **Hopkins, Lake** *imp. l.* Austr.
140 B3 **Hopkinsville** U.S.A.
134 B1 **Hoquiam** U.S.A.
81 C1 **Horasan** Turkey
93 F4 **Hörby** Sweden

91	C2	Horishni Plavni Ukr.
89	D3	Horki Belarus
91	C2	Horlivka Ukr.
79	D2	Hormak Iran
79	C2	Hormuz, Strait of Iran/Oman
103	D2	Horn Austria
92	□A2	Horn c. Iceland
153	B6	Horn, Cape Chile
141	D2	Hornell U.S.A.
130	B2	Hornepayne Can.
98	C2	Hornsea U.K.
90	B2	Horodenka Ukr.
91	C1	Horodnya Ukr.
90	B2	Horodok Khmel'nyts'ka Oblast' Ukr.
90	A2	Horodok L'vivs'ka Oblast' Ukr.
90	A1	Horokhiv Ukr.
		Horqin Youyi Qianqi China see Ulanhot
131	E1	Horse Islands Can.
52	B3	Horsham Austr.
126	C2	Horton r. Can.
117	B4	Hosa'ina Eth.
74	A2	Hoshab Pak.
74	B1	Hoshiarpur India
77	E3	Hotan China
122	B2	Hotazel S. Africa
142	B2	Hot Springs AR U.S.A.
136	C2	Hot Springs SD U.S.A.
128	C1	Hottah Lake Can.
62	B1	Houayxay Laos
100	B2	Houffalize Belgium
70	B2	Houma China
142	B3	Houma U.S.A.
128	B2	Houston Can.
139	D3	Houston U.S.A.
122	B3	Houwater S. Africa
68	C1	Hovd Mongolia
99	C3	Hove U.K.
68	C1	Hövsgöl Nuur l. Mongolia
116	A3	Howar, Wadi watercourse Sudan
53	C3	Howe, Cape Austr.
49	G2	Howland Island N. Pacific Ocean
53	C3	Howlong Austr.
101	D2	Höxter Ger.
96	C1	Hoy i. U.K.
93	E3	Høyanger Norway
102	C1	Hoyerswerda Ger.
62	A2	Hpapun Myanmar
103	D1	Hradec Králové Czechia
109	C2	Hrasnica Bos. & Herz.
91	C1	Hrebinka Ukr.
88	B3	Hrodna/Grodno Belarus
62	A1	Hsi-hseng Myanmar
71	C3	Hsinchu Taiwan
62	A1	Hsipaw Myanmar
70	A2	Huachi China
150	A3	Huacho Peru
69	D2	Huade China
65	B1	Huadian China
70	B2	Huai'an China
71	A3	Huaihua China
70	B2	Huainan China
70	B2	Huaiyang China
145	C3	Huajuápan de León Mex.
		Hualian Taiwan see Hualien
71	C3	Hualien Taiwan
150	A2	Huallaga r. Peru
120	A2	Huambo Angola
150	A3	Huancayo Peru
		Huangcaoba China see Xingyi
70	B2	Huangchuan China
		Huang Hai sea N. Pacific Ocean see Yellow Sea
		Huang He r. China see Yellow River
71	A4	Huangliu China
70	B3	Huangshan China
70	B2	Huangshi China
70	A2	Huangtu Gaoyuan plat. China
71	C3	Huangyan China
65	B1	Huanren China
150	A2	Huánuco Peru
152	B2	Huanuni Bol.
150	A2	Huaraz Peru
150	A3	Huarmey Peru
152	A3	Huasco Chile
152	A3	Huasco r. Chile
144	B2	Huatabampo Mex.
145	C3	Huatusco Mex.
71	A3	Huayuan China
73	B3	Hubballi India
70	B2	Hubei prov. China
		Hubli India see Hubballi
100	C2	Hückelhoven Ger.
98	C2	Hucknall U.K.
98	C2	Huddersfield U.K.
93	G3	Hudiksvall Sweden
141	E2	Hudson r. U.S.A.
129	D2	Hudson Bay Can.
127	F3	Hudson Bay sea Can.
128	B2	Hudson's Hope Can.
127	G2	Hudson Strait Can.
63	B2	Huê Vietnam
146	A3	Huehuetenango Guat.
144	B2	Huehueto, Cerro mt. Mex.
145	C2	Huejutla Mex.
106	B2	Huelva Spain
107	C2	Huércal-Overa Spain
107	C1	Huesca Spain
106	C2	Huéscar Spain
50	B3	Hughes (abandoned) Austr.
139	D2	Hugo U.S.A.
122	B2	Huhudi S. Africa
122	A2	Huib-Hoch Plateau Namibia
71	B3	Huichang China
65	B1	Huich'ŏn N. Korea
120	A2	Huíla, Planalto da Angola
71	B3	Huilai China
62	B1	Huili China
65	B1	Huinan China
93	H3	Huittinen Fin.
145	C3	Huixtla Mex.
		Huiyang China see Huizhou
62	B1	Huize China
71	B3	Huizhou China
78	B2	Hujr Saudi Arabia
122	B1	Hukuntsi Botswana
78	B2	Hulayfah Saudi Arabia
66	B1	Hulin China
130	C2	Hull Can.
		Hull China see Hulun Buir
69	D1	Hulun Buir China
69	D1	Hulun Nur l. China
91	D2	Hulyaypole Ukr.
69	E1	Huma China
150	B2	Humaitá Brazil
122	B3	Humansdorp S. Africa
98	C2	Humber est. U.K.
126	D3	Humboldt Can.
142	C1	Humboldt U.S.A.
135	C2	Humboldt r. U.S.A.
103	E2	Humenné Slovakia
53	C3	Hume Reservoir Austr.
138	A1	Humphreys Peak U.S.A.
92	□A2	Húnaflói b. Iceland
71	B3	Hunan prov. China
65	C1	Hunchun China
110	B1	Hunedoara Romania
101	D2	Hünfeld Ger.
103	D2	Hungary country Europe
52	B1	Hungerford Austr.
65	B2	Hüngnam N. Korea
65	A1	Hun He r. China
99	D2	Hunstanton U.K.
101	D1	Hunte r. Ger.
51	D4	Hunter Islands Austr.
99	C2	Huntingdon U.K.
140	B2	Huntington IN U.S.A.
140	C3	Huntington WV U.S.A.
54	C1	Huntly N.Z.
96	C2	Huntly U.K.
130	C2	Huntsville Can.
142	C2	Huntsville AL U.S.A.
139	D2	Huntsville TX U.S.A.
59	D3	Huon Peninsula P.N.G.
70	B2	Huozhou China
116	B2	Hurghada Egypt
137	D2	Huron U.S.A.
140	C2	Huron, Lake Can./U.S.A.
135	D3	Hurricane U.S.A.
92	□B2	Húsavík Iceland
110	C1	Huşi Romania
126	A2	Huslia U.S.A.
78	B3	Ḩuşn Al 'Abr Yemen
102	B1	Husum Ger.
69	C1	Hutag-Öndör Mongolia
60	A1	Hutanopan Indon.
137	D3	Hutchinson U.S.A.
70	C2	Huzhou China
92	□C3	Hvalnes Iceland
92	□B3	Hvannadalshnúkur vol. Iceland
109	C2	Hvar i. Croatia
120	B2	Hwange Zimbabwe
136	C2	Hyannis U.S.A.
68	C1	Hyargas Nuur salt l. Mongol.
50	A3	Hyden Austr.
73	B3	Hyderabad India
74	A2	Hyderabad Pak.
105	D3	Hyères France
105	D3	Hyères, Îles d' is France
65	B1	Hyesan N. Korea
128	B2	Hyland Post Can.
67	B3	Hyōno-sen mt. Japan
99	D3	Hythe U.K.
93	H3	Hyvinkää Fin.

I

150	B2	Iaco r. Brazil
110	C2	Ialomiţa r. Romania
110	C1	Ianca Romania
110	C1	Iaşi Romania
64	A1	Iba Phil.
115	C4	Ibadan Nigeria
150	A1	Ibagué Col.
150	A1	Ibarra Ecuador
78	B3	Ibb Yemen
100	C1	Ibbenbüren Ger.
115	C4	Ibi Nigeria
155	C1	Ibiá Brazil
155	D1	Ibiraçu Brazil
107	D2	Ibiza Spain
107	D2	Ibiza i. Spain
151	D3	Ibotirama Brazil
79	C2	Ibrā' Oman
79	C2	Ibrī Oman
150	A3	Ica Peru
92	□B2	Iceland country Europe
66	D3	Ichinoseki Japan
91	C1	Ichki Ukr.
91	C1	Ichnya Ukr.
65	B2	Ich'ŏn N. Korea
139	E2	Idabel U.S.A.
134	D2	Idaho state U.S.A.
134	D2	Idaho Falls U.S.A.
100	C3	Idar-Oberstein Ger.
116	B2	Idfū Egypt
118	B3	Idiofa Dem. Rep. Congo

80 B2 **Idlib** Syria
154 B2 **Iepê** Brazil
100 A2 **Ieper** Belgium
119 D3 **Ifakara** Tanz.
121 □D3 **Ifanadiana** Madag.
115 C4 **Ife** Nigeria
114 C3 **Ifôghas, Adrar des** *hills* Mali
61 C1 **Igan** *Sarawak* Malaysia
154 C2 **Igarapava** Brazil
82 G2 **Igarka** Russia
74 B3 **Igatpuri** India
81 C2 **Iğdır** Turkey
108 A3 **Iglesias** *Sardinia* Italy
127 F2 **Igloolik** Can.
Igluligaarjuk Can. *see* **Chesterfield Inlet**
130 A2 **Ignace** Can.
88 C2 **Ignalina** Lith.
110 C2 **İğneada** Turkey
111 B3 **Igoumenitsa** Greece
86 E3 **Igra** Russia
86 F2 **Igrim** Russia
154 B3 **Iguaçu** *r.* Brazil
154 B3 **Iguaçu Falls** Arg./Brazil
145 C3 **Iguala** Mex.
107 D1 **Igualada** Spain
154 C2 **Iguape** Brazil
154 B2 **Iguatemi** Brazil
154 B2 **Iguatemi** *r.* Brazil
151 E2 **Iguatu** Brazil
118 A3 **Iguéla** Gabon
119 D3 **Igunga** Tanz.
121 □D3 **Ihosy** Madag.
110 B2 **Ihtiman** Bulg.
92 I3 **Iisalmi** Fin.
115 C4 **Ijebu-Ode** Nigeria
100 B1 **IJmuiden** Neth.
100 B1 **IJssel** *r.* Neth.
100 B1 **IJsselmeer** *l.* Neth.
123 C2 **Ikageng** S. Africa
111 C3 **Ikaria** *i.* Greece
118 C3 **Ikela** Dem. Rep. Congo
67 A4 **Iki-shima** *i.* Japan
121 □D3 **Ikongo** Madag.
65 B2 **Iksan** S. Korea
64 B1 **Ilagan** Phil.
81 C2 **Īlām** Iran
75 C2 **Ilam** Nepal
103 D1 **Iława** Pol.
79 C2 **Ilazārān, Kūh-e** *mt.* Iran
129 D2 **Île-à-la-Crosse** Can.
129 D2 **Île-à-la-Crosse, Lac** *l.* Can.
118 C3 **Ilebo** Dem. Rep. Congo
124 H6 **Île Clipperton** *terr.* N. Pacific Ocean
119 D2 **Ileret** Kenya
113 K11 **Îles Crozet** *is* Indian Ocean
49 I3 **Îles du Désappointement** *is* Fr. Polynesia
49 I4 **Îles Gambier** *is* Fr. Polynesia
99 D3 **Ilford** U.K.
99 A3 **Ilfracombe** U.K.
154 B2 **Ilha Grande** *resr* Brazil
155 D2 **Ilha Grande, Baía da** *b.* Brazil
154 B2 **Ilha Solteíra, Represa** *resr* Brazil
106 B1 **Ílhavo** Port.
151 E3 **Ilhéus** Brazil
64 B2 **Iligan** Phil.
152 A4 **Illapel** Chile
Illichivs'k Ukr. *see* **Chornomors'k**
140 A3 **Illinois** *r.* U.S.A.
140 B3 **Illinois** *state* U.S.A.
90 B2 **Illintsi** Ukr.
115 C2 **Illizi** Alg.
89 D2 **Il'men', Ozero** *l.* Russia
101 E2 **Ilmenau** Ger.
150 A3 **Ilo** Peru
64 B1 **Iloilo** Phil.
92 J3 **Ilomantsi** Fin.
115 C4 **Ilorin** Nigeria
53 D1 **Iluka** Austr.
127 H2 **Ilulissat** Greenland
59 C3 **Ilwaki** Indon.
67 A4 **Imari** Japan
117 C4 **Īmī** Eth.
108 B2 **Imola** Italy
151 D2 **Imperatriz** Brazil
136 C2 **Imperial** U.S.A.
118 B2 **Impfondo** Congo
62 A1 **Imphal** India
111 C2 **İmroz** Turkey
150 B3 **Inambari** *r.* Peru
115 C2 **In Aménas** Alg.
59 C3 **Inanwatan** Indon.
92 I2 **Inari** Fin.
92 I2 **Inarijärvi** *l.* Fin.
67 D3 **Inawashiro-ko** *l.* Japan
80 B1 **İnce Burun** *pt* Turkey
65 B2 **Incheon** S. Korea
123 D2 **Incomati** *r.* Moz.
78 A3 **Inda Silasē** Eth.
144 B2 **Indé** Mex.
135 C3 **Independence** *CA* U.S.A.
137 E2 **Independence** *IA* U.S.A.
137 D3 **Independence** *KS* U.S.A.
137 E3 **Independence** *MO* U.S.A.
134 C2 **Independence Mountains** U.S.A.
76 B2 **Inderbor** Kazakh.
72 B2 **India** *country* Asia
141 D2 **Indiana** U.S.A.
140 B2 **Indiana** *state* U.S.A.
140 B3 **Indianapolis** U.S.A.
129 D2 **Indian Head** Can.
159 **Indian Ocean** World
137 E2 **Indianola** *IA* U.S.A.
142 B2 **Indianola** *MS* U.S.A.
135 C3 **Indian Springs** U.S.A.
86 D2 **Indiga** Russia
83 K2 **Indigirka** *r.* Russia
109 D1 **Inđija** Serbia
135 C4 **Indio** U.S.A.
74 B2 **Indira Gandhi Nahar** India
58 B3 **Indonesia** *country* Asia
74 B2 **Indore** India
61 B2 **Indramayu, Tanjung** *pt* Indon.
104 C2 **Indre** *r.* France
74 A2 **Indus** *r.* China/Pak.
74 A2 **Indus, Mouths of the** Pak.
80 B1 **İnebolu** Turkey
111 C2 **İnegöl** Turkey
144 B3 **Infiernillo, Presa** *resr* Mex.
53 D1 **Inglewood** Austr.
102 C2 **Ingolstadt** Ger.
75 C2 **Ingraj Bazar** India
123 D2 **Inhaca** Moz.
121 C3 **Inhambane** Moz.
150 B1 **Inírida** Col.
97 A2 **Inishbofin** *i.* Ireland
97 B2 **Inishmore** *i.* Ireland
97 C1 **Inishowen** *pen.* Ireland
54 B2 **Inland Kaikoura Range** *mts* N.Z.
102 C2 **Inn** *r.* Europe
127 G1 **Innaanganeq** *c.* Greenland
Inner Mongolia *aut. reg.* China *see* **Nei Mongol Zizhiqu**
96 B2 **Inner Sound** *sea chan.* U.K.
51 D1 **Innisfail** Austr.
102 C2 **Innsbruck** Austria
154 B1 **Inocência** Brazil
118 B3 **Inongo** Dem. Rep. Congo
103 D1 **Inowrocław** Pol.
114 C2 **In Salah** Alg.
62 A2 **Insein** Myanmar
86 F2 **Inta** Russia
137 E1 **International Falls** U.S.A.
130 C1 **Inukjuak** Can.
126 C2 **Inuvik** Can.
96 B2 **Inveraray** U.K.
54 A3 **Invercargill** N.Z.
53 D1 **Inverell** Austr.
96 B2 **Invergordon** U.K.
128 C2 **Invermere** Can.
131 D2 **Inverness** Can.
96 B2 **Inverness** U.K.
96 C2 **Inverurie** U.K.
52 A3 **Investigator Strait** Austr.
77 E1 **Inya** Russia
119 D3 **Inyonga** Tanz.
87 D3 **Inza** Russia
111 B3 **Ioannina** Greece
137 D3 **Iola** U.S.A.
96 A2 **Iona** *i.* U.K.
111 B3 **Ionian Islands** Greece
109 C3 **Ionian Sea** Greece/Italy
Ionioi Nisoi *is* Greece *see* **Ionian Islands**
111 C3 **Ios** *i.* Greece
137 E2 **Iowa** *state* U.S.A.
137 E2 **Iowa City** U.S.A.
154 C1 **Ipameri** Brazil
155 D1 **Ipatinga** Brazil
81 C1 **Ipatovo** Russia
123 C2 **Ipelegeng** S. Africa
150 A1 **Ipiales** Col.
154 B3 **Ipiranga** Brazil
60 B1 **Ipoh** Malaysia
154 B1 **Iporá** Brazil
118 C2 **Ippy** C.A.R.
111 C2 **İpsala** Turkey
53 D1 **Ipswich** Austr.
99 D2 **Ipswich** U.K.
127 G2 **Iqaluit** Can.
152 A3 **Iquique** Chile
150 A2 **Iquitos** Peru
Irakleio Greece *see* **Iraklion**
111 C3 **Iraklion** Greece
76 B3 **Iran** *country* Asia
61 C1 **Iran, Pegunungan** *mts* Indon.
79 D2 **Īrānshahr** Iran
144 B2 **Irapuato** Mex.
81 C2 **Iraq** *country* Asia
154 B3 **Irati** Brazil
88 B2 **Irbe Strait** *sea chan.* Estonia/Latvia
80 B2 **Irbid** Jordan
86 F3 **Irbit** Russia
151 D3 **Irecê** Brazil
97 C2 **Ireland** *country* Europe
118 C3 **Irema** Dem. Rep. Congo
114 B3 **Irîgui** *reg.* Mali/Maur.
119 D3 **Iringa** Tanz.
151 C2 **Iriri** *r.* Brazil
95 B3 **Irish Sea** Ireland/U.K.
69 C1 **Irkutsk** Russia
52 A2 **Iron Knob** Austr.
140 B1 **Iron Mountain** U.S.A.
140 A1 **Ironwood** U.S.A.
64 B1 **Irosin** Phil.
67 C4 **Irō-zaki** *pt* Japan
90 C1 **Irpin'** Ukr.
62 A2 **Irrawaddy** *r.* Myanmar
63 A2 **Irrawaddy, Mouths of the** Myanmar
86 F2 **Irtysh** *r.* Kazakh./Russia
107 C1 **Irun** Spain
Iruña Spain *see* **Pamplona/Iruña**
96 B3 **Irvine** U.K.
64 B2 **Isabela** Phil.
146 B3 **Isabelia, Cordillera** *mts* Nic.

92	□A2	Ísafjörður Iceland
67	B4	Isahaya Japan
105	C2	Isar r. Ger.
96	□	Isbister U.K.
108	B2	Ischia, Isola d' i. Italy
67	C4	Ise Japan
118	C2	Isengi Dem. Rep. Congo
100	C2	Iserlohn Ger.
101	D1	Isernhagen Ger.
67	C4	Ise-wan b. Japan
114	C4	Iseyin Nigeria
		Isfahan Iran see Eşfahān
66	D2	Ishikari-wan b. Japan
66	D3	Ishinomaki Japan
67	D3	Ishioka Japan
140	B1	Ishpeming U.S.A.
111	C2	Işıklar Dağı mts Turkey
111	C3	Işıklı Turkey
123	D2	Isipingo S. Africa
119	C3	Isiro Dem. Rep. Congo
110	B2	Iskar r. Bulg.
80	B2	İskenderun Turkey
82	G3	Iskitim Russia
128	A2	Iskut r. Can.
74	B1	Islamabad Pak.
52	A2	Island Lagoon imp. l. Austr.
129	E2	Island Lake Can.
54	B1	Islands, Bay of N.Z.
		Islas Malvinas terr.
		S. Atlantic Ocean see
		Falkland Islands
96	A3	Islay i. U.K.
98	A1	Isle of Man i. Irish Sea
91	D2	Islyam-Terek Ukr.
77	D3	Ismoili Somoní, Qullai mt.
		Tajik.
109	C3	Isola di Capo Rizzuto Italy
110	C2	Isperih Bulg.
80	B2	Israel country Asia
105	C2	Issoire France
111	C2	İstanbul Turkey
		İstanbul Boğazı str. Turkey see
		Bosporus
111	B3	Istiaia Greece
105	D3	Istres France
108	B1	Istria pen. Croatia
151	D3	Itaberaba Brazil
155	D1	Itabira Brazil
155	D2	Itabirito Brazil
151	E3	Itabuna Brazil
150	C2	Itacoatiara Brazil
154	B2	Itaguajé Brazil
154	C2	Itaí Brazil
154	B3	Itaipu, Represa de resr Brazil
151	C2	Itaituba Brazil
152	D3	Itajaí Brazil
155	C2	Itajubá Brazil
108	B2	Italy country Europe
155	D1	Itamarandiba Brazil
155	D1	Itambacuri Brazil
155	D1	Itambé, Pico de mt. Brazil
62	A1	Itanagar India
154	C2	Itanhaém Brazil
155	D1	Itanhém Brazil
155	D1	Itaobím Brazil
154	C1	Itapajipe Brazil
155	E1	Itapebi Brazil
155	D2	Itapecuru Mirim Brazil
155	D2	Itapemirim Brazil
154	C2	Itaperuna Brazil
154	B2	Itapetinga Brazil
154	C2	Itapetininga Brazil
154	C2	Itapeva Brazil
151	E3	Itapicuru r. Brazil
154	C1	Itapuranga Brazil
154	C2	Itararé Brazil
75	B2	Itarsi India
154	B1	Itarumã Brazil

155	D2	Itaúna Brazil
71	C3	Itbayat i. Phil.
141	D2	Ithaca U.S.A.
101	D1	Ith Hils ridge Ger.
118	C2	Itimbiri r. Dem. Rep. Congo
155	D1	Itinga Brazil
154	B1	Itiquira Brazil
154	A1	Itiquira r. Brazil
67	C4	Itō Japan
154	C2	Itu Brazil
150	A2	Ituí r. Brazil
154	C1	Ituiutaba Brazil
119	C3	Itula Dem. Rep. Congo
154	C1	Itumbiara Brazil
151	C3	Iturama Brazil
101	D1	Itzehoe Ger.
83	N2	Iul'tin Russia
92	I2	Ivai r. Brazil
92	I2	Ivalo Fin.
88	C3	Ivanava Belarus
52	B2	Ivanhoe Austr.
90	B1	Ivankiv Ukr.
90	A2	Ivano-Frankivs'k Ukr.
89	F2	Ivanovo Russia
88	C3	Ivatsevichy Belarus
111	C2	Ivaylovgrad Bulg.
86	F2	Ivdel' Russia
154	B2	Ivinheima r. Brazil
154	B2	Ivinhema Brazil
127	H2	Ivittuut Greenland
		Ivory Coast country Africa see
		Côte d'Ivoire
108	A1	Ivrea Italy
111	C3	İvrindi Turkey
127	F2	Ivujivik Can.
67	D3	Iwaki Japan
67	B4	Iwakuni Japan
66	D2	Iwamizawa Japan
66	D2	Iwanai Japan
88	C3	Iwye Belarus
123	D3	Ixopo S. Africa
144	B2	Ixtlán Mex.
145	D2	Izamal Mex.
81	C1	Izberbash Russia
86	F3	Izhevsk Russia
86	F2	Izhma Russia
89	E3	Izmalkovo Russia
90	B2	Izmayil Ukr.
111	C3	İzmir Turkey
111	C2	İznik Gölü l. Turkey
152	B2	Izozog, Bañados del swamp Bol.
67	B3	Izumo Japan
90	B1	Izyaslav Ukr.
91	D2	Izyum Ukr.

J

		Jabal, Bahr el r. South Sudan/ Uganda see White Nile
106	C2	Jabalón r. Spain
75	B2	Jabalpur India
50	C1	Jabiru Austr.
109	C2	Jablanica Bos. & Herz.
151	E2	Jaboatão dos Guararapes Brazil
154	C2	Jaboticabal Brazil
107	C1	Jaca Spain
145	C2	Jacala Mex.
151	C2	Jacareacanga Brazil
155	C2	Jacareí Brazil
155	D1	Jacinto Brazil
141	E1	Jackman U.S.A.
142	C2	Jackson AL U.S.A.
140	C2	Jackson MI U.S.A.
142	B2	Jackson MS U.S.A.
142	C1	Jackson TN U.S.A.
136	A2	Jackson WY U.S.A.

54	A2	Jackson Head N.Z.
142	B2	Jacksonville AR U.S.A.
143	D2	Jacksonville FL U.S.A.
140	A3	Jacksonville IL U.S.A.
143	E2	Jacksonville NC U.S.A.
139	D2	Jacksonville TX U.S.A.
147	C3	Jacmel Haiti
74	A2	Jacobabad Pak.
151	D3	Jacobina Brazil
131	D2	Jacques-Cartier, Mont mt. Can.
151	D2	Jacundá Brazil
154	C2	Jacupiranga Brazil
109	C2	Jadovnik mt. Bos. & Herz.
150	A2	Jaén Peru
106	C2	Jaén Spain
52	A3	Jaffa, Cape Austr.
73	B4	Jaffna Sri Lanka
73	C3	Jagdalpur India
123	C2	Jagersfontein S. Africa
154	C2	Jaguariaíva Brazil
79	C2	Jahrom Iran
74	B2	Jaipur India
74	B2	Jaisalmer India
75	C2	Jajarkot Nepal
109	C2	Jajce Bos. & Herz.
60	B2	Jakarta Indon.
128	A1	Jakes Corner Can.
92	H3	Jäkkvik Sweden
93	H3	Jakobstad Fin.
77	D3	Jalālābād Afgh.
77	D3	Jalal-Abad Kyrg.
74	B1	Jalandhar India
		Jalapa Mex. see Xalapa
154	B2	Jales Brazil
74	B2	Jalgaon India
115	D4	Jalingo Nigeria
75	B3	Jalna India
144	B2	Jalpa Mex.
75	C2	Jalpaiguri India
145	C2	Jalpan Mex.
		Jalta i. Tunisia see La Galite, Île de
115	E2	Jālū Libya
146	C3	Jamaica country West Indies
146	C3	Jamaica Channel Haiti/ Jamaica
75	C2	Jamalpur Bangl.
60	B2	Jambi Indon.
137	D2	James r. ND/SD U.S.A.
141	D3	James r. VA U.S.A.
130	B1	James Bay Can.
61	C1	James Shoal S. China Sea
52	A2	Jamestown Austr.
137	D1	Jamestown ND U.S.A.
141	D2	Jamestown NY U.S.A.
74	B1	Jammu India
74	B1	Jammu and Kashmir state India
74	B2	Jamnagar India
93	I3	Jämsä Fin.
75	C2	Jamshedpur India
75	C2	Jamuna r. Bangl.
75	C2	Janakpur Nepal
155	D1	Janaúba Brazil
81	D2	Jandaq Iran
140	B2	Janesville U.S.A.
65	B3	Jangheung S. Korea
65	B3	Jangseong S. Korea
80	B2	Janin West Bank
114	A3	Janjanbureh Gambia
84	F1	Jan Mayen terr. Arctic Ocean
81	D1	Jañña Turkm.
122	B3	Jansenville S. Africa
155	D1	Januária Brazil
74	B2	Jaora India
67	C3	Japan country Asia
156	C3	Japan, Sea of N. Pacific Ocean

50 B2 **Japurá** *r.* Brazil
54 C1 **Jaraguá** Brazil
54 B2 **Jaraguari** Brazil
70 A2 **Jarantai** China
52 C3 **Jardim** Brazil
03 D1 **Jarocin** Pol.
03 E1 **Jarosław** Pol.
92 F3 **Järpen** Sweden
50 B3 **Jaru** Brazil
Jarud China *see* **Lubei**
49 H3 **Jarvis Island** S. Pacific Ocean
03 E2 **Jasło** Pol.
28 C2 **Jasper** Can.
40 B3 **Jasper** *IN* U.S.A.
39 E2 **Jasper** *TX* U.S.A.
03 D2 **Jastrzębie-Zdrój** Pol.
03 D2 **Jászberény** Hungary
54 B1 **Jataí** Brazil
74 A2 **Jati** Pak.
54 C2 **Jaú** Brazil
50 B2 **Jaú** *r.* Brazil
45 C2 **Jaumave** Mex.
75 C2 **Jaunpur** India
54 B1 **Jauru** Brazil
61 B2 **Java** *i.* Indon.
Java Sea Indon. *see* **Jawa, Laut**
Jawa *i.* Indon. *see* **Java**
59 D4 **Jawa, Laut** *sea* Indon.
17 C4 **Jawhar** Somalia
03 D1 **Jawor** Pol.
03 D1 **Jaworzno** Pol.
59 D3 **Jaya, Puncak** *mt.* Indon.
59 D3 **Jayapura** Indon.
78 B3 **Jāzān** Saudi Arabia
79 C2 **Jaz Mūrīān, Hāmūn-e** *imp. l.* Iran
28 B1 **Jean Marie River** Can.
31 D1 **Jeannin, Lac** *l.* Can.
16 A3 **Jebel Abyad Plateau** Sudan
65 B2 **Jecheon** S. Korea
96 C3 **Jedburgh** U.K.
78 A2 **Jeddah** Saudi Arabia
01 E1 **Jeetze** *r.* Ger.
35 C3 **Jefferson, Mount** U.S.A.
37 E3 **Jefferson City** U.S.A.
65 B3 **Jeju** S. Korea
65 B3 **Jeju-do** *i.* S. Korea
65 B3 **Jeju-haehyeop** *sea chan.* S. Korea
88 C2 **Jēkabpils** Latvia
03 D1 **Jelenia Góra** Pol.
88 B2 **Jelgava** Latvia
61 C2 **Jember** Indon.
01 E2 **Jena** Ger.
58 B3 **Jeneponto** Indon.
Jengish Chokusu *mt.* China/Kyrg. *see* **Pobeda Peak**
42 B2 **Jennings** U.S.A.
65 B2 **Jeonju** S. Korea
51 D3 **Jequié** Brazil
55 D1 **Jequitaí** Brazil
55 D1 **Jequitinhonha** Brazil
55 E1 **Jequitinhonha** *r.* Brazil
47 C3 **Jérémie** Haiti
44 B2 **Jerez** Mex.
06 B2 **Jerez de la Frontera** Spain
15 C1 **Jerid, Chott el** *salt l.* Tunisia
34 D2 **Jerome** U.S.A.
95 C4 **Jersey** *terr.* Channel Is
51 D2 **Jerumenha** Brazil
80 B2 **Jerusalem** Israel/West Bank
53 D3 **Jervis Bay Territory** *admin. div.* Austr.
08 B1 **Jesenice** Slovenia
08 B2 **Jesi** Italy
01 F2 **Jessen (Elster)** Ger.
75 C2 **Jessore** Bangl.
43 D2 **Jesup** U.S.A.
145 C3 **Jesús Carranza** Mex.
109 C2 **Jezercë, Maja** *mt.* Albania
74 B2 **Jhalawar** India
74 B1 **Jhang** Pak.
75 B2 **Jhansi** India
75 C2 **Jharsuguda** India
74 B1 **Jhelum** Pak.
70 C2 **Jiading** China
69 E1 **Jiamusi** China
71 B3 **Ji'an** *Jiangxi* China
65 B1 **Ji'an** *Jilin* China
62 A1 **Jianchuan** China
Jiandaoyu China *see* **Guojiaba**
70 B2 **Jiangsu** *prov.* China
71 B3 **Jiangxi** *prov.* China
70 A2 **Jiangyou** China
70 B3 **Jianli** China
70 B2 **Jianqiao** China
71 B3 **Jianyang** *Fujian* China
70 A2 **Jianyang** *Sichuan* China
70 C2 **Jiaozhou** China
70 B2 **Jiaozuo** China
70 C2 **Jiaxing** China
71 C3 **Jiayi** Taiwan
68 C2 **Jiayuguan** China
Jiddah Saudi Arabia *see* **Jeddah**
92 G2 **Jiehkkevárri** *mt.* Norway
70 B2 **Jiexiu** China
68 C2 **Jigzhi** China
103 D2 **Jihlava** Czechia
117 C4 **Jijiga** Eth.
116 A2 **Jilf al Kabīr, Haḍabat al** *plat.* Egypt
117 C4 **Jilib** Somalia
69 E2 **Jilin** China
65 B1 **Jilin** *prov.* China
65 A1 **Jilin Hada Ling** *mts* China
117 B4 **Jīma** Eth.
144 B2 **Jiménez** *Chihuahua* Mex.
145 C2 **Jiménez** *Tamaulipas* Mex.
70 B2 **Jinan** China
70 B2 **Jincheng** China
53 C3 **Jindabyne** Austr.
65 B3 **Jin-do** *i.* S. Korea
103 D2 **Jindřichův Hradec** Czechia
71 B3 **Jingdezhen** China
70 B2 **Jinghang Yunhe** *canal* China
62 B1 **Jinghong** China
70 B2 **Jingmen** China
70 A2 **Jingning** China
70 A2 **Jingtai** China
71 A3 **Jingxi** China
65 B1 **Jingyu** China
70 A2 **Jingyuan** China
70 B2 **Jingzhou** China
65 B2 **Jinhae** S. Korea
71 B3 **Jinhua** China
70 B2 **Jining** China
119 D2 **Jinja** Uganda
117 B4 **Jinka** Eth.
Jinmen Taiwan *see* **Kinmen**
146 B3 **Jinotepe** Nic.
71 A3 **Jinping** China
Jinsha Jiang *r.* China *see* **Yangtze**
70 B3 **Jinshi** China
70 B2 **Jinzhong** China
70 C1 **Jinzhou** China
150 B2 **Ji-Paraná** *r.* Brazil
75 C1 **Jirang** China
65 B2 **Jiri-san** *mt.* S. Korea
79 C2 **Jīroft** Iran
71 A3 **Jishou** China
110 B2 **Jiu** *r.* Romania
70 A2 **Jiuding Shan** *mt.* China
70 B3 **Jiujiang** China
66 B1 **Jixi** China
77 C2 **Jizzax** Uzbek.
151 E2 **João Pessoa** Brazil
155 C1 **João Pinheiro** Brazil
74 B2 **Jodhpur** India
92 I3 **Joensuu** Fin.
67 C3 **Jōetsu** Japan
121 C3 **Jofane** Moz.
88 C2 **Jõgeva** Estonia
123 C2 **Johannesburg** S. Africa
134 C2 **John Day** U.S.A.
134 B1 **John Day** *r.* U.S.A.
128 C2 **John D'Or Prairie** Can.
143 E1 **John H. Kerr Reservoir** U.S.A.
96 C1 **John o' Groats** U.K.
143 D1 **Johnson City** U.S.A.
128 A1 **Johnson's Crossing** Can.
49 H1 **Johnston Atoll** N. Pacific Ocean
96 B3 **Johnstone** U.K.
141 D2 **Johnstown** U.S.A.
60 B1 **Johor Bahru** Malaysia
88 C2 **Jõhvi** Estonia
154 C3 **Joinville** Brazil
105 D2 **Joinville** France
92 G2 **Jokkmokk** Sweden
92 □B2 **Jökulsá á Fjöllum** *r.* Iceland
140 B2 **Joliet** U.S.A.
130 C2 **Joliette** Can.
64 B2 **Jolo** Phil.
64 B2 **Jolo** *i.* Phil.
61 C2 **Jombang** Indon.
75 C2 **Jomsom** Nepal
88 B2 **Jonava** Lith.
142 B1 **Jonesboro** *AR* U.S.A.
142 B2 **Jonesboro** *LA* U.S.A.
127 F1 **Jones Sound** *sea chan.* Can.
93 F4 **Jönköping** Sweden
131 C2 **Jonquière** Can.
145 C3 **Jonuta** Mex.
137 E3 **Joplin** U.S.A.
80 B2 **Jordan** *country* Asia
80 B2 **Jordan** *r.* Asia
136 B1 **Jordan** U.S.A.
134 C2 **Jordan Valley** U.S.A.
109 D3 **Jorgucat** Albania
62 A1 **Jorhat** India
93 E4 **Jørpeland** Norway
115 C4 **Jos** Nigeria
145 C3 **José Cardel** Mex.
131 D1 **Joseph, Lac** *l.* Can.
50 B1 **Joseph Bonaparte Gulf** Austr.
115 C4 **Jos Plateau** Nigeria
93 E3 **Jotunheimen** *mts* Norway
122 B3 **Joubertina** S. Africa
123 C2 **Jouberton** S. Africa
93 I3 **Joutseno** Fin.
134 B1 **Juan de Fuca Strait** Can./U.S.A.
Juanshui China *see* **Tongcheng**
145 B2 **Juárez** Mex.
151 D2 **Juazeiro** Brazil
151 E2 **Juazeiro do Norte** Brazil
117 B4 **Juba** South Sudan
117 C4 **Jubaland** *reg.* Somalia
117 C5 **Jubba** *r.* Somalia
78 B2 **Jubbah** Saudi Arabia
145 C3 **Juchitán** Mex.
102 C2 **Judenburg** Austria
101 D2 **Jühnde** Ger.
146 B3 **Juigalpa** Nic.
100 C1 **Juist** *i.* Ger.
155 D2 **Juiz de Fora** Brazil
150 A3 **Juliaca** Peru
75 C2 **Jumla** Nepal
74 B2 **Junagadh** India
139 D2 **Junction** U.S.A.
137 D3 **Junction City** U.S.A.
154 C2 **Jundiaí** Brazil

128 A2 **Juneau** U.S.A.
53 C2 **Junee** Austr.
105 D2 **Jungfrau** *mt.* Switz.
141 D2 **Juniata** *r.* U.S.A.
92 G3 **Junsele** Sweden
134 C2 **Juntura** U.S.A.
154 C2 **Juquiá** Brazil
117 A4 **Jur** *r.* South Sudan
105 D2 **Jura** *mts* France/Switz.
96 B2 **Jura** *i.* U.K.
96 B3 **Jura, Sound of** *sea chan.* U.K.
88 B2 **Jurbarkas** Lith.
88 B2 **Jūrmala** Latvia
150 B2 **Juruá** *r.* Brazil
150 C2 **Juruena** *r.* Brazil
150 B2 **Jutaí** *r.* Brazil
101 F2 **Jüterbog** Ger.
146 B2 **Juventud, Isla de la** *i.* Cuba
70 B2 **Juxian** China
79 C2 **Jūyom** Iran
122 B1 **Jwaneng** Botswana
93 I3 **Jyväskylä** Fin.

K

74 B1 **K2** *mt.* China/Pak.
119 C3 **Kabalo** Dem. Rep. Congo
119 C3 **Kabare** Dem. Rep. Congo
130 B2 **Kabinakagami Lake** Can.
118 C3 **Kabinda** Dem. Rep. Congo
118 B2 **Kabo** C.A.R.
120 B2 **Kabompo** Zambia
119 C3 **Kabongo** Dem. Rep. Congo
77 C3 **Kābul** Afgh.
64 B2 **Kaburuang** *i.* Indon.
121 B2 **Kabwe** Zambia
74 A2 **Kachchh, Gulf of** India
74 B2 **Kachchh, Rann of** *marsh* India
83 I3 **Kachug** Russia
81 C1 **Kaçkar Dağı** *mt.* Turkey
73 B3 **Kadapa** India
111 C2 **Kadıköy** Turkey
114 B3 **Kadiolo** Mali
91 D2 **Kadiyivka** Ukr.
73 B3 **Kadmat** *atoll* India
121 B2 **Kadoma** Zimbabwe
63 A2 **Kadonkani** Myanmar
117 A3 **Kadugli** Sudan
115 C3 **Kaduna** Nigeria
89 E2 **Kaduy** Russia
86 E2 **Kadzherom** Russia
114 A3 **Kaédi** Maur.
118 B1 **Kaélé** Cameroon
65 B2 **Kaesŏng** N. Korea
114 A3 **Kaffrine** Senegal
121 B2 **Kafue** Zambia
120 B2 **Kafue** *r.* Zambia
118 B2 **Kaga Bandoro** C.A.R.
91 E2 **Kagal'nitskaya** Russia
67 B4 **Kagoshima** Japan
90 C2 **Kaharlyk** Ukr.
61 C2 **Kahayan** *r.* Indon.
118 B3 **Kahemba** Dem. Rep. Congo
101 E2 **Kahla** Ger.
79 C2 **Kahnūj** Iran
92 H2 **Kahperusvaarat** *mts* Fin.
80 B2 **Kahramanmaraş** Turkey
79 C2 **Kahūrak** Iran
59 C3 **Kai, Kepulauan** *is* Indon.
115 C4 **Kaiama** Nigeria
54 B2 **Kaiapoi** N.Z.
59 C3 **Kai Besar** *i.* Indon.
59 C3 **Kai Kecil** *i.* Indon.
70 B2 **Kaifeng** China
Kaihua China *see* **Wenshan**
122 B2 **Kaiingveld** *reg.* S. Africa
54 B2 **Kaikoura** N.Z.
114 A4 **Kailahun** Sierra Leone
71 A3 **Kaili** China
59 C3 **Kaimana** Indon.
54 C1 **Kaimanawa Mountains** N.Z.
67 C4 **Kainan** Japan
115 C3 **Kainji Reservoir** Nigeria
54 B1 **Kaipara Harbour** N.Z.
74 B2 **Kairana** India
115 D1 **Kairouan** Tunisia
54 B1 **Kaitaia** N.Z.
54 C1 **Kaitawa** N.Z.
Kaitong China *see* **Tongyu**
59 C3 **Kaiwatu** Indon.
65 A1 **Kaiyuan** *Liaoning* China
62 B1 **Kaiyuan** *Yunnan* China
92 I3 **Kajaani** Fin.
51 D2 **Kajabbi** Austr.
122 B2 **Kakamas** S. Africa
119 D2 **Kakamega** Kenya
91 C2 **Kakhovka** Ukr.
91 C2 **Kakhovs'ke Vodoskhovyshche** *resr* Ukr.
73 C3 **Kakinada** India
128 C1 **Kakisa** Can.
119 C3 **Kakoswa** Dem. Rep. Congo
126 B2 **Kaktovik** U.S.A.
Kalaallit Nunaat *terr.* N. America *see* **Greenland**
59 C3 **Kalabahi** Indon.
120 B2 **Kalabo** Zambia
73 B3 **Kalaburagi** India
91 E1 **Kalach** Russia
119 D2 **Kalacha Dida** Kenya
62 A1 **Kaladan** *r.* India/Myanmar
120 B3 **Kalahari Desert** Africa
92 H3 **Kalajoki** Fin.
111 B2 **Kalamaria** Greece
111 B3 **Kalamata** Greece
140 B2 **Kalamazoo** U.S.A.
111 B3 **Kalampaka** Greece
91 C2 **Kalanchak** Ukr.
115 E1 **Kalanshiyū ar Ramlī al Kabīr, Sarīr** *des.* Libya
63 B2 **Kalasin** Thai.
79 C2 **Kalāt** Iran
74 A2 **Kalat** Pak.
50 A2 **Kalbarri** Austr.
111 C3 **Kale** Turkey
80 B1 **Kalecik** Turkey
118 C3 **Kalema** Dem. Rep. Congo
119 C3 **Kalemie** Dem. Rep. Congo
62 A1 **Kalemyo** Myanmar
Kalgan China *see* **Zhangjiakou**
50 B3 **Kalgoorlie** Austr.
109 C2 **Kali** Croatia
110 C2 **Kaliakra, Nos** *pt* Bulg.
119 C3 **Kalima** Dem. Rep. Congo
61 C2 **Kalimantan** *reg.* Indon.
88 B3 **Kaliningrad** Russia
91 D2 **Kalininskaya** Russia
88 C3 **Kalinkavichy** Belarus
134 D1 **Kalispell** U.S.A.
103 D1 **Kalisz** Pol.
91 E2 **Kalitva** *r.* Russia
92 H2 **Kalix** Sweden
92 H2 **Kalixälven** *r.* Sweden
111 C3 **Kalkan** Turkey
120 A3 **Kalkfeld** Namibia
92 I3 **Kallavesi** *l.* Fin.
92 F3 **Kallsjön** *l.* Sweden
93 G4 **Kalmar** Sweden
93 G4 **Kalmarsund** *sea chan.* Sweden
120 B2 **Kalomo** Zambia
128 B2 **Kalone Peak** Can.
75 B1 **Kalpa** India
73 B3 **Kalpeni** *atoll* India
75 B2 **Kalpi** India
101 D1 **Kaltenkirchen** Ger.
89 E3 **Kaluga** Russia
93 F4 **Kalundborg** Denmark
90 A2 **Kalush** Ukr.
89 E2 **Kalyazin** Russia
111 C3 **Kalymnos** *i.* Greece
119 C3 **Kama** Dem. Rep. Congo
62 A2 **Kama** Myanmar
86 E3 **Kama** *r.* Russia
66 D3 **Kamaishi** Japan
80 B2 **Kaman** Turkey
120 A2 **Kamanjab** Namibia
78 B3 **Kamarān** *i.* Yemen
74 A2 **Kamarod** Pak.
50 B3 **Kambalda** Austr.
119 C4 **Kambove** Dem. Rep. Congo
183 L3 **Kamchatka Peninsula** Russia
110 C2 **Kamchia** *r.* Bulg.
110 B2 **Kamenitsa** *mt.* Bulg.
108 B2 **Kamenjak, Rt** *pt* Croatia
91 D1 **Kamenka** Russia
91 E2 **Kamenolomni** Russia
83 M2 **Kamenskoye** Russia
91 E2 **Kamensk-Shakhtinskiy** Russ
86 F3 **Kamensk-Ural'skiy** Russia
122 A3 **Kamiesberge** *mts* S. Africa
122 A3 **Kamieskroon** S. Africa
129 D1 **Kamilukuak Lake** Can.
119 C3 **Kamina** Dem. Rep. Congo
129 E1 **Kaminak Lake** Can.
90 A1 **Kamin'-Kashyrs'kyy** Ukr.
128 B2 **Kamloops** Can.
118 C3 **Kamonia** Dem. Rep. Congo
119 D2 **Kampala** Uganda
60 B1 **Kampar** Malaysia
100 B1 **Kampen** Neth.
119 C3 **Kampene** Dem. Rep. Congo
63 A2 **Kamphaeng Phet** Thai.
63 B2 **Kâmpóng Cham** Cambodia
63 B2 **Kâmpóng Chhnăng** Camboc
Kâmpóng Saôm Cambodia s **Sihanoukville**
63 B2 **Kâmpóng Spœ** Cambodia
63 B2 **Kâmpôt** Cambodia
129 D2 **Kamsack** Can.
86 E3 **Kamskoye Vodokhranilishch** *resr* Russia
117 C4 **Kamsuuma** Somalia
90 B2 **Kam"yanets'-Podil's'kyy** Uk
90 A1 **Kam"yanka-Buz'ka** Ukr.
91 C2 **Kam"yans'ke** Ukr.
88 B3 **Kamyanyets** Belarus
91 D2 **Kamyshevatskaya** Russia
87 D3 **Kamyshin** Russia
135 D3 **Kanab** U.S.A.
118 C3 **Kananga** Dem. Rep. Congo
87 D3 **Kanash** Russia
140 C3 **Kanawha** *r.* U.S.A.
67 C3 **Kanazawa** Japan
62 A1 **Kanbalu** Myanmar
63 A2 **Kanchanaburi** Thai.
73 B3 **Kanchipuram** India
77 C3 **Kandahār** Afgh.
86 C2 **Kandalaksha** Russia
61 C2 **Kandangan** Indon.
74 A2 **Kandh Kot** Pak.
114 C3 **Kandi** Benin
74 B2 **Kandla** India
53 C2 **Kandos** Austr.
121 □D2 **Kandreho** Madag.
73 C4 **Kandy** Sri Lanka
76 B2 **Kandyagash** Kazakh.
127 G1 **Kane Bassin** *b.* Greenland
91 D2 **Kanevskaya** Russia
122 B1 **Kang** Botswana
127 H2 **Kangaatsiaq** Greenland
114 B3 **Kangaba** Mali
80 B2 **Kangal** Turkey
60 B1 **Kangar** Malaysia
52 A3 **Kangaroo Island** Austr.

75 C2 **Kangchenjunga** mt. India/
Nepal
65 D2 **Kangdong** N. Korea
61 C2 **Kangean** is Indon.
127 I2 **Kangeq** c. Greenland
127 H2 **Kangerlussuaq** inlet
Greenland
127 I2 **Kangersuatsiaq** Greenland
65 B1 **Kanggye** N. Korea
131 D1 **Kangiqsualujjuaq** Can.
127 G2 **Kangiqsujuaq** Can.
127 G2 **Kangirsuk** Can.
65 A1 **Kangping** China
72 D2 **Kangto** mt. China/India
62 A1 **Kani** Myanmar
86 D2 **Kanin, Poluostrov** pen. Russia
86 D2 **Kanin Nos** Russia
91 C2 **Kaniv** Ukr.
93 H3 **Kankaanpää** Fin.
140 B3 **Kankakee** U.S.A.
114 B3 **Kankan** Guinea
75 C2 **Kanker** India
115 C3 **Kannur** India
115 C3 **Kano** Nigeria
122 B3 **Kanonpunt** pt S. Africa
67 B4 **Kanoya** Japan
75 C2 **Kanpur** India
136 C3 **Kansas** r. U.S.A.
137 D3 **Kansas** state U.S.A.
137 E3 **Kansas City** U.S.A.
83 H3 **Kansk** Russia
114 C3 **Kantchari** Burkina Faso
91 D2 **Kantemirovka** Russia
97 B2 **Kanturk** Ireland
123 D2 **Kanyamazane** S. Africa
123 C1 **Kanye** Botswana
63 B2 **Kaôh Kŏng** Cambodia
73 C1 **Kaohsiung** Taiwan
120 A2 **Kaokoveld** plat. Namibia
114 A3 **Kaolack** Senegal
118 B2 **Kaoma** Zambia
118 C3 **Kapanga** Dem. Rep. Congo
100 B2 **Kapellen** Belgium
121 B2 **Kapiri Mposhi** Zambia
127 H2 **Kapisillit** Greenland
130 B1 **Kapiskau** r. Can.
61 C1 **Kapit** Sarawak Malaysia
63 A3 **Kapoe** Thai.
114 B4 **Kapoeta** South Sudan
103 D2 **Kaposvár** Hungary
77 D2 **Kapshagay** Kazakh.
77 D2 **Kapshagay,
Vodokhranilishche** resr
Kazakh.
61 B2 **Kapuas** r. Indon.
52 A2 **Kapunda** Austr.
130 B2 **Kapuskasing** Can.
103 D2 **Kapuvár** Hungary
88 C3 **Kapyl'** Belarus
114 C4 **Kara** Togo
111 C3 **Kara Ada** i. Turkey
76 C1 **Karabalyk** Kazakh.
80 B1 **Karabük** Turkey
76 C2 **Karabutak** Kazakh.
110 C2 **Karacaköy** Turkey
89 D3 **Karachev** Russia
74 A2 **Karachi** Pak.
Kara Deniz sea Asia/Europe
see **Black Sea**
77 D2 **Karagandy** Kazakh.
77 D2 **Karagayly** Kazakh.
83 L3 **Karaginskiy Zaliv** b. Russia
81 B2 **Karaj** Iran
64 B2 **Karakelong** i. Indon.
77 D2 **Kara-Köl** Kyrg.
77 D2 **Karakol** Kyrg.
74 B1 **Karakoram Range** mts Asia

Karakum, Peski des. Kazakh.
see **Karakum Desert**
76 B2 **Karakum Desert** Kazakh.
76 C3 **Karakum Desert** Turkm.
Karakumy, Peski des. Turkm.
see **Karakum Desert**
80 B2 **Karaman** Turkey
77 E2 **Karamay** China
54 B2 **Karamea** N.Z.
54 B2 **Karamea Bight** b. N.Z.
80 B2 **Karapınar** Turkey
122 A2 **Karasburg** Namibia
86 F1 **Kara Sea** Russia
92 I2 **Karasjok** Norway
82 G3 **Karasuk** Russia
77 D2 **Karatau** Kazakh.
86 F2 **Karatau, Khrebet** mts Kazakh.
Karatayka Russia
67 A4 **Karatsu** Japan
60 B2 **Karawang** Indon.
81 C2 **Karbalā'** Iraq
103 E2 **Karcag** Hungary
111 B3 **Karditsa** Greece
88 B2 **Kärdla** Estonia
110 C2 **Kardzhali** Bulg.
122 B3 **Kareeberge** mts S. Africa
91 C2 **Kareli** Russia
74 B1 **Kargil** India
121 B2 **Kariba** Zimbabwe
121 B2 **Kariba, Lake** resr Zambia/
Zimbabwe
61 B2 **Karimata, Kepulauan** is Indon.
61 B2 **Karimata, Selat** str. Indon.
73 B3 **Karimnagar** India
61 C2 **Karimunjawa, Pulau-pulau** is
Indon.
91 C2 **Karkinits'ka Zatoka** g. Ukr.
91 D2 **Karlivka** Ukr.
109 C1 **Karlovac** Croatia
102 C1 **Karlovy Vary** Czechia
93 F4 **Karlshamn** Sweden
93 G4 **Karlskrona** Sweden
102 B2 **Karlsruhe** Ger.
93 F4 **Karlstad** Sweden
101 D3 **Karlstadt** Ger.
89 D3 **Karma** Belarus
93 E4 **Karmøy** i. Norway
74 B2 **Karnal** India
75 D2 **Karnaphuli Reservoir** Bangl.
110 C2 **Karnobat** Bulg.
74 A2 **Karodi** Pak.
121 B2 **Karoi** Zimbabwe
121 C1 **Karonga** Malawi
116 B3 **Karora** Eritrea
111 C3 **Karpathos** i. Greece
111 B3 **Karpenisi** Greece
86 D2 **Karpogory** Russia
50 A2 **Karratha** Austr.
81 C1 **Kars** Turkey
88 C2 **Kārsava** Latvia
86 E2 **Karskiye Vorota, Proliv** str.
Russia
Karskoye More sea Russia see
Kara Sea
101 E1 **Karstädt** Ger.
111 C3 **Kartal** Turkey
87 F3 **Kartaly** Russia
73 B3 **Karwar** India
83 I3 **Karymskoye** Russia
111 B3 **Karystos** Greece
80 A2 **Kaş** Turkey
130 B1 **Kasabonika Lake** Can.
118 C4 **Kasaji** Dem. Rep. Congo
121 C2 **Kasama** Zambia
120 B2 **Kasane** Botswana
118 B3 **Kasangulu** Dem. Rep. Congo
73 B3 **Kasaragod** India
129 D1 **Kasba Lake** Can.

120 B2 **Kasempa** Zambia
119 C4 **Kasenga** Dem. Rep. Congo
119 C3 **Kasese** Dem. Rep. Congo
119 D2 **Kasese** Uganda
81 D2 **Kāshān** Iran
Kashgar China see **Kashi**
77 D3 **Kashi** China
67 D3 **Kashima-nada** b. Japan
89 E2 **Kashin** Russia
89 E3 **Kashira** Russia
89 E3 **Kashirskoye** Russia
67 C3 **Kashiwazaki** Japan
76 B3 **Kāshmar** Iran
74 B1 **Kashmir** reg. Asia
74 A2 **Kashmore** Pak.
119 C3 **Kashyukulu** Dem. Rep. Congo
87 D3 **Kasimov** Russia
93 H3 **Kaskinen** Fin.
119 C3 **Kasongo** Dem. Rep. Congo
118 B3 **Kasongo-Lunda**
Dem. Rep. Congo
111 C3 **Kasos** i. Greece
Kaspiyskoye More l. Asia/
Europe see **Caspian Sea**
116 B3 **Kassala** Sudan
101 D2 **Kassel** Ger.
80 B1 **Kastamonu** Turkey
111 B2 **Kastoria** Greece
89 D3 **Kastsyukovichy** Belarus
119 D3 **Kasulu** Tanz.
121 C2 **Kasungu** Malawi
141 F1 **Katahdin, Mount** U.S.A.
118 C3 **Katako-Kombe**
Dem. Rep. Congo
50 A3 **Katanning** Austr.
63 A3 **Katchall** i. India
111 B2 **Katerini** Greece
128 A2 **Kate's Needle** mt. Can./U.S.A.
121 C2 **Katete** Zambia
62 A1 **Katha** Myanmar
50 C1 **Katherine** r. Austr.
74 B2 **Kathiawar** pen. India
75 C2 **Kathmandu** Nepal
122 B2 **Kathu** S. Africa
74 B1 **Kathua** India
114 B3 **Kati** Mali
75 C2 **Katihar** India
54 C1 **Katikati** N.Z.
123 C3 **Katikati** S. Africa
120 B2 **Katima Mulilo** Namibia
Ka Tiritiri o te Moana mts
N.Z. see **Southern Alps/
Ka Tiritiri o te Moana**
52 A1 **Kati Thanda-Lake Eyre
(North)** imp. l. Austr.
123 C2 **Katlehong** S. Africa
75 C2 **Katni** India
111 B3 **Kato Achaïa** Greece
53 D2 **Katoomba** Austr.
103 D1 **Katowice** Pol.
78 A2 **Kātrīnā, Jabal** mt. Egypt
93 G4 **Katrineholm** Sweden
115 C3 **Katsina** Nigeria
115 C4 **Katsina-Ala** Nigeria
77 C3 **Kattaqo'rg'on** Uzbek.
93 F4 **Kattegat** str. Denmark/Sweden
100 B1 **Katwijk aan Zee** Neth.
124 E5 **Kaua'i** i. U.S.A.
93 H3 **Kauhajoki** Fin.
88 B3 **Kaunas** Lith.
115 C3 **Kaura-Namoda** Nigeria
92 H2 **Kautokeino** Norway
111 B2 **Kavala** Greece
66 C2 **Kavalerovo** Russia
73 C3 **Kavali** India
73 B3 **Kavaratti** atoll India
110 C2 **Kavarna** Bulg.
81 D2 **Kavīr, Dasht-e** des. Iran

67 C3 **Kawagoe** Japan
54 B1 **Kawakawa** N.Z.
67 C3 **Kawanishi** Japan
130 C2 **Kawartha Lakes** Can.
67 C3 **Kawasaki** Japan
54 C1 **Kawerau** N.Z.
63 A2 **Kawkareik** Myanmar
62 A1 **Kawlin** Myanmar
63 A2 **Kawmapyin** Myanmar
63 A2 **Kawthaung** Myanmar
77 D3 **Kaxgar He** *r.* China
114 B3 **Kaya** Burkina Faso
61 C1 **Kayan** *r.* Indon.
136 B2 **Kaycee** U.S.A.
138 A1 **Kayenta** U.S.A.
114 A3 **Kayes** Mali
77 D2 **Kaynar** Kazakh.
80 B2 **Kayseri** Turkey
81 D1 **Kazakhskiy Zaliv** *b.* Kazakh.
76 C2 **Kazakhstan** *country* Asia
87 D3 **Kazan'** Russia
80 A1 **Kazanlak** Bulg.
76 A2 **Kazbek** *mt.* Georgia/Russia
81 D3 **Kāzerūn** Iran
103 E2 **Kazincbarcika** Hungary
86 F2 **Kazym-Mys** Russia
111 B3 **Kea** *i.* Greece
97 C1 **Keady** U.K.
137 D2 **Kearney** U.S.A.
138 A2 **Kearny** U.S.A.
116 A3 **Kebkabiya** Sudan
92 G2 **Kebnekaise** *mt.* Sweden
117 C4 **K'ebrī Dehar** Eth.
61 C1 **Kebuang** Indon.
61 B2 **Kebumen** Indon.
128 B2 **Kechika** *r.* Can.
103 D2 **Kecskemét** Hungary
88 B2 **Kėdainiai** Lith.
114 A3 **Kédougou** Senegal
103 D1 **Kędzierzyn-Koźle** Pol.
128 B1 **Keele** *r.* Can.
128 A1 **Keele Peak** Can.
keeling Taiwan *see* **Chilung**
141 E2 **Keene** U.S.A.
122 A2 **Keetmanshoop** Namibia
129 E3 **Keewatin** Can.
Kefallonia *i.* Greece *see* **Cephalonia**
59 C3 **Kefamenanu** Indon.
92 □A3 **Keflavík** Iceland
77 D2 **Kegen** Kazakh.
128 C2 **Keg River** Can.
62 A1 **Kehsi Mansam** Myanmar
98 C2 **Keighley** U.K.
88 B2 **Keila** Estonia
122 B2 **Keimoes** S. Africa
92 I3 **Keitele** *l.* Fin.
52 B3 **Keith** Austr.
103 E2 **Kékes** *mt.* Hungary
92 J2 **Kelesuayv, Gora** *h.* Russia
102 C2 **Kelheim** Ger.
80 B1 **Kelkit** *r.* Turkey
128 B1 **Keller Lake** Can.
134 C1 **Kellogg** U.S.A.
92 I2 **Kelloselkä** Fin.
97 C2 **Kells** Ireland
88 B2 **Kelmė** Lith.
115 D4 **Kélo** Chad
128 C3 **Kelowna** Can.
96 C3 **Kelso** U.K.
134 B1 **Kelso** U.S.A.
60 B1 **Keluang** Malaysia
129 D2 **Kelvington** Can.
86 C2 **Kem'** Russia
128 B2 **Kemano (abandoned)** Can.
111 C3 **Kemer** Turkey
82 G3 **Kemerovo** Russia
92 H2 **Kemi** Fin.
92 I2 **Kemijärvi** Fin.
92 I2 **Kemijoki** *r.* Fin.
136 A2 **Kemmerer** U.S.A.
92 I3 **Kempele** Fin.
53 D2 **Kempsey** Austr.
130 C2 **Kempt, Lac** *l.* Can.
102 C2 **Kempten (Allgäu)** Ger.
123 C2 **Kempton Park** S. Africa
61 C2 **Kemujan** *i.* Indon.
129 D2 **Kenaston** Can.
98 B1 **Kendal** U.K.
59 C3 **Kendari** Indon.
61 C2 **Kendawangan** Indon.
115 D3 **Kendégué** Chad
75 C2 **Kendujhargarh** India
114 A4 **Kenema** Sierra Leone
118 B3 **Kenge** Dem. Rep. Congo
62 A1 **Kengtung** Myanmar
122 B2 **Kenhardt** S. Africa
114 B1 **Kénitra** Morocco
97 B3 **Kenmare** Ireland
136 C1 **Kenmare** U.S.A.
97 A3 **Kenmare River** *inlet* Ireland
100 C3 **Kenn** Ger.
137 E3 **Kennett** U.S.A.
134 C1 **Kennewick** U.S.A.
129 E3 **Kenora** Can.
140 B2 **Kenosha** U.S.A.
138 C2 **Kent** U.S.A.
77 C2 **Kentau** Kazakh.
140 B3 **Kentucky** *r.* U.S.A.
140 C3 **Kentucky** *state* U.S.A.
140 B3 **Kentucky Lake** U.S.A.
119 D2 **Kenya** *country* Africa
119 D3 **Kenya, Mount** Kenya
137 E2 **Keokuk** U.S.A.
111 C3 **Kepsut** Turkey
52 B3 **Kerang** Austr.
91 D2 **Kerch** Ukr.
59 D3 **Kerema** P.N.G.
128 C3 **Keremeos** Can.
116 B3 **Keren** Eritrea
81 C2 **Kerend-e Gharb** Iran
Kerepakupai Merú Venez. *see* **Angel Falls**
159 C7 **Kerguelen Plateau** Indian Ocean
119 D3 **Kericho** Kenya
54 B1 **Kerikeri** N.Z.
60 B2 **Kerinci, Gunung** *vol.* Indon.
111 A3 **Kerkyra** Greece
Kerkyra *i.* Greece *see* **Corfu**
116 B3 **Kerma** Sudan
49 G4 **Kermadec Islands** S. Pacific Ocean
79 C1 **Kermān** Iran
81 C2 **Kermānshāh** Iran
139 C2 **Kermit** U.S.A.
135 C3 **Kern** *r.* U.S.A.
100 C2 **Kerpen** Ger.
129 D2 **Kerrobert** Can.
139 D2 **Kerrville** U.S.A.
Keryneia Cyprus *see* **Kyrenia**
130 B1 **Kesagami Lake** Can.
111 C2 **Keşan** Turkey
66 D3 **Kesennuma** Japan
74 B2 **Keshod** India
100 C2 **Kessel** Neth.
98 B1 **Keswick** U.K.
103 D2 **Keszthely** Hungary
82 G3 **Ket'** *r.* Russia
61 C2 **Ketapang** Indon.
128 A2 **Ketchikan** U.S.A.
134 D2 **Ketchum** U.S.A.
99 C2 **Kettering** U.K.
93 H3 **Keuruu** Fin.
100 C2 **Kevelaer** Ger.
140 B2 **Kewanee** U.S.A.
140 B1 **Keweenaw Bay** U.S.A.
140 B1 **Keweenaw Peninsula** U.S.A.
143 D3 **Key Largo** U.S.A.
141 D3 **Keyser** U.S.A.
143 D4 **Key West** U.S.A.
123 C2 **Kgotsong** S. Africa
69 E1 **Khabarovsk** Russia
80 B1 **Khadyzhensk** Russia
62 A1 **Khagrachhari** Bangl.
74 A2 **Khairpur** Pak.
122 B1 **Khakhea** Botswana
68 C1 **Khamar-Daban, Khrebet** *mts* Russia
74 B2 **Khambhat** India
73 B3 **Khambhat, Gulf of** India
74 B2 **Khamgaon** India
78 B3 **Khamis Mushayṭ** Saudi Arabi
78 B3 **Khamr** Yemen
77 C3 **Khānābād** Afgh.
74 B2 **Khandwa** India
83 K2 **Khandyga** Russia
74 B1 **Khanewal** Pak.
66 B2 **Khanka, Lake** China/Russia
74 B2 **Khanpur** Pak.
77 D2 **Khantau** Kazakh.
83 H2 **Khantayskoye, Ozero** *l.* Russia
86 F2 **Khanty-Mansiysk** Russia
63 A3 **Khao Chum Thong** Thai.
63 A2 **Khao Laem, Ang Kep Nam** Thai.
87 D4 **Kharabali** Russia
75 C2 **Kharagpur** India
81 D3 **Kharāmeh** Iran
79 C2 **Khārān** *r.* Iran
116 B2 **Khārijah, Wāḥāt al** *oasis* Egypt
91 D2 **Kharkiv** Ukr.
Khar'kov Ukr. *see* **Kharkiv**
86 D3 **Kharovsk** Russia
116 B3 **Khartoum** Sudan
87 D4 **Khasavyurt** Russia
79 D2 **Khāsh** Iran
78 A3 **Khashm el Girba** Sudan
78 A3 **Khashm el Girba Dam** Sudan
74 D2 **Khasi Hills** India
123 C3 **Khayamnandi** S. Africa
78 A2 **Khaybar** Saudi Arabia
122 A3 **Khayelitsha** S. Africa
107 D2 **Khemis Miliana** Alg.
63 B2 **Khemmarat** Thai.
115 C1 **Khenchela** Alg.
91 C2 **Kherson** Ukr.
83 H2 **Kheta** *r.* Russia
69 D1 **Khilok** Russia
89 E2 **Khimki** Russia
74 A2 **Khipro** Pak.
89 E3 **Khlevnoye** Russia
90 B2 **Khmel'nyts'kyy** Ukr.
89 E3 **Khokhol'skiy** Russia
74 B2 **Khokhropar** Pak.
89 D2 **Kholm** Russia
89 D2 **Kholm-Zhirkovskiy** Russia
79 C2 **Khonj** Iran
63 B2 **Khon Kaen** Thai.
62 A1 **Khonsa** India
83 K2 **Khonuu** Russia
86 E2 **Khorey-Ver** Russia
69 D1 **Khorinsk** Russia
91 C2 **Khorol** Ukr.
90 B1 **Khoroshiv** Ukr.
81 C2 **Khorramābād** Iran
81 C2 **Khorramshahr** Iran
77 D3 **Khorugh** Tajik.
74 A1 **Khōst** Afgh.
62 A1 **Khreum** Myanmar
76 B1 **Khromtau** Kazakh.
87 C4 **Khrustal'nyy** Ukr.
90 B2 **Khrystynivka** Ukr.
77 C2 **Khŭjand** Tajik.

63	B2	Khu Khan Thai.
78	A2	Khulays Saudi Arabia
75	C2	Khulna Bangl.
79	B2	Khurays Saudi Arabia
81	H3	Khushab Pak.
90	A2	Khust Ukr.
23	C2	Khutsong S. Africa
74	A2	Khuzdar Pak.
81	D2	Khvānsār Iran
79	C2	Khvormūj Iran
81	D2	Khvoy Iran
89	D2	Khvoynaya Russia
81	H3	Khyber Pass Afgh./Pak.
53	D2	Kiama Austr.
19	C3	Kiambi Dem. Rep. Congo
19	D3	Kibiti Tanz.
09	D2	Kičevo Macedonia
14	C3	Kidal Mali
99	B2	Kidderminster U.K.
14	A3	Kidira Senegal
54	C1	Kidnappers, Cape N.Z.
02	C2	Kiel Ger.
03	E1	Kielce Pol.
98	B1	Kielder Water U.K.
90	C1	Kiev Ukr.
14	A3	Kiffa Maur.
19	D3	Kigali Rwanda
19	C3	Kigoma Tanz.
88	B2	Kihnu i. Estonia
92	I2	Kiiminki Fin.
67	B4	Kii-suidō sea chan. Japan
09	D1	Kikinda Serbia
19	C3	Kikondja Dem. Rep. Congo
59	D3	Kikori P.N.G.
59	D3	Kikori r. P.N.G.
18	B3	Kikwit Dem. Rep. Congo
65	B1	Kilchu N. Korea
18	B3	Kilembe Dem. Rep. Congo
39	E2	Kilis Turkey
19	D3	Kilimanjaro vol. Tanz.
80	B2	Kilis Turkey
90	B2	Kiliya Ukr.
97	B2	Kilkee Ireland
97	D1	Kilkeel U.K.
97	C2	Kilkenny Ireland
11	B2	Kilkis Greece
97	B1	Killala Bay Ireland
97	B2	Killaloe Ireland
29	C2	Killam Can.
97	C2	Killarney Ireland
39	D2	Killeen U.S.A.
96	B2	Killin U.K.
97	B1	Killybegs Ireland
96	B3	Kilmarnock U.K.
52	A3	Kilmore Austr.
19	D3	Kilosa Tanz.
97	B2	Kilrush Ireland
19	C3	Kilwa Dem. Rep. Congo
19	D3	Kilwa Masoko Tanz.
19	D3	Kimambi Tanz.
51	A3	Kimba Austr.
36	C2	Kimball U.S.A.
28	C2	Kimberley Can.
22	B2	Kimberley S. Africa
50	B1	Kimberley Plateau Austr.
65	B2	Kimch'aek N. Korea
27	G2	Kimmirut Can.
89	E3	Kimovsk Russia
18	B3	Kimpese Dem. Rep. Congo
89	E2	Kimry Russia
61	C1	Kinabalu, Gunung mt. Sabah Malaysia
28	C2	Kinbasket Lake Can.
30	B2	Kincardine Can.
62	A1	Kinchang Myanmar
19	C3	Kinda Dem. Rep. Congo
98	C2	Kinder Scout h. U.K.
29	D2	Kindersley Can.
114	A3	Kindia Guinea
119	C3	Kindu Dem. Rep. Congo
86	D3	Kineshma Russia
78	A2	King Abdullah Economic City Saudi Arabia
51	E2	Kingaroy Austr.
135	B3	King City U.S.A.
130	C1	King George Islands Can.
88	C2	Kingisepp Russia
51	D3	King Island Austr.
50	B1	King Leopold Ranges hills Austr.
138	A1	Kingman U.S.A.
135	B3	Kings r. U.S.A.
52	A3	Kingscote Austr.
99	D2	King's Lynn U.K.
48	F3	Kingsmill Group is Kiribati
50	B1	King Sound b. Austr.
134	D2	Kings Peak U.S.A.
143	D1	Kingsport U.S.A.
130	C2	Kingston Can.
146	C3	Kingston Jamaica
141	E2	Kingston U.S.A.
52	A3	Kingston South East Austr.
98	C2	Kingston upon Hull U.K.
147	D3	Kingstown St Vincent
139	D3	Kingsville U.S.A.
99	B3	Kingswood U.K.
96	B2	Kingussie U.K.
126	E2	King William Island Can.
123	C3	King William's Town S. Africa
67	D3	Kinka-san i. Japan
71	B3	Kinmen Taiwan
93	F4	Kinna Sweden
97	B3	Kinsale Ireland
118	B3	Kinshasa Dem. Rep. Congo
143	E1	Kinston U.S.A.
88	B2	Kintai Lith.
114	B4	Kintampo Ghana
96	B3	Kintyre pen. U.K.
62	A1	Kin-U Myanmar
130	C2	Kipawa, Lac l. Can.
83	I3	Kirensk Russia
89	E3	Kireyevsk Russia
		Kirghizia country Asia see Kyrgyzstan
49	G3	Kiribati country Pacific Ocean
80	B2	Kırıkkale Turkey
89	E2	Kirillov Russia
		Kirin China see Jilin
		Kirinyaga mt. Kenya see Kenya, Mount
89	D2	Kirishi Russia
49	H2	Kiritimati atoll Kiribati
111	C3	Kırkağaç Turkey
96	C2	Kirkcaldy U.K.
96	B3	Kirkcudbright U.K.
92	J2	Kirkenes Norway
130	B2	Kirkland Lake Can.
137	E2	Kirksville U.S.A.
81	C2	Kirkūk Iraq
96	C1	Kirkwall U.K.
89	D3	Kirov Kaluzhskaya Oblast' Russia
86	D3	Kirov Kirovskaya Oblast' Russia
		Kirovabad Azer. see Gäncä
86	E3	Kirovo-Chepetsk Russia
		Kirovohrad Ukr. see
86	C2	Kropyvnyts'kyy
96	C2	Kirovsk Russia
86	E3	Kirriemuir U.K.
74	A2	Kirs Russia
92	H2	Kirthar Range mts Pak.
67	C3	Kiruna Sweden
89	E2	Kiryū Japan
119	C2	Kirzhach Russia
118	B3	Kisangani Dem. Rep. Congo
		Kisantu Dem. Rep. Congo
60	A1	Kisaran Indon.
82	G3	Kiselevsk Russia
75	C2	Kishanganj India
115	C4	Kishi Nigeria
		Kishinev Moldova see Chişinău
77	D1	Kishkenekol' Kazakh.
74	B2	Kishtwar India
119	D3	Kisii Kenya
103	D2	Kiskunfélegyháza Hungary
103	D2	Kiskunhalas Hungary
87	D4	Kislovodsk Russia
117	C5	Kismaayo Somalia
119	D3	Kisoro Uganda
111	A3	Kissamos Greece
114	A4	Kissidougou Guinea
143	D3	Kissimmee U.S.A.
143	D3	Kissimmee, Lake U.S.A.
129	D2	Kississing Lake Can.
119	D3	Kisumu Kenya
114	B3	Kita Mali
66	D3	Kitakami Japan
66	D3	Kitakami-gawa r. Japan
67	B4	Kita-Kyūshū Japan
119	D2	Kitale Kenya
66	D2	Kitami Japan
130	B2	Kitchener Can.
93	J3	Kitee Fin.
119	D2	Kitgum Uganda
128	B2	Kitimat Can.
118	B3	Kitona Dem. Rep. Congo
119	D3	Kitunda Tanz.
128	B2	Kitwanga Can.
121	B2	Kitwe Zambia
101	E3	Kitzingen Ger.
92	I3	Kiuruvesi Fin.
119	C3	Kivu, Lac l. Dem. Rep. Congo/ Rwanda
110	C2	Kıyıköy Turkey
86	E3	Kizel Russia
111	C3	Kızılca Dağ mt. Turkey
87	D4	Kizlyar Russia
92	I1	Kjøllefjord Norway
92	G2	Kjøpsvik Norway
102	C1	Kladno Czechia
102	C2	Klagenfurt am Wörthersee Austria
88	B2	Klaipėda Lith.
94	B1	Klaksvík Faroe Is
134	B2	Klamath r. U.S.A.
134	B2	Klamath Falls U.S.A.
134	B2	Klamath Mountains U.S.A.
60	B1	Klang Malaysia
102	C2	Klatovy Czechia
122	A3	Klawer S. Africa
128	A2	Klawock U.S.A.
128	B2	Kleena Kleene Can.
122	B2	Kleinbegin S. Africa
122	A2	Kleinsee S. Africa
123	C2	Klerksdorp S. Africa
89	D3	Kletnya Russia
100	C2	Kleve Ger.
89	D3	Klimavichy Belarus
89	E2	Klimovo Russia
89	E2	Klimovsk Russia
89	E2	Klin Russia
101	F2	Klínovec mt. Czechia
93	G4	Klintehamn Sweden
89	D3	Klintsy Russia
109	C2	Ključ Bos. & Herz.
103	D1	Kłodzko Pol.
100	C1	Kloosterhaar Neth.
103	D2	Klosterneuburg Austria
101	E1	Klötze (Altmark) Ger.
103	D1	Kluczbork Pol.
128	A2	Klukwan U.S.A.
88	C3	Klyetsk Belarus
98	C1	Knaresborough U.K.

93 F3 **Knästen** *h.* Sweden
129 E2 **Knee Lake** Can.
101 E1 **Knesebeck** Ger.
101 E3 **Knetzgau** Ger.
109 C2 **Knin** Croatia
103 C2 **Knittelfeld** Austria
109 D2 **Knjaževac** Serbia
100 A2 **Knokke-Heist** Belgium
143 D1 **Knoxville** U.S.A.
122 B3 **Knysna** S. Africa
76 B1 **Kobda** Kazakh.
67 C4 **Kōbe** Japan
København Denmark *see* **Copenhagen**
100 C2 **Koblenz** Ger.
59 C3 **Kobroor** *i.* Indon.
88 B3 **Kobryn** Belarus
109 D2 **Kočani** Macedonia
111 C2 **Kocasu** *r.* Turkey
75 C2 **Koch Bihar** India
73 B4 **Kochi** India
67 B4 **Kōchi** Japan
87 D4 **Kochubey** Russia
75 C2 **Kodarma** India
117 B4 **Kodok** South Sudan
90 B2 **Kodyma** Ukr.
111 C2 **Kodzhaele** *mt.* Bulg./Greece
122 A2 **Koës** Namibia
122 C2 **Koffiefontein** S. Africa
114 B4 **Koforidua** Ghana
67 C3 **Kōfu** Japan
131 D1 **Kogaluk** *r.* Can.
117 B5 **Kogelo** Kenya
74 B1 **Kohat** Pak.
62 A1 **Kohima** India
88 C2 **Kohtla-Järve** Estonia
114 A4 **Koidu-Sefadu** Sierra Leone
92 H3 **Kokkola** Fin.
140 B2 **Kokomo** U.S.A.
77 E2 **Kokpekty** Kazakh.
77 C1 **Kokshetau** Kazakh.
131 D1 **Koksoak** *r.* Can.
123 C3 **Kokstad** S. Africa
Koktokay China *see* **Fuyun**
58 C3 **Kolaka** Indon.
86 C2 **Kola Peninsula** Russia
92 H2 **Kolari** Fin.
114 A3 **Kolda** Senegal
93 E4 **Kolding** Denmark
107 D2 **Koléa** Alg.
86 D2 **Kolguyev, Ostrov** *i.* Russia
73 B3 **Kolhapur** India
88 B2 **Kolkasrags** *pt* Latvia
75 C2 **Kolkata** India
73 B4 **Kollam** India
Köln Ger. *see* **Cologne**
103 D1 **Kołobrzeg** Pol.
114 B3 **Kolokani** Mali
89 E2 **Kolomna** Russia
90 B2 **Kolomyya** Ukr.
122 B2 **Kolonkwaneng** Botswana
82 G3 **Kolpashevo** Russia
89 E3 **Kolpny** Russia
Kol'skiy Poluostrov *pen.* Russia *see* **Kola Peninsula**
78 B3 **Koluli** Eritrea
119 C4 **Kolwezi** Dem. Rep. Congo
83 L2 **Kolyma** *r.* Russia
83 L2 **Kolymskaya Nizmennost'** *lowland* Russia
83 M2 **Kolymskiy, Khrebet** *mts* Russia
67 C3 **Komaki** Japan
83 M3 **Komandorskiye Ostrova** *is* Russia
103 D2 **Komárno** Slovakia
123 D2 **Komati** *r.* S. Africa/Swaziland
67 C3 **Komatsu** Japan
119 C3 **Kombe** Dem. Rep. Congo
109 C2 **Komiža** Croatia
103 D2 **Komló** Hungary
118 B3 **Komono** Congo
111 C2 **Komotini** Greece
122 B3 **Komsberg** *mts* S. Africa
83 H1 **Komsomolets, Ostrov** *i.* Russia
89 F2 **Komsomol'sk** Russia
Komsomol's'k Ukr. *see* **Horishni Plavni**
87 D4 **Komsomol'skiy** Russia
69 E1 **Komsomol'sk-na-Amure** Russia
89 E2 **Konakovo** Russia
75 C3 **Kondagaon** India
86 F2 **Kondinskoye** Russia
119 D3 **Kondoa** Tanz.
86 C2 **Kondopoga** Russia
89 E3 **Kondrovo** Russia
127 I2 **Kong Christian IX Land** *reg.* Greenland
127 I2 **Kong Frederik VI Kyst** *coastal area* Greenland
119 C3 **Kongolo** Dem. Rep. Congo
93 E4 **Kongsberg** Norway
93 F3 **Kongsvinger** Norway
77 D3 **Kongur Shan** *mt.* China
100 C2 **Königswinter** Ger.
103 D1 **Konin** Pol.
109 C2 **Konjic** Bos. & Herz.
122 A2 **Konkiep** *watercourse* Namibia
91 C1 **Konotop** Ukr.
102 B2 **Konstanz** Ger.
115 C3 **Kontagora** Nigeria
63 B2 **Kon Tum** Vietnam
63 B2 **Kon Tum, Cao Nguyên** *plat.* Vietnam
80 B2 **Konya** Turkey
100 C3 **Konz** Ger.
86 E3 **Konzhakovskiy Kamen', Gora** *mt.* Russia
134 C1 **Kooskia** U.S.A.
128 C3 **Kootenay Lake** Can.
122 B3 **Kootjieskolk** S. Africa
92 □B2 **Kópasker** Iceland
108 B1 **Koper** Slovenia
93 G4 **Kopparberg** Sweden
109 C1 **Koprivnica** Croatia
89 F3 **Korablino** Russia
73 C3 **Koraput** India
101 D2 **Korbach** Ger.
109 D2 **Korçë** Albania
109 C2 **Korčula** Croatia
109 C2 **Korčula** *i.* Croatia
65 B1 **Korea, North** *country* Asia
65 B2 **Korea, South** *country* Asia
70 C2 **Korea Bay** *g.* China/N. Korea
65 B3 **Korea Strait** Japan/S. Korea
91 D2 **Korenovsk** Russia
90 B1 **Korets'** Ukr.
111 C2 **Körfez** Turkey
114 B4 **Korhogo** Côte d'Ivoire
Korinthos Greece *see* **Corinth**
103 D2 **Kőris-hegy** *h.* Hungary
109 D2 **Koritnik** *mt.* Albania/Kosovo
67 D3 **Kōriyama** Japan
80 B2 **Korkuteli** Turkey
68 B2 **Korla** China
103 D2 **Körmend** Hungary
114 B3 **Koro** Mali
131 D1 **Koroc** *r.* Can.
91 D1 **Korocha** Russia
119 D3 **Korogwe** Tanz.
59 C2 **Koror** Palau
90 B1 **Korosten'** Ukr.
90 B1 **Korostyshiv** Ukr.
115 D3 **Koro Toro** Chad
91 C2 **Korsun'-Shevchenkivs'kyy** Ukr.
103 E1 **Korsze** Pol.
100 A2 **Kortrijk** Belgium
83 L3 **Koryakskaya Sopka, Vulkan** *vol.* Russia
83 M2 **Koryakskoye Nagor'ye** *mts* Russia
86 D2 **Koryazhma** Russia
91 C1 **Koryukivka** Ukr.
111 C3 **Kos** Greece
111 C3 **Kos** *i.* Greece
65 B2 **Kosan** N. Korea
103 D1 **Kościan** Pol.
53 C3 **Kosciuszko, Mount** Austr.
68 B1 **Kosh-Agach** Russia
103 E2 **Košice** Slovakia
92 H2 **Koskullskulle** Sweden
65 B2 **Kosŏng** N. Korea
109 D2 **Kosovo** *country* Europe
Kosovska Mitrovica Kosovo *see* **Mitrovicë**
48 E2 **Kosrae** *atoll* Micronesia
114 B4 **Kossou, Lac de** *l.* Côte d'Ivoi
76 C1 **Kostanay** Kazakh.
110 B2 **Kostenets** Bulg.
123 C2 **Koster** S. Africa
117 B3 **Kosti** Sudan
86 C2 **Kostomuksha** Russia
90 B1 **Kostopil'** Ukr.
89 F2 **Kostroma** Russia
89 F2 **Kostroma** *r.* Russia
102 C1 **Kostrzyn nad Odrą** Pol.
103 D1 **Koszalin** Pol.
103 D2 **Kőszeg** Hungary
74 B2 **Kota** India
60 B2 **Kotaagung** Indon.
61 C2 **Kotabaru** Indon.
61 C1 **Kota Belud** *Sabah* Malaysia
60 B1 **Kota Bharu** Malaysia
60 B2 **Kotabumi** Indon.
61 C1 **Kota Kinabalu** *Sabah* Malays
61 C1 **Kota Samarahan** *Sarawak* Malaysia
86 D3 **Kotel'nich** Russia
87 D4 **Kotel'nikovo** Russia
83 K1 **Kotel'nyy, Ostrov** *i.* Russia
101 E2 **Köthen (Anhalt)** Ger.
93 I3 **Kotka** Fin.
86 D2 **Kotlas** Russia
109 C2 **Kotor Varoš** Bos. & Herz.
87 D3 **Kotovo** Russia
91 E1 **Kotovsk** Russia
Kotovs'k Ukr. *see* **Podil's'k**
83 H2 **Kotuy** *r.* Russia
100 A2 **Koudekerke** Neth.
114 B3 **Koudougou** Burkina Faso
122 B3 **Kougaberge** *mts* S. Africa
118 B3 **Koulamoutou** Gabon
114 B3 **Koulikoro** Mali
114 A3 **Koundâra** Guinea
151 C1 **Kourou** Fr. Guiana
114 B3 **Kouroussa** Guinea
115 D3 **Kousséri** Cameroon
114 B3 **Koutiala** Mali
93 I3 **Kouvola** Fin.
92 J2 **Kovdor** Russia
90 A1 **Kovel'** Ukr.
89 F2 **Kovrov** Russia
54 B2 **Kowhitirangi** N.Z.
Koyamutthoor India *see* **Coimbatore**
111 C3 **Köyceğiz** Turkey
86 D2 **Koyda** Russia
126 A2 **Koyukuk** *r.* U.S.A.
111 B2 **Kozani** Greece
90 C1 **Kozelets'** Ukr.
89 E3 **Kozel'sk** Russia

73 B3 **Kozhikode** India
90 B2 **Kozyatyn** Ukr.
63 A3 **Krabi** Thai.
63 A2 **Kra Buri** Thai.
63 B2 **Krâchéh** Cambodia
93 E4 **Kragerø** Norway
100 B1 **Kraggenburg** Neth.
109 D2 **Kragujevac** Serbia
60 B2 **Krakatau** *i.* Indon.
103 D1 **Kraków** Pol.
91 D2 **Kramators'k** Ukr.
93 G3 **Kramfors** Sweden
111 B3 **Kranidi** Greece
86 E1 **Krasino** Russia
88 C2 **Krāslava** Latvia
101 F2 **Kraslice** Czechia
89 D3 **Krasnapollye** Belarus
89 D3 **Krasnaya Gora** Russia
87 D3 **Krasnoarmeysk** Russia
Krasnoarmiys'k Ukr. *see* **Pokrovs'k**
86 D2 **Krasnoborsk** Russia
91 D2 **Krasnodar** Russia
91 D2 **Krasnodarskoye Vodokhranilishche** *resr* Russia
Krasnodon Ukr. *see* **Sorokine**
88 C2 **Krasnogorodsk** Russia
91 D2 **Krasnohrad** Ukr.
86 E3 **Krasnokamsk** Russia
89 D2 **Krasnomayskiy** Russia
87 D3 **Krasnoslobodsk** Russia
86 E3 **Krasnoufimsk** Russia
83 H3 **Krasnoyarsk** Russia
89 F2 **Krasnoye-na-Volge** Russia
89 D3 **Krasnyy** Russia
89 E2 **Krasnyy Kholm** Russia
Krasnyy Luch Ukr. *see* **Khrustal'nyy**
91 E2 **Krasnyy Sulin** Russia
90 B2 **Krasyliv** Ukr.
100 C2 **Krefeld** Ger.
91 C2 **Kremenchuk** Ukr.
91 C2 **Kremenchuts'ke Vodoskhovyshche** *resr* Ukr.
103 D2 **Křemešník** *h.* Czechia
91 D2 **Kreminna** Ukr.
103 D2 **Krems an der Donau** Austria
89 D2 **Kresttsy** Russia
88 B2 **Kretinga** Lith.
100 C2 **Kreuzau** Ger.
100 C2 **Kreuztal** Ger.
118 A2 **Kribi** Cameroon
111 B3 **Krikellos** Greece
66 D1 **Kril'on, Mys** *c.* Russia
73 C3 **Krishna** *r.* India
73 C3 **Krishna, Mouths of the** India
75 C2 **Krishnanagar** India
93 E4 **Kristiansand** Norway
93 F4 **Kristianstad** Sweden
92 E3 **Kristiansund** Norway
93 F4 **Kristinehamn** Sweden
Kriti *i.* Greece *see* **Crete**
111 C3 **Kritiko Pelagos** *sea* Greece
Krivoy Rog Ukr. *see* **Kryvyy Rih**
109 C1 **Križevci** Croatia
108 B1 **Krk** *i.* Croatia
92 F3 **Krokom** Sweden
91 C1 **Krolevets'** Ukr.
101 E2 **Kronach** Ger.
127 I2 **Kronprins Frederik Bjerge** *nunataks* Greenland
123 C2 **Kroonstad** S. Africa
87 D4 **Kropotkin** Russia
91 C2 **Kropyvnyts'kyy** Ukr.
103 E2 **Krosno** Pol.
103 D1 **Krotoszyn** Pol.
60 B2 **Krui** Indon.
109 C2 **Krujë** Albania
111 C2 **Krumovgrad** Bulg.
Krung Thep Thai. *see* **Bangkok**
88 C3 **Krupki** Belarus
109 D2 **Kruševac** Serbia
101 F2 **Krušné hory** *mts* Czechia
128 A2 **Kruzof Island** U.S.A.
89 D3 **Krychaw** Belarus
91 D3 **Krymsk** Russia
91 C2 **Kryvyy Rih** Ukr.
114 B2 **Ksabi** Alg.
107 D2 **Ksar el Boukhari** Alg.
114 B1 **Ksar el Kebir** Morocco
89 E3 **Kshenskiy** Russia
78 B2 **Kū', Jabal al** *h.* Saudi Arabia
61 C1 **Kuala Belait** Brunei
60 B1 **Kuala Kerai** Malaysia
60 B1 **Kuala Lipis** Malaysia
60 B1 **Kuala Lumpur** Malaysia
61 C2 **Kualapembuang** Indon.
60 B1 **Kuala Terengganu** Malaysia
60 B2 **Kualatungkal** Indon.
61 C1 **Kuamut** *Sabah* Malaysia
65 A1 **Kuandian** China
60 B1 **Kuantan** Malaysia
91 D2 **Kuban'** *r.* Russia
89 E2 **Kubenskoye, Ozero** *l.* Russia
110 C2 **Kubrat** Bulg.
61 C1 **Kuching** *Sarawak* Malaysia
109 C2 **Kuçovë** Albania
61 C1 **Kudat** *Sabah* Malaysia
61 C2 **Kudus** Indon.
102 C2 **Kufstein** Austria
127 F2 **Kugaaruk** Can.
126 D2 **Kugluktuk** Can.
92 I3 **Kuhmo** Fin.
79 C2 **Kūhrān, Kūh-e** *mt.* Iran
Kuitin China *see* **Kuytun**
120 A2 **Kuito** Angola
92 I2 **Kuivaniemi** Fin.
65 B2 **Kujang** N. Korea
109 D2 **Kukës** Albania
111 C3 **Kula** Turkey
75 D2 **Kula Kangri** *mt.* Bhutan/China
76 B2 **Kulandy** Kazakh.
88 B2 **Kuldīga** Latvia
122 B1 **Kule** Botswana
101 E2 **Kulmbach** Ger.
77 C3 **Kŭlob** Tajik.
76 B2 **Kul'sary** Kazakh.
77 D1 **Kulunda** Russia
127 I2 **Kulusuk** Greenland
67 C3 **Kumagaya** Japan
67 B4 **Kumamoto** Japan
109 D2 **Kumanovo** Macedonia
114 B4 **Kumasi** Ghana
118 A2 **Kumba** Cameroon
78 B2 **Kumdah** Saudi Arabia
87 E3 **Kumertau** Russia
93 G4 **Kumla** Sweden
115 D3 **Kumo** Nigeria
62 A1 **Kumon Range** *mts* Myanmar
62 B2 **Kumphawapi** Thai.
Kumul China *see* **Hami**
66 D2 **Kunashir, Ostrov** *i.* Russia
120 A2 **Kunene** *r.* Angola/Namibia
77 D2 **Kungei Alatau** *mts* Kazakh./Kyrg.
93 F4 **Kungsbacka** Sweden
118 B2 **Kungu** Dem. Rep. Congo
86 E3 **Kungur** Russia
62 A1 **Kunhing** Myanmar
77 D3 **Kunlun Shan** *mts* China
62 B1 **Kunming** China
50 B1 **Kununurra** Austr.
92 I3 **Kuopio** Fin.
109 C1 **Kupa** *r.* Croatia/Slovenia
59 C3 **Kupang** Indon.
88 B2 **Kupiškis** Lith.
111 C2 **Küplü** Turkey
128 A2 **Kupreanof Island** U.S.A.
91 D2 **Kup''yans'k** Ukr.
77 E2 **Kuqa** China
67 B4 **Kurashiki** Japan
67 B3 **Kurayoshi** Japan
89 E3 **Kurchatov** Russia
81 C2 **Kurdistan** *reg.* Asia
67 B4 **Kure** Japan
88 B2 **Kuressaare** Estonia
86 F3 **Kurgan** Russia
93 H3 **Kurikka** Fin.
156 C3 **Kuril Trench** N. Pacific Ocean
89 E3 **Kurkino** Russia
91 C2 **Kurman** Ukr.
117 B3 **Kurmuk** Sudan
73 B3 **Kurnool** India
53 D2 **Kurri Kurri** Austr.
89 E3 **Kursk** Russia
122 B2 **Kuruman** S. Africa
122 B2 **Kuruman** *watercourse* S. Africa
67 B4 **Kurume** Japan
83 I3 **Kurumkan** Russia
73 C4 **Kurunegala** Sri Lanka
111 C3 **Kuşadası** Turkey
111 C3 **Kuşadası, Gulf of** *b.* Turkey
111 C2 **Kuş Gölü** *l.* Turkey
91 D2 **Kushchëvskaya** Russia
66 D2 **Kushiro** Japan
75 C2 **Kushtia** Bangl.
76 C1 **Kusmuryn** Kazakh.
66 D2 **Kussharo-ko** *l.* Japan
111 C3 **Kütahya** Turkey
81 C1 **Kutaisi** Georgia
109 C1 **Kutjevo** Croatia
103 D1 **Kutno** Pol.
118 B3 **Kutu** Dem. Rep. Congo
126 D2 **Kuujjua** *r.* Can.
131 D1 **Kuujjuaq** Can.
130 C1 **Kuujjuarapik** Can.
92 I2 **Kuusamo** Fin.
120 A2 **Kuvango** Angola
89 D2 **Kuvshinovo** Russia
78 B2 **Kuwait** *country* Asia
79 B2 **Kuwait** Kuwait
Kuybyshev Russia *see* **Samara**
Kuybysheve Ukr. *see* **Bil'mak**
87 D3 **Kuybyshevskoye Vodokhranilishche** *resr* Russia
77 E2 **Kuytun** China
111 C3 **Kuyucak** Turkey
87 D3 **Kuznetsk** Russia
Kuznetsovs'k Ukr. *see* **Varash**
92 H1 **Kvalsund** Norway
123 D2 **KwaDukuza** S. Africa
123 D2 **KwaMashu** S. Africa
Kwangju S. Korea *see* **Gwangju**
65 B1 **Kwanmo-bong** *mt.* N. Korea
123 C3 **KwaNobuhle** S. Africa
122 B3 **KwaNonzame** S. Africa
123 C3 **Kwatinidubu** S. Africa
123 C2 **KwaZamokuhle** S. Africa
123 D2 **KwaZulu-Natal** *prov.* S. Africa
121 B2 **Kwekwe** Zimbabwe
118 B3 **Kwenge** *r.* Dem. Rep. Congo
103 D1 **Kwidzyn** Pol.
118 B3 **Kwilu** *r.* Angola/Dem. Rep. Congo
53 C3 **Kyabram** Austr.
62 A2 **Kyaikto** Myanmar
69 D1 **Kyakhta** Russia
52 A2 **Kyancutta** Austr.
62 A1 **Kyaukpadaung** Myanmar
62 A2 **Kyaukpyu** Myanmar
88 B3 **Kybartai** Lith.
62 A2 **Kyebogyi** Myanmar
62 A2 **Kyeintali** Myanmar
74 B1 **Kyelang** India

Kyiv Ukr. *see* **Kiev**
90 C1 **Kyivs'ke Vodoskhovyshche** *resr* Ukr.
Kyklades *is* Greece *see* **Cyclades**
129 D2 **Kyle** Can.
96 B2 **Kyle of Lochalsh** U.K.
100 C3 **Kyll** *r.* Ger.
111 B3 **Kyllini** *mt.* Greece
111 B3 **Kymi** Greece
52 B3 **Kyneton** Austr.
119 D2 **Kyoga, Lake** Uganda
53 D1 **Kyogle** Austr.
67 C4 **Kyōto** Japan
111 B3 **Kyparissia** Greece
111 B3 **Kyra Panagia** *i.* Greece
80 B2 **Kyrenia** Cyprus
77 D2 **Kyrgyzstan** *country* Asia
101 F1 **Kyritz** Ger.
92 H3 **Kyrönjoki** *r.* Fin.
86 E2 **Kyrta** Russia
86 D2 **Kyssa** Russia
111 B3 **Kythira** *i.* Greece
111 B3 **Kythnos** *i.* Greece
128 B2 **Kyuquot** Can.
67 B4 **Kyūshū** *i.* Japan
110 B2 **Kyustendil** Bulg.
92 H3 **Kyyjärvi** Fin.
68 C1 **Kyzyl** Russia
76 C2 **Kyzylkum Desert** Kazakh./Uzbek.
77 C2 **Kyzylorda** Kazakh.

L

145 C3 **La Angostura, Presa de** *resr* Mex.
117 C4 **Laascaanood** Somalia
150 B1 **La Asunción** Venez.
114 A2 **Laâyoune** Western Sahara
87 D4 **Laba** *r.* Russia
144 B2 **La Babia** Mex.
146 B3 **La Bahía, Islas de** *is* Hond.
152 B3 **La Banda** Arg.
104 B2 **La Baule-Escoublac** France
114 A3 **Labé** Guinea
128 A1 **Laberge, Lake** Can.
129 C2 **La Biche, Lac** *l.* Can.
87 D4 **Labinsk** Russia
64 B1 **Labo** Phil.
104 B3 **Labouheyre** France
131 D1 **Labrador** *reg.* Can.
131 D1 **Labrador City** Can.
158 C1 **Labrador Sea** Can./Greenland
150 B2 **Lábrea** Brazil
61 C1 **Labuan** Malaysia
59 C3 **Labuha** Indon.
60 B1 **Labuhanbilik** Indon.
63 A2 **Labutta** Myanmar
86 F2 **Labytnangi** Russia
109 C2 **Laç** Albania
105 C2 **La Capelle** France
Laccadive Islands India *see* **Lakshadweep**
129 E2 **Lac du Bonnet** Can.
146 B3 **La Ceiba** Hond.
53 B2 **Lachlan** *r.* Austr.
141 E1 **Lachute** Can.
105 D3 **La Ciotat** France
129 C2 **Lac La Biche** Can.
Lac la Martre Can. *see* **Whatî**
141 E1 **Lac-Mégantic** Can.
128 C2 **Lacombe** Can.
146 B4 **La Concepción** Panama
145 C3 **La Concordia** Mex.
108 A3 **Laconi** *Sardinia* Italy
141 E2 **Laconia** U.S.A.
128 C2 **La Crete** Can.
140 A2 **La Crosse** U.S.A.
144 B2 **La Cruz** Mex.
144 B2 **La Cuesta** Mex.
75 B1 **Ladakh Range** *mts* India/Pak.
122 B3 **Ladismith** S. Africa
79 D2 **Lādīz** Iran
86 C2 **Ladoga, Lake** Russia
Ladozhskoye Ozero *l.* Russia *see* **Ladoga, Lake**
128 B3 **Ladysmith** Can.
123 C2 **Ladysmith** S. Africa
59 D3 **Lae** P.N.G.
152 B3 **La Esmeralda** Bol.
93 F4 **Læsø** *i.* Denmark
143 C2 **LaFayette** U.S.A.
140 B2 **Lafayette** *IN* U.S.A.
142 B2 **Lafayette** *LA* U.S.A.
115 C4 **Lafia** Nigeria
104 B2 **La Flèche** France
143 D1 **LaFollette** U.S.A.
131 C1 **Laforge** Can.
79 C2 **Lāft** Iran
108 A3 **La Galite, Île de** *i.* Tunisia
81 C1 **Lagan'** Russia
118 B2 **Lagdo, Lac de** *l.* Cameroon
152 C3 **Lages** Brazil
115 C1 **Laghouat** Alg.
155 D1 **Lagoa Santa** Brazil
114 A2 **La Gomera** *i.* Canary Islands
114 C4 **Lagos** Nigeria
106 B2 **Lagos** Port.
134 C1 **La Grande** U.S.A.
130 C1 **La Grande 3, Réservoir** *resr* Can.
131 C1 **La Grande 4, Réservoir** *resr* Can.
50 B1 **La Grange** Austr.
143 C2 **La Grange** U.S.A.
150 B1 **La Gran Sabana** *plat.* Venez.
152 D3 **Laguna** Brazil
144 A2 **Laguna, Picacho de la** *mt.* Mex.
150 A2 **Lagunas** Peru
La Habana Cuba *see* **Havana**
61 C1 **Lahad Datu** *Sabah* Malaysia
60 B2 **Lahat** Indon.
78 B3 **Laḩij** Yemen
81 C2 **Lāhījān** Iran
100 C2 **Lahnstein** Ger.
74 B1 **Lahore** Pak.
74 A2 **Lahri** Pak.
93 I3 **Lahti** Fin.
115 D4 **Laï** Chad
53 D1 **Laidley** Austr.
104 C2 **L'Aigle** France
111 B3 **Laimos, Akrotirio** *pt* Greece
122 B3 **Laingsburg** S. Africa
92 H2 **Lainioälven** *r.* Sweden
96 B1 **Lairg** U.K.
108 B1 **Laives** Italy
70 B2 **Laiwu** China
70 C2 **Laiyang** China
70 B2 **Laizhou** China
70 B2 **Laizhou Wan** *b.* China
50 C1 **Lajamanu** Austr.
144 B2 **La Junta** Mex.
136 C3 **La Junta** U.S.A.
121 C2 **Lake Cabora Bassa** *resr* Moz.
53 C2 **Lake Cargelligo** Austr.
53 D2 **Lake Cathie** Austr.
142 B2 **Lake Charles** U.S.A.
143 D2 **Lake City** *FL* U.S.A.
143 E2 **Lake City** *SC* U.S.A.
108 A1 **Lake Como** Italy
128 B3 **Lake Cowichan** Can.
108 B1 **Lake Garda** Italy
138 A2 **Lake Havasu City** U.S.A.
143 D3 **Lakeland** U.S.A.
128 C2 **Lake Louise** Can.
134 B1 **Lake Oswego** U.S.A.
54 A2 **Lake Paringa** N.Z.
142 B2 **Lake Providence** U.S.A.
53 C3 **Lakes Entrance** Austr.
134 B2 **Lakeview** U.S.A.
136 B3 **Lakewood** *CO* U.S.A.
141 E2 **Lakewood** *NJ* U.S.A.
143 D3 **Lake Worth** U.S.A.
74 A2 **Lakhpat** India
74 B1 **Lakki Marwat** Pak.
111 B3 **Lakonikos Kolpos** *b.* Greece
92 H1 **Lakselv** Norway
73 B3 **Lakshadweep** India
107 C1 **L'Alcora** Spain
145 C3 **La Libertad** Guat.
106 B1 **Lalín** Spain
75 B2 **Lalitpur** India
129 D2 **La Loche** Can.
100 B2 **La Louvière** Belgium
108 A2 **La Maddalena** *Sardinia* Italy
61 C1 **Lamag** *Sabah* Malaysia
La Manche *str.* France/U.K. **English Channel**
136 C3 **Lamar** U.S.A.
108 A3 **La Marmora, Punta** *mt.* *Sardinia* Italy
128 C1 **La Martre, Lac** *l.* Can.
118 B3 **Lambaréné** Gabon
122 A3 **Lambert's Bay** S. Africa
92 □A2 **Lambeyri** Iceland
106 B1 **Lamego** Port.
150 A3 **La Merced** Peru
79 C2 **Lāmerd** Iran
52 B3 **Lameroo** Austr.
139 C2 **Lamesa** U.S.A.
111 B3 **Lamia** Greece
137 E2 **Lamoni** U.S.A.
62 A2 **Lampang** Thai.
139 D2 **Lampasas** U.S.A.
145 B2 **Lampazos** Mex.
99 A2 **Lampeter** U.K.
62 A2 **Lamphun** Thai.
119 E3 **Lamu** Kenya
62 A2 **Lan, Loi** *mt.* Myanmar/Tha
96 C3 **Lanark** U.K.
63 A2 **Lanbi Kyun** *i.* Myanmar
Lancang Jiang *r.* China *see* **Mekong**
98 B1 **Lancaster** U.K.
135 C4 **Lancaster** *CA* U.S.A.
140 C3 **Lancaster** *OH* U.S.A.
141 D2 **Lancaster** *PA* U.S.A.
143 D2 **Lancaster** *SC* U.S.A.
127 F2 **Lancaster Sound** *str.* Can.
Lanchow China *see* **Lanzho**
102 C2 **Landeck** Austria
136 B2 **Lander** U.S.A.
99 A3 **Land's End** *pt* U.K.
102 C2 **Landshut** Ger.
93 F4 **Landskrona** Sweden
143 C2 **Lanett** U.S.A.
122 B2 **Langberg** *mts* S. Africa
137 D1 **Langdon** U.S.A.
93 F4 **Langeland** *i.* Denmark
101 D1 **Langen** Ger.
100 C1 **Langeoog** Ger.
100 C1 **Langeoog** *i.* Ger.
101 D2 **Langgöns** Ger.
92 □A3 **Langjökull** Iceland
105 C3 **Langogne** France
104 B3 **Langon** France
105 D2 **Langres** France
60 A1 **Langsa** Indon.
62 B1 **Lang Sơn** Vietnam
101 D1 **Langwedel** Ger.
129 D2 **Lanigan** Can.
153 A4 **Lanín, Volcán** *vol.* Arg./Chi

81 C2 **Länkäran** Azer.
104 B2 **Lannion** France
140 C2 **Lansing** U.S.A.
71 B3 **Lanxi** China
117 B4 **Lanya** South Sudan
114 A2 **Lanzarote** *i.* Canary Islands
70 A2 **Lanzhou** China
64 B1 **Laoag City** Phil.
62 B1 **Lao Cai** Vietnam
70 B2 **Laohekou** China
68 C2 **Laojunmiao** China
65 B1 **Laoling** China
65 B1 **Lao Ling** *mts* China
68 C2 **Lao Mangnai** China
105 C2 **Laon** France
62 B2 **Laos** *country* Asia
65 B1 **Laotougou** China
154 C3 **Lapa** Brazil
114 A2 **La Palma** *i.* Canary Islands
146 C4 **La Palma** Panama
150 B1 **La Paragua** Venez.
152 B2 **La Paz** Bol.
144 A2 **La Paz** Mex.
150 B2 **La Pedrera** Col.
66 D1 **La Pérouse Strait** Japan/Russia
145 C2 **La Pesca** Mex.
144 B2 **La Piedad** Mex.
153 C4 **La Plata** Arg.
153 C4 **La Plata, Río de** *sea chan.* Arg./Uru.
106 B1 **La Pola** Spain
93 I3 **Lappeenranta** Fin.
92 G2 **Lappland** *reg.* Europe
111 C2 **Lâpseki** Turkey
83 J1 **Laptev Sea** Russia
Laptevykh, More *sea* Russia *see* **Laptev Sea**
92 H3 **Lapua** Fin.
152 B3 **La Quiaca** Arg.
79 C2 **Lār** Iran
114 B1 **Larache** Morocco
136 B2 **Laramie** U.S.A.
136 B2 **Laramie Mountains** U.S.A.
154 B3 **Laranjeiras do Sul** Brazil
59 C3 **Larantuka** Indon.
59 C3 **Larat** *i.* Indon.
107 D2 **Larba** Alg.
106 C1 **Laredo** Spain
139 D3 **Laredo** U.S.A.
96 B3 **Largs** U.K.
152 B3 **La Rioja** Arg.
111 B3 **Larisa** Greece
74 A2 **Larkana** Pak.
80 B2 **Larnaca** Cyprus
97 D1 **Larne** U.K.
100 B2 **La Roche-en-Ardenne** Belgium
104 B2 **La Rochelle** France
104 B2 **La Roche-sur-Yon** France
107 C2 **La Roda** Spain
147 D3 **La Romana** Dom. Rep.
129 D2 **La Ronge** Can.
129 D2 **La Ronge, Lac** *l.* Can.
50 C1 **Larrimah** Austr.
55 P3 **Larsen Ice Shelf** Antarctica
93 F4 **Larvik** Norway
130 C2 **La Sarre** Can.
138 B2 **Las Cruces** U.S.A.
153 C4 **Las Flores** Arg.
153 B4 **Las Heras** Arg.
62 A1 **Lashio** Myanmar
74 A1 **Lashkar Gāh** Afgh.
109 C3 **La Sila** *reg.* Italy
152 B3 **Las Lomitas** Arg.
144 B2 **Las Nieves** Mex.
114 A2 **Las Palmas de Gran Canaria** Canary Islands
108 A2 **La Spezia** Italy
153 B5 **Las Plumas** Arg.
129 D2 **Last Mountain Lake** Can.
118 B3 **Lastoursville** Gabon
109 C2 **Lastovo** *i.* Croatia
144 A2 **Las Tres Vírgenes, Volcán** *vol.* Mex.
146 C2 **Las Tunas** Cuba
144 B2 **Las Varas** *Chihuahua* Mex.
144 B2 **Las Varas** *Nayarit* Mex.
138 B1 **Las Vegas** *NM* U.S.A.
135 C3 **Las Vegas** *NV* U.S.A.
131 E1 **La Tabatière** Can.
80 B2 **Latakia** Syria
104 B3 **La Teste-de-Buch** France
108 B2 **Latina** Italy
147 D3 **La Tortuga, Isla** *i.* Venez.
64 B1 **La Trinidad** Phil.
89 E2 **Latskoye** Russia
131 C2 **La Tuque** Can.
88 B2 **Latvia** *country* Europe
102 C1 **Lauchhammer** Ger.
106 C1 **Laudio/Llodio** Spain
101 E3 **Lauf an der Pegnitz** Ger.
105 D2 **Laufen** Switz.
51 D4 **Launceston** Austr.
99 A3 **Launceston** U.K.
62 A1 **Launggyaung** Myanmar
51 D1 **Laura** Austr.
142 C2 **Laurel** *MS* U.S.A.
134 E1 **Laurel** *MT* U.S.A.
109 C2 **Lauria** Italy
143 E2 **Laurinburg** U.S.A.
105 D2 **Lausanne** Switz.
61 C2 **Laut** *i.* Indon.
61 C2 **Laut Bali** *sea* Indon.
101 D2 **Lauterbach (Hessen)** Ger.
61 C2 **Laut Kecil, Kepulauan** *is* Indon.
100 C1 **Lauwersmeer** *l.* Neth.
104 B2 **Laval** France
107 C2 **La Vall d'Uixó** Spain
50 B2 **Laverton** Austr.
155 D2 **Lavras** Brazil
123 D2 **Lavumisa** Swaziland
61 C1 **Lawas** *Sarawak* Malaysia
62 A1 **Lawksawk** Myanmar
114 B3 **Lawra** Ghana
137 D3 **Lawrence** U.S.A.
142 C1 **Lawrenceburg** U.S.A.
139 D2 **Lawton** U.S.A.
78 A2 **Lawz, Jabal al** *mt.* Saudi Arabia
93 F4 **Laxå** Sweden
74 B1 **Layyah** Pak.
109 D2 **Lazarevac** Serbia
144 A1 **Lázaro Cárdenas** *Baja California* Mex.
144 B3 **Lázaro Cárdenas** *Michoacán* Mex.
88 B3 **Lazdijai** Lith.
136 C2 **Lead** U.S.A.
129 D2 **Leader** Can.
136 B3 **Leadville** U.S.A.
Leaf Bay Can. *see* **Tasiujaq**
129 D2 **Leaf Rapids** Can.
97 B2 **Leane, Lough** *l.* Ireland
137 E3 **Leavenworth** U.S.A.
80 B2 **Lebanon** *country* Asia
137 E3 **Lebanon** *MO* U.S.A.
141 E2 **Lebanon** *NH* U.S.A.
134 B2 **Lebanon** *OR* U.S.A.
141 D2 **Lebanon** *PA* U.S.A.
89 E3 **Lebedyan'** Russia
91 C1 **Lebedyn** Ukr.
104 C2 **Le Blanc** France
103 D1 **Lębork** Pol.
123 C1 **Lebowakgomo** S. Africa
106 B2 **Lebrija** Spain
153 A4 **Lebu** Chile
104 C3 **Le Bugue** France
109 C2 **Lecce** Italy
108 A1 **Lecco** Italy
102 C2 **Lech** *r.* Austria/Ger.
111 B3 **Lechaina** Greece
71 B3 **Lechang** China
102 B1 **Leck** Ger.
104 C3 **Lectoure** France
106 B1 **Ledesma** Spain
104 C2 **Le Dorat** France
128 C2 **Leduc** Can.
137 E1 **Leech Lake** U.S.A.
98 C2 **Leeds** U.K.
98 B2 **Leek** U.K.
100 C1 **Leer (Ostfriesland)** Ger.
143 D3 **Leesburg** U.S.A.
142 B2 **Leesville** U.S.A.
53 C2 **Leeton** Austr.
122 B3 **Leeu-Gamka** S. Africa
100 B1 **Leeuwarden** Neth.
50 A3 **Leeuwin, Cape** Austr.
147 D3 **Leeward Islands** Caribbean Sea
111 B3 **Lefkada** Greece
111 B3 **Lefkada** *i.* Greece
Lefkosia Cyprus *see* **Nicosia**
64 B1 **Legazpi** Phil.
108 B1 **Legnago** Italy
103 D1 **Legnica** Pol.
75 B1 **Leh** India
104 C2 **Le Havre** France
122 B1 **Lehututu** Botswana
103 D2 **Leibnitz** Austria
99 C2 **Leicester** U.K.
51 C1 **Leichhardt** *r.* Austr.
100 B1 **Leiden** Neth.
100 A2 **Leie** *r.* Belgium
52 A2 **Leigh Creek** Austr.
93 E3 **Leikanger** Norway
101 D1 **Leine** *r.* Ger.
97 C2 **Leinster** *reg.* Ireland
101 F2 **Leipzig** Ger.
92 F2 **Leiranger** Norway
106 B2 **Leiria** Port.
93 E4 **Leirvik** Norway
97 C2 **Leixlip** Ireland
71 B3 **Leiyang** China
71 B3 **Leizhou** China
71 A3 **Leizhou Bandao** *pen.* China
118 B3 **Lékana** Congo
100 B1 **Lelystad** Neth.
153 B6 **Le Maire, Estrecho de** *sea chan.* Arg.
Léman, Lac *l.* France/Switz. *see* **Geneva, Lake**
104 C2 **Le Mans** France
137 D2 **Le Mars** U.S.A.
154 C2 **Leme** Brazil
Lemesos Cyprus *see* **Limassol**
101 D1 **Lemförde** Ger.
127 G2 **Lemieux Islands** Can.
136 C1 **Lemmon** U.S.A.
135 C3 **Lemoore** U.S.A.
131 D1 **Le Moyne, Lac** *l.* Can.
62 A1 **Lemro** *r.* Myanmar
109 C2 **Le Murge** *hills* Italy
83 J2 **Lena** *r.* Russia
100 C1 **Lengerich** Ger.
71 B3 **Lengshuijiang** China
Leningrad Russia *see* **St Petersburg**
91 D2 **Leningradskaya** Russia
77 D3 **Lenin Peak** Kyrg./Tajik.
Leninsk Kazakh. *see* **Baykonyr**
89 E3 **Leninskiy** Russia
100 A2 **Lens** Belgium
104 C1 **Lens** France
83 I2 **Lensk** Russia

103 D2 **Lenti** Hungary
109 C3 **Lentini** *Sicily* Italy
114 B3 **Léo** Burkina Faso
103 D2 **Leoben** Austria
99 B2 **Leominster** U.K.
144 B2 **León** Mex.
146 B3 **León** Nic.
106 B1 **León** Spain
122 A1 **Leonardville** Namibia
155 D2 **Leopoldina** Brazil
123 C1 **Lephalale** S. Africa
123 C1 **Lephepe** Botswana
123 C3 **Lephoi** S. Africa
71 B3 **Leping** China
105 C2 **Le Puy-en-Velay** France
150 A2 **Lérida** Col.
106 C1 **Lerma** Spain
111 C3 **Leros** *i.* Greece
130 C1 **Le Roy, Lac** *l.* Can.
93 F4 **Lerum** Sweden
96 □ **Lerwick** U.K.
111 C3 **Lesbos** *i.* Greece
147 C3 **Les Cayes** Haiti
69 C3 **Leshan** China
86 D2 **Leshukonskoye** Russia
109 D2 **Leskovac** Serbia
104 B2 **Lesneven** France
89 E2 **Lesnoye** Russia
83 H3 **Lesosibirsk** Russia
123 C2 **Lesotho** *country* Africa
66 B1 **Lesozavodsk** Russia
104 B2 **Les Sables-d'Olonne** France
147 D3 **Lesser Antilles** *is* Caribbean Sea
81 C1 **Lesser Caucasus** *mts* Asia
128 C2 **Lesser Slave Lake** Can.
58 B3 **Lesser Sunda Islands** *is* Indon.
105 C3 **Les Vans** France
Lesvos *i.* Greece *see* **Lesbos**
103 D1 **Leszno** Pol.
99 C3 **Letchworth Garden City** U.K.
128 C3 **Lethbridge** Can.
150 C1 **Lethem** Guyana
59 C3 **Leti, Kepulauan** *is* Indon.
150 B2 **Leticia** Col.
123 C1 **Letlhakeng** Botswana
104 C1 **Le Touquet-Paris-Plage** France
99 D3 **Le Tréport** France
63 A2 **Letsok-aw Kyun** *i.* Myanmar
123 C2 **Letsopa** S. Africa
97 C1 **Letterkenny** Ireland
105 C3 **Leucate, Étang de** *l.* France
60 A1 **Leuser, Gunung** *mt.* Indon.
100 B2 **Leuven** Belgium
92 F3 **Levanger** Norway
139 C2 **Levelland** U.S.A.
50 B1 **Lévêque, Cape** Austr.
100 C2 **Leverkusen** Ger.
103 D2 **Levice** Slovakia
54 C2 **Levin** N.Z.
131 C2 **Lévis** Can.
89 E3 **Lev Tolstoy** Russia
99 D3 **Lewes** U.K.
96 A1 **Lewis, Isle of** *i.* U.K.
140 C3 **Lewisburg** U.S.A.
134 D1 **Lewis Range** *mts* U.S.A.
134 C1 **Lewiston** *ID* U.S.A.
141 E2 **Lewiston** *ME* U.S.A.
134 E1 **Lewistown** U.S.A.
140 C3 **Lexington** *KY* U.S.A.
136 D2 **Lexington** *NE* U.S.A.
141 D3 **Lexington** *VA* U.S.A.
64 B1 **Leyte** *i.* Phil.
109 C2 **Lezhë** Albania
89 F2 **Lezhnevo** Russia
89 E3 **L'gov** Russia
68 C2 **Lharigarbo** China
75 D2 **Lhasa** China
75 C2 **Lhazê** China
60 A1 **Lhokseumawe** Indon.
111 B3 **Liakoura** *mt.* Greece
67 B3 **Liancourt Rocks** *i.* N. Pacific Ocean
71 B3 **Lianhua** China
71 B3 **Lianjiang** China
70 C1 **Lianshan** China
70 B2 **Lianyungang** China
71 B3 **Lianzhou** China
70 B2 **Liaocheng** China
70 C1 **Liaodong Bandao** *pen.* China
70 C1 **Liaodong Wan** *b.* China
65 A1 **Liao He** *r.* China
70 C1 **Liaoning** *prov.* China
65 A1 **Liaoyang** China
65 B1 **Liaoyuan** China
128 B1 **Liard** *r.* Can.
134 C1 **Libby** U.S.A.
118 B2 **Libenge** Dem. Rep. Congo
136 C3 **Liberal** U.S.A.
103 D1 **Liberec** Czechia
114 B4 **Liberia** *country* Africa
146 B3 **Liberia** Costa Rica
150 B1 **Libertad** Venez.
100 B3 **Libin** Belgium
104 B3 **Libourne** France
118 A2 **Libreville** Gabon
115 D2 **Libya** *country* Africa
115 E2 **Libyan Desert** Egypt/Libya
116 A1 **Libyan Plateau** Egypt/Libya
108 B3 **Licata** *Sicily* Italy
Licheng China *see* **Lipu**
121 C2 **Lichinga** Moz.
101 E2 **Lichte** Ger.
123 C2 **Lichtenburg** S. Africa
101 E2 **Lichtenfels** Ger.
88 C3 **Lida** Belarus
93 F4 **Lidköping** Sweden
50 C2 **Liebig, Mount** Austr.
105 D2 **Liechtenstein** *country* Europe
100 B2 **Liège** Belgium
92 J3 **Lieksa** Fin.
119 C2 **Lienart** Dem. Rep. Congo
63 B2 **Liên Nghia** Vietnam
102 C2 **Lienz** Austria
88 B2 **Liepāja** Latvia
102 C2 **Liezen** Austria
97 C2 **Liffey** *r.* Ireland
97 C1 **Lifford** Ireland
53 C1 **Lightning Ridge** Austr.
121 C2 **Ligonha** *r.* Moz.
105 D3 **Ligurian Sea** France/Italy
119 C4 **Likasi** Dem. Rep. Congo
128 B2 **Likely** Can.
89 E2 **Likhoslavl'** Russia
61 B1 **Liku** Indon.
105 D3 **L'Île-Rousse** *Corsica* France
71 B3 **Liling** China
93 F4 **Lilla Edet** Sweden
100 B2 **Lille** Belgium
105 C1 **Lille** France
Lille Bælt *sea chan.* Denmark *see* **Little Belt**
93 F3 **Lillehammer** Norway
93 F4 **Lillestrøm** Norway
128 B2 **Lillooet** Can.
121 C2 **Lilongwe** Malawi
64 B2 **Liloy** Phil.
150 A3 **Lima** Peru
140 C2 **Lima** U.S.A.
80 B2 **Limassol** Cyprus
97 C1 **Limavady** U.K.
153 B4 **Limay** *r.* Arg.
101 F2 **Limbach-Oberfrohna** Ger.
88 B2 **Limbaži** Latvia
118 A2 **Limbe** Cameroon
100 D2 **Limburg an der Lahn** Ger.
122 B2 **Lime Acres** S. Africa
154 C2 **Limeira** Brazil
97 B2 **Limerick** Ireland
93 E4 **Limfjorden** *sea chan.* Denmar
111 C3 **Limnos** *i.* Greece
104 C2 **Limoges** France
136 C3 **Limon** U.S.A.
104 C3 **Limoux** France
123 C1 **Limpopo** *prov.* S. Africa
121 C3 **Limpopo** *r.* S. Africa/Zimbabwe
64 A1 **Linapacan** *i.* Phil.
153 A4 **Linares** Chile
145 C2 **Linares** Mex.
106 C2 **Linares** Spain
62 B1 **Lincang** China
Linchuan China *see* **Fuzhou**
98 C2 **Lincoln** U.K.
140 B2 **Lincoln** *IL* U.S.A.
141 F1 **Lincoln** *ME* U.S.A.
137 D2 **Lincoln** *NE* U.S.A.
151 C1 **Linden** Guyana
142 C1 **Linden** U.S.A.
119 C2 **Lindi** *r.* Dem. Rep. Congo
119 D3 **Lindi** Tanz.
Lindisfarne *i.* U.K. *see* **Holy Island**
80 A2 **Lindos** Greece
141 D2 **Lindsay** Can.
49 H2 **Line Islands** Kiribati
70 B2 **Linfen** China
64 B1 **Lingayen** Phil.
70 B2 **Lingbao** China
123 C3 **Lingelethu** S. Africa
123 C3 **Lingelihle** S. Africa
100 C1 **Lingen (Ems)** Ger.
60 B2 **Lingga, Kepulauan** *is* Indon.
71 B3 **Lingling** China
71 A3 **Lingshan** China
71 A4 **Lingshui** China
114 A3 **Linguère** Senegal
63 B2 **Linh, Ngok** *mt.* Vietnam
155 D1 **Linhares** Brazil
93 G4 **Linköping** Sweden
66 B1 **Linkou** China
70 B2 **Linqing** China
154 C2 **Lins** Brazil
136 C1 **Linton** U.S.A.
69 D2 **Linxi** China
69 C2 **Linxia** China
70 B2 **Linyi** *Shandong* China
70 B2 **Linyi** *Shandong* China
70 B2 **Linying** China
102 C2 **Linz** Austria
105 C3 **Lion, Golfe du** *g.* France
109 B3 **Lipari** *Sicily* Italy
108 B3 **Lipari, Isole** *is* Italy
89 E3 **Lipetsk** Russia
110 B1 **Lipova** Romania
101 D2 **Lippstadt** Ger.
71 B3 **Lipu** China
76 C1 **Lisakovsk** Kazakh.
118 C2 **Lisala** Dem. Rep. Congo
Lisboa Port. *see* **Lisbon**
106 B2 **Lisbon** Port.
97 C1 **Lisburn** U.K.
97 B2 **Liscannor Bay** Ireland
104 C2 **Lisieux** France
99 A3 **Liskeard** U.K.
89 E3 **Liski** Russia
53 D1 **Lismore** Austr.
97 C1 **Lisnaskea** U.K.
97 B2 **Listowel** Ireland
71 A3 **Litang** *Guangxi* China
68 C2 **Litang** *Sichuan* China
140 B3 **Litchfield** *IL* U.S.A.

137 E1 **Litchfield** *MN* U.S.A.
53 D2 **Lithgow** Austr.
111 B3 **Lithino, Akrotirio** *pt* Greece
88 B2 **Lithuania** *country* Europe
102 C1 **Litoměřice** Czechia
146 C2 **Little Abaco** *i.* Bahamas
73 D3 **Little Andaman** *i.* India
93 E4 **Little Belt** *sea chan.* Denmark
137 E1 **Little Falls** U.S.A.
139 C2 **Littlefield** U.S.A.
99 C3 **Littlehampton** U.K.
122 A2 **Little Karas Berg** *plat.* Namibia
122 B3 **Little Karoo** *plat.* S. Africa
96 A2 **Little Minch** *sea chan.* U.K.
136 C1 **Little Missouri** *r.* U.S.A.
63 A3 **Little Nicobar** *i.* India
142 B2 **Little Rock** U.S.A.
141 E2 **Littleton** U.S.A.
70 B2 **Liujiachang** China
71 A3 **Liupanshui** China
71 A3 **Liuzhou** China
111 B3 **Livadeia** Greece
88 C2 **Līvāni** Latvia
50 B1 **Liveringa** Austr.
138 C2 **Livermore, Mount** U.S.A.
131 D2 **Liverpool** Can.
98 B2 **Liverpool** U.K.
127 F2 **Liverpool, Cape** Can.
53 C2 **Liverpool Range** *mts* Austr.
134 D1 **Livingston** *MT* U.S.A.
139 E2 **Livingston** *TX* U.S.A.
139 D2 **Livingston, Lake** U.S.A.
120 B2 **Livingstone** Zambia
109 C2 **Livno** Bos. & Herz.
89 E3 **Livny** Russia
140 C2 **Livonia** U.S.A.
108 B2 **Livorno** Italy
119 D3 **Liwale** Tanz.
70 B2 **Liyang** China
99 A4 **Lizard Point** U.K.
Lizarra Spain *see* **Estella/Lizarra**
108 B1 **Ljubljana** Slovenia
93 G3 **Ljungan** *r.* Sweden
93 F4 **Ljungby** Sweden
93 G3 **Ljusdal** Sweden
93 G3 **Ljusnan** *r.* Sweden
99 B3 **Llandeilo** U.K.
99 B3 **Llandovery** U.K.
99 B2 **Llandrindod Wells** U.K.
98 B2 **Llandudno** U.K.
99 A3 **Llanelli** U.K.
98 A2 **Llangefni** U.K.
139 C2 **Llano Estacado** *plain* U.S.A.
150 B1 **Llanos** *plain* Col./Venez.
107 D1 **Lleida** Spain
99 A2 **Lleyn Peninsula** U.K.
107 C2 **Llíria** Spain
Llodio Spain *see* **Laudio/Llodio**
128 B2 **Lloyd George, Mount** Can.
129 D2 **Lloyd Lake** Can.
129 C2 **Lloydminster** Can.
152 B3 **Llullaillaco, Volcán** *vol.* Chile
123 C2 **Lobatse** Botswana
120 A2 **Lobito** Angola
101 F1 **Loburg** Ger.
96 B2 **Lochaber** *reg.* U.K.
104 C2 **Loches** France
96 B2 **Lochgilphead** U.K.
96 B1 **Lochinver** U.K.
96 A2 **Lochmaddy** U.K.
96 C2 **Lochnagar** *mt.* U.K.
52 A2 **Lock** Austr.
96 C3 **Lockerbie** U.K.
139 D3 **Lockhart** U.S.A.
141 D2 **Lock Haven** U.S.A.
141 D2 **Lockport** U.S.A.
63 B2 **Lôc Ninh** Vietnam
105 C3 **Lodève** France
86 C2 **Lodeynoye Pole** Russia
92 F2 **Løding** Norway
119 D2 **Lodwar** Kenya
103 D1 **Łódź** Pol.
62 B2 **Loei** Thai.
122 A3 **Loeriesfontein** S. Africa
92 F2 **Lofoten** *is* Norway
134 D2 **Logan** U.S.A.
126 B2 **Logan, Mount** Can.
140 B2 **Logansport** U.S.A.
108 B1 **Logatec** Slovenia
106 C1 **Logroño** Spain
101 D1 **Löhne** Ger.
101 D1 **Lohne (Oldenburg)** Ger.
62 A2 **Loikaw** Myanmar
104 B2 **Loire** *r.* France
150 A2 **Loja** Ecuador
106 C2 **Loja** Spain
92 I2 **Lokan tekojärvi** *resr* Fin.
74 B1 **Lōkār** Afgh.
100 B2 **Lokeren** Belgium
122 B1 **Lokgwabe** Botswana
119 D2 **Lokichar** Kenya
119 D2 **Lokichokio** Kenya
89 D2 **Loknya** Russia
115 C4 **Lokoja** Nigeria
89 D3 **Lokot'** Russia
88 C2 **Loksa** Estonia
127 G2 **Loks Land** *i.* Can.
119 D3 **Loliondo** Tanz.
93 F4 **Lolland** *i.* Denmark
122 B2 **Lolwane** S. Africa
110 B2 **Lom** Bulg.
93 E3 **Lom** Norway
119 C2 **Lomami** *r.* Dem. Rep. Congo
153 C4 **Lomas de Zamora** Arg.
61 C2 **Lombok** *i.* Indon.
61 C2 **Lombok, Selat** *sea chan.* Indon.
114 C4 **Lomé** Togo
118 C3 **Lomela** *r.* Dem. Rep. Congo
100 B2 **Lommel** Belgium
96 B2 **Lomond, Loch** *l.* U.K.
88 C2 **Lomonosov** Russia
135 B4 **Lompoc** U.S.A.
63 B2 **Lom Sak** Thai.
103 E1 **Łomża** Pol.
130 B2 **London** Can.
99 C3 **London** U.K.
140 C3 **London** U.S.A.
97 C1 **Londonderry** U.K.
50 B1 **Londonderry, Cape** Austr.
154 B2 **Londrina** Brazil
83 M2 **Longa, Proliv** *sea chan.* Russia
61 C1 **Long Akah** *Sarawak* Malaysia
143 E2 **Long Bay** U.S.A.
135 C4 **Long Beach** U.S.A.
97 C2 **Longford** Ireland
61 C2 **Longiram** Indon.
147 C2 **Long Island** Bahamas
130 C1 **Long Island** Can.
59 D3 **Long Island** P.N.G.
141 E2 **Long Island** U.S.A.
130 B2 **Longlac** Can.
130 B2 **Long Lake** Can.
136 B2 **Longmont** U.S.A.
70 A2 **Longnan** China
140 C2 **Long Point** Can.
71 B3 **Longquan** China
131 E2 **Long Range Mountains** Can.
51 D2 **Longreach** Austr.
99 D2 **Long Stratton** U.K.
98 B1 **Longtown** U.K.
105 D2 **Longuyon** France
139 E2 **Longview** *TX* U.S.A.
134 B1 **Longview** *WA* U.S.A.
70 A2 **Longxi** China
71 B3 **Longxi Shan** *mt.* China
63 B2 **Long Xuyên** Vietnam
71 B3 **Longyan** China
82 C1 **Longyearbyen** Svalbard
102 B2 **Lons-le-Saunier** France
143 E2 **Lookout, Cape** U.S.A.
97 B2 **Loop Head** Ireland
63 B2 **Lop Buri** Thai.
64 B1 **Lopez** Phil.
68 C2 **Lop Nur** *salt flat* China
118 B2 **Lopori** *r.* Dem. Rep. Congo
74 A2 **Lora, Hāmūn-i-** *dry lake* Afgh./Pak.
106 B2 **Lora del Río** Spain
140 C2 **Lorain** U.S.A.
74 A1 **Loralai** Pak.
107 C2 **Lorca** Spain
48 E5 **Lord Howe Island** Austr.
138 B2 **Lordsburg** U.S.A.
155 C2 **Lorena** Brazil
152 B2 **Loreto** Bol.
144 A2 **Loreto** Mex.
104 B2 **Lorient** France
96 B2 **Lorn, Firth of** *est.* U.K.
52 B3 **Lorne** Austr.
138 B1 **Los Alamos** U.S.A.
139 D3 **Los Aldamas** Mex.
153 A4 **Los Ángeles** Chile
135 C4 **Los Angeles** U.S.A.
135 B3 **Los Banos** U.S.A.
152 B3 **Los Blancos** Arg.
91 E1 **Losevo** Russia
108 B2 **Lošinj** *i.* Croatia
144 B2 **Los Mochis** Mex.
118 B2 **Losombo** Dem. Rep. Congo
147 D3 **Los Roques, Islas** *is* Venez.
96 C2 **Lossiemouth** U.K.
150 B1 **Los Teques** Venez.
152 A4 **Los Vilos** Chile
104 C3 **Lot** *r.* France
119 D2 **Lotagipi Swamp** Kenya/Sudan
96 C1 **Loth** U.K.
118 C3 **Loto** Dem. Rep. Congo
89 E2 **Lotoshino** Russia
62 B1 **Louangnamtha** Laos
62 B2 **Louangphabang** Laos
118 B3 **Loubomo** Congo
104 B2 **Loudéac** France
71 B3 **Loudi** China
118 B3 **Loudima** Congo
114 A3 **Louga** Senegal
99 C2 **Loughborough** U.K.
97 B2 **Loughrea** Ireland
105 D2 **Louhans** France
97 B2 **Louisburgh** Ireland
142 B2 **Louisiana** *state* U.S.A.
140 B3 **Louisville** *KY* U.S.A.
142 C2 **Louisville** *MS* U.S.A.
86 C2 **Loukhi** Russia
130 C1 **Loups Marins, Lacs des** *lakes* Can.
104 B3 **Lourdes** France
151 C1 **Lourenço** Brazil
106 B1 **Lousã** Port.
53 C2 **Louth** Austr.
98 C2 **Louth** U.K.
Louvain Belgium *see* **Leuven**
89 D2 **Lovat'** *r.* Russia
110 B2 **Lovech** Bulg.
136 B2 **Loveland** U.S.A.
135 C2 **Lovelock** U.S.A.
139 C2 **Lovington** U.S.A.
119 C3 **Lowa** Dem. Rep. Congo
141 E2 **Lowell** U.S.A.
128 C3 **Lower Arrow Lake** Can.
54 B2 **Lower Hutt** N.Z.
97 C1 **Lower Lough Erne** *l.* U.K.

128 B2 **Lower Post** Can.
99 D2 **Lowestoft** U.K.
103 D1 **Łowicz** Pol.
141 D2 **Lowville** U.S.A.
52 B2 **Loxton** Austr.
Loyang China *see* **Luoyang**
48 F4 **Loyauté, Îles** *is* New Caledonia
89 D3 **Loyew** Belarus
109 C2 **Loznica** Serbia
91 D2 **Lozova** Ukr.
120 B2 **Luacano** Angola
70 B2 **Lu'an** China
120 A1 **Luanda** Angola
121 C2 **Luangwa** *r.* Zambia
121 B2 **Luanshya** Zambia
106 B1 **Luarca** Spain
120 B2 **Luau** Angola
103 E1 **Lubaczów** Pol.
120 A2 **Lubango** Angola
119 C3 **Lubao** Dem. Rep. Congo
103 E1 **Lubartów** Pol.
101 D1 **Lübbecke** Ger.
139 C2 **Lubbock** U.S.A.
101 E1 **Lübeck** Ger.
69 E2 **Lubei** China
87 E3 **Lubenka** Kazakh.
103 D1 **Lubin** Pol.
103 E1 **Lublin** Pol.
91 C1 **Lubny** Ukr.
61 C1 **Lubok Antu** *Sarawak* Malaysia
101 E1 **Lübow** Ger.
101 E1 **Lübtheen** Ger.
119 C3 **Lubudi** Dem. Rep. Congo
60 B2 **Lubuklinggau** Indon.
119 C4 **Lubumbashi** Dem. Rep. Congo
120 B2 **Lubungu** Zambia
119 C3 **Lubutu** Dem. Rep. Congo
120 A1 **Lucala** Angola
97 C2 **Lucan** Ireland
120 B1 **Lucapa** Angola
96 B3 **Luce Bay** U.K.
154 B2 **Lucélia** Brazil
64 B1 **Lucena** Phil.
106 C2 **Lucena** Spain
103 D2 **Lučenec** Slovakia
109 C2 **Lucera** Italy
105 D2 **Lucerne** Switz.
101 E1 **Lüchow (Wendland)** Ger.
120 A2 **Lucira** Angola
101 F1 **Luckenwalde** Ger.
122 B2 **Luckhoff** S. Africa
75 C2 **Lucknow** India
120 B2 **Lucusse** Angola
Lüda China *see* **Dalian**
100 C2 **Lüdenscheid** Ger.
101 E1 **Lüder** Ger.
120 A3 **Lüderitz** Namibia
74 B1 **Ludhiana** India
140 B2 **Ludington** U.S.A.
99 B2 **Ludlow** U.K.
135 C4 **Ludlow** U.S.A.
110 C2 **Ludogorie** *reg.* Bulg.
93 G3 **Ludvika** Sweden
102 B2 **Ludwigsburg** Ger.
101 F1 **Ludwigsfelde** Ger.
101 D3 **Ludwigshafen am Rhein** Ger.
101 E1 **Ludwigslust** Ger.
88 C2 **Ludza** Latvia
118 C3 **Luebo** Dem. Rep. Congo
120 A2 **Luena** Angola
70 A2 **Lüeyang** China
71 B3 **Lufeng** China
139 E2 **Lufkin** U.S.A.
88 C2 **Luga** Russia
88 C2 **Luga** *r.* Russia
105 D2 **Lugano** Switz.
121 C2 **Lugenda** *r.* Moz.
97 C2 **Lugnaquilla** *h.* Ireland
106 B1 **Lugo** Spain
110 B1 **Lugoj** Romania
91 D2 **Luhans'k** Ukr.
119 D3 **Luhombero** Tanz.
90 B1 **Luhyny** Ukr.
120 B2 **Luiana** Angola
118 C3 **Luilaka** *r.* Dem. Rep. Congo
105 D2 **Luino** Italy
92 I2 **Luiro** *r.* Fin.
118 C3 **Luiza** Dem. Rep. Congo
70 B2 **Lujiang** China
109 C2 **Lukavac** Bos. & Herz.
118 B3 **Lukenie** *r.* Dem. Rep. Congo
138 A2 **Lukeville** U.S.A.
89 E3 **Lukhovitsy** Russia
103 E1 **Łuków** Pol.
120 B2 **Lukulu** Zambia
92 H2 **Luleå** Sweden
92 H2 **Luleälven** *r.* Sweden
110 C2 **Lüleburgaz** Turkey
70 B2 **Lüliang Shan** *mts* China
61 C2 **Lumajang** Indon.
75 C1 **Lumajangdong Co** *salt l.* China
120 B2 **Lumbala Kaquengue** Angola
120 B2 **Lumbala N'guimbo** Angola
143 E2 **Lumberton** U.S.A.
61 C1 **Lumbis** Indon.
106 B1 **Lumbrales** Spain
63 B2 **Lumphăt** Cambodia
129 D2 **Lumsden** Can.
54 A3 **Lumsden** N.Z.
93 F4 **Lund** Sweden
121 C2 **Lundazi** Zambia
99 A3 **Lundy** *i.* U.K.
101 E1 **Lüneburg** Ger.
101 E1 **Lüneburger Heide** *reg.* Ger.
100 C2 **Lünen** Ger.
105 D2 **Lunéville** France
120 B2 **Lunga** *r.* Zambia
114 A4 **Lungi** Sierra Leone
62 A1 **Lunglei** India
120 B2 **Lungwebungu** *r.* Zambia
74 B2 **Luni** *r.* India
88 C3 **Luninyets** Belarus
114 A4 **Lunsar** Sierra Leone
77 E2 **Luntai** China
71 A3 **Luodian** China
71 B3 **Luoding** China
70 B2 **Luohe** China
70 B2 **Luoyang** China
121 B2 **Lupane** Zimbabwe
110 B1 **Lupeni** Romania
121 C2 **Lupilichi** Moz.
101 F2 **Luppa** Ger.
121 D2 **Lúrio** Moz.
121 D2 **Lurio** *r.* Moz.
121 B2 **Lusaka** Zambia
118 C3 **Lusambo** Dem. Rep. Congo
109 C2 **Lushnjë** Albania
136 C2 **Lusk** U.S.A.
76 B3 **Lūt, Kavīr-e** *des.* Iran
99 C3 **Luton** U.K.
61 C1 **Lutong** *Sarawak* Malaysia
129 C1 **Łutselk'e** Can.
90 B1 **Luts'k** Ukr.
122 B2 **Lutzputs** S. Africa
122 A3 **Lutzville** S. Africa
117 C4 **Luuq** Somalia
137 D2 **Luverne** U.S.A.
119 C3 **Luvua** *r.* Dem. Rep. Congo
123 D1 **Luvuvhu** *r.* S. Africa
119 D2 **Luwero** Uganda
59 C3 **Luwuk** Indon.
100 C3 **Luxembourg** *country* Europe
100 C3 **Luxembourg** Lux.
105 D2 **Luxeuil-les-Bains** France
123 C3 **Luxolweni** S. Africa
116 B2 **Luxor** Egypt
100 B2 **Luyksgestel** Neth.
86 D2 **Luza** Russia
Luzern Switz. *see* **Lucerne**
71 A3 **Luzhou** China
154 C1 **Luziânia** Brazil
151 D2 **Luzilândia** Brazil
64 B1 **Luzon** *i.* Phil.
71 C3 **Luzon Strait** Phil./Taiwan
90 A2 **L'viv** Ukr.
L'vov Ukr. *see* **L'viv**
88 C3 **Lyakhavichy** Belarus
92 G3 **Lycksele** Sweden
88 C3 **Lyel'chytsy** Belarus
88 C3 **Lyepyel'** Belarus
99 B3 **Lyme Bay** U.K.
141 D3 **Lynchburg** U.S.A.
129 D2 **Lynn Lake** Can.
129 D1 **Lynx Lake** Can.
105 C2 **Lyon** France
89 D2 **Lyozna** Belarus
86 E3 **Lys'va** Russia
91 D2 **Lysychans'k** Ukr.
98 B2 **Lytham St Anne's** U.K.
88 C3 **Lyuban'** Belarus
89 E2 **Lyubertsy** Russia
90 B1 **Lyubeshiv** Ukr.
89 F2 **Lyubim** Russia
91 D2 **Lyubotyn** Ukr.
89 D2 **Lyubytino** Russia
89 D3 **Lyudinovo** Russia

M

80 B2 **Ma'ān** Jordan
88 C2 **Maardu** Estonia
100 B2 **Maas** *r.* Neth.
100 B2 **Maaseik** Belgium
64 B1 **Maasin** Phil.
100 B2 **Maastricht** Neth.
121 C3 **Mabalane** Moz.
150 C1 **Mabaruma** Guyana
121 C3 **Mabote** Moz.
122 B2 **Mabule** Botswana
122 B1 **Mabutsane** Botswana
155 D2 **Macaé** Brazil
121 C2 **Macaloge** Moz.
126 E2 **MacAlpine Lake** Can.
71 B3 **Macao** *aut. reg.* China
151 C1 **Macapá** Brazil
150 A2 **Macará** Ecuador
155 D1 **Macarani** Brazil
123 D1 **Macarretane** Moz.
151 E2 **Macau** Brazil
98 B2 **Macclesfield** U.K.
50 B2 **Macdonald, Lake** *imp. l.* Aus
50 C2 **MacDonnell Ranges** *mts* Austr.
130 A1 **MacDowell Lake** Can.
106 B1 **Macedo de Cavaleiros** Port.
52 B3 **Macedon** *mt.* Austr.
109 D2 **Macedonia** *country* Europe
151 E2 **Maceió** Brazil
108 B2 **Macerata** Italy
52 A2 **Macfarlane, Lake** *imp. l.* Aus
97 B3 **Macgillycuddy's Reeks** *mts* Ireland
74 A2 **Mach** Pak.
155 C2 **Machado** Brazil
121 C3 **Machaila** Moz.
119 D3 **Machakos** Kenya
150 A2 **Machala** Ecuador
68 C2 **Machali** China
121 C3 **Machanga** Moz.
70 B2 **Macheng** China
141 F2 **Machias** U.S.A.

150 A1	Machiques Venez.	
150 A3	Machu Picchu tourist site Peru	
123 D2	Macia Moz.	
110 C1	Măcin Romania	
114 B3	Macina Mali	
53 L2	Macintyre r. Austr.	
51 D2	Mackay Austr.	
50 B2	Mackay, Lake imp. l. Austr.	
129 C1	MacKay Lake Can.	
128 B2	Mackenzie Can.	
128 C2	Mackenzie r. Can.	
126 D1	Mackenzie Bay Can.	
126 D1	Mackenzie King Island Can.	
128 C2	Mackenzie Mountains Can.	
129 D2	Macklin Can.	
53 D1	Macksville Austr.	
53 D1	Maclean Austr.	
51 D2	MacLeod, Lake dry lake Austr.	
140 A2	Macomb U.S.A.	
108 A2	Macomer Sardinia Italy	
105 C2	Mâcon France	
143 D2	Macon GA U.S.A.	
137 E3	Macon MO U.S.A.	
53 D2	Macquarie r. Austr.	
48 E6	Macquarie Island S. Pacific Ocean	
53 C2	Macquarie Marshes Austr.	
97 B3	Macroom Ireland	
45 A1	Macumba watercourse Austr.	
45 C3	Macuspana Mex.	
44 B2	Macuzari, Presa resr Mex.	
123 D2	Madadeni S. Africa	
121 □D3	Madagascar country Africa	
115 D2	Madama Niger	
111 B2	Madan Bulg.	
59 D3	Madang P.N.G.	
151 E4	Madeira r. Brazil	
114 A1	Madeira terr. N. Atlantic Ocean	
131 D2	Madeleine, Îles de la is Can.	
44 B2	Madera Mex.	
135 B3	Madera U.S.A.	
18 B3	Madingou Congo	
137 E2	Madison IN U.S.A.	
137 D2	Madison SD U.S.A.	
140 A2	Madison WI U.S.A.	
140 C3	Madison WV U.S.A.	
140 B3	Madison r. U.S.A.	
140 A3	Madisonville U.S.A.	
61 C2	Madiun Indon.	
19 D2	Mado Gashi Kenya	
88 C2	Madona Latvia	
78 A2	Madrakah Saudi Arabia	
	Madras India see Chennai	
34 B2	Madras U.S.A.	
45 C2	Madre, Laguna lag. Mex.	
45 B3	Madre del Sur, Sierra mts Mex.	
44 B2	Madre Occidental, Sierra mts Mex.	
45 B2	Madre Oriental, Sierra mts Mex.	
106 C1	Madrid Spain	
106 C2	Madridejos Spain	
61 C2	Madura i. Indon.	
61 C2	Madura, Selat sea chan. Indon.	
73 B4	Madurai India	
62 A2	Maebashi Japan	
62 A2	Mae Hong Son Thai.	
62 A1	Mae Sai Thai.	
62 A2	Mae Sariang Thai.	
62 A2	Mae Suai Thai.	
23 C2	Mafeteng Lesotho	
19 D3	Mafia Island Tanz.	
19 D3	Mafinga Tanz.	
54 C3	Mafra Brazil	
83 L3	Magadan Russia	
47 C4	Magangué Col.	
144 A1	Magdalena Mex.	
138 B2	Magdalena U.S.A.	
144 A2	Magdalena, Bahía b. Mex.	
101 E1	Magdeburg Ger.	
153 A6	Magellan, Strait of Chile	
97 C1	Magherafelt U.K.	
87 E3	Magnitogorsk Russia	
142 B2	Magnolia U.S.A.	
131 D1	Magpie, Lac l. Can.	
114 A3	Magta' Lahjar Maur.	
151 D2	Maguarinho, Cabo c. Brazil	
123 D2	Magude Moz.	
	Magway Myanmar see Magwe	
62 A1	Magwe Myanmar	
81 C2	Mahābād Iran	
74 B2	Mahajan India	
121 □D2	Mahajanga Madag.	
61 C2	Mahakam r. Indon.	
123 C1	Mahalapye Botswana	
121 □D2	Mahalevona Madag.	
75 C2	Mahanadi r. India	
121 □D2	Mahanoro Madag.	
63 B2	Maha Sarakham Thai.	
121 □D2	Mahavavy r. Madag.	
78 B2	Mahd adh Dhahab Saudi Arabia	
150 C1	Mahdia Guyana	
113 K7	Mahé i. Seychelles	
74 B2	Mahesana India	
54 C1	Mahia Peninsula N.Z.	
123 C2	Mahikeng S. Africa	
89 D3	Mahilyow/Mogilev Belarus	
74 B2	Mahi Sagar r. India	
74 B2	Mahuva India	
110 C2	Mahya Daği mt. Turkey	
74 A1	Maidān Shahr Afgh.	
129 D2	Maidstone Can.	
99 D3	Maidstone U.K.	
115 D3	Maiduguri Nigeria	
75 C2	Mailani India	
114 A3	Maimanah Afgh.	
101 D2	Main r. Ger.	
118 B3	Mai-Ndombe, Lac l. Dem. Rep. Congo	
101 E3	Main-Donau-Kanal canal Ger.	
141 F1	Maine state U.S.A.	
62 A1	Maingkwan Myanmar	
96 C1	Mainland i. Scotland U.K.	
96 □	Mainland i. Scotland U.K.	
121 □D2	Maintirano Madag.	
101 D2	Mainz Ger.	
150 B1	Maiquetía Venez.	
53 D2	Maitland N.S.W. Austr.	
52 A2	Maitland S.A. Austr.	
146 B3	Maíz, Islas del is Nic.	
67 C3	Maizuru Japan	
61 C2	Majene Indon.	
107 D2	Majorca i. Spain	
48 F2	Majuro atoll Marshall Is	
123 C2	Majwemasweu S. Africa	
118 B3	Makabana Congo	
58 B3	Makale Indon.	
77 E2	Makanshy Kazakh.	
109 C2	Makarska Croatia	
58 B3	Makassar Indon.	
61 C2	Makassar, Selat str. Indon.	
	Makassar Strait Indon. see Makassar, Selat	
76 B2	Makat Kazakh.	
54 A3	Makati c. N.Z.	
123 D2	Makatini Flats lowland S. Africa	
114 A4	Makeni Sierra Leone	
120 B3	Makgadikgadi depr. Botswana	
87 D4	Makhachkala Russia	
123 C1	Makhado S. Africa	
76 B2	Makhambet Kazakh.	
119 D3	Makindu Kenya	
77 D1	Makinsk Kazakh.	
91 D2	Makiyivka Ukr.	
	Makkah Saudi Arabia see Mecca	
131 E1	Makkovik Can.	
103 E2	Makó Hungary	
118 B2	Makokou Gabon	
119 D3	Makongolosi Tanz.	
122 B2	Makopong Botswana	
79 D2	Makran reg. Iran/Pak.	
74 A2	Makran Coast Range mts Pak.	
89 E2	Maksatikha Russia	
81 C2	Mākū Iran	
62 A1	Makum India	
67 B4	Makurazaki Japan	
115 C4	Makurdi Nigeria	
92 G2	Malå Sweden	
146 B4	Mala, Punta pt Panama	
118 A2	Malabo Equat. Guinea	
60 A1	Malacca, Strait of Indon./Malaysia	
134 D2	Malad City U.S.A.	
88 C3	Maladzyechna Belarus	
106 C2	Málaga Spain	
97 B1	Málainn Mhóir Ireland	
48 E3	Malaita i. Solomon Is	
117 B4	Malakal South Sudan	
48 F4	Malakula i. Vanuatu	
61 C2	Malang Indon.	
120 A1	Malanje Angola	
93 G4	Mälaren l. Sweden	
153 B4	Malargüe Arg.	
80 B2	Malatya Turkey	
121 C2	Malawi country Africa	
	Malawi, Lake Africa see Nyasa, Lake	
64 B2	Malaya Vishera Russia	
64 B2	Malaybalay Phil.	
71 B1	Malāyer Iran	
60 B1	Malaysia country Asia	
81 C2	Malazgirt Turkey	
103 E1	Malbork Pol.	
101 F1	Malchin Ger.	
100 A2	Maldegem Belgium	
49 H3	Malden Island Kiribati	
56 G6	Maldives country Indian Ocean	
153 C4	Maldonado Uru.	
56 G6	Male Maldives	
111 B3	Maleas, Akrotirio pt Greece	
103 D2	Malé Karpaty hills Slovakia	
134 C2	Malheur Lake U.S.A.	
114 B3	Mali country Africa	
114 A3	Mali Guinea	
58 C3	Malili Indon.	
119 E3	Malindi Kenya	
97 C1	Malin Head Ireland	
111 C2	Malkara Turkey	
88 C3	Mal'kavichy Belarus	
110 C2	Malko Tarnovo Bulg.	
53 C3	Mallacoota Austr.	
53 C3	Mallacoota Inlet b. Austr.	
96 B2	Mallaig U.K.	
129 E1	Mallery Lake Can.	
	Mallorca i. Spain see Majorca	
97 B2	Mallow Ireland	
92 H2	Malmberget Sweden	
100 C2	Malmedy Belgium	
122 A3	Malmesbury S. Africa	
93 F4	Malmö Sweden	
62 B1	Malong China	
118 C4	Malonga Dem. Rep. Congo	
93 E3	Måløy Norway	
89 E2	Maloyaroslavets Russia	
89 E2	Maloye Borisovo Russia	
85 H5	Malta country Europe	
88 C2	Malta Latvia	
134 E1	Malta U.S.A.	

122 A1 **Maltahöhe** Namibia
98 C1 **Malton** U.K.
Maluku *is* Indon. *see* **Moluccas**
59 C3 **Maluku, Laut** *sea* Indon.
93 F3 **Malung** Sweden
123 C2 **Maluti Mountains** Lesotho
73 B3 **Malvan** India
142 B2 **Malvern** U.S.A.
90 B1 **Malyn** Ukr.
83 L2 **Malyy Anyuy** *r.* Russia
83 K2 **Malyy Lyakhovskiy, Ostrov** *i.* Russia
123 C2 **Mamafubedu** S. Africa
119 C2 **Mambasa** Dem. Rep. Congo
118 B2 **Mambéré** *r.* C.A.R.
123 C2 **Mamelodi** S. Africa
150 B3 **Mamoré** *r.* Bol./Brazil
114 A3 **Mamou** Guinea
61 C2 **Mamuju** Indon.
114 B4 **Man** Côte d'Ivoire
98 A1 **Man, Isle of** *i.* Irish Sea
150 B2 **Manacapuru** Brazil
107 D2 **Manacor** Spain
59 C2 **Manado** Indon.
146 B3 **Managua** Nic.
121 □D3 **Manakara** Madag.
78 B3 **Manākhah** Yemen
79 C2 **Manama** Bahrain
59 D3 **Manam Island** P.N.G.
121 □D3 **Mananara** *r.* Madag.
121 □D2 **Mananara Avaratra** Madag.
121 □D3 **Mananjary** Madag.
114 A3 **Manantali, Lac de** *l.* Mali
77 E2 **Manas Hu** *l.* China
59 C3 **Manatuto** East Timor
62 A2 **Man-aung Kyun** *i.* Myanmar
150 B2 **Manaus** Brazil
80 B2 **Manavgat** Turkey
98 B2 **Manchester** U.K.
141 E2 **Manchester** U.S.A.
121 □D3 **Mandabe** Madag.
93 E4 **Mandal** Norway
59 D3 **Mandala, Puncak** *mt.* Indon.
62 A1 **Mandalay** Myanmar
69 D1 **Mandalgovĭ** Mongolia
136 C1 **Mandan** U.S.A.
118 B1 **Mandara Mountains** Cameroon/Nigeria
108 A3 **Mandas** *Sardinia* Italy
100 C2 **Manderscheid** Ger.
74 B1 **Mandi** India
114 B3 **Mandiana** Guinea
75 C2 **Mandla** India
121 □D2 **Mandritsara** Madag.
74 B2 **Mandsaur** India
50 A3 **Mandurah** Austr.
73 B3 **Mandya** India
108 B1 **Manerbio** Italy
90 B1 **Manevychi** Ukr.
109 C2 **Manfredonia** Italy
114 B3 **Manga** Burkina Faso
118 B3 **Mangai** Dem. Rep. Congo
54 C1 **Mangakino** N.Z.
110 C2 **Mangalia** Romania
Mangalore India *see* **Mangaluru**
73 B3 **Mangaluru** India
123 C2 **Mangaung** S. Africa
61 B2 **Manggar** Indon.
76 B2 **Mangistau** Kazakh.
121 C2 **Mangochi** Malawi
59 C3 **Mangole** *i.* Indon.
154 B3 **Mangueirinha** Brazil
69 E1 **Mangui** China
137 D3 **Manhattan** U.S.A.
121 C3 **Manhica** Moz.
155 D2 **Manhuaçu** Brazil
121 □D2 **Mania** *r.* Madag.
108 B1 **Maniago** Italy
150 B2 **Manicoré** Brazil
131 D2 **Manicouagan** *r.* Can.
131 D1 **Manicouagan, Petit Lac** *l.* Can.
131 D1 **Manicouagan, Réservoir** *resr* Can.
79 B2 **Manīfah** Saudi Arabia
64 B1 **Manila** Phil.
53 D2 **Manilla** Austr.
111 C3 **Manisa** Turkey
140 B2 **Manistee** U.S.A.
129 E2 **Manitoba** *prov.* Can.
129 E2 **Manitoba, Lake** Can.
140 B1 **Manitou Islands** U.S.A.
130 B2 **Manitoulin Island** Can.
140 B2 **Manitowoc** U.S.A.
130 C2 **Maniwaki** Can.
150 A1 **Manizales** Col.
137 E2 **Mankato** U.S.A.
114 B4 **Mankono** Côte d'Ivoire
129 D3 **Mankota** Can.
73 C4 **Mankulam** Sri Lanka
74 B2 **Manmad** India
73 B4 **Mannar, Gulf of** India/Sri Lanka
101 D3 **Mannheim** Ger.
128 C2 **Manning** Can.
52 A2 **Mannum** Austr.
129 C2 **Mannville** Can.
59 C3 **Manokwari** Indon.
119 C3 **Manono** Dem. Rep. Congo
63 A2 **Manoron** Myanmar
105 D3 **Manosque** France
131 C1 **Manouane, Lac** *l.* Can.
107 D1 **Manresa** Spain
121 B2 **Mansa** Zambia
127 F2 **Mansel Island** Can.
92 I2 **Mansel'kya** *ridge* Fin./Russia
53 C3 **Mansfield** Austr.
98 C2 **Mansfield** U.K.
142 B2 **Mansfield** *LA* U.S.A.
140 C2 **Mansfield** *OH* U.S.A.
141 D2 **Mansfield** *PA* U.S.A.
150 A2 **Manta** Ecuador
143 E1 **Manteo** U.S.A.
104 C2 **Mantes-la-Jolie** France
155 C2 **Mantiqueira, Serra da** *mts* Brazil
Mantova Italy *see* **Mantua**
108 B1 **Mantua** Italy
151 C2 **Manuelzinho** Brazil
59 C3 **Manui** *i.* Indon.
54 B1 **Manukau** N.Z.
142 B2 **Many** U.S.A.
119 D3 **Manyoni** Tanz.
106 C2 **Manzanares** Spain
144 B3 **Manzanillo** Mex.
69 D1 **Manzhouli** China
123 D2 **Manzini** Swaziland
115 D3 **Mao** Chad
107 D2 **Maó** Spain
59 D3 **Maoke, Pegunungan** *mts* Indon.
123 C2 **Maokeng** S. Africa
65 A1 **Maokui Shan** *mt.* China
71 B3 **Maoming** China
121 C3 **Mapai** Moz.
75 C1 **Mapam Yumco** *l.* China
145 C3 **Mapastepec** Mex.
144 B2 **Mapimí** Mex.
144 B2 **Mapimí, Bolsón de** *des.* Mex.
121 C3 **Mapinhane** Moz.
129 D3 **Maple Creek** Can.
121 C3 **Maputo** Moz.
123 D2 **Maputo** *r.* Moz./S. Africa
120 A1 **Maquela do Zombo** Angola
153 B5 **Maquinchao** Arg.
137 E2 **Maquoketa** U.S.A.
150 B2 **Maraã** Brazil
151 D2 **Marabá** Brazil
151 C1 **Maracá, Ilha de** *i.* Brazil
150 A1 **Maracaibo** Venez.
150 A1 **Maracaibo, Lake** Venez.
152 C3 **Maracaju, Serra de** *hills* Bra
150 B1 **Maracay** Venez.
115 D2 **Marādah** Libya
115 C3 **Maradi** Niger
81 C2 **Marāgheh** Iran
151 D2 **Marajó, Baía de** *est.* Brazil
151 C2 **Marajó, Ilha de** *i.* Brazil
79 C2 **Marākī** Iran
119 D2 **Maralal** Kenya
50 C3 **Maralinga** Austr.
81 C2 **Marand** Iran
150 A2 **Marañón** *r.* Peru
130 B2 **Marathon** Can.
143 D4 **Marathon** U.S.A.
106 C2 **Marbella** Spain
50 A2 **Marble Bar** Austr.
123 C1 **Marble Hall** S. Africa
101 D2 **Marburg** Ger.
123 D3 **Marburg** S. Africa
99 D2 **March** U.K.
100 B2 **Marche-en-Famenne** Belgi
106 B2 **Marchena** Spain
152 B4 **Mar Chiquita, Laguna** *l.* Ar
141 E2 **Marcy, Mount** U.S.A.
74 B1 **Mardan** Pak.
153 C4 **Mar del Plata** Arg.
81 C2 **Mardin** Turkey
96 B2 **Maree, Loch** *l.* U.K.
108 B3 **Marettimo, Isola** *i.* *Sicily* Ita
89 D2 **Marevo** Russia
138 C2 **Marfa** U.S.A.
73 B3 **Margao** India
50 A3 **Margaret River** Austr.
147 D3 **Margarita, Isla de** *i.* Venez.
123 D3 **Margate** S. Africa
99 D3 **Margate** U.K.
Margherita Peak Dem. Rep. Congo/Uganda
Stanley, Mount
76 C3 **Mārgō, Dasht-e** *des.* Afgh.
91 C2 **Marhanets'** Ukr.
62 A1 **Mari** Myanmar
152 B3 **María Elena** Chile
156 C5 **Mariana Trench** N. Pacific Ocean
142 B2 **Marianna** *AR* U.S.A.
143 C2 **Marianna** *FL* U.S.A.
102 C2 **Mariánské Lázně** Czechia
144 B2 **Marías, Islas** *is* Mex.
78 B3 **Ma'rib** Yemen
109 C1 **Maribor** Slovenia
117 A4 **Maridi** *watercourse* South Sudan
55 M2 **Marie Byrd Land** *reg.* Antarctica
147 D3 **Marie-Galante** *i.* Guadelou
93 G3 **Mariehamn** Fin.
122 A1 **Mariental** Namibia
93 F4 **Mariestad** Sweden
143 D2 **Marietta** *GA* U.S.A.
140 C3 **Marietta** *OH* U.S.A.
105 D3 **Marignane** France
83 K3 **Marii, Mys** *pt* Russia
88 B3 **Marijampolė** Lith.
154 C2 **Marília** Brazil
106 B1 **Marín** Spain
109 C3 **Marina di Gioiosa Ionica** I
88 C3 **Mar"ina Horka** Belarus
140 B1 **Marinette** U.S.A.
154 B2 **Maringá** Brazil
106 B2 **Marinha Grande** Port.
140 B2 **Marion** *IN* U.S.A.

140 C2 **Marion** *OH* U.S.A.
143 E2 **Marion** *SC* U.S.A.
140 C3 **Marion** *VA* U.S.A.
143 D2 **Marion, Lake** U.S.A.
52 A3 **Marion Bay** Austr.
152 B3 **Mariscal José Félix Estigarribia** Para.
110 C2 **Maritsa** *r.* Bulg.
91 D2 **Mariupol'** Ukr.
117 C4 **Marka** Somalia
123 C1 **Marken** S. Africa
100 B1 **Markermeer** *l.* Neth.
83 I2 **Markha** *r.* Russia
91 D2 **Markivka** Ukr.
142 B2 **Marksville** U.S.A.
101 D3 **Marktheidenfeld** Ger.
101 F2 **Marktredwitz** Ger.
100 C2 **Marl** Ger.
100 A3 **Marle** France
139 D2 **Marlin** U.S.A.
104 C3 **Marmande** France
111 C2 **Marmara, Sea of** *g.* Turkey
Marmara Denizi *g.* Turkey *see* **Marmara, Sea of**
111 C3 **Marmaris** Turkey
104 C2 **Marne-la-Vallée** France
121 □D2 **Maroantsetra** Madag.
101 E2 **Maroldsweisach** Ger.
121 □D2 **Maromokotro** *mt.* Madag.
121 C2 **Marondera** Zimbabwe
151 C1 **Maroni** *r.* Fr. Guiana
118 B1 **Maroua** Cameroon
121 □D2 **Marovoay** Madag.
49 I3 **Marquesas Islands** *is* Fr. Polynesia
140 B1 **Marquette** U.S.A.
117 A3 **Marra, Jebel** *mt.* Sudan
117 A3 **Marra, Jebel** *plat.* Sudan
123 D2 **Marracuene** Moz.
114 B1 **Marrakech** Morocco
52 A1 **Marree** Austr.
121 C2 **Marromeu** Moz.
121 C2 **Marrupa** Moz.
116 B2 **Marsá al 'Alam** Egypt
115 D1 **Marsá al Burayqah** Libya
119 D2 **Marsabit** Kenya
108 B3 **Marsala** *Sicily* Italy
116 A1 **Marsá Maṭrūḥ** Egypt
101 D2 **Marsberg** Ger.
108 B2 **Marsciano** Italy
53 C2 **Marsden** Austr.
105 D3 **Marseille** France
137 D2 **Marshall** *MN* U.S.A.
137 E3 **Marshall** *MO* U.S.A.
139 E2 **Marshall** *TX* U.S.A.
48 F2 **Marshall Islands** *country* N. Pacific Ocean
137 E2 **Marshalltown** U.S.A.
140 A2 **Marshfield** U.S.A.
143 E3 **Marsh Harbour** Bahamas
142 B3 **Marsh Island** U.S.A.
88 A2 **Märsta** Sweden
61 C2 **Martapura** *Kalimantan Selatan* Indon.
60 B2 **Martapura** *Sumatera Selatan* Indon.
141 E2 **Martha's Vineyard** *i.* U.S.A.
105 D2 **Martigny** Switz.
103 D2 **Martin** Slovakia
136 C2 **Martin** U.S.A.
145 C2 **Martínez** Mex.
147 D3 **Martinique** *terr.* West Indies
141 D3 **Martinsburg** U.S.A.
140 D3 **Martinsville** U.S.A.
76 B1 **Martok** Kazakh.
54 C2 **Marton** N.Z.
107 D1 **Martorell** Spain
106 C2 **Martos** Spain
105 C3 **Marvejols** France
76 C3 **Mary** Turkm.
51 E2 **Maryborough** Austr.
122 B2 **Marydale** S. Africa
141 D3 **Maryland** *state* U.S.A.
137 D3 **Marysville** U.S.A.
137 E2 **Maryville** *MO* U.S.A.
143 D1 **Maryville** *TN* U.S.A.
119 D3 **Masai Steppe** *plain* Tanz.
119 D3 **Masaka** Uganda
65 B2 **Masan** S. Korea
119 D4 **Masasi** Tanz.
64 B1 **Masbate** Phil.
64 B1 **Masbate** *i.* Phil.
123 C2 **Maseru** Lesotho
76 B3 **Mashhad** Iran
123 D2 **Mashishing** S. Africa
74 A2 **Mashkel, Hamun-i-** *salt flat* Pak.
123 C3 **Masibambane** S. Africa
79 C3 **Masīlah, Wādī al** *watercourse* Yemen
123 C2 **Masilo** S. Africa
119 D2 **Masindi** Uganda
79 C2 **Maṣīrah, Jazīrat** *i.* Oman
79 C3 **Maṣīrah, Khalīj** *b.* Oman
81 C2 **Masjed Soleymān** Iran
97 B2 **Mask, Lough** *l.* Ireland
121 □E2 **Masoala, Tanjona** *c.* Madag.
137 E2 **Mason City** U.S.A.
Masqaṭ Oman *see* **Muscat**
108 B2 **Massa** Italy
141 E2 **Massachusetts** *state* U.S.A.
141 E2 **Massachusetts Bay** U.S.A.
121 C3 **Massangena** Moz.
120 A1 **Massango** Angola
116 B3 **Massawa** Eritrea
141 E2 **Massena** U.S.A.
128 A2 **Masset** Can.
105 C2 **Massif Central** *mts* France
140 C2 **Massillon** U.S.A.
121 C3 **Massinga** Moz.
123 D1 **Massingir** Moz.
78 A2 **Mastābah** Saudi Arabia
54 C2 **Masterton** N.Z.
74 A2 **Mastung** Pak.
78 A2 **Mastūrah** Saudi Arabia
88 B3 **Masty** Belarus
67 B4 **Masuda** Japan
Masuku Gabon *see* **Franceville**
121 C3 **Masvingo** Zimbabwe
69 D1 **Matad** Mongolia
118 B3 **Matadi** Dem. Rep. Congo
146 B3 **Matagalpa** Nic.
130 C2 **Matagami** Can.
130 C2 **Matagami, Lac** *l.* Can.
139 D3 **Matagorda Island** U.S.A.
120 A2 **Matala** Angola
114 A3 **Matam** Senegal
144 B2 **Matamoros** *Coahuila* Mex.
145 C2 **Matamoros** *Tamaulipas* Mex.
119 D3 **Matandu** *r.* Tanz.
131 D2 **Matane** Can.
146 B2 **Matanzas** Cuba
73 C4 **Matara** Sri Lanka
61 C2 **Mataram** Indon.
50 C1 **Mataranka** Austr.
107 D1 **Mataró** Spain
123 C3 **Matatiele** S. Africa
54 A3 **Mataura** N.Z.
49 G3 **Matā'utu** Wallis and Futuna Is
54 C1 **Matawai** N.Z.
152 B2 **Mategua** Bol.
145 B2 **Matehuala** Mex.
109 C2 **Matera** Italy
139 D3 **Mathis** U.S.A.
75 B2 **Mathura** India
64 B2 **Mati** Phil.
98 C2 **Matlock** U.K.
123 D2 **Matola** Moz.
Matou China *see* **Pingguo**
67 B3 **Matsue** Japan
66 D2 **Matsumae** Japan
67 C4 **Matsusaka** Japan
67 B4 **Matsuyama** Japan
130 B1 **Mattagami** *r.* Can.
105 D2 **Matterhorn** *mt.* Italy/Switz.
134 C2 **Matterhorn** *mt.* U.S.A.
140 B3 **Mattoon** U.S.A.
150 B1 **Maturín** Venez.
123 C2 **Matwabeng** S. Africa
100 A2 **Maubeuge** France
104 C3 **Maubourguet** France
124 E5 **Maui** *i.* U.S.A.
140 C2 **Maumee** *r.* U.S.A.
120 B2 **Maun** Botswana
62 A1 **Maungdaw** Myanmar
50 C2 **Maurice, Lake** *imp. l.* Austr.
114 A3 **Mauritania** *country* Africa
113 K9 **Mauritius** *country* Indian Ocean
78 B2 **Māwān, Khashm** *mt.* Saudi Arabia
118 B3 **Mawanga** Dem. Rep. Congo
71 B3 **Mawei** China
62 A1 **Mawkmai** Myanmar
62 A1 **Mawlaik** Myanmar
Mawlamyaing Myanmar *see* **Moulmein**
78 B2 **Mawqaq** Saudi Arabia
78 B3 **Mawza'** Yemen
108 A3 **Maxia, Punta** *mt. Sardinia* Italy
83 J2 **Maya** *r.* Russia
147 C2 **Mayaguana** *i.* Bahamas
96 B3 **Maybole** U.K.
104 B2 **Mayenne** France
104 B2 **Mayenne** *r.* France
128 C2 **Mayerthorpe** Can.
140 B3 **Mayfield** U.S.A.
87 D4 **Maykop** Russia
126 B2 **Mayo** Can.
118 B3 **Mayoko** Congo
121 D2 **Mayotte** *terr.* Africa
83 J3 **Mayskiy** Russia
140 C3 **Maysville** U.S.A.
118 B3 **Mayumba** Gabon
137 D1 **Mayville** U.S.A.
151 C2 **Mazagão** Brazil
104 C3 **Mazamet** France
77 D3 **Mazar** China
108 B3 **Mazara del Vallo** *Sicily* Italy
77 C3 **Mazār-e Sharīf** Afgh.
144 A2 **Mazatán** Mex.
146 A3 **Mazatenango** Guat.
144 B2 **Mazatlán** Mex.
88 B2 **Mažeikiai** Lith.
88 B2 **Mazirbe** Latvia
121 B3 **Mazunga** Zimbabwe
88 C3 **Mazyr** Belarus
123 D2 **Mbabane** Swaziland
118 B2 **Mbaïki** C.A.R.
121 C1 **Mbala** Zambia
119 D2 **Mbale** Uganda
118 B2 **Mbalmayo** Cameroon
118 B3 **Mbandaka** Dem. Rep. Congo
118 A2 **Mbanga** Cameroon
120 A1 **M'banza Congo** Angola
119 D3 **Mbeya** Tanz.
119 D4 **Mbinga** Tanz.
123 D2 **Mbombela** S. Africa
118 B2 **Mbomo** Congo
118 B2 **Mbouda** Cameroon
114 A3 **Mbour** Senegal
114 A3 **Mbout** Maur.
118 C3 **Mbuji-Mayi** Dem. Rep. Congo
119 D3 **Mbuyuni** Tanz.

139 D2 **McAlester** U.S.A.
139 D3 **McAllen** U.S.A.
128 B2 **McBride** Can.
134 C2 **McCall** U.S.A.
126 E2 **McClintock Channel** Can.
126 D2 **McClure Strait** Can.
142 B2 **McComb** U.S.A.
136 C2 **McConaughy, Lake** U.S.A.
136 C2 **McCook** U.S.A.
134 C2 **McDermitt** U.S.A.
134 D1 **McDonald Peak** U.S.A.
134 D1 **McGuire, Mount** U.S.A.
McKinley, Mount U.S.A. *see* **Denali**
128 C2 **McLennan** Can.
128 B2 **McLeod Lake** Can.
134 B1 **McMinnville** *OR* U.S.A.
142 C1 **McMinnville** *TN* U.S.A.
137 D3 **McPherson** U.S.A.
123 C3 **Mdantsane** S. Africa
135 D3 **Mead, Lake** *resr* U.S.A.
129 D2 **Meadow Lake** Can.
140 C2 **Meadville** U.S.A.
66 D2 **Meaken-dake** *vol.* Japan
106 B1 **Mealhada** Port.
131 E1 **Mealy Mountains** Can.
128 C2 **Meander River** Can.
78 A2 **Mecca** Saudi Arabia
100 B2 **Mechelen** Belgium
100 B2 **Mechelen** Neth.
100 C2 **Mechernich** Ger.
100 C2 **Meckenheim** Ger.
106 B1 **Meda** Port.
60 A1 **Medan** Indon.
153 B5 **Medanosa, Punta** *pt* Arg.
73 C4 **Medawachchiya** Sri Lanka
107 D2 **Médéa** Alg.
150 A1 **Medellín** Col.
115 D1 **Médenine** Tunisia
134 B2 **Medford** U.S.A.
110 C2 **Medgidia** Romania
110 B1 **Mediaş** Romania
136 B2 **Medicine Bow Mountains** U.S.A.
136 B2 **Medicine Bow Peak** U.S.A.
129 C2 **Medicine Hat** Can.
137 D3 **Medicine Lodge** U.S.A.
155 D1 **Medina** Brazil
78 A2 **Medina** Saudi Arabia
106 C1 **Medinaceli** Spain
106 C1 **Medina del Campo** Spain
106 B1 **Medina de Rioseco** Spain
75 C2 **Medininagar** India
84 G5 **Mediterranean Sea** World
129 C2 **Medley** Can.
87 E3 **Mednogorsk** Russia
83 L2 **Medvezh'i, Ostrova** *is* Russia
86 C2 **Medvezh'yegorsk** Russia
50 A2 **Meekatharra** Austr.
136 B2 **Meeker** U.S.A.
75 B2 **Meerut** India
100 A2 **Meetkerke** Belgium
111 B3 **Megalopoli** Greece
75 C2 **Meghasani** *mt.* India
80 A2 **Megisti** *i.* Greece
92 I1 **Mehamn** Norway
50 A2 **Meharry, Mount** Austr.
79 C2 **Mehrān** *watercourse* Iran
76 C3 **Mehrestān** Iran
74 B1 **Mehtar Lām** Afgh.
154 C1 **Meia Ponte** *r.* Brazil
118 B2 **Meiganga** Cameroon
65 B1 **Meihekou** China
Meijiang China *see* **Ningdu**
62 A1 **Meiktila** Myanmar
101 E2 **Meiningen** Ger.
102 C1 **Meißen** Ger.
71 B3 **Meizhou** China
152 B3 **Mejicana** *mt.* Arg.
152 A3 **Mejillones** Chile
117 B3 **Mek'elē** Eth.
114 C2 **Mekerrhane, Sebkha** *salt pan* Alg.
114 B1 **Meknès** Morocco
63 B2 **Mekong** *r.* Asia
63 B3 **Mekong, Mouths of the** Vietnam
60 B1 **Melaka** Malaysia
53 B3 **Melbourne** Austr.
143 D3 **Melbourne** U.S.A.
108 A2 **Mele, Capo** *c.* Italy
131 C1 **Mélèzes, Rivière aux** *r.* Can.
115 D3 **Melfi** Chad
109 C2 **Melfi** Italy
129 D2 **Melfort** Can.
92 F3 **Melhus** Norway
106 B1 **Melide** Spain
114 B1 **Melilla** N. Africa
91 D2 **Melitopol'** Ukr.
101 D1 **Melle** Ger.
93 F4 **Mellerud** Sweden
101 E2 **Mellrichstadt** Ger.
100 D1 **Mellum** *i.* Ger.
152 C4 **Melo** Uru.
115 C1 **Melrhir, Chott** *salt l.* Alg.
99 C2 **Melton Mowbray** U.K.
104 C2 **Melun** France
129 D2 **Melville** Can.
51 D1 **Melville, Cape** Austr.
131 E1 **Melville, Lake** Can.
50 C1 **Melville Island** Austr.
126 D1 **Melville Island** Can.
127 F2 **Melville Peninsula** Can.
102 C2 **Memmingen** Ger.
61 B1 **Mempawah** Indon.
80 B3 **Memphis** *tourist site* Egypt
142 B1 **Memphis** *TN* U.S.A.
139 C2 **Memphis** *TX* U.S.A.
91 C1 **Mena** Ukr.
142 B2 **Mena** U.S.A.
114 C3 **Ménaka** Mali
Mènam Khong *r.* Laos/Thai. *see* **Mekong**
105 C3 **Mende** France
116 B3 **Mendefera** Eritrea
145 C2 **Méndez** Mex.
119 D2 **Mendī** Eth.
59 D3 **Mendi** P.N.G.
99 B3 **Mendip Hills** U.K.
153 B4 **Mendoza** Arg.
111 C3 **Menemen** Turkey
60 B2 **Menggala** Indon.
62 B1 **Mengzi** China
131 D1 **Menihek** Can.
52 B2 **Menindee** Austr.
52 B2 **Menindee Lake** Austr.
52 A3 **Meningie** Austr.
104 C2 **Mennecy** France
140 B1 **Menominee** U.S.A.
120 A2 **Menongue** Angola
Menorca *i.* Spain *see* **Minorca**
60 A2 **Mentawai, Kepulauan** *is* Indon.
60 B2 **Mentok** Indon.
50 B2 **Menzies** Austr.
100 C1 **Meppel** Neth.
100 C1 **Meppen** Ger.
123 D1 **Mepuze** Moz.
123 C2 **Meqheleng** S. Africa
108 B1 **Merano** Italy
59 D3 **Merauke** Indon.
52 B2 **Merbein** Austr.
135 B3 **Merced** U.S.A.
152 C3 **Mercedes** Arg.
127 G2 **Mercy, Cape** Can.
139 C1 **Meredith, Lake** U.S.A.
91 D2 **Merefa** Ukr.
116 A3 **Merga Oasis** Sudan
63 A2 **Mergui Archipelago** *is* Myanmar
110 C2 **Meriç** *r.* Greece/Turkey
145 D2 **Mérida** Mex.
106 B2 **Mérida** Spain
150 A1 **Mérida** Venez.
142 C2 **Meridian** U.S.A.
53 C3 **Merimbula** Austr.
116 B3 **Merowe** Sudan
50 A3 **Merredin** Austr.
96 B3 **Merrick** *h.* U.K.
140 B1 **Merrill** U.S.A.
140 B2 **Merrillville** U.S.A.
128 B2 **Merritt** Can.
53 C2 **Merrygoen** Austr.
116 C3 **Mersa Fatma** Eritrea
100 C3 **Mersch** Lux.
101 E2 **Merseburg** Ger.
98 B2 **Mersey** *r.* U.K.
80 B2 **Mersin** Turkey
60 B1 **Mersing** Malaysia
99 D3 **Mers-les-Bains** France
74 B2 **Merta** India
99 B3 **Merthyr Tydfil** U.K.
106 B2 **Mértola** Port.
76 B2 **Mertvyy Kultuk, Sor** *dry lake* Kazakh.
119 D3 **Meru** *vol.* Tanz.
100 C3 **Merzig** Ger.
138 A2 **Mesa** U.S.A.
109 C2 **Mesagne** Italy
101 D2 **Meschede** Ger.
89 E3 **Meshchovsk** Russia
91 E2 **Meshkovskaya** Russia
111 B2 **Mesimeri** Greece
111 B3 **Mesolongi** Greece
121 D2 **Messalo** *r.* Moz.
109 C3 **Messina** *Sicily* Italy
109 C3 **Messina, Strait of** Italy
111 B3 **Messiniakos Kolpos** *g.* Gree
110 B2 **Mesta** *r.* Bulg.
150 B1 **Meta** *r.* Col./Venez.
127 G2 **Meta Incognita Peninsula** Can.
152 B3 **Metán** Arg.
111 B3 **Methoni** Greece
109 C2 **Metković** Croatia
60 B2 **Metro** Indon.
117 B4 **Metu** Eth.
105 D2 **Metz** France
100 B2 **Meuse** *r.* Belgium/France
139 D2 **Mexia** U.S.A.
144 A1 **Mexicali** Mex.
144 B2 **Mexico** *country* Central America
137 E3 **Mexico** U.S.A.
125 I5 **Mexico, Gulf of** Mex./U.S.A.
145 C3 **Mexico City** Mex.
101 F1 **Meyenburg** Ger.
86 D2 **Mezen'** Russia
86 D2 **Mezen'** *r.* Russia
86 E1 **Mezhdusharskiy, Ostrov** *i.* Russia
103 E2 **Mezőtúr** Hungary
144 B2 **Mezquitic** Mex.
88 C2 **Mežvidi** Latvia
121 C2 **Mfuwe** Zambia
123 D2 **Mhlume** Swaziland
74 B2 **Mhow** India
145 C3 **Miahuatlán** Mex.
106 B2 **Miajadas** Spain
143 D3 **Miami** *FL* U.S.A.
139 E1 **Miami** *OK* U.S.A.
143 D3 **Miami Beach** U.S.A.
81 C2 **Mīāndoāb** Iran
121 D2 **Miandrivazo** Madag.

81 C2 **Mīāneh** Iran
74 B1 **Mianwali** Pak.
70 A2 **Mianyang** China
121 ▫D2 **Miarinarivo** Madag.
87 F3 **Miass** Russia
128 C2 **Mica Creek** Can.
103 E2 **Michalovce** Slovakia
140 B1 **Michigan** *state* U.S.A.
140 B2 **Michigan, Lake** U.S.A.
140 B2 **Michigan City** U.S.A.
130 B2 **Michipicoten Island** Can.
130 B2 **Michipicoten River** Can.
89 F3 **Michurinsk** Russia
48 D2 **Micronesia, Federated States of** *country* N. Pacific Ocean
100 A2 **Middelburg** Neth.
123 C3 **Middelburg** *E. Cape* S. Africa
123 C2 **Middelburg** *Mpumalanga* S. Africa
100 B2 **Middelharnis** Neth.
134 B2 **Middle Alkali Lake** U.S.A.
73 D3 **Middle Andaman** *i.* India
136 D2 **Middle Loup** *r.* U.S.A.
140 C3 **Middlesboro** U.S.A.
98 C1 **Middlesbrough** U.K.
141 E2 **Middletown** *NY* U.S.A.
140 C3 **Middletown** *OH* U.S.A.
78 B3 **Mīdī** Yemen
130 C2 **Midland** Can.
140 C2 **Midland** *MI* U.S.A.
139 C2 **Midland** *TX* U.S.A.
97 B3 **Midleton** Ireland
94 B1 **Miðvágur** Faroe Is
109 D2 **Midzhur** *mt.* Bulgaria/Serbia
103 E1 **Mielec** Pol.
110 C1 **Miercurea Ciuc** Romania
106 B1 **Mieres del Camín** Spain
101 E1 **Mieste** Ger.
145 C3 **Miguel Alemán, Presa** *resr* Mex.
144 B2 **Miguel Auza** Mex.
144 B2 **Miguel Hidalgo, Presa** *resr* Mex.
63 A2 **Migyaunglaung** Myanmar
89 E3 **Mikhaylov** Russia
Mikhaylovgrad Bulg. *see* **Montana**
66 B2 **Mikhaylovka** Russia
77 D1 **Mikhaylovskoye** Russia
93 I3 **Mikkeli** Fin.
86 E2 **Mikun'** Russia
67 C3 **Mikuni-sanmyaku** *mts* Japan
108 A1 **Milan** Italy
121 C2 **Milange** Moz.
Milano Italy *see* **Milan**
111 C3 **Milas** Turkey
137 D1 **Milbank** U.S.A.
99 D2 **Mildenhall** U.K.
52 B2 **Mildura** Austr.
62 B1 **Mile** China
136 B1 **Miles City** U.S.A.
141 D3 **Milford** *DE* U.S.A.
135 D3 **Milford** *UT* U.S.A.
99 A3 **Milford Haven** U.K.
54 A2 **Milford Sound** N.Z.
107 D2 **Miliana** Alg.
116 B3 **Milk, Wadi el** *watercourse* Sudan
83 L3 **Mil'kovo** Russia
129 C3 **Milk River** Can.
105 C3 **Millau** France
143 D2 **Milledgeville** U.S.A.
137 E1 **Mille Lacs** *lakes* U.S.A.
130 A2 **Mille Lacs, Lac des** *l.* Can.
137 D2 **Miller** U.S.A.
91 E2 **Millerovo** Russia
52 A2 **Millers Creek** Austr.
52 B3 **Millicent** Austr.
141 F1 **Millinocket** U.S.A.
53 D1 **Millmerran** Austr.
98 B1 **Millom** U.K.
128 C1 **Mills Lake** Can.
111 B3 **Milos** *i.* Greece
89 E3 **Miloslavskoye** Russia
91 E2 **Milove** Ukr.
52 B1 **Milparinka** Austr.
54 A3 **Milton** N.Z.
99 C2 **Milton Keynes** U.K.
140 B2 **Milwaukee** U.S.A.
104 B3 **Mimizan** France
118 B3 **Mimongo** Gabon
79 C2 **Mīnāb** Iran
58 C2 **Minahasa, Semenanjung** *pen.* Indon.
79 C2 **Mīnā' Jabal 'Alī** U.A.E.
60 B1 **Minas** Indon.
153 C4 **Minas** Uru.
155 D1 **Minas Novas** Brazil
145 C3 **Minatitlán** Mex.
62 A1 **Minbu** Myanmar
64 B2 **Mindanao** *i.* Phil.
101 D1 **Minden** Ger.
142 B2 **Minden** *LA* U.S.A.
137 D2 **Minden** *NE* U.S.A.
64 B1 **Mindoro** *i.* Phil.
64 A1 **Mindoro Strait** Phil.
118 B3 **Mindouli** Congo
99 B3 **Minehead** U.K.
154 B1 **Mineiros** Brazil
139 D2 **Mineral Wells** U.S.A.
77 E3 **Minfeng** China
119 C4 **Minga** Dem. Rep. Congo
81 C1 **Mingäçevir** Azer.
131 D1 **Mingan** Can.
52 B2 **Mingary** Austr.
70 B2 **Mingguang** China
62 A1 **Mingin** Myanmar
107 C2 **Minglanilla** Spain
119 D4 **Mingoyo** Tanz.
69 E1 **Mingshui** China
71 B3 **Mingxi** China
73 B4 **Minicoy** *atoll* India
50 A2 **Minilya** Austr.
131 D1 **Minipi Lake** Can.
130 A1 **Miniss Lake** Can.
115 C4 **Minna** Nigeria
137 E2 **Minneapolis** U.S.A.
129 E2 **Minnedosa** Can.
137 E2 **Minnesota** *r.* U.S.A.
137 E1 **Minnesota** *state* U.S.A.
106 B1 **Miño** *r.* Port./Spain
107 D1 **Minorca** *i.* Spain
136 C1 **Minot** U.S.A.
88 C3 **Minsk** Belarus
103 E1 **Mińsk Mazowiecki** Pol.
131 D2 **Minto** Can.
130 C1 **Minto, Lac** *l.* Can.
70 A2 **Minxian** China
155 D1 **Mirabela** Brazil
155 D1 **Miralta** Brazil
131 D2 **Miramichi** Can.
111 C3 **Mirampellou, Kolpos** *b.* Greece
152 C3 **Miranda** Brazil
152 C2 **Miranda** *r.* Brazil
106 C1 **Miranda de Ebro** Spain
106 B1 **Mirandela** Port.
154 B2 **Mirandópolis** Brazil
79 C3 **Mirbāţ** Oman
61 C1 **Miri** *Sarawak* Malaysia
153 C4 **Mirim, Lagoa** *l.* Brazil/Uru.
79 D2 **Mīrjāveh** Iran
83 I2 **Mirnyy** Russia
101 F1 **Mirow** Ger.
74 A2 **Mirpur Khas** Pak.
111 B3 **Mirtoö Pelagos** *sea* Greece
65 B2 **Miryang** S. Korea
75 C2 **Mirzapur** India
66 B1 **Mishan** China
146 B3 **Miskitos, Cayos** *is* Nic.
103 E2 **Miskolc** Hungary
59 C3 **Misool** *i.* Indon.
115 D1 **Mişrātah** Libya
130 B1 **Missinaibi** *r.* Can.
130 B2 **Missinaibi Lake** Can.
128 B3 **Mission** Can.
130 B1 **Missisa Lake** Can.
142 C3 **Mississippi** *r.* U.S.A.
142 C2 **Mississippi** *state* U.S.A.
142 C3 **Mississippi Delta** U.S.A.
134 D1 **Missoula** U.S.A.
137 E3 **Missouri** *r.* U.S.A.
137 E3 **Missouri** *state* U.S.A.
131 C2 **Mistassibi** *r.* Can.
130 C1 **Mistassini, Lac** *l.* Can.
131 D1 **Mistastin Lake** Can.
103 D2 **Mistelbach** Austria
131 D1 **Mistinibi, Lac** *l.* Can.
130 C1 **Mistissini** Can.
51 D2 **Mitchell** Austr.
51 D1 **Mitchell** *r.* Austr.
137 D2 **Mitchell** U.S.A.
97 B2 **Mitchelstown** Ireland
74 A2 **Mithi** Pak.
67 D3 **Mito** Japan
119 D3 **Mitole** Tanz.
109 D2 **Mitrovicë** Kosovo
53 D2 **Mittagong** Austr.
101 E2 **Mittelhausen** Ger.
101 D1 **Mittellandkanal** *canal* Ger.
101 F3 **Mitterteich** Ger.
150 A1 **Mitú** Col.
119 C4 **Mitumba, Chaîne des** *mts* Dem. Rep. Congo
119 C3 **Mitumba, Monts** *mts* Dem. Rep. Congo
118 B2 **Mitzic** Gabon
78 B2 **Miyah, Wādī al** *watercourse* Saudi Arabia
67 C4 **Miyake-jima** *i.* Japan
66 D3 **Miyako** Japan
67 B4 **Miyakonojō** Japan
76 B2 **Miyaly** Kazakh.
Miyang China *see* **Mile**
67 B4 **Miyazaki** Japan
115 D1 **Mizdah** Libya
97 B3 **Mizen Head** Ireland
90 A2 **Mizhhirr"ya** Ukr.
93 G4 **Mjölby** Sweden
93 F3 **Mjøsa** *l.* Norway
119 D3 **Mkomazi** Tanz.
103 C1 **Mladá Boleslav** Czechia
109 D2 **Mladenovac** Serbia
103 E1 **Mława** Pol.
123 C3 **Mlungisi** S. Africa
90 B1 **Mlyniv** Ukr.
123 C2 **Mmabatho** S. Africa
123 C2 **Mmathethe** Botswana
135 E3 **Moab** U.S.A.
123 D2 **Moamba** Moz.
119 C3 **Moba** Dem. Rep. Congo
118 C2 **Mobayi-Mbongo** Dem. Rep. Congo
137 E3 **Moberly** U.S.A.
142 C2 **Mobile** U.S.A.
142 C2 **Mobile Bay** U.S.A.
136 C1 **Mobridge** U.S.A.
121 D2 **Moçambique** Moz.
62 B1 **Môc Châu** Vietnam
78 B3 **Mocha** Yemen
123 C1 **Mochudi** Botswana
121 D2 **Mocimboa da Praia** Moz.
150 A1 **Mocoa** Col.
154 C2 **Mococa** Brazil

Mocorito

144	B2	Mocorito Mex.
144	B1	Moctezuma *Chihuahua* Mex.
145	B2	Moctezuma *San Luis Potosí* Mex.
144	B2	Moctezuma *Sonora* Mex.
121	C2	Mocuba Moz.
105	D2	Modane France
122	B2	Modder r. S. Africa
108	B2	Modena Italy
135	B3	Modesto U.S.A.
123	C1	Modimolle S. Africa
123	D1	Modjadjiskloof S. Africa
53	C3	Moe Austr.
100	C2	Moers Ger.
96	C3	Moffat U.K.
117	C4	Mogadishu Somalia
123	C1	Mogalakwena r. S. Africa
62	A1	Mogaung Myanmar
155	C2	Mogi das Cruzes Brazil
		Mogilev Belarus *see*
		Mahilyow/Mogilev
154	C2	Mogi Mirim Brazil
83	I3	Mogocha Russia
62	A1	Mogok Myanmar
103	D2	Mohács Hungary
123	C3	Mohale's Hoek Lesotho
		Mohali India *see*
		S. A. S. Nagar
79	C2	Mohammadābād Iran
107	D2	Mohammadia Alg.
141	E2	Mohawk r. U.S.A.
119	D3	Mohoro Tanz.
90	B2	Mohyliv-Podil's'kyy Ukr.
110	C1	Moinești Romania
92	F2	Mo i Rana Norway
104	C3	Moissac France
135	C3	Mojave U.S.A.
135	C3	Mojave Desert U.S.A.
62	B1	Mojiang China
154	C2	Moji-Guaçu r. Brazil
54	B1	Mokau N.Z.
123	C2	Mokhotlong Lesotho
123	C1	Mokopane S. Africa
65	B3	Mokpo S. Korea
145	C2	Molango Mex.
		Moldavia country Europe *see*
		Moldova
92	E3	Molde Norway
90	B2	Moldova country Europe
110	B1	Moldoveanu, Vârful mt. Romania
90	B2	Moldovei Centrale, Podişul plat. Moldova
123	C1	Molepolole Botswana
88	C2	Molėtai Lith.
109	C2	Molfetta Italy
107	C1	Molina de Aragón Spain
150	A3	Mollendo Peru
53	C2	Molong Austr.
122	B2	Molopo watercourse Botswana/S. Africa
118	B2	Moloundou Cameroon
59	C3	Moluccas is Indon.
		Molucca Sea Indon. *see*
		Maluku, Laut
52	B2	Momba Austr.
119	D3	Mombasa Kenya
154	B1	Mombuca, Serra da hills Brazil
93	F4	Møn i. Denmark
105	D3	Monaco country Europe
96	B2	Monadhliath Mountains U.K.
97	C1	Monaghan Ireland
89	D3	Monastyrshchina Russia
90	B2	Monastyryshche Ukr.
66	D2	Monbetsu Japan
108	A1	Moncalieri Italy
107	C1	Moncayo mt. Spain
86	C2	Monchegorsk Russia

100	C2	Mönchengladbach Ger.
144	B2	Monclova Mex.
131	D2	Moncton Can.
106	B1	Mondego r. Port.
108	A2	Mondovì Italy
111	B3	Monemvasia Greece
66	C1	Moneron, Ostrov i. Russia
137	E3	Monett U.S.A.
108	B1	Monfalcone Italy
106	B1	Monforte de Lemos Spain
62	B1	Mông Cai Vietnam
62	B1	Mong Lin Myanmar
68	C1	Mongolia country Asia
62	A1	Mong Pawk Myanmar
62	A1	Mong Ping Myanmar
120	B2	Mongu Zambia
135	C3	Monitor Range mts U.S.A.
114	C4	Mono r. Benin/Togo
135	C3	Mono Lake U.S.A.
109	C2	Monopoli Italy
107	C1	Monreal del Campo Spain
142	B2	Monroe LA U.S.A.
140	B2	Monroe WI U.S.A.
142	C2	Monroeville U.S.A.
114	A4	Monrovia Liberia
100	A2	Mons Belgium
122	B3	Montagu S. Africa
109	C3	Montalto mt. Italy
110	B2	Montana Bulg.
134	E1	Montana state U.S.A.
104	C2	Montargis France
104	C3	Montauban France
141	E2	Montauk Point U.S.A.
123	C2	Mont-aux-Sources mt. Lesotho
105	C2	Montbard France
105	C2	Montbrison France
100	B3	Montcornet France
104	B3	Mont-de-Marsan France
104	C2	Montdidier France
151	C2	Monte Alegre Brazil
105	D3	Monte-Carlo Monaco
152	C4	Monte Caseros Arg.
146	C3	Montego Bay Jamaica
105	C3	Montélimar France
109	C2	Montella Italy
145	C2	Montemorelos Mex.
104	C2	Montendre France
109	C2	Montenegro country Europe
121	C2	Montepuez Moz.
108	B2	Montepulciano Italy
135	B3	Monterey U.S.A.
135	B3	Monterey Bay U.S.A.
150	A1	Montería Col.
152	B2	Montero Bol.
145	B2	Monterrey Mex.
109	C2	Montesano sulla Marcellana Italy
109	C2	Monte Sant'Angelo Italy
151	E3	Monte Santo Brazil
108	A2	Monte Santu, Capo di c. Sardinia Italy
155	D1	Montes Claros Brazil
153	C4	Montevideo Uru.
137	D2	Montevideo U.S.A.
136	B3	Monte Vista U.S.A.
142	C2	Montgomery U.S.A.
105	D2	Monthey Switz.
142	B2	Monticello AR U.S.A.
135	E3	Monticello UT U.S.A.
104	C2	Montignac France
105	C2	Montigny-le-Roi France
106	C2	Montilla Spain
130	C2	Mont-Joli Can.
130	C2	Mont-Laurier Can.
131	C2	Montluçon France
104	C2	Montmagny Can.
104	C2	Montmorillon France

51	E2	Monto Austr.
134	D2	Montpelier ID U.S.A.
141	E2	Montpelier VT U.S.A.
105	C3	Montpellier France
130	C2	Montréal Can.
129	D2	Montreal Lake Can.
129	D2	Montreal Lake l. Can.
99	D3	Montreuil France
105	D2	Montreux Switz.
96	C2	Montrose U.K.
136	B3	Montrose U.S.A.
147	D3	Montserrat terr. West Indies
62	A1	Monywa Myanmar
108	A1	Monza Italy
107	D1	Monzón Spain
123	C1	Mookane Botswana
123	C1	Mookgophong S. Africa
53	D1	Moonie Austr.
53	C1	Moonie r. Austr.
52	A2	Moonta Austr.
50	A2	Moore, Lake imp. l. Austr.
137	D1	Moorhead U.S.A.
53	C3	Mooroopna Austr.
122	A3	Moorreesburg S. Africa
130	B1	Moose r. Can.
130	B1	Moose Factory Can.
141	F1	Moosehead Lake U.S.A.
129	D2	Moose Jaw Can.
137	E1	Moose Lake U.S.A.
129	D2	Moosomin Can.
130	B1	Moosonee Can.
52	B2	Mootwingee Austr.
123	C1	Mopane S. Africa
114	B3	Mopti Mali
150	A3	Moquegua Peru
93	F3	Mora Sweden
137	E1	Mora U.S.A.
75	B2	Moradabad India
121	□D2	Moramanga Madag.
103	D2	Morava r. Europe
96	B2	Moray Firth b. U.K.
100	C3	Morbach Ger.
74	B2	Morbi India
104	B3	Morcenx France
69	E1	Mordaga China
129	E3	Morden Can.
91	E1	Mordovo Russia
98	B1	Morecambe U.K.
98	B1	Morecambe Bay U.K.
53	C1	Moree Austr.
59	D3	Morehead P.N.G.
140	C3	Morehead U.S.A.
143	E2	Morehead City U.S.A.
145	B3	Morelia Mex.
107	C1	Morella Spain
106	B2	Morena, Sierra mts Spain
110	C2	Moreni Romania
128	A2	Moresby, Mount Can.
138	B2	Morgan City U.S.A.
143	D1	Morganton U.S.A.
140	C3	Morgantown U.S.A.
105	D2	Morges Switz.
77	C3	Morghāb, Daryā-ye r. Afgh.
66	D2	Mori Japan
128	B2	Morice Lake Can.
66	D3	Morioka Japan
53	D2	Morisset Austr.
104	B2	Morlaix France
51	C1	Mornington Island Austr.
59	D3	Morobe P.N.G.
114	B1	Morocco country Africa
119	D3	Morogoro Tanz.
64	B2	More Gulf Phil.
122	B2	Morokweng S. Africa
121	□D3	Morombe Madag.
68	C1	Mörön Mongolia
121	□D3	Morondava Madag.
121	D2	Moroni Comoros

216

59 C2 **Morotai** *i.* Indon.
119 D2 **Moroto** Uganda
98 C1 **Morpeth** U.K.
86 F2 **Morrasale** Russia
154 C1 **Morrinhos** Brazil
129 E3 **Morris** Can.
137 D1 **Morris** U.S.A.
143 D1 **Morristown** U.S.A.
87 D3 **Morshansk** Russia
154 B1 **Mortes, Rio das** *r.* Brazil
52 B3 **Mortlake** Austr.
53 D3 **Moruya** Austr.
96 B2 **Morvern** *reg.* U.K.
53 C3 **Morwell** Austr.
102 B2 **Mosbach** Ger.
89 E2 **Moscow** Russia
134 C1 **Moscow** U.S.A.
100 C2 **Mosel** *r.* Ger.
105 D2 **Moselle** *r.* France
134 C1 **Moses Lake** U.S.A.
92 □A3 **Mosfellsbær** Iceland
54 B3 **Mosgiel** N.Z.
89 D2 **Moshenskoye** Russia
119 D3 **Moshi** Tanz.
92 F2 **Mosjøen** Norway
Moskva Russia *see* **Moscow**
103 D2 **Mosonmagyaróvár** Hungary
146 B3 **Mosquitos, Costa de** *coastal area* Nic.
146 B4 **Mosquitos, Golfo de los** *b.* Panama
93 F4 **Moss** Norway
122 B3 **Mossel Bay** S. Africa
122 B3 **Mossel Bay** S. Africa
118 B3 **Mossendjo** Congo
52 B2 **Mossgiel** Austr.
51 D1 **Mossman** Austr.
151 E2 **Mossoró** Brazil
53 D2 **Moss Vale** Austr.
102 C1 **Most** Czechia
114 C1 **Mostaganem** Alg.
109 C2 **Mostar** Bos. & Herz.
152 C4 **Mostardas** Brazil
81 C2 **Mosul** Iraq
93 G4 **Motala** Sweden
96 C3 **Motherwell** U.K.
107 C2 **Motilla del Palancar** Spain
122 B1 **Motokwe** Botswana
106 C2 **Motril** Spain
110 B2 **Motru** Romania
63 A2 **Mottama, Gulf of** Myanmar
Motu Ihupuku N.Z. *see* **Campbell Island/ Motu Ihupuku**
145 D2 **Motul** Mex.
111 C3 **Moudros** Greece
118 B3 **Mouila** Gabon
52 B3 **Moulamein** Austr.
105 C2 **Moulins** France
63 A2 **Moulmein** Myanmar
143 D2 **Moultrie** U.S.A.
143 E2 **Moultrie, Lake** U.S.A.
140 B3 **Mound City** U.S.A.
115 D4 **Moundou** Chad
137 E3 **Mountain Grove** U.S.A.
142 B1 **Mountain Home** *AR* U.S.A.
134 C2 **Mountain Home** *ID* U.S.A.
143 D1 **Mount Airy** U.S.A.
52 A3 **Mount Barker** Austr.
53 C3 **Mount Beauty** Austr.
121 C2 **Mount Darwin** Zimbabwe
141 F2 **Mount Desert Island** U.S.A.
123 C3 **Mount Fletcher** S. Africa
123 C3 **Mount Frere** S. Africa
52 B3 **Mount Gambier** Austr.
59 D3 **Mount Hagen** P.N.G.
53 C2 **Mount Hope** Austr.
51 C2 **Mount Isa** Austr.
50 A2 **Mount Magnet** Austr.
52 B2 **Mount Manara** Austr.
54 C1 **Mount Maunganui** N.Z.
111 B2 **Mount Olympus** Greece
137 E2 **Mount Pleasant** *IA* U.S.A.
140 C2 **Mount Pleasant** *MI* U.S.A.
139 E2 **Mount Pleasant** *TX* U.S.A.
99 A3 **Mount's Bay** U.K.
134 B2 **Mount Shasta** U.S.A.
140 B3 **Mount Vernon** *IL* U.S.A.
140 C2 **Mount Vernon** *OH* U.S.A.
134 B1 **Mount Vernon** *WA* U.S.A.
51 D2 **Moura** Austr.
115 E3 **Mourdi, Dépression du** *depr.* Chad
97 C1 **Mourne Mountains** *hills* U.K.
100 A2 **Mouscron** Belgium
115 D3 **Moussoro** Chad
58 C2 **Moutong** Indon.
115 C2 **Mouydir, Monts du** *plat.* Alg.
100 B3 **Mouzon** France
97 B1 **Moy** *r.* Ireland
117 B4 **Moyale** Eth.
123 C3 **Moyeni** Lesotho
76 B2 **Mo'ynoq** Uzbek.
77 D2 **Moyynty** Kazakh.
121 C3 **Mozambique** *country* Africa
113 I9 **Mozambique Channel** Africa
89 E2 **Mozhaysk** Russia
119 D3 **Mpanda** Tanz.
121 C2 **Mpika** Zambia
121 C1 **Mporokoso** Zambia
123 C2 **Mpumalanga** *prov.* S. Africa
62 A1 **Mrauk-U** Myanmar
88 C2 **Mshinskaya** Russia
107 D2 **M'Sila** Alg.
89 D2 **Msta** *r.* Russia
89 D2 **Mstinskiy Most** Russia
89 D3 **Mstsislaw** Belarus
123 C3 **Mthatha** S. Africa
89 E3 **Mtsensk** Russia
119 E4 **Mtwara** Tanz.
118 B3 **Muanda** Dem. Rep. Congo
63 B2 **Muang Không** Laos
62 B1 **Muang Ngoy** Laos
62 B2 **Muang Pakbeng** Laos
62 B1 **Muang Sing** Laos
62 B2 **Muang Vangviang** Laos
60 B1 **Muar** Malaysia
60 B2 **Muarabungo** Indon.
60 B2 **Muaradua** Indon.
61 C2 **Muaralaung** Indon.
60 A2 **Muarasiberut** Indon.
60 B2 **Muaratembesi** Indon.
61 C2 **Muarateweh** Indon.
119 D2 **Mubende** Uganda
115 D3 **Mubi** Nigeria
120 B2 **Muconda** Angola
155 E1 **Mucuri** Brazil
155 E1 **Mucuri** *r.* Brazil
66 A2 **Mudanjiang** China
66 A1 **Mudan Jiang** *r.* China
111 C2 **Mudanya** Turkey
101 E1 **Müden (Örtze)** Ger.
53 C2 **Mudgee** Austr.
63 A2 **Mudon** Myanmar
80 B1 **Mudurnu** Turkey
121 C2 **Mueda** Moz.
121 B2 **Mufulira** Zambia
120 B2 **Mufumbwe** Zambia
111 C3 **Muğla** Turkey
116 B2 **Muhammad Qol** Sudan
101 F2 **Mühlberg/Elbe** Ger.
101 E2 **Mühlhausen/Thüringen** Ger.
121 C2 **Muite** Moz.
65 B2 **Muju** S. Korea
90 A2 **Mukacheve** Ukr.
61 C1 **Mukah** *Sarawak* Malaysia
79 B3 **Mukalla** Yemen
63 B2 **Mukdahan** Thai.
50 A3 **Mukinbudin** Austr.
60 B2 **Mukomuko** Indon.
121 C2 **Mulanje, Mount** Malawi
101 F2 **Mulde** *r.* Ger.
144 A2 **Mulegé** Mex.
139 C2 **Muleshoe** U.S.A.
106 C2 **Mulhacén** *mt.* Spain
100 C2 **Mülheim an der Ruhr** Ger.
105 D2 **Mulhouse** France
66 B2 **Muling** China
66 B1 **Muling He** *r.* China
96 B2 **Mull** *i.* U.K.
53 C2 **Mullaley** Austr.
136 C2 **Mullen** U.S.A.
61 C1 **Muller, Pegunungan** *mts* Indon.
50 A2 **Mullewa** Austr.
97 C2 **Mullingar** Ireland
96 B3 **Mull of Galloway** *c.* U.K.
96 B3 **Mull of Kintyre** *hd* U.K.
96 A3 **Mull of Oa** *hd* U.K.
120 B2 **Mulobezi** Zambia
74 B1 **Multan** Pak.
73 B3 **Mumbai** India
120 B2 **Mumbwa** Zambia
145 D2 **Muna** Mex.
101 E2 **Münchberg** Ger.
München Ger. *see* **Munich**
140 B2 **Muncie** U.S.A.
50 B3 **Mundrabilla** Austr.
119 C2 **Mungbere** Dem. Rep. Congo
75 C2 **Munger** India
52 A1 **Mungeranie** Austr.
53 C1 **Mungindi** Austr.
102 C2 **Munich** Ger.
155 D2 **Muniz Freire** Brazil
101 E1 **Munster** Ger.
100 C2 **Münster** Ger.
97 B2 **Munster** *reg.* Ireland
100 C2 **Münsterland** *reg.* Ger.
62 B1 **Mương Nhe** Vietnam
92 H2 **Muonio** Fin.
92 H2 **Muonioälven** *r.* Fin./Sweden
Muqdisho Somalia *see* **Mogadishu**
103 D2 **Mur** *r.* Austria
119 C3 **Muramvya** Burundi
119 D3 **Murang'a** Kenya
81 B2 **Murat** *r.* Turkey
111 C2 **Muratlı** Turkey
50 A2 **Murchison** *watercourse* Austr.
107 C2 **Murcia** Spain
111 C2 **Mürefte** Turkey
110 B1 **Mureşul** *r.* Romania
104 C3 **Muret** France
142 C1 **Murfreesboro** U.S.A.
77 D3 **Murghob** Tajik.
155 D2 **Muriaé** Brazil
120 B1 **Muriege** Angola
101 F1 **Müritz** *l.* Ger.
86 C2 **Murmansk** Russia
87 D3 **Murom** Russia
66 D2 **Muroran** Japan
106 B1 **Muros** Spain
67 B4 **Muroto** Japan
67 B4 **Muroto-zaki** *pt* Japan
143 D1 **Murphy** U.S.A.
53 C1 **Murra Murra** Austr.
52 A3 **Murray** *r.* Austr.
128 B2 **Murray** *r.* Can.
140 B3 **Murray** U.S.A.
143 D2 **Murray, Lake** U.S.A.
52 A3 **Murray Bridge** Austr.
122 B3 **Murraysburg** S. Africa
52 B3 **Murrayville** Austr.
52 B2 **Murrumbidgee** *r.* Austr.

121 C2 **Murrupula** Moz.
53 D2 **Murrurundi** Austr.
109 C1 **Murska Sobota** Slovenia
54 C1 **Murupara** N.Z.
49 I4 **Mururoa** *atoll* Fr. Polynesia
Murwara India *see* **Katni**
53 D1 **Murwillumbah** Austr.
115 D2 **Murzūq** Libya
115 D2 **Murzuq, Idhān** *des.* Libya
81 C2 **Muş** Turkey
110 B2 **Musala** *mt.* Bulg.
65 B1 **Musan** N. Korea
78 B3 **Musaymir** Yemen
79 C2 **Muscat** Oman
137 E2 **Muscatine** U.S.A.
50 C2 **Musgrave Ranges** *mts* Austr.
118 B3 **Mushie** Dem. Rep. Congo
60 B2 **Musi** *r.* Indon.
123 D1 **Musina** S. Africa
140 B2 **Muskegon** U.S.A.
139 D1 **Muskogee** U.S.A.
128 B2 **Muskwa** *r.* Can.
74 A1 **Muslimbagh** Pak.
78 A3 **Musmar** Sudan
119 D3 **Musoma** Tanz.
96 C3 **Musselburgh** U.K.
88 B2 **Mustjala** Estonia
53 D2 **Muswellbrook** Austr.
116 A2 **Mūţ** Egypt
121 C2 **Mutare** Zimbabwe
66 D2 **Mutsu** Japan
121 C2 **Mutuali** Moz.
92 I2 **Muurola** Fin.
70 A2 **Mu Us Shadi** *des.* China
120 A1 **Muxaluando** Angola
86 C2 **Muyezerskiy** Russia
119 D3 **Muyinga** Burundi
74 B1 **Muzaffargarh** Pak.
75 C2 **Muzaffarpur** India
144 B2 **Múzquiz** Mex.
75 C1 **Muz Shan** *mt.* China
119 C3 **Mwanza** Dem. Rep. Congo
119 D3 **Mwanza** Tanz.
118 C3 **Mweka** Dem. Rep. Congo
121 B2 **Mwenda** Zambia
118 C3 **Mwene-Ditu** Dem. Rep. Congo
121 C3 **Mwenezi** Zimbabwe
119 C3 **Mweru, Lake** Dem. Rep. Congo/Zambia
118 C3 **Mwimba** Dem. Rep. Congo
120 B2 **Mwinilunga** Zambia
88 C3 **Myadzyel** Belarus
62 A2 **Myanaung** Myanmar
62 A1 **Myanmar** *country* Asia
63 A2 **Myaungmya** Myanmar
63 A2 **Myeik** Myanmar
Myeik Kyunzu *is* Myanmar *see* **Mergui Archipelago**
62 A1 **Myingyan** Myanmar
62 A1 **Myitkyina** Myanmar
91 C2 **Mykolayiv** Ukr.
111 C3 **Mykonos** Greece
111 C3 **Mykonos** *i.* Greece
86 E2 **Myla** Russia
75 D2 **Mymensingh** Bangl.
67 C3 **Myōkō** Japan
65 B1 **Myŏnggan** N. Korea
88 C2 **Myory** Belarus
92 □B3 **Mýrdalsjökull** Iceland
91 C2 **Myrhorod** Ukr.
91 D2 **Myrnohrad** Ukr.
90 C2 **Myronivka** Ukr.
143 E2 **Myrtle Beach** U.S.A.
53 C3 **Myrtleford** Austr.
134 B2 **Myrtle Point** U.S.A.
89 E2 **Myshkin** Russia
103 C1 **Myślibórz** Pol.
Mysore India *see* **Mysuru**
83 N2 **Mys Shmidta** Russia
73 B3 **Mysuru** India
63 B2 **My Tho** Vietnam
111 C3 **Mytilini** Greece
89 E3 **Mytishchi** Russia
123 C3 **Mzamomhle** S. Africa
121 C2 **Mzimba** Malawi
121 C2 **Mzuzu** Malawi

N

97 C2 **Naas** Ireland
122 A2 **Nababeep** S. Africa
87 E3 **Naberezhnyye Chelny** Russia
59 D3 **Nabire** Indon.
80 B2 **Nāblus** West Bank
121 D2 **Nacala** Moz.
63 A2 **Nachuge** India
139 E2 **Nacogdoches** U.S.A.
144 B1 **Nacozari de García** Mex.
74 B2 **Nadiad** India
90 A2 **Nadvirna** Ukr.
86 C2 **Nadvoitsy** Russia
86 G2 **Nadym** Russia
93 F4 **Næstved** Denmark
111 B3 **Nafpaktos** Greece
111 B3 **Nafplio** Greece
115 D1 **Nafūsah, Jabal** *hills* Libya
78 B2 **Nafy** Saudi Arabia
64 B1 **Naga** Phil.
130 B1 **Nagagami** *r.* Can.
67 C3 **Nagano** Japan
67 C3 **Nagaoka** Japan
75 D2 **Nagaon** India
74 B1 **Nagar** India
74 B2 **Nagar Parkar** Pak.
67 A4 **Nagasaki** Japan
67 B4 **Nagato** Japan
74 B2 **Nagaur** India
73 B4 **Nagercoil** India
74 A2 **Nagha Kalat** Pak.
75 B2 **Nagina** India
67 C3 **Nagoya** Japan
75 B2 **Nagpur** India
68 C2 **Nagqu** China
103 D2 **Nagyatád** Hungary
103 D2 **Nagykanizsa** Hungary
128 B1 **Nahanni Butte** Can.
76 A3 **Nahāvand** Iran
101 E1 **Nahrendorf** Ger.
153 A5 **Nahuel Huapí, Lago** *l.* Arg.
131 D1 **Nain** Can.
81 D2 **Nā'īn** Iran
96 C2 **Nairn** U.K.
119 D3 **Nairobi** Kenya
119 D3 **Naivasha** Kenya
81 D2 **Najafābād** Iran
78 B2 **Najd** *reg.* Saudi Arabia
106 C1 **Nájera** Spain
65 C1 **Najin** N. Korea
78 B3 **Najrān** Saudi Arabia
Nakambé *r.* Burkina Faso/Ghana *see* **White Volta**
67 C3 **Nakatsugawa** Japan
78 A3 **Nakfa** Eritrea
66 B2 **Nakhodka** Russia
63 B2 **Nakhon Pathom** Thai.
63 B2 **Nakhon Ratchasima** Thai.
63 B2 **Nakhon Sawan** Thai.
63 A3 **Nakhon Si Thammarat** Thai.
130 B1 **Nakina** Can.
121 C1 **Nakonde** Zambia
93 F4 **Nakskov** Denmark
119 D3 **Nakuru** Kenya
128 C2 **Nakusp** Can.
75 D2 **Nalbari** India
87 D4 **Nal'chik** Russia
115 D1 **Nālūt** Libya
123 C2 **Namahadi** S. Africa
77 D2 **Namangan** Uzbek.
122 A2 **Namaqualand** *reg.* S. Africa
51 E2 **Nambour** Austr.
53 D2 **Nambucca Heads** Austr.
75 D1 **Nam Co** *salt l.* China
62 B1 **Nam Định** Vietnam
120 A3 **Namib Desert** Namibia
120 A2 **Namibe** Angola
120 A3 **Namibia** *country* Africa
72 D2 **Namjagbarwa Feng** *mt.* Chin
59 C3 **Namlea** Indon.
53 C2 **Namoi** *r.* Austr.
134 C2 **Nampa** U.S.A.
114 B3 **Nampala** Mali
65 B2 **Namp'o** N. Korea
121 C2 **Nampula** Moz.
62 A1 **Namrup** India
62 A1 **Namsang** Myanmar
92 F3 **Namsos** Norway
63 A2 **Nam Tok** Thai.
83 J2 **Namtsy** Russia
62 A1 **Namtu** Myanmar
100 B2 **Namur** Belgium
120 B2 **Namwala** Zambia
65 B2 **Namwon** S. Korea
62 A1 **Namya Ra** Myanmar
62 B2 **Nan** Thai.
128 B3 **Nanaimo** Can.
71 B3 **Nan'an** China
122 A1 **Nananib Plateau** Namibia
67 C3 **Nanao** Japan
71 B3 **Nanchang** *Jiangxi* China
71 B3 **Nanchang** *Jiangxi* China
70 A2 **Nanchong** China
63 A3 **Nancowry** *i.* India
105 D2 **Nancy** France
75 C1 **Nanda Devi** *mt.* India
71 A3 **Nandan** China
73 B3 **Nanded** India
74 B2 **Nandurbar** India
73 B3 **Nandyal** India
71 B3 **Nanfeng** China
118 B2 **Nanga Eboko** Cameroon
71 C3 **Nangan Island** *i.* Taiwan
74 B1 **Nanga Parbat** *mt.* Pak.
61 C2 **Nangapinoh** Indon.
61 C2 **Nangatayap** Indon.
70 B2 **Nangong** China
119 D3 **Nangulangwa** Tanz.
70 C2 **Nanhui** China
70 B2 **Nanjing** China
Nanking China *see* **Nanjing**
120 A2 **Nankova** Angola
71 B3 **Nan Ling** *mts* China
71 A3 **Nanning** China
127 H2 **Nanortalik** Greenland
71 A3 **Nanpan Jiang** *r.* China
75 C2 **Nanpara** India
71 B3 **Nanping** China
Nansei-shotō *is* Japan *see* **Ryukyu Islands**
104 B2 **Nantes** France
70 C2 **Nantong** China
141 F2 **Nantucket Island** U.S.A.
155 D1 **Nanuque** Brazil
64 B2 **Nanusa, Kepulauan** *is* Indon.
71 B3 **Nanxiong** China
70 B2 **Nanyang** China
70 B2 **Nanzhang** China
131 C1 **Naococane, Lac** *l.* Can.
135 B3 **Napa** U.S.A.
126 D2 **Napaktulik Lake** Can.
127 H2 **Napasoq** Greenland
54 C1 **Napier** N.Z.
108 B2 **Naples** Italy
143 D3 **Naples** U.S.A.

150 A2 **Napo** *r.* Ecuador/Peru
Napoli Italy *see* **Naples**
114 B3 **Nara** Mali
93 I4 **Narach** Belarus
52 B3 **Naracoorte** Austr.
145 C2 **Naranjos** Mex.
63 B3 **Narathiwat** Thai.
105 C3 **Narbonne** France
63 A2 **Narcondam Island** India
127 G1 **Nares Strait** Can./Greenland
122 A1 **Narib** Namibia
87 D4 **Narimanov** Russia
67 D3 **Narita** Japan
74 B2 **Narmada** *r.* India
74 B2 **Narnaul** India
108 B2 **Narni** Italy
90 B1 **Narodychi** Ukr.
89 E2 **Naro-Fominsk** Russia
53 D3 **Narooma** Austr.
88 C3 **Narowlya** Belarus
53 C2 **Narrabri** Austr.
53 C2 **Narrandera** Austr.
53 C2 **Narromine** Austr.
88 C2 **Narva** Estonia
88 C2 **Narva Bay** Estonia/Russia
92 G2 **Narvik** Norway
88 C2 **Narvskoye Vodokhranilishche** *resr* Estonia/Russia
86 E2 **Nar'yan-Mar** Russia
77 D2 **Naryn** Kyrg.
74 B2 **Nashik** India
141 E2 **Nashua** U.S.A.
142 C1 **Nashville** U.S.A.
49 I5 **Nasinu** Fiji
117 B4 **Nasir** South Sudan
128 B2 **Nass** *r.* Can.
146 C2 **Nassau** Bahamas
116 B2 **Nasser, Lake** *resr* Egypt
93 F4 **Nässjö** Sweden
130 C1 **Nastapoca** *r.* Can.
130 C1 **Nastapoka Islands** Can.
67 D3 **Nasushiobara** Japan
120 B3 **Nata** Botswana
151 E2 **Natal** Brazil
131 D1 **Natashquan** Can.
131 D1 **Natashquan** *r.* Can.
142 B2 **Natchez** U.S.A.
142 B2 **Natchitoches** U.S.A.
53 C3 **Nathalia** Austr.
107 D1 **Nati, Punta** *pt* Spain
114 C3 **Natitingou** Benin
151 D3 **Natividade** Brazil
67 D3 **Natori** Japan
131 D1 **Natuashish** Can.
61 B1 **Natuna, Kepulauan** *is* Indon.
61 B1 **Natuna Besar** *i.* Indon.
107 D2 **Nau, Cap de la** *c.* Spain
120 A3 **Nauchas** Namibia
101 F1 **Nauen** Ger.
127 F2 **Naujaat** Can.
88 B2 **Naujoji Akmenė** Lith.
74 A2 **Naukot** Pak.
101 E2 **Naumburg (Saale)** Ger.
48 F3 **Nauru** *country* S. Pacific Ocean
145 C2 **Nautla** Mex.
88 C3 **Navahrudak** Belarus
106 B2 **Navalmoral de la Mata** Spain
106 B2 **Navalvillar de Pela** Spain
97 C2 **Navan** Ireland
88 C2 **Navapolatsk** Belarus
83 M2 **Navarin, Mys** *c.* Russia
153 B6 **Navarino, Isla** *i.* Chile
96 B1 **Naver** *r.* U.K.
73 B3 **Navi Mumbai** India
89 D3 **Navlya** Russia
110 C2 **Năvodari** Romania
77 C2 **Navoiy** Uzbek.
144 B2 **Navojoa** Mex.
144 B2 **Navolato** Mex.
74 A2 **Nawabshah** Pak.
62 A1 **Nawnghkio** Myanmar
62 A1 **Nawngleng** Myanmar
81 C2 **Naxçıvan** Azer.
111 C3 **Naxos** *i.* Greece
144 B2 **Nayar** Mex.
66 D2 **Nayoro** Japan
144 B2 **Nazas** Mex.
144 B2 **Nazas** *r.* Mex.
150 A3 **Nazca** Peru
80 B2 **Nazerat** Israel
111 C3 **Nazilli** Turkey
117 B4 **Nazrēt** Eth.
79 C2 **Nazwá** Oman
121 B1 **Nchelenge** Zambia
122 B1 **Ncojane** Botswana
120 A1 **N'dalatando** Angola
118 C2 **Ndélé** C.A.R.
118 B3 **Ndendé** Gabon
115 D3 **Ndjamena** Chad
121 B2 **Ndola** Zambia
97 C1 **Neagh, Lough** *l.* U.K.
50 C2 **Neale, Lake** *imp. l.* Austr.
111 B2 **Nea Roda** Greece
99 B3 **Neath** U.K.
53 C1 **Nebine Creek** *r.* Austr.
150 B1 **Neblina, Pico da** *mt.* Brazil
89 D2 **Nebolchi** Russia
136 C2 **Nebraska** *state* U.S.A.
137 D2 **Nebraska City** U.S.A.
108 B3 **Nebrodi, Monti** *mts Sicily* Italy
153 C4 **Necochea** Arg.
131 C1 **Nedlouc, Lac** *l.* Can.
135 D4 **Needles** U.S.A.
129 E2 **Neepawa** Can.
87 E3 **Neftekamsk** Russia
82 F2 **Nefteyugansk** Russia
120 A1 **Negage** Angola
117 B4 **Negēlē** Eth.
150 A2 **Negra, Punta** *pt* Peru
63 A2 **Negrais, Cape** Myanmar
153 B5 **Negro** *r.* Arg.
150 C2 **Negro** *r.* S. America
152 C4 **Negro** *r.* Uru.
106 B2 **Negro, Cabo** *c.* Morocco
64 B2 **Negros** *i.* Phil.
69 E1 **Nehe** China
70 A3 **Neijiang** China
129 D2 **Neilburg** Can.
70 A1 **Nei Mongol Zizhiqu** *aut. reg.* China
150 A1 **Neiva** Col.
129 E2 **Nejanilini Lake** Can.
117 B4 **Nek'emtē** Eth.
89 F2 **Nekrasovskoye** Russia
89 D2 **Nelidovo** Russia
73 B3 **Nellore** India
128 C3 **Nelson** Can.
129 E2 **Nelson** *r.* Can.
54 B2 **Nelson** N.Z.
52 B3 **Nelson, Cape** Austr.
53 D2 **Nelson Bay** Austr.
129 E2 **Nelson House** Can.
134 E1 **Nelson Reservoir** U.S.A.
114 B3 **Néma** Maur.
88 B2 **Neman** Russia
104 C2 **Nemours** France
66 D2 **Nemuro** Japan
90 B2 **Nemyriv** Ukr.
97 B2 **Nenagh** Ireland
99 D2 **Nene** *r.* U.K.
69 E1 **Nenjiang** China
137 E3 **Neosho** U.S.A.
75 C2 **Nepal** *country* Asia
75 C2 **Nepalganj** Nepal
135 D3 **Nephi** U.S.A.
97 B1 **Nephin** *h.* Ireland
97 B1 **Nephin Beg Range** *hills* Ireland
131 D2 **Nepisiguit** *r.* Can.
119 C2 **Nepoko** *r.* Dem. Rep. Congo
104 C3 **Nérac** France
53 D1 **Nerang** Austr.
69 D1 **Nerchinsk** Russia
89 F2 **Nerekhta** Russia
109 C2 **Neretva** *r.* Bos. & Herz./Croatia
120 B2 **Neriquinha** Angola
88 B3 **Neris** *r.* Lith.
89 E2 **Nerl'** *r.* Russia
86 F2 **Nerokhi** Russia
154 C1 **Nerópolis** Brazil
83 J3 **Neryungri** Russia
92 □C2 **Neskaupstaður** Iceland
96 B2 **Ness, Loch** *l.* U.K.
136 D3 **Ness City** U.S.A.
111 B2 **Nestos** *r.* Greece
100 B1 **Netherlands** *country* Europe
127 G2 **Nettilling Lake** Can.
101 F1 **Neubrandenburg** Ger.
105 D2 **Neuchâtel** Switz.
100 C2 **Neuerburg** Ger.
100 B3 **Neufchâteau** Belgium
105 D2 **Neufchâteau** France
104 C2 **Neufchâtel-en-Bray** France
101 D2 **Neuhof** Ger.
102 B1 **Neumünster** Ger.
102 B2 **Neunkirchen** Ger.
153 B4 **Neuquén** Arg.
153 B4 **Neuquén** *r.* Arg.
101 F1 **Neuruppin** Ger.
100 C2 **Neuss** Ger.
101 D1 **Neustadt am Rübenberge** Ger.
101 E3 **Neustadt an der Aisch** Ger.
101 F1 **Neustrelitz** Ger.
100 C2 **Neuwied** Ger.
137 E3 **Nevada** U.S.A.
135 C3 **Nevada** *state* U.S.A.
106 C2 **Nevada, Sierra** *mts* Spain
135 B2 **Nevada, Sierra** *mts* U.S.A.
88 C2 **Nevel'** Russia
105 C2 **Nevers** France
53 C2 **Nevertire** Austr.
109 C2 **Nevesinje** Bos. & Herz.
87 D4 **Nevinnomyssk** Russia
128 B2 **New Aiyansh** Can.
140 B3 **New Albany** U.S.A.
151 C1 **New Amsterdam** Guyana
141 E2 **Newark** *NJ* U.S.A.
140 C2 **Newark** *OH* U.S.A.
98 C2 **Newark-on-Trent** U.K.
141 E2 **New Bedford** U.S.A.
143 E1 **New Bern** U.S.A.
143 D2 **Newberry** U.S.A.
139 E2 **New Boston** U.S.A.
139 D3 **New Braunfels** U.S.A.
97 C2 **Newbridge** Ireland
48 E3 **New Britain** *i.* P.N.G.
131 D2 **New Brunswick** *prov.* Can.
99 C3 **Newbury** U.K.
64 A1 **New Busuanga** Phil.
48 E4 **New Caledonia** *terr.* S. Pacific Ocean
53 D2 **Newcastle** Austr.
123 C2 **Newcastle** S. Africa
97 D1 **Newcastle** U.K.
140 C2 **New Castle** U.S.A.
136 C2 **Newcastle** U.S.A.
98 B2 **Newcastle-under-Lyme** U.K.
98 C1 **Newcastle upon Tyne** U.K.
97 B2 **Newcastle West** Ireland
74 B2 **New Delhi** India
128 C3 **New Denver** Can.
53 D2 **New England Range** *mts* Austr.

131 E2 **Newfoundland** *i.* Can.
131 E1 **Newfoundland and Labrador** *prov.* Can.
131 D2 **New Glasgow** Can.
59 D3 **New Guinea** *i.* Indon./P.N.G.
141 E2 **New Hampshire** *state* U.S.A.
141 E2 **New Haven** U.S.A.
128 B2 **New Hazelton** Can.
New Hebrides *country* S. Pacific Ocean *see* **Vanuatu**
142 B2 **New Iberia** U.S.A.
48 E3 **New Ireland** *i.* P.N.G.
141 E3 **New Jersey** *state* U.S.A.
130 C2 **New Liskeard** Can.
50 A2 **Newman** Austr.
138 B2 **New Mexico** *state* U.S.A.
142 B3 **New Orleans** U.S.A.
140 C2 **New Philadelphia** U.S.A.
54 B1 **New Plymouth** N.Z.
99 C3 **Newport** *England* U.K.
99 B3 **Newport** *Wales* U.K.
142 B1 **Newport** *AR* U.S.A.
134 B2 **Newport** *OR* U.S.A.
141 E2 **Newport** *RI* U.S.A.
141 E2 **Newport** *VT* U.S.A.
134 C1 **Newport** *WA* U.S.A.
141 D3 **Newport News** U.S.A.
143 E3 **New Providence** *i.* Bahamas
99 A3 **Newquay** U.K.
142 B2 **New Roads** U.S.A.
97 C2 **New Ross** Ireland
97 C1 **Newry** U.K.
83 K1 **New Siberia Islands** Russia
52 B2 **New South Wales** *state* Austr.
137 E2 **Newton** *IA* U.S.A.
137 D3 **Newton** *KS* U.S.A.
99 B3 **Newton Abbot** U.K.
96 B3 **Newton Stewart** U.K.
97 B2 **Newtown** Ireland
99 B2 **Newtown** U.K.
136 C1 **New Town** U.S.A.
97 D1 **Newtownabbey** U.K.
97 D1 **Newtownards** U.K.
96 C3 **Newtown St Boswells** U.K.
97 C1 **Newtownstewart** U.K.
137 E2 **New Ulm** U.S.A.
141 E2 **New York** U.S.A.
141 D2 **New York** *state* U.S.A.
54 B2 **New Zealand** *country* Oceania
79 C2 **Neyrīz** Iran
76 B3 **Neyshābūr** Iran
145 C3 **Nezahualcóyotl, Presa** *resr* Mex.
61 B1 **Ngabang** Indon.
75 C2 **Ngamring** China
75 C1 **Ngangla Ringco** *salt l.* China
77 E3 **Nganglong Kangri** *mt.* China
75 C1 **Nganglong Kangri** *mts* China
75 C1 **Ngangzê Co** *salt l.* China
62 A2 **Ngao** Thai.
118 B2 **Ngaoundéré** Cameroon
54 C1 **Ngaruawahia** N.Z.
62 A2 **Ngathainggyaung** Myanmar
121 D2 **Ngazidja** *i.* Comoros
118 B3 **Ngo** Congo
115 D4 **Ngol Bembo** Nigeria
68 C2 **Ngoring Hu** *l.* China
115 D3 **Ngourti** Niger
115 D3 **Nguigmi** Niger
59 D2 **Ngulu** *atoll* Micronesia
115 D3 **Nguru** Nigeria
123 D2 **Ngwelezana** S. Africa
121 C2 **Nhamalabué** Moz.
63 B2 **Nha Trang** Vietnam
52 B3 **Nhill** Austr.
123 D2 **Nhlangano** Swaziland
51 C1 **Nhulunbuy** Austr.
141 D2 **Niagara Falls** Can.
114 C3 **Niamey** Niger
119 C2 **Niangara** Dem. Rep. Congo
114 B3 **Niangay, Lac** *l.* Mali
60 A1 **Nias** *i.* Indon.
146 B3 **Nicaragua** *country* Central America
146 B3 **Nicaragua, Lake** Nic.
105 D3 **Nice** France
73 D4 **Nicobar Islands** India
80 B2 **Nicosia** Cyprus
146 B4 **Nicoya, Golfo de** *b.* Costa Rica
88 B2 **Nida** Lith.
103 E1 **Nidzica** Pol.
102 B1 **Niebüll** Ger.
101 D2 **Niederaula** Ger.
118 B2 **Niefang** Equat. Guinea
101 F1 **Niemegk** Ger.
101 D1 **Nienburg (Weser)** Ger.
100 B1 **Nieuwe Niedorp** Neth.
151 C1 **Nieuw Nickerie** Suriname
122 A3 **Nieuwoudtville** S. Africa
100 A2 **Nieuwpoort** Belgium
80 B2 **Niğde** Turkey
115 C3 **Niger** *country* Africa
115 C4 **Niger** *r.* Africa
115 C4 **Niger, Mouths of the** Nigeria
115 C4 **Nigeria** *country* Africa
130 B2 **Nighthawk Lake** Can.
111 B2 **Nigrita** Greece
67 C3 **Niigata** Japan
67 B4 **Niihama** Japan
67 C4 **Nii-jima** *i.* Japan
67 C3 **Niitsu** Japan
100 B2 **Nijmegen** Neth.
100 C1 **Nijverdal** Neth.
92 J2 **Nikel'** Russia
91 D2 **Nikol's'ke** Ukr.
83 M3 **Nikol'skoye** Russia
91 C2 **Nikopol'** Ukr.
80 B1 **Niksar** Turkey
79 D2 **Nīkshahr** Iran
109 C2 **Nikšić** Montenegro
116 B1 **Nile** *r.* Africa
140 B2 **Niles** U.S.A.
74 A1 **Nīlī** Afgh.
74 B2 **Nimach** India
105 C3 **Nîmes** France
53 C3 **Nimmitabel** Austr.
117 B4 **Nimule** Sudan
53 C1 **Nindigully** Austr.
73 B4 **Nine Degree Channel** India
53 C3 **Ninety Mile Beach** Austr.
54 B1 **Ninety Mile Beach** N.Z.
70 C3 **Ningbo** China
71 B3 **Ningde** China
71 B3 **Ningdu** China
70 B2 **Ningguo** China
71 C3 **Ninghai** China
Ningjiang China *see* **Songyuan**
68 C2 **Ningjing Shan** *mts* China
70 A2 **Ningxia Huizu Zizhiqu** *aut. reg.* China
70 B2 **Ningyang** China
62 B1 **Ninh Binh** Vietnam
63 B2 **Ninh Hoa** Vietnam
66 D2 **Ninohe** Japan
137 D2 **Niobrara** *r.* U.S.A.
114 B3 **Niono** Mali
114 B3 **Nioro** Mali
104 B2 **Niort** France
129 D2 **Nipawin** Can.
130 B2 **Nipigon** Can.
130 B2 **Nipigon, Lake** Can.
131 D1 **Nipishish Lake** Can.
130 C2 **Nipissing, Lake** Can.
135 C3 **Nipton** U.S.A.
151 D3 **Niquelândia** Brazil
73 B3 **Nirmal** India
109 D2 **Niš** Serbia
109 D2 **Nišava** *r.* Serbia
108 B3 **Niscemi** *Sicily* Italy
67 B4 **Nishino-omote** Japan
155 D2 **Niterói** Brazil
96 C3 **Nith** *r.* U.K.
103 D2 **Nitra** Slovakia
49 G4 **Niue** *terr.* S. Pacific Ocean
92 H3 **Nivala** Fin.
100 B2 **Nivelles** Belgium
73 B3 **Nizamabad** India
87 E3 **Nizhnekamsk** Russia
83 H3 **Nizhneudinsk** Russia
82 G2 **Nizhnevartovsk** Russia
89 F3 **Nizhniy Kislyay** Russia
87 D3 **Nizhniy Lomov** Russia
87 D3 **Nizhniy Novgorod** Russia
86 E2 **Nizhniy Odes** Russia
86 E3 **Nizhniy Tagil** Russia
83 G2 **Nizhnyaya Tunguska** *r.* Russia
91 C1 **Nizhyn** Ukr.
119 D3 **Njinjo** Tanz.
119 D3 **Njombe** Tanz.
121 C2 **Nkhotakota** Malawi
118 A2 **Nkongsamba** Cameroon
123 C3 **Nkululeko** S. Africa
123 C3 **Nkwenkwezi** S. Africa
67 B4 **Nobeoka** Japan
52 B1 **Noccundra** Austr.
144 A1 **Nogales** Mex.
138 A2 **Nogales** U.S.A.
104 C2 **Nogent-le-Rotrou** France
89 E2 **Noginsk** Russia
74 B2 **Nohar** India
100 C3 **Nohfelden** Ger.
104 B2 **Noirmoutier, Île de** *i.* France
104 B2 **Noirmoutier-en-l'Île** France
67 C4 **Nojima-zaki** *c.* Japan
74 B2 **Nokha** India
93 H3 **Nokia** Fin.
74 A2 **Nok Kundi** Pak.
118 B2 **Nola** C.A.R.
86 D3 **Nolinsk** Russia
123 C3 **Nomonde** S. Africa
123 D2 **Nondweni** S. Africa
62 B2 **Nong Khai** Thai.
52 A2 **Nonning** Austr.
144 B2 **Nonoava** Mex.
65 B2 **Nonsan** S. Korea
63 B2 **Nonthaburi** Thai.
122 B3 **Nonzwakazi** S. Africa
77 C3 **Norak** Tajik.
141 D1 **Noranda** Can.
82 C1 **Nordaustlandet** *i.* Svalbard
128 C2 **Nordegg** Can.
100 C1 **Norden** Ger.
83 H1 **Nordenshel'da, Arkhipelag** *is* Russia
100 C1 **Norderney** Ger.
100 C1 **Norderney** *i.* Ger.
101 E1 **Norderstedt** Ger.
93 E3 **Nordfjordeid** Norway
101 E2 **Nordhausen** Ger.
101 D1 **Nordholz** Ger.
100 C1 **Nordhorn** Ger.
Nordkapp *c.* Norway *see* **North Cape**
92 F3 **Nordli** Norway
102 C2 **Nördlingen** Ger.
92 G3 **Nordmaling** Sweden
94 B1 **Norðoyar** *is* Faroe Is
97 C2 **Nore** *r.* Ireland
137 D2 **Norfolk** *NE* U.S.A.
141 D3 **Norfolk** *VA* U.S.A.
48 F4 **Norfolk Island** *terr.* S. Pacific Ocean
93 E3 **Norheimsund** Norway

82 G2 Noril'sk Russia
75 C2 Norkyung China
139 D1 Norman U.S.A.
Normandes, Îles is
English Chan. see
Channel Islands
51 D1 Normanton Austr.
93 G4 Norrköping Sweden
93 G3 Norrtälje Sweden
50 B3 Norseman Austr.
93 G3 Norsjö Sweden
98 C1 Northallerton U.K.
92 A2 Northampton Austr.
99 C2 Northampton U.K.
73 D3 North Andaman i. India
129 D2 North Battleford Can.
130 C2 North Bay Can.
130 C1 North Belcher Islands Can.
96 C2 North Berwick U.K.
92 I1 North Cape Norway
54 B1 North Cape N.Z.
130 C1 North Caribou Lake Can.
143 E1 North Carolina state U.S.A.
130 B2 North Channel lake channel Can.
96 A3 North Channel U.K.
128 B3 North Cowichan Can.
136 C1 North Dakota state U.S.A.
99 C3 North Downs hills U.K.
143 E3 Northeast Providence Channel Bahamas
101 D2 Northeim Ger.
122 A2 Northern Cape prov. S. Africa
129 E2 Northern Indian Lake Can.
97 C1 Northern Ireland prov. U.K.
48 D1 Northern Mariana Islands terr. N. Pacific Ocean
50 C1 Northern Territory admin. div. Austr.
96 C2 North Esk r. U.K.
137 E2 Northfield U.S.A.
99 D3 North Foreland c. U.K.
54 B1 North Island N.Z.
129 E2 North Knife Lake Can.
65 B1 North Korea country Asia
62 A1 North Lakhimpur India
128 B1 North Nahanni r. Can.
136 C2 North Platte U.S.A.
136 C2 North Platte r. U.S.A.
96 C1 North Ronaldsay i. U.K.
94 D2 North Sea Europe
130 A1 North Spirit Lake Can.
53 D1 North Stradbroke Island Austr.
54 B1 North Taranaki Bight b. N.Z.
130 C1 North Twin Island Can.
98 B1 North Tyne r. U.K.
96 A2 North Uist i. U.K.
131 D2 Northumberland Strait Can.
122 C2 North West prov. S. Africa
54 A2 North West Cape Austr.
143 E3 Northwest Providence Channel Bahamas
131 E1 North West River Can.
128 B1 Northwest Territories admin. div. Can.
98 C1 North York Moors moorland U.K.
140 C3 Norton U.S.A.
121 C2 Norton Zimbabwe
140 C2 Norwalk U.S.A.
93 F3 Norway country Europe
129 E2 Norway House Can.
160 A3 Norwegian Sea N. Atlantic Ocean
99 D2 Norwich U.K.
141 E2 Norwich CT U.S.A.
141 D2 Norwich NY U.S.A.

66 D2 Noshiro Japan
91 C1 Nosivka Ukr.
122 B2 Nosop watercourse Africa
86 E2 Nosovaya Russia
79 C2 Noşratābād Iran
Nossob watercourse Africa see Nosop
103 D1 Noteć r. Pol.
93 E4 Notodden Norway
67 C3 Noto-hantō pen. Japan
131 D2 Notre-Dame, Monts mts Can.
131 E2 Notre Dame Bay Can.
130 C1 Nottaway r. Can.
99 C2 Nottingham U.K.
114 A2 Nouadhibou Maur.
114 A3 Nouakchott Maur.
114 A3 Nouâmghâr Maur.
48 F4 Nouméa New Caledonia
114 B3 Nouna Burkina Faso
154 B2 Nova Esperança Brazil
154 B2 Nova Friburgo Brazil
109 C1 Nova Gradiška Croatia
154 C2 Nova Granada Brazil
155 D2 Nova Iguaçu Brazil
91 C2 Nova Kakhovka Ukr.
155 D1 Nova Lima Brazil
154 B2 Nova Londrina Brazil
91 C2 Nova Odesa Ukr.
131 D2 Nova Scotia prov. Can.
155 D1 Nova Venécia Brazil
83 K1 Novaya Sibir', Ostrov i. Russia
86 E1 Novaya Zemlya is Russia
103 D2 Nové Zámky Slovakia
91 C1 Novhorod-Sivers'kyy Ukr.
110 B2 Novi Iskar Bulg.
108 A2 Novi Ligure Italy
109 D2 Novi Pazar Serbia
109 C1 Novi Sad Serbia
87 D3 Novoanninskiy Russia
150 B2 Novo Aripuanã Brazil
91 D2 Novoazovs'k Ukr.
91 E2 Novocherkassk Russia
86 D2 Novodvinsk Russia
152 C3 Novo Hamburgo Brazil
154 C2 Novo Horizonte Brazil
90 B1 Novohrad-Volyns'kyy Ukr.
103 D2 Novo mesto Slovenia
91 D3 Novomikhaylovskiy Russia
89 E3 Novomoskovsk Russia
91 D2 Novomoskovs'k Ukr.
91 C2 Novomyrhorod Ukr.
91 C2 Novooleksiyivka Ukr.
150 B1 Novo Paraíso Brazil
91 D2 Novopskov Ukr.
91 D3 Novorossiysk Russia
88 C2 Novorzhev Russia
87 E3 Novosergiyevka Russia
91 D1 Novoshakhtinsk Russia
82 G3 Novosibirsk Russia
Novosibirskiye Ostrova is Russia see New Siberia Islands
89 E3 Novosil' Russia
89 D2 Novosokol'niki Russia
91 C2 Novotroyits'ke Ukr.
91 C2 Novoukrayinka Ukr.
90 A1 Novovolyns'k Ukr.
89 D3 Novozybkov Russia
103 D2 Nový Jičín Czechia
86 E2 Novyy Bor Russia
91 D1 Novyy Oskol Russia
86 G2 Novyy Port Russia
82 G2 Novyy Urengoy Russia
69 E1 Novyy Urgal Russia
103 D1 Nowogard Pol.
53 D2 Nowra Austr.
81 D2 Now Shahr Iran
74 B1 Nowshera Pak.
103 E2 Nowy Sącz Pol.

103 E2 Nowy Targ Pol.
87 G2 Noyabr'sk Russia
105 C2 Noyon France
68 C2 Noyon Mongolia
121 C2 Nsanje Malawi
118 B3 Ntandembele Dem. Rep. Congo
111 B3 Ntoro, Kavo pt Greece
119 D3 Ntungamo Uganda
79 C2 Nu'aym reg. Oman
116 B2 Nubian Desert Sudan
129 E1 Nueltin Lake Can.
153 A5 Nueva Lubecka Arg.
145 B2 Nueva Rosita Mex.
144 B1 Nuevo Casas Grandes Mex.
144 B2 Nuevo Ideal Mex.
145 C2 Nuevo Laredo Mex.
117 C4 Nugaal watercourse Somalia
117 C4 Nugaaleed, Dooxo val. Somalia
105 C2 Nuits-St-Georges France
Nu Jiang r. China/Myanmar see Salween
49 G4 Nuku'alofa Tonga
49 I3 Nuku Hiva i. Fr. Polynesia
76 B2 Nukus Uzbek.
50 B2 Nullagine Austr.
50 B3 Nullarbor Plain Austr.
115 D4 Numan Nigeria
67 C3 Numazu Japan
93 E3 Numedal val. Norway
59 C3 Numfoor i. Indon.
53 C3 Numurkah Austr.
Nunap Isua c. Greenland see Farewell, Cape
127 G3 Nunavik reg. Can.
129 E1 Nunavut admin. div. Can.
99 C2 Nuneaton U.K.
106 B1 Nuñomoral Spain
108 A2 Nuoro Sardinia Italy
78 B2 Nuqrah Saudi Arabia
101 E3 Nuremberg Ger.
52 A2 Nuriootpa Austr.
92 I3 Nurmes Fin.
Nürnberg Ger. see Nuremberg
62 A1 Nu Shan mts China
74 A2 Nushki Pak.
127 H2 Nuuk Greenland
127 H2 Nuussuaq Greenland
127 H2 Nuussuaq pen. Greenland
78 A2 Nuwaybi' al Muzayyinah Egypt
122 B3 Nuweveldberge mts S. Africa
86 F2 Nyagan' Russia
75 D1 Nyainqêntanglha Feng mt. China
75 D2 Nyainqêntanglha Shan mts China
117 A3 Nyala Sudan
86 D2 Nyandoma Russia
118 B3 Nyanga r. Gabon
121 C2 Nyanga Zimbabwe
Nyang'oma Kenya see Kogelo
121 C1 Nyasa, Lake Africa
93 F4 Nyborg Denmark
92 I1 Nyborg Norway
93 G4 Nybro Sweden
119 D3 Nyeri Kenya
68 C3 Nyingchi China
103 E2 Nyíregyháza Hungary
93 F4 Nykøbing Falster Denmark
93 G4 Nyköping Sweden
53 C2 Nymagee Austr.
93 G4 Nynäshamn Sweden
53 C2 Nyngan Austr.
88 B3 Nyoman r. Belarus/Lith.
105 D3 Nyons France
86 E2 Nyrob Russia

134 C2 **Nyssa** U.S.A.
119 C3 **Nyunzu** Dem. Rep. Congo
91 C2 **Nyzhn'ohirs'kyy** Ukr.
119 D3 **Nzega** Tanz.
114 B4 **Nzérékoré** Guinea
120 A1 **N'zeto** Angola

O

136 C2 **Oahe, Lake** U.S.A.
124 E5 **O'ahu** *i.* U.S.A.
52 B2 **Oakbank** Austr.
142 B2 **Oakdale** U.S.A.
53 D1 **Oakey** Austr.
134 B1 **Oak Harbor** U.S.A.
140 C3 **Oak Hill** U.S.A.
135 B3 **Oakland** U.S.A.
50 B2 **Oakover** *r.* Austr.
134 B2 **Oakridge** U.S.A.
143 D1 **Oak Ridge** U.S.A.
54 B3 **Oamaru** N.Z.
64 B1 **Oas** Phil.
145 C3 **Oaxaca** Mex.
86 F2 **Ob'** *r.* Russia
118 B2 **Obala** Cameroon
96 B2 **Oban** U.K.
106 B1 **O Barco** Spain
53 C2 **Oberon** Austr.
101 F3 **Oberpfälzer Wald** *mts* Ger.
101 F3 **Oberviechtach** Ger.
59 C3 **Obi** *i.* Indon.
151 C2 **Óbidos** Brazil
66 D2 **Obihiro** Japan
69 E1 **Obluch'ye** Russia
89 E2 **Obninsk** Russia
119 C2 **Obo** C.A.R.
117 C3 **Obock** Djibouti
118 B3 **Obouya** Congo
89 E3 **Oboyan'** Russia
144 B2 **Obregón, Presa** *resr* Mex.
109 D2 **Obrenovac** Serbia
87 E3 **Obshchiy Syrt** *hills* Kazakh./Russia
86 G2 **Obskaya Guba** *sea chan.* Russia
114 B4 **Obuasi** Ghana
90 C1 **Obukhiv** Ukr.
86 D2 **Ob"yachevo** Russia
143 D3 **Ocala** U.S.A.
144 B2 **Ocampo** Mex.
106 C2 **Ocaña** Spain
150 A1 **Occidental, Cordillera** *mts* Col.
150 A3 **Occidental, Cordillera** *mts* Peru
141 D3 **Ocean City** U.S.A.
128 B2 **Ocean Falls** Can.
135 C4 **Oceanside** U.S.A.
91 C2 **Ochakiv** Ukr.
86 E3 **Ocher** Russia
101 E3 **Ochsenfurt** Ger.
143 D2 **Oconee** *r.* U.S.A.
145 C3 **Ocosingo** Mex.
58 C3 **Ocussi** *enclave* East Timor
116 B2 **Oda, Jebel** *mt.* Sudan
66 D2 **Ōdate** Japan
67 C3 **Odawara** Japan
93 E3 **Odda** Norway
106 B2 **Odemira** Port.
111 C3 **Ödemiş** Turkey
93 F4 **Odense** Denmark
101 D3 **Odenwald** *reg.* Ger.
Odesa Ukr. *see* **Odessa**
90 C2 **Odessa** Ukr.
139 C2 **Odessa** U.S.A.
114 B4 **Odienné** Côte d'Ivoire
103 D2 **Odra** *r.* Ger./Pol.
151 D2 **Oeiras** Brazil
100 D2 **Oelde** Ger.
136 C2 **Oelrichs** U.S.A.
101 F2 **Oelsnitz/Vogtland** Ger.
100 B1 **Oenkerk** Neth.
109 C2 **Ofanto** *r.* Italy
101 D2 **Offenbach am Main** Ger.
102 B2 **Offenburg** Ger.
117 C4 **Ogadēn** *reg.* Eth.
66 C3 **Oga-hantō** *pen.* Japan
67 C3 **Ōgaki** Japan
136 C2 **Ogallala** U.S.A.
115 C4 **Ogbomoso** Nigeria
134 D2 **Ogden** U.S.A.
141 D2 **Ogdensburg** U.S.A.
126 B2 **Ogilvie** *r.* Can.
126 B2 **Ogilvie Mountains** Can.
143 D2 **Oglethorpe, Mount** U.S.A.
130 B1 **Ogoki** *r.* Can.
130 B1 **Ogoki Reservoir** Can.
88 B2 **Ogre** Latvia
109 C1 **Ogulin** Croatia
140 B3 **Ohio** *r.* U.S.A.
140 C2 **Ohio** *state* U.S.A.
101 E2 **Ohrdruf** Ger.
109 D2 **Ohrid** Macedonia
111 B2 **Ohrid, Lake** Albania/Macedonia
151 C1 **Oiapoque** Brazil
141 D2 **Oil City** U.S.A.
100 A3 **Oise** *r.* France
67 B4 **Ōita** Japan
144 B2 **Ojinaga** Mex.
152 B3 **Ojos del Salado, Cerro** *mt.* Arg./Chile
89 F2 **Oka** *r.* Russia
120 A3 **Okahandja** Namibia
120 A3 **Okakarara** Namibia
128 C3 **Okanagan Falls** Can.
128 C3 **Okanagan Lake** Can.
134 C1 **Okanogan** U.S.A.
134 C1 **Okanogan** *r.* U.S.A.
74 B1 **Okara** Pak.
120 B2 **Okavango** *r.* Africa
120 B2 **Okavango Delta** *swamp* Botswana
67 C3 **Okaya** Japan
67 B4 **Okayama** Japan
67 C4 **Okazaki** Japan
143 D3 **Okeechobee, Lake** U.S.A.
143 D2 **Okefenokee Swamp** U.S.A.
99 A3 **Okehampton** U.K.
74 A2 **Okha** India
83 K3 **Okha** Russia
75 C2 **Okhaldhunga** Nepal
83 K3 **Okhota** *r.* Russia
83 K3 **Okhotsk** Russia
156 C2 **Okhotsk, Sea of** Japan/Russia
91 C1 **Okhtyrka** Ukr.
69 E3 **Okinawa** *i.* Japan
67 B3 **Oki-shotō** *is* Japan
139 D1 **Oklahoma** *state* U.S.A.
139 D1 **Oklahoma City** U.S.A.
139 D1 **Okmulgee** U.S.A.
78 A2 **Oko, Wadi** *watercourse* Sudan
118 B3 **Okondja** Gabon
128 C2 **Okotoks** Can.
89 D3 **Okovskiy Les** *for.* Russia
118 B3 **Okoyo** Congo
92 H1 **Øksfjord** Norway
62 A2 **Oktwin** Myanmar
86 D2 **Oktyabr'skiy** *Arkhangel'skaya Oblast'* Russia
83 L3 **Oktyabr'skiy** *Kamchatskiy Kray* Russia
87 E3 **Oktyabr'skiy** *Respublika Bashkortostan* Russia
86 F2 **Oktyabr'skoye** Russia
83 H1 **Oktyabr'skoy Revolyutsii, Ostrov** *i.* Russia
89 D2 **Okulovka** Russia
66 C2 **Okushiri-tō** *i.* Japan
92 □A3 **Ólafsvík** Iceland
93 G4 **Öland** *i.* Sweden
52 B2 **Olary** Austr.
153 B4 **Olavarría** Arg.
103 D1 **Oława** Pol.
108 A2 **Olbia** *Sardinia* Italy
126 B2 **Old Crow** Can.
101 D1 **Oldenburg** Ger.
102 C1 **Oldenburg in Holstein** Ger.
100 C1 **Oldenzaal** Neth.
97 B3 **Old Head of Kinsale** Ireland
128 C2 **Olds** Can.
129 D2 **Old Wives Lake** Can.
141 D2 **Olean** U.S.A.
103 E1 **Olecko** Pol.
83 J2 **Olekminsk** Russia
91 C2 **Oleksandriya** Ukr.
86 C2 **Olenegorsk** Russia
83 I2 **Olenek** Russia
83 I2 **Olenek** *r.* Russia
89 D2 **Olenino** Russia
91 C2 **Oleshky** Ukr.
90 B1 **Olevs'k** Ukr.
106 B2 **Olhão** Port.
122 A2 **Olifants** *watercourse* Namibia
123 D1 **Olifants** S. Africa
123 D1 **Olifants** *r. Limpopo* S. Africa
122 A3 **Olifants** *r. W. Cape* S. Africa
122 B2 **Olifantshoek** S. Africa
154 C2 **Olímpia** Brazil
151 E2 **Olinda** Brazil
123 C1 **Oliphants Drift** Botswana
107 C2 **Oliva** Spain
155 D2 **Oliveira** Brazil
106 B2 **Olivenza** Spain
152 B3 **Ollagüe** Chile
150 A2 **Olmos** Peru
140 B3 **Olney** U.S.A.
103 D2 **Olomouc** Czechia
64 B1 **Olongapo** Phil.
104 B3 **Oloron-Ste-Marie** France
107 D1 **Olot** Spain
69 D1 **Olovyannaya** Russia
83 L2 **Oloy** *r.* Russia
100 C2 **Olpe** Ger.
103 E1 **Olsztyn** Pol.
110 B2 **Olt** *r.* Romania
81 C1 **Oltu** Turkey
111 B3 **Olympia** *tourist site* Greece
134 B1 **Olympia** U.S.A.
134 B1 **Olympus, Mount** U.S.A.
83 M3 **Olyutorskiy, Mys** *c.* Russia
97 C1 **Omagh** U.K.
137 D2 **Omaha** U.S.A.
79 C2 **Oman** *country* Asia
79 C2 **Oman, Gulf of** Asia
120 A3 **Omaruru** Namibia
120 B2 **Omatako** *watercourse* Namibia
116 B3 **Omdurman** Sudan
53 C3 **Omeo** Austr.
145 C3 **Ometepec** Mex.
78 A3 **Om Hajēr** Eritrea
128 B2 **Omineca Mountains** Can.
67 C3 **Ōmiya** Japan
100 C1 **Ommen** Neth.
83 L2 **Omolon** *r.* Russia
100 B3 **Omont** France
82 F3 **Omsk** Russia
83 L2 **Omsukchan** Russia
110 C1 **Omu, Vârful** *mt.* Romania
67 A4 **Ōmura** Japan
141 D3 **Onancock** U.S.A.
140 C1 **Onaping Lake** Can.
131 C2 **Onatchiway, Lac** *l.* Can.
120 A2 **Oncócua** Angola
122 B3 **Onderstedorings** S. Africa

120 A2 **Ondjiva** Angola
86 C2 **Onega** Russia
86 C2 **Onega** r. Russia
141 D2 **Oneida Lake** U.S.A.
137 D2 **O'Neill** U.S.A.
141 D2 **Oneonta** U.S.A.
110 C1 **Onesti** Romania
Onezhskoye, Ozero l. Russia *see* **Onezhskoye Ozero**
122 B2 **Onezhskoye Ozero** l. Russia
65 B2 **Ongers** watercourse S. Africa
73 C3 **Ongjin** N. Korea
121 □D3 **Ongole** India
115 C4 **Onilahy** r. Madag.
50 A2 **Onitsha** Nigeria
143 E2 **Onseepkans** S. Africa
50 A2 **Onslow** Austr.
130 A1 **Onslow Bay** U.S.A.
134 C2 **Ontario** prov. Can.
134 C2 **Ontario** U.S.A.
51 C2 **Ontario, Lake** Can./U.S.A.
Oodnadatta Austr.
Oostende Belgium *see* **Ostend**
100 B2 **Oosterhout** Neth.
100 A1 **Oosterschelde** est. Neth.
128 B1 **Oost-Vlieland** Neth.
128 B2 **Ootsa Lake** Can.
128 B2 **Ootsa Lake** Can.
118 C3 **Opala** Dem. Rep. Congo
130 C1 **Opataca, Lac** l. Can.
143 D2 **Opava** Czechia
143 C2 **Opelika** U.S.A.
142 B2 **Opelousas** U.S.A.
131 D1 **Opinaca, Réservoir** resr Can.
Opiscótéo, Lac l. Can.
88 C2 **Opochka** Russia
144 A2 **Opodepe** Mex.
131 C2 **Opole** Pol.
106 B1 **Oporto** Port.
54 B1 **Opotiki** N.Z.
93 E3 **Oppdal** Norway
54 B2 **Opunake** N.Z.
120 A2 **Opuwo** Namibia
110 B1 **Oradea** Romania
Orahovac Kosovo *see* **Rahovec**
114 B1 **Oran** Alg.
152 B3 **Orán** Arg.
65 B1 **Örang** N. Korea
53 C2 **Orange** Austr.
105 C3 **Orange** France
122 A2 **Orange** r. Namibia/S. Africa
139 E2 **Orange** U.S.A.
143 D2 **Orangeburg** U.S.A.
140 C2 **Orangeville** Can.
101 F1 **Oranienburg** Ger.
122 A2 **Oranjemund** Namibia
120 B3 **Orapa** Botswana
110 C1 **Orăştie** Romania
108 B2 **Orbetello** Italy
53 C3 **Orbost** Austr.
50 B1 **Ord, Mount** N. Austr.
106 B1 **Ordes** Spain
Ordos China *see* **Dongsheng**
80 B1 **Ordu** Turkey
Ordzhonikidze Russia *see* **Vladikavkaz**
Ordzhonikidze Ukr. *see* **Pokrov**
93 G4 **Örebro** Sweden
134 B2 **Oregon** state U.S.A.
134 B1 **Oregon City** U.S.A.
87 C3 **Orekhovo-Zuyevo** Russia
89 E3 **Orël** Russia
83 K3 **Orel', Ozero** l. Russia
135 D2 **Orem** U.S.A.
111 C3 **Ören** Turkey
87 E3 **Orenburg** Russia
54 A3 **Orepuki** N.Z.

93 F4 **Öresund** str. Denmark/Sweden
99 D2 **Orford Ness** hd U.K.
111 C3 **Orhaneli** Turkey
111 C2 **Orhangazi** Turkey
83 I3 **Orhon Gol** r. Mongolia
152 B2 **Oriental, Cordillera** mts Bol.
150 A3 **Oriental, Cordillera** mts Col.
107 C2 **Oriental, Cordillera** mts Peru
Orihuela Spain
91 D2 **Orikhiv** Ukr.
130 C2 **Orillia** Can.
150 B1 **Orinoco** r. Col./Venez.
150 B1 **Orinoco, Delta del** Venez.
93 H4 **Orissaare** Estonia
108 A3 **Oristano** Sardinia Italy
93 I3 **Orivesi** l. Fin.
151 C2 **Oriximiná** Brazil
145 C3 **Orizaba** Mex.
145 C3 **Orizaba, Pico de** vol. Mex.
92 E3 **Orkanger** Norway
93 F4 **Örkelljunga** Sweden
92 E3 **Orkla** r. Norway
96 C1 **Orkney Islands** U.K.
154 C2 **Orlândia** Brazil
143 D3 **Orlando** U.S.A.
104 C2 **Orléans** France
74 A2 **Ormara** Pak.
64 B1 **Ormoc** Phil.
98 B2 **Ormskirk** U.K.
92 G3 **Örnsköldsvik** Sweden
114 B3 **Orodara** Burkina Faso
134 C1 **Orofino** U.S.A.
Oroqen Zizhiqi China *see* **Alihe**
64 B2 **Oroquieta** Phil.
108 A2 **Orosei** Sardinia Italy
108 A2 **Orosei, Golfo di** b. Sardinia Italy
103 E2 **Orosháza** Hungary
135 B3 **Oroville** U.S.A.
52 A2 **Orroroo** Austr.
89 D3 **Orsha** Belarus
87 E3 **Orsk** Russia
93 E3 **Ørsta** Norway
106 B1 **Ortegal, Cabo** c. Spain
104 B3 **Orthez** France
106 B1 **Ortiguera** Spain
137 D1 **Ortonville** U.S.A.
83 J2 **Orulgan, Khrebet** mts Russia
Orūmīyeh, Daryācheh-ye salt l. Iran *see* **Urmia, Lake**
152 B2 **Oruro** Bol.
108 B2 **Orvieto** Italy
146 B4 **Osa, Península de** pen. Costa Rica
137 E3 **Osage** r. U.S.A.
67 C4 **Ōsaka** Japan
66 D3 **Ōsaki** Japan
110 B2 **Osam** r. Bulg.
101 E1 **Oschersleben (Bode)** Ger.
108 A2 **Oschiri** Sardinia Italy
89 E3 **Osetr** r. Russia
77 D2 **Osh** Kyrg.
120 A2 **Oshakati** Namibia
130 C2 **Oshawa** Can.
66 C2 **Ō-shima** i. Japan
67 C4 **Ō-shima** i. Japan
140 B2 **Oshkosh** U.S.A.
81 C2 **Oshnavīyeh** Iran
118 B3 **Oshwe** Dem. Rep. Congo
109 C1 **Osijek** Croatia
128 C2 **Osilinka** r. Can.
108 B2 **Osimo** Italy
123 D2 **oSizweni** S. Africa
137 E2 **Oskaloosa** U.S.A.
93 G4 **Oskarshamn** Sweden
89 E3 **Oskol** r. Russia

93 F4 **Oslo** Norway
93 F4 **Oslofjorden** sea chan. Norway
80 B1 **Osmancık** Turkey
111 C2 **Osmaneli** Turkey
80 B2 **Osmaniye** Turkey
88 C2 **Os'mino** Russia
100 D1 **Osnabrück** Ger.
115 C4 **Osogbo** Nigeria
153 A5 **Osorno** Chile
106 C1 **Osorno** Spain
128 C3 **Osoyoos** Can.
24 Neth. **Oss** Neth.
51 D4 **Ossa, Mount** Austr.
83 L3 **Ossora** Russia
89 D2 **Ostashkov** Russia
101 D1 **Oste** r. Ger.
100 A2 **Ostend** Belgium
101 E1 **Osterburg (Altmark)** Ger.
93 F3 **Österdalälven** r. Sweden
101 D1 **Osterholz-Scharmbeck** Ger.
101 E2 **Osterode am Harz** Ger.
92 F3 **Östersund** Sweden
Ostfriesische Inseln is Ger. *see* **East Frisian Islands**
100 C1 **Ostfriesland** reg. Ger.
93 G3 **Osthammar** Sweden
103 D2 **Ostrava** Czechia
103 D1 **Ostróda** Pol.
89 E3 **Ostrogozhsk** Russia
103 E1 **Ostrołęka** Pol.
101 F2 **Ostrov** Czechia
88 C2 **Ostrov** Russia
103 E1 **Ostrowiec Świętokrzyski** Pol.
103 E1 **Ostrów Mazowiecka** Pol.
103 D1 **Ostrów Wielkopolski** Pol.
67 B4 **Ōsumi-kaikyō** sea chan. Japan
67 B4 **Ōsumi-shotō** is Japan
106 B2 **Osuna** Spain
141 D2 **Oswego** U.S.A.
99 B2 **Oswestry** U.K.
67 C3 **Ōta** Japan
54 B3 **Otago Peninsula** N.Z.
54 C2 **Otaki** N.Z.
66 D2 **Otaru** Japan
120 A2 **Otavi** Namibia
134 C1 **Othello** U.S.A.
120 A3 **Otjiwarongo** Namibia
117 B3 **Otoro, Jebel** mt. Sudan
93 E4 **Otra** r. Norway
109 C2 **Otranto, Strait of** Albania/Italy
67 C3 **Ōtsu** Japan
93 E3 **Otta** Norway
130 C2 **Ottawa** Can.
130 C2 **Ottawa** r. Can.
140 B2 **Ottawa** IL. U.S.A.
137 D3 **Ottawa** KS U.S.A.
130 B1 **Otter Rapids** Can.
100 B2 **Ottignies** Belgium
137 E2 **Ottumwa** U.S.A.
115 C4 **Otuzco** Peru
52 B3 **Otway, Cape** Austr.
142 B2 **Ouachita** r. U.S.A.
142 B2 **Ouachita, Lake** U.S.A.
142 B2 **Ouachita Mountains** U.S.A.
118 C2 **Ouadda** C.A.R.
115 D3 **Ouaddaï** reg. Chad
114 B3 **Ouagadougou** Burkina Faso
114 B3 **Ouahigouya** Burkina Faso
114 B3 **Oualâta** Maur.
118 C2 **Ouanda Djallé** C.A.R.
114 B2 **Ouarâne** reg. Maur.
115 C1 **Ouargla** Alg.
114 B1 **Ouarzazate** Morocco
100 A2 **Oudenaarde** Belgium
122 B3 **Oudtshoorn** S. Africa
107 C2 **Oued Tlélat** Alg.
104 A2 **Ouessant, Île d'** i. France

118 B2 **Ouesso** Congo
114 B1 **Oujda** Morocco
107 D2 **Ouled Farès** Alg.
92 I2 **Oulu** Fin.
92 I3 **Oulujärvi** *l.* Fin.
108 A1 **Oulx** Italy
115 E3 **Oum-Chalouba** Chad
115 D3 **Oum-Hadjer** Chad
115 E3 **Ounianga Kébir** Chad
100 B2 **Oupeye** Belgium
106 B1 **Ourense** Spain
154 C2 **Ourinhos** Brazil
155 D2 **Ouro Preto** Brazil
100 B2 **Ourthe** *r.* Belgium
98 C2 **Ouse** *r.* U.K.
131 D2 **Outardes, Rivière aux** *r.* Can.
131 D1 **Outardes Quatre, Réservoir** *resr* Can.
96 A2 **Outer Hebrides** *is* U.K.
120 A3 **Outjo** Namibia
129 D2 **Outlook** Can.
92 I3 **Outokumpu** Fin.
52 B3 **Ouyen** Austr.
106 B1 **Ovar** Port.
92 H2 **Överkalix** Sweden
135 D3 **Overton** U.S.A.
92 H2 **Övertorneå** Sweden
106 B1 **Oviedo** Spain
93 E3 **Øvre Årdal** Norway
93 F3 **Øvre Rendal** Norway
90 B1 **Ovruch** Ukr.
118 B3 **Owando** Congo
67 C4 **Owase** Japan
137 E2 **Owatonna** U.S.A.
140 B3 **Owensboro** U.S.A.
135 C3 **Owens Lake** U.S.A.
130 B2 **Owen Sound** Can.
115 C4 **Owerri** Nigeria
140 C2 **Owosso** U.S.A.
134 C2 **Owyhee** U.S.A.
134 C2 **Owyhee** *r.* U.S.A.
54 B2 **Oxford** N.Z.
99 C3 **Oxford** U.K.
142 C2 **Oxford** U.S.A.
129 E2 **Oxford Lake** Can.
52 B2 **Oxley** Austr.
97 B1 **Ox Mountains** *hills* Ireland
135 C4 **Oxnard** U.S.A.
67 C3 **Oyama** Japan
118 B2 **Oyem** Gabon
129 C2 **Oyen** Can.
105 D2 **Oyonnax** France
64 B2 **Ozamis** Phil.
142 C2 **Ozark** U.S.A.
137 E3 **Ozark Plateau** U.S.A.
137 E3 **Ozarks, Lake of the** U.S.A.
83 L3 **Ozernovskiy** Russia
88 B3 **Ozersk** Russia
89 E3 **Ozery** Russia
87 D3 **Ozinki** Russia

P

127 H2 **Paamiut** Greenland
122 A3 **Paarl** S. Africa
103 D1 **Pabianice** Pol.
75 C2 **Pabna** Bangl.
74 A2 **Pab Range** *mts* Pak.
109 C3 **Pachino** *Sicily* Italy
145 C2 **Pachuca** Mex.
156 **Pacific Ocean** World
103 D1 **Paczków** Pol.
60 B2 **Padang** Indon.
60 B1 **Padang Endau** Malaysia
60 B2 **Padangpanjang** Indon.
60 A1 **Padangsidempuan** Indon.
101 D2 **Paderborn** Ger.
Padova Italy *see* **Padua**
139 D3 **Padre Island** U.S.A.
52 B3 **Padthaway** Austr.
108 B1 **Padua** Italy
140 B3 **Paducah** *KY* U.S.A.
139 C2 **Paducah** *TX* U.S.A.
65 B1 **Paegam** N. Korea
Paengnyŏng-do *i.* S. Korea *see* **Baengnyeong-do**
54 C1 **Paeroa** N.Z.
Pafos Cyprus *see* **Paphos**
109 C2 **Pag** Croatia
64 B2 **Pagadian** Phil.
60 B2 **Pagai Selatan** *i.* Indon.
60 B2 **Pagai Utara** *i.* Indon.
59 D1 **Pagan** *i.* N. Mariana Is
61 C2 **Pagatan** Indon.
138 A1 **Page** U.S.A.
88 B2 **Pagėgiai** Lith.
136 B3 **Pagosa Springs** U.S.A.
88 C2 **Paide** Estonia
93 I3 **Päijänne** *l.* Fin.
75 C2 **Paikü Co** *l.* China
138 A1 **Painted Desert** U.S.A.
96 B3 **Paisley** U.K.
92 H2 **Pajala** Sweden
150 B1 **Pakaraima Mountains** S. America
74 A2 **Pakistan** *country* Asia
62 A1 **Pakokku** Myanmar
88 B2 **Pakruojis** Lith.
103 D2 **Paks** Hungary
130 A1 **Pakwash Lake** Can.
62 B2 **Pakxan** Laos
63 B2 **Pakxé** Laos
115 D4 **Pala** Chad
60 B2 **Palabuhanratu, Teluk** *b.* Indon.
111 C3 **Palaikastro** Greece
111 B3 **Palaiochora** Greece
122 B1 **Palamakoloi** Botswana
107 D1 **Palamós** Spain
83 L3 **Palana** Russia
64 B1 **Palanan** Phil.
61 C2 **Palangkaraya** Indon.
74 B2 **Palanpur** India
120 B3 **Palapye** Botswana
83 L2 **Palatka** Russia
143 D3 **Palatka** U.S.A.
59 C2 **Palau** *country* N. Pacific Ocean
63 A2 **Palaw** Myanmar
64 A2 **Palawan** *i.* Phil.
93 H4 **Paldiski** Estonia
60 B2 **Palembang** Indon.
106 C1 **Palencia** Spain
145 C3 **Palenque** Mex.
108 B3 **Palermo** *Sicily* Italy
139 D2 **Palestine** U.S.A.
62 A1 **Paletwa** Myanmar
74 B2 **Pali** India
48 E2 **Palikir** Micronesia
109 C2 **Palinuro, Capo** *c.* Italy
111 B3 **Paliouri, Akrotirio** *pt* Greece
100 B3 **Paliseul** Belgium
92 I3 **Paljakka** *h.* Fin.
88 C2 **Palkino** Russia
73 B4 **Palk Strait** India/Sri Lanka
54 C2 **Palliser, Cape** N.Z.
49 I3 **Palliser, Îles** *is* Fr. Polynesia
106 B2 **Palma del Río** Spain
107 D2 **Palma de Mallorca** Spain
154 B3 **Palmas** *Paraná* Brazil
151 D3 **Palmas** *Tocantins* Brazil
114 B4 **Palmas, Cape** Liberia
154 C3 **Palmeira** Brazil
151 D2 **Palmeirais** Brazil
55 P2 **Palmer Land** *reg.* Antarctica
54 C2 **Palmerston North** N.Z.
109 C3 **Palmi** Italy
145 C2 **Palmillas** Mex.
150 A1 **Palmira** Col.
135 C4 **Palm Springs** U.S.A.
49 H2 **Palmyra Atoll** N. Pacific Ocean
117 B3 **Paloich** South Sudan
145 C3 **Palomares** Mex.
107 C2 **Palos, Cabo de** *c.* Spain
92 I3 **Paltamo** Fin.
58 B3 **Palu** Indon.
83 M2 **Palyavaam** *r.* Russia
104 C3 **Pamiers** France
77 D3 **Pamir** *mts* Asia
143 E1 **Pamlico Sound** *sea chan.* U.S.A.
152 B2 **Pampa Grande** Bol.
153 B4 **Pampas** *reg.* Arg.
150 A1 **Pamplona** Col.
107 C1 **Pamplona/Iruña** Spain
111 D2 **Pamukova** Turkey
60 B2 **Panaitan** *i.* Indon.
73 B3 **Panaji** India
146 B4 **Panama** *country* Central America
146 C4 **Panama, Gulf of** Panama
146 C4 **Panama Canal** Panama
146 C4 **Panama City** Panama
142 C2 **Panama City** U.S.A.
135 C3 **Panamint Range** *mts* U.S.A.
64 B1 **Panay** *i.* Phil.
109 D2 **Pančevo** Serbia
64 B1 **Pandan** Phil.
75 C2 **Pandaria** India
73 B3 **Pandharpur** India
88 B2 **Panevėžys** Lith.
61 C2 **Pangkalanbuun** Indon.
60 A1 **Pangkalansusu** Indon.
60 B2 **Pangkalpinang** Indon.
127 G2 **Pangnirtung** Can.
86 G2 **Pangody** Russia
89 F3 **Panino** Russia
74 B2 **Panipat** India
74 A2 **Panjgur** Pak.
65 C1 **Pan Ling** *mts* China
75 C2 **Panna** India
50 A2 **Pannawonica** Austr.
154 B2 **Panorama** Brazil
65 B1 **Panshi** China
145 C2 **Pánuco** Mex.
62 B1 **Panzhihua** China
109 C3 **Paola** Italy
63 B2 **Paôy Pêt** Cambodia
103 D2 **Pápa** Hungary
54 B1 **Papakura** N.Z.
145 C2 **Papantla** Mex.
49 I4 **Papeete** Fr. Polynesia
100 C1 **Papenburg** Ger.
80 B2 **Paphos** Cyprus
59 D3 **Papua, Gulf of** P.N.G.
59 D3 **Papua New Guinea** *country* Oceania
50 A2 **Paraburdoo** Austr.
154 C1 **Paracatu** Brazil
155 C1 **Paracatu** *r.* Brazil
52 A2 **Parachilna** Austr.
109 D2 **Paraćin** Serbia
155 D1 **Pará de Minas** Brazil
135 B3 **Paradise** U.S.A.
142 B1 **Paragould** U.S.A.
151 C3 **Paraguai** *r.* Brazil
152 C3 **Paraguay** *r.* Arg./Para.
152 C3 **Paraguay** *country* S. Americ
155 D2 **Paraíba do Sul** *r.* Brazil
154 B1 **Paraíso** Brazil
145 C3 **Paraíso** Mex.
114 C4 **Parakou** Benin
151 C1 **Paramaribo** Suriname
83 L3 **Paramushir, Ostrov** *i.* Russ

152 B4 **Paraná** Arg.
154 A3 **Paraná** r. S. America
154 B2 **Paraguá** Brazil
154 B1 **Paranaíba** Brazil
154 B1 **Paranaíba** r. Brazil
154 B2 **Paranapanema** r. Brazil
154 B2 **Paranapiacaba, Serra** mts Brazil
152 B2 **Paranavaí** Brazil
54 B2 **Paraparaumu** N.Z.
155 D2 **Parati** Brazil
154 B1 **Paraúna** Brazil
105 C2 **Paray-le-Monial** France
73 B3 **Parbhani** India
151 E1 **Parchim** Ger.
155 E1 **Pardo** r. Bahia Brazil
154 E2 **Pardo** r. Mato Grosso do Sul Brazil
154 C2 **Pardo** r. São Paulo Brazil
103 D1 **Pardubice** Czechia
150 B3 **Parecis, Serra dos** hills Brazil
128 D1 **Parent, Lac** l. Can.
58 B3 **Parepare** Indon.
89 D2 **Parfino** Russia
111 B3 **Parga** Greece
109 C2 **Parghelia** Italy
147 D3 **Paria, Gulf of** Trin. and Tob./Venez.
154 B2 **Parima, Serra** mts Brazil
151 C2 **Parintins** Brazil
104 C2 **Paris** France
142 C1 **Paris** TN U.S.A.
139 D2 **Paris** TX U.S.A.
93 H3 **Parkano** Fin.
77 C2 **Parker** U.S.A.
140 C3 **Parkersburg** U.S.A.
53 C2 **Parkes** Austr.
140 A1 **Park Falls** U.S.A.
137 D1 **Park Rapids** U.S.A.
108 B2 **Parma** Italy
151 D2 **Parnaíba** Brazil
151 D2 **Parnaíba** r. Brazil
54 B2 **Parnassus** N.Z.
111 B3 **Parnonas** mts Greece
88 B2 **Pärnu** Estonia
65 B2 **Paro-ho** i. S. Korea
52 B2 **Paroo** watercourse Austr.
         Paropamisus mts Afgh. see Safēd Kōh, Silsilah-ye
111 C3 **Paros** i. Greece
144 B2 **Parras** Mex.
126 C2 **Parry, Cape** Can.
126 C2 **Parry Islands** Can.
130 B2 **Parry Sound** Can.
79 C2 **Pārsīān** Iran
137 D3 **Parsons** U.S.A.
101 D2 **Partenstein** Ger.
104 B2 **Parthenay** France
97 B1 **Partry Mountains** hills Ireland
151 C2 **Paru** r. Brazil
135 C4 **Pasadena** U.S.A.
62 A2 **Pasawng** Myanmar
142 C2 **Pascagoula** U.S.A.
110 C1 **Paşcani** Romania
134 C1 **Pasco** U.S.A.
101 F1 **Pasewalk** Ger.
129 D2 **Pasfield Lake** Can.
64 B1 **Pasig** Phil.
60 B1 **Pasir Putih** Malaysia
74 A2 **Pasni** Pak.
135 B3 **Paso Robles** U.S.A.
155 C2 **Passa Tempo** Brazil
102 C2 **Passau** Ger.
152 C3 **Passo Fundo** Brazil
155 C2 **Passos** Brazil
88 C2 **Pastavy** Belarus
150 A2 **Pastaza** r. Peru
150 A1 **Pasto** Col.

61 C2 **Pasuruan** Indon.
88 B2 **Pasvalys** Lith.
153 A6 **Patagonia** reg. Arg.
75 C2 **Patan** Nepal
54 B1 **Patea** N.Z.
141 E2 **Paterson** U.S.A.
         Pathein Myanmar see Bassein
136 B2 **Pathfinder Reservoir** U.S.A.
61 C2 **Pati** Indon.
62 A1 **Patkai Bum** mts India/Myanmar
111 C3 **Patmos** i. Greece
75 C2 **Patna** India
81 C2 **Patnos** Turkey
154 B3 **Pato Branco** Brazil
155 C1 **Patos, Lagoa dos** l. Brazil
152 B4 **Patos de Minas** Brazil
152 B4 **Patquía** Arg.
111 B3 **Patras** Greece
75 C2 **Patratu** India
154 C1 **Patrocínio** Brazil
63 B3 **Pattani** Thai.
63 B2 **Pattaya** Thai.
128 B2 **Pattullo, Mount** Can.
129 D2 **Patuanak** Can.
144 B3 **Pátzcuaro** Mex.
104 B3 **Pau** France
104 B3 **Pauillac** France
62 A1 **Pauk** Myanmar
151 D2 **Paulistana** Brazil
151 E2 **Paulo Afonso** Brazil
123 D2 **Paulpietersburg** S. Africa
139 D2 **Pauls Valley** U.S.A.
62 A2 **Paungde** Myanmar
155 D1 **Pavão** Brazil
108 A1 **Pavia** Italy
88 B2 **Pāvilosta** Latvia
110 C2 **Pavlikeni** Bulg.
77 D1 **Pavlodar** Kazakh.
91 D2 **Pavlohrad** Ukr.
91 E1 **Pavlovsk** Russia
91 D2 **Pavlovskaya** Russia
60 B2 **Payakumbuh** Indon.
134 C2 **Payette** U.S.A.
134 C2 **Payette** r. U.S.A.
86 F2 **Pay-Khoy, Khrebet** hills Russia
152 C4 **Paysandú** Uru.
81 C1 **Pazar** Turkey
110 B2 **Pazardzhik** Bulg.
111 C3 **Pazarköy** Turkey
108 B1 **Pazin** Croatia
63 A2 **Pe** Myanmar
128 C2 **Peace** r. Can.
128 C2 **Peace River** Can.
135 E3 **Peale, Mount** U.S.A.
142 C2 **Pearl** r. U.S.A.
139 D3 **Pearsall** U.S.A.
121 C2 **Pebane** Moz.
         Peć Kosovo see Pejë
155 D1 **Peçanha** Brazil
86 E2 **Pechora** Russia
86 E2 **Pechora** r. Russia
88 C2 **Pechory** Russia
139 C2 **Pecos** U.S.A.
139 C3 **Pecos** r. U.S.A.
103 D2 **Pécs** Hungary
155 D1 **Pedra Azul** Brazil
154 C2 **Pedregulho** Brazil
151 D2 **Pedreiras** Brazil
73 C4 **Pedro, Point** Sri Lanka
151 D2 **Pedro Afonso** Brazil
154 B1 **Pedro Gomes** Brazil
152 C3 **Pedro Juan Caballero** Para.
96 C3 **Peebles** U.K.
143 E2 **Pee Dee** r. U.S.A.
126 C2 **Peel** r. Can.
98 A1 **Peel** Isle of Man
128 C2 **Peerless Lake** Can.

54 B2 **Pegasus Bay** N.Z.
101 E2 **Pegnitz** Ger.
62 A2 **Pegu** Myanmar
61 C1 **Pegunungan Sambaliung** mts Indon.
62 A2 **Pegu Yoma** mts Myanmar
153 B4 **Pehuajó** Arg.
101 E1 **Peine** Ger.
88 C2 **Peipus, Lake** Estonia/Russia
154 B2 **Peixe** r. Brazil
109 D2 **Pejë** Kosovo
         Pekalongan Indon.
130 B2 **Pelee Island** Can.
60 B1 **Pekan** Malaysia
60 B1 **Pekanbaru** Indon.
         Peking China see **Beijing**
130 B2 **Pelee Island** Can.
59 C3 **Peleng** i. Indon.
92 I2 **Pelkosenniemi** Fin.
122 A2 **Pella** S. Africa
59 D3 **Pelleluhu Islands** P.N.G.
92 H2 **Pello** Fin.
128 A1 **Pelly** r. Can.
128 A1 **Pelly Mountains** Can.
152 C4 **Pelotas** Brazil
152 C3 **Pelotas, Rio das** r. Brazil
141 F1 **Pemadumcook Lake** U.S.A.
61 B1 **Pemangkat** Indon.
60 A1 **Pematangsiantar** Indon.
121 D2 **Pemba** Moz.
120 B2 **Pemba** Zambia
119 D3 **Pemba Island** Tanz.
128 B2 **Pemberton** Can.
137 D1 **Pembina** r. Can./U.S.A.
130 C2 **Pembroke** Can.
99 A3 **Pembroke** U.K.
145 B2 **Peña Nevada, Cerro** mt. Mex.
154 B2 **Penápolis** Brazil
106 B1 **Peñaranda de Bracamonte** Spain
61 B1 **Penarik** Indon.
107 C1 **Peñarroya** mt. Spain
106 B2 **Peñarroya-Pueblonuevo** Spain
106 B1 **Peñas, Cabo de** c. Spain
153 A5 **Penas, Golfo de** g. Chile
134 C1 **Pendleton** U.S.A.
128 B2 **Pendleton Bay** Can.
134 C1 **Pend Oreille Lake** U.S.A.
74 B3 **Penganga** r. India
123 D1 **Penge** S. Africa
70 C2 **Penglai** China
71 A3 **Pengshui** China
106 B2 **Peniche** Port.
98 B1 **Penicuik** U.K.
108 B2 **Penne** Italy
98 B1 **Pennines** hills U.K.
141 D2 **Pennsylvania** state U.S.A.
127 G2 **Penny Icecap** Can.
141 F2 **Penobscot** r. U.S.A.
52 B3 **Penola** Austr.
50 C3 **Penong** Austr.
49 H3 **Penrhyn** atoll Cook Is
98 B1 **Penrith** U.K.
142 C2 **Pensacola** U.S.A.
55 Q1 **Pensacola Mountains** Antarctica
61 C1 **Pensiangan** Sabah Malaysia
128 C3 **Penticton** Can.
96 C1 **Pentland Firth** sea chan. U.K.
99 B2 **Penygadair** h. U.K.
87 D3 **Penza** Russia
99 A3 **Penzance** U.K.
140 B2 **Peoria** U.S.A.
60 B2 **Perabumulih** Indon.
107 C1 **Perales del Alfambra** Spain
51 E2 **Percy Isles** Austr.
86 F2 **Peregrebnoye** Russia
150 A1 **Pereira** Col.
154 B2 **Pereira Barreto** Brazil

90 A2 **Peremyshlyany** Ukr.
89 E2 **Pereslavl'-Zalesskiy** Russia
91 C1 **Pereyaslav-Khmel'nyts'kyy** Ukr.
153 B4 **Pergamino** Arg.
92 H3 **Perhonjoki** *r.* Fin.
131 C1 **Péribonka, Lac** *l.* Can.
152 B3 **Perico** Arg.
144 B2 **Pericos** Mex.
104 C2 **Périgueux** France
147 C4 **Perijá, Sierra de** *mts* Venez.
153 A5 **Perito Moreno** Arg.
101 E1 **Perleberg** Ger.
86 E3 **Perm'** Russia
52 A2 **Pernatty Lagoon** *imp. l.* Austr.
105 C2 **Péronne** France
145 C3 **Perote** Mex.
104 C3 **Perpignan** France
99 A3 **Perranporth** U.K.
143 D2 **Perry** *FL* U.S.A.
143 D2 **Perry** *GA* U.S.A.
137 E2 **Perry** *IA* U.S.A.
139 C1 **Perryton** U.S.A.
137 F3 **Perryville** U.S.A.
99 B2 **Pershore** U.K.
91 D2 **Pershotravens'k** Ukr.
Persian Gulf Asia *see* **The Gulf**
50 A3 **Perth** Austr.
96 C2 **Perth** U.K.
105 D3 **Pertuis** France
108 A2 **Pertusato, Capo** *c. Corsica* France
150 A2 **Peru** *country* S. America
157 H4 **Peru-Chile Trench** S. Pacific Ocean
108 B2 **Perugia** Italy
154 C2 **Peruíbe** Brazil
100 A2 **Péruwelz** Belgium
90 C2 **Pervomays'k** Ukr.
91 C2 **Pervomays'ke** Ukr.
89 F3 **Pervomayskiy** Russia
91 D2 **Pervomays'kyy** Ukr.
108 B2 **Pesaro** Italy
108 B2 **Pescara** Italy
108 B2 **Pescara** *r.* Italy
74 B1 **Peshawar** Pak.
109 D2 **Peshkopi** Albania
109 C1 **Pesnica** Slovenia
89 E2 **Pestovo** Russia
144 B3 **Petatlán** Mex.
140 B2 **Petenwell Lake** U.S.A.
52 A2 **Peterborough** Austr.
130 C2 **Peterborough** Can.
99 C2 **Peterborough** U.K.
96 D2 **Peterhead** U.K.
50 B2 **Petermann Ranges** *mts* Austr.
129 D2 **Peter Pond Lake** Can.
128 A2 **Petersburg** *AK* U.S.A.
141 D3 **Petersburg** *VA* U.S.A.
101 D1 **Petershagen** Ger.
131 E1 **Petit Mécatina** *r.* Can.
145 D2 **Peto** Mex.
140 C1 **Petoskey** U.S.A.
80 B2 **Petra** *tourist site* Jordan
66 B2 **Petra Velikogo, Zaliv** *b.* Russia
111 B2 **Petrich** Bulg.
151 D2 **Petrolina** Brazil
83 L3 **Petropavlovsk-Kamchatskiy** Russia
77 C1 **Petropavlovskoye** Kazakh.
110 B1 **Petroşani** Romania
89 F3 **Petrovskoye** Russia
86 C2 **Petrozavodsk** Russia
123 C2 **Petrusburg** S. Africa
123 C2 **Petrus Steyn** S. Africa
122 B3 **Petrusville** S. Africa
89 E2 **Petushki** Russia
60 A1 **Peureulak** Indon.
83 M2 **Pevek** Russia
102 B2 **Pforzheim** Ger.
102 C2 **Pfunds** Austria
101 D3 **Pfungstadt** Ger.
123 C2 **Phahameng** S. Africa
123 D1 **Phalaborwa** S. Africa
74 B2 **Phalodi** India
63 B2 **Phang Hoei, San Khao** *mts* Thai.
63 A3 **Phangnga** Thai.
62 B1 **Phăng Xi Păng** *mt.* Vietnam
63 B2 **Phan Rang-Thap Cham** Vietnam
63 B2 **Phan Thiêt** Vietnam
63 B3 **Phatthalung** Thai.
62 A2 **Phayao** Thai.
129 D2 **Phelps Lake** Can.
143 C2 **Phenix City** U.S.A.
63 A2 **Phet Buri** Thai.
63 B2 **Phichit** Thai.
141 D3 **Philadelphia** U.S.A.
136 C2 **Philip** U.S.A.
100 B2 **Philippeville** Belgium
100 A2 **Philippine** Neth.
64 B1 **Philippines** *country* Asia
64 B1 **Philippine Sea** N. Pacific Ocean
126 B2 **Philip Smith Mountains** U.S.A.
122 B3 **Philipstown** S. Africa
53 C3 **Phillip Island** Austr.
137 D3 **Phillipsburg** U.S.A.
123 C2 **Phiritona** S. Africa
63 B2 **Phitsanulok** Thai.
63 B2 **Phnom Penh** Cambodia
Phnum Pénh Cambodia *see* **Phnom Penh**
138 A2 **Phoenix** U.S.A.
49 G3 **Phoenix Islands** Kiribati
63 B2 **Phon** Thai.
62 B1 **Phôngsali** Laos
62 B2 **Phônsavan** Laos
62 B2 **Phônsavan** *mt.* Laos
62 B2 **Phrae** Thai.
63 A3 **Phuket** Thai.
62 A2 **Phumiphon, Khuan** Thai.
123 C2 **Phuthaditjhaba** S. Africa
62 A2 **Phyu** Myanmar
108 A1 **Piacenza** Italy
110 C1 **Piatra Neamţ** Romania
151 D2 **Piauí** *r.* Brazil
108 B1 **Piave** *r.* Italy
117 B4 **Pibor** South Sudan
117 B4 **Pibor** *r.* South Sudan
142 C2 **Picayune** U.S.A.
152 B3 **Pichanal** Arg.
144 A2 **Pichilingue** Mex.
98 C1 **Pickering** U.K.
130 A1 **Pickle Lake** Can.
151 D2 **Picos** Brazil
153 B5 **Pico Truncado** Arg.
53 D2 **Picton** Austr.
150 B3 **Piedras, Río de las** *r.* Peru
145 C3 **Piedras Negras** Guat.
145 B2 **Piedras Negras** Mex.
93 I3 **Pieksämäki** Fin.
92 I3 **Pielinen** *l.* Fin.
136 C2 **Pierre** U.S.A.
105 C3 **Pierrelatte** France
123 D2 **Pietermaritzburg** S. Africa
110 B1 **Pietrosa** *mt.* Romania
128 C2 **Pigeon Lake** Can.
153 B4 **Pigüé** Arg.
92 I3 **Pihtipudas** Fin.
145 C3 **Pijijiapan** Mex.
136 C3 **Pikes Peak** U.S.A.
122 A3 **Piketberg** S. Africa
140 C3 **Pikeville** U.S.A.
103 D1 **Piła** Pol.
153 C4 **Pilar** Arg.
152 C3 **Pilar** Para.
50 A2 **Pilbara** *reg.* Austr.
53 C2 **Pilliga** Austr.
154 C1 **Pilões, Serra dos** *mts* Brazi
150 B3 **Pimenta Bueno** Brazil
153 C4 **Pinamar** Arg.
80 B2 **Pınarbaşı** Turkey
146 B2 **Pinar del Río** Cuba
103 E1 **Pińczów** Pol.
151 D2 **Pindaré** *r.* Brazil
Pindos *mts* Greece *see* **Pindus Mountains**
111 B2 **Pindus Mountains** Greece
142 B2 **Pine Bluff** U.S.A.
50 C1 **Pine Creek** Austr.
136 B2 **Pinedale** U.S.A.
86 D2 **Pinega** Russia
129 D2 **Pinehouse Lake** Can.
111 B3 **Pineios** *r.* Greece
128 C1 **Pine Point (abandoned)** Ca
136 C2 **Pine Ridge** U.S.A.
123 D2 **Pinetown** S. Africa
70 B2 **Pingdingshan** China
71 A3 **Pingguo** China
71 B3 **Pingjiang** China
70 A2 **Pingliang** China
71 C3 **P'ingtung** Taiwan
71 A3 **Pingxiang** *Guangxi* China
71 B3 **Pingxiang** *Jiangxi* China
70 B2 **Pingyin** China
151 D2 **Pinheiro** Brazil
101 D1 **Pinneberg** Ger.
145 C3 **Pinotepa Nacional** Mex.
88 C3 **Pinsk** Belarus
135 D3 **Pioche** U.S.A.
119 C3 **Piodi** Dem. Rep. Congo
103 E1 **Pionki** Pol.
103 D1 **Piotrków Trybunalski** Pol.
137 D2 **Pipestone** U.S.A.
131 C2 **Pipmuacan, Réservoir** *resr* Can.
154 B2 **Piquiri** *r.* Brazil
154 C1 **Piracanjuba** Brazil
154 C2 **Piracicaba** Brazil
155 D1 **Piracicaba** *r.* Brazil
111 B3 **Piraeus** Greece
154 C2 **Piraí do Sul** Brazil
154 C2 **Pirajuí** Brazil
154 B1 **Piranhas** Brazil
151 E2 **Piranhas** *r.* Brazil
155 D1 **Pirapora** Brazil
154 C2 **Pirassununga** Brazil
154 C1 **Pires do Rio** Brazil
151 D2 **Piripiri** Brazil
59 C3 **Piru** Indon.
108 B2 **Pisa** Italy
152 A2 **Pisagua** Chile
150 A3 **Pisco** Peru
102 C2 **Písek** Czechia
79 D2 **Pīshīn** Iran
145 D2 **Pisté** Mex.
109 C2 **Pisticci** Italy
108 B2 **Pistoia** Italy
106 C1 **Pisuerga** *r.* Spain
134 B2 **Pit** *r.* U.S.A.
154 B2 **Pitanga** Brazil
155 D1 **Pitangui** Brazil
49 J4 **Pitcairn Island** *i.* Pitcairn Is
92 H2 **Piteå** Sweden
92 H2 **Piteälven** *r.* Sweden
110 B2 **Piteşti** Romania
75 C2 **Pithoragarh** India
96 C2 **Pitlochry** U.K.
128 B2 **Pitt Island** Can.
137 E3 **Pittsburg** U.S.A.
141 D2 **Pittsburgh** U.S.A.
141 E2 **Pittsfield** U.S.A.

53 D1 **Pittsworth** Austr.
155 C2 **Piumhi** Brazil
150 A2 **Piura** Peru
90 C2 **Pivdennyy Buh** *r.* Ukr.
131 E2 **Placentia** Can.
135 B3 **Placerville** U.S.A.
146 C2 **Placetas** Cuba
139 C2 **Plainview** U.S.A.
154 C1 **Planaltina** Brazil
142 B2 **Plaquemine** U.S.A.
106 B1 **Plasencia** Spain
147 C4 **Plato** Col.
137 D2 **Platte** *r.* U.S.A.
141 E2 **Plattsburgh** U.S.A.
101 F1 **Plau am See** Ger.
101 F2 **Plauen** Ger.
101 F1 **Plauer See** *l.* Ger.
89 E3 **Plavsk** Russia
129 E2 **Playgreen Lake** Can.
63 B2 **Plây Ku** Vietnam
153 B4 **Plaza Huincul** Arg.
139 D3 **Pleasanton** U.S.A.
54 B2 **Pleasant Point** N.Z.
104 C2 **Pleaux** France
130 B1 **Pledger Lake** Can.
54 C1 **Plenty, Bay of** *g.* N.Z.
136 C1 **Plentywood** U.S.A.
86 D2 **Plesetsk** Russia
131 C1 **Plétipi, Lac** *l.* Can.
100 C2 **Plettenberg** Ger.
122 B3 **Plettenberg Bay** S. Africa
110 B2 **Pleven** Bulg.
109 C2 **Pljevlja** Montenegro
109 C2 **Ploče** Croatia
103 D1 **Płock** Pol.
109 C2 **Počno** *mt.* Bos. & Herz.
104 B2 **Ploemeur** France
110 C2 **Ploiești** Romania
89 F2 **Ploskoye** Russia
104 B2 **Plouzané** France
110 B2 **Plovdiv** Bulg.
88 B2 **Plungė** Lith.
88 C3 **Plyeshchanitsy** Belarus
99 A3 **Plymouth** U.K.
140 B2 **Plymouth** U.S.A.
147 D3 **Plymouth (abandoned)** Montserrat
88 C2 **Plyussa** Russia
102 C2 **Plzeň** Czechia
114 B3 **Pô** Burkina Faso
108 B1 **Po** *r.* Italy
77 E2 **Pobeda Peak** China/Kyrg.
142 B1 **Pocahontas** U.S.A.
134 D2 **Pocatello** U.S.A.
90 B1 **Pochayiv** Ukr.
89 D3 **Pochep** Russia
89 D3 **Pochinok** Russia
145 C3 **Pochutla** Mex.
141 D3 **Pocomoke City** U.S.A.
155 C2 **Poços de Caldas** Brazil
89 D2 **Poddor'ye** Russia
91 D1 **Podgorenskiy** Russia
109 C2 **Podgorica** Montenegro
82 G3 **Podgornoye** Russia
90 B2 **Podil's'k** Ukr.
83 H2 **Podkamennaya Tunguska** *r.* Russia
89 E2 **Podol'sk** Russia
109 D2 **Podujevë** Kosovo
Podujevo Kosovo *see* **Podujevë**
122 A2 **Pofadder** S. Africa
89 D3 **Pogar** Russia
109 D2 **Pogradec** Albania
65 B2 **Pohang** S. Korea
48 E2 **Pohnpei** *atoll* Micronesia
110 B2 **Poiana Mare** Romania
118 C3 **Poie** Dem. Rep. Congo
118 B3 **Pointe-Noire** Congo
126 D2 **Point Lake** Can.
140 C3 **Point Pleasant** U.S.A.
104 C2 **Poitiers** France
74 B2 **Pokaran** India
75 C2 **Pokhara** Nepal
91 C2 **Pokrov** Ukr.
83 J2 **Pokrovsk** Russia
91 D2 **Pokrovs'k** Ukr.
91 D2 **Pokrovskoye** Russia
138 A1 **Polacca** U.S.A.
103 D1 **Poland** *country* Europe
88 C2 **Polatsk** Belarus
61 C2 **Polewali** Indon.
118 B2 **Poli** Cameroon
102 C1 **Police** Pol.
109 C2 **Policoro** Italy
105 D2 **Poligny** France
64 B1 **Polillo Islands** Phil.
90 B1 **Polis'ke (abandoned)** Ukr.
103 D1 **Polkowice** Pol.
109 C3 **Pollino, Monte** *mt.* Italy
91 D2 **Polohy** Ukr.
123 C1 **Polokwane** S. Africa
123 D1 **Polokwane** *r.* S. Africa
90 B1 **Polonne** Ukr.
134 D1 **Polson** U.S.A.
91 C2 **Poltava** Ukr.
66 B2 **Poltavka** Russia
91 D2 **Poltavskaya** Russia
88 C2 **Põlva** Estonia
111 B2 **Polygyros** Greece
106 B2 **Pombal** Port.
102 C1 **Pomeranian Bay** *b.* Ger.
102 C1 **Pomeranian Bay** Ger./Pol.
108 B2 **Pomezia** Italy
92 I2 **Pomokaira** *reg.* Fin.
110 C2 **Pomorie** Bulg.
Pomorska, Zatoka *b.* Ger./Pol. *see* **Pomeranian Bay**
155 D1 **Pompéu** Brazil
139 D1 **Ponca City** U.S.A.
147 D3 **Ponce** Puerto Rico
127 F2 **Pond Inlet** Can.
106 B1 **Ponferrada** Spain
117 A4 **Pongo** *watercourse* South Sudan
123 D2 **Pongola** *r.* S. Africa
128 C2 **Ponoka** Can.
84 D5 **Ponta Delgada** Azores
154 B3 **Ponta Grossa** Brazil
154 C1 **Pontalina** Brazil
105 D2 **Pont-à-Mousson** France
105 D2 **Pontarlier** France
102 B2 **Pontcharra** France
142 B2 **Pontchartrain, Lake** U.S.A.
106 B2 **Ponte de Sor** Port.
129 D3 **Ponteix** Can.
150 C3 **Pontes e Lacerda** Brazil
106 B1 **Pontevedra** Spain
140 B2 **Pontiac** *IL* U.S.A.
140 C2 **Pontiac** *MI* U.S.A.
61 B2 **Pontianak** Indon.
104 B2 **Pontivy** France
151 C1 **Pontoetoe** Suriname
129 E2 **Ponton** Can.
99 B3 **Pontypool** U.K.
108 B2 **Ponziane, Isole** *is* Italy
99 C3 **Poole** U.K.
Poona India *see* **Pune**
52 B2 **Pooncarie** Austr.
152 B2 **Poopó, Lago de** *l.* Bol.
150 A1 **Popayán** Col.
83 I2 **Popigay** *r.* Russia
52 B2 **Popiltah** Austr.
129 E2 **Poplar** *r.* Can.
137 E3 **Poplar Bluff** U.S.A.
118 B3 **Popokabaka** Dem. Rep. Congo
110 C2 **Popovo** Bulg.
103 E2 **Poprad** Slovakia
151 D3 **Porangatu** Brazil
74 A2 **Porbandar** India
126 B2 **Porcupine** *r.* Can./U.S.A.
108 B1 **Poreč** Croatia
93 H3 **Pori** Fin.
54 B2 **Porirua** N.Z.
88 C2 **Porkhov** Russia
104 B2 **Pornic** France
83 K3 **Poronaysk** Russia
111 B3 **Poros** Greece
93 E4 **Porsgrunn** Norway
97 C1 **Portadown** U.K.
97 D1 **Portaferry** U.K.
140 B2 **Portage** U.S.A.
129 E3 **Portage la Prairie** Can.
128 B3 **Port Alberni** Can.
106 B2 **Portalegre** Port.
139 C2 **Portales** U.S.A.
128 A2 **Port Alexander** U.S.A.
128 B2 **Port Alice** Can.
134 B1 **Port Angeles** U.S.A.
51 D4 **Port Arthur** Austr.
139 E3 **Port Arthur** U.S.A.
96 A3 **Port Askaig** U.K.
52 A2 **Port Augusta** Austr.
147 C3 **Port-au-Prince** Haiti
131 E1 **Port aux Choix** Can.
73 D3 **Port Blair** India
52 B3 **Port Campbell** Austr.
54 B3 **Port Chalmers** N.Z.
143 D3 **Port Charlotte** U.S.A.
147 C3 **Port-de-Paix** Haiti
128 A2 **Port Edward** Can.
155 D1 **Porteirinha** Brazil
151 C2 **Portel** Brazil
130 B2 **Port Elgin** Can.
123 C3 **Port Elizabeth** S. Africa
96 A3 **Port Ellen** U.K.
98 A1 **Port Erin** Isle of Man
122 A3 **Porterville** S. Africa
135 C3 **Porterville** U.S.A.
52 B3 **Port Fairy** Austr.
54 C1 **Port Fitzroy** N.Z.
118 A3 **Port-Gentil** Gabon
115 C4 **Port Harcourt** Nigeria
128 B2 **Port Hardy** Can.
Port Harrison Can. *see* **Inukjuak**
131 D2 **Port Hawkesbury** Can.
50 A2 **Port Hedland** Austr.
99 A2 **Porthmadog** U.K.
131 E1 **Port Hope Simpson** Can.
140 C2 **Port Huron** U.S.A.
106 B2 **Portimão** Port.
53 C2 **Portland** *N.S.W.* Austr.
52 B3 **Portland** *Vic.* Austr.
141 E2 **Portland** *ME* U.S.A.
134 B1 **Portland** *OR* U.S.A.
128 A2 **Portland Canal** *inlet* Can.
97 C2 **Portlaoise** Ireland
139 D3 **Port Lavaca** U.S.A.
52 A2 **Port Lincoln** Austr.
114 A4 **Port Loko** Sierra Leone
113 K9 **Port Louis** Mauritius
53 D2 **Port Macquarie** Austr.
128 B2 **Port McNeill** Can.
131 D2 **Port-Menier** Can.
59 D3 **Port Moresby** P.N.G.
122 A2 **Port Nolloth** S. Africa
Port-Nouveau-Québec Can. *see* **Kangiqsualujjuaq**
Porto Port. *see* **Oporto**
150 B2 **Porto Acre** Brazil
152 C4 **Porto Alegre** Brazil
151 C3 **Porto Artur** Brazil
151 C3 **Porto dos Gaúchos Óbidos** Brazil

150 C3 **Porto Esperidião** Brazil
108 B2 **Portoferraio** Italy
96 A1 **Port of Ness** U.K.
151 D2 **Porto Franco** Brazil
147 D3 **Port of Spain** Trin. and Tob.
108 B1 **Portogruaro** Italy
108 B2 **Portomaggiore** Italy
154 B2 **Porto Mendes** Brazil
152 C3 **Porto Murtinho** Brazil
151 D3 **Porto Nacional** Brazil
114 C4 **Porto-Novo** Benin
154 B2 **Porto Primavera, Represa** *resr* Brazil
155 E1 **Porto Seguro** Brazil
108 B2 **Porto Tolle** Italy
108 A2 **Porto Torres** *Sardinia* Italy
105 D3 **Porto-Vecchio** *Corsica* France
150 B2 **Porto Velho** Brazil
150 A2 **Portoviejo** Ecuador
52 B3 **Port Phillip Bay** Austr.
52 A2 **Port Pirie** Austr.
96 A2 **Portree** U.K.
128 B3 **Port Renfrew** Can.
97 C1 **Portrush** U.K.
116 B1 **Port Said** Egypt
143 C3 **Port St Joe** U.S.A.
123 C3 **Port St Johns** S. Africa
123 D3 **Port Shepstone** S. Africa
99 C3 **Portsmouth** U.K.
141 E2 **Portsmouth** *NH* U.S.A.
140 C3 **Portsmouth** *OH* U.S.A.
141 D3 **Portsmouth** *VA* U.S.A.
97 C1 **Portstewart** U.K.
116 B3 **Port Sudan** Sudan
142 C3 **Port Sulphur** U.S.A.
99 B3 **Port Talbot** U.K.
106 B2 **Portugal** *country* Europe
97 B2 **Portumna** Ireland
105 C3 **Port-Vendres** France
48 F4 **Port Vila** Vanuatu
93 I3 **Porvoo** Fin.
152 C3 **Posadas** Arg.
89 E2 **Poshekhon'ye** Russia
92 I2 **Posio** Fin.
58 C3 **Poso** Indon.
151 D3 **Posse** Brazil
101 E2 **Pößneck** Ger.
139 C2 **Post** U.S.A.
Poste-de-la-Baleine Can. *see* **Kuujjuarapik**
122 B2 **Postmasburg** S. Africa
109 C2 **Posušje** Bos. & Herz.
139 E1 **Poteau** U.S.A.
109 C2 **Potenza** Italy
151 D2 **Poti** *r.* Brazil
81 C1 **Poti** Georgia
115 D3 **Potiskum** Nigeria
141 D3 **Potomac, South Branch** *r.* U.S.A.
152 B2 **Potosí** Bol.
64 B1 **Pototan** Phil.
138 C3 **Potrero del Llano** Mex.
101 F1 **Potsdam** Ger.
141 E2 **Potsdam** U.S.A.
141 D2 **Pottstown** U.S.A.
141 D2 **Pottsville** U.S.A.
131 E2 **Pouch Cove** Can.
141 E2 **Poughkeepsie** U.S.A.
98 B2 **Poulton-le-Fylde** U.K.
155 C2 **Pouso Alegre** Brazil
63 B2 **Poŭthĭsăt** Cambodia
103 D2 **Považská Bystrica** Slovakia
109 C2 **Povlen** *mt.* Serbia
106 B1 **Póvoa de Varzim** Port.
136 B2 **Powell** U.S.A.
135 D3 **Powell, Lake** *resr* U.S.A.
128 B3 **Powell River** Can.
154 B1 **Poxoréo** Brazil
71 B3 **Poyang** China
71 B3 **Poyang Hu** *l.* China
109 D2 **Požarevac** Serbia
145 C2 **Poza Rica** Mex.
109 C1 **Požega** Croatia
109 D2 **Požega** Serbia
79 D2 **Pozm Tīāb** Iran
103 D1 **Poznań** Pol.
106 C2 **Pozoblanco** Spain
108 B2 **Pozzuoli** Italy
102 C2 **Prachatice** Czechia
63 A2 **Prachuap Khiri Khan** Thai.
155 E1 **Prado** Brazil
102 C1 **Prague** Czechia
Praha Czechia *see* **Prague**
112 C5 **Praia** Cape Verde
139 C2 **Prairie Dog Town Fork** *r.* U.S.A.
140 A2 **Prairie du Chien** U.S.A.
60 A1 **Prapat** Indon.
154 C1 **Prata** Brazil
105 E3 **Prato** Italy
137 D3 **Pratt** U.S.A.
61 C2 **Praya** Indon.
63 B2 **Preăh Vihéar** Cambodia
89 F2 **Prechistoye** Russia
129 D2 **Preeceville** Can.
88 C2 **Preiļi** Latvia
53 C2 **Premer** Austr.
105 C2 **Prémery** France
101 F1 **Premnitz** Ger.
102 C1 **Prenzlau** Ger.
63 A2 **Preparis Island** Cocos Is
63 A2 **Preparis North Channel** Cocos Is
63 A2 **Preparis South Channel** Cocos Is
103 D2 **Přerov** Czechia
138 A2 **Prescott** U.S.A.
109 D2 **Preševo** Serbia
152 B3 **Presidencia Roque Sáenz Peña** Arg.
151 D2 **Presidente Dutra** Brazil
154 B2 **Presidente Epitácio** Brazil
64 B2 **Presidente Manuel A Roxas** Phil.
154 B2 **Presidente Prudente** Brazil
138 C3 **Presidio** U.S.A.
103 E2 **Prešov** Slovakia
141 F1 **Presque Isle** U.S.A.
101 F2 **Pressel** Ger.
98 B2 **Preston** U.K.
134 D2 **Preston** U.S.A.
96 B3 **Prestwick** U.K.
155 C1 **Preto** *r.* Brazil
123 C2 **Pretoria** S. Africa
111 B3 **Preveza** Greece
63 B2 **Prey Vêng** Cambodia
109 C2 **Priboj** Serbia
135 D3 **Price** U.S.A.
88 B3 **Prienai** Lith.
122 B2 **Prieska** S. Africa
103 D2 **Prievidza** Slovakia
109 C2 **Prijedor** Bos. & Herz.
Prikaspiyskaya Nizmennost' *lowland* Kazakh./Russia *see* **Caspian Lowland**
109 D2 **Prilep** Macedonia
91 D2 **Primorsko-Akhtarsk** Russia
129 D2 **Primrose Lake** Can.
129 D2 **Prince Albert** Can.
122 B3 **Prince Albert** S. Africa
126 D2 **Prince Albert Peninsula** Can.
122 B3 **Prince Albert Road** S. Africa
126 C2 **Prince Alfred, Cape** Can.
122 A3 **Prince Alfred Hamlet** S. Africa
127 F2 **Prince Charles Island** Can.
55 E2 **Prince Charles Mountains** Antarctica
131 D2 **Prince Edward Island** *prov.* Can.
113 I11 **Prince Edward Islands** Indian Ocean
128 B2 **Prince George** Can.
126 E2 **Prince of Wales Island** Can.
128 A2 **Prince of Wales Island** U.S.A.
126 D2 **Prince of Wales Strait** Can.
126 D1 **Prince Patrick Island** Can.
126 E2 **Prince Regent Inlet** *sea chan.* Can.
128 A2 **Prince Rupert** Can.
51 D1 **Princess Charlotte Bay** Austr.
128 B2 **Princess Royal Island** Can.
128 B3 **Princeton** Can.
134 B2 **Prineville** U.S.A.
90 B1 **Pripet** *r.* Belarus/Ukr.
90 A1 **Pripet Marshes** Belarus/Ukr.
Prishtinë Kosovo *see* **Pristina**
109 D2 **Pristina** Kosovo
101 F1 **Pritzwalk** Ger.
109 C2 **Privlaka** Croatia
89 F2 **Privolzhsk** Russia
109 D2 **Prizren** Kosovo
151 C1 **Professor van Blommestein Meer** *resr* Suriname
145 D2 **Progreso** Mex.
81 C1 **Prokhladnyy** Russia
109 D2 **Prokuplje** Serbia
87 D4 **Proletarskoye Vodokhranilishche** *l.* Russia
126 C3 **Prophet** *r.* Can.
128 B2 **Prophet River** Can.
51 D2 **Proserpine** Austr.
89 E3 **Protvino** Russia
110 C2 **Provadia** Bulg.
141 E2 **Providence** U.S.A.
146 B3 **Providencia, Isla de** *i.* Caribbean Sea
83 N2 **Provideniya** Russia
135 D2 **Provo** U.S.A.
129 C2 **Provost** Can.
154 B3 **Prudentópolis** Brazil
126 B2 **Prudhoe Bay** U.S.A.
100 C2 **Prüm** Ger.
105 D3 **Prunelli-di-Fiumorbo** *Corsica* France
103 E1 **Pruszków** Pol.
110 C1 **Prut** *r.* Europe
91 C1 **Pryluky** Ukr.
91 D2 **Prymors'k** Ukr.
139 D1 **Pryor** U.S.A.
Prypyats' *r.* Belarus *see* **Pripet**
103 E2 **Przemyśl** Pol.
111 C3 **Psara** *i.* Greece
81 C1 **Psebay** Russia
91 D3 **Pshekha** *r.* Russia
88 C2 **Pskov** Russia
88 C2 **Pskov, Lake** Estonia/Russia
111 B2 **Ptolemaïda** Greece
109 C1 **Ptuj** Slovenia
150 A2 **Pucallpa** Peru
71 B3 **Pucheng** China
103 D1 **Puck** Pol.
92 I2 **Pudasjärvi** Fin.
86 C2 **Pudozh** Russia
Puduchcheri India *see* **Puducherry**
73 B3 **Puducherry** India
145 C3 **Puebla** Mex.
136 C3 **Pueblo** U.S.A.
153 B4 **Puelén** Arg.
106 C2 **Puente Genil** Spain
152 B2 **Puerto Alegre** Bol.
145 C3 **Puerto Ángel** Mex.
146 B4 **Puerto Armuelles** Panama

150 B1 Puerto Ayacucho Venez.
153 A5 Puerto Aysén Chile
146 B3 Puerto Cabezas Nic.
150 B1 Puerto Carreño Col.
153 A5 Puerto Cisnes Chile
144 A2 Puerto Cortés Mex.
153 B5 Puerto Deseado Arg.
145 C3 Puerto Escondido Mex.
152 B2 Puerto Frey Bol.
152 C2 Puerto Isabel Bol.
150 A2 Puerto Leguízamo Col.
144 A2 Puerto Libertad Mex.
146 B3 Puerto Limón Costa Rica
106 C2 Puertollano Spain
153 B5 Puerto Madryn Arg.
150 B3 Puerto Maldonado Peru
153 A5 Puerto Montt Chile
153 A6 Puerto Natales Chile
150 B1 Puerto Nuevo Col.
144 A1 Puerto Peñasco Mex.
152 C3 Puerto Pinasco Para.
147 C3 Puerto Plata Dom. Rep.
150 A2 Puerto Portillo Peru
64 A2 Puerto Princesa Phil.
147 D3 Puerto Rico terr. West Indies
158 B3 Puerto Rico Trench Caribbean Sea
146 A3 Puerto San José Guat.
153 B5 Puerto San Julián Arg.
153 B6 Puerto Santa Cruz Arg.
144 B2 Puerto Vallarta Mex.
87 D3 Pugachev Russia
74 B2 Pugal India
54 B2 Pukaki, Lake N.Z.
129 D2 Pukatawagan Can.
65 B1 Pukchin N. Korea
65 B1 Pukch'ŏng N. Korea
54 B1 Pukekohe N.Z.
65 B1 Puksubaek-san mt. N. Korea
108 B2 Pula Croatia
108 A3 Pula Sardinia Italy
152 B3 Pulacayo Bol.
60 A2 Pulautelo Indon.
77 C3 Pul-e Khumrī Afgh.
92 I3 Pulkkila Fin.
134 C1 Pullman U.S.A.
64 B1 Pulog, Mount Phil.
150 A2 Puná, Isla i. Ecuador
54 B2 Punakaiki N.Z.
123 D1 Punda Maria S. Africa
73 B3 Pune India
65 B1 P'ungsan N. Korea
121 C2 Púnguè r. Moz.
153 B4 Punta Alta Arg.
153 A6 Punta Arenas Chile
146 B3 Puntarenas Costa Rica
117 C4 Puntland reg. Somalia
150 A1 Punto Fijo Venez.
92 I3 Puolanka Fin.
82 G2 Pur r. Russia
75 C3 Puri India
100 B1 Purmerend Neth.
75 C2 Purnia India
75 C2 Puruliya India
150 B2 Purus r. Brazil/Peru
61 B2 Purwakarta Indon.
65 B1 Puryŏng N. Korea
Pusan S. Korea see Busan
88 C2 Pushkinskiye Gory Russia
88 C2 Pustoshka Russia
62 A1 Putao Myanmar
71 B3 Putian China
Puting China see De'an
61 C2 Puting, Tanjung pt Indon.
101 F1 Putlitz Ger.
58 A2 Putrajaya Malaysia
102 C1 Puttgarden Ger.
150 A2 Putumayo r. Col.
61 C1 Putussibau Indon.
91 C1 Putyvl' Ukr.
127 F2 Puvirnituq Can.
70 B2 Puyang China
104 C3 Puylaurens France
99 A2 Pwllheli U.K.
63 A2 Pyapon Myanmar
82 G2 Pyasina r. Russia
87 D4 Pyatigorsk Russia
91 C2 P"yatykhatky Ukr.
62 A2 Pyè Myanmar
88 C3 Pyetrykaw Belarus
93 H3 Pyhäjärvi l. Fin.
92 H3 Pyhäjoki r. Fin.
92 I3 Pyhäsalmi Fin.
62 A2 Pyinmana Myanmar
65 B2 Pyŏksŏng N. Korea
65 B2 P'yŏnggang N. Korea
65 B2 P'yŏngsan N. Korea
65 B2 P'yŏngyang N. Korea
135 C2 Pyramid Lake U.S.A.
80 B3 Pyramids of Giza tourist site Egypt
107 D1 Pyrenees mts Europe
111 B3 Pyrgos Greece
91 C1 Pyryatyn Ukr.
103 C1 Pyrzyce Pol.
88 C2 Pytalovo Russia
111 B3 Pyxaria mt. Greece

Q

127 G1 Qaanaaq Greenland
123 C3 Qacha's Nek Lesotho
68 C2 Qaidam Pendi basin China
74 A1 Qalāt Afgh.
78 B2 Qal'at Bīshah Saudi Arabia
129 E1 Qamanirjuaq Lake Can.
Qamanittuaq Can. see Baker Lake
79 C3 Qamar, Ghubbat al b. Yemen
78 B3 Qam Hadīl Saudi Arabia
77 C3 Qarshi Uzbek.
78 B2 Qaryat al Ulyā Saudi Arabia
127 H2 Qasigiannguit Greenland
79 D2 Qaşr-e Qand Iran
81 C2 Qaşr-e Shīrīn Iran
127 H2 Qassimiut Greenland
78 B3 Qa'tabah Yemen
79 C2 Qatar country Asia
116 A2 Qattara Depression Egypt
81 C1 Qazax Azer.
81 C2 Qazvīn Iran
127 H2 Qeqertarsuaq i. Greenland
127 H2 Qeqertarsuatsiaat Greenland
127 H2 Qeqertarsuup Tunua b. Greenland
79 C2 Qeshm Iran
70 A3 Qianjiang Chongqing China
70 B2 Qianjiang Hubei China
65 A1 Qian Shan mts China
70 C2 Qidong China
68 B2 Qiemo China
71 A3 Qijiang China
68 C2 Qijiaojing China
127 G2 Qikiqtarjuaq Can.
74 A2 Qila Ladgasht Pak.
68 C2 Qilian Shan mts China
127 I2 Qillak i. Greenland
70 B3 Qimen China
127 G1 Qimusseriarsuaq b. Greenland
116 B2 Qinā Egypt
70 C2 Qingdao China
68 C2 Qinghai Hu salt l. China
68 C2 Qinghai Nanshan mts China
70 A2 Qingyang China
71 B3 Qingyuan Guangdong China
65 A1 Qingyuan Liaoning China
Qingzang Gaoyuan plat. China see Tibet, Plateau of
70 B2 Qingzhou China
70 B2 Qinhuangdao China
70 A2 Qin Ling mts China
Qinting China see Lianhua
70 B2 Qinyang China
71 A3 Qinzhou China
71 B4 Qionghai China
68 C2 Qionglai Shan mts China
71 B4 Qiongshan China
69 E1 Qiqihar China
79 C2 Qīr Iran
66 B1 Qitaihe China
70 B2 Qixian China
Qogir Feng mt. China/Pak. see K2
81 D2 Qom Iran
Qomolangma Feng mt. China/Nepal see Everest, Mount
76 B2 Qo'ng'irot Uzbek.
Qoqek China see Tacheng
77 D2 Qo'qon Uzbek.
76 B2 Qoraqalpog'iston Uzbek.
100 C1 Quakenbrück Ger.
63 B2 Quang Ngai Vietnam
63 B2 Quang Tri Vietnam
71 B3 Quanzhou Fujian China
71 B3 Quanzhou Guangxi China
108 A3 Quartu Sant'Elena Sardinia Italy
138 A2 Quartzsite U.S.A.
81 C1 Quba Azer.
53 C3 Queanbeyan Austr.
131 C2 Québec Can.
130 C1 Québec prov. Can.
101 E2 Quedlinburg Ger.
128 A2 Queen Charlotte Can.
128 B2 Queen Charlotte Sound sea chan. Can.
128 B2 Queen Charlotte Strait Can.
126 D1 Queen Elizabeth Islands Can.
55 A1 Queen Elizabeth Land reg. Antarctica
126 E2 Queen Maud Gulf Can.
55 B2 Queen Maud Land reg. Antarctica
55 N1 Queen Maud Mountains Antarctica
52 B1 Queensland state Austr.
51 D4 Queenstown Austr.
54 A3 Queenstown N.Z.
123 C3 Queenstown S. Africa
121 C2 Quelimane Moz.
138 B2 Quemado U.S.A.
154 B2 Querência do Norte Brazil
145 B2 Querétaro Mex.
101 E2 Querfurt Ger.
128 B2 Quesnel Can.
128 B2 Quesnel Lake Can.
74 A1 Quetta Pak.
64 A2 Quezon Phil.
64 B1 Quezon City Phil.
120 A2 Quibala Angola
150 A1 Quibdó Col.
104 B2 Quiberon France
104 C3 Quillan France
153 C4 Quilmes Arg.
Quilon India see Kollam
51 D2 Quilpie Austr.
153 A4 Quilpué Chile
120 A1 Quimbele Angola
152 B3 Quimilí Arg.
104 B2 Quimper France
104 B2 Quimperlé France
137 E3 Quincy IL U.S.A.
141 E2 Quincy MA U.S.A.

107 C1 **Quinto** Spain
121 D2 **Quionga** Moz.
53 D2 **Quirindi** Austr.
120 A2 **Quitapa** Angola
150 A2 **Quito** Ecuador
151 E2 **Quixadá** Brazil
71 A3 **Qujing** China
52 A2 **Quorn** Austr.
79 C2 **Qurayat** Oman
77 C3 **Qŭrghonteppa** Tajik.
63 B2 **Quy Nhơn** Vietnam
71 B3 **Quzhou** China

R

103 D2 **Raab** *r.* Austria
92 H3 **Raahe** Fin.
100 C1 **Raalte** Neth.
61 C2 **Raas** *i.* Indon.
61 C2 **Raba** Indon.
114 B1 **Rabat** Morocco
48 E3 **Rabaul** P.N.G.
78 A2 **Rābigh** Saudi Arabia
131 E2 **Race, Cape** Can.
142 B3 **Raceland** U.S.A.
63 B3 **Rach Gia** Vietnam
140 B2 **Racine** U.S.A.
78 B3 **Radā'** Yemen
110 C1 **Rădăuți** Romania
140 B3 **Radcliff** U.S.A.
74 B2 **Radhanpur** India
130 C1 **Radisson** Can.
103 E1 **Radom** Pol.
103 D1 **Radomsko** Pol.
90 B1 **Radomyshl'** Ukr.
109 D2 **Radoviš** Macedonia
88 B2 **Radviliškis** Lith.
78 A2 **Raḍwá, Jabal** *mt.* Saudi Arabia
90 B1 **Radyvyliv** Ukr.
75 C2 **Rae Bareli** India
100 C2 **Raeren** Belgium
54 C1 **Raetihi** N.Z.
152 B4 **Rafaela** Arg.
118 C2 **Rafaï** C.A.R.
78 B2 **Rafḥā'** Saudi Arabia
79 C1 **Rafsanjān** Iran
64 B2 **Ragang, Mount** *vol.* Phil.
109 B3 **Ragusa** *Sicily* Italy
59 C3 **Raha** Indon.
88 D3 **Rahachow** Belarus
74 B2 **Rahimyar Khan** Pak.
109 D2 **Rahovec** Kosovo
73 B3 **Raichur** India
75 C2 **Raigarh** India
128 C2 **Rainbow Lake** Can.
134 B1 **Rainier, Mount** *vol.* U.S.A.
130 A2 **Rainy Lake** Can./U.S.A.
129 E3 **Rainy River** Can.
75 C2 **Raipur** India
93 H3 **Raisio** Fin.
73 C3 **Rajahmundry** India
61 C1 **Rajang** *r.* *Sarawak* Malaysia
74 B2 **Rajanpur** Pak.
73 B4 **Rajapalaiyam** India
Rajasthan Canal India *see* **Indira Gandhi Nahar**
74 B2 **Rajgarh** India
74 B2 **Rajkot** India
74 B2 **Rajpur** India
75 C2 **Rajshahi** Bangl.
54 B2 **Rakaia** *r.* N.Z.
90 A2 **Rakhiv** Ukr.
91 D1 **Rakitnoye** Russia
Rakiura N.Z. *see* **Stewart Island/Rakiura**
88 C2 **Rakke** Estonia
88 C2 **Rakvere** Estonia
143 E1 **Raleigh** U.S.A.
48 F2 **Ralik Chain** *is* Marshall Is
117 B4 **Ramciel** South Sudan
74 B2 **Ramgarh** India
81 C2 **Rāmhormoz** Iran
Ramlat Rabyānah *des.* Libya *see* **Rebiana Sand Sea**
110 C1 **Râmnicu Sărat** Romania
110 B1 **Râmnicu Vâlcea** Romania
89 E3 **Ramon'** Russia
123 C1 **Ramotswa** Botswana
75 B2 **Rampur** India
62 A2 **Ramree Island** Myanmar
98 A1 **Ramsey** Isle of Man
99 D3 **Ramsgate** U.K.
75 C2 **Ranaghat** India
61 C1 **Ranau** *Sabah* Malaysia
153 A4 **Rancagua** Chile
75 C2 **Ranchi** India
93 F4 **Randers** Denmark
54 B2 **Rangiora** N.Z.
54 C1 **Rangitaiki** *r.* N.Z.
54 B2 **Rangitoto ke te Tonga** N.Z.
62 A2 **Rangoon** Myanmar
75 C2 **Rangpur** Bangl.
129 E1 **Rankin Inlet** Can.
53 C2 **Rankins Springs** Austr.
96 B2 **Rannoch Moor** *moorland* U.K.
63 A3 **Ranong** Thai.
59 C3 **Ransiki** Indon.
61 C2 **Rantaupanjang** Indon.
60 A1 **Rantauprapat** Indon.
92 I2 **Ranua** Fin.
78 B2 **Ranyah, Wādī** *watercourse* Saudi Arabia
49 I4 **Rapa** *i.* Fr. Polynesia
136 C2 **Rapid City** U.S.A.
88 B2 **Rapla** Estonia
74 A2 **Rapur** India
49 H4 **Rarotonga** *i.* Cook Is
153 B5 **Rasa, Punta** *pt* Arg.
79 C2 **Ra's al Khaymah** U.A.E.
117 B3 **Ras Dejen** *mt.* Eth.
88 B2 **Raseiniai** Lith.
81 C2 **Rasht** Iran
74 A2 **Ras Koh** *mt.* Pak.
88 C2 **Rasony** Belarus
87 D3 **Rasskazovo** Russia
79 C2 **Ras Tannūrah** Saudi Arabia
101 D1 **Rastede** Ger.
93 F3 **Rätan** Sweden
74 B2 **Ratangarh** India
63 A2 **Rat Buri** Thai.
62 A1 **Rathedaung** Myanmar
101 F1 **Rathenow** Ger.
97 C1 **Rathlin Island** U.K.
74 B2 **Ratlam** India
73 B3 **Ratnagiri** India
73 C4 **Ratnapura** Sri Lanka
90 A1 **Ratne** Ukr.
138 C1 **Raton** U.S.A.
96 D2 **Rattray Head** U.K.
101 E1 **Ratzeburg** Ger.
92 □B2 **Raufarhöfn** Iceland
54 C1 **Raukumara Range** *mts* N.Z.
75 C2 **Raulakela** India
93 H3 **Rauma** Fin.
61 C2 **Raung, Gunung** *vol.* Indon.
134 D1 **Ravalli** U.S.A.
81 C2 **Ravānsar** Iran
108 B2 **Ravenna** Italy
102 B2 **Ravensburg** Ger.
74 B1 **Ravi** *r.* Pak.
74 B1 **Rawalpindi** Pak.
103 D1 **Rawicz** Pol.
50 B3 **Rawlinna** Austr.
136 B2 **Rawlins** U.S.A.
153 B5 **Rawson** Arg.
73 C3 **Rayagarha** India
69 E1 **Raychikhinsk** Russia
78 B3 **Raydah** Yemen
87 E3 **Rayevskiy** Russia
134 B1 **Raymond** U.S.A.
53 D2 **Raymond Terrace** Austr.
139 D3 **Raymondville** U.S.A.
145 C2 **Rayón** Mex.
63 B2 **Rayong** Thai.
78 A2 **Rayyis** Saudi Arabia
104 B2 **Raz, Pointe du** *pt* France
81 C2 **Razāzah, Buḥayrat ar** *l.* Iraq
110 C2 **Razgrad** Bulg.
110 C2 **Razim, Lacul** *lag.* Romania
110 B2 **Razlog** Bulg.
104 B2 **Ré, Île de** *i.* France
99 C3 **Reading** U.K.
141 D2 **Reading** U.S.A.
115 E2 **Rebiana Sand Sea** *des.* Libya
66 D1 **Rebun-tō** *i.* Japan
50 B3 **Recherche, Archipelago of the** *is* Austr.
89 D3 **Rechytsa** Belarus
151 E2 **Recife** Brazil
123 C3 **Recife, Cape** S. Africa
100 C2 **Recklinghausen** Ger.
152 C3 **Reconquista** Arg.
142 B2 **Red** *r.* U.S.A.
131 E1 **Red Bay** Can.
135 B2 **Red Bluff** U.S.A.
98 C1 **Redcar** U.K.
129 C2 **Redcliff** Can.
52 B2 **Red Cliffs** Austr.
128 C2 **Red Deer** Can.
126 D3 **Red Deer** *r.* Can.
129 D2 **Red Deer Lake** Can.
134 B2 **Redding** U.S.A.
99 C2 **Redditch** U.K.
137 D2 **Redfield** U.S.A.
130 A1 **Red Lake** Can.
137 E1 **Red Lakes** U.S.A.
134 E1 **Red Lodge** U.S.A.
134 B2 **Redmond** U.S.A.
137 D2 **Red Oak** U.S.A.
106 B2 **Redondo** Port.
159 B2 **Red Sea** Africa/Asia
128 B1 **Redstone** *r.* Can.
100 B1 **Reduzum** Neth.
137 E2 **Red Wing** U.S.A.
137 D2 **Redwood Falls** U.S.A.
97 C2 **Ree, Lough** *l.* Ireland
134 B2 **Reedsport** U.S.A.
54 B2 **Reefton** N.Z.
102 C2 **Regen** Ger.
155 E1 **Regência** Brazil
102 C2 **Regensburg** Ger.
114 C2 **Reggane** Alg.
109 C3 **Reggio di Calabria** Italy
108 B2 **Reggio nell'Emilia** Italy
110 B1 **Reghin** Romania
129 D2 **Regina** Can.
122 A1 **Rehoboth** Namibia
101 F2 **Reichenbach im Vogtland** Ger.
143 E1 **Reidsville** U.S.A.
99 C3 **Reigate** U.K.
105 C2 **Reims** France
101 E1 **Reinbek** Ger.
129 D2 **Reindeer** *r.* Can.
129 E2 **Reindeer Island** Can.
129 D2 **Reindeer Lake** Can.
92 F2 **Reine** Norway
100 C3 **Reinsfeld** Ger.
123 C2 **Reitz** S. Africa
122 B2 **Reivilo** S. Africa
129 D1 **Reliance** Can.
107 D2 **Relizane** Alg.
79 C2 **Remeshk** Iran
105 D2 **Remiremont** France

00 C2 Remscheid Ger.
02 B1 Rendsburg Ger.
41 D1 Renfrew Can.
60 B2 Rengat Indon.
90 B2 Reni Ukr.
52 B2 Renmark Austr.
04 D2 Rennerod Ger.
04 B2 Rennes France
29 D1 Rennie Lake Can.
08 B2 Reno r. Italy
95 C3 Reno U.S.A.
70 A3 Renshou China
40 B2 Rensselaer U.S.A.
75 C2 Renukut India
00 B1 Renwick N.Z.
58 C3 Reo Indon.
86 D3 Republican r. U.S.A.
Repulse Bay Can. see Naujaat
50 A2 Requena Peru
07 C2 Requena Spain
54 B2 Reserva Brazil
54 C2 Resistencia Arg.
40 B1 Reşiţa Romania
34 D2 Resolute Can.
27 G2 Resolution Island Can.
05 C2 Rethel France
11 B3 Rethymno Greece
43 K9 Réunion terr. Indian Ocean
07 D1 Reus Spain
02 C2 Reutlingen Ger.
23 E2 Revelstoke Can.
44 A3 Revillagigedo, Islas is Mex.
22 A2 Revillagigedo Island U.S.A.
75 C2 Rewa India
34 D2 Rexburg U.S.A.
92 □A3 Reykjanestá pt Iceland
92 □A2 Reykjavík Iceland
45 C2 Reynosa Mex.
88 C2 Rēzekne Latvia
Rhein r. Ger. see Rhine
00 C1 Rheine Ger.
01 F1 Rheinsberg Ger.
Rhin r. France see Rhine
Rhine r. Europe
.00 C1 Rhine r. Europe
.40 B1 Rhinelander U.S.A.
.01 F1 Rhinluch marsh Ger.
.01 F1 Rhinow Ger.
.41 E2 Rhode Island state U.S.A.
.11 C3 Rhodes Greece
.11 C3 Rhodes i. Greece
.10 B2 Rhodope Mountains Bulg./Greece
.05 C2 Rhône r. France/Switz.
Rhuthun U.K. see Ruthin
98 B2 Rhyl U.K.
.54 C1 Rianápolis Brazil
60 B1 Riau, Kepulauan is Indon.
.06 B1 Ribadeo Spain
.06 B1 Ribadesella/Ribeseya Spain
.54 B2 Ribas do Rio Pardo Brazil
.21 C2 Ribáuè Moz.
98 B2 Ribble r. U.K.
.54 C2 Ribeira r. Brazil
.54 C2 Ribeirão Preto Brazil
.04 C2 Ribérac France
.52 B2 Riberalta Bol.
Ribeseya Spain see Ribadesella/Ribeseya
90 B2 Ribnita Moldova
.02 C1 Ribnitz-Damgarten Ger.
.40 A1 Rice Lake U.S.A.
.23 D2 Richards Bay S. Africa
.26 B2 Richardson Mountains Can.
.35 D3 Richfield U.S.A.
.34 C1 Richland U.S.A.
.40 A2 Richland Center U.S.A.
53 D2 Richmond N.S.W. Austr.
51 D2 Richmond Qld Austr.

54 B2 Richmond N.Z.
122 B3 Richmond S. Africa
98 C1 Richmond U.K.
140 C3 Richmond IN U.S.A.
140 C3 Richmond KY U.S.A.
141 D3 Richmond VA U.S.A.
130 C2 Rideau Lakes Can.
135 C3 Ridgecrest U.S.A.
102 C1 Riesa Ger.
100 D1 Rieste Ger.
123 B2 Riet r. S. Africa
101 D2 Rietberg Ger.
108 B2 Rieti Italy
136 B3 Rifle U.S.A.
88 B2 Riga Latvia
88 B2 Riga, Gulf of Estonia/Latvia
134 D2 Rigby U.S.A.
131 E1 Rigolet Can.
93 H3 Riihimäki Fin.
108 B1 Rijeka Croatia
134 C2 Riley U.S.A.
78 B2 Rimah, Wādī ar watercourse Saudi Arabia
103 E2 Rimavská Sobota Slovakia
128 C2 Rimbey Can.
108 B2 Rimini Italy
131 D2 Rimouski Can.
93 F3 Ringebu Norway
93 E4 Ringkøbing Denmark
92 G2 Ringvassøya i. Norway
101 D1 Rinteln Ger.
150 A2 Riobamba Ecuador
150 B3 Rio Branco Brazil
154 C3 Rio Branco do Sul Brazil
154 B2 Rio Brilhante Brazil
154 C2 Río Claro Brazil
153 B4 Río Colorado Arg.
153 B4 Río Cuarto Arg.
155 D2 Rio de Janeiro Brazil
153 B6 Río Gallegos Arg.
153 B6 Río Grande Arg.
152 C4 Rio Grande Brazil
144 B2 Río Grande Mex.
139 D3 Rio Grande r. Mex./U.S.A.
139 D3 Rio Grande City U.S.A.
150 A1 Riohacha Col.
150 A2 Rioja Peru
145 D2 Río Lagartos Mex.
105 C2 Riom France
153 A5 Río Mayo Arg.
152 B2 Río Mulatos Bol.
154 C3 Río Negro Brazil
155 D1 Rio Pardo de Minas Brazil
138 B1 Rio Rancho U.S.A.
150 A2 Río Tigre Ecuador
154 B1 Rio Verde Brazil
145 C2 Río Verde Mex.
154 B1 Rio Verde de Mato Grosso Brazil
90 C1 Ripky Ukr.
98 C2 Ripley U.K.
107 D1 Ripoll Spain
98 C1 Ripon U.K.
66 D1 Rishiri-tō i. Japan
93 E4 Risør Norway
122 B3 Ritchie S. Africa
63 A2 Ritchie's Archipelago is India
134 C1 Ritzville U.S.A.
152 B3 Rivadavia Arg.
108 B1 Riva del Garda Italy
146 B3 Rivas Nic.
152 C4 Rivera Uru.
129 C2 Riverhurst Can.
52 B2 Riverina reg. Austr.
122 B3 Riversdale S. Africa
135 C4 Riverside U.S.A.
136 B2 Riverton U.S.A.
131 D2 Riverview Can.

104 C3 Rivesaltes France
131 D2 Rivière-du-Loup Can.
90 B1 Rivne Ukr.
54 B2 Riwaka N.Z.
78 B2 Riyadh Saudi Arabia
81 C1 Rize Turkey
70 B2 Rizhao China
105 C2 Roanne France
141 D3 Roanoke U.S.A.
143 E1 Roanoke r. U.S.A.
143 E1 Roanoke Rapids U.S.A.
52 A3 Robe Austr.
101 F1 Röbel/Müritz Ger.
130 C2 Robert-Bourassa, Réservoir resr Can.
92 H3 Robertsfors Sweden
122 A3 Robertson S. Africa
114 A4 Robertsport Liberia
131 C2 Roberval Can.
50 A2 Robinson Ranges hills Austr.
52 B2 Robinvale Austr.
129 D2 Roblin Can.
128 C2 Robson, Mount Can.
153 C4 Rocha Uru.
98 B2 Rochdale U.K.
154 B1 Rochedo Brazil
100 B2 Rochefort Belgium
104 B2 Rochefort France
137 E2 Rochester MN U.S.A.
141 E2 Rochester NH U.S.A.
141 D2 Rochester NY U.S.A.
140 B2 Rockford U.S.A.
51 E2 Rockhampton Austr.
143 D2 Rock Hill U.S.A.
50 A3 Rockingham Austr.
140 A2 Rock Island U.S.A.
136 B1 Rock Springs MT U.S.A.
139 C3 Rocksprings U.S.A.
136 B2 Rock Springs WY U.S.A.
136 C3 Rocky Ford U.S.A.
143 E1 Rocky Mount U.S.A.
128 C2 Rocky Mountain House Can.
124 G3 Rocky Mountains Can./U.S.A.
100 B3 Rocroi France
102 C1 Rødbyhavn Denmark
131 E1 Roddickton Can.
104 C3 Rodez France
89 F2 Rodniki Russia
Rodos Greece see Rhodes
Rodos i. Greece see Rhodes
50 A2 Roebourne Austr.
50 B1 Roebuck Bay Austr.
123 C1 Roedtan S. Africa
100 B2 Roermond Neth.
100 A2 Roeselare Belgium
127 F2 Roes Welcome Sound sea chan. Can.
142 B1 Rogers U.S.A.
122 B3 Roggeveldberge esc. S. Africa
92 E3 Rognan Norway
134 B2 Rogue r. U.S.A.
88 B2 Roja Latvia
88 C2 Rokiškis Lith.
90 B1 Rokytne Ukr.
137 E3 Rolândia Brazil
137 E3 Rolla U.S.A.
51 D2 Roma Austr.
Roma Italy see Rome
123 C2 Roma Lesotho
139 D3 Roma U.S.A.
143 E2 Romain, Cape U.S.A.
110 C1 Roman Romania
59 C3 Romang, Pulau i. Indon.
110 B1 Romania country Europe
91 C2 Roman-Kosh mt. Ukr.
69 D1 Romanovka Russia
105 D2 Rombas France
64 B1 Romblon Phil.

Rome

108 B2 Rome Italy
143 C2 Rome GA U.S.A.
141 D2 Rome NY U.S.A.
99 D3 Romford U.K.
105 C2 Romilly-sur-Seine France
91 C1 Rommy Ukr.
104 C2 Romorantin-Lanthenay France
99 C3 Romsey U.K.
96 □ Ronas Hill U.K.
151 C3 Roncador, Serra do hills Brazil
106 B2 Ronda Spain
154 B2 Rondon Brazil
154 B1 Rondonópolis Brazil
74 B1 Rondu Pak.
71 A3 Rong'an China
71 A3 Rongjiang China
62 A1 Rongklang Range mts Myanmar
Rongmei China see Hefeng
93 F4 Rønne Denmark
55 P2 Ronne Ice Shelf Antarctica
101 D1 Ronnenberg Ger.
100 A2 Ronse Belgium
75 D4 Roorkee India
100 B2 Roosendaal Neth.
135 E2 Roosevelt U.S.A.
128 B2 Roosevelt, Mount Can.
55 K2 Roosevelt Sub-glacial Island Antarctica
104 B3 Roquefort France
150 B1 Roraima, Mount Guyana
93 F3 Røros Norway
153 B4 Rosario Arg.
144 A1 Rosario Baja California Mex.
144 B2 Rosario Sinaloa Mex.
144 B2 Rosario Sonora Mex.
151 C3 Rosário Oeste Brazil
144 A2 Rosarito Mex.
109 C3 Rosarno Italy
104 B2 Roscoff France
97 C2 Roscommon Ireland
97 C2 Roscrea Ireland
147 D3 Roseau Dominica
137 D1 Roseau U.S.A.
134 B2 Roseburg U.S.A.
139 D3 Rosenberg U.S.A.
101 D1 Rosengarten Ger.
102 C2 Rosenheim Ger.
129 D2 Rosetown Can.
122 A2 Rosh Pinah Namibia
110 C2 Roşiori de Vede Romania
93 F4 Roskilde Denmark
89 D3 Roslavl' Russia
109 C3 Rossano Italy
97 B1 Rossan Point Ireland
55 K1 Ross Ice Shelf Antarctica
131 D2 Rossignol, Lake Can.
128 C3 Rossland Can.
97 C3 Rosslare Ireland
114 A3 Rosso Maur.
105 D3 Rosso, Capo c. Corsica France
99 B3 Ross-on-Wye U.K.
91 D1 Rossosh' Russia
128 A1 Ross River Can.
55 K2 Ross Sea Antarctica
92 F2 Røssvatnet l. Norway
79 C2 Rostāq Iran
129 D2 Rosthern Can.
102 C1 Rostock Ger.
89 E2 Rostov Russia
91 D2 Rostov-na-Donu Russia
92 H2 Rosvik Sweden
138 C2 Roswell U.S.A.
59 D2 Rota i. N. Mariana Is
59 C3 Rote i. Indon.
101 D1 Rotenburg (Wümme) Ger.
102 C2 Roth Ger.

98 C1 Rothbury U.K.
98 C2 Rotherham U.K.
96 B3 Rothesay U.K.
53 C2 Roto Austr.
105 D3 Rotondo, Monte mt. Corsica France
54 C1 Rotorua N.Z.
54 C1 Rotorua, Lake N.Z.
101 E2 Rottenbach Ger.
102 C2 Rottenmann Austria
100 B2 Rotterdam Neth.
102 B2 Rottweil Ger.
49 F3 Rotuma i. Fiji
105 C1 Roubaix France
104 C2 Rouen France
Roulers Belgium see Roeselare
53 D2 Round Mountain Austr.
131 E2 Round Pond l. Can.
139 D2 Round Rock U.S.A.
134 E1 Roundup U.S.A.
96 C1 Rousay i. U.K.
130 C2 Rouyn-Noranda Can.
92 I2 Rovaniemi Fin.
91 D2 Roven'ki Russia
91 D2 Roven'ky Ukr.
108 B1 Rovereto Italy
63 B2 Rôviĕng Cambodia
108 B1 Rovigo Italy
108 B1 Rovinj Croatia
53 C1 Rowena Austr.
64 B1 Roxas Capiz Phil.
64 B1 Roxas Oriental Mindoro Phil.
64 A1 Roxas Palawan Phil.
52 A2 Roxby Downs Austr.
138 C1 Roy U.S.A.
140 B1 Royale, Isle i. U.S.A.
99 D3 Royal Tunbridge Wells U.K.
104 B2 Royan France
99 C2 Royston U.K.
90 C2 Rozdil'na Ukr.
91 C2 Rozdol'ne Ukr.
100 B3 Rozoy-sur-Serre France
87 D3 Rtishchevo Russia
54 C1 Ruapehu, Mount vol. N.Z.
54 A3 Ruapuke Island N.Z.
78 B3 Rub' al Khālī des. Saudi Arabia
91 D2 Rubizhne Ukr.
77 E1 Rubtsovsk Russia
135 C2 Ruby Mountains U.S.A.
66 C2 Rudnaya Pristan' Russia
89 D3 Rudnya Russia
76 C1 Rudnyy Kazakh.
82 E1 Rudol'fa, Ostrov i. Russia
101 E2 Rudolstadt Ger.
119 D3 Rufiji r. Tanz.
153 B4 Rufino Arg.
121 B2 Rufunsa Zambia
70 C2 Rugao China
99 C2 Rugby U.K.
136 C1 Rugby U.S.A.
102 C1 Rügen i. Ger.
101 E2 Ruhla Ger.
88 B2 Ruhnu i. Estonia
100 C2 Ruhr r. Ger.
71 C3 Rui'an China
138 B2 Ruidoso U.S.A.
144 B2 Ruiz Mex.
119 D3 Rukwa, Lake Tanz.
96 A2 Rum i. U.K.
109 C1 Ruma Serbia
78 B2 Rumāh Saudi Arabia
117 A4 Rumbek South Sudan
105 D2 Rumilly France
50 C1 Rum Jungle (abandoned) Austr.
54 B2 Runanga N.Z.
98 B2 Runcorn U.K.
120 A2 Rundu Namibia

68 B2 Ruoqiang China
130 C1 Rupert r. Can.
130 C1 Rupert Bay Can.
121 C2 Rusape Zimbabwe
110 C2 Ruse Bulg.
77 D3 Rūshon Tajik.
136 C2 Rushville U.S.A.
53 C3 Rushworth Austr.
129 D2 Russell Can.
54 B1 Russell N.Z.
142 C2 Russellville AL U.S.A.
142 B1 Russellville AR U.S.A.
140 B3 Russellville KY U.S.A.
101 D2 Rüsselsheim Ger.
Russia country Asia/Europe
123 C2 Rustenburg S. Africa
142 B2 Ruston U.S.A.
98 B2 Ruthin U.K.
141 E2 Rutland U.S.A.
119 E4 Ruvuma r. Moz./Tanz.
79 C2 Ruweis U.A.E.
77 C1 Ruzayevka Kazakh.
87 D3 Ruzayevka Russia
119 C3 Rwanda country Africa
89 E3 Ryazan' Russia
89 F3 Ryazhsk Russia
86 C2 Rybachiy, Poluostrov pen. Russia
89 E2 Rybinsk Russia
89 E2 Rybinskoye Vodokhranilishche resr Russia
103 D1 Rybnik Pol.
89 E3 Rybnoye Russia
99 D3 Rye U.K.
89 D3 Ryl'sk Russia
67 C3 Ryōtsu Japan
69 E3 Ryukyu Islands Japan
103 E1 Rzeszów Pol.
89 D2 Rzhev Russia

S

79 C2 Sa'ādatābād Iran
101 E2 Saale r. Ger.
101 E2 Saalfeld/Saale Ger.
102 B2 Saarbrücken Ger.
88 B2 Saaremaa i. Estonia
92 I2 Saarenkylä Fin.
93 I3 Saarijärvi Fin.
102 B2 Saarlouis Ger.
80 B2 Sab' Ābār Syria
107 D1 Sabadell Spain
61 C1 Sabah state Malaysia
61 C2 Sabalana i. Indon.
155 D1 Sabará Brazil
108 B2 Sabaudia Italy
115 D2 Sabhā Libya
123 D2 Sabie r. Moz./S. Africa
145 B2 Sabinas Mex.
145 B2 Sabinas Hidalgo Mex.
131 D2 Sable, Cape Can.
143 D3 Sable, Cape U.S.A.
131 E2 Sable Island Can.
106 B1 Sabugal Port.
78 B3 Şabyā Saudi Arabia
81 C2 Sabzevār Iran
120 A2 Sachanga Angola
65 B3 Sacheon S. Korea
130 A1 Sachigo Lake Can.
126 C2 Sachs Harbour Can.
135 B3 Sacramento U.S.A.
138 B2 Sacramento Mountains U.S.A.
135 B2 Sacramento Valley U.S.A.
123 C3 Sada S. Africa
107 C1 Sádaba Spain
78 B3 Şa'dah Yemen
62 A1 Sadiya India
67 C3 Sadoga-shima i. Japan

107 D2 **Sa Dragonera** *i.* Spain
76 C3 **Safēd Kōh, Silsilah-ye** *mts* Afgh.
93 F4 **Säffle** Sweden
138 B2 **Safford** U.S.A.
99 D2 **Saffron Walden** U.K.
114 B1 **Safi** Morocco
86 D2 **Safonovo** *Arkhangel'skaya Oblast'* Russia
89 D2 **Safonovo** *Smolenskaya Oblast'* Russia
75 C2 **Saga** China
67 B4 **Saga** Japan
62 A1 **Sagaing** Myanmar
67 C3 **Sagamihara** Japan
75 B2 **Sagar** India
140 C2 **Saginaw** U.S.A.
140 C2 **Saginaw Bay** U.S.A.
106 B2 **Sagres** Port.
146 B2 **Sagua la Grande** Cuba
141 F1 **Saguenay** *r.* Can.
       Sagunt Spain *see* Sagunto/ Sagunt
107 C2 **Sagunto/Sagunt** Spain
76 B2 **Sagyndyk, Mys** *pt* Kazakh.
114 C3 **Sahara** *des.* Africa
       Saharan Atlas *mts* Alg. *see* Atlas Saharien
75 B2 **Saharanpur** India
73 **Saharsa** India
114 B3 **Sahel** *reg.* Africa
144 B2 **Sahuayo** Mex.
78 B2 **Şāḥuq** *reg.* Saudi Arabia
       Saïda Lebanon *see* Sidon
75 C2 **Saidpur** Bangl.
       Saigon Vietnam *see* Ho Chi Minh City
62 A1 **Saiha** India
69 D2 **Saihan Tal** China
67 B4 **Saiki** Japan
93 I3 **Saimaa** *l.* Fin.
144 B2 **Sain Alto** Mex.
99 C3 **St Abb's Head** U.K.
99 C3 **St Albans** U.K.
99 B3 **St Aldhelm's Head** U.K.
96 C3 **St Andrews** U.K.
131 E1 **St Anthony** Can.
134 D2 **St Anthony** U.S.A.
52 B3 **St Arnaud** Austr.
131 E1 **St-Augustin** Can.
131 E1 **St Augustin** *r.* Can.
143 D3 **St Augustine** U.S.A.
99 A3 **St Austell** U.K.
104 C2 **St-Avertin** France
98 B1 **St Bees Head** U.K.
105 D3 **St-Bonnet-en-Champsaur** France
99 A3 **St Bride's Bay** U.K.
104 B2 **St-Brieuc** France
99 C3 **St Catharines** France
99 C3 **St Catherine's Point** U.K.
137 E3 **St Charles** U.S.A.
140 C2 **St Clair, Lake** Can./U.S.A.
105 D2 **St-Claude** France
137 E1 **St Cloud** U.S.A.
104 A1 **St Croix** *r.* U.S.A.
147 D3 **St Croix** *i.* Virgin Is (U.S.A.)
105 C2 **St-Dizier** France
131 D2 **Ste-Anne-des-Monts** Can.
105 D2 **St-Égrève** France
137 E3 **St Elias Mountains** Can.
131 D1 **Ste-Marguerite** *r.* Can.
129 E2 **Sainte Rose du Lac** Can.
104 C2 **Saintes** France
105 D2 **St-Étienne** France
108 A2 **St-Florent** Corsica France
105 C2 **St-Flour** France

136 C3 **St Francis** U.S.A.
104 C3 **St-Gaudens** France
53 C1 **St George** Austr.
135 D3 **St George** U.S.A.
143 D3 **St George Island** U.S.A.
131 C2 **St-Georges** Can.
147 D3 **St George's** Grenada
97 C3 **St George's Channel** Ireland/ U.K.
105 C2 **St Gotthard Pass** Switz.
113 E8 **St Helena** *i.* S. Atlantic Ocean
113 D8 **St Helena, Ascension and Tristan da Cunha** *terr.* S. Atlantic Ocean
122 A3 **St Helena Bay** S. Africa
122 A3 **St Helena Bay** S. Africa
98 B2 **St Helens** U.K.
134 B1 **St Helens, Mount** *vol.* U.S.A.
95 C4 **St Helier** Channel Is
100 B2 **St-Hubert** Belgium
141 E1 **St-Hyacinthe** Can.
140 C1 **St Ignace** U.S.A.
130 B2 **St Ignace Island** Can.
99 A3 **St Ives** U.K.
128 A2 **St James, Cape** Can.
131 C2 **St-Jean, Lac** *l.* Can.
104 B2 **St-Jean-d'Angély** France
104 B2 **St-Jean-de-Monts** France
130 C2 **St-Jean-sur-Richelieu** Can.
141 E1 **St-Jérôme** Can.
134 C1 **St Joe** *r.* U.S.A.
131 D2 **Saint John** Can.
141 F1 **St John** *r.* U.S.A.
147 D3 **St John's** Antigua
131 E2 **St John's** Can.
138 B2 **St Johns** U.S.A.
141 E2 **St Johnsbury** U.S.A.
137 E3 **St Joseph** U.S.A.
130 A1 **St Joseph, Lake** Can.
130 B2 **St Joseph Island** Can.
104 C2 **St-Junien** France
94 B2 **St Kilda** *i.* U.K.
147 D3 **St Kitts and Nevis** *country* West Indies
       St-Laurent, Golfe du *g.* Can. *see* St Lawrence, Gulf of
151 C1 **St-Laurent-du-Maroni** Fr. Guiana
131 D2 **St Lawrence** *inlet* Can.
131 D2 **St Lawrence, Gulf of** Can.
83 N2 **St Lawrence Island** U.S.A.
104 B2 **St-Lô** France
114 A3 **St-Louis** Senegal
137 E3 **St Louis** *r.* U.S.A.
137 E3 **St Louis** U.S.A.
147 D3 **St Lucia** *country* West Indies
123 D2 **St Lucia Estuary** S. Africa
104 B2 **St-Malo** France
104 B2 **St-Malo, Golfe de** *g.* France
122 A3 **St Martin, Cape** S. Africa
141 D2 **St Marys** U.S.A.
130 C2 **St-Maurice** *r.* Can.
104 B2 **St-Nazaire** France
104 C1 **St-Omer** France
129 C2 **St Paul** Can.
137 E2 **St Paul** U.S.A.
137 E2 **St Peter** U.S.A.
95 C4 **St Peter Port** Channel Is
89 D2 **St Petersburg** Russia
143 D3 **St Petersburg** U.S.A.
131 E2 **St-Pierre** St Pierre and Miquelon
131 E2 **St Pierre and Miquelon** *terr.* N. America
104 B2 **St-Pierre-d'Oléron** France
105 C2 **St-Pourçain-sur-Sioule** France
131 D2 **St Quentin** Can.
105 C2 **St-Quentin** France

131 D2 **St-Siméon** Can.
129 E2 **St Theresa Point** Can.
130 B2 **St Thomas** Can.
105 D3 **St-Tropez** France
105 D3 **St-Tropez, Cap de** *c.* France
52 A3 **St Vincent, Gulf** Austr.
147 D3 **St Vincent and the Grenadines** *country* West Indies
100 C2 **St-Vith** Belgium
129 C2 **St Walburg** Can.
104 C2 **St-Yrieix-la-Perche** France
59 D1 **Saipan** *i.* N. Mariana Is
152 B2 **Sajama, Nevado** *mt.* Bol.
122 B2 **Sak** *watercourse* S. Africa
67 C4 **Sakai** Japan
67 B4 **Sakaide** Japan
78 B2 **Sakākā** Saudi Arabia
136 C1 **Sakakawea, Lake** U.S.A.
111 D2 **Sakarya** *r.* Turkey
66 C3 **Sakata** Japan
65 B1 **Sakchu** N. Korea
83 K3 **Sakhalin** *i.* Russia
123 C2 **Sakhile** S. Africa
81 C1 **Şäki** Azer.
88 B3 **Šakiai** Lith.
69 E3 **Sakishima-shotō** *is* Japan
62 B2 **Sakon Nakhon** Thai.
122 B3 **Sakrivier** S. Africa
67 D3 **Sakura** Japan
91 C2 **Saky** Ukr.
93 G4 **Sala** Sweden
130 C2 **Salaberry-de-Valleyfield** Can.
88 B2 **Salacgrīva** Latvia
109 C2 **Sala Consilina** Italy
135 C4 **Salada, Laguna** *salt l.* Mex.
152 B4 **Salado** *r.* Arg.
145 C2 **Salado** *r.* Mex.
114 B4 **Salaga** Ghana
122 B1 **Salajwe** Botswana
115 D3 **Salal** Chad
78 A2 **Salālā** Sudan
79 C3 **Şalālah** Oman
145 B2 **Salamanca** Mex.
106 B1 **Salamanca** Spain
106 B1 **Salas** Spain
63 B2 **Salavan** Laos
59 C3 **Salawati** *i.* Indon.
58 C3 **Salayar** *i.* Indon.
104 C2 **Salbris** France
88 C3 **Šalčininkai** Lith.
106 C1 **Saldaña** Spain
122 A3 **Saldanha** S. Africa
88 B2 **Saldus** Latvia
53 C3 **Sale** Austr.
86 F2 **Salekhard** Russia
73 B3 **Salem** India
137 E3 **Salem** MO U.S.A.
134 B2 **Salem** OR U.S.A.
96 B2 **Salen** U.K.
109 B2 **Salerno** Italy
98 B2 **Salford** U.K.
151 E2 **Salgado** *r.* Brazil
103 D2 **Salgótarján** Hungary
151 E2 **Salgueiro** Brazil
136 B3 **Salida** U.S.A.
111 C3 **Salihli** Turkey
88 C3 **Salihorsk** Belarus
121 C2 **Salima** Malawi
121 C2 **Salimo** Moz.
137 D3 **Salina** U.S.A.
108 B3 **Salina, Isola** *i.* Italy
145 C3 **Salina Cruz** Mex.
155 D1 **Salinas** Brazil
144 B2 **Salinas** Mex.
135 B3 **Salinas** U.S.A.
107 D2 **Salines, Cap de ses** *c.* Spain
151 D2 **Salinópolis** Brazil

Salisbury

99 C3 Salisbury U.K.
141 D3 Salisbury MD U.S.A.
143 D1 Salisbury NC U.S.A.
99 B3 Salisbury Plain U.K.
151 D2 Salitre r. Brazil
92 I2 Salla Fin.
127 F2 Salluit Can.
75 C2 Sallyana Nepal
81 C2 Salmās Iran
134 D1 Salmon U.S.A.
134 C1 Salmon r. U.S.A.
128 C2 Salmon Arm Can.
134 C2 Salmon River Mountains U.S.A.
100 C3 Salmtal Ger.
93 H3 Salo Fin.
87 D4 Sal'sk Russia
122 B3 Salt watercourse S. Africa
138 A2 Salt r. U.S.A.
152 B3 Salta Arg.
145 B2 Saltillo Mex.
134 D2 Salt Lake City U.S.A.
154 C2 Salto Brazil
154 C2 Salto Uru.
155 E1 Salto da Divisa Brazil
154 B2 Salto del Guairá Para.
135 C4 Salton Sea salt l. U.S.A.
143 D2 Saluda U.S.A.
108 A2 Saluzzo Italy
151 E3 Salvador Brazil
79 C2 Salwah Saudi Arabia
62 A2 Salween r. China/Myanmar
81 C2 Salyan Azer.
102 C2 Salzburg Austria
101 E1 Salzgitter Ger.
101 D2 Salzkotten Ger.
101 E1 Salzwedel Ger.
144 B1 Samalayuca Mex.
66 D2 Samani Japan
64 B1 Samar i. Phil.
87 E3 Samara Russia
61 C2 Samarinda Indon.
77 C3 Samarqand Uzbek.
81 C2 Sāmarrā' Iraq
81 C1 Şamaxı Azer.
119 C3 Samba Dem. Rep. Congo
75 C2 Sambalpur India
61 B1 Sambar, Tanjung pt Indon.
61 B1 Sambas Indon.
121 DE2 Sambava Madag.
90 A2 Sambir Ukr.
153 C4 Samborombón, Bahía b. Arg.
65 B2 Samcheok S. Korea
81 C2 Samdi Dag mt. Turkey
119 D3 Same Tanz.
78 B2 Samirah Saudi Arabia
65 B1 Samjiyŏn N. Korea
49 G3 Samoa country
S. Pacific Ocean
109 C1 Samobor Croatia
111 C3 Samos i. Greece
111 C3 Samothraki Greece
111 C3 Samothraki i. Greece
61 C2 Sampit Indon.
119 C3 Sampwe Dem. Rep. Congo
63 B2 Sâmraông Cambodia
139 E2 Sam Rayburn Reservoir U.S.A.
80 B1 Samsun Turkey
81 C1 Samt'redia Georgia
63 B3 Samui, Ko i. Thai.
63 B2 Samut Songkhram Thai.
114 B3 San Mali
78 B3 Şan'ā' Yemen
118 A2 Sanaga r. Cameroon
81 C2 Sanandaj Iran
146 B3 San Andrés, Isla de i. Caribbean Sea
138 B2 San Andres Mountains U.S.A.

145 C3 San Andrés Tuxtla Mex.
139 C2 San Angelo U.S.A.
139 D3 San Antonio U.S.A.
135 C4 San Antonio, Mount U.S.A.
152 B3 San Antonio de los Cobres Arg.
153 B5 San Antonio Oeste Arg.
108 A2 San Benedetto del Tronto Italy
144 A3 San Benedicto, Isla i. Mex.
135 C4 San Bernardino U.S.A.
135 C4 San Bernardino Mountains U.S.A.
143 C3 San Blas, Cape U.S.A.
152 B2 San Borja Bol.
144 B2 San Buenaventura Mex.
64 B1 San Carlos Phil.
147 D4 San Carlos Venez.
153 A5 San Carlos de Bariloche Arg.
147 C4 San Carlos del Zulia Venez.
153 A5 San Clemente, Monte mt. Chile
135 C4 San Clemente Island U.S.A.
104 C2 Sancoins France
150 A1 San Cristóbal Venez.
145 C3 San Cristóbal de las Casas Mex.
146 C2 Sancti Spíritus Cuba
61 C1 Sandakan Sabah Malaysia
93 E3 Sandane Norway
111 B2 Sandanski Bulg.
96 C1 Sanday i. U.K.
139 C2 Sanderson U.S.A.
150 B3 Sandia Peru
135 C4 San Diego U.S.A.
80 B2 Sandıklı Turkey
93 E4 Sandnes Norway
92 F2 Sandnessjøen Norway
118 C3 Sandoa Dem. Rep. Congo
103 E1 Sandomierz Pol.
89 E2 Sandovo Russia
94 B1 Sandoy i. Faroe Is
134 C1 Sandpoint U.S.A.
71 B3 Sandu China
94 B1 Sandur Faroe Is
140 C2 Sandusky U.S.A.
122 A3 Sandveld mts S. Africa
93 F4 Sandvika Norway
93 G3 Sandviken Sweden
131 E1 Sandwich Bay Can.
129 D2 Sandy Bay Can.
51 E2 Sandy Cape Austr.
130 A1 Sandy Lake Can.
130 A1 Sandy Lake l. Can.
144 A1 San Felipe Baja California Mex.
145 B2 San Felipe Guanajuato Mex.
150 B1 San Felipe Venez.
144 A2 San Fernando Baja California Mex.
145 C2 San Fernando Tamaulipas Mex.
64 B1 San Fernando La Union Phil.
64 B1 San Fernando Pampanga Phil.
106 B2 San Fernando Spain
147 D3 San Fernando Trin. and Tob.
150 B1 San Fernando de Apure Venez.
143 D3 Sanford FL U.S.A.
141 E2 Sanford ME U.S.A.
152 B4 San Francisco Arg.
138 A2 San Francisco U.S.A.
74 B3 Sangamner India
83 J2 Sangar Russia
108 A3 San Gavino Monreale Sardinia Italy
101 E2 Sangerhausen Ger.
61 C1 Sanggau Indon.

118 B3 Sangha r. Congo
59 C2 Sangihe, Kepulauan is Indon.
64 B2 Sangihe Besar i. Indon.
109 C3 San Giovanni in Fiore Italy
65 B2 Sangju S. Korea
61 C1 Sangkulirang Indon.
73 B3 Sangli India
118 B2 Sangmélima Cameroon
121 C3 Sango Zimbabwe
136 B3 Sangre de Cristo Range mts U.S.A.
75 C2 Sangsang China
144 A2 San Hipólito, Punta pt Mex.
144 A2 San Ignacio Mex.
130 C1 Sanikiluaq Can.
71 A3 Sanjiang China
135 B3 San Joaquin r. U.S.A.
153 B5 San Jorge, Golfo de g. Arg.
146 B4 San José Costa Rica
64 B1 San Jose Nueva Ecija Phil.
64 B1 San Jose Occidental Mindoro Phil.
135 B3 San Jose U.S.A.
144 A2 San José, Isla i. Mex.
144 B2 San José de Bavicora Mex.
64 B1 San José de Buenavista Phil.
144 A2 San José de Comondú Mex.
144 B2 San José del Cabo Mex.
150 A1 San José del Guaviare Col.
152 B4 San Juan Arg.
146 B3 San Juan r. Costa Rica/Nic.
147 D3 San Juan Puerto Rico
135 D3 San Juan r. U.S.A.
145 C3 San Juan Bautista Tuxtepec Mex.
134 B1 San Juan Islands U.S.A.
152 B4 San Juanito Mex.
136 B3 San Juan Mountains U.S.A.
75 C2 Sankh r. India
105 D2 Sankt Gallen Switz.
105 D2 Sankt Moritz Switz.
Sankt-Peterburg Russia see St Petersburg
102 C2 Sankt Veit an der Glan Austria
100 C3 Sankt Wendel Ger.
80 B2 Şanlıurfa Turkey
138 B3 San Lorenzo Mex.
106 B2 Sanlúcar de Barrameda Spain
153 B4 San Luis Arg.
145 B2 San Luis de la Paz Mex.
138 A2 San Luisito Mex.
135 B3 San Luis Obispo U.S.A.
145 B2 San Luis Potosí Mex.
144 A1 San Luis Río Colorado Mex.
139 D3 San Marcos U.S.A.
108 B2 San Marino country Europe
108 B2 San Marino San Marino
144 B2 San Martín de Bolaños Mex.
153 A5 San Martín de los Andes Arg.
153 B5 San Matías, Golfo g. Arg.
70 B2 Sanmenxia China
146 B3 San Miguel El Salvador
152 B3 San Miguel de Tucumán Arg.
145 C3 San Miguel Sola de Vega Mex.
71 B3 Sanming China
153 B4 San Nicolás de los Arroyos Arg.
135 C4 San Nicolas Island U.S.A.
123 C2 Sannieshof S. Africa
103 E2 Sanok Pol.
64 B1 San Pablo Phil.
144 B2 San Pablo Balleza Mex.
152 B3 San Pedro Arg.
152 B2 San Pedro Bol.
114 B4 San Pedro Côte d'Ivoire
144 A2 San Pedro Mex.
138 A2 San Pedro watercourse U.S.A.

06 B2 San Pedro, Sierra de mts Spain
44 B2 San Pedro de las Colonias Mex.
46 B3 San Pedro Sula Hond.
08 A3 San Pietro, Isola di i. Sardinia Italy
44 A1 San Quintín, Cabo c. Mex.
53 B4 San Rafael Arg.
08 A2 Sanremo Italy
46 B3 San Salvador El Salvador
52 B3 San Salvador de Jujuy Arg.
San Sebastián Spain see Donostia/San Sebastián
09 C2 San Severo Italy
09 C2 Sanski Most Bos. & Herz.
52 B2 Santa Ana Bol.
46 B3 Santa Ana El Salvador
44 A1 Santa Ana Mex.
35 C4 Santa Ana U.S.A.
44 B2 Santa Bárbara Mex.
35 C4 Santa Barbara U.S.A.
54 B2 Santa Bárbara, Serra de hills Brazil
50 B2 Santa Clara Col.
46 C2 Santa Clara Cuba
35 C4 Santa Clarita U.S.A.
09 C3 Santa Croce, Capo c. Sicily Italy
53 B6 Santa Cruz r. Arg.
52 B2 Santa Cruz Bol.
64 B1 Santa Cruz Phil.
35 B3 Santa Cruz U.S.A.
45 C3 Santa Cruz Barillas Guat.
55 E1 Santa Cruz Cabrália Brazil
07 C2 Santa Cruz de Moya Spain
14 A2 Santa Cruz de Tenerife Canary Islands
35 C4 Santa Cruz Island U.S.A.
48 F3 Santa Cruz Islands Solomon Is
52 B4 Santa Fe Arg.
38 B1 Santa Fe U.S.A.
54 B1 Santa Helena de Goiás Brazil
53 B4 Santa Isabel Arg.
54 B1 Santa Luisa, Serra de hills Brazil
52 B3 Santa María Brazil
44 B1 Santa María r. Mex.
35 B4 Santa María U.S.A.
23 D2 Santa María, Cabo de c. Moz.
06 B2 Santa Maria, Cabo de c. Port.
51 D2 Santa Maria das Barreiras Brazil
09 C3 Santa Maria di Leuca, Capo c. Italy
50 A1 Santa Marta Col.
35 C4 Santa Monica U.S.A.
51 C2 Santana Amapá Brazil
51 C3 Santana Bahia Brazil
06 C1 Santander Spain
08 A3 Sant'Antioco Sardinia Italy
08 A3 Sant'Antioco, Isola di i. Sardinia Italy
07 D2 Sant Antoni de Portmany Spain
51 C2 Santarém Brazil
06 B2 Santarém Port.
54 B1 Santa Rita do Araguaia Brazil
53 B4 Santa Rosa Arg.
52 C3 Santa Rosa Brazil
35 B3 Santa Rosa CA U.S.A.
38 C2 Santa Rosa NM U.S.A.
46 B3 Santa Rosa de Copán Hond.
35 B4 Santa Rosa Island U.S.A.
08 A3 Santa Rosalía Mex.
07 D2 Sant Francesc de Formentera Spain

152 C3 Santiago Brazil
153 A4 Santiago Chile
147 C3 Santiago Dom. Rep.
144 B2 Santiago Mex.
146 B4 Santiago Panama
64 B1 Santiago Phil.
106 B1 Santiago de Compostela Spain
144 B2 Santiago Ixcuintla Mex.
144 B2 Santiago Papasquiaro Mex.
107 D2 Sant Joan de Labritja Spain
107 D1 Sant Jordi, Golf de g. Spain
155 D2 Santo Amaro de Campos Brazil
155 D2 Santo André Brazil
152 C3 Santo Ângelo Brazil
154 B2 Santo Antônio da Platina Brazil
151 E3 Santo Antônio de Jesus Brazil
150 B2 Santo Antônio do Içá Brazil
155 C2 Santo Antônio do Monte Brazil
147 D3 Santo Domingo Dom. Rep.
138 B1 Santo Domingo Pueblo U.S.A.
111 C3 Santorini i. Greece
155 C2 Santos Brazil
152 C3 Santo Tomé Brazil
146 B3 San Vicente El Salvador
144 A1 San Vicente Mex.
150 A3 San Vicente de Cañete Peru
108 B2 San Vincenzo Italy
108 B3 San Vito, Capo c. Sicily Italy
71 A4 Sanya China
155 C2 São Bernardo do Campo Brazil
152 C3 São Borja Brazil
152 C3 São Carlos Brazil
151 C3 São Félix do Araguaia Brazil
151 C2 São Félix do Xingu Brazil
155 D2 São Fidélis Brazil
155 D1 São Francisco Brazil
151 E3 São Francisco r. Brazil
154 C3 São Francisco, Ilha de i. Brazil
154 C3 São Francisco do Sul Brazil
152 C4 São Gabriel Brazil
150 B2 São Gabriel da Cachoeira Brazil
155 D2 São Gonçalo Brazil
155 C1 São Gotardo Brazil
155 C2 São João da Barra Brazil
155 C2 São João de Boa Vista Brazil
106 B1 São João da Madeira Port.
155 D1 São João do Paraíso Brazil
155 C2 São João Nepomuceno Brazil
155 D1 São Joaquim da Barra Brazil
154 C3 São José do Rio Preto Brazil
155 C2 São José dos Campos Brazil
154 C3 São José dos Pinhais Brazil
155 C2 São Lourenço Brazil
151 D2 São Luís Brazil
154 C2 São Manuel Brazil
154 C1 São Marcos r. Brazil
151 D2 São Marcos, Baía de b. Brazil
155 E1 São Mateus Brazil
155 C2 São Paulo Brazil
151 D2 São Raimundo Nonato Brazil
155 C1 São Romão Brazil
154 C2 São Sebastião, Ilha do i. Brazil
154 C3 São Sebastião do Paraíso Brazil
154 B1 São Simão Brazil
154 B1 São Simão, Barragem de resr Brazil
113 F6 São Tomé São Tomé and Príncipe
155 D2 São Tomé, Cabo de c. Brazil
113 F6 São Tomé and Príncipe country Africa

155 C2 São Vicente Brazil
106 B2 São Vicente, Cabo de c. Port.
59 C3 Saparua Indon.
89 F3 Sapozhok Russia
66 D2 Sapporo Japan
109 C2 Sapri Italy
81 C2 Saqqez Iran
81 C2 Sarāb Iran
63 B2 Sara Buri Thai.
109 C2 Sarajevo Bos. & Herz.
76 B1 Saraktash Russia
141 E2 Saranac Lake U.S.A.
109 D3 Sarandë Albania
64 B2 Sarangani Islands Phil.
87 D3 Saransk Russia
87 E3 Sarapul Russia
143 D3 Sarasota U.S.A.
90 B2 Sarata Ukr.
136 B2 Saratoga U.S.A.
141 E2 Saratoga Springs U.S.A.
61 C1 Saratok Sarawak Malaysia
87 D3 Saratov Russia
79 D2 Sarāvān Iran
61 C1 Sarawak state Malaysia
110 C2 Saray Turkey
111 C3 Sarayköy Turkey
79 D2 Sarbāz Iran
74 B2 Sardarshahr India
Sardegna i. Italy see Sardinia
108 A2 Sardinia i. Italy
92 G2 Sarektjåkkå mt. Sweden
77 C3 Sar-e Pul Afgh.
158 B3 Sargasso Sea N. Atlantic Ocean
74 B1 Sargodha Pak.
115 D4 Sarh Chad
81 D2 Sarhad reg. Iran
81 D2 Sārī Iran
111 C3 Sangöl Turkey
81 C1 Sarıkamış Turkey
61 C1 Sarikei Sarawak Malaysia
51 D2 Sarina Austr.
65 B2 Sariwŏn N. Korea
111 C2 Sarıyer Turkey
78 B2 Sark, Safrā' as esc. Saudi Arabia
77 D2 Sarkand Kazakh.
111 C2 Şarköy Turkey
59 D3 Sarmi Indon.
140 C2 Sarnia Can.
90 B1 Sarny Ukr.
60 B2 Sarolangun Indon.
111 B3 Saronikos Kolpos g. Greece
111 C2 Saros Körfezi b. Turkey
87 D3 Sarov Russia
105 D2 Sarrebourg France
106 B1 Sarria Spain
107 C1 Sarrión Spain
105 D3 Sartène Corsica France
103 D2 Sárvár Hungary
77 D1 Saryarka plain Kazakh.
76 B2 Sarykamysh, Lake salt l. Turkm./Uzbek.
77 D2 Saryozek Kazakh.
77 D2 Saryshagan Kazakh.
82 F3 Sarysu watercourse Kazakh.
77 D3 Sary-Tash Kyrg.
75 C2 Sasaram India
67 A4 Sasebo Japan
129 D2 Saskatchewan prov. Can.
129 D2 Saskatchewan r. Can.
129 D2 Saskatoon Can.
83 I2 Saskylakh Russia
74 B1 S. A. S. Nagar India
123 C2 Sasolburg S. Africa
87 D3 Sasovo Russia
114 B4 Sassandra Côte d'Ivoire
108 A2 Sassari Sardinia Italy

102 C1 **Sassnitz** Ger.
114 A3 **Satadougou** Mali
123 D1 **Satara** S. Africa
75 C2 **Satna** India
74 B2 **Satpura Range** *mts* India
67 B4 **Satsuma-Sendai** Japan
63 B2 **Sattahip** Thai.
110 B1 **Satu Mare** Romania
63 B3 **Satun** Thai.
144 B2 **Saucillo** Mex.
93 E4 **Sauda** Norway
92 □B2 **Sauðárkrókur** Iceland
78 B2 **Saudi Arabia** *country* Asia
105 C3 **Saugues** France
105 C2 **Saulieu** France
130 B2 **Sault Sainte Marie** Can.
140 C1 **Sault Sainte Marie** U.S.A.
77 C1 **Saumalkol'** Kazakh.
59 C3 **Saumlaki** Indon.
104 B2 **Saumur** France
120 B1 **Saurimo** Angola
109 D2 **Sava** *r.* Europe
49 G3 **Savai'i** *i.* Samoa
91 E1 **Savala** *r.* Russia
143 D2 **Savannah** *GA* U.S.A.
142 C1 **Savannah** *TN* U.S.A.
143 D2 **Savannah** *r.* U.S.A.
63 B2 **Savannakhét** Laos
130 A1 **Savant Lake** Can.
111 C3 **Savaştepe** Turkey
89 F2 **Savino** Russia
86 D2 **Savinskiy** Russia
108 A2 **Savona** Italy
93 I3 **Savonlinna** Fin.
92 I2 **Savukoski** Fin.
Savu Sea Indon. *see* **Sawu, Laut**
74 B2 **Sawai Madhopur** India
62 A2 **Sawankhalok** Thai.
136 B3 **Sawatch Range** *mts* U.S.A.
53 D2 **Sawtell** Austr.
59 C3 **Sawu, Laut** *sea* Indon.
79 C3 **Sayḩūt** Yemen
69 D2 **Saynshand** Mongolia
141 D2 **Sayre** U.S.A.
144 B3 **Sayula** *Jalisco* Mex.
145 C3 **Sayula** *Veracruz* Mex.
128 B2 **Sayward** Can.
89 E2 **Sazonovo** Russia
114 B2 **Sbaa** Alg.
98 B1 **Scafell Pike** *h.* U.K.
109 C3 **Scalea** Italy
96 C1 **Scapa Flow** *inlet* U.K.
130 C2 **Scarborough** Can.
147 D3 **Scarborough** Trin. and Tob.
98 C1 **Scarborough** U.K.
64 A1 **Scarborough Reef** *sea feature* S. China Sea
96 A2 **Scarinish** U.K.
Scarpanto *i.* Greece *see* **Karpathos**
105 D2 **Schaffhausen** Switz.
100 B1 **Schagen** Neth.
102 C2 **Schärding** Austria
100 A2 **Scharendijke** Neth.
101 D1 **Scharhörn** *i.* Ger.
101 D1 **Scheeßel** Ger.
131 D1 **Schefferville** Can.
135 D3 **Schell Creek Range** *mts* U.S.A.
141 E2 **Schenectady** U.S.A.
101 E3 **Scheßlitz** Ger.
100 C1 **Schiermonnikoog** *i.* Neth.
108 B1 **Schio** Italy
101 F2 **Schkeuditz** Ger.
101 E1 **Schladen** Ger.
101 E2 **Schleiz** Ger.
102 B1 **Schleswig** Ger.
101 D2 **Schloß Holte-Stukenbrock** Ger.
101 D2 **Schlüchtern** Ger.
101 E3 **Schlüsselfeld** Ger.
101 D2 **Schmallenberg** Ger.
101 D1 **Schneverdingen** Ger.
101 E1 **Schönebeck (Elbe)** Ger.
101 E1 **Schöningen** Ger.
100 B2 **Schoonhoven** Neth.
59 D3 **Schouten Islands** P.N.G.
102 B2 **Schwäbische Alb** *mts* Ger.
102 C2 **Schwandorf** Ger.
61 C2 **Schwaner, Pegunungan** *mts* Indon.
101 E1 **Schwarzenbek** Ger.
101 F2 **Schwarzenberg/Erzgebirge** Ger.
122 A2 **Schwarzrand** *mts* Namibia
Schwarzwald *mts* Ger. *see* **Black Forest**
102 C2 **Schwaz** Austria
102 C1 **Schwedt/Oder** Ger.
101 E2 **Schweinfurt** Ger.
101 E1 **Schwerin** Ger.
101 E1 **Schweriner See** *l.* Ger.
105 D2 **Schwyz** Switz.
108 B3 **Sciacca** *Sicily* Italy
95 B4 **Scilly, Isles of** U.K.
140 C3 **Scioto** *r.* U.S.A.
136 B1 **Scobey** U.S.A.
53 D2 **Scone** Austr.
55 R3 **Scotia Ridge** S. Atlantic Ocean
158 C8 **Scotia Sea** S. Atlantic Ocean
96 C2 **Scotland** *admin. div.* U.K.
128 B2 **Scott, Cape** Can.
123 D3 **Scottburgh** S. Africa
136 C3 **Scott City** U.S.A.
136 C2 **Scottsbluff** U.S.A.
142 C2 **Scottsboro** U.S.A.
96 B1 **Scourie** U.K.
141 D2 **Scranton** U.S.A.
98 C2 **Scunthorpe** U.K.
105 E2 **Scuol** Switz.
129 E2 **Seal** *r.* Can.
122 B3 **Seal, Cape** S. Africa
52 B3 **Sea Lake** Austr.
139 D3 **Sealy** U.S.A.
142 B1 **Searcy** U.S.A.
98 B1 **Seascale** U.K.
134 B1 **Seattle** U.S.A.
141 E2 **Sebago Lake** U.S.A.
144 A2 **Sebastián Vizcaíno, Bahía** *b.* Mex.
110 B1 **Sebeş** Romania
60 B2 **Sebesi** *i.* Indon.
88 C2 **Sebezh** Russia
80 B1 **Şebinkarahisar** Turkey
143 D3 **Sebring** U.S.A.
128 B3 **Sechelt** Can.
150 A2 **Sechura** Peru
73 B3 **Secunderabad** India
137 E3 **Sedalia** U.S.A.
105 C2 **Sedan** France
54 B2 **Seddon** N.Z.
138 A2 **Sedona** U.S.A.
101 E2 **Seeburg** Ger.
101 E1 **Seehausen (Altmark)** Ger.
122 A2 **Seeheim** Namibia
104 C2 **Sées** France
101 E2 **Seesen** Ger.
101 E1 **Seevetal** Ger.
123 C1 **Sefare** Botswana
60 B1 **Segamat** Malaysia
86 C2 **Segezha** Russia
114 B3 **Ségou** Mali
106 C1 **Segovia** Spain
115 D2 **Séguédine** Niger
114 B4 **Séguéla** Côte d'Ivoire
139 D3 **Seguin** U.S.A.
107 C2 **Segura** *r.* Spain
106 C2 **Segura, Sierra de** *mts* Spain
120 B3 **Sehithwa** Botswana
93 H3 **Seinäjoki** Fin.
104 C2 **Seine** *r.* France
104 B2 **Seine, Baie de** *b.* France
103 E1 **Sejny** Pol.
60 B2 **Sekayu** Indon.
114 B4 **Sekondi** Ghana
59 C3 **Selaru** *i.* Indon.
61 C2 **Selatan, Tanjung** *pt* Indon.
126 A2 **Selawik** U.S.A.
98 C2 **Selby** U.K.
120 B3 **Selebi-Phikwe** Botswana
105 D2 **Sélestat** France
92 □A3 **Selfoss** Iceland
114 A3 **Sélibabi** Maur.
138 A1 **Seligman** U.S.A.
116 A2 **Selîma Oasis** Sudan
111 C3 **Selimiye** Turkey
114 B3 **Sélingué, Lac de** *l.* Mali
89 D2 **Selizharovo** Russia
93 E4 **Seljord** Norway
129 E2 **Selkirk** Can.
96 C3 **Selkirk** U.K.
128 C2 **Selkirk Mountains** Can.
142 C2 **Selma** *AL* U.S.A.
135 C3 **Selma** *CA* U.S.A.
89 D3 **Sel'tso** Russia
150 A2 **Selvas** *reg.* Brazil
134 C1 **Selway** *r.* U.S.A.
129 D1 **Selwyn Lake** Can.
128 A1 **Selwyn Mountains** Can.
51 C2 **Selwyn Range** *hills* Austr.
60 B2 **Semangka, Teluk** *b.* Indon.
61 C2 **Semarang** Indon.
61 B1 **Sematan** *Sarawak* Malaysia
118 B2 **Sembé** Congo
81 C2 **Şemdinli** Turkey
91 C1 **Semenivka** Ukr.
86 D3 **Semenov** Russia
61 C2 **Semeru, Gunung** *vol.* Indon.
77 E1 **Semey** Kazakh.
89 E3 **Semiluki** Russia
136 B2 **Seminoe Reservoir** U.S.A.
139 C2 **Seminole** U.S.A.
143 D2 **Seminole, Lake** U.S.A.
61 C1 **Semitau** Indon.
81 D2 **Semnān** Iran
61 C1 **Semporna** *Sabah* Malaysia
105 C2 **Semur-en-Auxois** France
150 B2 **Sena Madureira** Brazil
120 B2 **Senanga** Zambia
67 D3 **Sendai** Japan
114 A3 **Senegal** *country* Africa
114 A3 **Sénégal** *r.* Maur./Senegal
102 C1 **Senftenberg** Ger.
119 D3 **Sengerema** Tanz.
151 D3 **Senhor do Bonfim** Brazil
108 B2 **Senigallia** Italy
109 B2 **Senj** Croatia
92 G2 **Senja** *i.* Norway
122 B2 **Senlac** S. Africa
104 C2 **Senlis** France
63 B2 **Sênmônoŭrôm** Cambodia
117 B3 **Sennar** Sudan
130 C2 **Senneterre** Can.
123 C3 **Senqu** *r.* Lesotho
105 C2 **Sens** France
109 D1 **Senta** Serbia
128 B2 **Sentinel Peak** Can.
123 C1 **Senwabarwana** S. Africa
65 B2 **Seocheon** S. Korea
65 B2 **Seongnam** S. Korea
75 B2 **Seoni** India
65 B2 **Seosan** S. Korea
65 B2 **Seoul** S. Korea
155 D2 **Sepetiba, Baía de** *b.* Brazil
59 D3 **Sepik** *r.* P.N.G.

61 C1 **Sepinang** Indon.
131 D1 **Sept-Îles** Can.
59 C3 **Seram** *i.* Indon.
59 C3 **Seram, Laut** *sea* Indon.
60 B2 **Serang** Indon.
109 D2 **Serbia** *country* Europe
109 D2 **Serbia and Montenegro** Europe
76 B3 **Serdar** Turkm.
89 E3 **Serebryanyye Prudy** Russia
60 B1 **Seremban** Malaysia
119 D3 **Serengeti Plain** Tanz.
87 D3 **Sergach** Russia
89 E2 **Sergiyev Posad** Russia
74 A1 **Serhetabat** Turkm.
61 C1 **Seria** Brunei
61 C1 **Serian** *Sarawak* Malaysia
111 B3 **Serifos** *i.* Greece
80 B2 **Serik** Turkey
59 C3 **Sermata, Kepulauan** *is* Indon.
86 F3 **Serov** Russia
120 B3 **Serowe** Botswana
106 B2 **Serpa** Port.
89 E3 **Serpukhov** Russia
151 D3 **Serra da Mesa, Represa** *resr* Brazil
154 B1 **Serranópolis** Brazil
100 A3 **Serre** *r.* France
111 B2 **Serres** Greece
151 E3 **Serrinha** Brazil
155 D1 **Serro** Brazil
154 C2 **Sertãozinho** Brazil
61 C2 **Seruyan** *r.* Indon.
68 C2 **Sêrxü** China
120 A2 **Sesfontein** Namibia
108 B2 **Sessa Aurunca** Italy
108 A2 **Sestri Levante** Italy
105 C3 **Sète** France
155 D1 **Sete Lagoas** Brazil
92 G2 **Setermoen** Norway
93 E4 **Setesdal** *val.* Norway
115 C1 **Sétif** Alg.
67 B4 **Seto-naikai** *sea* Japan
114 B1 **Settat** Morocco
98 B1 **Settle** U.K.
106 B2 **Setúbal** Port.
106 B2 **Setúbal, Baía de** *b.* Port.
130 A1 **Seul, Lac** *l.* Can.
76 A2 **Sevan, Lake** Armenia
Sevana Lich *l.* Armenia *see* **Sevan, Lake**
91 C3 **Sevastopol'** Ukr.
105 C3 **Sévérac-le-Château** France
130 B1 **Severn** *r.* Can.
122 B2 **Severn** S. Africa
99 B3 **Severn** *r.* U.K.
86 D2 **Severnaya Dvina** *r.* Russia
83 H1 **Severnaya Zemlya** *is* Russia
86 D2 **Severnyy** *Nenetskiy Avtonomnyy Okrug* Russia
86 F2 **Severnyy** *Respublika Komi* Russia
82 E1 **Severnyy, Ostrov** *i.* Russia
86 C2 **Severodvinsk** Russia
86 C2 **Severomorsk** Russia
91 D3 **Severskaya** Russia
135 D3 **Sevier** *r.* U.S.A.
135 D3 **Sevier Lake** U.S.A.
Sevilla Spain *see* **Seville**
106 B2 **Seville** Spain
128 A2 **Sewell Inlet** Can.
128 C2 **Sexsmith** Can.
144 B2 **Sextín** *r.* Mex.
86 G1 **Seyakha** Russia
113 J7 **Seychelles** *country* Indian Ocean
92 □C2 **Seyðisfjörður** Iceland
91 C1 **Seym** *r.* Russia/Ukr.
83 L2 **Seymchan** Russia
53 C3 **Seymour** Austr.
140 B3 **Seymour** *IN* U.S.A.
139 D2 **Seymour** *TX* U.S.A.
105 C2 **Sézanne** France
110 C1 **Sfântu Gheorghe** Romania
115 D1 **Sfax** Tunisia
's-Gravenhage Neth. *see* **The Hague**
96 A2 **Sgurr Alasdair** *h.* U.K.
70 A2 **Shaanxi** *prov.* China
91 D2 **Shabel'skoye** Russia
77 D3 **Shache** China
55 R1 **Shackleton Range** *mts* Antarctica
99 B3 **Shaftesbury** U.K.
75 C2 **Shahdol** India
77 C3 **Shāh Fōlād** *mt.* Afgh.
75 B2 **Shahjahanpur** India
81 D2 **Shahr-e Kord** Iran
81 D2 **Shahreẕā** Iran
77 C3 **Shahrisabz** Uzbek.
81 D2 **Shāhrūd** Iran
89 E2 **Shakhovskaya** Russia
91 E2 **Shakhty** Russia
86 D3 **Shakhun'ya** Russia
66 D2 **Shakotan-misaki** *c.* Japan
76 B2 **Shalkar** Kazakh.
68 C2 **Shaluli Shan** *mts* China
129 E2 **Shamattawa** Can.
139 C1 **Shamrock** U.S.A.
70 B2 **Shancheng** China
68 C2 **Shandan** China
70 B2 **Shandong** *prov.* China
70 C2 **Shandong Bandao** *pen.* China
121 B2 **Shangani** *r.* Zimbabwe
70 C2 **Shanghai** China
70 C2 **Shanghai** *mun.* China
71 B3 **Shanghang** China
70 A2 **Shangluo** China
71 B3 **Shangrao** China
70 B2 **Shangshui** China
70 C2 **Shangyu** China
69 E1 **Shangzhi** China
97 B2 **Shannon** *r.* Ireland
97 B2 **Shannon, Mouth of the** Ireland
71 B3 **Shantou** China
70 B2 **Shanxi** *prov.* China
71 B3 **Shaoguan** China
71 B3 **Shaowu** China
70 C2 **Shaoxing** China
71 B3 **Shaoyang** China
116 C2 **Shaqrā'** Saudi Arabia
90 B2 **Sharhorod** Ukr.
79 C2 **Sharjah** U.A.E.
88 C2 **Sharkawshchyna** Belarus
50 A2 **Shark Bay** Austr.
78 A2 **Sharm ash Shaykh** Egypt
140 C2 **Sharon** U.S.A.
86 D3 **Shar'ya** Russia
121 B3 **Shashe** *r.* Botswana/Zimbabwe
117 B4 **Shashemenē** Eth.
134 B2 **Shasta, Mount** *vol.* U.S.A.
134 B2 **Shasta Lake** U.S.A.
156 D3 **Shatsky Rise** *sea feature* N. Pacific Ocean
89 E2 **Shatura** Russia
129 D3 **Shaunavon** Can.
140 B2 **Shawano** U.S.A.
131 C2 **Shawinigan** Can.
139 D1 **Shawnee** U.S.A.
50 B2 **Shay Gap (abandoned)** Austr.
89 E3 **Shchekino** Russia
89 E2 **Shchelkovo** Russia
89 E3 **Shchigry** Russia
Shchors Ukr. *see* **Snovs'k**
88 B3 **Shchuchyn** Belarus
91 D1 **Shebekino** Russia
117 C4 **Shebelē Wenz, Wabē** *r.* Eth./Somalia
140 B2 **Sheboygan** U.S.A.
91 D3 **Shebsh** *r.* Russia
97 C2 **Sheelin, Lough** *l.* Ireland
98 C2 **Sheffield** U.K.
89 E2 **Sheksna** Russia
89 E2 **Sheksninskoye Vodokhranilishche** *resr* Russia
83 M2 **Shelagskiy, Mys** *pt* Russia
131 D2 **Shelburne** Can.
134 D1 **Shelby** U.S.A.
140 B3 **Shelbyville** *IN* U.S.A.
142 C1 **Shelbyville** *TN* U.S.A.
83 L2 **Shelikhova, Zaliv** *g.* Russia
129 D2 **Shellbrook** Can.
134 B1 **Shelton** U.S.A.
137 D2 **Shenandoah** U.S.A.
141 D3 **Shenandoah** *r.* U.S.A.
141 D3 **Shenandoah Mountains** U.S.A.
118 A2 **Shendam** Nigeria
86 D2 **Shenkursk** Russia
65 A1 **Shenyang** China
71 B3 **Shenzhen** China
90 B1 **Shepetivka** Ukr.
53 C3 **Shepparton** Austr.
99 D3 **Sheppey, Isle of** *i.* U.K.
131 D2 **Sherbrooke** *N.S.* Can.
131 C2 **Sherbrooke** *Que.* Can.
116 B3 **Shereiq** Sudan
136 B2 **Sheridan** U.S.A.
139 D2 **Sherman** U.S.A.
100 B2 **'s-Hertogenbosch** Neth.
96 □ **Shetland Islands** U.K.
76 B2 **Shetpe** Kazakh.
Shevchenko Kazakh. *see* **Aktau**
137 D1 **Sheyenne** *r.* U.S.A.
79 B3 **Shibām** Yemen
66 D2 **Shibetsu** Japan
77 C3 **Shibirghān** Afgh.
71 B3 **Shicheng** China
96 B2 **Shiel, Loch** *l.* U.K.
77 E2 **Shihezi** China
Shijiao China *see* **Fogang**
70 B2 **Shijiazhuang** China
74 A2 **Shikarpur** Pak.
67 B4 **Shikoku** *i.* Japan
66 D2 **Shikotsu-ko** *l.* Japan
86 D2 **Shilega** Russia
75 C2 **Shiliguri** India
75 D2 **Shillong** India
89 F3 **Shilovo** Russia
117 C3 **Shimbiris** *mt.* Somalia
67 C3 **Shimizu** Japan
Shimoga India *see* **Shivamogga**
67 B4 **Shimonoseki** Japan
96 B1 **Shin, Loch** *l.* U.K.
67 C4 **Shingū** Japan
123 D1 **Shingwedzi** S. Africa
123 D1 **Shingwedzi** *r.* S. Africa
119 D3 **Shinyanga** Tanz.
67 C4 **Shiono-misaki** *c.* Japan
138 B1 **Shiprock** U.S.A.
71 A3 **Shiqian** China
70 A2 **Shiquan** China
Shiquanhe China *see* **Gar**
Shiquan He *r.* China/Pak. *see* **Indus**
67 C3 **Shirane-san** *mt.* Japan
81 D3 **Shīrāz** Iran
66 D2 **Shiretoko-misaki** *c.* Japan
66 D2 **Shiriya-zaki** *c.* Japan
74 B2 **Shiv** India
73 B3 **Shivamogga** India
69 D1 **Shiveegovĭ** Mongolia

75 B2 **Shivpuri** India
70 B2 **Shiyan** China
70 B2 **Shizhong** China
70 A2 **Shizuishan** China
67 C4 **Shizuoka** Japan
89 D3 **Shklow** Belarus
109 C2 **Shkodër** Albania
83 H1 **Shmidta, Ostrov** *i.* Russia
135 C3 **Shoshone** U.S.A.
135 C3 **Shoshone Mountains** U.S.A.
123 C1 **Shoshong** Botswana
91 C1 **Shostka** Ukr.
70 B2 **Shouxian** China
138 A2 **Show Low** U.S.A.
91 C2 **Shpola** Ukr.
142 B2 **Shreveport** U.S.A.
99 B2 **Shrewsbury** U.K.
62 A1 **Shuangjiang** China
87 E4 **Shubarkudyk** Kazakh.
116 B1 **Shubrā al Khaymah** Egypt
89 D2 **Shugozero** Russia
120 B2 **Shumba** Zimbabwe
110 C2 **Shumen** Bulg.
88 C2 **Shumilina** Belarus
89 D3 **Shumyachi** Russia
126 A2 **Shungnak** U.S.A.
78 B3 **Shuqrah** Yemen
89 F2 **Shushkodom** Russia
81 C2 **Shūshtar** Iran
128 C2 **Shuswap Lake** Can.
89 F2 **Shuya** Russia
89 F2 **Shuyskoye** Russia
62 A1 **Shwebo** Myanmar
62 A1 **Shwedwin** Myanmar
62 A2 **Shwegyin** Myanmar
77 D2 **Shyganak** Kazakh.
77 C2 **Shymkent** Kazakh.
91 C2 **Shyroke** Ukr.
59 C3 **Sia** Indon.
74 A2 **Siahan Range** *mts* Pak.
74 B1 **Sialkot** Pak.
64 B2 **Siargao** *i.* Phil.
88 B2 **Šiauliai** Lith.
109 C2 **Šibenik** Croatia
83 I2 **Siberia** *reg.* Russia
60 A2 **Siberut** *i.* Indon.
74 A2 **Sibi** Pak.
110 B1 **Sibiu** Romania
60 A1 **Sibolga** Indon.
62 A1 **Sibsagar** India
61 C1 **Sibu** *Sarawak* Malaysia
118 B2 **Sibut** C.A.R.
64 B1 **Sibuyan** *i.* Phil.
64 B1 **Sibuyan Sea** Phil.
128 C2 **Sicamous** Can.
63 A3 **Sichon** Thai.
70 A2 **Sichuan** *prov.* China
70 A3 **Sichuan Pendi** *basin* China
105 D3 **Sicié, Cap** *c.* France
Sicilia *i.* Italy *see* **Sicily**
108 B3 **Sicilian Channel** Italy/Tunisia
108 B3 **Sicily** *i.* Italy
150 A3 **Sicuani** Peru
74 B2 **Siddhapur** India
111 C3 **Sideros, Akrotirio** *pt* Greece
107 D2 **Sidi Aïssa** Alg.
107 D2 **Sidi Ali** Alg.
114 B1 **Sidi Bel Abbès** Alg.
114 A2 **Sidi Ifni** Morocco
60 A1 **Sidikalang** Indon.
96 C2 **Sidlaw Hills** U.K.
99 B3 **Sidmouth** U.K.
134 B1 **Sidney** Can.
136 C1 **Sidney** *MT* U.S.A.
136 C2 **Sidney** *NE* U.S.A.
140 C2 **Sidney** *OH* U.S.A.
143 D2 **Sidney Lanier, Lake** U.S.A.
80 B2 **Sidon** Lebanon
154 B2 **Sidrolândia** Brazil
103 E1 **Siedlce** Pol.
100 C2 **Sieg** *r.* Ger.
100 D2 **Siegen** Ger.
63 B2 **Siĕm Réab** Cambodia
108 B2 **Siena** Italy
103 D1 **Sieradz** Pol.
153 B5 **Sierra Grande** Arg.
114 A4 **Sierra Leone** *country* Africa
144 B2 **Sierra Mojada** Mex.
138 A2 **Sierra Vista** U.S.A.
105 D2 **Sierre** Switz.
111 B3 **Sifnos** *i.* Greece
107 C2 **Sig** Alg.
127 H2 **Sigguup Nunaa** *pen.* Greenland
103 E2 **Sighetu Marmației** Romania
110 B1 **Sighișoara** Romania
60 A1 **Sigli** Indon.
92 □B2 **Siglufjörður** Iceland
102 B2 **Sigmaringen** Ger.
100 B3 **Signy-l'Abbaye** France
106 C1 **Sigüenza** Spain
114 B3 **Siguiri** Guinea
88 B2 **Sigulda** Latvia
63 B2 **Sihanoukville** Cambodia
92 I3 **Siilinjärvi** Fin.
81 C2 **Siirt** Turkey
60 B2 **Sijunjung** Indon.
74 B2 **Sikar** India
114 B3 **Sikasso** Mali
137 F3 **Sikeston** U.S.A.
66 B2 **Sikhote-Alin'** *mts* Russia
111 C3 **Sikinos** *i.* Greece
75 C2 **Sikkim** *state* India
144 B2 **Silao** Mex.
75 D2 **Silchar** India
77 D1 **Siletyteniz, Ozero** *salt l.* Kazakh.
75 C2 **Silgarhi** Nepal
80 B2 **Silifke** Turkey
75 C1 **Siling Co** *salt l.* China
110 C2 **Silistra** Bulg.
80 A1 **Silivri** Turkey
93 F3 **Siljan** *l.* Sweden
93 E4 **Silkeborg** Denmark
88 C2 **Sillamäe** Estonia
142 B1 **Siloam Springs** U.S.A.
123 D2 **Silobela** S. Africa
88 B2 **Šilutė** Lith.
81 C2 **Silvan** Turkey
138 B2 **Silver City** U.S.A.
136 B3 **Silverton** U.S.A.
62 B1 **Simao** China
130 C2 **Simard, Lac** *l.* Can.
111 C3 **Simav** Turkey
111 C3 **Simav Dağları** *mts* Turkey
118 C2 **Simba** Dem. Rep. Congo
141 D2 **Simcoe, Lake** Can.
60 A1 **Simeulue** *i.* Indon.
91 C3 **Simferopol'** Ukr.
110 B1 **Şimleu Silvaniei** Romania
100 C3 **Simmern/Hunsrück** Ger.
129 D2 **Simonhouse** Can.
51 C2 **Simpson Desert** Austr.
93 F4 **Simrishamn** Sweden
60 A1 **Sinabang** Indon.
116 B2 **Sinai** *pen.* Egypt
71 A3 **Sinan** China
65 B2 **Sinanju** N. Korea
62 A1 **Sinbo** Myanmar
150 A1 **Sincelejo** Col.
111 C3 **Sındırgı** Turkey
86 E2 **Sindor** Russia
111 C2 **Sinekçi** Turkey
106 B2 **Sines** Port.
106 B2 **Sines, Cabo de** *c.* Port.
75 C2 **Singahi** India
60 B1 **Singapore** *country* Asia
61 C2 **Singaraja** Indon.
119 D3 **Singida** Tanz.
62 A1 **Singkaling Hkamti** Myanm
61 B1 **Singkawang** Indon.
60 A1 **Singkil** Indon.
53 D2 **Singleton** Austr.
62 A1 **Singu** Myanmar
108 A2 **Siniscola** *Sardinia* Italy
109 C2 **Sinj** Croatia
116 B3 **Sinkat** Sudan
Sinkiang Uighur Autonom Region *aut. reg.* China *see* **Xinjiang Uygur Zizhiqu**
80 B1 **Sinop** Turkey
65 B1 **Sinp'o** N. Korea
61 C1 **Sintang** Indon.
100 B2 **Sint Anthonis** Neth.
100 A2 **Sint-Laureins** Belgium
147 D3 **Sint Maarten** *i.* West Indies
147 D3 **Sint Maarten** *terr.* West Ind
100 B2 **Sint-Niklaas** Belgium
139 D3 **Sinton** U.S.A.
65 A1 **Sinŭiju** N. Korea
103 D2 **Siófok** Hungary
105 D2 **Sion** Switz.
137 D2 **Sioux Center** U.S.A.
137 D2 **Sioux City** U.S.A.
137 D2 **Sioux Falls** U.S.A.
130 A1 **Sioux Lookout** Can.
65 A1 **Siping** China
129 E2 **Sipiwesk Lake** Can.
60 A2 **Sipura** *i.* Indon.
93 E4 **Sira** *r.* Norway
Siracusa *Sicily* Italy *see* **Syracuse**
51 C1 **Sir Edward Pellew Group** *is* Austr.
116 B1 **Sirhān, Wādī an** *watercourse* Saudi Arabia
79 C2 **Sīrīk** Iran
62 B2 **Siri Kit, Khuan** Thai.
128 B1 **Sir James MacBrien, Moun** Can.
79 C2 **Sīrjān** Iran
81 C2 **Şırnak** Turkey
74 B2 **Sirohi** India
74 B2 **Sirsa** India
115 D1 **Sirte** Libya
115 D1 **Sirte, Gulf of** Libya
88 B2 **Širvintos** Lith.
145 C2 **Sisal** Mex.
122 B2 **Sishen** S. Africa
81 C2 **Sisian** Armenia
129 D2 **Sisipuk Lake** Can.
63 B2 **Sisŏphŏn** Cambodia
105 D3 **Sisteron** France
75 C2 **Sitapur** India
123 D2 **Siteki** Swaziland
128 A2 **Sitka** U.S.A.
100 B2 **Sittard** Neth.
62 A2 **Sittaung** *r.* Myanmar
Sittwe Myanmar *see* **Akyab**
61 C2 **Situbondo** Indon.
80 B2 **Sivas** Turkey
111 C3 **Sivaslı** Turkey
80 B2 **Siverek** Turkey
80 B2 **Sivrihisar** Turkey
116 A2 **Sīwah** Egypt
74 B1 **Siwalik Range** *mts* India/Nepal
105 D3 **Six-Fours-les-Plages** France
70 B2 **Sixian** China
123 C2 **Siyabuswa** S. Africa
Sjælland *i.* Denmark *see* **Zealand**
109 D2 **Sjenica** Serbia
92 G2 **Sjøvegan** Norway

91 C2 **Skadovs'k** Ukr.
93 F4 **Skagen** Denmark
93 E4 **Skagerrak** *str.* Denmark/Norway
134 B1 **Skagit** *r.* U.S.A.
128 A2 **Skagway** U.S.A.
74 B1 **Skardu** Pak.
103 E1 **Skarżysko-Kamienna** Pol.
103 D2 **Skawina** Pol.
128 B2 **Skeena** *r.* Can.
128 B2 **Skeena Mountains** Can.
98 D2 **Skegness** U.K.
92 H3 **Skellefteå** Sweden
92 H3 **Skellefteälven** *r.* Sweden
97 C2 **Skerries** Ireland
111 B3 **Skiathos** *i.* Greece
97 B3 **Skibbereen** Ireland
92 □B2 **Skíðadals-jökull** *glacier* Iceland
98 B1 **Skiddaw** *h.* U.K.
93 E4 **Skien** Norway
103 E1 **Skierniewice** Pol.
115 C1 **Skikda** Alg.
52 B3 **Skipton** Austr.
98 B2 **Skipton** U.K.
93 E4 **Skive** Denmark
92 H1 **Skjervøy** Norway
111 B3 **Skopelos** *i.* Greece
89 E3 **Skopin** Russia
109 D2 **Skopje** Macedonia
93 F4 **Skövde** Sweden
141 F2 **Skowhegan** U.S.A.
88 B2 **Skrunda** Latvia
128 A1 **Skukum, Mount** Can.
123 D1 **Skukuza** S. Africa
88 B2 **Skuodas** Lith.
96 A2 **Skye** *i.* U.K.
111 B3 **Skyros** Greece
111 B3 **Skyros** *i.* Greece
93 F4 **Slagelse** Denmark
97 C2 **Slaney** *r.* Ireland
88 C2 **Slantsy** Russia
109 C1 **Slatina** Croatia
110 B2 **Slatina** Romania
129 C1 **Slave** *r.* Can.
114 C4 **Slave Coast** Africa
128 C2 **Slave Lake** Can.
82 G3 **Slavgorod** Russia
109 C1 **Slavonski Brod** Croatia
90 B1 **Slavuta** Ukr.
90 C1 **Slavutych** Ukr.
91 D2 **Slavyansk-na-Kubani** Russia
89 D3 **Slawharad** Belarus
103 D1 **Sławno** Pol.
97 A2 **Slea Head** Ireland
130 C1 **Sleeper Islands** Can.
Slêmanî Iraq *see* **As Sulaymānīyah/Slêmanî**
97 D1 **Slieve Donard** *h.* U.K.
Slieve Gamph *hills* Ireland *see* **Ox Mountains**
97 B1 **Sligo** Ireland
97 B1 **Sligo Bay** Ireland
93 G4 **Slite** Sweden
110 C2 **Sliven** Bulg.
110 C2 **Slobozia** Romania
128 C3 **Slocan** Can.
88 C3 **Slonim** Belarus
100 B1 **Sloten** Neth.
99 C3 **Slough** U.K.
103 D2 **Slovakia** *country* Europe
108 B1 **Slovenia** *country* Europe
91 D2 **Slov"yans'k** Ukr.
90 B1 **Sluch** *r.* Ukr.
103 D1 **Słupsk** Pol.
88 C3 **Slutsk** Belarus
97 A2 **Slyne Head** Ireland
131 D1 **Smallwood Reservoir** Can.
88 C3 **Smalyavichy** Belarus
88 C3 **Smarhon'** Belarus
129 D2 **Smeaton** Can.
109 D2 **Smederevo** Serbia
109 D2 **Smederevska Palanka** Serbia
91 C2 **Smila** Ukr.
88 C2 **Smiltene** Latvia
128 B2 **Smithers** Can.
143 E1 **Smithfield** U.S.A.
141 D3 **Smith Mountain Lake** U.S.A.
130 C2 **Smiths Falls** Can.
137 D3 **Smoky Hills** U.S.A.
92 E3 **Smøla** *i.* Norway
89 D3 **Smolensk** Russia
110 B2 **Smolyan** Bulg.
130 B2 **Smooth Rock Falls** Can.
Smyrna Turkey *see* **İzmir**
92 □B3 **Snæfell** *mt.* Iceland
98 A1 **Snaefell** *h.* Isle of Man
132 B2 **Snake** *r.* U.S.A.
134 D2 **Snake River Plain** U.S.A.
100 B1 **Sneek** Neth.
97 B3 **Sneem** Ireland
122 B3 **Sneeuberge** *mts* S. Africa
108 B1 **Snežnik** *mt.* Slovenia
91 C2 **Snihurivka** Ukr.
93 E3 **Snøhetta** *mt.* Norway
91 C1 **Snovs'k** Ukr.
129 D1 **Snowbird Lake** Can.
98 A2 **Snowdon** *mt.* U.K.
Snowdrift Can. *see* **Łutselk'e**
129 C1 **Snowdrift** *r.* Can.
138 A2 **Snowflake** U.S.A.
129 D2 **Snow Lake** Can.
52 A2 **Snowtown** Austr.
53 C3 **Snowy** *r.* Austr.
53 C3 **Snowy Mountains** Austr.
139 C2 **Snyder** U.S.A.
121 □D2 **Soalala** Madag.
59 C2 **Soasiu** Indon.
117 B4 **Sobat** *r.* South Sudan
89 F2 **Sobinka** Russia
151 D3 **Sobradinho, Barragem de** *resr* Brazil
151 D2 **Sobral** Brazil
87 C4 **Sochi** Russia
49 H4 **Society Islands** Fr. Polynesia
150 A1 **Socorro** Col.
138 B2 **Socorro** U.S.A.
144 A3 **Socorro, Isla** *i.* Mex.
56 F6 **Socotra** *i.* Yemen
63 B3 **Soc Trăng** Vietnam
106 C2 **Socuéllamos** Spain
92 I2 **Sodankylä** Fin.
134 D2 **Soda Springs** U.S.A.
93 G3 **Söderhamn** Sweden
93 G4 **Södertälje** Sweden
116 A3 **Sodiri** Sudan
117 B4 **Sodo** Eth.
93 G3 **Södra Kvarken** *str.* Fin./Sweden
100 D2 **Soest** Ger.
110 B2 **Sofia** Bulg.
Sofiya Bulg. *see* **Sofia**
68 C2 **Sog** China
93 E3 **Sognefjorden** *inlet* Norway
111 D2 **Söğüt** Turkey
100 B2 **Soignies** Belgium
105 C2 **Soissons** France
90 A1 **Sokal'** Ukr.
111 C3 **Söke** Turkey
81 C1 **Sokhumi** Georgia
114 C4 **Sokodé** Togo
89 F2 **Sokol** Russia
101 F2 **Sokolov** Czechia
115 C3 **Sokoto** Nigeria
115 C3 **Sokoto** *r.* Nigeria
90 B2 **Sokyryany** Ukr.
73 B3 **Solapur** India
135 B3 **Soledad** U.S.A.
89 F2 **Soligalich** Russia
99 C2 **Solihull** U.K.
86 E3 **Solikamsk** Russia
87 E3 **Sol'-Iletsk** Russia
100 C2 **Solingen** Ger.
92 G3 **Sollefteå** Sweden
93 G4 **Sollentuna** Sweden
101 D2 **Solling** *hills* Ger.
89 E2 **Solnechnogorsk** Russia
60 B2 **Solok** Indon.
48 E3 **Solomon Islands** *country* S. Pacific Ocean
48 E3 **Solomon Sea** S. Pacific Ocean
105 D2 **Solothurn** Switz.
101 D1 **Soltau** Ger.
89 D2 **Sol'tsy** Russia
96 C3 **Solway Firth** *est.* U.K.
120 B2 **Solwezi** Zambia
111 C3 **Soma** Turkey
117 C4 **Somalia** *country* Africa
117 A4 **Somaliland** *disp. terr.* Somalia
120 B1 **Sombo** Angola
109 C1 **Sombor** Serbia
144 B2 **Sombrerete** Mex.
140 C3 **Somerset** U.S.A.
123 C3 **Somerset East** S. Africa
126 E2 **Somerset Island** Can.
122 A3 **Somerset West** S. Africa
101 E2 **Sömmerda** Ger.
75 C2 **Son** *r.* India
65 C1 **Sŏnbong** N. Korea
93 E4 **Sønderborg** Denmark
101 E2 **Sondershausen** Ger.
Søndre Strømfjord *inlet* Greenland *see* **Kangerlussuaq**
62 B1 **Sông Đa, Hô** *resr* Vietnam
119 D4 **Songea** Tanz.
65 B1 **Sŏnggan** N. Korea
65 B1 **Songhua Hu** *resr* China
Sŏngjin N. Korea *see* **Kimch'aek**
63 B3 **Songkhla** Thai.
65 B2 **Songnim** N. Korea
120 A1 **Songo** Angola
121 C2 **Songo** Moz.
69 E1 **Songyuan** China
Sonid Youqi China *see* **Saihan Tal**
89 E2 **Sonkovo** Russia
62 B1 **Sơn La** Vietnam
74 A2 **Sonmiani** Pak.
101 E2 **Sonneberg** Ger.
138 A2 **Sonoita** Mex.
144 A2 **Sonora** *r.* Mex.
135 B3 **Sonora** *CA* U.S.A.
139 C2 **Sonora** *TX* U.S.A.
117 A4 **Sopo** *watercourse* South Sudan
103 D2 **Sopron** Hungary
108 B2 **Sora** Italy
130 C2 **Sorel** Can.
51 D4 **Sorell** Austr.
106 C1 **Soria** Spain
90 B2 **Soroca** Moldova
154 C2 **Sorocaba** Brazil
87 E3 **Sorochinsk** Russia
91 D2 **Sorokine** Ukr.
59 D2 **Sorol** *atoll* Micronesia
59 C3 **Sorong** Indon.
119 D2 **Soroti** Uganda
92 H1 **Sørøya** *i.* Norway
92 G2 **Sorsele** Sweden
64 B1 **Sorsogon** Phil.
86 C2 **Sortavala** Russia
92 G2 **Sortland** Norway
123 C2 **Soshanguve** S. Africa
89 E3 **Sosna** *r.* Russia
153 B4 **Sosneado** *mt.* Arg.

Sosnogorsk

86 E2	Sosnogorsk Russia	
86 D2	Sosnovka Russia	
88 C2	Sosnovyy Bor Russia	
103 D1	Sosnowiec Pol.	
91 D2	Sosyka r. Russia	
145 C2	Soto la Marina Mex.	
118 B2	Souanké Congo	
104 C3	Souillac France	
	Sŏul S. Korea see Seoul	
104 B2	Soulac-sur-Mer France	
104 B3	Soulom France	
	Soûr Lebanon see Tyre	
107 D2	Sour el Ghozlane Alg.	
129 D3	Souris Man. Can.	
131 D2	Souris P.E.I. Can.	
129 E3	Souris r. Can.	
151 E2	Sousa Brazil	
115 D1	Sousse Tunisia	
104 B3	Soustons France	
122 B3	South Africa country Africa	
99 C3	Southampton U.K.	
127 F2	Southampton Island Can.	
73 D3	South Andaman i. India	
52 A1	South Australia state Austr.	
130 B3	South Baymouth Can.	
140 B2	South Bend U.S.A.	
143 D2	South Carolina state U.S.A.	
156 B4	South China Sea N. Pacific Ocean	
136 C2	South Dakota state U.S.A.	
99 C3	South Downs hills U.K.	
129 D2	Southend Can.	
99 D3	Southend-on-Sea U.K.	
54 B2	Southern Alps/Ka Tiritiri o te Moana mts N.Z.	
50 A3	Southern Cross Austr.	
129 E2	Southern Indian Lake Can.	
159	Southern Ocean World	
143 E1	Southern Pines U.S.A.	
96 B3	Southern Uplands hills U.K.	
149 F6	South Georgia and the South Sandwich Islands terr. S. Atlantic Ocean	
96 A2	South Harris pen. U.K.	
129 E1	South Henik Lake Can.	
54 B2	South Island N.Z.	
65 B2	South Korea country Asia	
135 B3	South Lake Tahoe U.S.A.	
55 Q4	South Orkney Islands S. Atlantic Ocean	
81 C1	South Ossetia disp. terr. Georgia	
136 C2	South Platte r. U.S.A.	
98 B2	Southport U.K.	
143 E2	Southport U.K.	
96 C1	South Ronaldsay i. U.K.	
123 D3	South Sand Bluff pt S. Africa	
129 D2	South Saskatchewan r. Can.	
129 E2	South Seal r. Can.	
55 P3	South Shetland Islands Antarctica	
98 C1	South Shields U.K.	
117 A4	South Sudan country Africa	
54 B1	South Taranaki Bight b. N.Z.	
130 C1	South Twin Island Can.	
96 A2	South Uist i. U.K.	
53 D2	South West Rocks Austr.	
99 C2	Southwold U.K.	
109 C3	Soverato Italy	
88 B2	Sovetsk Russia	
86 F2	Sovetskiy Russia	
123 C2	Soweto S. Africa	
66 D1	Sōya-misaki c. Japan	
90 C1	Sozh r. Russia	
110 C2	Sozopol Bulg.	
106 C1	Spain country Europe	
99 C2	Spalding U.K.	
135 D2	Spanish Fork U.S.A.	

97 B2	Spanish Point Ireland	
108 B3	Sparagio, Monte mt. Sicily Italy	
135 C3	Sparks U.S.A.	
140 A2	Sparta U.S.A.	
143 D2	Spartanburg U.S.A.	
111 B3	Sparti Greece	
109 C3	Spartivento, Capo c. Italy	
89 D3	Spas-Demensk Russia	
89 F2	Spas-Klepiki Russia	
66 B2	Spassk-Dal'niy Russia	
89 F3	Spassk-Ryazanskiy Russia	
111 B3	Spatha, Akrotirio pt Greece	
136 C2	Spearfish U.S.A.	
139 C1	Spearman U.S.A.	
137 D2	Spencer U.S.A.	
52 A2	Spencer Gulf est. Austr.	
98 C1	Spennymoor U.K.	
54 B2	Spenser Mountains N.Z.	
101 D3	Spessart reg. Ger.	
96 C2	Spey r. U.K.	
102 B2	Speyer Ger.	
100 C1	Spiekeroog i. Ger.	
100 B2	Spijkenisse Neth.	
128 C2	Spirit River Can.	
103 E2	Spišská Nová Ves Slovakia	
82 C1	Spitsbergen i. Svalbard	
102 C2	Spittal an der Drau Austria	
109 C2	Split Croatia	
129 E2	Split Lake Can.	
129 E2	Split Lake Can.	
134 C1	Spokane U.S.A.	
140 A1	Spooner U.S.A.	
101 F2	Spree r. Ger.	
122 A2	Springbok S. Africa	
131 E2	Springdale Can.	
142 B1	Springdale U.S.A.	
101 D1	Springe Ger.	
138 C1	Springer U.S.A.	
138 B2	Springerville U.S.A.	
136 C3	Springfield CO U.S.A.	
140 B3	Springfield IL U.S.A.	
141 E2	Springfield MA U.S.A.	
137 E3	Springfield MO U.S.A.	
140 C3	Springfield OH U.S.A.	
134 B2	Springfield OR U.S.A.	
123 C3	Springfontein S. Africa	
131 D2	Springhill Can.	
143 D3	Spring Hill U.S.A.	
54 B2	Springs Junction N.Z.	
98 D2	Spurn Head U.K.	
128 B3	Squamish Can.	
109 C3	Squillace, Golfo di g. Italy	
	Srbija country Europe see Serbia	
109 C2	Srebrenica Bos. & Herz.	
110 C2	Sredets Bulg.	
83 L3	Sredinnyy Khrebet mts Russia	
83 L2	Srednekolymsk Russia	
	Sredne-Russkaya Vozvyshennost' hills Russia see Central Russian Upland	
	Sredne-Sibirskoye Ploskogor'ye plat. Russia see Central Siberian Plateau	
69 D1	Sretensk Russia	
61 C1	Sri Aman Sarawak Malaysia	
73 B4	Sri Jayewardenepura Kotte Sri Lanka	
73 C3	Srikakulam India	
73 C4	Sri Lanka country Asia	
74 B1	Srinagar India	
73 B3	Srivardhan India	
101 D1	Stade Ger.	
101 E1	Stadensen Ger.	
100 C1	Stadskanaal Neth.	
101 D2	Stadtallendorf Ger.	
101 D1	Stadthagen Ger.	

99 B2	Stafford U.K.	
99 C3	Staines-upon-Thames U.K.	
	Stakhanov Ukr. see Kadiyivka	
	Stalingrad Russia see Volgograd	
103 E1	Stalowa Wola Pol.	
99 C2	Stamford U.K.	
141 E2	Stamford CT U.S.A.	
139 D2	Stamford TX U.S.A.	
122 A1	Stampriet Namibia	
92 F2	Stamsund Norway	
123 C2	Standerton S. Africa	
140 C2	Standish U.S.A.	
153 C6	Stanley Falkland Is	
136 C1	Stanley U.S.A.	
119 C2	Stanley, Mount Dem. Rep. Congo/Uganda	
83 I3	Stanovoye Nagor'ye mts Russia	
83 J3	Stanovoy Khrebet mts Russia	
53 D1	Stanthorpe Austr.	
103 E1	Starachowice Pol.	
	Stara Planina mts Bulgaria/Serbia see Balkan Mountains	
89 D2	Staraya Russa Russia	
89 D2	Staraya Toropa Russia	
110 C2	Stara Zagora Bulg.	
103 D1	Stargard Szczeciński Pol.	
142 C2	Starkville U.S.A.	
91 D2	Starobil's'k Ukr.	
89 D3	Starodub Russia	
103 D1	Starogard Gdański Pol.	
90 B2	Starokostyantyniv Ukr.	
91 D2	Starominskaya Russia	
91 D2	Staroshcherbinovskaya Russia	
91 D2	Starotitarovskaya Russia	
89 F3	Staroyur'yevo Russia	
99 B3	Start Point U.K.	
88 C3	Staryya Darohi Belarus	
91 D2	Staryy Oskol Russia	
101 E2	Staßfurt Ger.	
141 D2	State College U.S.A.	
143 D2	Statesboro U.S.A.	
143 D1	Statesville U.S.A.	
93 E4	Stavanger Norway	
87 D4	Stavropol' Russia	
87 D4	Stavropol'skaya Vozvyshennost' hills Russia	
52 B3	Stawell Austr.	
123 C2	Steadville S. Africa	
136 B2	Steamboat Springs U.S.A.	
101 E2	Stedten Ger.	
128 B2	Steen River Can.	
134 C2	Steens Mountain U.S.A.	
100 C1	Steenwijk Neth.	
126 D2	Stefansson Island Can.	
101 E3	Steigerwald mts Ger.	
129 E3	Steinbach Can.	
100 C1	Steinfurt Ger.	
120 A3	Steinhausen Namibia	
92 F3	Steinkjer Norway	
122 A2	Steinkopf S. Africa	
122 B2	Stella S. Africa	
105 D2	Stenay France	
101 E1	Stendal Ger.	
	Stepanakert Azer. see Xankändi	
131 E2	Stephenville Can.	
139 D2	Stephenville U.S.A.	
122 B3	Sterling S. Africa	
136 C2	Sterling CO U.S.A.	
140 B2	Sterling IL U.S.A.	
87 E3	Sterlitamak Russia	
101 E1	Sternberg Ger.	
128 C2	Stettler Can.	
140 C2	Steubenville U.S.A.	
99 C3	Stevenage U.K.	
129 E2	Stevenson Lake Can.	

126 B2 **Stevens Village** U.S.A.
128 B2 **Stewart** Can.
126 B2 **Stewart** *r.* Can.
54 A3 **Stewart Island/Rakiura** N.Z.
127 F2 **Stewart Lake** Can.
102 C2 **Steyr** Austria
122 B3 **Steytlerville** S. Africa
128 A2 **Stikine** *r.* Can.
28 A2 **Stikine Plateau** Can.
22 B3 **Stilbaai** S. Africa
39 D1 **Stillwater** U.S.A.
09 D2 **Štip** Macedonia
96 C2 **Stirling** U.K.
92 F3 **Stjørdalshalsen** Norway
03 D2 **Stockerau** Austria
93 G4 **Stockholm** Sweden
98 B2 **Stockport** U.K.
35 B3 **Stockton** U.S.A.
98 C1 **Stockton-on-Tees** U.K.
63 B2 **Stœng Trêng** Cambodia
96 B1 **Stoer, Point of** U.K.
98 B2 **Stoke-on-Trent** U.K.
09 D2 **Stol** *mt.* Serbia
09 C2 **Stolac** Bos. & Herz.
00 C2 **Stolberg (Rheinland)** Ger.
88 C3 **Stolin** Belarus
01 F2 **Stollberg** Ger.
01 D1 **Stolzenau** Ger.
96 C2 **Stonehaven** U.K.
29 E2 **Stonewall** Can.
29 D2 **Stony Rapids** Can.
92 G2 **Storavan** *l.* Sweden
Store Bælt *sea chan.* Denmark *see* **Great Belt**
92 F3 **Støren** Norway
92 F2 **Storforshei** Norway
26 D2 **Storkerson Peninsula** Can.
37 D2 **Storm Lake** U.S.A.
93 E3 **Stornosa** *mt.* Norway
96 A1 **Stornoway** U.K.
86 E2 **Storozhevsk** Russia
90 B2 **Storozhynets'** Ukr.
92 F3 **Storsjön** *l.* Sweden
92 H2 **Storslett** Norway
92 G2 **Storuman** Sweden
99 C2 **Stour** *r. England* U.K.
99 C3 **Stour** *r. England* U.K.
30 A1 **Stout Lake** Can.
88 C3 **Stowbtsy** Belarus
97 C1 **Strabane** U.K.
02 C2 **Strakonice** Czechia
02 C1 **Stralsund** Ger.
22 A3 **Strand** S. Africa
93 E3 **Stranda** Norway
97 D1 **Strangford Lough** *inlet* U.K.
96 B3 **Stranraer** U.K.
05 D2 **Strasbourg** France
40 C2 **Stratford** Can.
54 B1 **Stratford** N.Z.
39 C1 **Stratford** U.S.A.
99 C2 **Stratford-upon-Avon** U.K.
28 C2 **Strathmore** Can.
96 C2 **Strathspey** *val.* U.K.
02 C2 **Straubing** Ger.
51 C3 **Streaky Bay** Austr.
40 B2 **Streator** U.S.A.
10 B2 **Strehaia** Romania
53 B5 **Stroeder** Arg.
01 D1 **Ströhen** Ger.
09 C3 **Stromboli, Isola** *i.* Italy
96 C1 **Stromness** U.K.
92 G3 **Strömsund** Sweden
96 C1 **Stronsay** *i.* U.K.
53 D2 **Stroud** Austr.
99 B3 **Stroud** U.K.
00 C1 **Strücklingen (Saterland)** Ger.
09 D2 **Struga** Macedonia
88 C2 **Strugi-Krasnyye** Russia
122 B3 **Struis Bay** S. Africa
109 D2 **Strumica** Macedonia
122 B2 **Strydenburg** S. Africa
111 B2 **Strymonas** *r.* Greece
90 A2 **Stryy** Ukr.
128 B2 **Stuart Lake** Can.
130 A1 **Stull Lake** Can.
89 E3 **Stupino** Russia
140 B2 **Sturgeon Bay** U.S.A.
130 C2 **Sturgeon Falls** Can.
130 A2 **Sturgeon Lake** Can.
140 B2 **Sturgis** *MI* U.S.A.
136 C2 **Sturgis** *SD* U.S.A.
50 B1 **Sturt Creek** *watercourse* Austr.
52 B1 **Sturt Stony Desert** Austr.
123 C3 **Stutterheim** S. Africa
102 B2 **Stuttgart** Ger.
142 B2 **Stuttgart** U.S.A.
92 □A2 **Stykkishólmur** Iceland
90 B1 **Styr** *r.* Belarus/Ukr.
155 D1 **Suaçuí Grande** *r.* Brazil
116 B3 **Suakin** Sudan
78 A3 **Suara** Eritrea
109 C1 **Subotica** Serbia
110 C1 **Suceava** Romania
97 B2 **Suck** *r.* Ireland
152 B2 **Sucre** Bol.
154 B2 **Sucuriú** *r.* Brazil
89 E2 **Suda** Russia
91 C3 **Sudak** Ukr.
117 A3 **Sudan** *country* Africa
130 B2 **Sudbury** Can.
117 A4 **Sudd** *swamp* South Sudan
89 F2 **Sudislavl'** Russia
89 F2 **Sudogda** Russia
94 B1 **Suðuroy** *i.* Faroe Is
107 C2 **Sueca** Spain
116 B2 **Suez** Egypt
116 B2 **Suez, Gulf of** Egypt
80 B2 **Suez Canal** Egypt
141 D3 **Suffolk** U.S.A.
116 B2 **Sūhāj** Egypt
79 C2 **Şuḩār** Oman
69 D1 **Sühbaatar** Mongolia
101 E2 **Suhl** Ger.
109 C1 **Suhopolje** Croatia
70 B2 **Suide** China
66 B2 **Suifenhe** China
69 E1 **Suihua** China
70 A2 **Suining** China
70 B2 **Suiping** China
70 B2 **Suiyang** China
70 B2 **Suizhou** China
74 B2 **Sujangarh** India
74 B1 **Sujanpur** India
74 A2 **Sujawal** Pak.
60 B2 **Sukabumi** Indon.
61 B2 **Sukadana** Indon.
61 C2 **Sukaraja** Indon.
89 E3 **Sukhinichi** Russia
89 F2 **Sukhona** *r.* Russia
62 A2 **Sukhothai** Thai.
74 A2 **Sukkur** Pak.
89 E2 **Sukromny** Russia
59 C3 **Sula, Kepulauan** *is* Indon.
74 A1 **Sulaiman Range** *mts* Pak.
Sulawesi *i.* Indon. *see* **Celebes**
150 A2 **Sullana** Peru
137 E3 **Sullivan** U.S.A.
139 D2 **Sulphur Springs** U.S.A.
64 B2 **Sulu Archipelago** *is* Phil.
64 A2 **Sulu Sea** N. Pacific Ocean
101 E3 **Sulzbach-Rosenberg** Ger.
79 C2 **Sumāil** Oman
Sumatera *i.* Indon. *see* **Sumatra**
60 A1 **Sumatra** *i.* Indon.
58 C3 **Sumba** *i.* Indon.
61 C2 **Sumbawa** *i.* Indon.
61 C2 **Sumbawa Besar** Indon.
119 D3 **Sumbawanga** Tanz.
120 A2 **Sumbe** Angola
96 □ **Sumburgh** U.K.
96 □ **Sumburgh Head** U.K.
61 C2 **Sumenep** Indon.
67 D4 **Sumisu-jima** *i.* Japan
131 D2 **Summerside** Can.
140 C3 **Summersville** U.S.A.
128 B2 **Summit Lake** Can.
103 D2 **Šumperk** Czechia
81 C1 **Sumqayıt** Azer.
143 D2 **Sumter** U.S.A.
91 C1 **Sumy** Ukr.
75 D2 **Sunamganj** Bangl.
65 B2 **Sunan** N. Korea
79 C2 **Şunaynah** Oman
52 B3 **Sunbury** Austr.
141 D2 **Sunbury** U.S.A.
65 B3 **Suncheon** S. Korea
65 B2 **Sunch'ŏn** N. Korea
123 C2 **Sun City** S. Africa
60 B2 **Sunda, Selat** *str.* Indon.
136 C2 **Sundance** U.S.A.
75 C2 **Sundarbans** *coastal area* Bangl./India
98 C1 **Sunderland** U.K.
128 C2 **Sundre** Can.
93 G3 **Sundsvall** Sweden
123 D2 **Sundumbili** S. Africa
61 C2 **Sungai Barito** *r.* Indon.
59 D3 **Sungai Digul** *r.* Indon.
60 B1 **Sungai Kampar** *r.* Indon.
60 B2 **Sungailiat** Indon.
60 B2 **Sungaipenuh** Indon.
60 B1 **Sungai Petani** Malaysia
60 B1 **Sungai Rokan** *r.* Indon.
59 D3 **Sungai Taritatu** *r.* Indon.
80 B1 **Sungurlu** Turkey
93 E3 **Sunndalsøra** Norway
134 C1 **Sunnyside** U.S.A.
135 B3 **Sunnyvale** U.S.A.
83 I2 **Suntar** Russia
74 A2 **Suntsar** Pak.
114 B4 **Sunyani** Ghana
82 D2 **Suoyarvi** Russia
138 A2 **Superior** *AZ* U.S.A.
137 D2 **Superior** *NE* U.S.A.
140 A1 **Superior** *WI* U.S.A.
140 B1 **Superior, Lake** Can./U.S.A.
89 D3 **Suponevo** Russia
81 C2 **Sūq ash Shuyūkh** Iraq
70 B2 **Suqian** China
78 A2 **Sūq Suwayq** Saudi Arabia
79 C2 **Şūr** Oman
74 A2 **Surab** Pak.
61 C2 **Surabaya** Indon.
61 C2 **Surakarta** Indon.
74 B2 **Surat** India
74 B2 **Suratgarh** India
63 A3 **Surat Thani** Thai.
89 D3 **Surazh** Russia
109 D2 **Surdulica** Serbia
82 F2 **Surgut** Russia
64 B2 **Surigao** Phil.
63 B2 **Surin** Thai.
151 C1 **Suriname** *country* S. America
Surt Libya *see* **Sirte**
Surt, Khalīj *g.* Libya *see* **Sirte, Gulf of**
60 B2 **Surulangun** Indon.
89 F2 **Susanino** Russia
135 B2 **Susanville** U.S.A.
80 B1 **Suşehri** Turkey
131 D2 **Sussex** Can.
101 D1 **Süstedt** Ger.
100 C1 **Sustrum** Ger.

83 K2 **Susuman** Russia
111 C3 **Susurluk** Turkey
75 B1 **Sutak** India
122 B3 **Sutherland** S. Africa
99 C2 **Sutton Coldfield** U.K.
66 D2 **Suttsu** Japan
49 F4 **Suva** Fiji
89 E3 **Suvorov** Russia
103 E1 **Suwałki** Pol.
63 B2 **Suwannaphum** Thai.
143 D3 **Suwannee** *r.* U.S.A.
Suweis, Qanâ el *canal* Egypt *see* **Suez Canal**
65 B2 **Suwon** S. Korea
79 C2 **Sūzā** Iran
89 F2 **Suzdal'** Russia
70 B2 **Suzhou** *Anhui* China
70 C2 **Suzhou** *Jiangsu* China
67 C3 **Suzu** Japan
67 C3 **Suzu-misaki** *pt* Japan
82 B1 **Svalbard** *terr.* Arctic Ocean
91 D2 **Svatove** Ukr.
63 B2 **Svay Riĕng** Cambodia
93 F3 **Sveg** Sweden
88 C2 **Švenčionys** Lith.
93 F4 **Svendborg** Denmark
Sverdlovsk Russia *see* **Yekaterinburg**
109 D2 **Sveti Nikole** Macedonia
Svetlogorsk Belarus *see* **Svyetlahorsk/Svetlogorsk**
88 B3 **Svetlogorsk** Russia
88 B3 **Svetlyy** Russia
93 I3 **Svetogorsk** Russia
110 C2 **Svilengrad** Bulg.
110 B2 **Svinecea Mare, Vârful** *mt.* Romania
110 C2 **Svishtov** Bulg.
103 D2 **Svitavy** Czechia
91 C2 **Svitlovods'k** Ukr.
69 E1 **Svobodnyy** Russia
92 F2 **Svolvær** Norway
88 C3 **Svyetlahorsk/Svetlogorsk** Belarus
143 D2 **Swainsboro** U.S.A.
120 A3 **Swakopmund** Namibia
52 B3 **Swan Hill** Austr.
128 C2 **Swan Hills** Can.
129 D2 **Swan Lake** Can.
129 D2 **Swan River** Can.
53 D2 **Swansea** Austr.
99 B3 **Swansea** U.K.
123 C2 **Swartruggens** S. Africa
Swatow China *see* **Shantou**
123 D2 **Swaziland** *country* Africa
93 G3 **Sweden** *country* Europe
139 C2 **Sweetwater** U.S.A.
136 B2 **Sweetwater** *r.* U.S.A.
122 B3 **Swellendam** S. Africa
103 D1 **Świdnica** Pol.
103 D1 **Świdwin** Pol.
103 D1 **Świebodzin** Pol.
103 D1 **Świecie** Pol.
129 D2 **Swift Current** Can.
97 C1 **Swilly, Lough** *inlet* Ireland
99 C3 **Swindon** U.K.
102 C1 **Świnoujście** Pol.
105 D2 **Switzerland** *country* Europe
97 C2 **Swords** Ireland
88 C3 **Syanno** Belarus
89 D2 **Sychevka** Russia
53 D2 **Sydney** Austr.
131 D2 **Sydney** Can.
131 D2 **Sydney Mines** Can.
91 D2 **Syeverodonets'k** Ukr.
86 E2 **Syktyvkar** Russia
142 C2 **Sylacauga** U.S.A.
75 D2 **Sylhet** Bangl.
102 B1 **Sylt** *i.* Ger.
111 C3 **Symi** *i.* Greece
91 D2 **Synel'nykove** Ukr.
109 C3 **Syracuse** *Sicily* Italy
136 C3 **Syracuse** *KS* U.S.A.
141 D2 **Syracuse** *NY* U.S.A.
77 C2 **Syrdar'ya** *r.* Asia
80 B2 **Syria** *country* Asia
80 B2 **Syrian Desert** Asia
111 B3 **Syros** *i.* Greece
87 D3 **Syzran'** Russia
102 C1 **Szczecin** Pol.
103 D1 **Szczecinek** Pol.
103 E1 **Szczytno** Pol.
103 E2 **Szeged** Hungary
103 D2 **Székesfehérvár** Hungary
103 D2 **Szekszárd** Hungary
103 E2 **Szentes** Hungary
103 D2 **Szentgotthárd** Hungary
103 D2 **Szigetvár** Hungary
103 E2 **Szolnok** Hungary
103 D2 **Szombathely** Hungary

T

78 B2 **Tābah** Saudi Arabia
76 B3 **Ţabas** Iran
81 D3 **Tābask, Kūh-e** *mt.* Iran
150 B2 **Tabatinga** Brazil
114 B2 **Tabelbala** Alg.
129 C3 **Taber** Can.
102 C2 **Tábor** Czechia
119 D3 **Tabora** Tanz.
114 B4 **Tabou** Côte d'Ivoire
81 C2 **Tabrīz** Iran
78 A2 **Tabūk** Saudi Arabia
77 E2 **Tacheng** China
102 C2 **Tachov** Czechia
64 B1 **Tacloban** Phil.
150 A3 **Tacna** Peru
134 B1 **Tacoma** U.S.A.
152 C4 **Tacuarembó** Uru.
138 B3 **Tacupeto** Mex.
117 C3 **Tadjourah** Djibouti
80 B2 **Tadmur** Syria
129 E2 **Tadoule Lake** Can.
65 B2 **Taebaek** S. Korea
Taegu S. Korea *see* **Daegu**
Taejŏn S. Korea *see* **Daejeon**
107 C1 **Tafalla** Spain
152 B3 **Tafí Viejo** Arg.
79 D2 **Taftān, Kūh-e** *mt.* Iran
91 D2 **Taganrog** Russia
91 D2 **Taganrog, Gulf of** Russia/Ukr.
62 A1 **Tagaung** Myanmar
64 B1 **Tagaytay City** Phil.
64 B2 **Tagbilaran** Phil.
64 B1 **Tagudin** Phil.
64 B2 **Tagum** Phil.
106 B2 **Tagus** *r.* Port./Spain
60 B1 **Tahan, Gunung** *mt.* Malaysia
115 C2 **Tahat, Mont** *mt.* Alg.
69 E1 **Tahe** China
49 I4 **Tahiti** *i.* Fr. Polynesia
139 E1 **Tahlequah** U.S.A.
135 B3 **Tahoe, Lake** U.S.A.
135 B3 **Tahoe City** U.S.A.
126 D2 **Tahoe Lake** Can.
115 C3 **Tahoua** Niger
79 C2 **Tahrūd** Iran
128 B3 **Tahsis** Can.
70 B2 **Tai'an** China
Taibei Taiwan *see* **Taipei**
Taibus Qi China *see* **Baochang**
71 C3 **Taichung** Taiwan
54 C1 **Taihape** N.Z.
70 C2 **Tai Hu** *l.* China
52 A3 **Tailem Bend** Austr.
71 C3 **Tainan** Taiwan
155 D1 **Taiobeiras** Brazil
71 C3 **Taipei** Taiwan
60 B1 **Taiping** Malaysia
71 B3 **Taishan** China
153 A5 **Taitao, Península de** *pen.* Chile
71 C3 **Taitung** Taiwan
92 I2 **Taivalkoski** Fin.
92 H2 **Taivaskero** *h.* Fin.
71 C3 **Taiwan** *country* Asia
71 B3 **Taiwan Strait** China/Taiwa
70 B2 **Taiyuan** China
Taizhong Taiwan *see* **Taichung**
70 B2 **Taizhou** *Jiangsu* China
71 C3 **Taizhou** *Zhejiang* China
78 B3 **Ta'izz** Yemen
77 D3 **Tajikistan** *country* Asia
75 B2 **Taj Mahal** *tourist site* India
Tajo *r.* Port. *see* **Tagus**
58 A1 **Tak** Thai.
54 B2 **Takaka** N.Z.
67 B4 **Takamatsu** Japan
67 C3 **Takaoka** Japan
54 B1 **Takapuna** N.Z.
67 C3 **Takasaki** Japan
122 B1 **Takatokwane** Botswana
67 C3 **Takayama** Japan
Takefu Japan *see* **Echizen**
60 A1 **Takengon** Indon.
63 B2 **Ta Khmau** Cambodia
66 D2 **Takikawa** Japan
128 B2 **Takla Lake** Can.
128 B2 **Takla Landing** Can.
77 E3 **Taklimakan Desert** China
Taklimakan Shamo *des.* Cl *see* **Taklimakan Desert**
128 A2 **Taku** *r.* Can./U.S.A.
63 A3 **Takua Pa** Thai.
115 C4 **Takum** Nigeria
88 C3 **Talachyn** Belarus
74 B1 **Talagang** Pak.
150 A2 **Talara** Peru
59 C2 **Talaud, Kepulauan** *is* Indo
106 C2 **Talavera de la Reina** Spain
153 A4 **Talca** Chile
153 A4 **Talcahuano** Chile
89 E2 **Taldom** Russia
77 D2 **Taldykorgan** Kazakh.
59 C3 **Taliabu** *i.* Indon.
64 B1 **Talisay** Phil.
61 C2 **Taliwang** Indon.
81 C2 **Tall 'Afar** Iraq
97 C2 **Tallaght** Ireland
143 D2 **Tallahassee** U.S.A.
88 B2 **Tallinn** Estonia
142 B2 **Tallulah** U.S.A.
104 B2 **Talmont-St-Hilaire** France
90 C2 **Tal'ne** Ukr.
117 B3 **Talodi** Sudan
91 E1 **Talovaya** Russia
126 E2 **Taloyoak** Can.
88 B2 **Talsi** Latvia
152 A3 **Taltal** Chile
129 C1 **Taltson** *r.* Can.
60 A1 **Talu** Indon.
53 C1 **Talwood** Austr.
114 B4 **Tamale** Ghana
115 C2 **Tamanrasset** Alg.
99 A3 **Tamar** *r.* U.K.
145 C2 **Tamazunchale** Mex.
114 A3 **Tambacounda** Senegal
61 B1 **Tambelan, Kepulauan** *is* Indon.
91 E1 **Tambov** Russia
145 C2 **Tamiahua, Laguna de** *lag.* Mex.

143 D3 **Tampa** U.S.A.
143 D3 **Tampa Bay** U.S.A.
93 H3 **Tampere** Fin.
145 C2 **Tampico** Mex.
69 D1 **Tamsagbulag** Mongolia
102 C2 **Tamsweg** Austria
53 D2 **Tamworth** Austr.
99 C2 **Tamworth** U.K.
119 E3 **Tana** *r.* Kenya
117 B3 **Tana, Lake** Eth.
67 C4 **Tanabe** Japan
92 I1 **Tana Bru** Norway
61 C2 **Tanahgrogot** Indon.
58 C3 **Tanahjampea** *i.* Indon.
50 C1 **Tanami Desert** Austr.
126 A2 **Tanana** U.S.A.
108 A1 **Tanaro** *r.* Italy
65 B1 **Tanch'ŏn** N. Korea
64 B2 **Tandag** Phil.
110 C2 **Țăndărei** Romania
153 C4 **Tandil** Arg.
74 A2 **Tando Adam** Pak.
74 A2 **Tando Muhammad Khan** Pak.
114 B2 **Tanezrouft** *reg.* Alg./Mali
119 D3 **Tanga** Tanz.
119 C3 **Tanganyika, Lake** Africa
Tanger Morocco *see* **Tangier**
101 E1 **Tangermünde** Ger.
75 C1 **Tanggula Shan** *mts* China
114 B1 **Tangier** Morocco
75 C1 **Tangra Yumco** *salt l.* China
70 B2 **Tangshan** China
68 C2 **Taniantaweng Shan** *mts* China
59 C3 **Tanimbar, Kepulauan** *is* Indon.
64 B2 **Tanjay** Phil.
60 A1 **Tanjungbalai** Indon.
61 B2 **Tanjungpandan** Indon.
60 B1 **Tanjungpinang** Indon.
61 C1 **Tanjungredeb** Indon.
61 C1 **Tanjungselor** Indon.
74 B1 **Tank** Pak.
115 C3 **Tanout** Niger
75 C2 **Tansen** Nepal
116 B1 **Ţanţā** Egypt
119 D3 **Tanzania** *country* Africa
69 E1 **Taonan** China
138 B1 **Taos** U.S.A.
114 B2 **Taoudenni** Mali
88 C2 **Tapa** Estonia
145 C3 **Tapachula** Mex.
151 C2 **Tapajós** *r.* Brazil
60 A1 **Tapaktuan** Indon.
145 C3 **Tapanatepec** Mex.
150 B2 **Tapauá** Brazil
114 B4 **Tapeta** Liberia
141 D3 **Tappahannock** U.S.A.
74 B2 **Tapti** *r.* India
150 B2 **Tapurucuara** Brazil
154 A1 **Taquarí** *r.* Brazil
154 B1 **Taquari, Serra do** *hills* Brazil
154 C2 **Taquaritinga** Brazil
115 D4 **Taraba** *r.* Nigeria
Ţarābulus Libya *see* **Tripoli**
61 C1 **Tarakan** Indon.
88 A3 **Taran, Mys** *pt* Russia
54 B1 **Taranaki, Mount** *vol.* N.Z.
106 C1 **Tarancón** Spain
109 C2 **Taranto** Italy
109 C2 **Taranto, Golfo di** *g.* Italy
150 A2 **Tarapoto** Peru
91 E2 **Tarasovskiy** Russia
150 A2 **Tarauacá** Brazil
150 B2 **Tarauacá** *r.* Brazil
48 F2 **Tarawa** *atoll* Kiribati
77 D2 **Taraz** Kazakh.
107 C1 **Tarazona** Spain
77 E2 **Tarbagatay, Khrebet** *mts* Kazakh.
96 A2 **Tarbert** *Scotland* U.K.
96 B3 **Tarbert** *Scotland* U.K.
104 C3 **Tarbes** France
96 B2 **Tarbet** U.K.
51 C3 **Tarcoola** Austr.
53 D2 **Taree** Austr.
110 C2 **Târgovişte** Romania
110 B1 **Târgu Jiu** Romania
110 B1 **Târgu Mureş** Romania
110 C1 **Târgu Neamţ** Romania
79 C2 **Tarif** U.A.E.
152 B3 **Tarija** Bol.
79 B3 **Tarīm** Yemen
77 E3 **Tarim Basin** China
77 E2 **Tarim He** *r.* China
Tarim Pendi *basin* China *see* **Tarim Basin**
82 G2 **Tarko-Sale** Russia
114 B4 **Tarkwa** Ghana
64 B1 **Tarlac** Phil.
68 C2 **Tarlag** China
92 G2 **Tärnaby** Sweden
77 C3 **Tarnak Rōd** *r.* Afgh.
110 B1 **Târnăveni** Romania
103 E1 **Tarnobrzeg** Pol.
103 E1 **Tarnów** Pol.
75 C1 **Taro Co** *salt l.* China
114 B1 **Taroudannt** Morocco
69 E1 **Tarqi** China
108 B2 **Tarquinia** Italy
107 D1 **Tarragona** Spain
107 D1 **Tàrrega** Spain
80 B2 **Tarsus** Turkey
152 B3 **Tartagal** Arg.
104 B3 **Tartas** France
88 C2 **Tartu** Estonia
80 B2 **Ţarţūs** Syria
155 D1 **Tarumirim** Brazil
89 E3 **Tarusa** Russia
108 B1 **Tarvisio** Italy
81 D3 **Tashk, Daryācheh-ye** *l.* Iran
Tashkent Uzbek. *see* **Toshkent**
127 I2 **Tasiilaq** Greenland
131 D1 **Tasiujaq** Can.
76 B1 **Taskala** Kazakh.
77 E2 **Taskesken** Kazakh.
54 B2 **Tasman Bay** N.Z.
51 D4 **Tasmania** *state* Austr.
54 B2 **Tasman Mountains** N.Z.
156 D8 **Tasman Sea** S. Pacific Ocean
103 D2 **Tatabánya** Hungary
90 B2 **Tatarbunary** Ukr.
83 K3 **Tatarskiy Proliv** *str.* Russia
67 C4 **Tateyama** Japan
128 C1 **Tathlina Lake** Can.
78 B3 **Tathlīth** Saudi Arabia
78 B2 **Tathlīth, Wādī** *watercourse* Saudi Arabia
53 C3 **Tathra** Austr.
62 A1 **Tatkon** Myanmar
128 B2 **Tatla Lake** Can.
103 D2 **Tatra Mountains** *mts* Pol./Slovakia
Tatry *mts* Pol./Slovakia *see* **Tatra Mountains**
154 C2 **Tatuí** Brazil
139 C2 **Tatum** U.S.A.
81 C2 **Tatvan** Turkey
151 D2 **Tauá** Brazil
155 C2 **Taubaté** Brazil
101 D3 **Tauberbischofsheim** Ger.
54 C1 **Taumarunui** N.Z.
62 A1 **Taunggyi** Myanmar
62 A2 **Taung-ngu** Myanmar
62 A2 **Taungup** Myanmar
99 B3 **Taunton** U.K.
100 C2 **Taunus** *hills* Ger.
54 C1 **Taupo** N.Z.
54 C1 **Taupo, Lake** N.Z.
88 B2 **Tauragė** Lith.
54 C1 **Tauranga** N.Z.
80 B2 **Taurus Mountains** Turkey
111 C3 **Tavas** Turkey
86 F3 **Tavda** Russia
106 B2 **Tavira** Port.
99 A3 **Tavistock** U.K.
63 A2 **Tavoy** Myanmar
111 C3 **Tavşanlı** Turkey
99 A3 **Taw** *r.* U.K.
140 C2 **Tawas City** U.S.A.
61 C1 **Tawau** *Sabah* Malaysia
64 A2 **Tawi-Tawi** *i.* Phil.
145 C3 **Taxco** Mex.
76 B2 **Taxiatosh** Uzbek.
77 D3 **Taxkorgan** China
96 C2 **Tay** *r.* U.K.
96 C2 **Tay, Firth of** *est.* U.K.
96 B2 **Tay, Loch** *l.* U.K.
128 B2 **Taylor** Can.
139 D2 **Taylor** U.S.A.
140 B3 **Taylorville** U.S.A.
78 A2 **Taymā'** Saudi Arabia
83 H2 **Taymura** *r.* Russia
83 H2 **Taymyr, Ozero** *l.* Russia
Taymyr, Poluostrov *pen.* Russia *see* **Taymyr Peninsula**
83 G2 **Taymyr Peninsula** Russia
63 B2 **Tây Ninh** Vietnam
64 A1 **Taytay** Phil.
82 G2 **Taz** *r.* Russia
114 B1 **Taza** Morocco
129 D2 **Tazin Lake** Can.
86 G2 **Tazovskaya Guba** *sea chan.* Russia
81 C1 **Tbilisi** Georgia
91 E2 **Tbilisskaya** Russia
118 B3 **Tchibanga** Gabon
118 B2 **Tcholliré** Cameroon
103 D1 **Tczew** Pol.
144 B2 **Teacapán** Mex.
54 A3 **Te Anau** N.Z.
54 A3 **Te Anau, Lake** N.Z.
145 C3 **Teapa** Mex.
54 C1 **Te Awamutu** N.Z.
115 C1 **Tébessa** Alg.
60 B2 **Tebingtinggi** *Sumatera Selatan* Indon.
60 A1 **Tebingtinggi** *Sumatera Utara* Indon.
114 B4 **Techiman** Ghana
144 B3 **Tecomán** Mex.
144 B2 **Tecoripa** Mex.
145 B3 **Técpan** Mex.
144 B2 **Tecuala** Mex.
110 C1 **Tecuci** Romania
68 C1 **Teeli** Russia
98 C1 **Tees** *r.* U.K.
111 C3 **Tefenni** Turkey
61 B2 **Tegal** Indon.
146 B3 **Tegucigalpa** Hond.
115 C3 **Teguidda-n-Tessoumt** Niger
114 B4 **Téhini** Côte d'Ivoire
81 D2 **Tehrān** Iran
145 C3 **Tehuacán** Mex.
145 C3 **Tehuantepec, Gulf of** Mex.
145 C3 **Tehuantepec, Istmo de** *isth.* Mex.
99 A2 **Teifi** *r.* U.K.
Te Ika-a-Māui N.Z. *see* **North Island**
76 C3 **Tejen** Turkm.
76 C3 **Tejen** *r.* Turkm.
Tejo *r.* Spain *see* **Tagus**
145 B3 **Tejupilco** Mex.

54 B2 **Tekapo, Lake** N.Z.
145 D2 **Tekax** Mex.
116 B3 **Tekezē Wenz** *r.* Eritrea/Eth.
111 C2 **Tekirdağ** Turkey
54 C1 **Te Kuiti** N.Z.
75 C2 **Tel** *r.* India
81 C1 **Telavi** Georgia
80 B2 **Tel Aviv-Yafo** Israel
145 D2 **Telchac Puerto** Mex.
128 A2 **Telegraph Creek** Can.
154 B2 **Telêmaco Borba** Brazil
99 B2 **Telford** U.K.
86 E2 **Telpoziz, Gora** *mt.* Russia
88 B2 **Telšiai** Lith.
61 B2 **Telukbatang** Indon.
60 A1 **Telukdalam** Indon.
60 B1 **Teluk Intan** Malaysia
130 C2 **Temagami Lake** Can.
61 C2 **Temanggung** Indon.
123 C2 **Temba** S. Africa
60 B2 **Tembilahan** Indon.
120 A1 **Tembo Aluma** Angola
99 B2 **Teme** *r.* U.K.
60 B1 **Temerluh** Malaysia
77 D1 **Temirtau** Kazakh.
53 C2 **Temora** Austr.
139 D2 **Temple** U.S.A.
97 C2 **Templemore** Ireland
145 C2 **Tempoal** Mex.
91 D2 **Temryuk** Russia
153 A4 **Temuco** Chile
54 B2 **Temuka** N.Z.
145 C2 **Tenabo** Mex.
73 C3 **Tenali** India
63 A2 **Tenasserim** Myanmar
99 A3 **Tenby** U.K.
117 C3 **Tendaho** Eth.
105 D3 **Tende** France
108 A2 **Tende, Col de** *pass* France/Italy
73 D4 **Ten Degree Channel** India
67 D3 **Tendō** Japan
114 B3 **Ténenkou** Mali
115 D3 **Ténéré, Erg du** *des.* Niger
115 D2 **Ténéré du Tafassâsset** *des.* Niger
114 A2 **Tenerife** *i.* Canary Islands
107 D2 **Ténès** Alg.
61 C2 **Tengah, Kepulauan** *is* Indon.
62 A1 **Tengchong** China
61 C2 **Tenggarong** Indon.
70 A2 **Tengger Shamo** *des.* China
71 B3 **Tengxian** China
119 C4 **Tenke** Dem. Rep. Congo
114 B3 **Tenkodogo** Burkina Faso
51 C1 **Tennant Creek** Austr.
142 C1 **Tennessee** *r.* U.S.A.
142 C1 **Tennessee** *state* U.S.A.
145 C3 **Tenosique** Mex.
53 D1 **Tenterfield** Austr.
154 B2 **Teodoro Sampaio** Brazil
155 D1 **Teófilo Otoni** Brazil
145 C3 **Teopisca** Mex.
144 B2 **Tepache** Mex.
54 B1 **Te Paki** N.Z.
144 B3 **Tepalcatepec** Mex.
144 B2 **Tepatitlán** Mex.
144 B2 **Tepehuanes** Mex.
109 D2 **Tepelenë** Albania
144 B2 **Tepic** Mex.
102 C1 **Teplice** Czechia
89 E3 **Teploye** Russia
144 B2 **Tequila** Mex.
108 B2 **Teramo** Italy
89 E3 **Terbuny** Russia
90 B2 **Terebovlya** Ukr.
87 D4 **Terek** *r.* Russia
151 D2 **Teresina** Brazil
155 D2 **Teresópolis** Brazil
63 A3 **Teressa Island** India
80 B1 **Terme** Turkey
108 B3 **Termini Imerese** *Sicily* Italy
145 C3 **Términos, Laguna de** *lag.* Mex.
77 C3 **Termiz** Uzbek.
109 B2 **Termoli** Italy
59 C2 **Ternate** Indon.
100 A2 **Terneuzen** Neth.
108 B2 **Terni** Italy
90 B2 **Ternopil'** Ukr.
128 B2 **Terrace** Can.
130 B2 **Terrace Bay** Can.
122 B2 **Terra Firma** S. Africa
140 B3 **Terre Haute** U.S.A.
131 E2 **Terrenceville** Can.
100 B1 **Terschelling** *i.* Neth.
108 A3 **Tertenia** *Sardinia* Italy
107 C1 **Teruel** Spain
92 H2 **Tervola** Fin.
109 C2 **Tešanj** Bos. & Herz.
116 B3 **Teseney** Eritrea
66 D2 **Teshio-gawa** *r.* Japan
128 A1 **Teslin** Can.
128 A1 **Teslin Lake** Can.
154 B1 **Tesouro** Brazil
115 C3 **Tessaoua** Niger
121 C2 **Tete** Moz.
90 C1 **Teteriv** *r.* Ukr.
101 F1 **Teterow** Ger.
90 B2 **Tetiyiv** Ukr.
114 B1 **Tétouan** Morocco
109 D2 **Tetovo** Macedonia
152 B3 **Teuco** *r.* Arg.
144 B2 **Teul de González Ortega** Mex.
101 D1 **Teutoburger Wald** *hills* Ger.
Tevere *r.* Italy *see* **Tiber**
54 A3 **Teviot** N.Z.
Te Waipounamu N.Z. *see* **South Island**
51 E2 **Tewantin** Austr.
54 C2 **Te Wharau** N.Z.
139 E2 **Texarkana** U.S.A.
53 D1 **Texas** Austr.
139 D2 **Texas** *state* U.S.A.
139 E3 **Texas City** U.S.A.
100 B1 **Texel** *i.* Neth.
139 D2 **Texoma, Lake** U.S.A.
123 C2 **Teyateyaneng** Lesotho
89 F2 **Teykovo** Russia
89 F2 **Teza** *r.* Russia
75 D2 **Tezpur** India
62 A1 **Tezu** India
129 E1 **Tha-anne** *r.* Can.
123 C2 **Thabana-Ntlenyana** *mt.* Lesotho
123 C2 **Thaba Putsoa** *mt.* Lesotho
123 C1 **Thabazimbi** S. Africa
123 C2 **Thabong** S. Africa
63 A2 **Thagyettaw** Myanmar
62 B1 **Thai Binh** Vietnam
63 B2 **Thailand** *country* Asia
63 B2 **Thailand, Gulf of** Asia
62 B1 **Thai Nguyên** Vietnam
62 B2 **Thakhèk** Laos
63 A3 **Thalang** Thai.
74 B1 **Thal Desert** Pak.
101 E2 **Thale** Ger.
62 B2 **Tha Li** Thai.
123 C1 **Thamaga** Botswana
116 C3 **Thamar, Jabal** *mt.* Yemen
79 C3 **Thamarīt** Oman
130 B2 **Thames** *r.* Can.
54 C1 **Thames** N.Z.
99 D3 **Thames** *est.* U.K.
99 D3 **Thames** *r.* U.K.
63 A2 **Thanbyuzayat** Myanmar
62 A2 **Thandwe** Myanmar
62 B2 **Thanh Hoa** Vietnam
73 B3 **Thanjavur** India
63 A2 **Thanlyin** Myanmar
74 A2 **Thano Bula Khan** Pak.
62 B1 **Than Uyên** Vietnam
74 A2 **Thar Desert** India/Pak.
52 B1 **Thargomindah** Austr.
81 C2 **Tharthār, Buḩayrat ath** *l.* Iraq
111 B2 **Thasos** *i.* Greece
62 B1 **Thât Khê** Vietnam
62 A2 **Thaton** Myanmar
74 A2 **Thatta** Pak.
62 A1 **Thaungdut** Myanmar
62 A2 **Thayawadi** Myanmar
62 A2 **Thayetmyo** Myanmar
62 A1 **Thazi** Myanmar
146 C2 **The Bahamas** *country* West Indies
98 B1 **The Cheviot** *h.* U.K.
134 B1 **The Dalles** U.S.A.
99 C2 **The Fens** *reg.* U.K.
114 A3 **The Gambia** *country* Africa
The Great Oasis Egypt *see* **Khārijah, Wāḩāt al**
79 C2 **The Gulf** Asia
100 B1 **The Hague** Neth.
129 E1 **Thelon** *r.* Can.
101 E2 **Themar** Ger.
96 A1 **The Minch** *sea chan.* U.K.
150 B2 **Theodore Roosevelt** *r.* Brazil
129 D2 **The Pas** Can.
111 B2 **Thermaïkos Kolpos** *g.* Greece
136 B2 **Thermopolis** U.S.A.
53 C3 **The Rock** Austr.
130 B2 **Thessalon** Can.
111 B2 **Thessaloniki** Greece
99 D2 **Thetford** U.K.
131 C2 **Thetford Mines** Can.
62 A1 **The Triangle** *mts* Myanmar
131 D1 **Thévenet, Lac** *l.* Can.
99 D2 **The Wash** *b.* U.K.
139 D2 **The Woodlands** U.S.A.
142 B3 **Thibodaux** U.S.A.
129 E2 **Thicket Portage** Can.
137 D1 **Thief River Falls** U.S.A.
105 C2 **Thiers** France
119 D3 **Thika** Kenya
73 B4 **Thiladhunmathi** Maldives
75 C2 **Thimphu** Bhutan
105 D2 **Thionville** France
Thira *i.* Greece *see* **Santorini**
98 C1 **Thirsk** U.K.
73 B4 **Thiruvananthapuram** India
93 E4 **Thisted** Denmark
129 E1 **Thlewiaza** *r.* Can.
62 A2 **Thoen** Thai.
123 D1 **Thohoyandou** S. Africa
101 E1 **Thomasburg** Ger.
97 C2 **Thomastown** Ireland
143 D2 **Thomasville** U.S.A.
100 C2 **Thommen** Belgium
129 E2 **Thompson** Can.
128 E3 **Thompson** *r.* U.S.A.
134 C1 **Thompson Falls** U.S.A.
128 B2 **Thompson Sound** Can.
Thoothukudi India *see* **Tuticorin**
96 C3 **Thornhill** U.K.
55 C2 **Thorshavnheiane** *reg.* Antarctica
104 B2 **Thouars** France
128 C2 **Three Hills** Can.
63 A2 **Three Pagodas Pass** Myanmar/Thai.
114 B4 **Three Points, Cape** Ghana
73 B3 **Thrissur** India
63 B2 **Thu Dâu Môt** Vietnam

100 B2 Thuin Belgium
127 G1 Thule Air Base Greenland
121 B3 Thuli Zimbabwe
130 B2 Thunder Bay Can.
63 A3 Thung Song Thai.
101 E2 Thüringer Becken reg. Ger.
101 E2 Thüringer Wald mts Ger.
97 C2 Thurles Ireland
96 C1 Thurso U.K.
96 C1 Thurso r. U.K.
151 D2 Tianguá Brazil
70 B2 Tianjin China
70 B2 Tianjin mun. China
71 A1 Tianlin China
70 B2 Tianmen China
70 A2 Tianshui China
154 B2 Tibagi r. Brazil
118 B2 Tibati Cameroon
108 B2 Tiber r. Italy
Tiberias, Lake Israel see Galilee, Sea of
115 D2 Tibesti mts Chad
Tibet, Plateau of China see Xizang Zizhiqu
68 B2 Tibet reg. China
68 B2 Tibet, Plateau of China
115 D2 Tibisti, Sarīr des. Libya
52 B1 Tibooburra Austr.
144 A2 Tiburón, Isla i. Mex.
114 B3 Tichît Maur.
114 A2 Tichla Western Sahara
145 D2 Ticul Mex.
114 A3 Tidjikja Maur.
100 B2 Tiel Neth.
65 A1 Tieling China
100 A2 Tielt Belgium
100 B2 Tienen Belgium
68 B2 Tien Shan mts China/Kyrg.
Tientsin China see Tianjin
93 G3 Tierp Sweden
145 C3 Tierra Blanca Mex.
145 C3 Tierra Colorada Mex.
153 B6 Tierra del Fuego i. Arg./Chile
154 C2 Tietê Brazil
Tiflis Georgia see Tbilisi
143 D2 Tifton U.S.A.
Tighina Moldova see Bender
131 D2 Tignish Can.
150 A2 Tigre r. Ecuador/Peru
81 C2 Tigris r. Asia
145 C2 Tihuatlán Mex.
144 A1 Tijuana Mex.
Tikapa Moana N.Z. see Hauraki Gulf/Tikapa Moana
91 E2 Tikhoretsk Russia
89 D2 Tikhvin Russia
89 D2 Tikhvinskaya Gryada ridge Russia
54 C1 Tikokino N.Z.
81 C2 Tikrīt Iraq
83 J2 Tiksi Russia
100 B2 Tilburg Neth.
152 B3 Tilcara Arg.
115 C3 Tillabéri Niger
134 B1 Tillamook U.S.A.
63 A3 Tillanchong Island India
111 C3 Tilos i. Greece
52 B2 Tilpa Austr.
86 F2 Til'tim Russia
89 E3 Tim Russia
86 D2 Timanskiy Kryazh ridge Russia
54 B2 Timaru N.Z.
91 D2 Timashëvsk Russia
114 B3 Timbedgha Maur.
50 C1 Timber Creek Austr.
114 B3 Timbuktu Mali
114 C2 Timimoun Alg.

111 B2 Timiou Prodromou, Akrotirio pt Greece
110 B1 Timiş r. Romania
110 B1 Timişoara Romania
130 B2 Timmins Can.
89 E2 Timokhino Russia
151 D2 Timon Brazil
59 C3 Timor i. East Timor/Indon.
Timor-Leste country Asia see East Timor
58 C3 Timor Sea Austr./Indon.
93 G3 Timrå Sweden
114 B2 Tindouf Alg.
75 C2 Tingri China
93 F4 Tingsryd Sweden
59 D2 Tinian i. N. Mariana Is
152 B3 Tinogasta Arg.
111 C3 Tinos Greece
111 C3 Tinos i. Greece
115 C2 Tinrhert, Hamada de Alg.
62 A1 Tinsukia India
107 D2 Tipasa Alg.
97 B2 Tipperary Ireland
109 C2 Tirana Albania
Tiranë Albania see Tirana
108 B1 Tirano Italy
90 B2 Tiraspol Moldova
111 C3 Tire Turkey
96 A2 Tiree i. U.K.
74 B1 Tirich Mir mt. Pak.
73 B3 Tiruchchirappalli India
73 B4 Tirunelveli India
73 B3 Tirupati India
73 B3 Tiruppattur India
73 B3 Tiruppur India
109 D1 Tisa r. Serbia
129 D2 Tisdale Can.
107 D2 Tissemsilt Alg.
152 B2 Titicaca, Lake Bol./Peru
75 C2 Titlagarh India
110 C2 Titu Romania
143 D3 Titusville U.S.A.
99 B3 Tiverton U.K.
108 B2 Tivoli Italy
79 C2 Ţīwī Oman
75 C2 Tizimín Mex.
107 D2 Tizi Ouzou Alg.
114 B2 Tiznit Morocco
145 C3 Tlacotalpán Mex.
144 B2 Tlahualilo Mex.
145 C3 Tlapa Mex.
145 C3 Tlaxcala Mex.
145 C3 Tlaxiaco Mex.
114 B1 Tlemcen Alg.
123 C1 Tlokweng Botswana
128 B2 Toad River Can.
121 □D2 Toamasina Madag.
60 B1 Toba, Danau l. Indon.
74 A1 Toba and Kakar Ranges mts Pak.
147 D3 Tobago i. Trin. and Tob.
59 C3 Tobelo Indon.
130 B2 Tobermory Can.
96 A2 Tobermory U.K.
129 D2 Tobin Lake Can.
60 B2 Toboali Indon.
86 F3 Tobol'sk Russia
76 C1 Tobyl r. Kazakh./Russia
151 D2 Tocantinópolis Brazil
151 D2 Tocantins r. Brazil
143 D2 Toccoa U.S.A.
108 A1 Toce r. Italy
152 A3 Tocopilla Chile
53 C3 Tocumwal Austr.
144 A2 Todos Santos Mex.
128 B3 Tofino Can.
96 □ Toft U.K.
49 G4 Tofua i. Tonga

59 C3 Togian, Kepulauan is Indon.
114 C4 Togo country Africa
126 B2 Tohana India
125 D2 Tok U.S.A.
116 B3 Tokar Sudan
69 E3 Tokara-rettō is Japan
91 E1 Tokarevka Russia
49 G3 Tokelau terr. S. Pacific Ocean
91 D2 Tokmak Ukr.
77 D2 Tokmok Kyrg.
54 C1 Tokoroa N.Z.
68 B2 Toksun China
67 B4 Tokushima Japan
67 C3 Tōkyō Japan
121 □D3 Tôlañaro Madag.
154 B2 Toledo Brazil
106 C2 Toledo Spain
140 C2 Toledo U.S.A.
106 C2 Toledo, Montes de mts Spain
142 B2 Toledo Bend Reservoir U.S.A.
121 □D3 Toliara Madag.
58 C2 Tolitoli Indon.
108 B1 Tolmezzo Italy
104 B3 Tolosa Spain
145 C3 Toluca Mex.
87 D3 Tol'yatti Russia
140 A2 Tomah U.S.A.
66 D2 Tomakomai Japan
66 D2 Tomari Port.
103 E1 Tomaszów Lubelski Pol.
103 E1 Tomaszów Mazowiecki Pol.
144 B3 Tomatlán Mex.
142 C2 Tombigbee r. U.S.A.
155 D2 Tombos Brazil
Tombouctou Mali see Timbuktu
120 A2 Tombua Angola
123 C1 Tom Burke S. Africa
53 C2 Tomingley Austr.
58 C3 Tomini, Teluk g. Indon.
109 C2 Tomislavgrad Bos. & Herz.
50 A2 Tom Price Austr.
82 G3 Tomsk Russia
93 F4 Tomtabacken h. Sweden
145 C3 Tonalá Mex.
150 B2 Tonantins Brazil
59 C2 Tondano Indon.
49 G4 Tonga country S. Pacific Ocean
49 G4 Tongatapu Group is Tonga
71 B3 Tongcheng China
70 A2 Tongchuan China
71 A3 Tongdao China
100 B2 Tongeren Belgium
62 B1 Tonghai China
65 B1 Tonghua China
65 B2 Tongjosŏn-man b. N. Korea
62 B1 Tongking, Gulf of China/Vietnam
69 E2 Tongliao China
70 B2 Tongling China
52 B2 Tongo Austr.
71 A3 Tongren China
Tongshan China see Xuzhou
Tongtian He r. China see Yangtze
96 B1 Tongue U.K.
65 B3 Tongyeong S. Korea
65 A2 Tongyu China
65 A1 Tongyuanpu China
74 B2 Tonk India
63 B2 Tonle Sap l. Cambodia
135 C3 Tonopah U.S.A.
93 F4 Tønsberg Norway
135 D2 Tooele U.S.A.
52 B3 Tooleybuc Austr.
53 D1 Toowoomba Austr.
137 D3 Topeka U.S.A.
144 B2 Topia Mex.

144 B2 **Topolobampo** Mex.
86 C2 **Topozero, Ozero** *l.* Russia
134 B1 **Toppenish** U.S.A.
111 C3 **Torbalı** Turkey
76 B3 **Torbat-e Ḩeydarīyeh** Iran
76 C3 **Torbat-e Jām** Iran
106 C1 **Tordesillas** Spain
107 C1 **Tordesilos** Spain
107 D1 **Torelló** Spain
101 F2 **Torgau** Ger.
76 C2 **Torgay** Kazakh.
100 A2 **Torhout** Belgium
Torino Italy *see* **Turin**
154 B1 **Torixoréu** Brazil
106 B1 **Tormes** *r.* Spain
92 H2 **Torneälven** *r.* Sweden
127 G3 **Torngat Mountains** Can.
92 H2 **Tornio** Fin.
106 B1 **Toro** Spain
130 C2 **Toronto** Can.
119 D2 **Tororo** Uganda
Toros Dağları *mts* Turkey *see* **Taurus Mountains**
99 B3 **Torquay** U.K.
106 B2 **Torrão** Port.
106 B1 **Torre** *mt.* Port.
107 D1 **Torreblanca** Spain
106 C1 **Torrecerredo** *mt.* Spain
106 B1 **Torre de Moncorvo** Port.
106 C1 **Torrelavega** Spain
106 C2 **Torremolinos** Spain
52 A2 **Torrens, Lake** *imp. l.* Austr.
107 C2 **Torrent** Spain
144 B2 **Torreón** Mex.
106 B2 **Torres Novas** Port.
106 B2 **Torres Vedras** Port.
107 C2 **Torrevieja** Spain
96 B2 **Torridon** U.K.
106 C2 **Torrijos** Spain
141 E2 **Torrington** *CT* U.S.A.
136 C2 **Torrington** *WY* U.S.A.
107 D1 **Torroella de Montgrí** Spain
94 B1 **Tórshavn** Faroe Is
152 B3 **Tórtolas, Cerro de las** *mt.* Arg./Chile
108 A3 **Tortolì** *Sardinia* Italy
107 D1 **Tortosa** Spain
103 D1 **Toruń** Pol.
97 B1 **Tory Island** Ireland
89 D2 **Torzhok** Russia
122 B2 **Tosca** S. Africa
108 B2 **Toscano, Arcipelago** *is* Italy
77 C2 **Toshkent** Uzbek.
89 D2 **Tosno** Russia
152 B3 **Tostado** Arg.
101 D1 **Tostedt** Ger.
80 B1 **Tosya** Turkey
86 D3 **Tot'ma** Russia
67 B3 **Tottori** Japan
114 B4 **Touba** Côte d'Ivoire
114 B1 **Toubkal, Jebel** *mt.* Morocco
114 B3 **Tougan** Burkina Faso
115 C1 **Touggourt** Alg.
105 D2 **Toul** France
105 D3 **Toulon** France
104 C3 **Toulouse** France
100 A2 **Tournai** Belgium
105 C2 **Tournus** France
151 E2 **Touros** Brazil
104 C2 **Tours** France
115 D2 **Tousside, Pic** *mt.* Chad
122 B3 **Touwsrivier** S. Africa
66 D2 **Towada** Japan
134 D1 **Townsend** U.S.A.
51 D1 **Townsville** Austr.
77 E2 **Toxkan He** *r.* China
66 D2 **Tōya-ko** *l.* Japan
67 C3 **Toyama** Japan
67 C3 **Toyota** Japan
115 C1 **Tozeur** Tunisia
81 C1 **T'q'varcheli** Georgia
Trâblous Lebanon *see* **Tripoli**
80 B1 **Trabzon** Turkey
106 B2 **Trafalgar, Cabo** *c.* Spain
128 C3 **Trail** Can.
88 B3 **Trakai** Lith.
97 B2 **Tralee** Ireland
97 C2 **Tramore** Ireland
63 A3 **Trang** Thai.
59 C3 **Trangan** *i.* Indon.
55 I2 **Transantarctic Mountains** Antarctica
90 B2 **Transnistria** *disp. terr.* Moldova
110 B1 **Transylvanian Alps** *mts* Romania
108 B3 **Trapani** *Sicily* Italy
53 C3 **Traralgon** Austr.
63 B2 **Trat** Thai.
102 C2 **Traunstein** Ger.
140 B2 **Traverse City** U.S.A.
103 D2 **Třebíč** Czechia
109 C2 **Trebinje** Bos. & Herz.
103 E2 **Trebišov** Slovakia
109 C1 **Trebnje** Slovenia
153 C4 **Treinta y Tres** Uru.
153 B5 **Trelew** Arg.
93 F4 **Trelleborg** Sweden
130 C2 **Tremblant, Mont** *h.* Can.
109 C2 **Tremiti, Isole** *is* Italy
134 D2 **Tremonton** U.S.A.
107 D1 **Tremp** Spain
103 D2 **Trenčín** Slovakia
153 B4 **Trenque Lauquen** Arg.
98 C2 **Trent** *r.* U.K.
108 B1 **Trento** Italy
141 D2 **Trenton** Can.
137 E2 **Trenton** *MO* U.S.A.
141 E2 **Trenton** *NJ* U.S.A.
131 E2 **Trepassey** Can.
153 B4 **Tres Arroyos** Arg.
155 C2 **Três Corações** Brazil
154 B2 **Três Lagoas** Brazil
153 A5 **Tres Lagos** Arg.
155 C1 **Três Marias, Represa** *resr* Brazil
155 C2 **Três Pontas** Brazil
153 B5 **Tres Puntas, Cabo** *c.* Arg.
155 D2 **Três Rios** Brazil
101 F1 **Treuenbrietzen** Ger.
108 A1 **Treviglio** Italy
108 B1 **Treviso** Italy
99 A3 **Trevose Head** U.K.
109 C3 **Tricase** Italy
53 C2 **Trida** Austr.
100 C3 **Trier** Ger.
108 B1 **Trieste** Italy
108 B1 **Triglav** *mt.* Slovenia
59 D3 **Trikora, Puncak** *mt.* Indon.
97 C2 **Trim** Ireland
73 C4 **Trincomalee** Sri Lanka
154 C1 **Trindade** Brazil
152 B2 **Trinidad** Bol.
147 D3 **Trinidad** *i.* Trin. and Tob.
136 C3 **Trinidad** U.S.A.
147 D3 **Trinidad and Tobago** *country* West Indies
131 E2 **Trinity Bay** Can.
111 B3 **Tripoli** Greece
80 B2 **Tripoli** Lebanon
115 D1 **Tripoli** Libya
113 D10 **Tristan da Cunha** *i.* S. Atlantic Ocean
Trivandrum India *see* **Thiruvananthapuram**
108 B2 **Trivento** Italy
103 D2 **Trnava** Slovakia
109 C2 **Trogir** Croatia
109 C2 **Troia** Italy
100 C2 **Troisdorf** Ger.
131 C2 **Trois-Rivières** Can.
86 E2 **Troitsko-Pechorsk** Russia
151 C2 **Trombetas** *r.* Brazil
123 C3 **Trompsburg** S. Africa
92 G2 **Tromsø** Norway
92 F3 **Trondheim** Norway
128 C2 **Trout Lake** Can.
128 B1 **Trout Lake** *l. N.W.T.* Can.
130 A1 **Trout Lake** *l. Ont.* Can.
99 B3 **Trowbridge** U.K.
142 C2 **Troy** *AL* U.S.A.
141 E2 **Troy** *NY* U.S.A.
105 C2 **Troyes** France
109 D2 **Trstenik** Serbia
89 D3 **Trubchevsk** Russia
106 B1 **Truchas** Spain
79 C2 **Trucial Coast** U.A.E.
146 B3 **Trujillo** Hond.
150 A2 **Trujillo** Peru
106 B2 **Trujillo** Spain
147 C4 **Trujillo** Venez.
142 B1 **Trumann** U.S.A.
131 D2 **Truro** Can.
99 A3 **Truro** U.K.
138 B2 **Truth or Consequences** U.S.A.
103 D1 **Trutnov** Czechia
93 F3 **Trysil** Norway
103 D1 **Trzebiatów** Pol.
68 B1 **Tsagaannuur** Mongolia
121 □D2 **Tsaratanana, Massif du** *mts* Madag.
110 C2 **Tsarevo** Bulg.
122 A2 **Tses** Namibia
122 B1 **Tsetseng** Botswana
68 C1 **Tsetserleg** *Arhangay* Mongolia
68 C1 **Tsetserleg** *Hövsgöl* Mongolia
122 B2 **Tshabong** Botswana
122 B1 **Tshane** Botswana
118 B3 **Tshela** Dem. Rep. Congo
118 C3 **Tshikapa** Dem. Rep. Congo
118 C3 **Tshikapa** *r.* Dem. Rep. Congo
123 D1 **Tshipise** S. Africa
118 C3 **Tshitanzu** Dem. Rep. Congo
118 C3 **Tshuapa** *r.* Dem. Rep. Congo
Tshwane S. Africa *see* **Pretoria**
87 D4 **Tsimlyanskoye Vodokhranilishche** *resr* Russia
Tsingtao China *see* **Qingdao**
Tsining China *see* **Ulan Qab**
121 □D2 **Tsiroanomandidy** Madag.
123 C3 **Tsomo** S. Africa
67 C4 **Tsu** Japan
67 D3 **Tsuchiura** Japan
66 D2 **Tsugarū-kaikyō** *str.* Japan
120 A2 **Tsumeb** Namibia
122 A1 **Tsumis Park** Namibia
120 B2 **Tsumkwe** Namibia
67 C3 **Tsuruga** Japan
66 C3 **Tsuruoka** Japan
67 A4 **Tsushima** *is* Japan
Tsushima-kaikyō *str.* Japan/S. Korea *see* **Korea Strait**
67 B3 **Tsuyama** Japan
123 C2 **Tswelelang** S. Africa
Tsyurupyns'k Ukr. *see* **Oleshky**
Tthenaagoo Can. *see* **Nahanni Butte**
59 C3 **Tual** Indon.
97 B2 **Tuam** Ireland
91 D3 **Tuapse** Russia
54 A3 **Tuatapere** N.Z.
96 A1 **Tuath, Loch a'** *b.* U.K.
138 A1 **Tuba City** U.S.A.
61 C2 **Tuban** Indon.

52 D3 **Tubarão** Brazil
02 B2 **Tübingen** Ger.
15 E1 **Tubruq** Libya
49 H4 **Tubuai** *i.* Fr. Polynesia
49 I4 **Tubuai Islands** *is* Fr. Polynesia
44 A1 **Tubutama** Mex.
52 C2 **Tucavaca** Bol.
28 B1 **Tuchitua** Can.
38 A2 **Tucson** U.S.A.
39 C1 **Tucumcari** U.S.A.
50 B1 **Tucupita** Venez.
51 D2 **Tucuruí** Brazil
51 D2 **Tucuruí, Represa de** *resr* Brazil
07 C1 **Tudela** Spain
06 B1 **Tuela** *r.* Port.
62 A1 **Tuensang** India
64 B1 **Tuguegarao** Phil.
06 B1 **Tui** Spain
59 C3 **Tukangbesi, Kepulauan** *is* Indon.
26 C2 **Tuktoyaktuk** Can.
88 B2 **Tukums** Latvia
45 C2 **Tula** Mex.
89 E3 **Tula** Russia
45 C2 **Tulancingo** Mex.
35 C3 **Tulare** U.S.A.
38 B2 **Tularosa** U.S.A.
10 C1 **Tulcea** Romania
90 B2 **Tul'chyn** Ukr.
29 E1 **Tulemalu Lake** Can.
39 C2 **Tulia** U.S.A.
42 C1 **Tullahoma** U.S.A.
97 C2 **Tullamore** Ireland
04 C2 **Tulle** France
51 D1 **Tully** Austr.
39 D1 **Tulsa** U.S.A.
50 A1 **Tumaco** Col.
23 C2 **Tumahole** S. Africa
73 B3 **Tumakuru** India
93 G4 **Tumba** Sweden
18 B3 **Tumba, Lac** *l.* Dem. Rep. Congo
53 C3 **Tumbarumba** Austr.
50 A2 **Tumbes** Peru
28 B2 **Tumbler Ridge** Can.
52 A2 **Tumby Bay** Austr.
65 B1 **Tumen** China
50 B1 **Tumereng** Guyana
64 A2 **Tumindao** *i.* Phil.
Tumkur India *see* **Tumakuru**
74 A2 **Tump** Pak.
51 C1 **Tumucumaque, Serra** *hills* Brazil
53 C3 **Tumut** Austr.
80 B2 **Tunceli** Turkey
53 D2 **Tuncurry** Austr.
19 D4 **Tunduru** Tanz.
10 C2 **Tundzha** *r.* Bulg.
28 B1 **Tungsten (abandoned)** Can.
15 D1 **Tunis** Tunisia
15 C1 **Tunisia** *country* Africa
50 A1 **Tunja** Col.
92 F3 **Tunnsjøen** *l.* Norway
Tunxi China *see* **Huangshan**
54 B2 **Tupã** Brazil
54 C1 **Tupaciguara** Brazil
42 C2 **Tupelo** U.S.A.
52 B3 **Tupiza** Bol.
76 B2 **Tupkaragan, Mys** *pt* Kazakh.
83 H2 **Tura** Russia
86 F3 **Tura** *r.* Russia
78 B2 **Turabah** Saudi Arabia
83 J3 **Turana, Khrebet** *mts* Russia
54 C1 **Turangi** N.Z.
76 B2 **Turan Lowland** Asia
78 A1 **Ţurayf** Saudi Arabia
88 B2 **Turba** Estonia
74 A2 **Turbat** Pak.
150 A1 **Turbo** Col.
110 B1 **Turda** Romania
Turfan China *see* **Turpan**
111 C3 **Turgutlu** Turkey
80 B1 **Turhal** Turkey
107 C2 **Turia, Riu** *r.* Spain
108 A1 **Turin** Italy
86 F3 **Turinsk** Russia
90 A1 **Turiys'k** Ukr.
119 D2 **Turkana, Lake** *salt l.* Eth./Kenya
80 B2 **Turkey** *country* Asia/Europe
77 C2 **Turkistan** Kazakh.
76 C3 **Türkmenabat** Turkm.
76 B2 **Türkmenbaşy** Turkm.
76 B2 **Turkmenistan** *country* Asia
147 C2 **Turks and Caicos Islands** *terr.* West Indies
93 H3 **Turku** Fin.
135 B3 **Turlock** U.S.A.
54 C2 **Turnagain, Cape** N.Z.
100 B2 **Turnhout** Belgium
129 D2 **Turnor Lake** Can.
110 B2 **Turnu Măgurele** Romania
68 B2 **Turpan** China
77 D2 **Turugart Pass** China/Kyrg.
142 C2 **Tuscaloosa** U.S.A.
142 C2 **Tuskegee** U.S.A.
73 B4 **Tuticorin** India
120 B3 **Tutume** Botswana
49 F3 **Tuvalu** *country* S. Pacific Ocean
78 B2 **Tuwayq, Jabal** *hills* Saudi Arabia
78 B2 **Tuwayq, Jabal** *mts* Saudi Arabia
78 A2 **Tuwwal** Saudi Arabia
144 B2 **Tuxpan** *Nayarit* Mex.
145 C2 **Tuxpan** *Veracruz* Mex.
145 C3 **Tuxtla Gutiérrez** Mex.
62 B1 **Tuyên Quang** Vietnam
63 B2 **Tuy Hoa** Vietnam
80 B2 **Tuz, Lake** *salt l.* Turkey
Tuz Gölü *salt l.* Turkey *see* **Tuz, Lake**
81 C2 **Ţūz Khurmātū** Iraq
109 C2 **Tuzla** Bos. & Herz.
91 E2 **Tuzlov** *r.* Russia
89 E2 **Tver'** Russia
98 B1 **Tweed** *r.* U.K.
122 A2 **Twee Rivier** Namibia
135 C4 **Twentynine Palms** U.S.A.
131 E2 **Twillingate** Can.
134 D2 **Twin Falls** U.S.A.
137 E1 **Two Harbors** U.S.A.
129 C2 **Two Hills** Can.
139 D2 **Tyler** U.S.A.
83 J3 **Tynda** Russia
93 F3 **Tynset** Norway
80 B2 **Tyre** Lebanon
111 B3 **Tyrnavos** Greece
52 B3 **Tyrrell, Lake** *dry lake* Austr.
108 B2 **Tyrrhenian Sea** France/Italy
87 E3 **Tyul'gan** Russia
86 F3 **Tyumen'** Russia
83 J2 **Tyung** *r.* Russia
99 A3 **Tywi** *r.* U.K.
123 D1 **Tzaneen** S. Africa

U

120 B2 **Uamanda** Angola
155 D2 **Ubá** Brazil
155 D1 **Ubaí** Brazil
151 E3 **Ubaitaba** Brazil
118 B3 **Ubangi** *r.* C.A.R./Dem. Rep. Congo
67 B4 **Ube** Japan
106 C2 **Úbeda** Spain
154 C1 **Uberaba** Brazil
154 C1 **Uberlândia** Brazil
106 B1 **Ubiña, Peña** *mt.* Spain
123 D2 **Ubombo** S. Africa
63 B2 **Ubon Ratchathani** Thai.
119 C3 **Ubundu** Dem. Rep. Congo
150 A2 **Ucayali** *r.* Peru
74 B2 **Uch** Pak.
66 D2 **Uchiura-wan** *b.* Japan
83 J3 **Uchur** *r.* Russia
128 B3 **Ucluelet** Can.
74 B2 **Udaipur** India
91 C1 **Uday** *r.* Ukr.
93 F4 **Uddevalla** Sweden
92 G2 **Uddjaure** *l.* Sweden
100 B2 **Uden** Neth.
74 B1 **Udhampur** India
108 B1 **Udine** Italy
89 E2 **Udomlya** Russia
62 B2 **Udon Thani** Thai.
73 B3 **Udupi** India
83 K3 **Udyl', Ozero** *l.* Russia
67 C3 **Ueda** Japan
58 C3 **Uekuli** Indon.
118 C2 **Uele** *r.* Dem. Rep. Congo
101 E1 **Uelzen** Ger.
119 C2 **Uere** *r.* Dem. Rep. Congo
87 E3 **Ufa** Russia
119 D3 **Ugalla** *r.* Tanz.
119 D2 **Uganda** *country* Africa
89 E2 **Uglich** Russia
89 D2 **Uglovka** Russia
89 D3 **Ugra** Russia
103 D2 **Uherské Hradiště** Czechia
101 E2 **Uichteritz** Ger.
96 A2 **Uig** U.K.
120 A1 **Uíge** Angola
65 B2 **Uijeongbu** S. Korea
135 D2 **Uinta Mountains** U.S.A.
65 B2 **Uiseong** S. Korea
120 A3 **Uis Mine** Namibia
123 C3 **Uitenhage** S. Africa
100 C1 **Uithuizen** Neth.
74 B2 **Ujjain** India
89 F3 **Ukholovo** Russia
62 A1 **Ukhrul** India
86 E2 **Ukhta** Russia
135 B3 **Ukiah** U.S.A.
127 H2 **Ukkusissat** Greenland
88 B2 **Ukmergė** Lith.
90 C2 **Ukraine** *country* Europe
Ulaanbaatar Mongolia *see* **Ulan Bator**
68 C1 **Ulaangom** Mongolia
69 D1 **Ulan Bator** Mongolia
Ulanhad China *see* **Chifeng**
69 E1 **Ulanhot** China
87 D4 **Ulan-Khol** Russia
70 B1 **Ulan Qab** China
69 D1 **Ulan-Ude** Russia
75 D1 **Ulan Ul Hu** *l.* China
Uleåborg Fin. *see* **Oulu**
88 C2 **Ülenurme** Estonia
69 D1 **Uliastai** China
68 C1 **Uliastay** Mongolia
59 D2 **Ulithi** *atoll* Micronesia
65 B2 **Uljin** S. Korea
53 D3 **Ulladulla** Austr.
96 B2 **Ullapool** U.K.
65 C2 **Ulleung-do** *i.* S. Korea
98 B1 **Ullswater** *l.* U.K.
102 B2 **Ulm** Ger.
65 B2 **Ulsan** S. Korea
96 □ **Ulsta** U.K.
97 C1 **Ulster** *reg.* Ireland/U.K.
52 B3 **Ultima** Austr.
111 C3 **Ulubey** Turkey

111 C2 **Uludağ** *mt.* Turkey
126 D2 **Ulukhaktok** Can.
123 D2 **Ulundi** S. Africa
77 E2 **Ulungur Hu** *l.* China
50 C2 **Uluru/Ayers Rock** *h.* Austr.
98 B1 **Ulverston** U.K.
87 D3 **Ul'yanovsk** Russia
136 C3 **Ulysses** U.S.A.
90 C2 **Uman'** Ukr.
86 C2 **Umba** Russia
59 D3 **Umboi** *i.* P.N.G.
92 H3 **Umeå** Sweden
92 H3 **Umeälven** *r.* Sweden
127 I2 **Umiiviip Kangertiva** *inlet* Greenland
126 D2 **Umingmaktok** Can.
123 D2 **Umlazi** S. Africa
117 A3 **Umm Keddada** Sudan
78 A2 **Umm Lajj** Saudi Arabia
117 B3 **Umm Ruwaba** Sudan
115 E1 **Umm Sa'ad** Libya
134 B2 **Umpqua** *r.* U.S.A.
120 A2 **Umpulo** Angola
154 B2 **Umuarama** Brazil
109 C1 **Una** *r.* Bos. & Herz./Croatia
155 E1 **Una** Brazil
154 C1 **Unaí** Brazil
78 B2 **'Unayzah** Saudi Arabia
136 C1 **Underwood** U.S.A.
89 D3 **Unecha** Russia
53 C2 **Ungarie** Austr.
52 A2 **Ungarra** Austr.
127 G2 **Ungava, Péninsule d'** *pen.* Can.
127 G3 **Ungava Bay** Can.
90 B2 **Ungheni** Moldova
Unguja *i.* Tanz. *see* **Zanzibar Island**
154 B3 **União da Vitória** Brazil
150 B2 **Unini** *r.* Brazil
142 C1 **Union City** U.S.A.
122 B3 **Uniondale** S. Africa
141 D3 **Uniontown** U.S.A.
79 C2 **United Arab Emirates** *country* Asia
95 C3 **United Kingdom** *country* Europe
132 D3 **United States of America** *country* N. America
129 D2 **Unity** Can.
96 □ **Unst** *i.* U.K.
101 E2 **Unstrut** *r.* Ger.
89 E3 **Upa** *r.* Russia
119 C3 **Upemba, Lac** *l.* Dem. Rep. Congo
122 B2 **Upington** S. Africa
134 B2 **Upper Alkali Lake** U.S.A.
128 C2 **Upper Arrow Lake** Can.
134 B2 **Upper Klamath Lake** U.S.A.
128 B1 **Upper Liard** Can.
97 C1 **Upper Lough Erne** *l.* U.K.
93 G4 **Uppsala** Sweden
78 B2 **'Uqlat aş Şuqūr** Saudi Arabia
Urad Qianqi China *see* **Xishanzui**
76 B2 **Ural** *r.* Kazakh./Russia
53 D2 **Uralla** Austr.
87 E3 **Ural Mountains** Russia
76 B1 **Ural'sk** Kazakh.
Ural'skiy Khrebet *mts* Russia *see* **Ural Mountains**
119 D3 **Urambo** Tanz.
53 C3 **Urana** Austr.
129 D2 **Uranium City** Can.
86 F2 **Uray** Russia
98 C1 **Ure** *r.* U.K.
86 D3 **Uren'** Russia
144 A2 **Ures** Mex.
76 C2 **Urganch** Uzbek.
100 B1 **Urk** Neth.
111 C3 **Urla** Turkey
81 C2 **Urmia, Lake** *salt l.* Iran
Uroševac Kosovo *see* **Ferizaj**
144 B2 **Uruáchic** Mex.
151 D3 **Uruaçu** Brazil
144 B3 **Uruapan** Mex.
150 A3 **Urubamba** *r.* Peru
151 C2 **Urucará** Brazil
151 D2 **Uruçuí** Brazil
151 C2 **Urucurituba** Brazil
152 C3 **Uruguaiana** Brazil
153 C4 **Uruguay** *country* S. America
Urumchi China *see* **Ürümqi**
68 B2 **Ürümqi** China
53 D2 **Urunga** Austr.
110 C2 **Urziceni** Romania
67 B4 **Usa** Japan
82 E2 **Usa** *r.* Russia
111 C3 **Uşak** Turkey
82 G1 **Ushakova, Ostrov** *i.* Russia
77 E2 **Usharal** Kazakh.
77 D2 **Ushtobe** Kazakh.
153 B6 **Ushuaia** Arg.
86 E2 **Usinsk** Russia
88 C3 **Uskhodni** Belarus
89 E3 **Usman'** Russia
86 D2 **Usogorsk** Russia
104 C2 **Ussel** France
66 B2 **Ussuriysk** Russia
108 B3 **Ustica, Isola di** *i. Sicily* Italy
83 H3 **Ust'-Ilimsk** Russia
86 E2 **Ust'-Ilych** Russia
103 D1 **Ustka** Pol.
83 L3 **Ust'-Kamchatsk** Russia
77 E2 **Ust'-Kamenogorsk** Kazakh.
86 F2 **Ust'-Kara** Russia
86 E2 **Ust'-Kulom** Russia
83 I3 **Ust'-Kut** Russia
91 D2 **Ust'-Labinsk** Russia
88 C2 **Ust'-Luga** Russia
86 E2 **Ust'-Nem** Russia
83 K2 **Ust'-Nera** Russia
83 K2 **Ust'-Omchug** Russia
83 H3 **Ust'-Ordynskiy** Russia
86 E2 **Ust'-Tsil'ma** Russia
86 D2 **Ust'-Ura** Russia
76 B2 **Ustyurt Plateau** Kazakh./Uzbek.
89 E2 **Ustyuzhna** Russia
89 D2 **Usvyaty** Russia
135 D3 **Utah** *state* U.S.A.
135 D2 **Utah Lake** U.S.A.
93 I4 **Utena** Lith.
123 D2 **uThukela** *r.* S. Africa
141 D2 **Utica** U.S.A.
107 C2 **Utiel** Spain
128 C2 **Utikuma Lake** Can.
100 B1 **Utrecht** Neth.
106 B2 **Utrera** Spain
92 I2 **Utsjoki** Fin.
67 C3 **Utsunomiya** Japan
87 D4 **Utta** Russia
62 B2 **Uttaradit** Thai.
127 H2 **Uummannaq Fjord** *inlet* Greenland
93 H3 **Uusikaupunki** Fin.
139 D3 **Uvalde** U.S.A.
119 D3 **Uvinza** Tanz.
68 C1 **Uvs Nuur** *salt l.* Mongolia
67 B4 **Uwajima** Japan
78 A2 **'Uwayriḍ, Ḥarrat al** *lava field* Saudi Arabia
116 A2 **Uweinat, Jebel** *mt.* Sudan
83 H3 **Uyar** Russia
115 C4 **Uyo** Nigeria
152 B3 **Uyuni, Salar de** *salt flat* Bol.
76 C2 **Uzbekistan** *country* Asia
104 C2 **Uzerche** France
105 C3 **Uzès** France
90 C1 **Uzh** *r.* Ukr.
90 A2 **Uzhhorod** Ukr.
109 C2 **Užice** Serbia
89 E3 **Uzlovaya** Russia
111 C3 **Üzümlü** Turkey
111 C2 **Uzunköprü** Turkey

V

123 B2 **Vaal** *r.* S. Africa
123 C2 **Vaal Dam** S. Africa
123 C1 **Vaalwater** S. Africa
92 H3 **Vaasa** Fin.
103 D2 **Vác** Hungary
152 C3 **Vacaria** Brazil
154 B2 **Vacaria, Serra** *hills* Brazil
135 B3 **Vacaville** U.S.A.
74 B2 **Vadodara** India
92 I1 **Vadsø** Norway
105 D2 **Vaduz** Liechtenstein
94 B1 **Vágar** *i.* Faroe Is
94 B1 **Vágur** Faroe Is
103 D2 **Váh** *r.* Slovakia
49 F3 **Vaiaku** Tuvalu
88 B2 **Vaida** Estonia
136 B3 **Vail** U.S.A.
79 C2 **Vakīlābād** Iran
108 B1 **Valdagno** Italy
89 D2 **Valday** Russia
89 D2 **Valdayskaya Vozvyshennost** *hills* Russia
106 B2 **Valdecañas, Embalse de** *res* Spain
93 G4 **Valdemarsvik** Sweden
106 C2 **Valdepeñas** Spain
153 B5 **Valdés, Península** *pen.* Arg.
153 A4 **Valdivia** Chile
130 C2 **Val-d'Or** Can.
143 D2 **Valdosta** U.S.A.
128 C2 **Valemount** Can.
105 C3 **Valence** France
107 C2 **Valencia** Spain
150 B1 **Valencia** Venez.
107 D2 **Valencia, Golfo de** *g.* Spain
100 A2 **Valenciennes** France
136 C2 **Valentine** U.S.A.
64 B1 **Valenzuela** Phil.
150 A1 **Valera** Venez.
109 C2 **Valjevo** Serbia
88 C2 **Valka** Latvia
93 H3 **Valkeakoski** Fin.
100 B2 **Valkenswaard** Neth.
91 D2 **Valky** Ukr.
55 D2 **Valkyrie Dome** Antarctica
145 D2 **Valladolid** Mex.
106 C1 **Valladolid** Spain
93 E4 **Valle** Norway
145 C2 **Vallecillos** Mex.
150 B1 **Valle de la Pascua** Venez.
150 A1 **Valledupar** Col.
145 C2 **Valle Hermoso** Mex.
135 B3 **Vallejo** U.S.A.
152 A3 **Vallenar** Chile
85 H5 **Valletta** Malta
137 D1 **Valley City** U.S.A.
134 B2 **Valley Falls** U.S.A.
128 C2 **Valleyview** Can.
107 D1 **Valls** Spain
129 D3 **Val Marie** Can.
88 C2 **Valmiera** Latvia
88 C3 **Valozhyn** Belarus
154 B2 **Valparaíso** Brazil
153 A4 **Valparaíso** Chile
105 C3 **Valréas** France
59 D3 **Vals, Tanjung** *c.* Indon.

74 B2 **Valsad** India
122 B2 **Valspan** S. Africa
91 D1 **Valuyki** Russia
106 B2 **Valverde del Camino** Spain
81 C2 **Van** Turkey
81 C2 **Van, Lake** *salt l.* Turkey
141 F1 **Van Buren** U.S.A.
128 B3 **Vancouver** Can.
134 B1 **Vancouver** U.S.A.
128 B3 **Vancouver Island** Can.
140 B3 **Vandalia** U.S.A.
123 C2 **Vanderbijlpark** S. Africa
128 B2 **Vanderhoof** Can.
88 C2 **Vändra** Estonia
93 F4 **Vänern** *l.* Sweden
93 F4 **Vänersborg** Sweden
121 □D3 **Vangaindrano** Madag.
Van Gölü *salt l.* Turkey *see* **Van, Lake**
138 C2 **Van Horn** U.S.A.
59 D3 **Vanimo** P.N.G.
83 K3 **Vanino** Russia
104 B2 **Vannes** France
59 D3 **Van Rees, Pegunungan** *mts* Indon.
122 A3 **Vanrhynsdorp** S. Africa
93 H3 **Vantaa** Fin.
49 F4 **Vanua Levu** *i.* Fiji
48 E3 **Vanuatu** *country* S. Pacific Ocean
140 C2 **Van Wert** U.S.A.
122 B3 **Van Wyksvlei** S. Africa
122 B2 **Van Zylsrus** S. Africa
75 C2 **Varanasi** India
92 I1 **Varangerfjorden** *sea chan.* Norway
92 I1 **Varangerhalvøya** *pen.* Norway
90 B1 **Varash** Ukr.
109 C1 **Varaždin** Croatia
93 F4 **Varberg** Sweden
109 D2 **Vardar** *r.* Macedonia
93 E4 **Varde** Denmark
92 J1 **Vardø** Norway
100 D1 **Varel** Ger.
88 B3 **Varėna** Lith.
108 A1 **Varese** Italy
155 C2 **Varginha** Brazil
93 I3 **Varkaus** Fin.
110 C2 **Varna** Bulg.
93 F4 **Värnamo** Sweden
155 D1 **Várzea da Palma** Brazil
86 C2 **Varzino** Russia
Vasa Fin. *see* **Vaasa**
88 C2 **Vasknarva** Estonia
110 C1 **Vaslui** Romania
93 G4 **Västerås** Sweden
93 G3 **Västerdalälven** *r.* Sweden
88 A2 **Västerhaninge** Sweden
93 G4 **Västervik** Sweden
108 B2 **Vasto** Italy
90 C1 **Vasyl'kiv** Ukr.
104 C2 **Vatan** France
108 B2 **Vatican City** Europe
92 □B3 **Vatnajökull** Iceland
110 C1 **Vatra Dornei** Romania
93 F4 **Vättern** *l.* Sweden
138 B2 **Vaughn** U.S.A.
105 C3 **Vauvert** France
49 G4 **Vava'u Group** *is* Tonga
88 B3 **Vawkavysk** Belarus
93 F4 **Växjö** Sweden
86 E1 **Vaygach, Ostrov** *i.* Russia
101 D1 **Vechta** Ger.
110 C2 **Vedea** *r.* Romania
100 C1 **Veendam** Neth.
100 B1 **Veenendaal** Neth.
129 C2 **Vegreville** Can.
106 B2 **Vejer de la Frontera** Spain
93 E4 **Vejle** Denmark
109 D2 **Velbŭzhdki Prokhod** *pass* Bulg./Macedonia
100 B2 **Veldhoven** Neth.
109 B2 **Velebit** *mts* Croatia
100 C2 **Velen** Ger.
109 C1 **Velenje** Slovenia
109 D2 **Veles** Macedonia
106 C2 **Vélez-Málaga** Spain
155 D1 **Velhas** *r.* Brazil
109 D2 **Velika Plana** Serbia
88 C2 **Velikaya** *r.* Russia
89 D2 **Velikiye Luki** Russia
89 D2 **Velikiy Novgorod** Russia
86 D2 **Velikiy Ustyug** Russia
110 C2 **Veliko Tarnovo** Bulg.
108 B2 **Veli Lošinj** Croatia
89 D2 **Velizh** Russia
86 D2 **Vel'sk** Russia
101 F1 **Velten** Ger.
91 D1 **Velykyy Burluk** Ukr.
108 B2 **Venafro** Italy
104 C2 **Vendôme** France
89 E3 **Venev** Russia
Venezia Italy *see* **Venice**
150 B1 **Venezuela** *country* S. America
150 A1 **Venezuela, Golfo de** *g.* Venez.
108 B1 **Venice** Italy
143 D3 **Venice** U.S.A.
108 B1 **Venice, Gulf of** Europe
100 C2 **Venlo** Neth.
100 B2 **Venray** Neth.
88 B2 **Venta** *r.* Latvia/Lith.
88 B2 **Venta** Lith.
123 C3 **Venterstad** S. Africa
99 C3 **Ventnor** U.K.
88 B2 **Ventspils** Latvia
135 C4 **Ventura** U.S.A.
139 C3 **Venustiano Carranza, Presa** *resr* Mex.
107 C2 **Vera** Spain
145 C3 **Veracruz** Mex.
74 B2 **Veraval** India
108 A1 **Verbania** Italy
108 A1 **Vercelli** Italy
105 D3 **Vercors** *reg.* France
92 F3 **Verdalsøra** Norway
154 B1 **Verde** *r. Goiás* Brazil
154 B2 **Verde** *r. Mato Grosso do Sul* Brazil
144 B2 **Verde** *r.* Mex.
138 A2 **Verde** *r.* U.S.A.
155 D1 **Verde Grande** *r.* Brazil
101 D1 **Verden (Aller)** Ger.
154 B1 **Verdinho, Serra do** *mts* Brazil
108 A2 **Verdon** *r.* France
105 D2 **Verdun** France
123 C2 **Vereeniging** S. Africa
106 B1 **Verín** Spain
91 D3 **Verkhnebakanskiy** Russia
92 J2 **Verkhnetulomskiy** Russia
91 E1 **Verkhniy Mamon** Russia
89 E3 **Verkhov'ye** Russia
90 A2 **Verkhovyna** Ukr.
83 J2 **Verkhoyanskiy Khrebet** *mts* Russia
129 C2 **Vermilion** Can.
137 D2 **Vermillion** U.S.A.
130 A2 **Vermillion Bay** Can.
141 E2 **Vermont** *state* U.S.A.
135 E2 **Vernal** U.S.A.
128 C2 **Vernon** Can.
139 D2 **Vernon** U.S.A.
143 D3 **Vero Beach** U.S.A.
111 B2 **Veroia** Greece
108 B1 **Verona** Italy
104 C2 **Versailles** France
104 B2 **Vertou** France
123 D2 **Verulam** S. Africa
100 B2 **Verviers** Belgium
105 C2 **Vervins** France
105 D3 **Vescovato** *Corsica* France
87 E3 **Veselaya, Gora** *mt.* Russia
91 C2 **Vesele** Ukr.
105 D2 **Vesoul** France
92 F2 **Vesterålen** *is* Norway
92 F2 **Vestfjorden** *sea chan.* Norway
94 B1 **Vestmanna** Faroe Is
93 E3 **Vestnes** Norway
108 B2 **Vesuvius** *vol.* Italy
89 E2 **Ves'yegonsk** Russia
93 G4 **Vetlanda** Sweden
86 D3 **Vetluga** Russia
100 A2 **Veurne** Belgium
105 D2 **Vevey** Switz.
91 D1 **Veydelevka** Russia
80 B1 **Vezirköprü** Turkey
151 D2 **Viana** Brazil
106 B1 **Viana do Castelo** Port.
Viangchan Laos *see* **Vientiane**
62 B1 **Viangphoukha** Laos
154 C1 **Vianópolis** Brazil
108 B2 **Viareggio** Italy
93 E4 **Viborg** Denmark
109 C3 **Vibo Valentia** Italy
107 D1 **Vic** Spain
144 A1 **Vicente Guerrero** Mex.
108 B1 **Vicenza** Italy
105 C2 **Vichy** France
142 B2 **Vicksburg** U.S.A.
155 D2 **Viçosa** Brazil
52 A3 **Victor Harbor** Austr.
50 C1 **Victoria** *r.* Austr.
52 B3 **Victoria** *state* Austr.
128 B3 **Victoria** Can.
153 A4 **Victoria** Chile
113 K7 **Victoria** Seychelles
139 D3 **Victoria** U.S.A.
119 D3 **Victoria, Lake** Africa
52 B2 **Victoria, Lake** Austr.
62 A1 **Victoria, Mount** Myanmar
59 D3 **Victoria, Mount** P.N.G.
120 B2 **Victoria Falls** Zambia/Zimbabwe
126 D2 **Victoria Island** Can.
50 C1 **Victoria River Downs** Austr.
122 B3 **Victoria West** S. Africa
135 C4 **Victorville** U.S.A.
110 C2 **Videle** Romania
92 □A2 **Víðidalsá** Iceland
153 B5 **Viedma** Arg.
153 A5 **Viedma, Lago** *l.* Arg.
100 B2 **Vielsalm** Belgium
101 E2 **Vienenburg** Ger.
103 D2 **Vienna** Austria
105 C2 **Vienne** France
104 C2 **Vienne** *r.* France
62 B2 **Vientiane** Laos
100 C2 **Viersen** Ger.
104 C2 **Vierzon** France
144 B2 **Viesca** Mex.
109 C2 **Vieste** Italy
62 B2 **Vietnam** *country* Asia
62 B1 **Viêt Tri** Vietnam
64 B1 **Vigan** Phil.
108 A1 **Vigevano** Italy
106 B1 **Vigo** Spain
73 C3 **Vijayawada** India
92 □B3 **Vík** Iceland
129 C2 **Viking** Can.
150 C3 **Vila Bela da Santíssima Trindade** Brazil
106 B2 **Vila Franca de Xira** Port.
106 B1 **Vilagarcía** Spain
106 B1 **Vilalba** Spain
106 B1 **Vila Nova de Gaia** Port.

107 D1 **Vilanova i la Geltrú** Spain
106 B1 **Vila Real** Port.
106 B1 **Vilar Formoso** Port.
155 D2 **Vila Velha** Brazil
150 A3 **Vilcabamba, Cordillera** *mts* Peru
92 G3 **Vilhelmina** Sweden
150 B3 **Vilhena** Brazil
88 C2 **Viljandi** Estonia
88 B3 **Vilkaviškis** Lith.
83 H1 **Vil'kitskogo, Proliv** *str.* Russia
144 B1 **Villa Ahumada** Mex.
106 B1 **Villablino** Spain
102 C2 **Villach** Austria
144 B2 **Villa de Cos** Mex.
152 B4 **Villa Dolores** Arg.
145 C3 **Villa Flores** Mex.
145 C2 **Villagrán** Mex.
145 C3 **Villahermosa** Mex.
152 B4 **Villa María** Arg.
152 B3 **Villa Montes** Bol.
144 B2 **Villanueva** Mex.
106 B2 **Villanueva de la Serena** Spain
106 C2 **Villanueva de los Infantes** Spain
152 C3 **Villa Ocampo** Arg.
108 A3 **Villaputzu** *Sardinia* Italy
152 C3 **Villarrica** Para.
106 C2 **Villarrobledo** Spain
152 B3 **Villa Unión** Arg.
144 B2 **Villa Unión** *Durango* Mex.
144 B2 **Villa Unión** *Sinaloa* Mex.
150 A1 **Villavicencio** Col.
152 B3 **Villazon** Bol.
107 C2 **Villena** Spain
104 C3 **Villeneuve-sur-Lot** France
142 B2 **Ville Platte** U.S.A.
105 C2 **Villeurbanne** France
102 B2 **Villingen** Ger.
88 C3 **Vilnius** Lith.
91 C2 **Vil'nohirs'k** Ukr.
91 D2 **Vil'nyans'k** Ukr.
100 B2 **Vilvoorde** Belgium
88 C3 **Vilyeyka** Belarus
83 J2 **Vilyuy** *r.* Russia
93 G4 **Vimmerby** Sweden
153 A4 **Viña del Mar** Chile
107 D1 **Vinaròs** Spain
140 B3 **Vincennes** U.S.A.
55 G3 **Vincennes Bay** Antarctica
141 D3 **Vineland** U.S.A.
62 B2 **Vinh** Vietnam
63 B2 **Vinh Long** Vietnam
139 D1 **Vinita** U.S.A.
90 B2 **Vinnytsya** Ukr.
55 O2 **Vinson, Mount** *mt.* Antarctica
93 E3 **Vinstra** Norway
108 B1 **Vipiteno** Italy
64 B1 **Virac** Phil.
129 D3 **Virden** Can.
104 B2 **Vire** France
120 A2 **Virei** Angola
155 D1 **Virgem da Lapa** Brazil
138 A1 **Virgin** *r.* U.S.A.
123 C2 **Virginia** S. Africa
137 E1 **Virginia** U.S.A.
141 D3 **Virginia** *state* U.S.A.
141 D3 **Virginia Beach** U.S.A.
135 C3 **Virginia City** U.S.A.
147 D3 **Virgin Islands (U.K.)** *terr.* West Indies
147 D3 **Virgin Islands (U.S.A.)** *terr.* West Indies
63 B2 **Virôchey** Cambodia
109 C1 **Virovitica** Croatia
100 B3 **Virton** Belgium
88 B2 **Virtsu** Estonia
109 C2 **Vis** *i.* Croatia
88 C2 **Visaginas** Lith.
135 C3 **Visalia** U.S.A.
74 B2 **Visavadar** India
64 B1 **Visayan Sea** Phil.
93 G4 **Visby** Sweden
126 D2 **Viscount Melville Sound** *sea chan.* Can.
151 D2 **Viseu** Brazil
106 B1 **Viseu** Port.
73 C3 **Vishakhapatnam** India
88 C2 **Viški** Latvia
109 C2 **Visoko** Bos. & Herz.
103 D1 **Vistula** *r.* Pol.
108 B2 **Viterbo** Italy
49 F4 **Viti Levu** *i.* Fiji
83 I3 **Vitim** *r.* Russia
155 D2 **Vitória** Brazil
151 D3 **Vitória da Conquista** Brazil
106 C1 **Vitoria-Gasteiz** Spain
104 B2 **Vitré** France
105 C2 **Vitry-le-François** France
89 D2 **Vitsyebsk** Belarus
105 D2 **Vittel** France
108 B3 **Vittoria** *Sicily* Italy
108 B1 **Vittorio Veneto** Italy
106 B1 **Viveiro** Spain
144 A2 **Vizcaíno, Sierra** *mts* Mex.
110 C2 **Vize** Turkey
73 C3 **Vizianagaram** India
100 B2 **Vlaardingen** Neth.
87 D4 **Vladikavkaz** Russia
89 F2 **Vladimir** Russia
66 B2 **Vladivostok** Russia
109 D2 **Vlasotince** Serbia
100 B1 **Vlieland** *i.* Neth.
100 A2 **Vlissingen** Neth.
109 C2 **Vlorë** Albania
102 C2 **Vöcklabruck** Austria
101 D2 **Vogelsberg** *hills* Ger.
119 D3 **Voi** Kenya
105 D2 **Voiron** France
131 D1 **Voisey's Bay** Can.
109 C1 **Vojvodina** *prov.* Serbia
92 J3 **Voknavolok** Russia
Volcano Bay Japan *see* **Uchiura-wan**
89 E2 **Volga** Russia
89 F2 **Volga** *r.* Russia
87 D4 **Volgodonsk** Russia
87 D4 **Volgograd** Russia
89 D2 **Volkhov** Russia
89 D1 **Volkhov** *r.* Russia
101 E2 **Volkstedt** Ger.
91 D2 **Volnovakha** Ukr.
90 B2 **Volochys'k** Ukr.
Volodars'ke Ukr. *see* **Nikol's'ke**
90 B1 **Volodymyrets'** Ukr.
90 A1 **Volodymyr-Volyns'kyy** Ukr.
89 E2 **Vologda** Russia
89 E2 **Volokolamsk** Russia
91 D1 **Volokonovka** Russia
111 B3 **Volos** Greece
88 C2 **Volosovo** Russia
89 D2 **Volot** Russia
89 E3 **Volovo** Russia
87 D3 **Vol'sk** Russia
114 C4 **Volta, Lake** *resr* Ghana
155 D2 **Volta Redonda** Brazil
87 D4 **Volzhskiy** Russia
92 □C2 **Vopnafjörður** Iceland
88 C3 **Voranava** Belarus
86 F2 **Vorkuta** Russia
88 B2 **Vormsi** *i.* Estonia
89 E3 **Voronezh** Russia
89 E3 **Voronezh** *r.* Russia
91 E1 **Vorontsovka** Russia
91 C2 **Vorskla** *r.* Russia
88 C2 **Võrtsjärv** *l.* Estonia
88 C2 **Võru** Estonia
122 B3 **Vosburg** S. Africa
105 D2 **Vosges** *mts* France
89 E2 **Voskresensk** Russia
93 E3 **Voss** Norway
83 H3 **Vostochnyy Sayan** *mts* Russia
86 E3 **Votkinsk** Russia
154 C2 **Votuporanga** Brazil
100 B3 **Vouziers** France
92 J2 **Voynitsa** Russia
91 C2 **Voznesens'k** Ukr.
93 E4 **Vrådal** Norway
66 B2 **Vrangel'** Russia
Vrangelya, Ostrov *i.* Russia *see* **Wrangel Island**
109 D2 **Vranje** Serbia
110 C2 **Vratnik** *pass* Bulg.
110 B2 **Vratsa** Bulg.
109 C1 **Vrbas** *r.* Bos. & Herz.
109 C1 **Vrbas** Serbia
122 A3 **Vredenburg** S. Africa
122 A3 **Vredendal** S. Africa
100 B3 **Vresse-sur-Semois** Belgium
109 D1 **Vršac** Serbia
122 B2 **Vryburg** S. Africa
123 D2 **Vryheid** S. Africa
89 D1 **Vsevolozhsk** Russia
Vučitrn Kosovo *see* **Vushtrri**
109 C1 **Vukovar** Croatia
86 E2 **Vuktyl** Russia
123 C2 **Vukuzakhe** S. Africa
109 B3 **Vulcano, Isola** *i.* Italy
63 B2 **Vung Tau** Vietnam
109 D2 **Vushtrri** Kosovo
74 B2 **Vyara** India
Vyatka Russia *see* **Kirov**
89 D2 **Vyaz'ma** Russia
93 I3 **Vyborg** Russia
88 C2 **Vyerkhnyadzvinsk** Belarus
87 D3 **Vyksa** Russia
90 B2 **Vylkove** Ukr.
90 A2 **Vynohradiv** Ukr.
89 D2 **Vypolzovo** Russia
89 D2 **Vyritsa** Russia
91 D2 **Vyselki** Russia
90 C1 **Vyshhorod** Ukr.
89 D2 **Vyshniy-Volochek** Russia
103 D2 **Vyškov** Czechia
86 C2 **Vytegra** Russia

W

114 B3 **Wa** Ghana
100 B2 **Waal** *r.* Neth.
100 B2 **Waalwijk** Neth.
128 C2 **Wabasca** *r.* Can.
128 C2 **Wabasca-Desmarais** Can.
140 B3 **Wabash** *r.* U.S.A.
129 E2 **Wabowden** Can.
143 D3 **Waccasassa Bay** U.S.A.
101 D2 **Wächtersbach** Ger.
139 D2 **Waco** U.S.A.
115 D2 **Waddān** Libya
Waddeneilanden *is* Neth. *see* **West Frisian Islands**
100 B1 **Waddenzee** *sea chan.* Neth.
128 B2 **Waddington, Mount** Can.
100 B1 **Waddinxveen** Neth.
129 D2 **Wadena** Can.
137 D1 **Wadena** U.S.A.
74 A2 **Wadh** Pak.
74 B2 **Wadhwan** India
116 B2 **Wadi Halfa** Sudan
116 B3 **Wad Madani** Sudan
70 C2 **Wafangdian** China
100 B2 **Wageningen** Neth.
127 F2 **Wager Bay** Can.

53 C3 **Wagga Wagga** Austr.
37 D2 **Wahoo** U.S.A.
37 D1 **Wahpeton** U.S.A.
Waiau N.Z. *see* **Franz Josef/ Waiau**
54 B2 **Waiau** *r.* N.Z.
59 C3 **Waigeo** *i.* Indon.
58 B3 **Waikabubak** Indon.
52 A2 **Waikerie** Austr.
54 B2 **Waimate** N.Z.
75 B3 **Wainganga** *r.* India
58 C3 **Waingapu** Indon.
29 C2 **Wainwright** Can.
54 C1 **Waiouru** N.Z.
54 B2 **Waipara** N.Z.
54 C1 **Waipawa** N.Z.
54 B2 **Wairau** *r.* N.Z.
54 C1 **Wairoa** N.Z.
54 B2 **Waitaki** *r.* N.Z.
54 B1 **Waitara** N.Z.
54 B1 **Waiuku** N.Z.
19 E2 **Wajir** Kenya
67 C3 **Wakasa-wan** *b.* Japan
54 A3 **Wakatipu, Lake** N.Z.
29 D2 **Wakaw** Can.
67 C4 **Wakayama** Japan
36 D3 **WaKeeney** U.S.A.
54 B2 **Wakefield** N.Z.
98 C2 **Wakefield** U.K.
48 F1 **Wake Island** N. Pacific Ocean
66 D1 **Wakkanai** Japan
23 D2 **Wakkerstroom** S. Africa
03 D1 **Wałbrzych** Pol.
53 D2 **Walcha** Austr.
00 C1 **Walchum** Ger.
03 D1 **Wałcz** Pol.
99 B2 **Wales** *admin. div.* U.K.
53 C2 **Walgett** Austr.
19 C3 **Walikale** Dem. Rep. Congo
35 C3 **Walker Lake** U.S.A.
52 A2 **Wallaroo** Austr.
98 B2 **Wallasey** U.K.
34 C1 **Walla Walla** U.S.A.
01 D3 **Walldürn** Ger.
53 C2 **Wallendbeen** Austr.
49 G3 **Wallis and Futuna** *terr.* S. Pacific Ocean
96 □ **Walls** U.K.
98 B1 **Walney, Isle of** *i.* U.K.
99 C2 **Walsall** U.K.
36 C3 **Walsenburg** U.S.A.
01 D1 **Walsrode** Ger.
43 D2 **Walterboro** U.S.A.
20 A3 **Walvis Bay** Namibia
19 C2 **Wamba** Dem. Rep. Congo
52 B1 **Wanaaring** Austr.
54 A2 **Wanaka** N.Z.
54 A2 **Wanaka, Lake** N.Z.
30 B2 **Wanapitei Lake** Can.
54 B3 **Wanda** Arg.
66 B1 **Wanda Shan** *mts* China
62 A1 **Wanding** China
54 C1 **Wanganui** N.Z.
53 C3 **Wangaratta** Austr.
65 B1 **Wangqing** China
62 A1 **Wan Hsa-la** Myanmar
71 B4 **Wanning** China
00 B2 **Wanroij** Neth.
99 C3 **Wantage** U.K.
70 A2 **Wanyuan** China
70 A2 **Wanzhou** China
73 B3 **Warangal** India
01 D2 **Warburg** Ger.
50 B2 **Warburton** Austr.
52 A1 **Warburton** *watercourse* Austr.
75 B2 **Wardha** India
96 C1 **Ward Hill** U.K.
28 B2 **Ware** Can.
101 F1 **Waren (Müritz)** Ger.
100 C2 **Warendorf** Ger.
53 D1 **Warialda** Austr.
122 A2 **Warmbad** Namibia
135 C3 **Warm Springs** U.S.A.
134 C2 **Warner Lakes** U.S.A.
143 D2 **Warner Robins** U.S.A.
152 B2 **Warnes** Bol.
52 B3 **Warracknabeal** Austr.
53 C2 **Warrego** *r.* Austr.
53 C2 **Warren** Austr.
142 B2 **Warren** *AR* U.S.A.
140 C2 **Warren** *OH* U.S.A.
141 D2 **Warren** *PA* U.S.A.
97 C1 **Warrenpoint** U.K.
137 E3 **Warrensburg** U.S.A.
122 B2 **Warrenton** S. Africa
115 C4 **Warri** Nigeria
98 B2 **Warrington** U.K.
52 B3 **Warrnambool** Austr.
103 E1 **Warsaw** Pol.
Warszawa Pol. *see* **Warsaw**
103 C1 **Warta** *r.* Pol.
53 D1 **Warwick** Austr.
99 C2 **Warwick** U.K.
135 C3 **Wasco** U.S.A.
136 C1 **Washburn** U.S.A.
141 D3 **Washington** *DC* U.S.A.
137 E2 **Washington** *IA* U.S.A.
140 B3 **Washington** *IN* U.S.A.
137 E3 **Washington** *MO* U.S.A.
143 E1 **Washington** *NC* U.S.A.
140 C2 **Washington** *PA* U.S.A.
134 B1 **Washington** *state* U.S.A.
141 E2 **Washington, Mount** U.S.A.
140 C3 **Washington Court House** U.S.A.
74 A2 **Washuk** Pak.
130 C1 **Waskaganish** Can.
129 E2 **Waskaiowaka Lake** Can.
122 A2 **Wasser** Namibia
130 C2 **Waswanipi, Lac** *l.* Can.
58 C3 **Watampone** Indon.
141 E2 **Waterbury** U.S.A.
129 D2 **Waterbury Lake** Can.
97 C2 **Waterford** Ireland
97 C2 **Waterford Harbour** Ireland
137 E2 **Waterloo** U.S.A.
123 C1 **Waterpoort** S. Africa
141 D2 **Watertown** *NY* U.S.A.
137 D2 **Watertown** *SD* U.S.A.
140 B2 **Watertown** *WI* U.S.A.
141 F2 **Waterville** U.S.A.
99 C3 **Watford** U.K.
136 C1 **Watford City** U.S.A.
129 D2 **Wathaman** *r.* Can.
139 D1 **Watonga** U.S.A.
129 D2 **Watrous** Can.
119 C2 **Watsa** Dem. Rep. Congo
140 B2 **Watseka** U.S.A.
118 C3 **Watsi Kengo** Dem. Rep. Congo
128 B1 **Watson Lake** Can.
135 B3 **Watsonville** U.S.A.
59 C3 **Watubela, Kepulauan** *is* Indon.
59 D3 **Wau** P.N.G.
117 A4 **Wau** South Sudan
53 D2 **Wauchope** Austr.
140 B2 **Waukegan** U.S.A.
139 D2 **Waurika** U.S.A.
140 B2 **Wausau** U.S.A.
99 D2 **Waveney** *r.* U.K.
137 E2 **Waverly** U.S.A.
143 D2 **Waycross** U.S.A.
137 D2 **Wayne** U.S.A.
143 D2 **Waynesboro** *GA* U.S.A.
141 D3 **Waynesboro** *VA* U.S.A.
143 D1 **Waynesville** U.S.A.
74 B1 **Wazirabad** Pak.
98 C1 **Wear** *r.* U.K.
139 D2 **Weatherford** U.S.A.
134 B2 **Weaverville** U.S.A.
130 B1 **Webequie** Can.
137 D1 **Webster** U.S.A.
137 E2 **Webster City** U.S.A.
55 Q2 **Weddell Sea** Antarctica
100 B2 **Weert** Neth.
53 C2 **Wee Waa** Austr.
100 C2 **Wegberg** Ger.
103 E1 **Węgorzewo** Pol.
101 F3 **Weiden in der Oberpfalz** Ger.
70 B2 **Weifang** China
70 C2 **Weihai** China
53 C1 **Weilmoringle** Austr.
101 E2 **Weimar** Ger.
70 A2 **Weinan** China
51 D1 **Weipa** Austr.
53 C1 **Weir** *r.* Austr.
140 C2 **Weirton** U.S.A.
62 B1 **Weishan** China
101 E2 **Weißenfels** Ger.
102 C2 **Weißkugel** *mt.* Austria/Italy
103 D1 **Wejherowo** Pol.
128 C1 **Wekweètì** Can.
140 C3 **Welch** U.S.A.
117 B3 **Weldiya** Eth.
123 C2 **Welkom** S. Africa
99 C2 **Welland** *r.* U.K.
51 C1 **Wellesley Islands** Austr.
53 C2 **Wellington** Austr.
54 B2 **Wellington** N.Z.
122 A3 **Wellington** S. Africa
137 D3 **Wellington** U.S.A.
153 A5 **Wellington, Isla** *i.* Chile
53 C3 **Wellington, Lake** Austr.
128 B2 **Wells** Can.
99 B3 **Wells** U.K.
134 D2 **Wells** U.S.A.
50 B2 **Wells, Lake** *imp. l.* Austr.
54 B1 **Wellsford** N.Z.
98 D2 **Wells-next-the-Sea** U.K.
102 C2 **Wels** Austria
99 B2 **Welshpool** U.K.
123 C2 **Wembesi** S. Africa
130 C1 **Wemindji** Can.
134 B1 **Wenatchee** U.S.A.
154 C2 **Wenceslau Braz** Brazil
71 B4 **Wencheng** China
114 B4 **Wenchi** Ghana
70 C2 **Wendeng** China
101 E1 **Wendisch Evern** Ger.
117 B4 **Wendo** Eth.
134 D2 **Wendover** U.S.A.
71 B3 **Wengyuan** China
71 C3 **Wenling** China
71 A3 **Wenshan** China
52 B2 **Wentworth** Austr.
71 C3 **Wenzhou** China
123 C2 **Wepener** S. Africa
122 B2 **Werda** Botswana
101 F2 **Werdau** Ger.
101 F1 **Werder (Havel)** Ger.
101 F3 **Wernberg-Köblitz** Ger.
101 E2 **Wernigerode** Ger.
101 D2 **Werra** *r.* Ger.
53 D2 **Werris Creek** Austr.
101 D3 **Wertheim** Ger.
100 C2 **Wesel** Ger.
101 E1 **Wesendorf** Ger.
101 D1 **Weser** *r.* Ger.
101 D1 **Weser** *sea chan.* Ger.
51 C1 **Wessel, Cape** Austr.
51 C1 **Wessel Islands** Austr.
123 C2 **Wesselton** S. Africa
80 B2 **West Bank** *disp. terr.* Asia

140 B2 **West Bend** U.S.A.
99 C2 **West Bromwich** U.K.
100 C2 **Westerburg** Ger.
100 C1 **Westerholt** Ger.
50 B2 **Western Australia** *state* Austr.
122 B3 **Western Cape** *prov.* S. Africa
116 A2 **Western Desert** Egypt
73 B3 **Western Ghats** *mts* India
114 A2 **Western Sahara** *disp. terr.* Africa
100 A2 **Westerschelde** *est.* Neth.
100 C1 **Westerstede** Ger.
100 C2 **Westerwald** *hills* Ger.
153 B6 **West Falkland** *i.* Falkland Is
140 B3 **West Frankfort** U.S.A.
100 B1 **West Frisian Islands** *is* Neth.
147 D2 **West Indies** *is* Caribbean Sea
96 A1 **West Loch Roag** *b.* U.K.
128 C2 **Westlock** Can.
100 B2 **Westmalle** Belgium
142 B1 **West Memphis** U.S.A.
140 C3 **Weston** U.S.A.
99 B3 **Weston-super-Mare** U.K.
143 D3 **West Palm Beach** U.S.A.
137 E3 **West Plains** U.S.A.
137 D2 **West Point** U.S.A.
97 B2 **Westport** Ireland
54 B2 **Westport** N.Z.
129 D2 **Westray** Can.
96 C1 **Westray** *i.* U.K.
100 B1 **West-Terschelling** Neth.
140 C3 **West Virginia** *state* U.S.A.
53 C2 **West Wyalong** Austr.
134 D2 **West Yellowstone** U.S.A.
59 C3 **Wetar** *i.* Indon.
128 C2 **Wetaskiwin** Can.
101 D2 **Wetzlar** Ger.
59 D3 **Wewak** P.N.G.
97 C2 **Wexford** Ireland
129 D2 **Weyakwin** Can.
129 D3 **Weyburn** Can.
101 D1 **Weyhe** Ger.
99 B3 **Weymouth** U.K.
54 C1 **Whakatane** N.Z.
129 E1 **Whale Cove** Can.
96 □ **Whalsay** *i.* U.K.
54 B1 **Whangarei** N.Z.
98 C2 **Wharfe** *r.* U.K.
139 D3 **Wharton** U.S.A.
128 C1 **Whatî** Can.
136 B2 **Wheatland** U.S.A.
138 B1 **Wheeler Peak** *NM* U.S.A.
135 D3 **Wheeler Peak** *NV* U.S.A.
140 C2 **Wheeling** U.S.A.
98 B1 **Whernside** *h.* U.K.
128 B2 **Whistler** Can.
98 C1 **Whitby** U.K.
142 B2 **White** *r.* U.S.A.
50 B2 **White, Lake** *imp. l.* Austr.
131 E2 **White Bay** Can.
136 C1 **White Butte** *mt.* U.S.A.
52 B2 **White Cliffs** Austr.
128 C2 **Whitecourt** Can.
134 D1 **Whitefish** U.S.A.
98 B1 **Whitehaven** U.K.
97 D1 **Whitehead** U.K.
128 A1 **Whitehorse** Can.
142 B3 **White Lake** U.S.A.
135 C3 **White Mountain Peak** U.S.A.
116 B3 **White Nile** *r.* South Sudan/Uganda
86 C2 **White Sea** Russia
134 D1 **White Sulphur Springs** U.S.A.
143 E2 **Whiteville** U.S.A.
114 B3 **White Volta** *r.* Burkina Faso/Ghana
138 B2 **Whitewater Baldy** *mt.* U.S.A.
130 B1 **Whitewater Lake** Can.
129 D2 **Whitewood** Can.
96 B3 **Whithorn** U.K.
54 C1 **Whitianga** N.Z.
135 C3 **Whitney, Mount** U.S.A.
51 D2 **Whitsunday Island** Austr.
52 A2 **Whyalla** Austr.
100 A2 **Wichelen** Belgium
137 D3 **Wichita** U.S.A.
139 D2 **Wichita Falls** U.S.A.
96 C1 **Wick** U.K.
138 A2 **Wickenburg** U.S.A.
97 C2 **Wicklow** Ireland
97 D2 **Wicklow Head** Ireland
97 C2 **Wicklow Mountains** Ireland
98 B2 **Widnes** U.K.
101 D1 **Wiehengebirge** *hills* Ger.
100 C2 **Wiehl** Ger.
103 D1 **Wieluń** Pol.
Wien Austria *see* **Vienna**
103 D2 **Wiener Neustadt** Austria
100 B1 **Wieringerwerf** Neth.
100 D2 **Wiesbaden** Ger.
100 C1 **Wiesmoor** Ger.
103 D1 **Wieżyca** *h.* Pol.
99 C3 **Wight, Isle of** *i.* U.K.
96 B3 **Wigtown** U.K.
100 B2 **Wijchen** Neth.
52 B2 **Wilcannia** Austr.
123 C3 **Wild Coast** S. Africa
123 C2 **Wilge** *r.* S. Africa
100 D1 **Wilhelmshaven** Ger.
141 D2 **Wilkes-Barre** U.S.A.
55 H3 **Wilkes Land** *reg.* Antarctica
129 D2 **Wilkie** Can.
138 B2 **Willcox** U.S.A.
100 B2 **Willebroek** Belgium
147 D3 **Willemstad** Curaçao
52 B3 **William, Mount** Austr.
52 A1 **William Creek** Austr.
138 A1 **Williams** U.S.A.
141 D3 **Williamsburg** U.S.A.
128 B2 **Williams Lake** Can.
140 C3 **Williamson** U.S.A.
141 D2 **Williamsport** U.S.A.
143 E1 **Williamston** U.S.A.
122 B3 **Williston** S. Africa
136 C1 **Williston** U.S.A.
128 B2 **Williston Lake** Can.
135 B3 **Willits** U.S.A.
137 D1 **Willmar** U.S.A.
122 B3 **Willowmore** S. Africa
123 C3 **Willowvale** S. Africa
50 B2 **Wills, Lake** *imp. l.* Austr.
52 A3 **Willunga** Austr.
52 A2 **Wilmington** Austr.
141 D3 **Wilmington** *DE* U.S.A.
143 E2 **Wilmington** *NC* U.S.A.
100 D2 **Wilnsdorf** Ger.
143 E1 **Wilson** U.S.A.
53 C3 **Wilson's Promontory** *pen.* Austr.
100 B3 **Wiltz** Lux.
50 B2 **Wiluna** Austr.
99 C3 **Winchester** U.K.
140 C3 **Winchester** *KY* U.S.A.
141 D3 **Winchester** *VA* U.S.A.
98 B1 **Windermere** *l.* U.K.
120 A3 **Windhoek** Namibia
137 D2 **Windom** U.S.A.
51 D2 **Windorah** Austr.
136 B2 **Wind River Range** *mts* U.S.A.
53 D2 **Windsor** Austr.
130 B2 **Windsor** Can.
147 D3 **Windward Islands** Caribbean Sea
147 C3 **Windward Passage** Cuba/Haiti
137 D3 **Winfield** U.S.A.
100 A2 **Wingene** Belgium
53 D2 **Wingham** Austr.
130 B1 **Winisk** *r.* Can.
130 B1 **Winisk (abandoned)** Can.
130 B1 **Winisk Lake** Can.
63 A2 **Winkana** Myanmar
129 E3 **Winkler** Can.
114 B4 **Winneba** Ghana
140 B2 **Winnebago, Lake** U.S.A.
134 C2 **Winnemucca** U.S.A.
136 C2 **Winner** U.S.A.
142 B2 **Winnfield** U.S.A.
137 E1 **Winnibigoshish, Lake** U.S.A.
129 E3 **Winnipeg** Can.
129 E2 **Winnipeg** *r.* Can.
129 E2 **Winnipeg, Lake** Can.
129 D2 **Winnipegosis, Lake** Can.
141 E2 **Winnipesaukee, Lake** U.S.A.
142 B2 **Winnsboro** U.S.A.
137 E2 **Winona** *MN* U.S.A.
142 C2 **Winona** *MS* U.S.A.
100 C1 **Winschoten** Neth.
101 D1 **Winsen (Aller)** Ger.
101 E1 **Winsen (Luhe)** Ger.
138 A1 **Winslow** U.S.A.
143 D1 **Winston-Salem** U.S.A.
101 D2 **Winterberg** Ger.
143 D3 **Winter Haven** U.S.A.
100 C2 **Winterswijk** Neth.
105 D2 **Winterthur** Switz.
51 D2 **Winton** Austr.
54 A3 **Winton** N.Z.
52 A2 **Wirrabara** Austr.
99 D2 **Wisbech** U.K.
140 A2 **Wisconsin** *r.* U.S.A.
140 B2 **Wisconsin** *state* U.S.A.
140 B2 **Wisconsin Rapids** U.S.A.
Wisła *r.* Pol. *see* **Vistula**
101 E1 **Wismar** Ger.
98 D2 **Withernsea** U.K.
100 B1 **Witmarsum** Neth.
99 C3 **Witney** U.K.
123 D2 **Witrivier** S. Africa
101 F2 **Wittenberg, Lutherstadt** Ge
101 E1 **Wittenberge** Ger.
101 E1 **Wittenburg** Ger.
101 E1 **Wittingen** Ger.
100 C3 **Wittlich** Ger.
100 C1 **Wittmund** Ger.
101 F1 **Wittstock/Dosse** Ger.
120 A3 **Witvlei** Namibia
101 D2 **Witzenhausen** Ger.
103 D1 **Władysławowo** Pol.
103 D1 **Włocławek** Pol.
53 C3 **Wodonga** Austr.
59 C3 **Wokam** *i.* Indon.
99 C3 **Woking** U.K.
101 F2 **Wolfen** Ger.
101 E1 **Wolfenbüttel** Ger.
101 D2 **Wolfhagen** Ger.
136 B1 **Wolf Point** U.S.A.
101 E1 **Wolfsburg** Ger.
100 C3 **Wolfstein** Ger.
131 D2 **Wolfville** Can.
102 C1 **Wolgast** Ger.
102 C1 **Wolin** Pol.
129 D2 **Wollaston Lake** Can.
129 D2 **Wollaston Lake** Can.
126 D2 **Wollaston Peninsula** Can.
53 D2 **Wollongong** Austr.
101 E2 **Wolmirsleben** Ger.
101 E1 **Wolmirstedt** Ger.
100 C1 **Wolvega** Neth.
99 B2 **Wolverhampton** U.K.
65 B2 **Wonju** S. Korea
128 B2 **Wonowon** Can.
65 B2 **Wŏnsan** N. Korea
53 C3 **Wonthaggi** Austr.
52 A2 **Woocalla** Austr.

51 C1 **Woodah, Isle** *i.* Austr.
99 D2 **Woodbridge** U.K.
136 B3 **Woodland Park** U.S.A.
50 C2 **Woodroffe, Mount** Austr.
51 C1 **Woods, Lake** *imp. l.* Austr.
129 E3 **Woods, Lake of the** Can./U.S.A.
53 C3 **Woods Point** Austr.
131 D2 **Woodstock** *N.B.* Can.
140 C2 **Woodstock** *Ont.* Can.
54 C2 **Woodville** N.Z.
139 D1 **Woodward** U.S.A.
53 D2 **Woolgoolga** Austr.
52 A2 **Woomera** Austr.
140 C2 **Wooster** U.S.A.
122 A3 **Worcester** S. Africa
99 B2 **Worcester** U.K.
141 E2 **Worcester** U.S.A.
102 C2 **Wörgl** Austria
98 B1 **Workington** U.K.
98 C2 **Worksop** U.K.
136 B2 **Worland** U.S.A.
101 D3 **Worms** Ger.
99 C3 **Worthing** U.K.
137 D2 **Worthington** U.S.A.
58 C3 **Wotu** Indon.
59 C3 **Wowoni** *i.* Indon.
83 N2 **Wrangel Island** Russia
128 A2 **Wrangell** U.S.A.
96 B1 **Wrath, Cape** U.K.
136 C2 **Wray** U.S.A.
122 A2 **Wreck Point** S. Africa
98 B2 **Wrexham** U.K.
136 B2 **Wright** U.S.A.
63 A2 **Wrightmyo** India
128 B1 **Wrigley** Can.
103 D1 **Wrocław** Pol.
103 D1 **Września** Pol.
70 B2 **Wu'an** China
70 A2 **Wuhai** China
70 B2 **Wuhan** China
70 B2 **Wuhu** China
Wujin China *see* **Changzhou**
115 C4 **Wukari** Nigeria
62 B1 **Wuliang Shan** *mts* China
59 C3 **Wuliaru** *i.* Indon.
71 A3 **Wumeng Shan** *mts* China
130 B1 **Wunnummin Lake** Can.
101 F2 **Wunsiedel** Ger.
101 D1 **Wunstorf** Ger.
62 A1 **Wuntho** Myanmar
100 C2 **Wuppertal** Ger.
122 A3 **Wuppertal** S. Africa
101 E2 **Wurzbach** Ger.
101 D3 **Würzburg** Ger.
101 F2 **Wurzen** Ger.
68 C2 **Wuwei** China
70 A2 **Wuxi** *Chongqing* China
70 C2 **Wuxi** *Jiangsu* China
Wuxing China *see* **Huzhou**
71 A3 **Wuxuan** China
Wuyang China *see* **Zhenyuan**
69 E1 **Wuyiling** China
71 B3 **Wuyishan** China
71 B3 **Wuyi Shan** *mts* China
70 A1 **Wuyuan** China
71 A4 **Wuzhishan** China
70 A2 **Wuzhong** China
71 B3 **Wuzhou** China
53 C2 **Wyangala Reservoir** Austr.
52 B3 **Wycheproof** Austr.
99 B3 **Wye** *r.* U.K.
50 B1 **Wyndham** Austr.
142 B1 **Wynne** U.S.A.
129 D2 **Wynyard** Can.
136 B2 **Wyoming** *state* U.S.A.
103 E1 **Wyszków** Pol.
140 C3 **Wytheville** U.S.A.

X

117 D3 **Xaafuun** Somalia
62 B2 **Xaignabouli** Laos
62 B2 **Xaisômboun** Laos
121 C3 **Xai-Xai** Moz.
145 C3 **Xalapa** Mex.
70 A1 **Xamba** China
62 A1 **Xamgyi'nyilha** China
62 B1 **Xam Nua** Laos
120 A2 **Xangongo** Angola
81 C2 **Xankändi** Azer.
111 B2 **Xanthi** Greece
150 B3 **Xapuri** Brazil
107 C2 **Xàtiva** Spain
Xiaguan China *see* **Dali**
71 B3 **Xiamen** China
70 A2 **Xi'an** China
70 A3 **Xianfeng** China
Xiangfan China *see* **Xiangyang**
Xianggang China *see* **Hong Kong**
Xianggang *aut. reg.* China *see* **Hong Kong**
Xiangjiang China *see* **Huichang**
71 B3 **Xiangtan** China
70 B2 **Xiangyang** China
70 B2 **Xiantao** China
70 A2 **Xianyang** China
70 B2 **Xiaogan** China
69 E1 **Xiao Hinggan Ling** *mts* China
70 C2 **Xiaoshan** China
62 B1 **Xichang** China
145 C2 **Xicohténcatl** Mex.
71 A3 **Xifeng** China
75 C2 **Xigazê** China
83 I4 **Xilinhot** China
70 B2 **Xincai** China
68 C2 **Xinghai** China
70 B2 **Xinghua** China
71 B3 **Xingning** China
70 A2 **Xingping** China
70 B2 **Xingtai** China
151 C2 **Xingu** *r.* Brazil
71 A3 **Xingyi** China
71 B3 **Xinhua** China
68 C2 **Xining** China
68 B2 **Xinjiang** *reg.* China
Xinjiang Uygur Autonomous Region *aut. reg.* China *see* **Xinjiang Uygur Zizhiqu**
75 C1 **Xinjiang Uygur Zizhiqu** *aut. reg.* China
Xinjing China *see* **Jingxi**
69 D2 **Xinkou** China
65 A1 **Xinmin** China
71 B3 **Xinning** China
70 B2 **Xintai** China
70 B2 **Xinxiang** China
70 B2 **Xinyang** China
70 B2 **Xinyi** China
71 C3 **Xinying** Taiwan
71 B3 **Xinyu** China
70 B2 **Xinzhou** China
Xinzhu Taiwan *see* **Hsinchu**
106 B1 **Xinzo de Limia** Spain
Xiongshan China *see* **Zhenghe**
68 C2 **Xiqing Shan** *mts* China
151 D3 **Xique-Xique** Brazil
70 A1 **Xishanzui** China
71 A3 **Xiushan** China
71 B3 **Xiuying** China
70 B2 **Xixia** China
Xixón Spain *see* **Gijón/Xixón**
75 C1 **Xizang Zizhiqu** *aut. reg.* China
76 B2 **Xo'jayli** Uzbek.
70 B2 **Xuancheng** China
71 A3 **Xuanwei** China
70 B2 **Xuchang** China
Xucheng China *see* **Xuwen**
117 C4 **Xuddur** Somalia
Xujiang China *see* **Guangchang**
71 B3 **Xun Jiang** *r.* China
71 B3 **Xunwu** China
107 C2 **Xúquer, Riu** *r.* Spain
71 B3 **Xuwen** China
71 A3 **Xuyong** China
70 B2 **Xuzhou** China
117 B4 **Yabēlo** Eth.

Y

69 D1 **Yablonovyy Khrebet** *mts* Russia
143 D1 **Yadkin** *r.* U.S.A.
75 C2 **Yadong** China
89 E2 **Yagnitsa** Russia
118 B1 **Yagoua** Cameroon
128 C3 **Yahk** Can.
144 B2 **Yahualica** Mex.
80 B2 **Yahyalı** Turkey
67 C4 **Yaizu** Japan
134 B1 **Yakima** U.S.A.
114 B3 **Yako** Burkina Faso
66 D2 **Yakumo** Japan
126 B3 **Yakutat** U.S.A.
83 J2 **Yakutsk** Russia
91 D2 **Yakymivka** Ukr.
63 B3 **Yala** Thai.
53 C3 **Yallourn** Austr.
111 C2 **Yalova** Turkey
91 C3 **Yalta** Ukr.
65 A1 **Yalu Jiang** *r.* China/N. Korea
67 D3 **Yamagata** Japan
67 B4 **Yamaguchi** Japan
Yamal, Poluostrov *pen.* Russia *see* **Yamal Peninsula**
86 F1 **Yamal Peninsula** Russia
53 D1 **Yamba** Austr.
117 A4 **Yambio** South Sudan
110 C2 **Yambol** Bulg.
86 G2 **Yamburg** Russia
62 A1 **Yamethin** Myanmar
114 B4 **Yamoussoukro** Côte d'Ivoire
90 B2 **Yampil'** Ukr.
75 C2 **Yamuna** *r.* India
75 D2 **Yamzho Yumco** *l.* China
83 K2 **Yana** *r.* Russia
70 A2 **Yan'an** China
150 A3 **Yanaoca** Peru
78 A2 **Yanbu' al Baḩr** Saudi Arabia
70 C2 **Yancheng** China
50 A3 **Yanchep** Austr.
70 B2 **Yangcheng** China
71 B3 **Yangchun** China
65 B2 **Yangdok** N. Korea
71 B3 **Yangjiang** China
Yangôn Myanmar *see* **Rangoon**
70 B2 **Yangquan** China
71 B3 **Yangshuo** China
70 C3 **Yangtze** *r.* China
69 E2 **Yangtze, Mouth of the** China
70 B2 **Yangzhou** China
65 B1 **Yanji** China
137 D2 **Yankton** U.S.A.
83 K2 **Yano-Indigirskaya Nizmennost'** *lowland* Russia
83 K2 **Yanskiy Zaliv** *g.* Russia
53 C1 **Yantabulla** Austr.
70 C2 **Yantai** China
91 C2 **Yany-Kapu** Ukr.
118 B2 **Yaoundé** Cameroon

59 D2 **Yap** *i.* Micronesia
59 D3 **Yapen** *i.* Indon.
59 D3 **Yapen, Selat** *sea chan.* Indon.
144 A2 **Yaqui** *r.* Mex.
51 D2 **Yaraka** Austr.
86 D3 **Yaransk** Russia
48 F2 **Yaren** Nauru
78 B3 **Yarīm** Yemen
77 D3 **Yarkant He** *r.* China
75 D2 **Yarlung Zangbo** *r.* China
131 D2 **Yarmouth** Can.
86 F2 **Yarono** Russia
89 E2 **Yaroslavl'** Russia
66 B2 **Yaroslavskiy** Russia
53 C3 **Yarram** Austr.
89 D2 **Yartsevo** Russia
89 E3 **Yasnogorsk** Russia
63 B2 **Yasothon** Thai.
53 C2 **Yass** Austr.
111 C3 **Yatağan** Turkey
129 E1 **Yathkyed Lake** Can.
67 B4 **Yatsushiro** Japan
150 B2 **Yavarí** *r.* Brazil/Peru
75 B2 **Yavatmal** India
90 A2 **Yavoriv** Ukr.
67 B4 **Yawatahama** Japan
81 D2 **Yazd** Iran
142 B2 **Yazoo City** U.S.A.
111 B3 **Ydra** *i.* Greece
63 A2 **Ye** Myanmar
77 D3 **Yecheng** China
144 B2 **Yécora** Mex.
91 D2 **Yedy-Kuyu** Ukr.
89 E3 **Yefremov** Russia
89 E2 **Yegor'yevsk** Russia
117 B4 **Yei** South Sudan
86 F3 **Yekaterinburg** Russia
77 D1 **Yekibastuz** Kazakh.
89 E3 **Yelets** Russia
114 A3 **Yélimané** Mali
96 □ **Yell** *i.* U.K.
128 C1 **Yellowknife** Can.
70 B2 **Yellow River** *r.* China
69 E2 **Yellow Sea** N. Pacific Ocean
136 C1 **Yellowstone** *r.* U.S.A.
136 A2 **Yellowstone Lake** U.S.A.
88 C3 **Yel'sk** Belarus
78 B3 **Yemen** *country* Asia
86 E2 **Yemva** Russia
91 D2 **Yenakiyeve** Ukr.
62 A1 **Yenangyaung** Myanmar
62 B1 **Yên Bai** Vietnam
114 B4 **Yendi** Ghana
111 C3 **Yenice** Turkey
111 C3 **Yenifoça** Turkey
68 C1 **Yenisey** *r.* Russia
65 B2 **Yeongdeok** S. Korea
53 C2 **Yeoval** Austr.
99 B3 **Yeovil** U.K.
51 E2 **Yeppoon** Austr.
83 I2 **Yerbogachen** Russia
81 C1 **Yerevan** Armenia
77 D1 **Yereymentau** Kazakh.
87 D3 **Yershov** Russia
Yertis *r.* Kazakh./Russia *see* **Irtysh**
65 B2 **Yesan** S. Korea
77 C1 **Yesil'** Kazakh.
77 D1 **Yesil'** *r.* Kazakh./Russia
111 C3 **Yeşilova** Turkey
99 A3 **Yes Tor** *h.* U.K.
53 D1 **Yetman** Austr.
62 A1 **Ye-U** Myanmar
104 B2 **Yeu, Île d'** *i.* France
91 C2 **Yevpatoriya** Ukr.
91 D2 **Yeya** *r.* Russia
91 D2 **Yeysk** Russia
88 C2 **Yezyaryshcha** Belarus
71 A3 **Yibin** China
70 B2 **Yichang** China
69 E1 **Yichun** *Heilong.* China
71 B3 **Yichun** *Jiangxi* China
110 C2 **Yıldız Dağları** *mts* Turkey
80 B2 **Yıldızeli** Turkey
70 A2 **Yinchuan** China
65 B1 **Yingchengzi** China
71 B3 **Yingde** China
70 C1 **Yingkou** China
70 B2 **Yingshan** *Hubei* China
70 A2 **Yingshan** *Sichuan* China
71 B3 **Yingtan** China
77 E2 **Yining** China
117 B4 **Yirga Alem** Eth.
70 B2 **Yishui** China
68 C2 **Yiwu** China
71 B3 **Yiyang** China
71 A3 **Yizhou** China
92 I2 **Yli-Kitka** *l.* Fin.
92 H2 **Ylitornio** Fin.
92 H3 **Ylivieska** Fin.
61 C2 **Yogyakarta** Indon.
118 B2 **Yoko** Cameroon
67 C3 **Yokohama** Japan
115 D4 **Yola** Nigeria
67 D3 **Yonezawa** Japan
71 B3 **Yong'an** China
71 B3 **Yongchun** China
70 A2 **Yongdeng** China
71 C3 **Yongkang** China
62 B1 **Yongsheng** China
71 B3 **Yongzhou** China
150 A1 **Yopal** Col.
50 A3 **York** Austr.
98 C2 **York** U.K.
137 D2 **York** *NE* U.S.A.
141 D3 **York** *PA* U.S.A.
51 D1 **York, Cape** Austr.
52 A3 **Yorke Peninsula** Austr.
52 A3 **Yorketown** Austr.
98 C2 **Yorkshire Wolds** *hills* U.K.
129 D2 **Yorkton** Can.
87 D3 **Yoshkar-Ola** Russia
97 C3 **Youghal** Ireland
53 C2 **Young** Austr.
52 A3 **Younghusband Peninsula** Austr.
140 C2 **Youngstown** U.S.A.
114 B3 **Youvarou** Mali
77 E2 **Youyi Feng** *mt.* China/Russia
80 B2 **Yozgat** Turkey
134 B2 **Yreka** U.S.A.
76 C2 **Yrgyz** Kazakh.
Yr Wyddfa *mt.* U.K. *see* **Snowdon**
105 C2 **Yssingeaux** France
93 F4 **Ystad** Sweden
Ysyk-Köl Kyrg. *see* **Balykchy**
77 D2 **Ysyk-Köl** *salt l.* Kyrg.
92 □A3 **Ytri-Rangá** *r.* Iceland
62 B1 **Yuanjiang** China
62 B1 **Yuan Jiang** *r.* China
62 B1 **Yuanmou** China
135 B3 **Yuba City** U.S.A.
66 D2 **Yūbari** Japan
145 C3 **Yucatán** *pen.* Mex.
146 B2 **Yucatan Channel** Cuba/Mex.
50 C2 **Yuendumu** Austr.
71 B3 **Yueyang** China
86 F2 **Yugorsk** Russia
83 L2 **Yukagirskoye Ploskogor'ye** *plat.* Russia
128 A1 **Yukon** *admin. div.* Can.
126 A2 **Yukon** *r.* Can./U.S.A.
71 B3 **Yulin** *Guangxi* China
70 A2 **Yulin** *Shaanxi* China
62 B1 **Yulong Xueshan** *mt.* China
138 A2 **Yuma** *AZ* U.S.A.
136 C2 **Yuma** *CO* U.S.A.
Yumen China *see* **Laojunm**
80 B2 **Yunak** Turkey
70 B2 **Yuncheng** China
71 B3 **Yunfu** China
62 B1 **Yunnan** *prov.* China
52 A2 **Yunta** Austr.
70 B2 **Yunyang** China
66 D3 **Yurihonjō** Japan
150 A2 **Yurimaguas** Peru
77 E3 **Yurungkax He** *r.* China
71 C3 **Yu Shan** *mt.* Taiwan
68 C2 **Yushu** China
Yushuwan China *see* **Huaib**
81 C1 **Yusufeli** Turkey
77 E3 **Yutian** China
62 B1 **Yuxi** China
66 D2 **Yuzhno-Kuril'sk** Russia
83 K3 **Yuzhno-Sakhalinsk** Russia
91 C2 **Yuzhnoukrayins'k** Ukr.
82 E2 **Yuzhnyy, Ostrov** *i.* Russia
69 D2 **Yuzhou** China
104 C2 **Yvetot** France

Z

100 B1 **Zaandam** Neth.
69 D1 **Zabaykal'sk** Russia
78 B3 **Zabīd** Yemen
Zābol Iran *see* **Mehrestān**
79 D2 **Zābolī** Iran
144 B3 **Zacapu** Mex.
144 B2 **Zacatecas** Mex.
145 C3 **Zacatepec** Mex.
145 C3 **Zacatlán** Mex.
111 B3 **Zacharo** Greece
144 B2 **Zacoalco** Mex.
145 C2 **Zacualtipán** Mex.
109 C2 **Zadar** Croatia
63 A3 **Zadetkyi Kyun** *i.* Myanmar
89 E3 **Zadonsk** Russia
106 B2 **Zafra** Spain
109 C1 **Zagreb** Croatia
Zagros, Kūhhā-ye *mts* Iran **Zagros Mountains**
81 C2 **Zagros Mountains** Iran
79 D2 **Zāhedān** Iran
80 B2 **Zahlé** Lebanon
78 B3 **Ẓahrān** Saudi Arabia
Zaire *country* Africa *see* **Con Democratic Republic of th**
109 D2 **Zaječar** Serbia
89 E3 **Zakharovo** Russia
81 C2 **Zākhū/Zaxo** Iraq
111 B3 **Zakynthos** Greece
111 B3 **Zakynthos** *i.* Greece
103 D2 **Zalaegerszeg** Hungary
110 B1 **Zalău** Romania
78 B2 **Ẓalim** Saudi Arabia
117 A3 **Zalingei** Sudan
78 A2 **Ẓalmā, Jabal aẓ** *mt.* Saudi Arabia
128 C2 **Zama City** Can.
120 C2 **Zambeze** *r.* Moz.
120 C2 **Zambezi** *r.* Africa
Zambezi *r.* Moz. *see* **Zambe**
120 B2 **Zambezi** Zambia
120 B2 **Zambia** *country* Africa
64 B2 **Zamboanga** Phil.
64 B2 **Zamboanga Peninsula** Phil
106 B1 **Zamora** Spain
144 B3 **Zamora de Hidalgo** Mex.
103 E1 **Zamość** Pol.
75 B1 **Zanda** China
100 B2 **Zandvliet** Belgium
140 C3 **Zanesville** U.S.A.
81 C2 **Zanjān** Iran

75	B1	Zanskar Mountains India
		Zante i. Greece see Zakynthos
119	D3	Zanzibar Tanz.
119	D3	Zanzibar Island Tanz.
89	E3	Zaokskiy Russia
115	C2	Zaouatallaz Alg.
89	D2	Zapadnaya Dvina r. Europe
89	D2	Zapadnaya Dvina Russia
68	B1	Zapadnyy Sayan reg. Russia
139	D3	Zapata U.S.A.
92	J2	Zapolyarnyy Russia
91	D2	Zaporizhzhya Ukr.
101	E2	Zappendorf Ger.
80	B2	Zara Turkey
145	B2	Zaragoza Mex.
107	C1	Zaragoza Spain
74	A1	Zarah Sharan Afgh.
76	B3	Zarand Iran
76	C3	Zaranj Afgh.
88	C2	Zarasai Lith.
89	E3	Zaraysk Russia
150	B1	Zaraza Venez.
115	C3	Zaria Nigeria
90	B1	Zarichne Ukr.
81	D3	Zarqān Iran
66	B2	Zarubino Russia
103	D1	Żary Pol.
115	D1	Zarzis Tunisia
123	C3	Zastron S. Africa
121	C3	Zavala Moz.
69	E1	Zavitinsk Russia
103	D1	Zawiercie Pol.
		Zaxo Iraq see Zākhū/Zaxo
77	E2	Zaysan, Lake Kazakh.
		Zaysan, Ozero l. Kazakh. see
		Zaysan, Lake
90	B1	Zdolbuniv Ukr.
93	F4	Zealand i. Denmark
100	A2	Zeebrugge Belgium
123	C2	Zeerust S. Africa
50	C2	Zeil, Mount Austr.
101	F2	Zeitz Ger.
88	B3	Zelenogradsk Russia
82	F1	Zemlya Aleksandry i. Russia
82	F1	Zemlya Vil'cheka i. Russia
107	D2	Zemmora Alg.
145	C3	Zempoaltépetl, Nudo de mt.
		Mex.
65	B1	Zengfeng Shan mt. China
105	D2	Zermatt Switz.
91	E2	Zernograd Russia
101	E2	Zeulenroda Ger.
101	D1	Zeven Ger.
100	C2	Zevenaar Neth.
83	J3	Zeya Russia
79	C2	Zeydābād Iran
83	J3	Zeyskoye Vodokhranilishche
		resr Russia
103	D1	Zgierz Pol.
88	B3	Zhabinka Belarus
76	A2	Zhalpaktal Kazakh.
77	C1	Zhaltyr Kazakh.
76	B2	Zhanakala Kazakh.
76	B2	Zhanaozen Kazakh.
		Zhangde China see Anyang
		Zhanghua Taiwan see
		Changhua
71	B3	Zhangjiajie China
70	B1	Zhangjiakou China
71	B3	Zhangping China
71	B3	Zhangshu China
68	C2	Zhangye China
71	B3	Zhangzhou China
87	D4	Zhanibek Kazakh.
71	B3	Zhanjiang China
71	B3	Zhao'an China
71	B3	Zhaoqing China
71	A3	Zhaotong China

75	C1	Zhari Namco salt l. China
77	E2	Zharkent Kazakh.
89	D2	Zharkovskiy Russia
77	E2	Zharma Kazakh.
90	C2	Zhashkiv Ukr.
		Zhayyk r. Kazakh./Russia see
		Ural
71	C3	Zhejiang prov. China
82	F1	Zhelaniya, Mys c. Russia
89	E3	Zheleznogorsk Russia
76	B2	Zhem r. Kazakh.
70	A2	Zhenba China
71	A3	Zheng'an China
71	B3	Zhenghe China
70	B2	Zhengzhou China
70	B2	Zhenjiang China
71	A3	Zhenyuan China
91	E1	Zherdevka Russia
86	D2	Zheshart Russia
77	D2	Zhetysuskiy Alatau mts China/
		Kazakh.
77	C2	Zhezkazgan Karagandinskaya
		Oblast' Kazakh.
77	C2	Zhezkazgan Karagandinskaya
		Oblast' Kazakh.
68	C3	Zhigang China
83	J2	Zhigansk Russia
		Zhi Qu r. China see Yangtze
		Zhishan China see Lingling
76	C1	Zhitikara Kazakh.
88	D3	Zhlobin Belarus
90	B2	Zhmerynka Ukr.
74	A1	Zhob Pak.
83	L1	Zhokhova, Ostrov i. Russia
75	C2	Zhongba China
		Zhonghe China see Xiushan
70	A2	Zhongning China
71	B3	Zhongshan Guangdong China
		Zhongshan Guizhou China see
		Liupanshui
70	A2	Zhongwei China
		Zhongxin China see
		Xamgyi'nyilha
76	C2	Zhosaly Kazakh.
70	B2	Zhoukou China
70	C2	Zhoushan China
91	C2	Zhovti Vody Ukr.
65	A2	Zhuanghe China
70	B2	Zhucheng China
89	D3	Zhukovka Russia
89	E2	Zhukovskiy Russia
70	B2	Zhumadian China
		Zhuoyang China see Suiping
71	B3	Zhuzhou Hunan China
71	B3	Zhuzhou Hunan China
90	A2	Zhydachiv Ukr.
88	C3	Zhytkavichy Belarus
90	B1	Zhytomyr Ukr.
103	D2	Žiar nad Hronom Slovakia
70	B2	Zibo China
103	D1	Zielona Góra Pol.
62	A1	Zigaing Myanmar
71	A3	Zigong China
114	A3	Ziguinchor Senegal
144	B3	Zihuatanejo Mex.
103	D2	Žilina Slovakia
83	H3	Zima Russia
145	C2	Zimapán Mex.
121	B2	Zimbabwe country Africa
114	A4	Zimmi Sierra Leone
110	C2	Zimnicea Romania
115	C3	Zinder Niger
78	B3	Zinjibār Yemen
103	D2	Zirc Hungary
62	A1	Ziro India
79	C2	Zīr Rūd Iran
103	D2	Zistersdorf Austria
145	B3	Zitácuaro Mex.

103	C1	Zittau Ger.
110	B2	Zlatitsa Bulg.
87	E3	Zlatoust Russia
103	D2	Zlín Czechia
89	D3	Zlynka Russia
89	E3	Zmiyevka Russia
91	D2	Zmiyiv Ukr.
89	E3	Znamenka Orlovskaya Oblast'
		Russia
91	E1	Znamenka Tambovskaya
		Oblast' Russia
91	C2	Znam"yanka Ukr.
103	D2	Znojmo Czechia
91	D1	Zolochiv Kharkivs'ka Oblast'
		Ukr.
90	A2	Zolochiv L'vivs'ka Oblast' Ukr.
91	C2	Zolotonosha Ukr.
89	E3	Zolotukhino Russia
121	C2	Zomba Malawi
80	B1	Zonguldak Turkey
105	D3	Zonza Corsica France
114	B4	Zorzor Liberia
115	C2	Zouar Chad
114	A2	Zouérat Maur.
109	C1	Zrenjanin Serbia
89	D2	Zubtsov Russia
105	D2	Zug Switz.
81	C1	Zugdidi Georgia
106	B2	Zújar r. Spain
100	C2	Zülpich Ger.
121	C2	Zumbo Moz.
145	C3	Zumpango Mex.
138	B1	Zuni Mountains U.S.A.
71	A3	Zunyi China
109	C1	Županja Croatia
105	D2	Zürich Switz.
100	C1	Zutphen Neth.
115	D1	Zuwārah Libya
90	C2	Zvenyhorodka Ukr.
121	C3	Zvishavane Zimbabwe
103	D2	Zvolen Slovakia
109	C2	Zvornik Bos. & Herz.
114	B4	Zwedru Liberia
123	C3	Zwelitsha S. Africa
103	D2	Zwettl Austria
101	F2	Zwickau Ger.
100	C1	Zwolle Neth.
83	L2	Zyryanka Russia

Acknowledgements

pages 34-35
Climatic map data:
Kottek, M., Grieser, J., Beck, C., Rudolf, B., and Rubel, F., 2006: World Map
of the Köppen-Geiger climate classification updated.
Meteorol. Z., 15, 259–263.
http://koeppen-geiger.vu-wien.ac.at

pages 36-37
World land cover map data:
© ESA 2010 and UCLouvain
Arino, O., Ramos, J., Kalogirou, V., Defourny, P., Achard, F., 2010.
GlobCover 2009. ESA Living Planet Symposium 2010, 28th June - 2nd July, Bergen, Norway, SP-686, ESA,
www.esa.int/due/globcover
http://due.esrin.esa.int/prjs/Results/20110202183257.pdf

pages 38-39
Population map data:
Center for International Earth Science Information Network (CIESIN), Columbia University; and Centro Internacional de Agricultura
Tropical (CIAT). 2005. Gridded Population of the World Version 3 (GPWv3). Palisades, NY: Socioeconomic
Data and Applications Center (SEDAC), Columbia University.
Available at: http://sedac.ciesin.columbia.edu/gpw
http://www.ciesin.columbia.edu

Cover
Paraná River, Argentina: © NASA/Science Photo Library

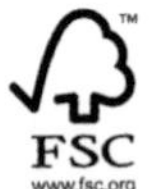

MIX
Paper from
responsible sources
FSC
www.fsc.org
FSC® C007454